THE STORY OF GRAPHIC DESIGN

GRAPHIC ARTS MESSAGE

EXHIBITION SEMINAR WORKSHOP

'92

TOKYO

THANKS FOR 73 YEARS CAMPAIGN

THE STORY OF
GRAPHIC DESIGN

From the Invention of Writing to the
Birth of Digital Design

PATRICK CRAMSIE

BRITISH LIBRARY

First published in 2010 by
The British Library
96 Euston Road
London NW1 2DB

British Library Cataloguing in Publication Data
A catalogue record for this publication is available
from The British Library

ISBN 978-0-7123-0696-6

Designed by Patrick Cramsie and Bobby Birchall
Colour reproduction by Dot Gradations Ltd, Essex
Printed in Hong Kong by Great Wall Printing Co. Ltd

Frontispiece: detail of 'Graphic Arts Message Tokyo'
poster designed by Neville Brody, 1992.

*This book is dedicated to my parents,
Rosy and Jim, my father-in-law, Adam,
and in loving memory of my mother-in-
law, Penelope.*

CONTENTS

continued ...

ACKNOWLEDGEMENTS

Zapf Dingbats is one of those enticingly perplexing names or phrases that pepper the lexicon of graphic design. Each of the symbols (dingbats) in this digital font was designed by Hermann Zapf, one of the most illustrious type designers of the twentieth century. Yet he is one among many other eminent designers, past and present, who have fallen victim to the concision required of a book like this. But while their names are not mentioned in the text, their influence runs through every page (visibly so in Zapf's case since he is also the designer of the typeface, Melior, in which this book is set). Similarly, there are a number of writers whose names do not appear in the bibliography or endnotes but who have greatly informed the text.

There are two individuals, both publishers, whose names deserve to appear here at the outset: David Way, at The British Library, and Eric Himmel, at Abrams. They placed an inordinate degree of faith in me as a first-time author and then maintained their faith during the years it took me to complete this book. Their patience and support set an example that everyone around them seemed to follow: at The British Library, Lara Speicher especially, who corralled the disparate group of editors, readers, researchers and designers with a calmness, geniality and persistence that few could match and many would wish to emulate; Jenny Lawson also, who took everything that came to her, often late, and always with the same degree of helpfulness and attention; Sally Nicholls and Kate Hampson, whose picture research was as complex and involving as any aspect of the production, yet who consistently did more than was required of them; Bernard Dod, Jenny Knight, Sarah Kane, Belinda Wilkinson, Beth Cleall, all of whom were similarly professional and supportive; so too Bobby Birchall, despite having to do as much work as any in helping lay out the book. I am very grateful to all of them. I am also grateful to those at Abrams: Andrea Colvin, Ankur Ghosh, Ashley Gillespie, Michelle Ishay, in particular, and Eric Klopfer. Outside of this group, Caroline Dawnay went far beyond what is normally expected of a literary agent.

I am indebted to those who read parts of the manuscript: Dan Antopolski, Francesca Beard especially, Mark Diaper and Niall Edworthy; and then to the many designers and other individuals who looked through relevant pieces of text and came back to me with clarifications and suggestions: Ken Garland, Milton Glaser, April Greiman, Willi Kunz, Romek Marber, John McConnell, Ootje Oxenaar, Michael Randle, Carol Schneider, Rosemarie Tissi, Niklaus Troxler, Rudy VanderLans, Rick Vermeulen, Paul White and Wes Wilson. I am especially grateful to Tom Geismar, Bill Longhauser, Katherine McCoy, Peter Saville and Massimo Vignelli, each of whom read more than their relevant pieces of text.

Those who helped in various ways with the pictures and text include: Chris Ashworth, Paul Bahn, Simon Beresford-Smith, Phil Cleaver, David Connor, Alison Cullingford, Kate Darby, Hattie Ellis, Matthew Engel, Ben and Emily Faccini, Charlie Fane, Marcus Fergusson, Simon Grant, Michael Graves, Richard Hollis, Richard and Florence Ingleby, John Marchant, Ian Mortimer, James Mosley, Penny Nagle, Babak Parviz, Sue Phillips, Stuart Proffitt, Ben Saltzman, Andrew Spira, Piers Taylor, Carl Williams, Andrew Wilson, and then the staff at St Bride Printing Library, especially Nigel Roche, whose knowledge and helpfulness were as invaluable to me as they have been to countless others. I should also like to acknowledge, in memoriam, Herbert Spencer, who encouraged me to write this book, and Alan Fletcher (an ex-pupil of Spencer's), who let me scour his library.

For practical support I am grateful to the Wingate Foundation, which awarded me a grant in 2003 that enabled me to begin researching this book. In a similar vein I owe a particular debt to Rosy and Jim Cramsie, Sinclair Cramsie, Matthew Darby, Adam and Poppet Fergusson, and David McDonald. No less deserving of my thanks are Tessa and Guy Baring, Saskia Bos, Steve Corry, Lara Cramsie, Flora Fremantle, Myra Hunt, Tam le Bailly, Mely Vera, Michael Phillips, Satyananda, Annie and John Spearman, and Hayley Williams.

There are others, most of them teachers, who have exerted an important, albeit indirect, influence on the book: Nicolas Barker, Tamasin Cole, Orna Frommer-Dawson especially, Eiichi Kono, Uli and Auri Schwartz, Martin Stringer and Peter Webb. As well as these individuals there are three others whose influence has been even more fundamental: Nick Hornby, who encouraged me to read (and listen to music); Holly Eley, who while at the *Times Literary Supplement* encouraged me to write; and Robin Child, who as my art master at secondary school, encouraged me to look. Any merit this book possesses has its roots in what I was privileged to learn in his classroom.

Petra, my wife, made similar kinds of contributions to those mentioned above and then many others besides. The acuteness of her editorial eye and the school-masterly admonishments that flowed from her correcting pen were partnered by her humour, patience, support and love. It will be a pleasure to repay in whatever way I can the devotion and forbearance she has shown this project.

INTRODUCTION
Graphic Design & Style

The impact of graphic design on our daily lives begins the moment we open our eyes each morning and continues until they close at night. The numbers on the display of an alarm clock, the design of a tube of toothpaste and the various washing and beauty products that form part of our early-morning ritual, the labels and logos on the clothes we pick out, the designs on the packets of cereal and other items we choose for breakfast; a morning paper perhaps and then the road signs and dashboard displays that silently guide us on our daily commute or journey to school; the hoardings, posters and shop signs that prick our consumerist urges; the money in our pockets and the embossed cards of plastic in our purses and wallets; the lettering and symbols that fleck the corridors and rooms of our place of work; the piles of papers that clutter our work spaces; the symbols and instructions that help us navigate through the screens on our computers and mobile phones; the sequence of words that annotate the latest news headlines on TV; and the books and magazines that fill snatched moments throughout the day or that tempt our tired eyes before lulling us to sleep; all these things, to name but a few, make up a realm of communication that is so deeply woven into our modern lives it is rarely considered as a single entity, let alone one that might be worthy of study. Printed words and pictures, and their modern equivalents on screen, are so commonplace and ubiquitous they seldom intrude on our consciousness. Their messages trump the medium that delivers them. And yet, taken as a whole, they are an integral part of our modern industrial culture.

Graphic forms have played a significant role in all large and complex societies. The social foundations of the first civilizations – their trade, their laws and their religion – were serviced and bolstered by a series of graphic marks (the word 'graphic' comes via Latin from the Greek *graphē* meaning writing or drawing). Symbols of provenance or logos, written records and receipts,

accounts, labels of goods and items of advertising were each taken on and developed over the centuries. They became essential components in the growth of commerce and technology prior to widespread industrialization. Similarly, legal codes, royal decrees and charters were first given permanence through carved writing 'set in stone' *(fig. i.1)*, before being scratched in ink onto pieces of parchment affixed with a seal, and then eventually printed and bound in large statute books. The importance of graphic forms to religion can be seen within shrines, temples and burial sites, whose surfaces were decorated with texts that set out the supernatural means by which people's earthly environment could be controlled and their route to the afterlife established. Through religious texts written in native languages, through scientific texts that used diagrams to reveal the planetary motion of the heavens or the workings of the human body, and through printed maps that charted the earth's land masses with a series of schematic pictures, printed graphic forms changed how people thought about their lives and, by extension, how they lived them.

For all graphic design's importance, it is only within the last three decades that the subject has been considered worth studying in the round (aspects of it, especially those relating to the history of books, have long been written about). It is now slowly filling the gaps in its history. Part of the reason for this lack of attention is that graphic design's role as a service provider masked whatever artistic merit it might have possessed. However much artistic skill was brought to a particular design, the design always had a job of work to do. It was either selling or informing, or sometimes doing a bit of both. This lack of clarity about the status of graphic design has been compounded by its ephemeral nature. Are posters really meant to be hung in galleries long after the events they promoted have passed? Is there really any social value in collecting beer mats or luggage labels? These sorts of questions bring us to the issue that makes it most difficult to consider graphic design as a single entity: its immense and unparalleled variety. The range of objects under its purview is vast and with every innovation in information technology the range only increases. These factors make graphic design a rich and rewarding area of study, but they also make it a difficult one.

The first known use of the term 'graphic design' appeared in August 1922 in an article from a newspaper supplement provided with the *Boston Evening Transcript* ('Advertising design is the only form of graphic design that gets home to everybody' was the line). The article had been written by an American graphic designer and writer W. A. Dwiggins (1880–1956). Six years later, when Dwiggins's influential *Layout in Advertising* was published – one of the earliest graphic design manuals – he had apparently forgotten the term. Dwiggins used similar phrases such as 'graphic advertising' or 'printing designer', but not 'graphic design'. Indeed, it was only very much later, during the early 1980s, that the term really became established, certainly outside the profession.

To some extent then the date of the term's first known use is a historical accident. It doesn't signify anything in particular. The beginning of graphic design as a profession – when designing became separated from making – was spread out over the decades that ended the nineteenth century and began the twentieth. The term's first use certainly doesn't mark the beginning of graphic design as a practice. The process of designing a piece of text for print first took place in the West almost 500 years before Dwiggins's article. Though it was a printer (or perhaps several people working together) who did the designing – that is, selecting and setting the type and then arranging for it to fall on a particular place on the page – the thought processes involved were similar to those that a designer would follow today.

Over the intervening centuries graphic design has become so multifarious it is hard to capture its full extent within a single, succinct definition. The variety of objects and media touched on above are partnered by a third element: graphic design's very varied styles of expression, which are so protean they are almost beyond the bounds of classification.

Rather than expecting a dictionary definition to do the term 'graphic design' justice, it is perhaps more useful to look at the fundamental characteristics of the subject. There are three, in particular, which form a sort of semantic centre of gravity. The main force of attraction is generated by the combination of words and pictures (and any of the visual elements in between, such as logos or symbols, which contain various word-like and picture-like qualities). Today, more than ever, both these things, words and pictures, appear alongside each other, working in unison. Many of the kinds of books, magazines and newspapers that were once exclusively typographic now include at least some kind of picture material.

This difference, the shift in prominence from words (in black and white) to pictures (in colour), represents the greatest change in the appearance of graphic design works (flick through Chapters 4 to 9 and compare them with the subsequent chapters). When Western graphic design emerged alongside the birth of printing with type, printed pictures had to be made by hand. Thus, they were relatively expensive and scarce. Throughout the following four centuries, they continued to need the close attention of various skilled craftsmen to draw, carve, etch or work on them in some fashion, so text remained the dominant graphic form. It was with the development of photography and the printing technique of lithography during the middle of the nineteenth century that a shift towards a more pictorial graphic design began. Today pictures are so easy to make (through digital photography, video and modern printing techniques) they are now as prevalent as words once were.

The second characteristic common to most forms of graphic design is its two-dimensionality. Whether printed onto paper or illuminated on a screen, graphic design usually exists on a flat surface. (An important corollary to this flatness is that invariably it is framed by the simple geometry of a rectangle, with all the compositional forces that this format brings to bear.) Stressing the significance of two dimensions in graphic design is not to deny the importance of the sculptural or tactile quality of a graphic work – the particular paper in a book, say, or even the perceptible thickness of silk-screened ink. But while these qualities make an important contribution to the character of a particular work, they do so much less than its two-dimensionality does. The contrasts of shape, tone, texture and colour thrown up by a single spatial plane help to define what is unique about a particular work. They make it recognizable.

The power of two dimensions is exploited by all forms of graphic reproduction. Whenever a design is photographed and reproduced in print – as the designs in this book are, for example – its identity or visual character is maintained even though some of its tactile or material qualities are lost. The retentive power of this kind of two-dimensional representation exerts an influence across the whole of the visual arts. In painting, sculpture and architecture, our knowledge of what we like and dislike, of the particular character of an artwork or building, is usually based on pictures in reproduction rather than first-hand experience. Similarly, few people will have seen any of the posters, book covers or printed pages included here in the original, and yet many of these works have become accepted as among the most significant items in graphic design's history. The same applies to those artworks or buildings that are held up as masterpieces within their respective fields. To a much greater extent than we credit, our knowledge and appreciation of all the visual arts is mediated through the power of graphic design's two dimensions.

The third essential characteristic of graphic design is that it is both geared towards and a product of a process of reproduction. Whether a design exists in print or on a screen-based display, its particular form will have been influenced by the technology used to reproduce it. The centrality of reproduction is what distinguishes graphic design from most forms of fine art. The pre-printed design or so-called 'artwork' for a poster, say, may be made entirely by hand (as it clearly was for the Atélier Populaire's posters *(>fig. 17.19, p.278)*, but the poster itself only really begins its life once the artwork has been reproduced in multiple copies and put in front of its audience. Whereas fine art is usually concerned with the uniqueness of an artefact, graphic design depends on an image's reproducibility (as the portrait of Che Guevara demonstrates, *>fig. 17.13, p.273*). Or to put it another way, fine artists are normally successful if they make a single object that is highly prized, whereas designers base much of their success on the number of times an image has been reproduced.

Most graphic design therefore is made with a particular method of reproduction in mind. The design is itself 'designed' to suit the method in question. A type designer might make small adjustments to the shape of his or (only relatively recently) her letters in order to avoid having ink fill in around the joins of two connecting letter strokes during the course of printing. The screen version of the letterforms needs a different set of alterations; arcane features such as 'hinting' and 'anti-aliasing'.

Some kinds of design have to be made for several reproductive processes. Logos often need to be designed to look as good on screen as they do on a printed page, and then also in small sizes on a mobile phone's display,

say, as well as in large sizes when projected onto a screen during a presentation. So in addition to the process-specific alterations mentioned above, they need to have some general features – mostly bold, simple shapes – if they are to fulfil the various demands made of them. In this way they too confirm the centrality of reproductive processes in graphic design.

This holy trinity of essential characteristics – words and pictures, two dimensions and reproduction – is exemplified by a particular graphic artefact, the poster. No other kind of object embodies these characteristics so completely. The poster's single rectangular surface and generous size (exemplified by its offshoot, the advertising hoarding) make it uniquely suited to communicating simple ideas with words and pictures. Because the poster can produce self-contained graphic statements, few of its qualities are lost in reproduction. Other items, such as book covers or web pages, say, are preludes or adjuncts to other bits of graphic information, but the poster relies on nothing other than its single solitary surface. It exists as a single flat plane rather than several planes bound together, as books or magazines are, or linked pages of information as in a screen-based display. It can be reproduced in other formats (as in a book like this, for example) without much loss of graphic power. Its completeness allows it to survive more or less intact.

The second half of this book contains a high proportion of posters. In light of the opening paragraph's emphasis on graphic design's immense variety, any bias in favour of a particular artefact might appear to be misplaced. Furthermore, letting this bias dominate the last few chapters in particular could also be criticized as wholly anachronistic. Ever since the late 1960s and early 1970s, when television first became a standard feature in people's homes, posters have played an increasingly marginal role in graphic design. The position they enjoyed throughout much of the previous century, as arguably the primary tool of communication, could not survive the arrival of moving pictures into people's living rooms. Though posters continued to be valued for their own aesthetic merits, as works of art as well as works of design, they were no longer the main advertising medium. The recent arrival of other screen-based methods of communication, such as computers and various hand-held devices, has increased this progressive marginalization. And yet, because of its ability to make self-contained graphic statements, the medium of the poster continues to pack a considerable graphic punch.

Despite all the new ways of receiving graphic information, posters are still climbing up the steps of the pantheon of graphic design works *(>fig. 20.20, p.325)*. Some among them, these examples of an apparently antiquated art form, have generated a buzz of interest as great as any by any other kind of graphic artefact. Even today, the poster's attributes allow it to influence graphic styles.

It is one thing to sketch out the essential characteristics of graphic design and then explain its special relationship with the poster format. It is quite another to describe how these characteristics evolved and the social forces that influenced their development. Fortunately, attempts have been made in both directions in several recent histories of graphic design. Though parts of this book touch on them too, that is not its main aim. As the title indicates, this is not meant to be a straightforward history of graphic design, with all the completeness that such a history would be expected to provide. No attempt has been made to include each of the most significant individuals in the field, or the entire range of related technologies, or a complete array of artefacts, or the most prominent periodicals or exhibitions. In varying ways and with varying degrees of success, each of these things has been attempted elsewhere.

The aim behind the 'story' being told here is to sketch out the main styles of Western graphic design. Just as there have been styles of architecture or painting – Renaissance buildings, Impressionist and Cubist pictures, and so forth – so there have been certain styles of graphic design. For most of its history, this has meant certain styles of printing. In fact there have been far too many styles for them all to be done justice within the pages of a single book. Each variant, however, has branched out from a number of main styles or else become entwined with others to produce hybrid forms. It is the main, broadest branches that concern this book. By setting them out clearly, it is hoped that anyone coming to the subject for the first time will be able to see its basic structure.

It should be made clear that by concentrating on styles of graphic design in the West – mainly central Europe, Britain and America – no suggestion is being made that graphic design in the rest of the world is any less interesting or deserving of study. (Having been studied less, it is really more deserving.) However, my own limitations force me to follow certain restrictions. It is enough of a conceit to cover the regions mentioned above, with whose cultures, languages and scripts I am at least partially familiar. It is not possible for me to do justice to those other regions whose cultures, languages and scripts are, in almost every instance, completely unknown to me.

Another self-imposed limitation concerns the kinds of objects or artefacts I have chosen to exclude from this story. Within graphic design as a whole, there are several areas with special attributes that set them apart from all others. To include them here would either have amounted to a series of token gestures or else have required the book to be extended dramatically. The items are as follows: information graphics and, in particular, the pictorial representation of statistics, which is an enormously extensive field, especially from the point of view of graphic style; packaging design and shop-front graphics, which have a special emphasis on three dimensions and even involve an element of small-scale structural engineering; cartoon strips or graphic novels, which would rightly require the kind of literary analysis given to novels; and then motion graphics, either within a film's title sequence, a TV programme or on the web. (The lack of an all-important temporal dimension makes the book an especially poor or difficult medium in which to discuss and analyse motion graphics.)

There are two main reasons for choosing to look at graphic design through the somewhat unfashionable prism of style. First, it is a very natural way of approaching any form of art. And second, it allows an important but neglected aspect of graphic design to be discussed. Style is a powerful organizing principle. Whenever we look at a work of art or design, we habitually make comparisons with other works: 'it looks a bit like such and such' or 'it's not as nice as so and so'. Comparing the formal aspects of works is as common among connoisseurs as novices. Graphic design is so very varied and complex, any opportunity to make it more straightforward by appealing to what comes naturally is worth taking. It is for this same reason that the examples of graphic design shown have been linked by a simple narrative, rather than being annotated through series of disconnected paragraphs whose proximity reflects only a general chronology, as is often the case in previous histories.

The word 'style' comes from the Latin *stilus*, the writing implement so named by the Romans but used earlier in Mesopotamia, Egypt and other parts of the ancient Near East. The Romans sometimes extended its meaning to refer to an author's manner of writing, but the activity with which they came to associate the word most closely, and explore most fully and subtly, was the ancient art of oratory or public speaking. The matching of the right words to a particular meaning in order to elicit a specific response from a certain audience was analysed in detail by Greek and Roman teachers of rhetoric. It was through the writings of figures such as Cicero, the Roman philosopher, statesman and lawyer, that certain doctrines of style were established – such as the doctrine of decorum, the use of a style appropriate to the occasion – and remained in use right up to the eighteenth century. It was during this same century that the history of art came to be looked at as a succession of period styles.

What was meant by this more recent use of the word 'style' was, put simply, any recognizable way of doing or making something. Art historians can learn to recognize the personal style of an artist by comparing examples of artworks. Equally, they can recognize shared characteristics between works produced by artists from a particular era, and so identify a period style. The Italian artist Michelangelo had a recognizable way of drawing which was different from that of his contemporary, Leonardo, though their similarities allow their work to be identified as Renaissance art. Added to these two ways of looking at style is the influence of the subject matter and the medium. The depiction of houses as opposed to flowers, say, or the use of photomontage rather than oil paint, influences the recognizability of a work in a way that is independent both of the person making it or the period in which it was made.

All these facets of style make it possible for us to pin down a work to a particular time and place. We can date it and say where it might have been made. By doing so, we begin to grasp its history. The more knowledge we gain, the better we will be at pinning down the time and place of other works, and so continues a cycle of enrichment and interest. As soon as we know the essential nature of a style, we have some common ground against which we can measure the uniqueness or the innovative quality of a particular work.

Innovations are especially relevant to the styles of graphic design discussed here. As well as allowing a design to stick out from the common herd, they also establish a set of benign associations – of originality, uniqueness or technological advancement – which can transfer to the product or service they promote. However, innovation does not, of itself, guarantee popularity. Not all of the styles included here were the most popular or dominant styles of their time. Many of the twentieth-century styles thrown up during the first wave of Modernism, such as Dada or De Stijl for example, were created by avant-garde artists who, by definition, were at the leading edge of developments in graphic design rather than sitting comfortably in its populist centre. After several decades, Modernist features achieved some popularity by being combined and placed within a more commercial context. But rather than their popularity, what makes them most relevant here is the contribution they made to the development of graphic forms. It is the setting out of these main evolutionary stages that is the aim of the book.

The second reason for focusing on style is to attempt to fill a hole at the heart of graphic design history. Most histories have focused on the social forces that prompted particular kinds of graphic design, or else on the influence of new technologies, or the swell of ideas that surrounded a particular group of designers or artists. All these approaches are valid, but they can only explain the appearance of a piece of work in a general way. Unlike in the fine arts, where the formal properties of artworks are scrutinized and discussed at length, there has been little graphic design history that tries to pin down what the salient features of a particular design are and then explain, with something more than generalizations, why they look the way they do. The impression given is that it is more important to understand the concerns that surrounded the creation of a design than the design itself.

Take the Coca-Cola logo, for example. This has a special status in Western graphic design since for a number of decades now it has been among the most recognized pieces of graphic design. Today perhaps no other logo is better known. In this sense it could be thought of as graphic design's equivalent of the *Mona Lisa*. And yet none of the existing histories has attempted to describe or explain its formal properties. In fact, oddly, almost without exception, no mention is made of the logo at all. Clearly, the amount of money that the Coca-Cola Company has put into marketing and distributing their product has helped make the logo highly recognizable. No doubt, the caffeine content and sugary flavour of the drink itself have made the product popular, and thereby increased the logo's exposure. But that doesn't mean that the logo hasn't contributed to its own popularity. Surely there are features within it that have added to its appeal. By looking at the style of the logo – that is, the elements that make up its form, the relationship between these elements, and the design's overall expression – it is possible

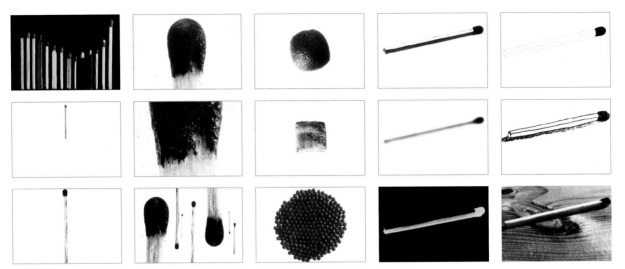

i.2: Variations on the theme of a match, Pentagram, 1967

to explain what some of these features might be and how they might work *(>p.154)*.

Most designs are the result of a long and considered process of experimentation and refinement. Graphic designers often make adjustments involving the tiniest margins, matters of millimetres or fractions of inches. To get some idea of the concerns behind any final form, therefore, it is necessary to look at the design in some detail. By looking closely at a design it is possible to enter into the work, and from this more intimate vantage point one can gain a greater understanding both of the work itself and of the subject as a whole. This looking inward to see more of what lies outside is one of the paradoxes of introspection. It allows us to consider the nature of superstition when we look at the use of photographs by the news media *(>p. 19)*; to engage with aspects of perceptual psychology when considering the legibility of letters *(>p.54)*; or to question the nature of identity in a consumerist society when confronted with recent works of graphic design-related art *(>p.308–9)*. These are just some of the issues that can be thrown up by this process.

In order to understand how styles of graphic design first developed, it is necessary to look at the conventions that were inherited by the first printers. A long tradition of writing out books by hand, far longer indeed than the current history of printing, had already established how a page should appear. It had organized text into words, sentences, paragraphs and chapters. It had established our mixed use of capitals and lowercase letters, as well as such things as the proportions of margins and the use of headings above columns of text. What the manuscript tradition itself had inherited, which has proven to be even more fundamental to Western graphic design, was the alphabet. The letters we use to make words are one of the essential building blocks of graphic design. Their particular form and the way they were developed are a vital part of graphic design's pre-history, and so it is with them that this book begins.

There is a path of history that leads from the origin of writing to the invention of the alphabet (*Chapter 1*). The shaping of this rudimentary alphabet into various practised scripts by the ancient Greeks and Romans (*Chapter 2*) was a necessary prelude to the copying of texts in handmade books during the Middle Ages (*Chapter 3*). During the middle of the fifteenth century, this important three-part pre-history provided the West's first type printers with models of design for the first items of graphic design (*Chapter 4*). These models were followed by a succession of *bona fide* printing styles over the next four centuries. Each one of them was a response to developments in printing and to some of the wider currents circulating in the arts: the Renaissance (*Chapter 5*), Baroque (*Chapter 6*) and Rococo styles were followed by Neo-classical forms (*Chapter 7*). During the nineteenth century, the growth of commerce saw a premium placed on novel historical or exotic styles, first in type and then across printed forms as a whole (*Chapter 8*).

Industrialization and the profusion of manufactured items that followed led some designers to look back at pre-industrial traditions of art and craft (*Chapter 9*). Towards the end of the century, a new influence from Japanese art combined with organic, curvilinear forms to create Art Nouveau, a style that spread throughout

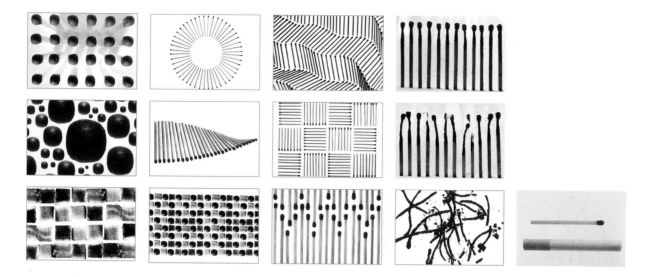

the decorative arts (*Chapter 10*) and to architecture. By contrast, the simplicity and directness that characterized a new kind of poster design during the first decades of the twentieth century was also applied to a range of designs dedicated to protecting both civilians and combatants during the First World War (*Chapter 11*). Leading up to the war and during the subsequent period of peace, numerous challenges to accepted artistic traditions were made by a series of art movements which later gathered under the banner of Modernism (*Chapter 12*). Especially influential for graphic design was a minimal and orderly style of Modernist design developed in the Bauhaus art school (*Chapter 13*). The style's abstract asymmetry contrasted with a strong preference for traditional styles of typography among the successors to the Arts and Crafts (*Chapter 14*). Following the Second World War, the growth in economic prosperity saw some of Modernism's methods and mannerisms applied to commercial ends which, through the use of photography in particular, gave them a popular appeal (*Chapter 15*). This paved the way for a rational mode of Modernist graphic design to be adopted as an international style (*Chapter 16*) serving the expanding needs of multinational corporations. The social revolution of the 1960s was expressed in an entirely opposite way; irrational or mystical forms were created by artist designers for the followers of a youth-based counterculture (*Chapter 17*). The influential Punk movement acted similarly a decade later (*Chapter 18*), though it was on a smaller scale and fuelled more by nihilism than expressions of peace and love. The vogue for rule-breaking led some designers to embrace complexity. This vision of Postmodernism (*Chapter 19*) seemed to

prefigure the novel digital forms that were made possible by the introduction of computers into graphic design during the mid-1980s (*Chapter 20*). From the 1990s onwards, new screen-based technologies combined with the connective power of the Internet, signaling a radical decline in the status of print. Both developments have pushed graphic design into a new, more egalitarian, uncertain and complex phase in its evolution (*Postscript*).

The complexity inherent in graphic design makes it interesting both as a practice and as a subject of study. But this complexity is not limited to the varied kinds of communication or the reproductive processes involved. Much of what makes it so fascinating, and difficult to do well indeed, comes down to the sheer range of possibilities that exist within any kind of visual representation. One of the most succinct demonstrations of just how extensive this range can be was provided by the British design company Pentagram in 1967 when they created a series of pictorial variations on the single theme of a match *(fig.i.2)*. The variations began with a photograph of several kinds of matches. One was then selected and shown at various sizes, with varied spatial dimensions, from various angles, in varying quantities, with different kinds of reproduction techniques, in different patterns, in a series of burning or broken arrangements, and then finally alongside its common adjunct, a cigarette. The caption to this last image reads: 'If we add another object we are again at the beginning'. The image represents a new beginning, and its appearance here alludes to the series of new beginnings that form the story set out in the following pages.

1 DESIGN AND SIGN

The Origin of the Alphabet, c. 34,000–1,100 BC

'He would not admit "civilization", but only "civility". With great deference to him I thought "civilization", from to "civilize", better ....' This mild and respectful complaint was written by James Boswell, the companion and biographer of the self-styled 'harmless drudge' Samuel Johnson, who during the middle years of the eighteenth century compiled the first authoritative English dictionary. Johnson did include 'civilization' in his dictionary, but only with a now archaic legal definition. When historians of early human societies use the word they, like Johnson, choose to ignore Boswell. Their definition of a civilization has nothing to do with whether the people concerned were well-behaved or not. For the historian, the hallmarks of a civilization lie in a community's size and social complexity. And a good guide to the existence of each is that the community had started to use writing.

Writing acts as a magnet. It generates a force of mutual attraction that binds the trader and the buyer, the priest and the layman, the master and the pupil in an ever-expanding mass. When early humans first made the transition from a life among scattered farming villages into larger and more socially complex groups, they usually did so around the same time that they started to write. This is not to say that the word 'civilization' can only be applied to communities in which writing took place. (It appears that the ancient inhabitants of the Norte Chico region in north-central Peru didn't write, yet few would deny them the title, not least because of their monumental architecture.) Whatever the case, it is rare for large and complex communities to remain free of writing's influence for long.

Today, writing can be found on almost anything; on roads and clothes, cars and buildings, as well as the succession of printed things that pass through our hands daily: newspapers, magazines, books, tickets, menus and the like. The written word connects us to others remote in time, the span of which can be measured in millennia; and then remote in space too, across distances that now extend right round the earth and beyond, out into the solar system. The modern world is wholly dependent on the series of little black marks that fleck the page or screen. Indeed, their influence on the way we think and feel is such that many people consider writing to be, if not the beating heart of a civilization, then, at least, its most resonant voice.

This visible voice is a uniquely human method of communication. No other animal passes on information or expresses emotion through a system of complex mark making. One species that has come close, in that it communicates through a system of visual signals, is bees. In certain instances, they use a patterned form of dance to 'talk' to each other. But what their dance doesn't do is give their communication any degree of permanence. This quality may be writing's greatest gift. The French eighteenth-century writer Voltaire alluded to it when he called writing 'the painting of the voice'. When reading writing, we do not have to rely on a single moment of interaction, as we do when hearing speech or, indeed, when seeing any of the other visible forms of human expression, such as a smile or a hand signal. Once writing has been put down on a durable surface, it can be read and reread over and over again. It becomes a kind of handmade time-machine, enabling the past to be preserved for the present, and the present for the future.

As well as preserving the past, writing provides us with some of the building blocks for our future expression. Initially, writing was used to represent parts of speech, or at the very least, it recorded information in a way that could be vocalized. But the more people wrote and read, the more they began to look on writing as distinct from speaking. They saw that writing had begun to find a voice of its own. Today, English speakers need only look at the early translations of the Bible or the writings of Shakespeare to see how the call and echo of literature has had as much impact on the way we speak as speech has had on our writing: a law unto themselves, a multitude of sins, at his wits end, bite the dust, born again, by the skin of your teeth, fall from grace, flesh and blood, give up the ghost, no rest for the wicked, scapegoat, sour grapes, etc., (King James Bible); a charmed life, a foregone conclusion, a sea change, a sorry sight, all corners of the world, love is blind, make your hair stand on end, the long and short of it, set your teeth on edge, vanish into thin air, wear your heart on your sleeve, wild goose chase, your heart's content, etc., (Shakespeare). We habitually pepper our conversation with a series of stock phrases or expressions that were first formed in writing.

Lurking behind both forms of expression, of writing and speech, is the shadowy but commanding presence of language itself. Without our facility for language we would be unable to write, nor could we think what to say. In this sense, what we write and speak is largely determined by how our language is structured. Unfortunately, language in all its aspects, from how we acquire it to how we express it, is so acutely subtle and complex that a complete understanding of its structure has eluded even the most able linguists and philosophers. From Plato in ancient Greece to the Viennese-born philosopher Ludwig Wittgenstein of the last century, thinkers of all ages have struggled to describe it accurately; and yet, almost magically, each one of us, with only very few exceptions, manages to learn the core of our mother tongue before we are five years old.

Some linguists have described this ability as existing in the form of an innate 'grammar'. Not the pedantic kind of grammar that tells us not to split an infinitive, but a more fundamental ability by which each of us is able to comprehend and create complex verbal relationships without any formal teaching. It is the cement that binds our spoken and written languages alike, and represents a part of our 'language instinct'. The actual act of writing, of making a particular letter shape, is obviously not instinctive in quite the same way – we all need to be taught how to do it – nonetheless, it certainly feels like second nature once we have mastered the skill. With a little practice, the 'how' of writing soon seems to take care of itself and we are free to concentrate on the 'what', the burden of our message.

To a literate person, communicating with visual symbols appears to be as natural as wings are to a bird, or fins to a fish ('as easy as ABC'), but when viewed over the incomprehensibly vast stretch of mankind's history, the invention of writing is a comparatively recent development – a drop in the ocean of time. Our early ancestors began to walk on two feet around six million years ago, while anatomically modern humans, modern *Homo sapiens*, appeared only 200,000 years ago, and we have only been writing in the last five-and-a-half thousand years. A better idea of this vast span of evolutionary history can be gauged if the time is condensed into a shorter period of, say, a year. Accordingly, our early ancestors would have appeared as modern *Homo sapiens* right at the end of the year, sometime around the third week of December, and we would have seen them invent writing only on the evening of the last day of the year. Moreover, writing would have only become commonplace during the last quarter of an hour.

Though writing is a relatively new human skill it has quickly become essential to our way of life. The importance we place on being able to give our communication a degree of permanence produced the very earliest forms of picture making, an activity from which writing is ultimately derived. The most dramatic examples of this early kind of information storage come from the prehistoric art of cave painting.

Among the numerous examples of painting found in subterranean caves in western Europe, perhaps the best known are those from the caves of Lascaux, in southwestern France, which have been dated to between 18,000 and 10,000 BC (<*fig.1.1*). When they were first discovered, in 1940, archaeologists did not believe them to be so old. But we now know that they are, in fact, relatively recent examples of a global explosion of human creativity that occurred between 40,000 and 10,000 BC. As well as cave paintings, other forms of art from this time, such as small figures of clay (usually female) and decorated objects (often weapons or tools) (*fig.1.2*) have been found. The origins of all these examples of prehistoric art are obscured by their having been made so very long ago, but while we may never know exactly when they were made, or by whom, we can be more certain about their status as works of art. Many display real skill and craftsmanship. Some of the paintings in Lascaux are delineated so boldly and fleshed out with such carefully modulated tones they clearly represent a highly developed style. Indeed, the Spanish painter Pablo Picasso (1881–1973), after catching first sight of them a year after their discovery, is reported to have exclaimed in awe, 'We have learnt nothing …'.

1.2: Decorated antler pin or spatula, Dordogne, France, c.38,000–24,000BC

In spite of their obvious beauty, it is not clear exactly why they were made. Whether the hunters of the Stone Age were acting on the simple impulse to make pictures for their own sake – that is, to make art – or whether the images of bison and deer were meant to conjure mystical powers over the prey they represented (which seems likely from what we know of later examples of tribal art), we cannot say for sure. Nevertheless, there they are, thousands of years later, a record of human thought as solid as the stone on which they appear. How strange and wonderful to know that we can stand where our ancient ancestors once stood and recognize, if only in a vague way, what must have passed through their minds as they made them.

From our own modern scientific and secular outlook, the superstition that may have guided Stone Age people in making their paintings might appear primitive, but when confronted with a potent image, modern humans are hardly paragons of rationality. Few of us could deface a favoured photograph of someone we loved without, at the very least, a pang of hesitation, despite our knowing the difference between a picture and a person. Investing images with our emotions in this way is hard to avoid. We may be able to see through the false promises of a fashion advertisement, yet it remains difficult for us not to succumb, at least on some level, to its seductive power. As much as we might like to resist, images of young, attractive people in sports cars do make us associate youth and attractiveness with these sorts of vehicles. This enormous potential for pictures to arouse our emotions is also exploited by the news media. How different our response to 9/11 might have been had New York been covered in low cloud, rather than exposed to view under a bright blue sky. The scale of the tragedy would have been the same, but without any clear pictorial input, our response to it would have been different. This is not to suggest that our own beliefs and those of Stone Age people are one and the same. What these examples do show, though, is that the differences between us are sometimes a matter of degree, not of kind. All of us are prey to the power of a potent image.

The simple methods used by our early ancestors to turn coloured earth and charcoal into vividly recognizable images on stone, solved one problem only to create another. Cave paintings managed to free language from the single moment of interaction that limited speech. But in doing so they bound language to the physical limitations of the picture surface. Cave paintings on stone walls are fixed in one place and, whether to escape from predators or from the cold, such places are often deeply inaccessible. They may be permanent, but they are hardly portable.

The material that gave Stone Age man his name also presented him with other difficulties in the task of communication. In addition to painting on it, marking stone by carving it with another stone (the metal tools of the Bronze Age were at least 8,000 years away) would not have been easy. It would have required intensive labour by a skilled hand with specific tools at the ready. The need for a more adaptable method of communication would have increased when, after the invention of farming and metallurgy, more settled and socially complex communities had begun to be established. Each of the earliest examples of writing was an attempt to meet this need.

The oldest civilization known to us appeared around the middle of the fourth millennium BC in the historical region called Sumer in the southernmost part of the larger historical region of Mesopotamia (Greek for 'land between the rivers'), which is now a part of modern Iraq. Sumer occupied a 1,000-km (600-mile) stretch of fertile land cradled between the dominating river valleys of the Euphrates and the Tigris. This rich and productive terrain lay at one end of a region often referred to as the 'Fertile Crescent', which arched westwards from Iraq, across southern Turkey, Syria and Lebanon, and down the coast of the Mediterranean Sea

1.3: Incised pottery cup, Ninevite 5, Iraq, c.2750–2500BC

1.4: Clay token, Iran, c.8000–3000BC

to Egypt. While the physical shape of the Middle East's land masses was much as it is today, the climate was markedly different and, hence, so was the vegetation. As indicated by its name, the Fertile Crescent was greener and the ground less dry. Years of flooding around the two great Mesopotamian river systems are thought to have produced a soil fertile enough for a relatively stable surplus of crops to be grown and traded. This, in turn, contributed to the transformation of an agrarian life among scattered villages into an urban life among settled towns.

Some indication of this transformation may be found in Mesopotamian pottery *(fig. 1.3)*. The features that make this example of grey, incised pottery less beautiful than much that preceded it – its regular pattern, shape and colour – suggest a degree of mass production. From this a number of inferences may be made: that technology had advanced far enough for complex tools, such as a potter's wheel, to be used; that the level of social cohesion allowed for some kind of regular workforce; that this workforce possessed the requisite level of skills to make and decorate the pots; that enough people had the means to trade the pottery; and that there was an ability to administer the whole process of production and distribution. There is a point at which the sheer mass of any production cannot be administered without a reliable method of recording information. Quantities of raw materials, items produced and sold, credits and debts, and a clear mark of ownership or provenance, all such particulars need to be accounted for. It was to these ends that the Mesopotamians turned to their most plentiful resource, the very ground on which they stood: clay.

From as far back as 8000BC coin-sized clay tokens etched with simple lines had been used in Sumer and other parts of the Middle East as a kind of counting stone or receipt *(fig. 1.4)*. The tokens' shapes and markings were simple enough to be duplicated but distinct enough to be recognizable. Each combination of shape and markings related to an amount of a particular commodity, usually one of something (such as one sheep or one flock of sheep). Quantities greater than one would be represented by the requisite number of tokens.

By about 4000BC some tokens began to be encased in clay 'envelopes' called *bullae (fig. 1.5)* ('bulletin' is derived from this word). Most of these hard, hollow balls of mud were then marked with a seal of ownership, though in some instances the markings gave a description of the contents. It is presumed that sealing the tokens and then labelling the contents was a way of archiving a transaction, but this apparently benign step is thought to have led to the tokens' extinction. By recording the contents graphically the tokens became redundant. The marks on the outside rather than the tokens on the inside could be used as a record for the initial transaction.

There is speculation that these new markings on the outside of the *bullae* then developed into, or at least influenced, a more graphically advanced set of impressions that began to be scratched onto larger flat blocks of clay *(fig. 1.6)*. The example shown here, which is believed to be from between 3100 and 3000BC, has been cut so as to fit in the hand, and then its surface has been divided into rows, before being etched with a series of numerical records, each of which is separated by vertical dividing lines. The shapes used to make up

1.5: Clay bullae, Iran, c.3300BC

1.6: Clay tablet, Iraq, c.3100–3000BC

these numerical records fall into two groups: punched circular or crescent-shaped numerals, and incised symbols of the items being counted. It is possible to pick out several instances of a beer symbol (beer was a popular drink at the time) which was made from a schematic depiction of an upright jar with a pointed base. Its inverted triangle shape is just one of at least 1500 pictographs or symbols that had been developed by this time.

Sumerian proto-writing was essentially a kind of picture-writing in which the characters were simple pictures of objects such as animals, tools or parts of the body. It is known, therefore, as 'pictographic' writing. All pictographic writing tends to mature into or be joined by another form called 'ideographic' writing (from the Greek word *idea* meaning 'notion' or 'pattern'), in which the range of meaning often extends from pictures of things to the ideas associated with them. The picture of a crying eye with a tear, for example, has commonly been used to represent the idea of 'sadness'. Both these kinds of writing are joined by, as well as subsumed into, a third category called 'logographic' writing (from the Greek *logos* meaning 'word'), in which characters are used to represent the words of a language. Some of these words are the important in-between words that don't relate directly to things or concepts, but most logographic characters are pictographs or ideographs.

Though Sumerian proto-writing is more simplified and schematized than the images that Stone Age people painted on the walls of their caves, there are some clear similarities. Both show simple objects delineated by dominating outlines. This similarity is not merely coincidental; both forms share a common function. The

task of each was to depict something in general, rather than any particular instance of a thing. The example mentioned earlier of the crying eye is not meant to be one person's representation of a particular eye at the particular moment that a tear fell. It stands for any crying eye and, by association, sorrow in general. Likewise, if we accept the credible hypothesis that cave art had some kind of magical function, the images on the cave walls were not meant to be eye-witness accounts of animals as they gambolled across the open plain, but rather symbolic representations of the kinds of animals that were perhaps the focus of a magical ritual. In order to be read as such, they needed to be both clear and iconic. Each of them proves that the true test of any image is not how faithfully it represents the world we see around us, but how well it performs a particular task within a particular context.

By around 2500BC the range of Sumerian marks had coalesced into a homogeneous size, style and set of shapes – in short, a true script *(>fig. 1.7)*. The script is known as 'cuneiform', from the Latin for 'wedge-shape', since each of its characters (a catch-all term for any of the symbols, be they pictures, letters or punctuation, that make up a script) is formed out of a cluster of wedge-shaped indentations pressed into the clay by a sharp edge which had been cut at one end of a stylus usually made out of reed. The angles of the indentations were standardized according to what was easiest for writing with the right hand: most pointed down or to the right, none pointed up or to the left. It lent the cuneiform script an angular, geometric quality, which combined with the soft, pliable clay to produce some tablets of

1.7: Clay cuneiform tablet, Iraq, c.2351–2342BC

great decorative richness and verve. Though the direction in which cuneiform was written underwent several changes, in this example it is written in short columns of horizontal lines from left to right, like the text in a newspaper. Though clay was its natural medium, cuneiform was also carved into stone or inscribed on metal, ivory, glass or wax, or even written in ink, though the last of these seems to have been rare.

Cuneiform's method of mark-making was straightforward and adaptable enough for it to be adopted by neighbouring peoples such as the Babylonians, Assyrians, the Akkadians, from northern Mesopotamia, and the Hittites. All were able to bring their own and, in some cases, quite different languages to it without having to change the script's essential character. What also contributed to the script being so adaptable to so many different languages was the development of a

phonetic component. At the same time as the characters were being abstracted away from recognizable pictures into stylized wedge shapes, so they moved from being tied to a particular object or idea to being tied to a particular sound.

The idea that helped to bring about this important phonetic transformation was the rebus principle. It allowed the same character to be used for words that sounded the same but had different meanings – so called homophones. An example of it applied to English would be, say, the pictograph of an eye, a can, the sea and a ewe, to write the sentence 'I can see you'. Today rebuses appear only in children's word games or as one of the graphic designer's methods of visual punning *(>fig.15.21, p.233)*, but around 3700BC, at the very beginning of Sumerian writing, the rebus played a key part in the development of complete writing. The increased application of this and other kinds of phonetic elements to the Sumerians, very homophonous language culminated *c.*2500BC in a uniform cuneiform script made almost entirely out of sound units.

Over cuneiform's near 3000-year-long history, which is longer than the history of our own Latin alphabet, the script is known to have served as many as 14 different languages. In doing so it helped to sustain the largest and most culturally diverse empire of the pre-Christian era, the Persian Empire. Its widespread adoption across the region caused the phonetic principle to spread both eastwards to the Indus and westwards to the Nile, where it was picked up by other emerging civilizations. It is even possible that the principle travelled much further afield, perhaps even as far as China and Central America, in which case we might be able to say that all of the world's writing systems were derived from a single original idea – the Sumerians' phonetic writing.

While it is easy to commend cuneiform for its usefulness, or its wicker-like beauty, we have to be more circumspect when crowning it with the title of the world's first writing. Not only is the material evidence difficult to date (it is harder to date something that has had its shape changed, as with carvings on rock or impressions made in clay, rather than something added to it, as with ink on parchment) but also, pinning down the point at which a group of symbols turned from being proto-writing used to supplement speech, to becoming complete writing used independently of speech, is not easy. None of man's early history can be plotted by a series of definite starting points. Like all other instances of early human activity, the first examples of writing can be taken only as indications of a process, parts of an evolving trend. Such examples have taken place in a number of different regions either via a common source or perhaps wholly independently.

Some palaeographers (from the Greek *palaeo,* 'old', and *graphe,* 'writing') are satisfied that by *c.*3700BC the pre-cuneiform proto-writing had evolved sufficiently for it to be accepted as complete writing, while others argue that recently dated Egyptian hieroglyphs from *c.*3400BC are more certain examples of the first writing. Evidence of scripts has also been found in the Indus valley (in what is now Pakistan, *c.*2600BC), Crete (*c.*1900BC), China (*c.*1400BC) and Central America (*c.*1100BC). While each of these dates is couched in uncertainties, what does seem likely is that it was in Mesopotamia that the seeds of writing were first sown.

If longevity is a guide to how successfully an image fulfilled the task assigned to it, few images have been as successful as the set of images that came from the only great civilization to rival Mesopotamia in scale and complexity. It too had to put down roots on the banks of a vast river, the river Nile, which stretches from central Africa northwards some 4000 miles, nearly twice the breadth of the United States, to the shores of the Mediterranean. Such a gargantuan flow provided the ancient Egyptians with a more dependable supply of water within a more uniform landscape than the busy network of river systems in Mesopotamia afforded the Sumerians. This more benign environment contributed to a culture which, in all the history of art, is unsurpassed in the constancy and duration of a unique style of image making. From the first stone carvings at the start of the third millennium BC, an unbroken tradition survived the changing rule of 30 dynasties over a period of two-and-a-half thousand years. When we think of the number of different styles that have filled thick books on Western art of the twentieth century alone, the constancy of Egyptian art is an awesome achievement.

Because the Egyptians considered writing to be a gift of the gods, they called the set of symbols that made up their script 'god's words'. The Greeks referred to them, similarly, as *hierogluphiká,* meaning 'sacred carvings', though their description was inspired by having first found Egyptian hieroglyphs in ancient temples. The Egyptians developed their hieroglyphs from the set of forms established within their tradition of monumental or ceremonial art. This large stone slab *(>fig.1.8)* from the tomb of Prince Rehotep, who died around 2600BC, shows hieroglyphs carved with the same care as the seated figure of the prince. Their orderly placement is as much a part of their appeal as their simple form, and yet their beauty is very different to that of the Sumerians' cuneiform. Instead of relying on the patterning potential of a single wedge-shaped mark, the Egyptians used a range of shapes for their hieroglyphs: geometric ones, various lines and dots, as well as the iconic pictorial signs – kestrels, snakes, hands, ox heads and the like – that have since become emblematic of their civilization.

It is tempting to believe that the Egyptian scribes were guided by the practised hands of their Sumerian cousins, for we have no better way of explaining how hundreds of Egyptian hieroglyphs appeared fully formed around 3400BC. Despite its different appearance, Egyptian writing shares some similarities with

1.8: Relief slab, Egypt, c.2600BC

Sumerian writing. As well as logography and linearity (text written in lines), hieroglyphs also contain signs that follow the rebus principle. This and other aspects of phonetic writing were to have a powerful effect on the development of hieroglyphs. Shortly before 2000 BC the scope of the rebus principle began to be limited so that only the first consonant of a word was represented rather than the whole word. This new phonetic device, known as 'acrophony' (in Greek *acro* means 'uppermost' and *phonos* 'sound'), was applied to 24 or so consonantal hieroglyphs *(fig. 1.9)*. Of all Egypt's considerable cultural achievements this small group of letters may have been its greatest, for it was with them that the first instance of alphabetic writing took place.

This is not the same as saying this was the first alphabet. Because the hieroglyphs were restricted to signifying consonants, they were unable to map out all the sounds in the Egyptian language (the vowel sounds had to be guessed at by the context of the words). Moreover, in almost every instance this consonantal alphabet was used in conjunction with logographic hieroglyphs.

Combining two systems in this way is not as unusual as it might seem. No script is ever quite 'pure' in the sense of strictly adhering to a single system of writing. The (phonetic) alphabet we use to write English relies

on a range of ideographic (punctuation) marks and logographic (numerical, mathematical) symbols for it to be read easily. The higher the proportion of phonetic signs within a script, the easier it is to guess the pronunciation. Yet phonetic signs (or phonograms) have a fundamental limitation. Because they are tied to a particular language, they can only be understood by those people who speak that language. The letter 'I' in English can only be understood as the first person singular pronoun by an English speaker. A pictorial/ ideographic sign, such as an arrow marked on a road sign, say, is not tied to any language. A reader does not need to know what language the sign writer spoke in order to work out its meaning. Like other pictorial signs, their supralingual nature makes them an ideal form of communication within a multilingual group.

Symbols such as these do not constitute 'writing' as the term is usually understood because they do not belong to a set of forms that, together, could represent a spoken language. For logographic signs more generally, the range of things they can communicate is limited. For pictograms to approach any kind of completeness in a writing system, there have to be many of them, and therein lies a disadvantage of a picture/idea-based

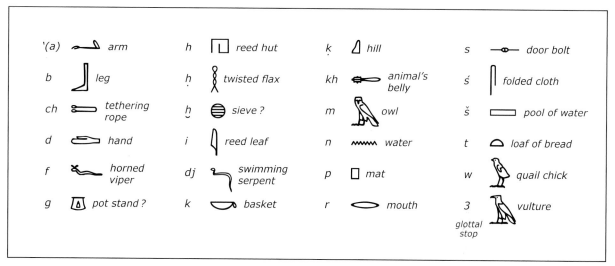

'(a)	arm	h	reed hut	ḳ	hill	s	door bolt
b	leg	ḥ	twisted flax	kh	animal's belly	ś	folded cloth
ch	tethering rope	ḫ	sieve ?	m	owl	š	pool of water
d	hand	i	reed leaf	n	water	t	loaf of bread
f	horned viper	dj	swimming serpent	p	mat	w	quail chick
g	pot stand ?	k	basket	r	mouth	3 glottal stop	vulture

1.9: Egyptian letters

(logographic) writing system. In Chinese, a knowledge of some 2000 characters is required for basic literacy, while the most complete Chinese dictionaries contain nearly 50,000 characters.

In spite of the large number of logographic hieroglyphs needed to write the Egyptian language, which even at its fewest numbered about 750, logographic writing dominated the Egyptians' writing system right up until the second century AD, when hieroglyphs began to be replaced by an alphabet based on Greek letters, called Coptic (>fig. 2.13, p.37). The logographic scripts were valuable not only for the way they fitted the Egyptians' language but also because they had embedded into their shape and meaning a great cultural richness. The enduring emphasis on tradition within Egyptian society may have blinded people to the full potential of its alphabetic writing, but there is speculation that the alphabet's potential was realized gradually through a whole sequence of influencing steps, from one script to another, which finally brought about some of the letters presented here on this page. Eleven of the letters in the modern Latin alphabet are thought to have Egyptian origins. The sounds may have changed significantly but some of the shapes have strong similarities, as a glance at some of the hieroglyphs underneath Prince Rehotep's table will attest. It is still possible to recognize in the eye shape (in line with his shoulder, and elsewhere) two of our current letters: 'O' (rounded) and 'M' (shortened). So, while the idea of complete writing itself may have been Sumerian, nearly half the letters of the Latin alphabet were derived from the Egyptians' alphabetic hieroglyphs.

As phoneticism was picked up by other scripts it was developed in three ways, each way corresponding to the main divisions of speech. The first, called 'syllabic' writing (known as a 'syllabary'), had each character representing a spoken syllable in-di-vi-du-al-ly. Though the syllable is not the smallest unit of speech, it is usually the most distinct, and this distinctiveness is likely to have prompted the Sumerians to develop their cuneiform in this direction. By about 2500BC, their script had become almost entirely phonographic or 'sound-based'. The Sumerians' syllabary comprised 100–150 different characters, which was not an unusually large number for this system of writing. Most syllabaries contain between 100 and 200 different characters. Today the Japanese *katakana* syllabary, for example, has 75 from which another 36 can be formed in combination.

The other two kinds of phonetic writing are both alphabetical, which is to say their characters, or letters (from the Greek word *elementum*), represent the smallest units of speech: either a single consonant or a single vowel. Alphabets generally require fewer characters than syllabaries, between 20 and 30 on average. The first kind of alphabetic writing, the Egyptians' consonantal alphabet, was rarely used on its own. The first example of a consonantal alphabet used singly was a kind of cuneiform script that appeared for a short period only, between 1450 and 1250BC, in the ancient port of Ugarit (now Ras Shamra on Syria's northern coast, opposite the island of Cyprus). It had the added distiction of being the first to include several vowel sounds, though they were never given equal status with the consonants, nor did they cater for every vowel sound in the Ugarits'

1.10: Red sandstone sphinx, Egypt, c.1800BC

Semitic language. Something of this consonantal bias is carried over into modern Semitic languages such as Arabic and Hebrew. As text messaging has proved, even nglsh cn b wrttn wtht vwls, thgh t s hrd t rd. (The word 'Semitic' here has a specific meaning well established by historians of language. It refers to a subgroup of Afro-Asiatic languages and scripts used by people who, the Bible says, are the descendants of Noah's son Shem. Semitic scripts therefore include a range of ancient and modern scripts from North Africa and the Middle East, such as Arabic, Aramaic, Ethiopic and Phoenician, as well as the ancient and modern forms of Hebrew.)

The second kind of phonetic system is an alphabet proper, sometimes called a full alphabet. It seems to have evolved from the consonantal form but, importantly, its vowel sounds were not subservient to the consonants. The full range of a language's sounds was represented graphically. This completeness has made it the most adaptable of the three phonetic scripts. Today the most prosperous member of the garrulous family of writing, the Latin alphabet, is a full alphabet.

It is thought that all alphabets in use today are linked to the Egyptians' consonantal alphabet through a Semitic source known as Proto-Sinaitic. The name refers to Egypt's Sinai peninsula, where the first few examples of the script were found. Though the script is thought to have been used there between 1800 and 1400BC, it originated north of the Sinai, in the historical region of Canaan, a strip of coastal land that covered much of modern Palestine, Israel and Lebanon. One of the best-known instances of the Proto-Sinaitic script is a set of crudely carved letters that appears on a small red sandstone sphinx from c.1800BC (fig.1.10). The shape of some of the letters, which are generally pictorial, are clearly adapted from Egyptian hieroglyphs and, indeed, they are accompanied by a few Egyptian hieroglyphs. The meaning of the script is not certain. Cuneiform and Cretan writing may have played some part in its creation, but because there are so few examples no clear judgement can be made. The general belief is that the script is an early consonantal alphabet, and if so it was the first that could be used as an independent system of writing.

1.11: Arrowhead, Phoenicia, c.1100BC

Similar kinds of pictorial, linear and consonantal writing were developed in Canaan during the millennium. Those that appeared before 1050 BC are referred to as Proto-Canaanite, while those that appeared after are known as Phoenician. It is around this time that a stable letter shape, a fixed sequence of letters and a single direction of writing was established. Moreover, as this bronze arrowhead shows *(fig.1.11)*, the pictorial quality of the Proto-Sinaitic letters had been replaced by an abstracted series of simple shapes, which for the first time approach the shape of our own letters. The inscription reads 'arrowhead of Ada, son of Ba'l'a' and the person who wrote it spoke a Semitic language and wrote the alphabet consonantally.

The Phoenician civilization that developed this northern Semitic writing derived its name from its success as a trading culture. *Phoinix* is Greek for 'purple', the colour of the expensive dye that the Phoenicians used to stain fabrics (it was secreted by a species of sea snail which then inhabited the waters of the Mediterranean). Their reputation as makers of tradable goods was rivalled by their reputation as sailors and colonizers. They established commercial centres throughout the eastern half of the Mediterranean, and even brought back tin from as far away as Britain. The organization required to trade and colonize successfully is likely to have been achieved through their simplified alphabet of 22 letters, considered to be the mother of all Western alphabets.

2 A CLASSICAL EDUCATION
Ancient Greece & Rome, c.2,000 BC– c.AD350

When the Phoenicians' fledgling alphabet made its way westward across the Mediterranean Sea to ancient Greece at the beginning of the first millennium BC, writing was already approaching the halfway stage in its 5500-year-long history. The alphabet's arrival in Greece coincided with, and contributed to, a period of dramatic change in the way life was lived throughout the Mediterranean region and many of its neighbouring territories. Of the cluster of eastern Mediterranean cultures that rose and fell during this period, it was the youngest of them, founded by the Greeks (or 'Hellenes' as they referred to themselves), that managed to break out beyond its immediate environment and establish its way of life in far-flung territories. At its greatest extent, c.323BC, the influence of Greek culture could be felt from the shores of southern Spain, across the Mediterranean basin and the whole breadth of the Middle East to the banks of the Indus, in what is now Pakistan. Though Greek control of these regions was often short-lived, the influence of its culture (a process referred to as 'Hellenization') was both enduring and wide-ranging. Over a 400-year period, from roughly 700 to 300BC, the Greeks laid the foundations for politics, philosophy, mathematics, poetry, drama, rhetoric and art on which Europe and much of the rest of the world were to build. The chief medium through which this cultural transmission was achieved was itself Greek in character. It was the first full alphabet.

This alphabet was not the earliest script in which the Greek language had been written. Perhaps even as early as 2000BC other non-alphabetic scripts had started to appear near the Greek mainland. Examples of a hieroglyphic script thought to have been used at around this time to write (Minoan) Greek have been found on the island of Crete. Its easterly location, like that of other early Greek scripts, suggests that contact with the Near East was important for the development of Greek writing, as indeed it was for Greek culture as a whole. Chief among the many littoral traders of the eastern Mediterranean, who diffused civilizing elements throughout the whole basin prior to the flowering of Greek culture, were the Phoenicians. It is possible that writing from the Phoenician city of Byblos inspired the Cretan hieroglyphic script via Cyprus. Both scripts used pictorial rebuses to stand for syllables in their languages.

The same system of writing is thought to have been used for the most notable and unusual of all the Aegean's early scripts: a spiral of symbols that were stamped onto both sides of a hand-sized disc of fired clay known as the Phaistos disc *(fig. 2.1)*. (Phaistos was the name of the ancient Cretan city where the disc was found.) The disc's 241 signs (or 242 – one of them has been obliterated), made with 45 different stamps, show Cretan hieroglyphs at their most elaborate and mysterious. Since the disc's discovery over a century ago, there has been no settled view on the meaning of its symbols, and indeed some even doubt the disc's authenticity. The sceptics point to the fact that no other examples of this stamped script have been found – it would be strange to establish a tool of mass production without ever mass producing – and that the shape of the disc's hieroglyphs are so singular. There is no close resemblance between them and other examples of Cretan writing. Apologists for the script claim that it is a consonantal alphabet of a Greek dialect, and that it spells out a text which starts from the right-hand side of the disc with the words 'Hear ye, Cretans and Danaans' before spiralling inwards. If the apologists are right and the script is authentic, then this circular document stands out as a singular landmark in the hazy terrain of early graphic design history. Though the disc is only made of clay, it would be the earliest example of printing with movable type (>p.70).

All the dates covered by the haze of early human history have to be qualified by phrases such as 'in and around' or 'circa', and those that mark the earliest moments of ancient Greek culture are no exception. However, with the arrival of the alphabet the haze begins to lift. One definite date stands out. In 776 BC a number of the 150 or so self-governing Greek city-states, then scattered along both shores of the Aegean Sea – the Greek to the east and the Turkish, as it is now, to the west – took part in the first Olympic games. (The event came to assume such significance that the Greeks chose it as the starting point for counting the years, much as those in the West have done with the birth of Christ.) A fundamental unifying force for those taking part was the language they shared. They all spoke Greek and had done so, albeit in a number of distinct dialects, for a long time. In addition to a common tongue, they had also begun to adopt a common method of writing.

During the early stages of the westward spread of alphabetic writing, a number of regional variations developed, though each is thought to have derived from a Phoenician source. The oldest known example of Greek letters appears around the shoulder of a now famous piece of pottery, the Dipylon jug of *c.*740 BC *(fig. 2.2)*, named after the area of ancient Athens known as the Dipylon gate, where the vessel was found. Its unbroken line of primitive letterforms are thought to be the first part of a two-line verse, and may be translated as 'whichever of the dancers now dances most lightly', suggesting that the jug might have been made as a prize. The shapes of the angular letters are similar to Phoenician letters (albeit a mirror image of them) and in reading from right to left they fit a Semitic convention that continues to this day. More telling of their Phoenician origins is that the names and the alphabetical sequence of the letters – *alpha, beta, gamma, delta ...* – are almost identical to those in the Phoenician alphabet – *aleph, bet, gimel, dalet ....*

We have seen how no single writing system can suit all languages. The relationship between the sounds of words and their meaning is just too varied. Nevertheless, no writing system has proved to be more adaptable than a full alphabet. The adaptation of the Phoenician alphabet by the Greeks is just one example among perhaps a hundred others. This Greek achievement involved two important acts of self-conscious planning and rationalization: the careful setting out of each of the main units of sound contained in the Greek language, and the assignment of a specific letter shape to each of these sounds. In spite of the fundamental difference between the sounds of the two

2.2: Dipylon jug, Athens, c.740BC

languages – Greek has strong Indo-European vowels (as English has), whereas the Phoenicians' Semitic language had vowels so weak they were barely marked in their alphabet – the task of fitting the Phoenicians' letters to Greek sounds was relatively straightforward. Those Phoenician letters that more or less matched the Greeks' own sounds could be taken over unchanged. Then some of the remaining Phoenician symbols were paired off with the exclusively Greek vowels. Last of all, the five remaining Greek sounds were attached to symbols from earlier Greek writing ('Υ' upsilon, 'Φ' phi, 'Χ' chi, 'Ψ' psi and 'Ω' omega). This Greek script was the very first instance of full, vowel-including, alphabetic writing. By 403 BC, a single variant of 24 letters, known as the Ionic alphabet (from a part of eastern Greece, then called Ionia, in what is now modern Turkey), was officially adopted as the standard Greek script, still used to this day. It is the world's oldest alphabet. The influence of the Greek alphabet spread far beyond the bounds of the Greek-speaking world. It was from two of its sub-branches, the Cyrillic and the Latin alphabets, that all modern Western writing developed.

With the advent of the Ionic alphabet, Greece did not suddenly become a nation of readers and writers. But, equally, literacy was no longer was the preserve of a small elite. To grasp the nature and extent of this rise in literacy, it is worth looking back at how writing was used in the first two great writing cultures of Mesopotamia and Egypt. At the beginning of the third millennium BC, only about one in 50 of the several thousand inhabitants in each of Mesopotamia's main cities were able to read and write. The rate of literacy in Egypt was even lower (though, as a consequence, literates were held in higher regard). In both civilizations most literates were professional scribes who had been handed the responsibility for administering the state by those in positions of superiority, be they priests, architects or kings, many of whom were themselves illiterate.

In both of these early civilizations, writing was used as a necessary adjunct for trade, civil administration, the law, and, to a varied extent, religion, but in every case it remained supplementary to the primary form of communication: word of mouth. The authority of the spoken word was paramount, and, indeed, writing was employed specifically to preserve that authority by being used as a means of recording speech. Thus, a Mesopotamian scribe's clay tablet was the medium for his (almost never her) master's message. Failure to write and then recite his master's voice faithfully was an offence punishable by law, so that a typical letter would start, 'To My Lord, say this ...' and end, '... thus speaks So-and so'. In so far as writing was used to pass one person's voice to another person's ear, its function was analogous to the telephone, a passive medium dedicated to extending the reach of the spoken word. Like the script of a play or a movie, words were written for speakers rather than silent readers.

The importance placed on who said what and when prompted Mesopotamian scribes to write in the last column of their text a colophon (this Greek word translates as 'finishing touch'), which comprised the title of the text – usually its first few words – followed by the scribe's own name, the date and then sometimes various other details such as the patron's name. A similar practice was also employed by Egyptian scribes, though in the case of a royal patron and other important

2.3: Egyptian scarab, c.1390–1352BC

individuals the scribe would often render the name in a form that could be seen as the forerunner of the publisher's logo (fig.2.3).

The forerunner of the stamped seal was the cylindrical seal, which was first developed in southern Mesopotamia around 3500BC, though during its 3200-year history it spread throughout the Near East. These 2.5cm (1in)-high carved cylinders of stone or fired clay were used for rolling out an impression onto clay (>fig.2.5) either in relief (a raised impression, as shown here) or hollow-relief (a sunken impression). As well as being used to verify the authenticity of a clay document, they were also used to mark ownership by being impressed onto small clay seals affixed to baskets, jars or storeroom doors. While the first seals were pictorial – mostly figurative depictions of kings, deities and animals – by the middle of the third millennium BC some illustrations began to be accompanied by text. The example shown here, which has been used to make a modern clay impression, includes a cuneiform text that spells out the name of the Mesopotamian scribe Adda, who owned the seal. The pointed hats with multiple horns on each of the figures show us that they are gods; the god of hunting (with a bow and arrow), of fertility and war (holding a cluster of dates and with weapons rising out of her wings), of the sun (with rays rising from his shoulders and slicing his way through the mountain to rise at dawn), of subterranean water and wisdom (with water and fish flowing from his shoulders) and a divine minister (with two faces, presumably a representation of solicitousness rather

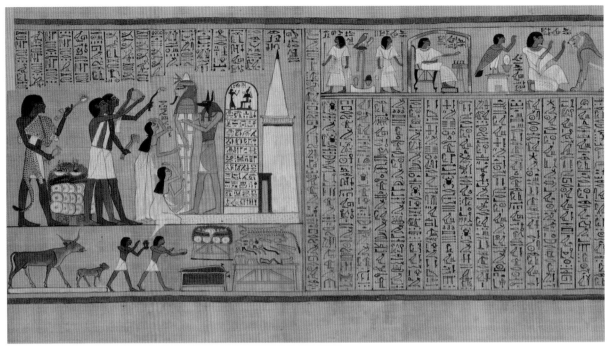

2.4: Book of the Dead, Egypt, c.1310BC

than insincerity). All these figures were carved into a valuable piece of green coloured rock which then had a hole put through it from top to bottom so that it could be carried around on a necklace. By being an essential part of a reproductive process of image making, albeit a very rudimentary one, such seals could be said to be the very first tools of graphic design.

The Egyptians also wore stamping seals as pendants, or else as rings on their fingers for impressing ink onto papyrus or for sealing scrolls rather than rolling on clay. The most emblematic shape of stamping seal was that of the dung beetle or scarab. This faeces-feeding creature had a special, sacred status in ancient Egypt. Its extended hemispherical shape was mimicked in the body of the seal, while its flat underside served as a surface on which to receive the carved imprint. The underside of the stone scarab shown (<fig.2.3) was carved between 1390 and 1352 BC. Its oval frame is filled with hieroglyphs for the Egyptian king Amenhotep III. A faint echo of its oval design can be seen thousands of years later in the logo of the publishers Penguin (>fig.14.19, p.216), whose hieroglyphic character, with its simple lines and a twisted head, is not entirely coincidental. The Penguin logo attempts to do what some of the animalistic hieroglyphs did: to show the parts of a creature at their most distinct. The webbed feet, two wings, rounded

body and beaked head of the penguin are combined to create an unnaturally disjointed creature, but not one that can be mistaken for any other kind of bird.

From the beginning of the second millennium BC, the scope of Egyptian texts was broadened to encompass more literary forms of writing rather than just administrative ones. The large number of hieroglyphs that had been used to record lists of funereal offerings or various religious decrees also began to describe events and tell stories. Funerary biographies became more than a series of names and dates, and by 1500 BC love poems were being written, as well as hymns, secular songs, myths and letters. One popular kind of literary form was the ubiquitous 'Book of the Dead' (fig.2.4), in which hymns and myths were included as spells to help a dead person pass through the underworld and be reborn into an afterlife. It was a kind of passport to eternity for the deceased. The lavishly illustrated version shown here was made for an important Egyptian official and scribe called Hunefer, who had lived with his wife Nasha around 1310 BC. The quality of the illustration reflects Hunefer's high status. As in other Egyptian papyri (the plural of papyrus) figures were used to illustrate the text. The scene in this example shows an important part of the Egyptians' funeral ritual called the 'Opening of the Mouth'. Hunefer's mummy is being

2.5: *Impression and cylinder of greenstone seal of Adda, Akkadia, c.2300BC*

2.6: *Scribal palette and brushes c.15,500–14,500BC*

2.7: *Quartzite statue, Egypt, c.750–712BC*

held up by a god, while three priests perform rituals on it in front of Hunefer's weeping wife and child.

Central to the development of all Egyptian writing, whether religious or literary, was the material on which it was written. Like the Mesopotamians with their abundance of clay, the Egyptians turned to a readily available raw material, the reed of the papyrus plant, which thrived in the marsh land of the Nile delta. Not long after the first hieroglyphs appeared *c.*3400BC, the Egyptians had devised a way of turning reeds into a lightweight and flexible writing surface. Strips were cut from the reed's stem, overlaid criss-cross fashion, beaten until they had fused through their own sap, dried and bleached in the sun, and finally polished with a pumice stone to produce a fine and smooth paper (the word 'paper' is derived from the Greek word *papyrus*). Usually 20 sheets were glued together to make a long strip, which could then be rolled into a scroll. After Egypt relinquished its hold on the production and export of papyrus, in the fourth century BC, the Greeks began to import it. In time, papyrus supplanted animal skins as the main writing medium, as it also did clay in the Near East.

As well as the Egyptians' writing material, the Greeks also adopted their writing implements. A red quartzite statue made in Egypt between 750 and 712BC *(fig.2.7)*, shows the classic pose of an Egyptian scribe: writing cross-legged with a partially unrolled scroll laid out on his lap. His high status is indicated by the two rolls of fat in his abdomen, an ancient sign of prosperity. The scribe would have written on the scroll either with a reed-pen stylus or else a brush made from the crushed or chewed end of a thin reed. Both implements would have been kept in a wooden palette *(fig.2.6)*. As shown above, many palettes had inkwells carved into them, mostly for the standard black ink that was made from a mixture of water, soot and gum arabic (the dried sap of the acacia tree), and a supplementary red ochre ink, which was used to highlight various bits of text such as titles and punctuation *(>fig.2.9)*. This standard form of palette was used as a badge of office so, as well as incising a shell-shaped inkwell container on the statue's left knee, the carver has also inscribed a hieroglyphic badge of two inkwells onto the statue's left shoulder.

The dominance of red as a second colour in Egyptian writing points to a pattern of dominance that has run through the whole history of printing and text reproduction. Stone-age cave painting shows mixed hues of reddish brown spread alongside charcoal black outlines. Ancient Egyptians favoured it on their papyri, as did successive generations of manuscript makers. Printers chose it as the standard accompaniment on their pages of black text, and groups of Modernist artists gave it a privileged position. Its early use was linked to its ready supply and ease of production. Clay tinted with ochre pigments can be found in soils around the world. It can be dug up, washed, dried and applied as paint, ink or dye. But there is more to our use of red than its availability. Like other primates, humans are genetically attracted to it. Glossy red lipstick is used as a sexual signal between humans in the same way that red heads, buttocks and skin are between the sexes of certain species of ape. But recent studies of primates have suggested that the origin of colour vision lies not in sex selection but foraging. The ability to pick out ripe fruit (which is more often red/orange than any other colour), gave those primates that had a relatively well developed sense of colour an evolutionary advantage over those that didn't. One can go further and speculate that the reason why fruit-eating animals were best able to pick out the colour red is because it stood out most against the surrounding green vegetation. It was thrown into relief by being the complementary colour of green. Red was the clearest signal of ripeness a fruit could give. And, importantly, the plants themselves benefited from having their fruit eaten because it led to a wider dispersal of their seeds. In this way fruiting plants and fruit-eating animals shared the evolutionary advantage that red brought to their symbiotic relationship. If this chain of hypothesis and speculation is correct then the most significant element in red being such a commanding colour for humans is the prevalence of its opposite colour, green. Ultimately, and curiously, it is chlorophyll, the green pigment in leaves and plants, that has influenced the red bias of so many graphic forms of design, be they the mastheads printed on newspapers and magazines or the texts written on ancient manuscripts.

The statue of the scribe above gives a clear indication of how the Egyptians wrote, but not what they wrote. After the fifth century AD exactly what they wrote became unknowable and remained so for the next 1400 years. The Roman annexation of Egypt in the first century AD strengthened the position of Greek as the language of officialdom, a position it had held for three centuries. Greek was chosen as an official language for the whole of the eastern half of the Roman empire. By the end of the third century Greek letters had been adapted to serve Egypt's vernacular language of Coptic (>fig. 2.13). Hieroglyphs were pushed to the margins of Egyptian society, finding refuge only in its ancient

2.8: The Rosetta Stone (detail)

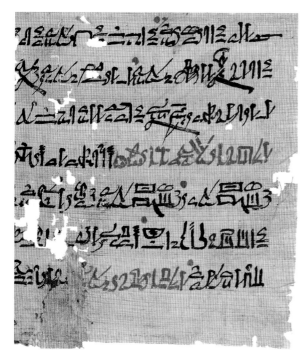

2.9: Hieratic script, c.1200–1194BC

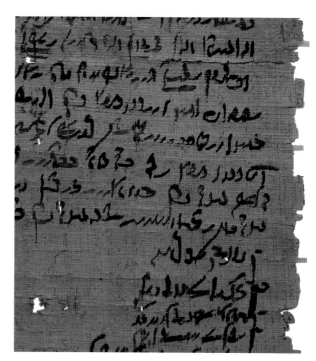

2.10: Demotic script, c.194BC

temples. By AD392, after Christianity had spread and non-Christian religions had suffered decades of persecution, the temples were forced either to adopt the new religion or close. With the demise of the Egyptians' religion, their 4000-year-old tradition of picture writing was lost to the world.

For successive generations of historians and palaeographers the Egyptians' hieroglyphs remained a fantastically compelling mystery. The hieroglyphs' pictorial allure led many people to try and decipher them, but most approached them as mystical symbols rather than the signs of a spoken language. It was only with the discovery of a remarkable, 1m (3ft) high fragment of dark grey, quartz-bearing stone (not basalt as had been thought) in a place known as Rosetta (today's el-Rashid) *(fig.2.8 & i.1)*, in the Nile delta, that the status of hieroglyphs could be firmly established, and the language and culture they represented brought back to life.

The Rosetta Stone has since become one of the most famous pieces of rock in the world. It was dug up by chance in 1799 by Napoleon Bonaparte's soldiers, during the French occupation of Egypt. Fortunately the officer who found it realized it was a significant artefact and immediately ensured its safe-keeping. What made it special was that it had the same bit

of text inscribed in three different scripts. The top section was written in formal hieroglyphs, which at the time they were carved, *c.*196BC had been the traditional script for stone inscriptions. The middle section was written in the everyday script of literate Egyptians, the informal 'demotic' hieroglyphs, and at the bottom was Egypt's then language of officialdom, Greek. When the initial shoulder-high slab of stone, or 'stela' (a decorated commemorative stone), had fallen from the temple wall, it broke in such a way that its bottom half included enough of the known Greek and the unknown Egyptian scripts for the correspondence between the scripts to be discovered. While parts of the surface were damaged, the bottom Greek script was able to provide some of the clues that eventually led the French scholar and philologist, Jean-François Champollion (1790–1832), to complete the hieroglyphs' decipherment in 1822. With the ancient language unlocked, a more informed study of Egyptian culture could begin.

The Rosetta Stone's two hieroglyphic scripts provide a vivid example of the tendency for all scripts to develop in two main directions, a formal script for ceremony or public display, and an informal one for everyday use. Writing is never solely utilitarian and commonplace, nor is it always beautiful and exclusive. Both sets of needs have to be served.

The first informal or 'cursive' hieroglyphic to be developed is called 'hieratic' (meaning 'priestly'). Its form was a response to the implements used and the surface it was written on. The fluid, linear and overtly handwritten shapes of hieratic were a natural consequence of ink flowing off the tip of the Egyptian scribes' pen or brush and onto the smooth sheets of papyrus. This example of a classic poem *(<fig. 2.9)*, which was made in around 1200 BC by a junior scribe called Inena, shows some of the vigour and intricacy of this cursive form. Where previously each hieroglyph would have stood out in splendid isolation, as in the 'Book of the Dead' *(<fig. 2.4)*, here many of the 'pictures' are run together, sometimes forming abbreviations or stark contractions of several symbols into smaller single shapes. The way the ink has been pushed and stroked across the papyrus suggests that Inena wrote quickly, though with enough control to set the series of complex word shapes and their dynamic swashes along a more or less even baseline (the imaginary line on which the writing appears to sit).

By using a red ink for headings and emphasis, or for the dots marking the ends of the lines of verse, Inena was following the conventions of the time; as he was by writing from right to left. The foundational form of writing, the inscribed hieroglyph, would have been easier to carve from the right when hammering with the right hand, and though this directional preference was less favourable for writing with ink on papyrus – smudging was likely when writing from the right with the right hand – it became the default direction for all kinds of Egyptian writing. (Most writing in North Africa and the Middle East continues to follow this right-to-left convention.) However, this directional preference was never a strong one. It could be ignored if doing so better served the needs of the overall design. On tombs and in illustrated papyri, hieroglyphs often appeared from left to right, or sometimes even in long vertical columns.

After nearly 2500 years of hieratic script, an ultra-cursive version, a sort of cursive cursive hieroglyph, became established as the everyday script *(<fig. 2.10)*. From the end of Egyptian dynastic rule, *c.*700 BC, this so-called 'demotic' (meaning 'in common use') script reduced the use of hieratic solely to the writing out of religious texts. The 'pictures' in the new demotic script were abstracted to the point of unrecognizability. They resemble the sort of writing that we might make if we were using similar writing materials. Though the formal hieroglyphs were replaced by other scripts for

2.11: Greek inscription, c.450BC

most uses, they remained the script for special texts, especially on illustrated and funerary papyri and those inscribed on stone.

Like the Egyptians, the Greeks also developed a cursive script from their formal inscriptional letters. By the middle of the fifth century BC Greek letters had evolved from being little more than graffiti, roughly scratched in short lines, to being carefully carved in longer chunks of text. The rise of Athenian democracy during the late sixth and early fifth centuries BC contributed to this development. It created the need for a series of decrees and treaties to be displayed publicly. Various laws or the terms of peace with a neighbouring city-state, say, were inscribed in marble blocks in a manner considered to be commensurate with the status of the message. (Athens was fortunate in having quarries of good-quality white marble close by, and there was enough of it to be used for inscriptions as well as sculptures and buildings.) Since most people could not read, the inscription was made to be seen as much as it was to be read. Its authority derived from its visual presence or style as much as its existence within an established system of legislature. This quest for a formal grandeur contributed to the development of an open and even layout called *stoichedon* (a military

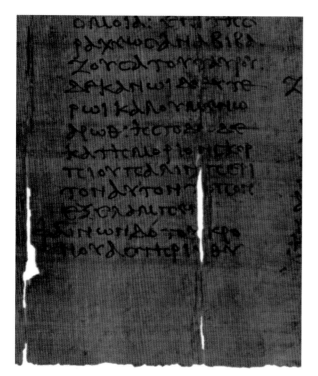

2.12: Greek uncial script, 450BC

2.13: Coptic writing on pottery, Egypt, 194BC

term meaning 'in files'), which required each letter to be arranged in a grid-like fashion, aligned vertically into columns as well as in horizontal rows.

Something of the geometric simplicity and austere beauty of this method is captured in this marble decree *(fig. 2.11)* from around 450BC. In order to make sure that the text would fit onto the stone, the carver counted the total number of letters and then used a piece of chalk to mark the position of each letter with a simple grid of horizontal and vertical lines. The grid also enabled the carver to meet the commercial imperative of speed, as indeed, did the simplicity and uniform thickness of the letter strokes. Simple lines and a definite placement allowed him to carve quickly.

The letters' regularly spaced pattern shows inscribed Greek capitals at their most characteristic. It is an arrangement that was partially echoed in more modern times by the even spaced lines of typewriter text *(>fig. 13.9, p.196)*. By being made with keys of equal width, its letters are also aligned vertically and horizontally. The difference between these two examples of 'mono-spaced' letters, though, is that the carving presents us with a continuous stream of letters uninterrupted by word spaces. Nor is this sequence of glyphs (linguistic symbols or carved shapes) flecked with punctuation marks. Some Greek stone inscriptions

do have small dots carved between words, or else small dashes called *paragraphoi* indicating a break in the sense of the writing, but, for the most part, ancient Greek texts offer a sparse and regular array of pure letterforms unmediated by spaces or markings. It is a condition rooted in their use; a visual record of an oral message which was meant to be read out loud.

A Greek orator was trained to work out where each word should start and finish during the act of speaking them. His ear would gauge the most likely sequence of words and, with practice, formulate his preferred phrasing and emphasis. Far be it for the scribe to impose his own interpretation on the correct phrasing for a piece of text. It was not within his remit to introduce unspoken matter into the text. Punctuation and capitalization are not vocalized parts of speech. Nor, indeed, are word spaces. A sentence is rarely spoken as a staccato series of words, like the kind we recite when learning a foreign language. Usually it is an uninterrupted flow of sound. Or, to put it another way: wenormallyspeaksentencesofoneword.

From at least the third century BC, the Greeks developed a cursive form of capital letter. This so-called 'uncial' form of Greek letter – also referred to as the 'literary' or 'book' hand – evolved out of writing with ink on papyrus. Unfortunately, no manuscript from the

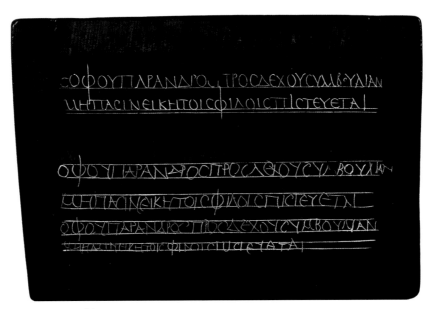

2.14: Wax tablet, AD2

Greek classical period (fifth and fourth centuries) has yet been found on Greek soil. Most of what we know of the physical appearance of Greek manuscripts has come from Egyptian sources, Greek being the language of Egyptian scholars and diplomats between the fourth and the seventh centuries AD. The preserving qualities of the Egyptian climate and the religious practice of sealing objects in tombs combined to ensure that some examples from this period survived. This Greek papyrus, from the fifth century BC *(<fig. 2.12)*, shows the Greek uncial in a single size and without word breaks. The direction of reading is from left to right, the opposite of most Egyptian and Mesopotamian texts. For a period the Greeks had even experimented with a quicker but more complicated *boustrophedon* (Greek for 'as the ox turns' in ploughing) method of alternating from right to left on one line to left to right on the next, but by *c.*350BC they appear to have settled on the left-to-right direction. The document itself is a copy of some notes that Aristotle, or perhaps one of his students, is thought to have made. The text gives an outline of the Athenian constitution, and as such it represents the first constitutional history of the first true democracy (provided we accept that the *demos,* i.e. the people that made up the Greek's *demokratia,* did not include women, slaves or immigrants).

Though Greek uncials developed into a more rounded, less formal, and highly cursive script, the distinction between straight and curved, or formal and informal, seems not to have been a hard and fast one.

The degree of formality or informality was as much a result of the wide range of writing implements and surfaces, such as papyrus, wax tablets or clay pottery, as of any predetermined status or design given to a piece of writing. Once bitten by the writing bug, humans have been compelled to scribble on most things. Beer mats, plaster casts and the backs of envelopes are some of the more unorthodox present-day items. Similarly, Greek letters were often jotted in ink on shards of stone or broken pottery *(<fig. 2.13)*, as other scripts seem to have been. (The Greek word for these broken fragments of writing is *ostracon,* plural *ostraca,* which has given us the word 'ostracize' in reference to the Athenian practice of using such items as voting slips when ridding the Assembly of an unwanted politician.)

Greek texts continued to serve the voice, but if one is to judge by the tone, the range and the depth of Greek writing, they also began to represent a true literature. The seeds of this flowering were contained in the first important works of Greek literature, the two books *The Iliad* and *The Odyssey* by Homer, *c.*700 BC. It is not certain that these books (which are in fact presumed to be early records of a long tradition of oral poetry) were the work of a single author, but they soon became standardized and accepted as an authoritative (albeit limited) history of Greece. Their status was such that generations of Greeks and, later, Romans, looked to them for moral guidance with a fervour and reverence more usually associated with sacred texts.

As works of history, however, they were eclipsed in the following century by the writing of Herodotus, the so-called 'Father of History', who wrote what has since been accepted as the first truly historical work in so far as it was both sufficiently empirical and analytical (the Greek word *historia* means 'inquiry'), rather than being narrative and mythological as its predecessors had been.

From *c.*400 BC the variety of genres expanded to include plays (tragedies and comedies), poems (epic, lyrical and choral) and epigrams, as well as much more substantial and rational works of history, rhetoric, literary criticism, philosophy, mathematics, astronomy and geography. At the end of the classical period, *c.*322 BC, when Greek became the official language of the Middle East, the influence of Greek literature spread wider still. It inspired the construction of the greatest shrine to writing in the ancient world, the Library of Alexandria, in Egypt. The library was built with the aim of housing the whole of Greek literature, and though this aim was never fulfilled, at its height the collection could boast around 500,000 papyrus scrolls.

Ancient Greece was not a literate society as such, or, at least, not as we would understand the term, but then neither was it a place where literacy remained the preserve of a small elite. By *c.*400 BC, the proportion of citizens in the larger city-states with some degree of literacy was perhaps as high as one in 20, and the social class of literates was diverse. Writing and reading were vocational skills. Literate slaves were used by their semi-literate masters so that the latter could involve themselves in a society that had become increasingly literate in character. Stories, plays and poetry would be recited and the written word also became a more conspicuous part of everyday life. Greek letters were stamped onto coins or inscribed on pottery, and by the second century BC many cities had stone monuments adorned with carved letters. The principal medium for ephemeral writing was the wax tablet or *tabula* (*fig.* 2.14). Wooden boards inlaid with a coating of beeswax, which could be wiped clear and reused, are also known to have been used by the ancient Assyrians and Egyptians. For each of these civilizations, the wax tablet was especially important in schools, for it was on such items that the young learnt the art of writing itself.

The word 'alphabet' is a story told in miniature: a Roman description of a Greek invention that had Phoenician origins. The word's Latin root, *alphabetum*, was derived from the first two letters of the Greek

2.15: *Etruscan alphabet on cockerel vase, 7th century BC*

alphabet, *alpha* and *beta*, which themselves had come from the Phoenician *aleph* and *beth*. This instance of the Roman adoption of a Greek invention was just one of the varied ways in which Romans lived their lives according to Greek example. The Roman conquest of Greece and its colonial territories by *c.*AD 100 only accelerated a process of cultural adoption (described by the trope 'Greece conquered, led Rome captive') that was already three centuries old. Greek remained the *lingua franca* in Rome's eastern provinces and all educated Romans were expected to be bilingual. They were schooled in the Greek classics and such books set the standards to which all Roman writers aspired.

The stamp of Greek cultural life on Rome was not total. Within the bounds of its empire, Rome managed to impress its own brand of culture on the lives of the people it governed. Whereas the Greeks' achievements had been predominantly conceptual and artistic, the Romans' were more practical and structural. The empire itself, perhaps Rome's greatest contribution to civilization, was underpinned by a developed legal system and methodical planning, both of which expressed something of the very Roman quality of sturdy vigour. At its height *c.*AD 117, Rome's empire encompassed nearly the whole of Europe west of the Rhine and south of the Danube, as well as Turkey, the north of Arabia, all the Middle East and the whole of Africa's Mediterranean coast. Moreover the empire became the cradle of Christianity, a world view that infused much of what was considered to be culturally valuable in Europe over the next 1500 years. In art the Romans more than matched the example of their mentors in portraiture, architecture and lettering, the last of which was used to adorn their grandest buildings. Constructions such as the Colosseum, Hadrian's Wall in Britain, and France's Pont-du-Gard aqueduct are impressively large, but there was much more to Roman building than sheer bulk. These examples are also admirably complex feats of structural engineering.

Within the art of writing Greek influence on Rome was absolute but indirect. During the eighth century BC, an early form of Greek alphabet from western Greece, known as Euboean, was adopted by the Etruscans, a culturally distinct group that earlier had settled in and dominated the region north of Rome. The Romans may have been introduced to their neighbours' alphabet (<*fig. 2.15*) after a period of Etruscan rule towards the end of the seventh century BC. They adopted 21 of the 26 Etruscan letters (as well as the Etruscan names *stylus,* for the writing implement, and *elementum,* for their letters). Early Roman writing looked similar to contemporary Etruscan writing; both were made with capitals scratched in crude diagonal lines. A period of adoption and adaption was needed for the Romans to establish some kind of standard shape and proportion, but by the first century BC, nearly every letter had acquired its own distinct form and sound, and by the fourth century AD, a canonical order of 23 Latin letters existed, all of which we can recognize today.

Three letters are notable by their absence, J, U and W. All of them were later additions: J only began to gain common acceptance as a variant of I in the seventeenth century, U was first used as a letter distinct from V in the sixteenth century, and W was introduced after the Norman conquest of Britain in the eleventh century. The letters K, Y and Z appear so seldom in Roman texts that one could be forgiven for assuming they too were among this list of absentees, but all were in fact part of the Roman alphabet. K was used for spelling some archaic words, and both Y and Z were adopted from the Greek alphabet for spelling Greek words.

Like the Greeks and Egyptians before them, the Romans established several styles of script. They

2.16: Trajan's Column, Rome, c.AD113

developed formal and cursive scripts, though within these two categories there were several subdivisions. This greater diversity partly reflects the large variety of Roman writing materials and methods – metal-tipped quills (called *pennae*) and broad-edged lettering brushes, both invented in Rome, were added to the range of inherited implements – and also the greater variety of uses Roman writing was put to. Letters appeared on wax tablets, papyrus, parchment, metal coins, stone walls, wooden boards and leather booklets.

The most visible and enduring examples of Roman lettering, however, were those that appeared on stone buildings and monuments. Such structures were built to impress on the empire's citizens the power and glory past emperors had brought the republic. One important monument was Trajan's Column *(fig. 2.16)*, which was built between AD106 and AD113 in the centre of Rome itself to celebrate Emperor Trajan's lucrative conquest of Dacia (in today's Romania). The design of the column, with its internal spiral staircase, its intricately carved depiction of the emperor's victory and its refined dedicatory inscription became a model for victory columns through the ages.

Roman lettering was also used to display the prestige and wealth of individuals in the privacy of their homes. Several famous examples appear in the partially preserved city of Pompeii, on the edge of

2.17: Square capitals, c.AD79

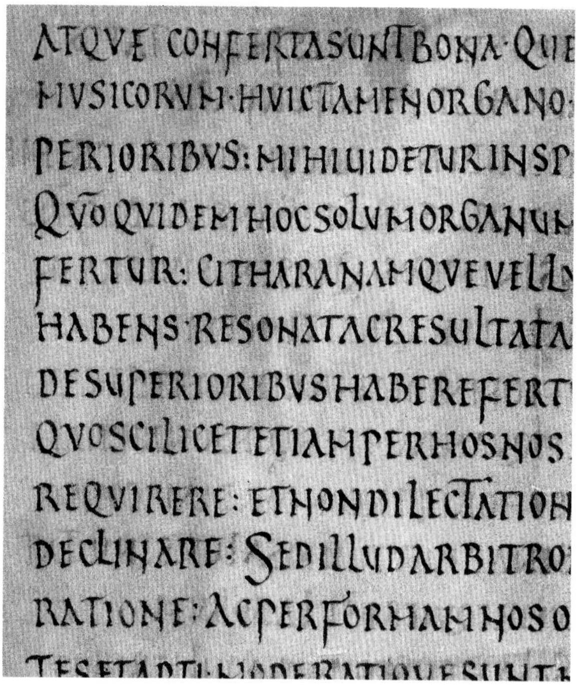

2.18: Rustic capitals, c.AD730

Naples. The entrances to a number of grand villas are adorned with intricately tiled mosaics of a barking dog, but in the most well-known example, the words 'Cave Canem' ('Beware of the Dog') have been included. Writing was also an important tool in commerce. Coins were stamped with letters giving the name of the portrait on one side and a dedication or mint mark or other short, often abbreviated, text on the other. More conspicuous than coins were the various hand-painted shop signs, 'for sale' signs, advertisements and public entertainment announcements, which were brushed onto walls in large capital letters (graffiti is a Latin word). Unfortunately, very few examples of this kind of public writing remain.

The wide range of materials and uses involved in Roman writing created a number of features which have since become fundamental to the appearance of the Latin alphabet: the carefully modulated thick-and-thin parts of letters; the pointed 'ticks' or serifs (from the Dutch word for 'stroke', *schreef*) that protrude from the ends of each stroke; and the establishment of the small-letter form. Each one of these developments came out of formal Roman writing, and specifically two kinds of formal capitals: square capitals *(fig. 2.17)* and rustic capitals *(fig. 2.18)*.

Square capitals, though never truly square, are the straighter and more static-looking of the two. It is likely

that they found their first form on soft materials, such as papyrus, but their appearance in Roman manuscripts was usually limited to titles, headings or initial letters. The example shown here is unusual for showing a full page of square capitals. But what makes this and other examples of square capitals strikingly different to any previous writing – be it Sumerian, Egyptian or Greek – is that each letter is made up of strokes of varying widths. The dramatic contrast between the thick and thin strokes is the result of having been written with a square-cut, broad-nibbed reed pen (a *calamus*). By giving their reed or quill pens a square tip rather than a pointed one, and then by holding the pen at an angle to the vertical and allowing the hand to move round as it wrote, Roman scribes were able to create letters that left a sinuous contrast between the thick and thin strokes. This contributed to a less even but visually richer trail of text across the page.

The most common kind of square capital were those painted or inscribed in large sizes on stone walls. Towards the end of the first century AD, inscribed square capitals (sometimes referred to as 'lapidary' from the Latin *lapis*, 'stone') had developed into a form that many consider to be the archetypal Roman letter, though it was never typical of Roman writing as a whole. The best-known instance is the aforementioned inscription at the base of Trajan's Column. Its lines of letters have

2.19: Trajan Column (detail)

long been revered as a model for the Latin alphabet *(fig. 2.19)*. During the latter half of the twentieth century especially, they were seen as providing a standard to which successive designers turned for education and edification.

The Trajan letters show how Roman square capitals differ from Greek capitals through the several simple contrasts of the letterforms. The calligraphic swelling and tapering of the Roman letters' strokes has already been outlined above, but another contrast is between the straight and the curved strokes of the letters. Roman square capitals were distinguished by a more consistent difference between the geometry of the square and the circle, both of which were used to guide the shape of the letters. Wide letters generally fitted into one or other shape, while the proportion of the narrow letters was guided by a half-square, as in 'E', 'F' and 'S'. The difference between these two widths, the full square and the half square, created an orderly spatial contrast, which became apparent as soon as the letters were run together in a line of text.

The geometrical shapes behind the construction of the square capital were only used as guides, not precise templates. They determined the general shape of each letter, not the strokes in detail. In the letters of the Trajan

2.20: Graffiti, Pompeii, c.AD79

Column, for example, the cutter has made small adjustments according to what suited his trained eye rather than geometric principles. The 'O', for example, is not perfectly round but slightly thinner than it is high; the 'M' has slightly splayed legs rather than perfectly vertical ones; and the 'E' has a central bar that is raised up from the centre of the vertical. As in other Roman inscriptions, they demonstrate the power of practice over theory.

A new contrast and, indeed, a new harmony could also be seen in the strokes of the letters. While the Greek's capitals had been monoline, the width of the square capitals' vertical strokes was roughly twice that of the horizontal ones. There was also a dimensional relationship between the width of the vertical and the height of each letter. Each letter was between eight to

2.21: Old Roman cursive, Roman letter, 1st–2nd century AD

ten stroke widths tall. The obvious care in the planning and execution of the Romans' square capitals extended to the angle of view presented to the readers. The carver of the Trajan capitals adjusted the relative size of the letters to compensate for their being read from below. The higher up the column the letters go, and hence the further from view they are, the larger the letters become.

Another significant feature of square capitals was the serifs. The origins of this enduring Roman feature are not clear. Serif-like shapes can be found in some later Greek inscriptions, but they are never as pronounced nor as integral to the letter as a whole as they are in Roman letters. Some historians have linked the invention of the Roman serif to the carver's chisel which, they argue, has to form some kind of serif when

terminating the end of a v-cut letter stroke. Another more recent theory has linked it to the invention of a square-cut writing implement; not a reed or quill, but a flat brush used by the letter-carver to mark out the letters before carving. Brushes were the standard implement for writing graffiti *(fig. 2.20)*, so it was perhaps natural that they should be incorporated into the process of making carved letters. In order to make a neat start and finish to each end of the brushed letter stroke – and to do so evenly along a line of letters – the paint would need to be slid in or slid out from one side of the stroke, rather than started or stopped abruptly (which could leave an unevenly wispy edge or, alternatively, a heavy splodge of ink). There are others still who deny that the serif has any practical origin and

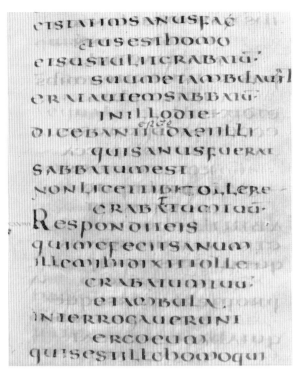

2.22: Uncial script, c.AD575

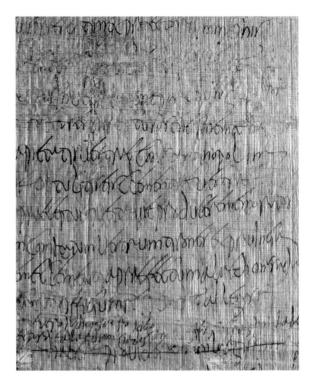

2.23: New Roman cursive, c.AD345

instead provide an aesthetic justification: the serif is an attempt to make the ends of each stroke look more definite and emphatically terminated.

Whatever its origin, the serif became such an accepted part of formal Roman letters it was soon taken up as a decorative element within a line of text. Some of the condensed, curved and fluid letter shapes of the Romans' rustic capitals were enlivened by large vigorous serifs, though others, as those shown here *(<fig.2.18)*, had serifs which are barely formed at all. For some 300 years, between the first and fourth centuries AD, rustic capitals were the standard formal writing hand, especially on soft materials such as papyrus, though they also came to be carved in stone.

Accompanying these two kinds of formal letters was an informal, cursive script called Old Roman cursive. It was barely deserving of the name, at least in the way it was written initially during the first century BC. Most of its letters were angular, not curved, and detached rather than joined up. These early aberrations hinted at the script's origins: the archaic square capital *(< fig.2.17)*. As the Old Roman cursive matured, it became capable of an astonishing variety. One of its more workaday guises appears on a letter *(<fig.2.21)* contained within the largest single collection of ancient Roman writing. It is one of several thousand letters and documents

that were found at the former Roman military base of Vindolanda, along Hadrian's Wall, the high stone-and-turf fortification that was built across the north of England. Vindolanda's hoard of wooden tablets dates from between AD85 and AD130, when Old Roman cursive was already two centuries old. The letter shown is from an entrepreneur called Octavius who had provided the Roman army with large quantities of supplies. He wrote it on one side of two thin wooden leaves which were folded together and then bound using the tie-holes on the leaves' outer edges, obviating the need for an envelope. As with today's hole-punched filing paper, these holes were punched into the leaves before the text was put down, a fact attested by the text, which has been written round them. It appears as though Octavius had been in a hurry. His writing looks rushed and there is also a faint 'offset' print on each page from the leaves having been folded before the ink had had time to dry. What is also evident is that Old Roman cursive, in all its utilitarian haste and profusion, was a true script. This is not calligraphy made in supplication to a deity or to uphold the honour of a king. There are no concessions to formality: the lines of writing are not straight, there are visible crossings out, and legibility seems to be coincidental rather than intentional. It is that immediate and intimate thing: lettering as handwriting.

2.24: New Roman half-uncial script, fifth century AD

The three Roman scripts mentioned above make up what is called the 'Old Roman System of Scripts'. By the fourth century AD, a 'New Roman System of Scripts' had been developed. Key to this new system was the creation of a new kind of formal capital, the Roman uncial, which for the first time hinted at the development of the small letters, or 'minuscules', of modern handwriting *(fig. 2.22)*. Most of these Latin minuscules are in fact a kind of 'quick' capital; a majuscule written at speed which has become deformed in the process. Naturally, this quicker writing forced some letters to break out of the vertical straitjacket that had bound their height and depth. As shown in this page of large letters, some have their terminal strokes extended into the free white space either above (as in 'd', 'h' and 'l') or below ('f', 'p' and 'q') the line of letters. Writing capitals more quickly also caused the internal structure of a number of letters to be simplified either by reducing the number of times the pen was lifted from the writing surface (three lifts for the capital 'A' became two for 'a') or by reducing the number of strokes used to write a letter (the four in the capital 'E' became three in 'e'). Those that weren't simplified retained their capital form and thereby contributed to the indecisive, albeit legible, mix of capitals and small letters. The intelligibility of the whole text was improved by an

early form of punctuation called *per cola et commata* (the plural forms of *colon* and *comma*, which at this time referred to the major and minor divisions respectively of a semantically coherent chunk of text – that is, a sequence of words that expressed a single idea, which itself was called a *periodus*). By marking the pauses in the rhetorical equivalent of a sentence with line breaks, *per cola et commata* was the first step towards a complete word separation.

The Old Roman cursive of the previous system of scripts seems to have been subject to a conscious reform during the third and fourth centuries. The result was a true minuscule in which nearly every letter had assumed its current small-letter form *(fig. 2.23)*. The shapes of this New Roman cursive were upright, flowing and, for the most part, joined up. In several instances, two letters were fused, creating what is known as a 'ligature'. It also featured for the first time the time-saving device of looped letter strokes (which here have a strong diagonal bias). It is the appearance of this new, simplified informal minuscule, rather than the earlier uncial, that is thought to have led to the development of a formal minuscule, known as half-uncial *(fig. 2.24)*. Its formality is expressed in its upright and unjoined letters. Both these latter minuscules, the informal New Roman cursive and the formal half-uncial, had replaced Old Roman cursive as the principal scripts for writing Latin by the fourth century AD. The short period of dominance by this new combination was the last time the Latin alphabet was to appear as a single set of scripts.

With the collapse of the western half of the Roman Empire at the end of the fifth century, out went a regional uniformity of lettering that had stretched from Britain's Hadrian's Wall to the shores of the Black Sea, on Europe's south-eastern fringe. It was at the entrance to the Black Sea, in the city of Byzantium (today's Istanbul), that a new capital was established for the eastern half of the empire in AD330. The city was renamed Constantinople in honour of the emperor, Constantine, who professed to have founded the capital as a rival to Rome 'on the command of God'. This profession of faith by the custodian of imperial power was new. No previous emperor had claimed to be a Christian. Once allied to imperial power, the Christian religion became the dominant cultural force in Europe, and its growth provided proto-graphic design with a new impetus: the birth of the book.

3 SPREADING THE WORD

Illuminated Manuscripts, c.350 – c.1500

'In the beginning was the Word.' These are the first words of the last of the four Gospels, the Gospel according to Saint John. If the number of surviving manuscripts is anything to go by, more manuscripts were made of the Gospels than of any other text during the Middle Ages. Such 'glad tidings' (*godspel* in Old English means 'good news') were central to the success of the early Christian missionaries in converting large sections of the old Roman Empire to the new religion. The Gospels' words were preached out loud and written down in the form of a book, and the stories they told were all the more affecting for being available in a visible form. A gospel manuscript was looked on as much more than the documentary evidence of a revered historical figure, Jesus of Nazareth. It was the word of God himself made manifest within a uniquely divine artefact, and thus richly deserving of all the skill, attention and expense their makers could bring to bear *(fig. 3.1)*. Not only are the covers of this French ninth-century gospel manuscript made from silver plate, the central figure of Christ is gilded and surrounded by jewels. The brilliance of the burnished gold and silver leaf that illuminates the pages of the most precious manuscripts cannot be simulated in today's most sophisticated facsimiles. While few of us would consider such manuscripts to be truly holy in quite the same way, many of us would consider the best of them to be among the greatest glories of Western art.

The unique book art displayed within their pages has a special place in graphic design's pre-history. The beginnings of almost all current typographic conventions can be found there. Our word spacing, punctuation, use of headings, margins, borders and annotations all became established during the making of the medieval manuscript. The conventions that surrounded their use have provided ample ammunition for the subsequent battles of graphic style.

The word 'manu-script' (from the Latin *manus* meaning 'hand', and *scriptum*, 'written') does not only refer to something that is handwritten, it almost invariably refers to writing presented in the form of a book – as pages that have been bound together along a common edge. This format has sustained western literary culture for almost 2000 years, yet its very success has stopped it from receiving the credit it deserves. The book must rank as one of man's greatest inventions, but seldom does it appear in any list of such things. (Nor does the alphabet.) Recently, however, the book has begun to receive more attention and respect. A degree of flattery has come through imitation as various attempts have been made to create digital books *(>fig. p1, p. 326)*. In fact these are more like digital wax tablets in that their single screens of text can be 'refreshed'. A closer approximation of the book would be an electronic device that used digital or electronic 'paper', but such a device has yet to appear. Explorations in digitization have combined with the newest mass-reading medium, the computer and the internet, to encourage talk of 'the paperless office' and 'the end of print'. Such warnings have turned out to be premature, coinciding as they do with year-on-year increases in paper use and rising quantities of production of nearly every kind of print medium – books, magazines, catalogues and so on. As a way of carrying substantial amounts of the same text in a portable and durable format, pages in book form have yet to be surpassed. This antique invention remains a standard method of storing and transmitting text-based information.

The impact of the manuscript on fourth-century Rome and subsequently throughout Europe increased the number of readers, and changed how and why people read. For a physician or lawyer or priest, the ability to refer to a portion of text easily and quickly, and then cross-reference it with other bits of text in the same

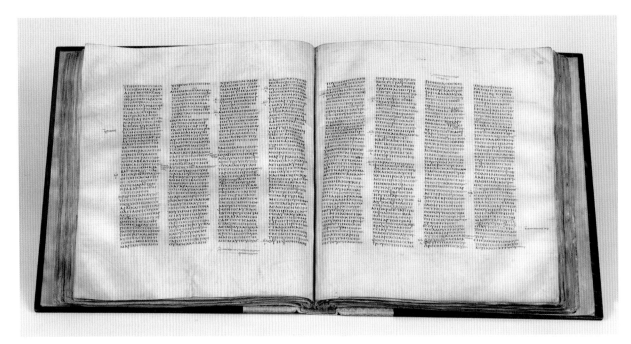

3.2: Codex Sinaiticus, eastern Mediterranean, mid-fourth century AD

volume, was becoming increasingly necessary. Such needs had been ill-served by the rolled scroll. When receiving information on separate bound pages, each of the kinds of readers mentioned above was able to compare the medical prescriptions, laws or biblical verses that concerned them. Furthermore, the book was eminently more portable than the scroll. A book could be easily carried and read in one hand, rather than two, and the amount of text it could hold easily exceeded its nearest rival in portability, the wax tablet.

The Romans' book or codex, as they called it (its plural is 'codices'), was an amalgam of two pre-existing Roman practices: first, the folding of papyrus sheets to form separate, portable pages (in the first century BC Julius Caesar is known to have used this device on the battlefield); and second, the binding of wooden wax tablets to make a kind of reusable notebook. It is these bound tablets that were first given the name *codex*, meaning literally 'block of wood'. (The English word 'book' has a similar derivation. It comes from the German word *boka* meaning 'beech', after the type of wood on which the Germanic indigenous runic script was written.) The earliest mention of the Romans' sheet-made codex appears at the end of the first century AD in the lines of the Roman poet Martial: 'The Iliad and all the adventures / of Ulysses, foe of Priam's kingdom, / all locked within a piece of skin / folded into several little sheets!'. The word 'skin' here is important. Animal skin

is known to have been used by the Egyptians as a surface for writing on as far back as the middle of the third millennium BC, but it was only when the eastern Greeks had learnt how to stretch skin thin enough and had passed this knowledge on to the Romans that animal skin began to rival papyrus as the dominant writing material. Sheep, lamb, cow, calf or goat skins were processed – soaked, scraped, stretched, dried and cleaned – to form a smooth writing surface known as parchment or vellum (the strict definition distinguishes vellum as being the skin of young animals – from a calf or kid – rather than mature ones). Though never cheap, parchment was less expensive than papyrus, and it was also more durable. The fact that it could withstand being used on both sides made it especially suitable for the book format. As the use of parchment in books increased, so the number of papyrus scrolls declined. The early adoption of the parchment codex by the burgeoning Christian religion is thought to have been decisive in the near-extinction of papyrus by the fourth century AD.

The pages of the earliest codices were based on the more-or-less square visible segment of an opened Roman scroll, the height of which was generally a little greater than that of a sheet of A4. In this fourth-century Greek codex of the Bible *(fig. 3.2)*, the text is written out in sparse lines of letters, with none of the variety of letter forms or colourful illumination that came to distinguish later manuscripts. Its aesthetic cue was

3.3: Codex Sinaiticus (detail)

done. The history of innovation in design, as elsewhere, is littered with examples of the straightforward mimicry of an established way of doing something: the first railway carriages looked like their horse-drawn predecessors; the subjects of early photographs, in portraits especially, were posed according to the established conventions of painted pictures; and, in the field of graphic design proper, the first printed books looked like manuscripts, as though they had been written out by hand (>fig. 4.10, p.73). In each case their creators had been intent on improving a particular aspect of the technology, rather than all of it. Had they considered the problem more broadly and been able to see the potential for creating wholly new forms, they might have chosen to do so. Yet, there are advantages in making something new look like something old. By retaining an element of continuity, the new thing can appear less threatening and/or confusing. Familiarity does not always breed contempt.

The invention of the codex went some way towards satisfying the appetite of the expanding mass of readers in Rome's empire. In the city of Rome itself, where this appetite was greatest, there was never a popular literature as such, not, at least, as we understand the term. Roman readers learnt the writings ascribed to the Greek author Homer and the only Roman author to rival him, Virgil, through dictation and recitation. Nevertheless, the demand for books was greater than it had ever been under the Greeks. Roman literature reached its peak in the first century BC with the writings of Caesar, the historian Livy, the orator Cicero and the poets Virgil and Horace. From the end of the first century AD, the literate classes had begun to depend on writing, as had, indeed, the empire itself. Letters, contracts, laws and votes – civil administration was firmly founded on the ability to read and write. While most Roman writing was still set down on the reusable wax tablet, manuscript books became commodified, and their ownership a status symbol.

The main period of manuscript making followed the fall of the empire in the fifth century and continued throughout the Middle Ages, ceasing only in the fifteenth century, during the late Renaissance. Thus, as things stand, the history of the handwritten book is twice as long as the currently 500-year history of the printed book.

The long life enjoyed by the manuscript did not just coincide with the Middle Ages; it helped to define the age. During the middle centuries of the first millennium, the so-called Dark Ages, the relative order and security

taken from the scroll, which apart from the expression of prestige in the choice of script had been a functional object rather than a decorative one. The scroll's main purpose had been to record speech, a task that writing remained wedded to throughout the life of the Roman Empire. Indeed, to some extent, the Romans held the human voice in even higher regard than the Greeks did. The great Roman orator Cicero (106–40 BC), who first articulated the doctrines of decorum and artistic style during the first century BC, became an idealized figure to later Romans on account of his speeches. They were copied down and circulated, and may still be read today. In order to serve the demands of speech, the text of a Roman scroll was laid out in an unbroken sequence of columns, usually running from left to right, so that by rolling and unrolling with his hands side by side the speaker could work his way through the text. This method contrasted with the Greek speaker, who usually held his scroll with one hand above the other in order to read from a continuous block of text that ran down the length of the scroll, in much the same way as we 'scroll' the text on a computer screen. Each of the columns in a Roman scroll had between 30 and 40 lines of roughly 20 to 30 letters, and, with the whole scroll being 6 to 10m (20 to 33ft) long when fully unrolled, the amount of text it contained was equivalent to that of a small novel.

By faithfully following the example of the Roman scroll, the early codex did as many new inventions have

in Europe that had been established under Roman rule was swept away by successive waves of marauding Germanic and Norse tribes. Yet by the fourteenth century, at the start of the Renaissance, Europeans had inherited an extraordinarily integrated civilization with bustling cities, towering cathedrals and thriving universities. Each was the fruit of a thoroughgoing Christian culture maintained from its centre, in Rome, by a powerful and wealthy pope; and via a 'civic' clergy, with its parish churches and bishoprics, as well as more marginal monasteries of monks and nuns. Much of the Church's power, like that of the Romans before it, was forged by the command and control of the written word, and it was in the monasteries that the word was first made flesh in the form of manuscripts.

The manuscript's development within the cloistered walls of the Church was linked to its role as an aid to learning. The Christian religion was founded on a thorough knowledge of its sacred texts. Divine reading combined with manual labour and public worship to form the tripartite basis of monastic life. Studying the scriptures was facilitated by two distinct methods of reading: reading out loud in a group and reading to oneself in silence or a low murmur. The most well-known description of the second kind of reading was given by one of the founding fathers of the early Church, Saint Augustine of Hippo, who in AD384 wrote a short but revealing description of his teacher Saint Ambrose thus: '… when he read, his eyes would travel across the pages, and his mind would explore the sense, but his voice and tongue were silent. … who would have the heart to interrupt such a man … guessing that in the brief time he had seized for the refreshment of this mind, he was resting from the din of other people's affairs … another and perhaps more cogent reason for his habit of reading silently was his need to conserve his voice, which was very prone to hoarseness. But whatever his reason, that man undoubtedly had a good one.' This passage has often been interpreted as signalling a sudden change from reading aloud to reading in silence. But Saint Ambrose was certainly not the first silent reader. It was practised throughout antiquity. What the description does emphasize is the importance of silent reading as a way of 'exploring the sense' of a text. This was not merely a matter of learning a story, but of taking it in fully so that it and all its implications become thoroughly familiar and personal. Saint Ambrose was one of a growing number of literates who had begun to use texts autodidactically, for their own

edification, rather than for sharing within a group.

This move away from public performance to private perusal had, in part, been influenced by the changed status of the language they were reading, an ecclesiastical form of Latin, which towards the end of the fourth century had become the language of literature and learning rather than a language of everyday speech. At one time, the same kind of Latin could be heard in any part of the Roman Empire, but after the fall of the empire classical Latin had fragmented into various regional dialects, the precursors of modern Italian, French and Spanish. Only in the Church, which had adopted Latin as the official language in the fourth century AD, was it preserved. Since most writing and manuscript production occurred in monasteries, the written word became closely identified with reading and learning rather than speaking, and as the number of silent readers steadily rose, so the feeling of being intimately connected to a text became more widespread. Not only could ideas be acquired more directly without having to listen to an intermediary, they also seemed to enter at a higher level of consciousness. This much more personal act of silently reading was further aided by the greater freedom provided by the manuscript to choose a favoured piece of text. The effect was such that by the end of the Middle Ages most readers had fallen silent.

The emancipation of the written word from the spoken one allowed some of the conventions inherited from the orator's scroll to be set aside. By the beginning of the fifth century the codex had become taller and narrower, so as to be more easily held in the hand, with two or sometimes only one column of text per page (>fig.3.10). In this it assumed the current literary format that now dominates the West: a rectangular page with horizontal lines of alphabetic text surrounded by four margins. Within these standard features a range of local styles of script and illumination were included, especially by monasteries on the fringes of the old empire. Some of the most distinct early examples of regional designs appear in the so-called 'insular' (Latin for 'island') manuscripts of the British Isles. From the middle of the fifth century, insular manuscripts began to be distinguished by two features that have since come to symbolize a Celtic style of design: a rounded script and an intricately woven style of decoration.

The three masterpieces of the insular manuscript are the Lindisfarne Gospels c.710–721, the Book of Durrow c.700 and the Book of Kells c.800. Each one is a gospel book, and their pages are filled with examples of

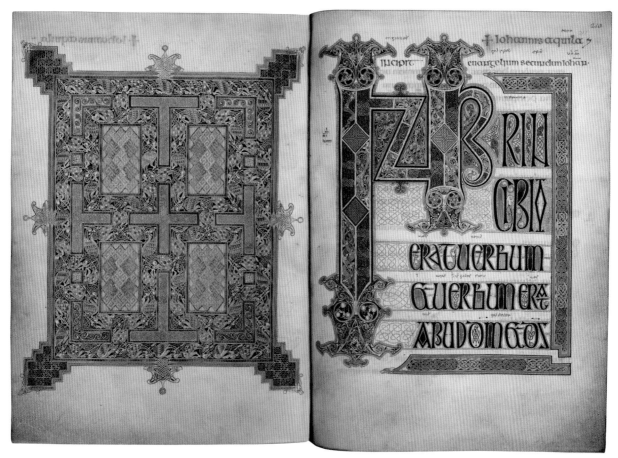

3.4: *Lindisfarne Gospels, England, c.710–721*

elaborately and skilfully hand-rendered illuminations. An involved patterning or decoration dominates all three, but it is among the pages of the Lindisfarne Gospels that the decoration is at its most fevered and mesmeric *(fig.3.4)*. This large book of Gospels was made in a monastery founded by Irish missionaries on an island off the north-east coast of England, which was then known as Lindisfarne but is now called Holy Island. The book's size and splendour suggests it was intended as a showpiece, a manuscript for religious ceremony rather than private study, and was likely therefore to have been read only on special festival days. Its large pages (340 x 250 mm, 13 3/8 x 9 7/8 in) and ornateness are instantly impressive. The richness of the detail invites a contemplative awe, which fits the description that a twelfth-century historian made about a similarly decorative insular manuscript, 'You will make out intricacies so delicate and subtle, so exact and compact, so full of knots and links, with colours so fresh and vivid, that you might say that all this was the work of an angel and not of a man'. The sense of wonder at the human endeavour

is increased by the knowledge that the 259 pages of script and decoration are thought to have been the work of a single scribe.

This Lindisfarne scribe did not write with the standard Roman uncial script favoured in continental and other less geographically remote English scriptoria. He used an Irish half-uncial letter *(>fig.3.5)*, in which nearly all the letters have developed our current small-letter or lowercase form (a clear exception being the letter 'R'). His steady and deliberate insular script is distinguished from the more common Roman half-uncial, by having especially thick and rounded letter shapes. They are shapes that have been written with a broad-nibbed pen held with the nib pointing straight up the page, and therefore with thin, almost hairline horizontal strokes and distinctive wedge-shaped serifs at the tops of the letters. Many of the horizontals are exaggeratedly extended, especially at the end of the lines of text. The text is written out *per cola et commata*, in lines of unbroken words the length of which is used to clarify the sense, although accompanying the classical method is a hint of word

3.5: Irish half-uncial, Lindisfarne Gospels

separation. Some of the text is written in red, or rubricated (from the Latin word *rubrica* meaning 'red earth').

What most forcibly distinguishes these insular books from previous manuscripts is their illustration. The inclusion of patterns and pictures in medieval manuscripts was actively promoted by the Church. As well as wanting to impress the reader with exuberant colours and intricate decoration, Christian missionaries were aware of the power of pictures to communicate something of the Christian message to an audience who, even if more literate than had previously been thought, would still have struggled to read an entire text. The sixth-century pope, Gregory the Great, explicitly encouraged pictures to be used in this way: 'Let pictures be words for those who cannot read'.

For those who could read, pictures were important in a different way. They were used as an aid to memorizing the text. The use of pictures as a memory device is known to have taken place in ancient Greece. It was a process that continued in the Middle Ages, though it had a particular cast in monasteries. Pictures were used not as a form of representation, as we understand the term, to show what something looked like. They were visual hooks on which to hang a story. Their form referred to a narrative which needed to be inwardly digested and remembered. In this way they were similar to words.

As well as helping memory, the pictures can also be seen as an elaborate and extended form of punctuation. They were often used to mark the major divisions within the text of a book, its chapters and the sections within them. Among the most emphatic visual divisions in the Lindisfarne Gospels are the introductory double-page spreads from each of the four Gospels *(< fig. 3.4)*. They are mostly ornamental – that is to say, non-figurative – and are filled with a dizzying array of intricately swirling lines and bright, flat colours. Their particular patterns are made from a fusion of influences: the Celtic (the spiralling knot interlaces) and the Germanic (the birds and beasts). On the left-hand or 'verso' pages of each spread a rich, linear style of pattern making is applied to the shape of a cross set within a densely decorated rectangle. No part of the pattern is left unfilled; no space is too small to decorate. The appearance of such solid ornamentation has led these sorts of pages to be described as 'carpet pages'. It is a resemblance that may have been intentional since prayer mats were certainly known in that part of England, as they were in Eastern Christianity and Islam. The carpet pages of the Lindisfarne Gospels are densely packed with a number of tightly and precisely interlaced heads and limbs of birds and other indistinguishable quadrupeds *(fig. 3.6)*. The animals and abstract shapes are woven together in busy and fluid rhythms, yet they are tethered to a simple geometrical grid. The compass and divider marks that can be seen on the back of the pages show how an ordered symmetry of repeated rectangular units underpins the page's apparently free-form design. In this the illuminator had observed the rules of sacred geometry, which were then associated with God's design for Creation.

The right hand or 'recto' page is equally dynamic, though its dynamism is not tied to a regular geometry in the same way. It is linked, instead, to the irregular forms of several large ornamental letters. Each recto page is an 'initial page', one in which the first few words (incipits) of the Gospel are illuminated with grand decorated initials that lead into a sequence of ornamental letters of diminishing sizes. The more angular set of ornamental letters has forms that appear to have been inspired by the German runic alphabet (the runic M of three vertical strokes and a horizontal appears). The text on the initial page of Saint John's Gospel reads 'In principio erat verbum et verbum erat apud d(eu)m et d(eu)s [erat verbum]' ('In the beginning was the word and the word was with God and God [was the word]'), and each

3.6: Carpet page (detail), Lindisfarne Gospels

3.7: Carolingian minuscule, France, ninth century

3.8: Winchester minuscule, England, tenth century

letter, as on the other incipit pages, is bordered by a buffer of tiny red drops of lead, carefully placed like a stippled kind of stitching. In other insular manuscripts they are only ever used as an adjunct to letters.

Almost a hundred years after the Lindisfarne Gospels was completed, the regional variety of scripts and decoration that had developed across western Europe was partially interrupted by a wholesale reform of the monasteries' scriptoria. The process of reform was part of a larger revival of classical learning, within the Church in particular, which historians refer to as the 'Carolingian Renaissance'. It was introduced by the devout Frankish king and emperor, Charlemagne (742–812) – whose family line came to be called the Carolingians – in an attempt to bring about a 'renewal of the Roman Empire' (as the legend on his personal seal put it) as well as a return to the standards of Christian worship achieved by the early Church Fathers. The territory under Charlemagne's rule was larger than any in the West since the Roman Empire (his successors, indeed, referred to their inherited dominions as 'the Holy Roman Empire'), and the effects of his reforms were wide ranging.

Central to the successful transmission of classical culture was the standardization of texts and the creation of a new, more legible script, the Carolingian (or Caroline) minuscule (fig.3.7). Though the form of this script was based on a Roman model, the half-uncial

(< fig.2.24, p.45), and, to a lesser extent, on the insular half-uncial (< fig.3.5), the clarity, efficiency and beauty of its letters were unprecedented. This very expert ninth-century example from France sets out the minuscule with a vibrant red ink. Its legibility is enhanced by its letter shapes, in particular the length of the strokes that rise above the main body of the letter, known as the 'ascenders' (as in the letters 'b', 'd' and 'h'), and then also the 'descenders' (those that fall below, as in 'g', 'p' and 'q'). The effect produces a much more consistent and recognizable word shape, which is also made more definite by the hint of word separation within the lines of text.

The shape of words is an important factor in legibility. When we read, our eyes pass over a line of text in a series of short jumps (called 'saccades', the fastest kind of movement in the human body), rather than an even sweep, and they absorb chunks of information at every pause. Within each chunk we register the overall shapes of the words (described by internal as well as external elements), rather than the shape of each letter separately. But clarity of word shape is not the only criterion. Legibility is not purely objective. We tend to read best the shapes we read most. Nor is legibility determined by word shape alone. There is always a degree of guesswork related to the context. It is spursingly easy to raed wodrs taht hvae thier itneranl lteres plcaed in the worng oredr bceuase tehy eixst in a cnotxet of maennig, of idoim and of smilair wrod sheaps. Nevertheless,

capitals (x26)	A B C D E F G H I J K L M N O P Q R S T U V W X Y Z
lowercase (x18)	a b c d e f g h i j k l m n o p q r s t u v w x y z
numerals (x9)	0 1 2 3 4 5 6 7 8 9
punctuation (x21)	, . ; : ... ' " ` " ' " ? ! ( ) [ ] - / * †
maths (x8)	+ - x ÷ = < > %
currency (x4)	£ $ € ¥
misc. (x5)	& # ° @ ©

3.9: Basic set of character shapes for reading English

the more distinct and consistent word shapes of the Carolingian minuscule do appear to be more legible than earlier scripts, and we may suppose that many readers at that time will have thought so too.

Within the controlled and hierarchical environment of Charlemagne's reformed scriptoria, every aspect of manuscript manufacture was codified (the word itself is derived from *codex* via 'code'). Features such as initials, headings, word spacing and punctuation began to be used more regularly and consistently. Accompanying the Carolingian minuscule script were square capitals, which were considered the correct form for writing headings or names, though not yet the letter at the start of a sentence. By formalizing the use of capitals with small-letters, the Carolingian reforms required writers of the Latin alphabet to learn many more than 26 letter shapes. The strict and often complex division of labour that now exists between lowercase and capitals when writing English, for example, means that the total number of letter shapes for everyday writing is around 44 (some caps and lowercase are the same). If we go on and add the basic set of non-alphabetic symbols – such as punctuation marks, units of currency and the like – the number rises to around 89 separate shapes *(fig. 3.9)*.

The legibility of a Carolingian manuscript was further enhanced by a reduction in the number of abbreviations, suspensions (omitted letters) and ligatures (two letters combined in a single shape). Each of these acts of compression had been necessary when whole words were expected to fit the straitjacket of so-called 'justified' text; that is, a column aligned on the right as well as the left. Such columns had been a common feature of many Roman codices. But the Carolingian reforms promoted the 'unjustified' column (otherwise descriptively called 'ragged-right' or 'ranged-left'). When using

this format, all the words within a text could be evenly spaced, and thus they contributed to a flowing and legible line of letters.

The effect of these reforms was to establish a common ground in many of the scriptoria in western Europe. Even when the Carolingian minuscule failed to dominate a particular region, due to the region's political independence or the existence of an established indigenous script, its influence was felt nevertheless. These lines *(fig. 3.8)* of a small British psalter (a book of Old Testament songs or psalms – *psalamoi* in Greek means 'songs sung with a harp'), from the tenth century, have some of the characteristics of the earlier insular script – its roundness and its exaggerated thick and thin strokes – but in its more exaggerated ascenders and descenders and its more distinct letter and word shapes the influence of the Carolingian is clear.

By the twelfth century, texts such as the Worms Bible *(>fig. 3.10)* carry the essential features of a modern page. We feel we are in familiar territory just by the way the page is presented. The contents are arranged within an ordered hierarchy which guides the reader through the different parts of the page. Its elementary signage system allows us, for example, to check which book of the Bible we are looking at by glancing at the top of the page, above the central margin, to the 'running head' or 'header' where the word 'Ezekiel' appears picked out in red. Our eye is then drawn down the page to the first line of the Book of Ezekiel by the large, decorated initial 'E' and the bearded figure of Ezekiel himself. As befits an important Old Testament prophet, he is crowned with a large, golden halo. In his left hand is an unrolled scroll revealing his prophecy ('Now it came to pass in the thirtieth year … that the heavens were opened, and I saw visions of God'). The swirling pattern that decorates the initial recalls the decoration of the earlier Lindisfarne Gospels, but the illuminator's inclusion of a figure from the text takes the decoration in a new direction. By using it to tell something of the story of the text, the illuminator is approaching the purpose of Pope Gregory's injunction, to provide pictures for the illiterate. But this approach is only one of several alternatives. Other manuscripts have no pictures at all, while some have illustrations that bear little relevance to the text. The subjects depicted might be chosen to display the illuminator's mastery (and enhance the owner's prestige) or they might be in response to a local fashion, or they may want to stand out by being comical or irreverent. Since pages were rarely numbered, part of the job of a picture was to provide a mental marker for the reader to pinpoint particular sections of text. The more irreverent the picture, the more likely a reader would remember it. Something of this nature occurs with the decorated initial 'I' in the left-hand column of text. At its base is the head of the prophet Ezekiel, whose words are being spoken with a grossly floriated tongue. Following the initial there is a gradual reduction in the size and complexity of the text's letters. The large black capital letters that come after the initial are themselves followed by a line of smaller capitals. Both kinds form a bridge between the initial and the main body of text. This hierarchical approach, which had been explicitly promoted by the Carolingian reforms, continues to be used at the start of many texts in books and magazines today.

An additional and more explicit way of separating sections of text was to have lines of rubricated capitals, beginning with the word *explicit* (meaning 'here ends', in reference to the preceding text), and towards the end of the capitals the word *incip* (an abbreviation of *incipit*, meaning 'here begins', in reference to the following text). A similar kind of 'incipit' text would sometimes appear at the beginning of each manuscript. It frequently bore the author's name and the title of the text, though what stopped it from being the equivalent to the modern-day title page was that it rarely appeared on a page of its own. Indeed, there was little need for a separate title page. Most books were made on commission so it was not necessary to display the contents so egregiously. Few owners would have had more than a handful of manuscripts on their shelves, so each would have been known intimately.

What makes the page most familiar is the main text. The words, clauses and sentences in the main body of text reveal themselves to be visually discrete units. A simple three-tiered hierarchy of word spaces, commas and full stops are used. Each is an emphatic confirmation of the changed role of writing away from being spoken and towards silent reading. The silent reader, being denied the vocal cues that came from reading out loud, would have welcomed the visual cues of word spaces and punctuation. The Church too would have welcomed the greater clarity that these elements brought to the sense of the text. An individual interpretation of the text was fundamental to good oratory, but it was anathema to the Church hierarchy. They wanted Christian readers to receive Christ's message clearly and unambiguously. Doctrinal differences could hang on the exact phrasing of a sentence. For example, the line from Matthew's Gospel, 'Judge not, that ye be not judged' ('Don't judge others, or they will judge you'), has an entirely different and more threatening meaning when the comma is removed: 'Judge not that ye be not judged' ('Don't think you won't be judged').

Punctuation, the text's most conspicuous sign system, was more limited and less uniform than it is today. Question, exclamation and quotation marks do not yet appear, partly because many of the parts of speech they signify are expressed within the Latin words themselves (suffixes added to the ends of words, or whole words placed at the beginning of a sentence – the clause *scriptum est*, for example, meaning 'as it is written', did the job of the modern quotation marks whenever it was placed in front of a quotation). The Carolingian reforms had also simplified the word order of Latin, bringing it closer to the native languages of its readers. By the thirteenth century, Latin had developed into a standardized tongue for scholars and theologians across western Europe (not that this changed the wording of the canonical texts). The galvanizing effect that these visual and linguistic reforms had on silent reading caused the voluble mutterings that had filled scriptoria during the early Middle Ages to gradually fade. By the late Middle Ages many monastic orders discouraged speaking entirely. For the new makers of the illuminated manuscript, silence was seen to be golden.

From around 1200, during the last 300 years of the Middle Ages, manuscripts were made increasingly outside the monasteries by professional book makers. The Church's long-standing monopoly was eroded by the rise of two new social groups: those within the new

EXPLICIT LIB· IEREM·
PPHE· IEREM· HABET
VERS? IIII· CCCC·
QNQGINTA· INCIP·
PLOG· INEZECHI

EZECHIEL· PPHA

EXPLIC· PLOG· SCI IER·
INCIP·LIB· EZEC
hIEL· PPHETE·

FACTVM EST

3.10: Manuscript page, Worms Bible, twelfth century

3.11: Documentary cursive, Magna Carta, England, 1215

universities who began to make books for students; and the wealthy merchant class, who, for the purposes of trade as well as for their own edification, had become increasingly literate. Both groups wanted secular books as well as religious ones and each expected to be able to buy books just like any other commercial item. Running parallel with the fledgling book trade was a separate category of non-literary manuscripts used for businesses and civil administration. Accounts, correspondence, laws and charters were serviced by a growing band of professional scribes and clerks.

One of the most significant secular documents of the age is a charter contract (a charter is a legal document in which one party grants permission to another) sealed in 1215 by the English king John (1166–1216), at the insistence of a rebellious group of barons *(fig.3.11)*. Apart from its size, Magna Carta (Latin for 'the Large Charter', a title bestowed some years later to distinguish it from a similar but smaller accompanying charter) looked like a typical legal document of the time. The script, a neat documentary cursive, was hurriedly written in a brownish ink with a typically thin-nibbed pen. Though not the grandest hand, there was some dressing up of the basic letters with various kinds of fancy looped ascenders. The document's importance has nothing to do with how it looks, nor much to do with the concessions contained in the text. What sets it apart is that it established, for the first time, that the power of the king could be limited by a written document; that he could be 'brought to book'. It is for this reason that some have claimed it to be the cornerstone of liberty in the English-speaking world.

Contrary to common parlance, 'the signing of Magna Carta' never happened. Neither party signed anything. The only authentication of the document was made with the king's principal royal seal, the Great Seal, which took on the standard design for English kings. On one side it showed an enthroned monarch dispensing justice, while on the other the monarch was mounted on his charger riding into battle. This wax seal might have been the only option available to this particular king, for there is no evidence that John was able to write at all. He, like other monarchs and members of the aristocracy of the time, may have thought it unbecoming to master this servile craft. It was an attitude that faded with the century. During the one that followed, the clerically influenced elite of western Europe were to claim reading and writing as their own.

The most popular secular literature of the late Middle Ages was a form of vernacular verse composed around episodic stories in rhyming couplets. The genre was supposed to be spoken out loud, and yet, popular performance literature of this kind was enjoyed as much by readers as by listeners. Two such works that continue to be read today are Dante's *The Divine Comedy* and Chaucer's *The Canterbury Tales*, but what was significant about them at the time they were written was that they appeared in their readers' native languages of Italian and English respectively, rather than in the ecclesiastical language of Latin. This made them immediately more accessible than any previous literature.

The enthusiasm for secular literature written in the vernacular did not at this stage threaten the existence of the ecclesiastical Latin manuscript. The importance placed on continuity within the traditional form of worship meant that it continued to remain popular. However, the situations in which it was read and the uses to which it was put became more varied. Both the formats and the layouts of this kind of manuscript reflected the greater variety of situations and uses. Pictures were added to various selections of biblical texts to create so-called Picture Bibles, among the most popular of which was the *Biblia Pauperum* (Bible of the Poor). It was one of the first to be made as a blockbook *(>fig.4.6, p.70)* – with text and illustrations printed from carved blocks of wood – in the fifteenth century, at around the time that printing with type was invented.

New kinds of textual arrangements appeared during the first half of the twelfth century in Bibles whose pages were extensively annotated, or 'glossed' (from the Greek *glossa* meaning 'tongue' or 'language'). Glosses were explanatory texts written by established authorities who had fleshed out the allegorical meaning or moral sense of the text (hence our word 'glossary'). Some attempts at laying out a formally glossed text had been made during the Carolingian period but more usually glosses were brief and informal often being confined to ad hoc translations of the text. Those that sit between the widely spaced lines of main text on the carpet page of the Lindisfarne Gospels *(<fig.3.4)*, for example, were added centuries after the manuscript had been completed. (They are Anglo-Saxon translations of the Latin text; the earliest surviving translation of the four Gospels into any form of English.) The columns of much more comprehensive glosses that surrounded the main text of a large French Bible from the thirteenth century *(fig.3.12, >3.13)* were written at the same time

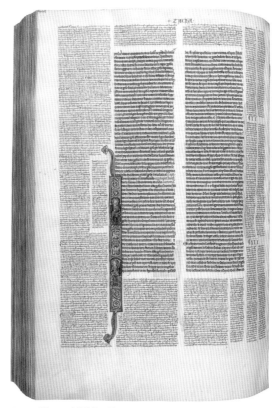

3.12: Glossed Bible, France, thirteenth century

as the main text. Both its gloss and the main text were planned and spaced on a grid of lines that ran across the entire area of text. The ruling that guided the writing of the gloss has been harmonized with the text-ruling in such a way that six lines of the gloss could be written in the space taken by four lines of main text.

Like the modern study aids that English students use when studying Shakespeare, for example, a clear difference between the commentary and the main text was maintained not just by the position of the texts but also by their different sizes and styles of script. The main text in this French Bible is written in a compressed script that had been developed out of the Carolingian minuscule by northern European scribes. The woven-wicker texture of its text caused it to be called *littera textualis* or textura (from the Latin for 'weaving'), though its prominence in German manuscripts in particular led later Italian scribes and historians to refer to it as 'Gothic' (the terms 'Blackletter', after its dense appearance on the page, and 'Old English', after its popularity in England, are now also used). Between the twelfth and sixteenth centuries textura evolved into a complex hierarchy of formal and cursive scripts. A set of formal book scripts were devised and priced according to the effort involved in writing them. The chief determinant in this system was the effort involved in terminating each of the letter strokes. In the example here the main text is written in *textualis rotunda*, which has strokes whose feet are rounded off with a natural uplift of the pen. The gloss is in a smaller, modified version of this script, though its letters have become extended with the speed of writing. It is further distinguished from the main text by being written in a lighter, browner ink. At the beginning of each commentary red ink is used to make a paragraph mark followed by the relevant word from the main text that is referred to by the commentary. Such large quantities of text often required large pages. The pages here are nearly half a metre high (49.5 x 32 cm, 19½ x 12⅝ in) and when set out on display in a handsome binding, they would have bolstered the prestige of any church or private patron. The book would have been considered of equal standing to an altar painting or sculpted cross.

By contrast, the carefully illuminated late-fifteenth century prayer book with its decorated clasp (*fig. 3.14*) is only 11cm (4⁵⁄₁₆in) high and 7.5cm (2¹⁵⁄₁₆in) wide. It was created for the private use of a wealthy individual and therefore needed to be small enough to carry or to hold in the hand for reading. It is a kind of manuscript known as a Book of Hours. The name refers to the practice of reading certain prayers and devotions during each of the eight periods or 'hours' of daily prayer required by monastic orders (in the Middle Ages 'hours' were periods devoted to religious duties rather than fixed units of time). They allowed ordinary people to take part in private prayer and meditation in their own home as well as in church.

Such books became popular in the early thirteenth century and by the fifteenth century they were bestsellers across Europe. As well as wealthy individuals acquiring their own personal copy, any household that could afford a book would have bought one (a whole Bible was too expensive). Because it was often the only book that people owned, many people first learnt to read from it (the word 'primer' comes from the office of Prime, the first set of morning prayers). Such books also allowed many people to engage directly with a religious text for the very first time, rather than having it mediated through a priest or parent. This change was especially significant for women. The role of women within early medieval literary culture was passive and peripheral. Some were involved as readers but very few as writers. As access to texts increased from the eleventh

3.13 Glossed Bible (detail), showing textual arrangement, thirteenth century

3.14: *Book of Hours, Bruges, c.1490–1500*

century, so a greater number of women became involved in making and writing books. For the first time in western European literature women were being celebrated both as authors (Julian [sic] of Norwich, 1342–*c*.1416, Christine de Pizan, 1363–*c*.1434) and theologians (Hildegard of Bingen, 1098–1179).

By allowing readers of both sexes to develop a close relationship with texts, manuscripts became cherished objects. The rich also used them as a means of displaying their wealth, status and taste and this demand for an overt demonstration of wealth created a series of more decorative and heavily illuminated manuscript pages. The large extended decorative initials that were already evident by the twelfth century were extended during the thirteenth into ever more elaborately foliated forms of decoration. They began to be painted around the main text and eventually came to envelop it completely. Whole figurative scenes were soon incorporated into the surround, especially on pages where a major division in the text needed to be marked. The subjects depicted in these illuminated miniatures included scenes from the life of the Virgin, Christ and the saints, as well as themes relating to death and judgment. The finest artists were commissioned to illustrate them with opulent colours and gilded decoration in the latest Gothic styles. Royal patronage encouraged artists to suffuse their subjects with the attitudes and conventions of the life of the court, which resulted in a special emphasis being placed on the depiction of elaborate folds in the elegant draperies worn by extenuated figures in swaying poses; such features defined a Gothic style of illustration.

The evident splendour of the Gothic illustrations, with their expensive pigments and touches of gold leaf, was joined during the fifteenth century by a new requirement, a demand for naturalism. Whereas splendour required wealth, naturalism depended on a more exclusive commodity, the skill of a master craftsman. In the Low Countries especially, naturalistic forms appeared in rich and colourful initials and borders. The border that appears in the manuscript of a popular French allegorical poem, the *Roman de la Rose (fig. 13.15)*, shows how the desire for naturalism had led the artist to turn the whole border into a wooden panel and then decorate it with plants, flowers, birds and butterflies. In its detail and realism it reflected the new standards of artistic skill that were being developed through the revolutionary techniques of oil painting and a more convincing illusion of space. Both developments made the studied charm of the Gothic style appear dated. The degree of naturalism in the border exceeds that contained in the more conventionalized Gothic illustration in the centre.

Accompanying the illustration is a style of Gothic script called *bâtarde*. It is a high grade cursive script that is particularly associated with manuscripts produced for the Burgundian court (which ruled over Belgium, the Netherlands and Luxembourg during the fifteenth century). It evolved out of a distinctively pointed cursive script called 'secretary', which had been developed in the French Chancery during the beginning of the fourteenth century. But instead of keeping the latter's hurried cursive form, *bâtarde* took on the upright letter shape of the textura to create a hybrid or bastard

3.15: Bâtarde script, 'Roman de la Rose', Bruges, c.1500

3.16: Pattern book, France, fifteenth century

3.17: Rotunda script, Milan, 1490-1504

form of letter. During the fifteenth and sixteenth centuries the script rose in status to become the standard script for luxurious editions of romances and histories, and all but replaced the textura scripts except in the very grandest books. Scribes appeared to enjoy the greater calligraphic verve and freedom of expression allowed by its arched and pointed strokes.

Not all manuscripts of the late Middle Ages were illuminated. Few readers of educational books could have afforded the expense involved. Grammars, text books, literary works (epics and romances), as well as many Books of Hours and psalters, were made with modest materials and within an increasingly rationalized method of production. The need to meet the growing demand for manuscripts encouraged their makers to standardize the production process. The most time-consuming aspect of manuscript manufacture was the writing and illuminating, and even a practised scribe or illuminator could benefit from using a pattern book which provided templates for various standard book features, such as decorative initials (fig.13.16).

As well as mastering the standard forms, manuscript makers also had to cater to local tastes. In Italy, where the influence of the Carolingian minuscule had remained strong, Italian scribes created a more rounded version of Gothic script, more so even than the

northern *texturalis rotunda*. The large, less compressed and angular letters of this Italian *rotunda (fig.3.17)*, though eclipsed in the late fourteenth century by a revival of the Roman tradition of lettering, continued to be used until the seventeenth century in service and devotional books.

The revival of classical lettering in Italy was part of a wider 'renaissance' of classical learning initiated by a group of Florentine writers and artists during the final years of the fourteenth century. They called themselves *umanisti* or 'humanists' because of the human values, as opposed to religious beliefs, to which they had been drawn by recently discovered art and writing from pre-Christian Greece and Rome. By studying classical texts and artefacts, they had learnt that artists need not only relate their work to the ancient scriptures or historical myths; they could also hold a mirror up to their own world, to the here-and-now. Something of this new attitude towards the potential of art and literature – the 'humanities' as they became known – spread to each of Europe's main cultural centres, though not all at the same time nor in the same way. Like all historical periods, the Middle Ages and its successor, the Renaissance, are blurred at the edges, and yet the dividing line was made a little less diffuse by a singular fact of history. That fact was the invention of printing with type in the West.

4 THE BLACK ART
The Birth of Printing & Early German Printing, c.1455–c.1530

'The pope has no power to remove guilt.' This provocative declamation was written in 1517 by the German monk and university lecturer Martin Luther. It was one of 95 points for debate, or 'theses', which he is said to have hammered onto a church door in his home town of Wittenberg in what is now central Germany. By choosing to make his views public in this way, Luther was following a convention of the time; the church door was a common forum for initiating public debate. But by challenging the authority of the pope so explicitly, he unwittingly set in train the destruction of a Christian unity which, for over a millennium, had bound its followers within a single, Catholic communion ('Catholic' comes from the Greek *katholikos*, meaning 'universal'). Luther's theses aroused a storm of sympathetic protest because they articulated a widely held view that, as an institution, the Church had become both self-serving and corrupt. By claiming for itself powers it did not possess and by seeking a wealth and status it ought not to covet, it had departed from one of the Church's founding principles, that of common justice. Pope Gregory the Great, one of the architects of the medieval papacy, had summed up the principle epigrammatically: 'What was given by a common God is only justly used when those who have received it use it for a common good.' The dispute that Luther and his followers set in train quickly grew into the revolutionary social, political and religious movement now called the Reformation. Over the next 200 years those who rose up in protest, the Protestant reformers, became engaged in a succession of bloody conflicts with Catholic counter-reformers. It was a period of conflict that ended with the Church emphatically divided.

Had Luther lived a generation earlier, his objections might have amounted to little more than a local religious squabble; as it was, they became part of a controversy that engaged the whole continent. The chief agent in spreading Luther's theses from what was then a relatively remote part of Europe was an invention that had been devised some 60 years earlier by a German merchant's son called Johannes Gensfleisch (literally 'Gooseflesh'). He is better known by another name which, in keeping with a local convention, was derived from the name of the house he grew up in. The house's name was Gutenberg.

What Johannes Gutenberg had invented was a special method of printing in which metal blocks of letters, called type *(fig. 4.1)*, were used to reproduce text faster and more faithfully than could ever be achieved by a scribe with a pen. The effect of Gutenberg's invention touched almost every aspect of European society. Not since the Greeks' invention of the alphabet had human communication been transformed so dramatically. Only a couple of decades after his invention, printers were able to produce 100 copies of a book in a day. Any comparable figure for scribal output can only be guessed at, but one contemporaneous account from the great Florentine manuscript dealer Vespasiano da Bisticci (1421–98) states that a team of 55 scribes took a full 12 months to complete 100 manuscripts, and even that figure is likely to have been an exaggeration. Before the arrival of Gutenberg's press, books were like paintings; unique artefacts which were precious and scarce. After 50 years of printing with type, they became much less so. It has been estimated that during this short period as many books were printed with Gutenberg's invention as had been written by hand during the whole of the previous millennium.

The fruits of printing are more easily grasped than the invention that bore them. To say that Gutenberg invented printing, or that he printed the first book, is to use a convenient shorthand. Neither statement is quite true. When Stone Age people marked the walls of their caves with hand prints, they were engaged

< 4.1: Forme of type for Mainz Psalter, 1463

in a rudimentary form of printing. We know that the
Egyptians used inked seals to impress their hieroglyphs
onto sheets of papyrus *(< fig. 2.3, p. 31)* and similarly, if
the Phaistos disc is indeed authentic *(< fig. 2.1, p. 28)*, its
repeated impressions are also an early form of printing. Each is an example of printing at its most basic,
and none of them was ever developed beyond its own
specific and limited uses. The same applies to the mass
printing of patterns on textiles *(>fig. 4.4)*, which were
first produced in Europe during the twelfth century,
though by being made from impressions from large
blocks of carved wood within a process that approached
mass production, such printing came closer to the subsequent method of printing text.

The first time that printing was used as an adjunct or
alternative to hand writing occurred in China. Its development there, in the eighth century, was linked to the
development of printing's favoured medium, the one
you have in front of you: paper. Whereas the Egyptians
had made papyrus out of beaten plant fibres, Chinese
paper was made from fibres soaked in water, a pulp.
Official Chinese records date the invention of paper to
AD 105, and, although recent archaeological evidence
suggests an even earlier date, perhaps as much as 200
years earlier, it was at the beginning of the second
century that Chinese scribes started to recognize paper
as an alternative to writing on silk and bamboo. For the
next thousand years the art of paper making was a secret
known only in the Far East and would have remained
so if, as legend has it, two Chinese paper makers had
not been captured in the prosperous silk-route city of
Samarkand, in today's Uzbekistan, and been forced to
reveal the secret of their trade. Having done so, they
were ordered by the city's governor to build and operate
a paper mill. From here paper made its slow journey
westward, through the Middle East and along the coast
of North Africa, until it reached Sicily and Spain in
the early 1100s. Despite becoming well established in
Moorish Spain, paper manufacture did not take root in
Christian Europe until the 1270s. This near 200-year delay had several causes. It was partly due to inertia: the
use of parchment (animal skin) was well established;
partly ignorance: at that time most of Europe was illiterate, much more so than in the Middle East; and partly
prejudice: paper was tainted in the eyes of the Church
by being a Muslim or Jewish artefact. Indeed, in 1221,
the Holy Roman Emperor, Frederick II, had issued a
declaration that no document written on paper could
be legally binding.

4.2: Watermark, Gutenberg Bible, Mainz, c.1455

Christian Europe finally began to make its own paper
in 1276, in the northern Italian town of Fabriano (beautiful handmade paper continues to be made there). To take
advantage of its paper's reputation for quality, its makers
developed a series of watermarks, an early form of logo,
to act as a guarantee of the paper's provenance *(fig. 4.2)*.
By the 1400s, paper making had become established
outside Italy, most notably in France, but also in Switzerland, Germany and the Low Countries. By this time, paper was being used in preference to parchment, for while
parchment was more durable, paper was easier to make
in large quantities and therefore cheaper. Furthermore, it
was easier to give paper a smooth and even surface.

While the Chinese had made their paper out of bark
and hemp, the main raw material for Europe's paper
was old rags. (One historian of the time noted that every
Frenchman, no matter how poor, owned several *chemis-
es de toile* ('vests'), and one particularly well-groomed
valet is reported to have had as many as 13; his master
would have owned more still.) The burgeoning demand
for rags to make paper established a new trade, that of
the rag-and-bone man, who would gather old clothes,
especially those made of linen (the woven fabric made

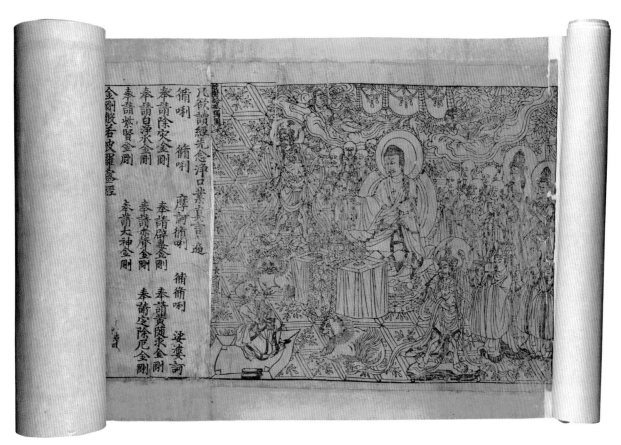

4.3: The Diamond Sutra, China, 868

from the bark of the flax plant) along with any bones, which he would boil down to make a glue for binding the linen's fibres during the paper-making process.

The attributes of cheapness and smoothness had earlier encouraged ancient Chinese scribes to take up the new medium and exploit it for whatever new methods of mark making it allowed. Not long after its invention they had used it to take rubbings from stone inscriptions, but it took a further 500 years or so before it was used for printing. Their first paper prints were made with carved blocks of wood. These woodblocks were made by cutting away the unprinted parts of the image from a short plank of wood so that a flat, uncut design was left raised 'in relief'. This technique allowed an unskilled hand to produce a primitive image with basic tools, but equally, as the earliest, dated and complete printed publication in the world, 'The Diamond Sutra' *(fig. 4.3)* attests, it was possible for a skilled hand to a create a subtle and skilfully rendered illustration. Along the length of this ancient Chinese paper scroll, all 5 m (16 ft) of it, a print was made out of seven separate woodblocks. In fact paper was used twice in the printing process: once by the artist, who painted

the image onto a thin paper before pasting it face-down onto the woodblock for the carver to cut out the image. This would have been especially helpful when cutting out the text in reverse, as is the case in all basic forms of relief printing. The second use of paper was for the scroll itself. The first part of the print shows a detailed and skilfully patterned picture of the Buddha, giving a sermon or 'sutra', as it is called in the ancient Indian language of Sanskrit. Along the remainder of the scroll, reading from right to left, are columns of Chinese text which spell out the sutra. Towards the end of the text, the Buddha gives his teaching a name, 'The Diamond of Transcendent Wisdom'. As he describes it, the teaching has the ability to cut like a diamond blade through the illusion of mankind's temporal existence to reveal what is real and everlasting. At the very end of the scroll is a colophon which gives the date when the block was cut, 11 May 868, and the instruction that the print was made 'for universal distribution'.

Printing with woodblocks is thought to have taken the same westward route into Europe as the invention of paper. It arrived in Europe in the twelfth century, before paper was commonplace and, as mentioned above, one

4.4: Sion textile (detail), Italy, after c.1350

of its earliest uses was on fabric *(fig. 4.4)*. In contrast to the more or less abstract designs that decorate most textiles today, the majority of the early woodblock prints depicted classical and biblical stories similar to those found on the pages of illuminated manuscripts.

The first instances of printing on paper were linked to pursuits then considered to be both sinful, as gambling with cards was, and saintly, as making pilgrimages to holy sites continues to be. Playing cards, like the processes that created them – paper making and printing – were a Chinese invention. Their introduction to Europe took place some time in the middle of the fourteenth century and was taken up by all classes in medieval Europe. Kings in their castles played with cards of ivory, merchants in market-places used cards engraved on silver, while everyone else played in taverns or on the roadside with cards printed on rough paper. Then, as now, after a hand was dealt a bet often followed close behind. The large number of records citing the restrictions imposed on gambling show us how popular card-playing was. One early fifteenth-century Italian priest, Saint Bernardino, is said to have delivered such a persuasive sermon against gambling that his audience took to burning their cards in the public square. A card-maker then complained to the priest that he would be destitute. The priest is said to have handed him a picture of Jesus and replied, 'If you know how to print, print this.' Perhaps it is this act that has led Saint Bernardino to be referred to on occasion as the patron saint of advertising and communications.

Many woodblock printers applied their knowledge in the direction of Saint Bernadino's injunction throughout the fourteenth century. Devotional pictures of saints or biblical figures were printed on single sheets of thick paper, and then sold at holy sites and shrines to pilgrims seeking souvenirs or holy charms. The most popular sites were often located within the massive stone walls of the new cathedrals (from the Greek *cathedra* meaning 'bishop's throne'), which rose up like great beacons of faith across Europe from the early twelfth century. The cathedral in Chartres, for example, just north of Paris, was popular on account of a piece of cloth it owned, which was said to have been part of the tunic worn by Mary when she gave birth to Jesus. Relics like this encouraged the devout to make pilgrimages as an act of piety, and the wrongdoers as an act of penitence. The sick did so in the hope that they might be made well, an all too common desire during the second half of the fourteenth century. During an initial four-year period, between 1347 and 1351, when the Black Death was at its height, a third of Europe's population is thought to have died from the plague.

Many of them, while on their sick-bed, would have prayed to a saint of uncertain origins, Saint Christopher. Though more commonly thought of as the patron saint of travellers, he is also the saint of the dying. Pictures of him in particular were sought because it was believed or hoped that, as the text in this early print puts it *(fig. 4.5)*, *Cristofori faciem die quacunque tueris, Illa nempe die morte mala non morieris* (Whoever looks on the face of Christopher shall not that day die an evil death). The

4.5: Buxheim St Christopher, Italy, after 1423

medieval art signifies the act of speaking (similar to the modern two-handed, double-finger gesture denoting 'in quotes'). To prove his identity, Christ performs a miracle by turning Christopher's staff into a fruiting palm tree.

Despite its early date, the woodcut was not the first of its kind. The quality of the cutting suggests it was made by a practised hand and its evident skill surpasses many of the prints that came after it. The tree, as well as Christopher's tunic and his pained expression, are drawn with a degree of realism that was new at that time. There are also naturalistic elements – neither the rabbit nor the mill add to the story line – which, as we have seen in some of the illuminated manuscripts, were then popular, and they too are skilfully rendered. The greater realism and the naturalistic setting may have enabled the viewer to identify with the story more closely. The addition of a colour wash would have increased this closer identification.

By the middle of the fifteenth century, woodcut printing on cards or single sheets had become sufficiently well established for it to be applied more concentratedly in book form. In the Netherlands and in Germany prints began to be bound into slim volumes of so-called 'block-books', which were often bundled together with a band and sold in sets. What is notable about the appearance of their printed pages *(>fig. 4.6)* is the greater prominence of the text. It has an almost equal standing with the pictures, somewhat like the modern comic book. The large amounts of text within one of the earliest and most popular kind of block-books, the *Biblia Pauperum* or 'Bible for the Poor', shown here, suggests that this name may have referred more to the class of relatively poor, though literate, clergy, rather than the poor and less literate laity. Most priests could not have afforded their own copy of the Bible, so this new version would have been invaluable in helping prepare sermons and establish theological doctrine.

The content of the *Biblia Pauperum* amounted to a potted history of biblical salvation (a special preoccupation of the Middle Ages). It presented a particular way of looking at biblical history. Its aim was to connect a story from the New Testament with stories of a similar theme from the Old, the implication being that the latter were prophecies fulfilled by the former. The text and pictures in each woodcut were combined according to a standardized arrangement derived from particular local variations of the book that had been established in manuscript form. Arches and windows were used to frame a story

quotation here is followed by the date 1423, which may be when the woodcut was made, rather than when it was printed. If it is the latter, this print would be the earliest dated European woodcut. The letters are carved in a regular Gothic script common to the southern German region where the print was found and is believed to have been made.

As with much early block-printing, the text is supplementary to the picture. The image tells the story of Saint Christopher and how he became identified with travellers (one of whom is shown towards the bottom left riding a donkey). Following his conversion to Christianity by a hermit (seen on the right holding a lantern – the light of Christianity) the saint dedicated himself to carrying people across a dangerous river. While carrying a boy across the river one day, Christopher felt the child getting heavier and heavier and had to lean hard on his staff for support. The child revealed himself to be Christ (the Greek word *Christophoros* means 'Christ-bearer') and explained his heaviness thus: 'I made the world, I redeemed the world, I bear the sins of the world'. In one hand Christ is carrying an orb, which signifies his global dominion, while the other is raised in a gesture that in

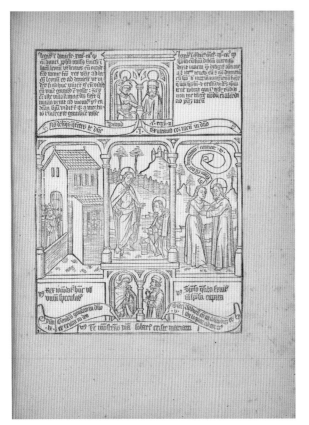

4.6: 'Biblia Pauperum' block-book, Netherlands, c.1470

from the New Testament in the middle – here, Mary Magdalene finding Christ after his resurrection – and two complementary stories from the Old Testament either side of it – King Nebuchadnezzar finding Daniel alive (on the left), and the daughter of Sion finding her spouse (on the right); Christ's injunction 'seek and ye shall find' is the uniting concept here. Above and below this triptych is a pair of prophets bearing witness to the biblical scenes. The page's text includes a verse from each of the four prophets set on two pairs of thin scroll-like banners, called banderoles, and then three rhymes of two lines each below the three pictures. In the top corners, two more substantial bits of text provide an interpretation of the pictures' meaning. Though block-books such as these were produced in large numbers, their authors and engravers are nearly all unknown.

Having established that printing, like its principal medium, paper, had come to Europe from China, and that it was already being used to make block-books by the middle of the fifteenth century, we can be forgiven for wondering what it was exactly that Gutenberg invented. The common description, beyond that of printing, is

that he invented printing with 'movable type'; that is, separate small metal blocks, each with a single letter shape carved on the end. By combining these blocks into lines and stacking the lines into columns it was possible to print pages of text. But even this claim is incorrect. Again, we have to look to China, for it is there that a blacksmith, alchemist and printer called Pi Sheng (990–1051) is said to have made type with fired blocks of clay between 1041 and 1048. There is no direct proof of his invention; no piece of type or printed artefact has survived. But the records of his work are sufficiently detailed for them to be accepted as true.

The earliest piece of printing made with metal type, as opposed to clay, was a Buddhist text dating from 1377. It had been printed at a provincial temple in South Korea, which suggests that Korean artisans had mastered the basic techniques of casting and setting type at least seven decades before Gutenberg produced his first book. The handsome Korean book shown here *(fig. 4.7)* was printed in 1434, two decades before Gutenberg, and yet the quality of its type, with letterforms based on the much-admired calligraphy of a contemporary Chinese scribe, shows how expertly Korean printers had perfected this printing technique.

So, since Gutenberg neither invented printing, nor printed the first book, nor invented movable type with whatever material, why is his name associated with the birth of printing? The answer is twofold. First, and most significantly, that by bringing together a series of previously unrelated technologies, Gutenberg was able to print text much faster and more efficiently than a scribe or a printer with a woodblock had ever done before. In so doing he changed the way Europeans read and, ultimately, what they thought. Medieval reading has been characterized as being a top-down flow of information from the author via the bishop or teacher to the passive layman or pupil. With Gutenberg's inaugural pull of the press, newly printed texts cut right across this literary hierarchy. The quantity and variety of newly printed material soon allowed readers to choose their own reading matter and then interpret it as they wished. Just as readers became more proactive, so did writers. Increasing numbers of literate people in Europe began to publish responses to what they had read, and these comments were themselves commented on. In this way, knowledge was accumulated and refined within an ever-widening public domain. It was the founding of the important process of 'peer review', which continues to lie at the heart of

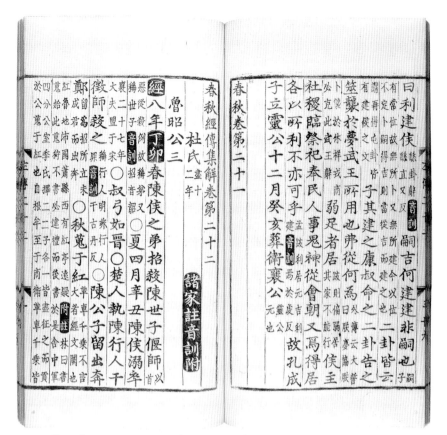

4.7: *Collected Commentaries on the Spring and Autumn Annals, Korea, 1434*

4.8: *Gold coins, Milan, c.1450*

modern scholarship and science. At the heart of this process was the concept of the 'edition'. A particular printed text could be relied on to exist in exactly the same form in every copy made during the same print run. Discussions of texts could be conducted in the knowledge that not only was the content the same but its appearance on particular pages was also the same. Neither of these could be guaranteed with a manuscript.

The second aspect of Gutenberg's contribution is less general and more technical. Gutenberg grew up in one of Germany's oldest and most prosperous cities, 'Golden' Mainz, whose location on the Rhine (then and still one of Europe's great trading routes) made it famous for its goldsmiths and jewellers. As a young man, it is thought that he spent some time working in the mint where for a period his father had some kind of managerial role. It is here that Gutenberg is likely to have gained an understanding of how letters were cut onto the ends of metal blocks, or 'punches' as they are called, in order to impress a design onto coins *(fig. 4.8)*. One of the hallmarks of the inventor is the ability to take a particular piece of knowledge or a set of skills and apply it to a new field. It was to Gutenberg's credit that he was

able to see how the minter's individual punches could be adapted to the process of printing text. By cutting letters individually onto the head of separate punches, rather than cutting whole lines of text on a single block of wood, as the carver of the picture of Saint Christopher had done, letters could be combined or 'set' in the requisite order and then held in a frame (known as a 'forme') before being covered in ink and impressed onto paper. Once printed they could then be broken up and reused in whatever new combination was needed. The time spent setting the type each time was as nothing compared to the woodcutter's task of carving each new page of text letter by letter on a fresh block of wood.

Another essential component in Gutenberg's act of creative synthesis was his adaptation of the minter's craft of casting metal from a mould. Legions of letters and punctuation marks were required to print a book. (This half page of text you are reading contains almost 2300 separate characters.) A single page from Gutenberg's first book, one page from a total of nearly 1300, contained about 3000 characters. But, instead of carving a separate punch for each of these thousands of characters, Gutenberg could make just one punch for

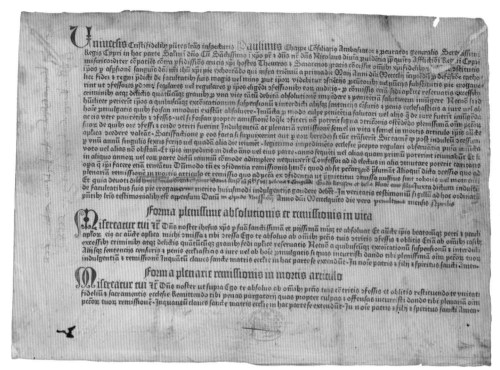

4.9: 31-line indulgence, printed by Johannes Gutenberg, Mainz, c.1454

each kind of character – one for the letter 'a', one for 'b', etc. – and then used the punch to make a mould from which any number of replica metal blocks, or 'types' could be cast. The fact that the alphabet contains a relatively small number of letters made the process of punch making and type casting economically viable. By contrast, Pi Sheng, the Chinese inventor of movable type, would have needed tens of thousands of punches to print his non-alphabetic system of writing. It is this fact, the sheer number of types required, that is likely to have inhibited the further development of this form of printing in the East.

Where Gutenberg was more straightforwardly innovative rather than adaptive was in designing a new kind of mould for casting his type. Like the conventional minter's mould, it had a small rectangular chamber with an upturned die as its base and an open top for pouring in an admixture of molten lead and tin, but instead of having sides of a fixed width, Gutenberg made them adjustable, so that type of various widths, from the narrow 'i's to the wide 'w's, could be cast. Having modified nearly all the constituent technologies of his printing method so successfully – he also found an unusually rich black ink, possibly the kind used by oil painters, that would adhere to the metal type – it seems justifiable to consider the entirety of his creation as a wholly new invention. It is a testament to its soundness and fitness that it remained the primary method of printing for the next 350 years.

Despite having described Gutenberg's achievement more precisely, we are still not free from the contention that plagues his status as an inventor. Gutenberg was not the only person from this time to be heralded as the inventor of printing. A few have argued that he stole the idea and the tools to execute it from a Dutch printer. Others have claimed that it was in fact Gutenberg's financial backer who invented the process. It seems unlikely that we shall ever know any more about who did what when, yet, with the facts as they stand today, what we *can* say is that nowhere else other than in Germany did the printed book first rival the manuscript, and with no one else can this fact be more closely associated than with Johannes Gutenberg.

It is a grand incongruity that printing, with its ability to record and disseminate action or thought, and as one of the greatest of all cultural achievements, first took place without any reliable witness or clear record. We know very little about Gutenberg as a man and we know even less about his works partly because Gutenberg wanted it this way. We do know that over the long period of testing and refining, Gutenberg tried to keep his activities secret. He had good reason to do so. Not

4.10: Gutenberg Bible, Mainz, c.1455

only had he borrowed large sums of money to fund the development of his invention, which made it imperative that no potential profits were lost to a rival printer, but also he would have been aware of how provocative his invention would be. It was likely to arouse considerable hostility from the powerful guilds of scribes and illuminators, whose livelihoods it would threaten.

Among the various early items thought to have been printed by Gutenberg, the first dated piece was a papal indulgence of 1454 *(fig. 4.9)*. An indulgence was an official pardon granted by the Church to sinners who had paid penance – fasting, going on pilgrimage or, most controversially, giving money to the Church – in an effort to shorten the time spent in purgatory (in Catholic doctrine, a sort of staging post to heaven or hell). It is not surprising that this kind of workaday item should appear among the very first pieces of printing. The granting of indulgences had grown into a small industry during the fourteenth and fifteenth centuries and could be as potentially lucrative for the printer as it was for the Church. Then as now the Church needed money to pay for the upkeep and beautification of Church buildings. Often, though, this money went directly into the clergy's pockets rather than their porches or pews. (In *The Canterbury Tales*, the long satirical poem by the medieval English author Geoffrey Chaucer, 1343–1400, the pardoner, a person who sells indulgences, says: 'And lightly it comth, so wol we spende.') It was this issue that had led Martin Luther to the church door. Indulgences could be issued in a written or a printed form, like a kind of receipt, with spaces left, as here, for the buyer's signature and the date. Its status as an essentially utilitarian, clerical document was reflected in its type and layout. Most of the type in this example is based on a semi-formal Gothic letter, *bâtarde (< fig. 3.15, p. 62)*. It contrasts with the decorated initials, the larger type at the beginning of the text and in the headings, which is set in a more formal textura. An informal script is used to complete and sign off the document. The long lines of tightly packed text give it the appearance of a legal document, like Magna Carta, rather than a formal book page.

The first book that Gutenberg printed with movable type was a large Latin Bible (*< fig. 4.10, 4.11*). Like the large manuscript Bibles, it was made for display or for communal reading rather than private study. Though it contains no date or place of printing, a copy was recorded as being bound by a Mainz bookbinder in 1456, which suggests that it was printed a year or two before. Bibliophiles refer to the book shown as 'the 42-line Bible' because most of its pages contain columns of text 42 lines long (in contrast to another similar Bible with 36 lines), but the name by which it is known generally is the Gutenberg Bible. It is understandably famous for being the first book of its kind, but its size, grandeur and beauty also contribute to its high status. Each page appears with two columns of text that together cover an area about the size of a sheet of A4 paper; the size of each page being twice as big, roughly A3 size (the size of a spread in this book). The earliest contemporary account describes the printed pages thus: 'All that has been written to me about that marvellous man seen at Frankfurt is true. [Evidently, someone, perhaps even Gutenberg, had taken them to sell at the book fair.] I have not seen complete Bibles but only a number of quires [unbound pages] of various books of the Bible. The script was very neat and legible, not at all difficult to follow – your grace would be able to read it without effort, and indeed without glasses.' Because we are less familiar with Gothic script, it is harder for us read the book's very regular and tightly spaced letters. Yet this deficiency might actually increase our appreciation of the pages. It heightens our sense of the tonal and spacial relationships that combine to make the pages so beautiful.

We see this Bible as the harbinger of a literary revolution, but for Gutenberg it was in many ways an extension of the manuscript tradition. He made it according to the conventions that governed the appearance of a large Bible. The form of the letters, their position on the page and the punctuation, all conform to the then current conventions of an ecclesiastical manuscript. Important among these was the sanctity of the text area and the evenness of the letter spacing within it. Each line of text has been forced to fit the rigidly fixed width of each column by using a large number of abbreviations and also by hanging out the hyphens (the diagonal equal signs) in the margins and gutter (the space between two columns of text). Combined letters, or 'ligatures' helped to create this justified setting. The rigid grid of letters was thrown into further relief by the glossy black ink on the stark white Italian paper, and then also by the contrasting swirls of multi-coloured illumination and dabs of (mostly) hand-painted rubrication. Following scribal practice, Gutenberg had left spaces in the columns of text for large hand-painted illuminated initials. He also supplied a separate list of headings to be written at the top of each page. Both the rubrication and illumination were to be added by or on behalf of each buyer. Of the 48 or so copies of Gutenberg's Bible still in existence, 20 of which are complete, all have been customized in this way. They each look different, but are all hybrids: printed manuscripts.

The Gutenberg Bible and the books that followed it during the second half of the fifteenth century are known to bibliophiles as 'incunabula' (Latin for 'swaddling clothes', 'cradle', 'birthplace' or 'origin') because they were made when the art of printing was still in its infancy. As a group, these books did not evolve seamlessly away from the appearance of a manuscript towards a clear and well-defined alternative. Their development proceeded in fits and starts. Innovations were abandoned by the printers who started them (Ratdolt's title page, *>fig.5.5, p.87*), and conventions were clung to long after they had served any useful purpose (the full point in a title on a title page, *>fig.5.13, p.94*). And yet, the uniformity of their printed texts made them visibly different. They could not escape the regimented cast of the new printing medium, with its rectangular types and text blocks. Mechanization imbued them with a new and subtle sense of order.

The difference in the appearance of printed type from a handwritten script may be seen by comparing the rubricated script at the top of a column of text on the Bible page and the text around it. Despite the efforts of the rubricator to match the script to the printed type, the red letters are unevenly spaced and they slope down the page slightly, whereas the printed letters are crisp and evenly spaced, and each line of text is uniformly horizontal. This new sense of order was not confined to the letterforms, it emanated from the whole page. The space between the lines of text, the alignment of the lines of text at the margins, and the position of the block of text on the page all looked tidier and more uniform than they did on a manuscript page. Shorthand scribbles and marginal notes disappeared, as did many of the ruled guidelines and illuminated sketches. The printed book began to look less and less like a handmade work of art and more like a mass-produced, machine-made artefact.

Incipit liber Bresith, quez nos Gene
sis. In principio creauit deus celū sin vō-
et terram. Terra autem erat inanis et
vacua: 7 tenebre erant sup faciē abissi:
et spiritus dūi ferebatur super aquas.
Dixitq; deus. Fiat lux. Et facta ē lux.
Et vidit deus lucem tp esset bona: et
diuisit lucem a tenebris. appellauitq;
lucem diem et tenebras noctem. Factū
tp est vespere 7 mane dies vnus. Dixit
quoq; deus. Fiat firmamentū in me-
dio aquarū: et diuidat aquas ab a-
quis. Et fecit deus firmamentū: diuisi-
sitq; aquas que erant sub firmamen-
to ab hijs que erant super firmamen-
tum: 7 factum est ita. Vocauitq; deus
firmamentū celū: 7 factum est vespere
et mane dies secundus. Dixit vero deus. Congregentur aque que sub celo
sunt in locum vnū et appareat arida.
Et factum est ita. Et vocauit deus ari-
dam terram: cōgregationésq; aquax
appellauit māria. Et vidit deus tp esset bonū. et ait. Germinet terra herbā
virentem et facientem semen: et lignū
pomiferū facietis fructum iuxta genus
suū: cuius semen in semetipo sit super
terram. Et factum est ita. Et protulit
terra herbam virentem et facientem semen iuxta getus suū: lignūq; faciens
fructū et habēs vnūqdq; sementē scdm
speciē suā. Et vidit deus tp esset bonū:
et factū ē vespere et mane dies tercius.
Dixitq; aūt deus. Fiant luminaria
in firmamēto celi · 7 diuidāt diem ac

pessent diei ac nocti: 7 diuiderō
ac tenebras. Et vidit de9 tp esse
et factū ē vespere et mane dies
Dixit etiam deus. Producan
reptile anime viuentis et volā
terram: sub firmamēto celi. Et
deus cete grandia. et omnē an
uentem atq; motabilem quā p
rant aque in species suas: 7 or
latile secundū genus suū. Et v
us tp esset bonū: benedixitq; ei
Crescite et multiplicamini. et r
quas maris: auesq; multipl
super terram. Et factū ē vespere 7
dies quitus. Dixit quoq; deu
dūcat terra animā viuentem i
re suo: iumenta 7 reptilia. 7 bes
re secundū species suas. Factū ē
fecit deus bestias terre iuxta spe
as: iumenta 7 omne reptile ter
nere suo. Et vidit deus tp esse
et ait. Faciam9 hominē ad yma
sikitudinē nostrā. 7 psit piscibz
7 volatilibz celi. 7 bestijs vniūse
oiūq; reptili qd mouet i terra.
uit deus hominē ad ymaginē
litudinē suam: ad ymaginem
uit illū: masculū et feminā crea
Benedixitq; illis deus · et ait. J
et multiplicamini 7 replete ter
subicite eam: 7 dominamini p
maris· 7 volatilibus celi: 7 vn
animātibus que mouentur s
Dixitq; deus. Ecce dedi vobis
herbam afferentem semen sup

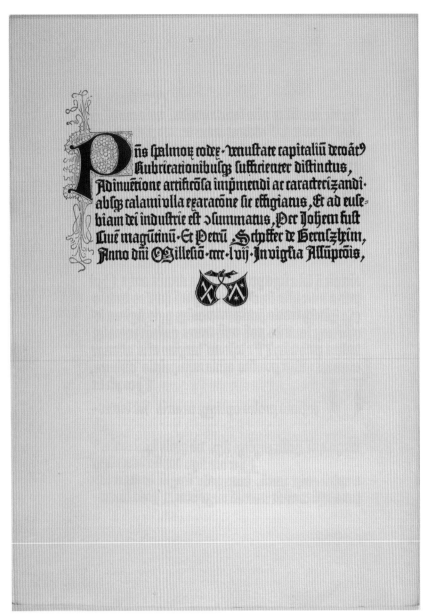

4.12: Colophon, Mainz Psalter (facsimile), Peter Schoeffer, 1457

The impact of the printing press on the appearance of books extended beyond the main pages of text and into a preliminary section which was first formed with and later dominated by a separate title page. We have seen already how manuscripts sometimes featured a short, often rubricated, introductory heading, or incipit *(<fig.3.10, p.57)*, which sat directly above the opening text. The incipit and a less common manuscript feature, the colophon, in which the name of the manuscript maker would be mentioned, can be thought of as the precursors to the title page by dint of their content. The first time the title appeared on a separate printed page

was in a collection of psalms, called the Mainz Psalter *(fig.4.12)*. The earlier of the two editions of this book is now believed to have been the second book printed, and, through its colophon, the first to include a printing date (1457). Above the date sits the name of the printer. In fact there are two names, neither of which is Gutenberg's, though both were well known to him. The first, Johann Fust (*c*.1400–66), was the name of his backer, and the second, Peter Schoeffer (*c*.1425–1503), his foreman and type designer. It seems that by the time the Psalter was being printed both men had stopped working with Gutenberg. We know that over a year earlier, in

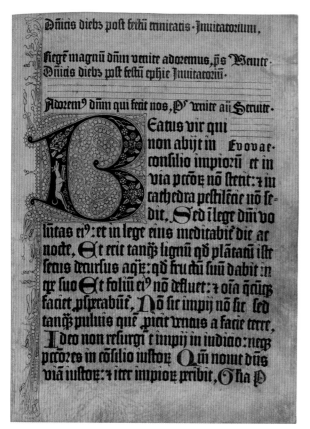

4.13: *Mainz Psalter, Peter Schoeffer, 1457*

1455, a court order had forced Gutenberg to hand over much of his printing equipment to Fust in lieu of an unpaid debt. Losing his invention immediately after he had printed his Bible must have been devastating. There is no clear evidence that he ever printed anything again, though there are several indications that he continued to be involved in the trade.

Fust and Schoeffer, by contrast, had a productive partnership that resulted in a number of fine books. The Mainz Psalter, their first, was one of the finest. Sitting underneath the Mainz Psalter's colophon is an early kind of printer's logo, or 'printer's device' *(fig. 4.12)*. It appeared in all their books, though the example here is thought to have been stamped by hand after the book was printed, as a sign of authenticity or quality. The shield symbols, each one decorated with their respective family designs, continued a heraldic tradition long established by medieval craftsmen. Having the shields hang from a branch was original though, and was imitated by subsequent German printers. It may have signified the union of the two families not only through their business activity but also through Schoeffer's marriage to Fust's daughter. The appeal of the device lay in the

beauty of the books it was associated with and then in the formal qualities of the device itself: its bold, simple shapes, its novel playfulness, and the ease with which it could be personalized.

The Mainz Psalter's most notable feature is its colour. It was the first and one of the few incunabula to have all its rubrication printed. Furthermore, the red incipits, initials and decoration were printed at the same time as the black text, under the same pull of the press. What was even more unique was the inclusion of a third colour, blue, or in some instances grey. The blue appeared alongside the red on the series of richly decorated initials that adorned the first page of each psalm; one colour for the letter itself (here, the blue), the other for the surrounding decoration. By printing the differently coloured parts simultaneously, Fust and Schoeffer were able to attain an extraordinarily precise fit *(fig.4.13)*. But the time, effort and skill involved in quickly applying different inks to precise bits of type dissuaded them from continuing this process. This attempt at a range of colour printing stands in splendid isolation. Its uniqueness indicated a trend in printing which continued for the next two centuries. There was little colour printing other than rubrication. For the most part, the printer's art was played out on a monochrome page.

Fust and Schoeffer continued to make innovations with their presses. They pioneered the printed title page, though it amounted to little more than a short label-like description. The block of text that begins their pamphlet of 1463, described as a papal bull (as in 'bulletin'), is the first known instance of this label form of title page *(fig. 4.14)*. In one sense it is undesigned. The text is set like a paragraph of main text. Its four lines of German text (a Latin version had two lines) set in large Gothic textura type describe the contents and give the author's name. Whereas manuscripts were usually made individually for and delivered directly to the person who had commissioned them, these early books were mass-produced speculatively and stored unbound before being sold. The need to protect the first page in particular prompted the addition of a blank cover page, which, from about 1480 began to have a small label-title printed on it so that the stored prints could be identified.

During printing's first two decades, books had been largely typographic. Any non-typographic matter was invariably part of a decorated initial or border. During the following three decades, in Germany especially,

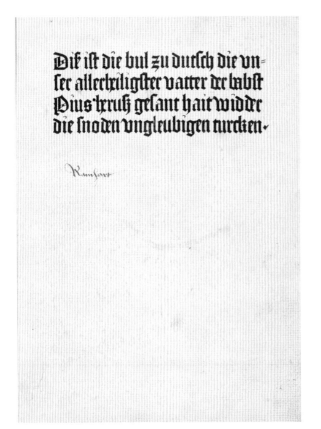

4.14: Papal bull, title page, Peter Schoeffer, Mainz, 1463

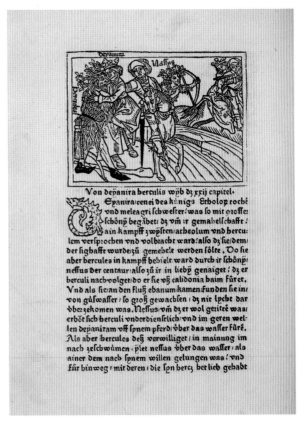

4.15: 'De mulieribus claris', printed by Johan Zainer, 1473

much greater emphasis was put on using woodcuts to illustrate the text. Printers there had become familiar with the new printing technology and had been able to work out how to incorporate the drawing and cutting of larger, subject-orientated woodcuts into the process of print production. They commissioned some of the greatest artists of the period to provide a range of varied effects to their book pages.

As early as 1460, the first non-decorative illustrations to be printed alongside type appeared in books printed by Albert Pfister (*c.*1420–*c.*1470), who worked in the city of Bamberg, about a hundred miles upstream of Mainz. Pfister printed both religious and secular texts. Fables and folk tales were rendered with the same kind of simple outlines and minimal shading that had appeared in contemporary block-book illustrations and they also took to being coloured by hand. A much more sophisticated page was produced by printing presses in Augsburg and Ulm, then the centres of religious picture production and playing card production respectively, though none were as refined as those produced by the Ulm printer, Johan Zainer (?–1523). It is in his edition of Boccaccio's *De mulieribus claris* ('Of Famous Women'),

printed in 1473, that a previously unrivalled marriage of woodcut and text was achieved *(fig. 4.15)*. The small, rounded Gothic type is less compact than the more angular and tighter Gothic of earlier incunabula. It lends the text area a lightness and an airiness, which is added to by the wider interline spacing. The visual weight of the block of type matches that of the illustration, which has been consciously filled out into the framed space with a rhythmical shading. The more even distribution of shading stops the illustration from being broken up by many large areas of uninked background space. The same visual weight was given to the woodcut initial. None of these three elements of type, illustration and initial are the best of their kind, but they have been brought together as harmoniously as any previous page design.

The most influential illustrated secular book of the period was the *Liber Chronicarum* (loosely translated as *The World Chronicle*), now more commonly known as 'The Nuremberg Chronicle', in reference to the city where it was first published. The book aims to provide an illustrated history of the world from the moment of Creation up to the year of publication, 1493. The

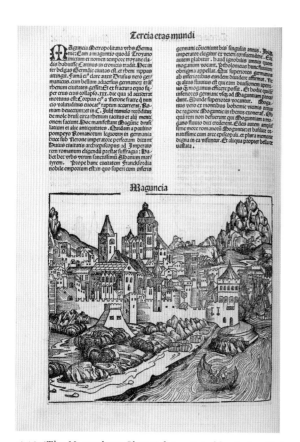

4.16: 'The Nuremberg Chronicle', printed by Anton Koberger, 1493

scholarly ambition of its author was matched by the logistical ambition of the printer, Anton Koberger (*c.*1440/5–1513), who organized the drawing – by at least 22 different illustrators – the cutting and then the printing of 652 woodcuts. The illustrations range from biblical and classical stories to portraits, genealogical trees, maps, panoramic landscapes and city views. But if we come to the book expecting it to be a faithful representation of how the world looked at the end of the fifteenth century, we shall be somewhat disappointed. The total number of illustrations is over 1800, almost three times the number of woodcuts. This is due to the large number of repeated images. The view of Mainz, for example, with its solid walls and flowing river, looks exactly like the views of Bologna and Lyon *(fig. 4.16)*. These last two cities were too far from Nuremberg for people to have much information about their actual appearance. Thus, rather than being topographically correct depictions, they served as a symbolic shorthand, indicating to the reader that each place was a city. Few people had travelled or would travel to such far flung places, so it was enough to show that they were of a certain size and import.

During the second quarter of the sixteenth century, printing with moveable type became established in most countries across Europe. The chronology of its introduction to some of Europe's major cities is as follows: Rome 1467, Venice 1469, Paris 1470, Budapest 1473, Cracow and Bruges 1474, London 1475, Geneva 1478, Antwerp 1481, Stockholm 1483. Many of the first practitioners in these cities were German nationals, who reinforced the strong influence that imported German books had brought to the appearance of the printed page. Gothic influences can be seen in the work of the English printer, William Caxton (*c.*1422–1492), who printed what is believed to be the first book in English, *The Recuyell [Collection] of the Histories of Troy* (> *fig. 4.17*). Caxton had translated it himself from French before printing it in Bruges around 1473/4. The text was printed with type that had been specially made for the book. Its design was based on the Gothic *bâtarde* script, which had been popular in manuscripts produced for the Burgundian court *(< fig. 3.15, p.62)*. The same style had been used by Gutenberg in his papal indulgence *(< fig. 4.9)*, though since Caxton was printing in English he

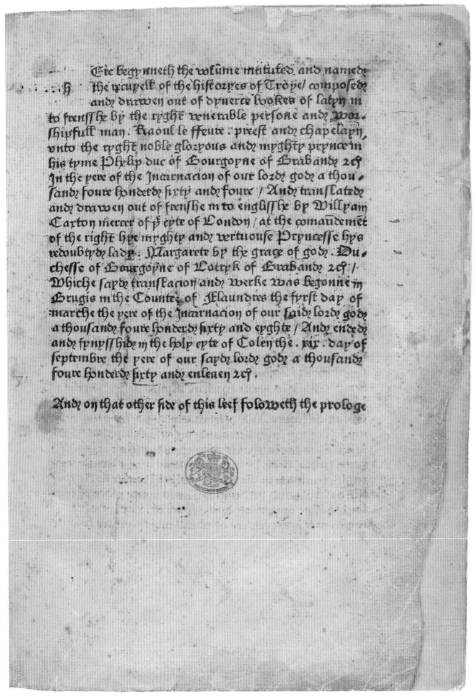

4.17: 'The Recuyell of the Histories of Troy', printed by William Caxton, Bruges, c.1473/4

incorporated features that were peculiar to the English language, such as the letters 'w' and 'k'.

Caxton's decision to print in English had a sound commercial basis. No other printer was catering to the English-speaking market. Yet he was only free to do so because his subject matter was secular. Had he wanted to print a Bible in English he would have had to apply for a special licence, without which he might have suffered as others had when caught in possession of English Bibles; they were tried for heresy and burnt at the stake. Leaders of the Church in England wished to avoid a situation in which, as one later commentator put it, 'every man, nay, every boy and wench that could read English, thought they spoke with God

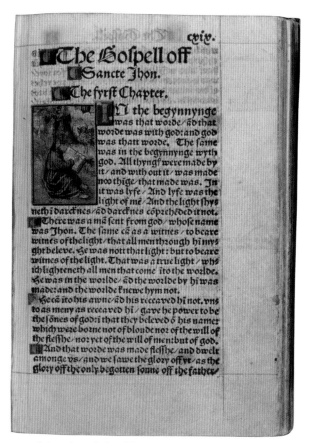

4.18: Printed English Bible, William Tyndale, Worms, 1526

which was printed with a Gothic type in a small format that was therefore easy to conceal. Once printed, his text could not be kept out of England nor, indeed, out of English. Tyndale's translation provided much of the text for the two most popular English Bibles prior to the modern versions of the twentieth century. One was the Geneva Bible of 1560, which dominated the sixteenth and seventeenth centuries (it was this verson that the Pilgrim Fathers and Puritans took to America), and the other was the King James Bible or 'Authorized Version' of 1611. Thus, as well as becoming known as 'the Father of the English Bible', Tyndale is also referred to by some as 'the Father of the English language' on account of the clarity and beauty of his translation. (Others argue that the title belongs to Thomas Cranmer whose prose masterpiece *The Book of Common Prayer*, of 1559, was both more widely used and closer to vernacular English.) Tyndale's language lives on even today in words such as 'beautiful', 'peacemaker' and 'scapegoat', and phrases such as 'the powers that be', 'the salt of the earth', 'a law unto themselves' and 'fight the good fight' *(< p.18)*.

The Gothic types and simple outline illustrations that had influenced printing in countries such as England were not adopted everywhere in Europe. In Italy especially, other influences were at work. In Italian painting, new techniques of shading, perspective and proportion had been discovered, and in architecture, sculpture and lettering a deliberate imitation of classical forms had taken hold. During a visit to Venice in 1506, the German painter and illustrator Albrecht Dürer sent news of these changes in Italian art back to Germany. He had seen for himself the greater freedom enjoyed by Italian artists compared to the restrictions he had had to endure as a member of the Nuremberg guilds. 'How I shall shiver for the sun' he wrote when contemplating his return.

Almighty and understood what he said'. The Church preferred to restrict Bible-reading to an elite group of Latin readers. It was a position that was supported initially by England's autocratic and opportunstic king, Henry VIII, who as 'Defender of the Faith' sought to maintain the primacy of the Latin Bible. However, after declaring independence from Rome Henry's attitude changed. Under the new, additional mantle of 'the only Supreme Head in Earth of the Church of England', he issued a command in 1538 that every church in England should own a copy of the Bible in English. This though was too late to save the life of an English scholar and translator, William Tyndale (1490/4–1536), who for the first time had translated the Bible into English directly from the original Hebrew and Greek (earlier translations had been made from the Latin). In an effort to get his outlawed English text printed, Tyndale fled to Germany and then to the Netherlands. Even there, Catholics caught up with him, and in 1536 he was strangled to death and his corpse burnt at the stake.

Tyndale though had managed to print his text. His first completed book was the New Testament *(fig. 4.18)*,

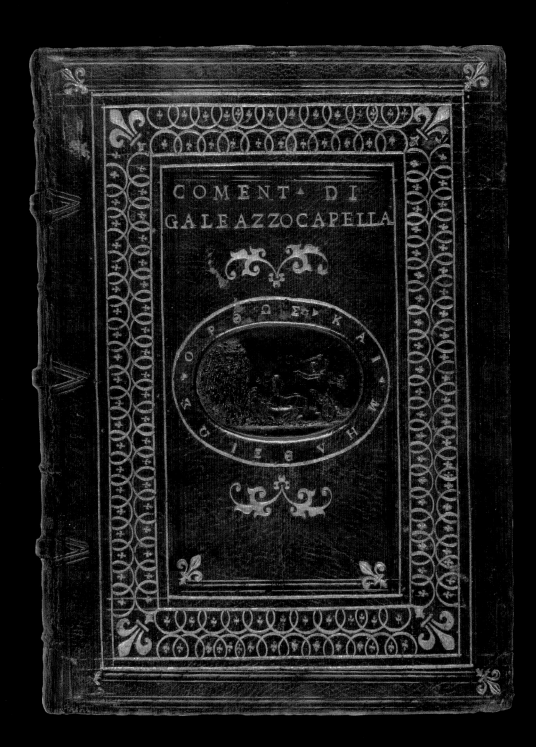

5 BACK TO THE FUTURE

Renaissance Italy & France, c.1460–c.1600

The first hundred years after Gutenberg's invention, from roughly 1455 to 1555, have been called the 'golden age' of printing. It is a title which recognizes both the large number of beautiful books that were printed during this period and the new kinds of beauty that sprang from their pages. Gothic type, which had so dominated the first printed books in Germany, was not the automatic choice of letterform for all printers elsewhere. In Italy a more rounded and open style of type was developed soon after printing first arrived there in 1465. The shape of these letters and the way they were placed on the page were linked to the 're-birth' – or renaissance, as later generations referred to it – of learning from ancient Greece and Rome. Books of Latin classics as well as some contemporary texts were set in a less angular, 'roman' style of type based on a script wrongly believed to have been written by the ancient Romans. The new roman types were set alongside exquisitely refined and, for the most part, unilluminated woodcuts of decorative initials and borders. The precision with which both type and decoration could be positioned on the page, and the uniformity with which ink could be impressed onto paper allowed the printed Renaissance page to look lighter and more refined than its manuscript equivalent. The very best Renaissance pages achieved a simplicity and grandeur not seen before and rarely matched since. The achievement is all the more remarkable since many of them were among the very first pages to pass through a printing press.

The revival of learning in Italy was largely based on books. Unlocking the ancient past required books in manuscript form to be studiously translated and annotated. From around the last quarter of the fifteenth century onwards, this newly recovered knowledge was transmitted by printed books. This critical mass of classical scholarship set off a series of chain reactions in almost every field of inquiry. Books on law, philosophy, art, mathematics, science, education and military warfare, among others seemed to find appropriate models or novel stimuli in classical texts. The production of indulgences, devotional prints and other forms of ephemera might have made up the bulk of printing during this time (so little exists its extent is difficult to gauge), but books were certainly the most prestigious form of print. The esteem in which the format and its often classical subject matter were held was reflected in the quality of the design. Buyers were willing to complement their elegant pages with solid bindings and handsome leather-clad protective covers *(fig. 5.1)*. This emphasis on the book's appearance made it the dominant format for exercises in the evolution of graphic style.

What is striking about the Renaissance printed book compared with the medieval manuscript is the almost complete loss of colour. Where once varied hues of illuminated initials and brightly painted borders had suffused book pages with a sense of depth and richness, there was now a resolutely two-dimensional surface of black and white. The loss of the polychrome page was not immediate, however, nor was it quite total. Many religious books in particular retained the rubricator's distinctive red and some illustrations continued to be coloured by hand. In Italy especially, printing underwent a significant period of transition during which some books were both printed and illuminated *(>fig. 5.2)*, just as copies of Gutenberg's Bible had been. But whereas many of the hand-painted decorations in that edition of the Bible had looked almost tokenistic in their sparseness, the illuminations in many of the early printed Italian books continued to be extremely highly wrought. The richness of the illuminator's palette was combined with a new mastery of the depiction of light and the new discovery of perspective to make ever more convincing *trompe l'oeil* effects. It was as though the Italian illuminators had been provoked into proving what skill and variety lay

5.2: *Printed and illuminated book, Milan, 1490*

within the human hand as compared to a block of type or a woodcut illustration.

For all its apparent attractions, the illuminated printed page did not fit with the process of mass production that so defined the printing press. Painted pages took too long to make. And yet, paradoxically, their old-fashioned traits of slowness and unrepeatability helped to preserve the art of illumination for a period. Wealthy patrons who wished to commemorate a special occasion or own a unique artefact would commission an illuminated manuscript specifically because it was not mass-produced. Those who could not afford such extravagances might also turn to a scribe when in need of a simple one-off document, a certificate of marriage say. It is likely that in these sorts of instances a scribe could write it more quickly than the printer could set, ink and print it. But examples of this kind were few. By 1500 the scribe had been pushed from his thousand-year-old position at the heart of the book to the very fringes of the book world.

Being devoid of hand-painted decoration and colour, the Renaissance book saw a new emphasis placed on the form of the text. Italy was the first country to receive the German invention of printing (two German printers set up a press in the town of Subiaco, outside Rome, in 1464), and the first to reject the Gothic types preferred by their northerly neighbours. Though the first printers in Italy were German, their customers were Italian, and many of them had firm ideas about the right kind of lettering for the books they wanted. The kind of lettering commonly wished for was a script known as humanist bookhand, or as the humanists themselves called it, *littera antiqua* ('letter of the ancients'), in contrast with the then current *littera moderna* or rotunda script.

Humanist scribes had developed their bookhand at the beginning of the century for new editions of classical texts. They had based it on a model which they believed to be ancient Roman. In fact, it was a Carolingian minuscule from the ninth century *(< fig.3.7, p.54)* (which indeed had been influenced by the Roman half-uncial). Being a 'minuscule', the model was without a fully developed set of capitals, so the humanist scribes combined it with a set of classical capital letters. The provenance of the capital form was beyond doubt. Roman inscriptional square capitals could be seen carved on a number of ancient buildings, monuments *(< fig.2.19, p.42)* and tombstones.

Just as humanist scholars had scoured monastery libraries for neglected classical manuscripts, so ancient monuments had been studied for examples of Roman lettering. The proportion of the letters were copied and imitated by calligraphers, painters and architects throughout the century. One of the first to make a thorough study of Roman inscriptional lettering was the calligrapher and *antiquarius* – a student of antiquity – Felice Feliciano (1433–79) of Verona. By going back to the principles of geometrical construction that had guided Roman stonecutters during the early years of the empire, Feliciano designed an alphabet of capitals using squares and circles, which he set down in manuscript form *c.*1460–3 *(fig.5.3)*. Each letter of his *Alphabetum Romanum* was made in outline with an interline shading indicating the 'v'-shaped cut of inscribed Roman letters. The proportion of the letters was guided by a square, and the width of the main stem of each letter was loosely a tenth of its height, in accordance with early Roman practice. Feliciano intended his letters to serve as models for stonecutters, but his treatise also encouraged scribes and printers, during the next century especially,

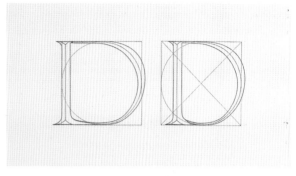

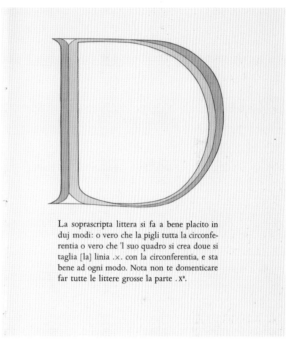

La soprascripta littera si fa a bene placito in duj modi: o vero che la pigli tutta la circonferentia o vero che 'l suo quadro si crea doue si taglia [la] linia .x. con la circonferentia, e sta bene ad ogni modo. Nota non te domenticare far tutte le littere grosse la parte . xª.

5.3: 'Alphabetum Romanum', Felice Feliciano, Verona, 1460–3

to investigate the effect of geometrical rules on the shape of capital letters. The influence of his treatise and others like it on printers and punch-cutters did not lead them to make shapes that were strictly proportional. The different requirements of type at different sizes didn't allow that. It was more a general sense of order that they picked up on, and perhaps too the germ of an idea that letters could be guided by criteria, geometrical or otherwise, that came from outside the physical act of carving or writing.

One of the first most complete transpositions of the humanist bookhand into roman type was a set of type made by the first non-German printer we know of, a Frenchman called Nicolas Jenson (1420–80). After learning how to print in Mainz, Jenson moved to Venice in 1467 to start his own printing workshop. He diligently sought out the best examples of incised capitals

nt templum:fecūdū legem diuinitus fupplicia
um per afpera fcanderet loca præcipité decidiffe:
m quum eques per littora ferretur in profundo
ɔ fuiffe aquis demerfum.Phaylum aūt alii facro
alii quū templū Inabis incéderet una cōcrematū
ɔ profecto hæc cafu nifi amés accidiffe putabit.
eifdem temporibus propter idem delictum non
olebat iure punitos non a fortuna & cafu fed di
us:Quod fi nōnulli rapaces & factiofi homines
nmodo populos fed patrias etiam fuas fubiece/
uidetur:mirandum non eft.Primum enim non
nines iudicant:homines enim de manifeftis tan
deus uero in aīum igreffus ipfū nudos uolūtatis
re nunq humana iudicia diuino tanq meliora &
ūnt.Multis eīm hoies fallunt fenfibus corporis
ni.Iudæo autem nihil eft quod fallat:fed fūma
ate cuncta geruntur.Deinde recte illud imprimis
lū tyrannos quod funt in lege fupplicia.Quádo
deo abundant ut nulla legum reuerétia fit:tunc
x ad uirtutem homines cōuertat crudelibus atq
uriam potentia præbet:uitiorum enim cumulus
ari nō poteft:& quéadmodū uindices publicas
ɔroditores & facrilegos interficiendos publice a/
hominis exercitium laudetur: fed quia populo
n profecto pacto huius mundi gubernator quafi
ios in ciuitates exfufcitat:ut iniuria atq; īpietaté
ɔ crudelitate iftorum puniat:qui quoniam non
d crudelitate cōmoti diuinæ uolūtati fubmiffæ/

5.4: Venetian type, Nicolas Jenson, Venice, 1470

and *littera antiqua* and then adapted them so expertly
that, despite his type being one of the earliest roman
types, it is still regarded as one of the finest *(fig. 5.4)*.
His metal punches captured more of the sharpness of
the incised capitals than the humanist scribes' had with
their pen-and-ink letters. From 1470 onwards, his 'Venetian' type (as all roman fonts made in Venice during this
early period are known) set the standard for subsequent
Venetian faces. Straight and strong, with only a slight
contrast between the thick and thin strokes, the letters
cohered into beautifully spaced words, which themselves combined to form soft and evenly textured lines
of text. The uniformly light and spacious impression
of one of Jenson's pages contrasted with the dark and
dense pages of Gothic type. Within the lines of evenly
spaced letters there were pleasant idiosyncrasies: the 'e'
had a calligraphic diagonal slant (a defining characteristic of Venetian type), and the serifs on top of the 'M'
pointed inwards as well as outwards. Jenson did not

disguise the different origins of his capital and lowercase letters by melding them into a harmonious union.
Relative to the lowercase letters, the capitals are wider
and larger than we are used to seeing today. It appears
as though the two cases are just good friends rather than
husband and wife.

Despite the close proximity of Italy's first printing
press to Rome, it was in Venice that the concentration
of printers was greatest prior to the turn of the century.
It was there too that early Italian printing was most
innovative and dynamic. The first decorated title page
(fig. 5.5) was printed there in 1476 by the German printer
Erhard Ratdolt (1442–1528), who had set up a press
with two partners earlier in the year. The book it appeared in was a 'Calendar' written by a German author
and printer referred to as Regiomontanus (a Latinized
term for his home town of Königsberg, or 'Kingsmoun-
tain'). The page's distinctive woodcut decoration is of
a kind more usually found on a page of text rather than
a title page, which was itself a rarity at this time. The
stylized outline of foliage and flowers, which extend
upwards from two vases on either side of the text, is a
typical Renaissance motif, as was the shield, though it
was placed somewhat unconventionally at the head of
the border rather than the foot. The visual tone of the
outline decoration is matched by Ratdolt's roman type,
and the dominance of the large initial 'A' is softened by
being printed in red.

Another 'first' for this page was the content of the
text. Unlike the label title page (<*fig. 4.14, p.78*), Ratdolt's decorated version corresponded more closely to
the modern title page in that it contained not only the
title of the book, 'kalendario' (line 2), and the author's
name, 'Ioannes opus regio de monte' (line 9), but also the
year (centred below the verse), and then, in three lines
along the bottom, the names of the three printers. In
other ways, though, Ratdolt's design was different from
a modern title page. As well as its unusual decoration,
most of its text is set as a poem, some of which praises
the book, much like a contemporary publisher's 'blurb'.
The design also differed from those that came after it. No
other decorated title page appeared before the 1490s and
even after then they were rare. Ratdolt never produced
another like it, but in other ways he continued to be innovative. He was the first to print mathematical figures,
which appeared in 1482 in a book on Euclid's geometry,
and was the first to print with gold ink, which he used
in the same edition. Further innovations saw him print
a type specimen sheet in 1486, the first piece of print

5.5: Title page, 'Calendarium', Erhard Ratdolt,
Venice, 1476

5.6: 'Hypnerotomachia Poliphili', Aldus Manutius,
Venice, 1499

dedicated to expounding the range of 14 type styles and sizes on offer. He was also the first to use Arabic numerals to date a book, and the first to list errata.

Ratdolt may have been the most experimental of the early Venetian printers and Jenson the first to master roman type, but the most celebrated and successful was the Italian scholar and publisher Aldus Manutius (1449/50–1515). His contribution to the Renaissance book was made through his skilful layouts, his introduction of 'italic' type and his making small-format books popular for non-religious texts. All Aldus's books were printed with types cut by a master punchcutter, Francesco Griffo of Bologna (1450–1518). Griffo's first 'Aldine' type was a roman based on Jenson's type, but with some of the calligraphic qualities removed. The letters were designed more on their own printerly terms, rather than being faithful transpositions of calligraphic and incised letters into type. It has been called the first real printed type, a

so-called 'Old Style' (or 'Old Face') type (i.e. 'post-Venetian', despite its being made in Venice). The cross-stroke of the 'e' is horizontal, not slanted. The capitals are less wide and less high, smaller than the ascenders even, and consequently they blend better with the lowercase letters. The lowercase is more condensed, but in no way mean or cramped. The straighter and thinner strokes and their neater serifs emphasize the common horizontal baseline along which the letters sit, giving the whole text a more settled and orderly feel. This supreme roman became the archetypal roman form for the next 250 years.

The type first appeared in 1495 in a book called *De Aetna* ('From Etna' – the mountain in Sicily) which had been written by the Italian scholar and cardinal Pietro Bembo. In what later became one of several loose conventions that guided the naming of type and typefaces, this type was given the name Bembo, in reference to its first use. Griffo recut it soon after and used this new and many consider to be better 'Bembo' in one of Aldus's most celebrated books, *Hypnerotomachia Poliphili* ('Poliphilo's Struggle for Love in a Dream') of 1499 (*< fig. 5.6*). The book is not without mistakes, misprints and haphazard corrections, but the new type is set within a highly distinguished and varied typographic layout. Sections of the text are set in lines of continuous capitals which evoke some of the grandeur of ancient stone inscriptions. What they lose in legibility, by being set in such tightly leaded lines, is made up for by the beauty of the letters' shapes. Dramatic outlines of wedge-shaped blocks of text, so arranged perhaps in an effort to fill the page when the amount of text was small, sit alongside well-balanced woodcut initials. Being neither too heavy nor too light, though often astonishingly intricate, the initials could stand on their own as objects worthy of close scrutiny. The illustrations are made from a delicate line of an almost uniform width and then anchored within a simple but weighty double-line border. The quality of the printing – its evenness and crispness – and the quality of the paper and binding are the best available. It is said that during the first quarter of the sixteenth century this book alone was responsible for making French printers change from using Gothic types to roman ones. Though with this masterpiece completed, Aldus never again produced a fully illustrated book. Instead his attention turned to scholarly printing, an area of publishing on which his influence was to be equally profound.

Aldus's greatest commercial success came with a series of classical texts published between 1501 and 1505. A scholar and businessman as well as a printer, Aldus understood that the expanding group of reading professionals – doctors, lawyers, scientists and teachers – wanted books that not only related to their work, but which could also be carried and used easily. Whereas previous printers had issued secular books such as the Latin classics in grand folio or quarto sizes, Aldus made them in the smaller octavo size, the size of a small modern paperback, and sold them at a price that even the moderately wealthy could afford. In this way, he made it possible for readers to carry secular books alongside their Books of Hours or breviaries. They became the 'prayer books of a lay culture'. By leaving out the commentaries that usually accompanied such texts, he established a sparse but intimate style of design (just you and the text). This attribute combined with their novel and uniform size to make the series highly collectable.

The standard book sizes available to Aldus were those inherited from centuries of manuscript production. A manuscript's size was determined largely by the size of the unfolded and uncut sheets supplied by the paper maker. The largest of the three most common manuscript sizes was called 'folio' (from *folium*, the Latin for 'leaf', sometimes abbreviated to 'fo'), which was made by folding a sheet once to give four pages equivalent in size to a modern, large coffee-table book or broadsheet newspaper. The middle book size was called 'quarto' (abbreviated to 'Qto' or '4to'), which was a quarter of the sheet size. This was made by folding the sheet twice, with the second fold at right angles to the first, to give eight pages, which were each roughly the size of a sheet of A4 paper. The smallest common book size, 'octavo' ('8vo'), an eighth the size of the sheet, was made by folding three times to give 16 pages of a size that was equivalent to a standard hardback novel. Some miniature books went down to a twelfth ('12mo' from 'duodecimo'), a sixteenth ('16mo' from 'sextodecimo'), a thirty-second ('32mo' from 'tricesimo-secundo'), or even a sixty-fourth size ('64mo' from 'sexagesimo-quarto'). Beyond this they rarely went. There appears to be a physical limit as to how many times a piece of paper can be folded. More than five times ('32mo') is very difficult, and beyond seven is apparently impossible, irrespective of how large and thin the paper is.

What had not become standardized was the size of the initial sheet. Thus one octavo book might be somewhat smaller or larger than another, depending on who had made the paper. Sheets supplied by Italian paper makers generally came in two sizes, one referred to as Royal (70 x 50cm or 28 x 20in) and the other as Median (50 x 30cm or 20 x 12in), but paper makers in Venice, for example, tended to supply a slightly larger sheet referred to as Super-Royal or Super-Median. Confusing matters further was that most pages needed to be trimmed after the sheet had been folded, so as to remove the folds (or 'bolts' as they are known) along one of the edges, which otherwise prevented the pages from being turned. Not all binders trimmed the pages by the same amount, so the conventional way of describing a book's size, by stating the sheet size (i.e. 'Royal' or 'Median') and then the number of times the sheet was folded (i.e. 'folio', 'quarto', etc.) could only ever be suggestive of a book's size. Aldus's scholarly series, for example, was 'Median octavo', that is to say roughly the size of an adult's hand, but clearly that's not the same as saying they were 15.4 x 8.7cm (6$\frac{1}{8}$ x 3$\frac{3}{8}$in), which is their precise size. (In printing, unlike Cartesian co-ordinates and map

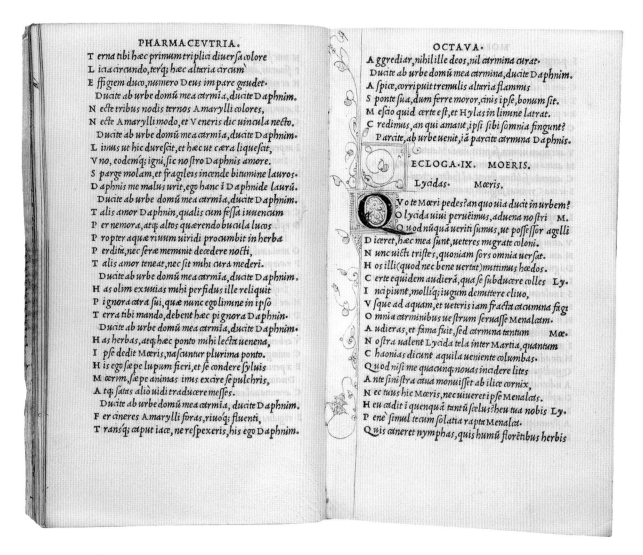

5.7: 'Opera' of Virgil, Aldus Manutius, Venice, 1501

references, the vertical measurement usually precedes the horizontal.)

The appeal of Aldus's portable octavos was added to by their new style of type. They were set with one of the very first italic types: a set of sloping calligraphic letters whose shapes were based on a popular cursive script which an earlier generation of humanists had developed for copying out classical texts. It has been thought that Aldus adopted this cursive humanist script as a space-saving device, but not only is there no quote or comment that supports this supposition, when the text is set in the same size of his roman type it does not increase in length. What is more certain is that his books benefited from the popularity of the humanist script, which was held as a model for handwriting among educated and literate Italians.

Aldus's use of italic type was not restricted to marking emphases or titles of books or paintings, as italic is today. Nor was it applied to both upper and lowercase letters. In accordance with the humanist model, his capitals remained upright. A page from the first Aldine octavo, an edition of verse by the classical Roman poet Virgil *(fig. 5.7)*, shows how the letters were not always evenly sloped – the 'c' slopes forward while the 'g' almost leans backward – and thus the lines of text were rather unevenly spaced. This unevenness was added to by the large number of combined letters or 'ligatures' that Aldus included in his range of type. This one spread alone has something like 130 of them (today, the same text set in a standard typeface would have no more than a handful: the odd combination of 'ff', 'fi' or 'fl'). To the modern reader, whose eyes are used to a more regular array of letters, the Aldine italic is not an easy read, but it bears close scrutiny – some of the ligatures, 'ct' for example, are beautifully combined. On publication Aldus's type was seen to have taken typographic elegance to a new height. In Italy it quickly gained an equal status with roman. During the first quarter of the sixteenth century, as many Italian books were printed in italic type (though still with more or less upright capitals) as in roman. As other parts of the Continent came to know of Aldus's new type, so italic ('of Italy') type came to replace roman as the type associated with classicism. Decades later books across Europe were being set in imitations of the Aldine italic.

The impact of printing on the livelihood of the scribe was not wholly negative. The production of cheaper reading material led to an increase in the number of readers, which in turn increased the demand for lessons in writing. Not just learning how to write, but also to develop a beautiful and mature handwriting. In the higher echelons of the expanding class of literates, good handwriting was seen as an important accomplishment. It was a marker of one's social standing. So as well as serving the traditional need for handwritten text in chanceries and in business and legal offices, scribes found work as writing masters. To advertise their expertise as well as provide models for readers to emulate, they published writing books showing samples of their scripts. Three well-known and influential Italian examples are the books by Ludovico Arrighi (1475–1527), Giovanni Palatino (c.1515–c.1575) and Giovantonio Tagliente (1465/70–after 1527). Each was a master, figuratively as well as literally (though Arrighi is often referred to as a writing master, it is not certain that he ever did teach).

The earliest of the three manuals was written by Arrighi and published in about 1522. His *La Operina da Imparare di scriuere littera Cancellarescha* ('A Learning Guide to Writing the Chancery Letter', *fig.5.8*) was only a little book of 32 pages, though like the other two, it is not quite what it seems. His flowing calligraphic scripts were actually printed letters which had been cut into a woodblock by an engraver with a gouging tool. Despite this different method of shape making and the fact that the letters had had to be cut in reverse, they carry something of the calligraphic verve of the original pen and ink forms. As the title indicates, the model put forward by Arrighi was the script used in the papal office, or chancery, at the Vatican, where he worked as a scribe. This *cancellarescha corsiva* or 'Chancery cursive' was a

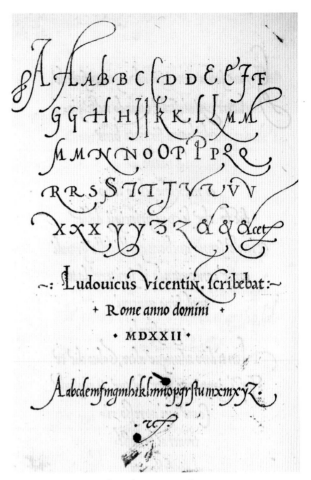

5.8: *Writing manual, Ludovico Arrighi, Rome, 1522*

stately, more decorative version of the humanist cursive that had guided Aldus's italics. Arrighi's upright roman capitals are distinguished by a set of variant 'swash' forms with exuberantly flourishing tails, and although these carved flourishes look a little static, they indicate the potential for expression that exists within a practised pen hand. The shape of Arrighi's cursive small-letters, at the bottom of the page, are only slightly inclined, yet they make a stark contrast with the upright capitals. Most of the ascenders and descenders have rounded billowing tails, which tip backwards on the down stroke and forwards on the up.

Where Arrighi's manual is a model of concentrated utility, with its clear and intimate instruction ('dear reader' was his mode of address), Palatino's is an exhibition in variety *(fig.5.9)*. Vastly more wide-ranging, it comes closer to the modern type-specimen book in that it contains not only Palatino's version of the Chancery script, but a plethora of letter styles of the Latin alphabet and, indeed, 'every sort of ancient and modern letters of

5.9: Writing manual, Giovanni Palatino, Rome 1561

5.10: Ornate Gothic letter, Paulus Franck, Germany, 1601

all nations': Arabic, Cyrillic and others. More influential than either Palatino's or Arrighi's though was Tagliente's writing manual. First published in 1524, it was reprinted in various editions until 1678. His own Chancery cursive is less expert than those of his compatriots, but the range of commercial scripts he provided and the more detailed instruction he gave contributed to the book's success. Many of his manual's historical and regional scripts have an angular bias, which might explain why his version of Chancery found favour in northern Europe, where the more angular Gothic letter was common.

The display of mastery between rival scribes created an inflationary pressure to outdo what had gone before. In northern Europe this pressure was directed towards an extreme form of decoration that rendered the letter all but illegible *(fig. 5.10)*. The initial spur to this super-abundance of decoration was a fractured form of Gothic letter or 'Fraktur', made with a number of individual letter strokes rather than a few joined-up ones. In some instances the separate nature of the strokes was visible.

Some barely touched their adjacent strokes (a sense of this is given in Tagliente's page of Gothic letters). The extent to which an elaborate decoration could be built onto the separate strokes of a letter is shown in this late example of the letter 'F' *(fig. 5.10)* from a series of capital initials that were penned by the German scribe Paulus Franck (*c.*1550–*c.*1610) in 1601. The rhythmical flourishes are organized into a series of contrasts: between thick and thin lines, parallel strokes and convergent ones, and between dense thickets of interlacing and light diaphanous swirls. The whole is suffused with an unbridled sense of exuberance, as though Franck was exulting in his mastery of the form. His extraordinary control and inventiveness were honed during his work as a chancery scribe, where a tradition of embellishing documents had been established. The skilful display of initial letters in particular was seen as proof of the document's prestige and authority.

In Italy the significance of classical models rather than recent home-grown traditions was demonstrated by

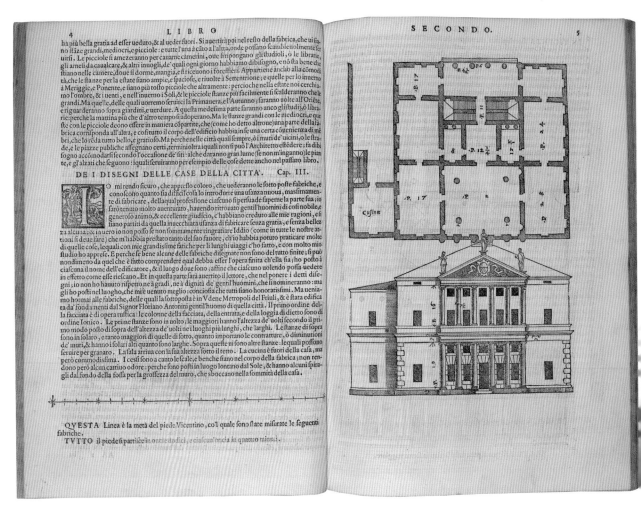

5.11: Andrea Palladio's 'I Quattro Libri dell' Architettura', Venice, 1570

the success of a treatise on architecture called *I Quattro Libri dell'Architettura* ('The Four Books of Architecture', *fig. 5.11*). It was written by the Italian architect Andrea Palladio (1508–80) and first published in 1570, though its popularity led it to be reprinted frequently and, indeed, it remains in print today. The book made Palladio famous and helped to define a style of architecture that bore his name, 'Palladian'. The style went on to influence the development of architecture across northern Europe, and later in North America. In the early nineteenth century, Thomas Jefferson, a some-time architect as well as a statesman, referred to Palladio's 'Four Books' as 'the Bible'.

Palladio's book was both a visual display of classical Roman architecture and a practical guide to building in the classical style. It was illustrated with a series of large schematic woodcuts, made from his own drawings, which filled out at least a page on almost every

spread. The woodcuts' simple lines showed plans and elevations of ancient buildings reconstructed as Palladio imagined they might have looked when first built. Also shown were new buildings that he had designed according to classical principles. Country houses, town houses, a monastery and even bridges were styled with pillars, capitals, arches, friezes and a panoply of attendant classical features.

The success of 'The Four Books' was founded on a combination of Palladio's clear and concise writing and the close correspondence of the writing with his illustrations. This clear and orderly fusion allowed readers to come away with a detailed understanding of the principles and methods of classical architecture. Palladio's own knowledge of classical forms had been guided by two important texts, one by the ancient Roman architect Vitruvius and the other by a fifteenth-century disciple of Vitruvius, Leon Battista Alberti. Both led Palladio to base his designs on mathematical proportions rather than the rich ornamental style that had characterized much early Renaissance architecture.

An important element in his explanation of the mathematical proportions behind his buildings was the printing of his unit of measure (which appears in the example opposite). Palladio was 'aware that units of measurement differ just as cities and regions do' – at that time the Venetian foot, for example, was different from the Vicentine foot (used in his home town of Vicenza) – but by actually printing his unit of measure readers were provided with a fixed point of reference. They could know the precise scale that Palladio was working on, and if they so wished, they could make the necessary adjustments when applying his designs to their own local unit of measure. (The text below the line says: 'This line, with which the following buildings have been measured, is half a Vicentine foot. The foot is divided into 12 inches, and each inch into four minutes.')

Most of the characteristics that defined this early period in graphic design were things made with ink: the formal clarity of the layout, the near monochrome palette and the rounded type. But there was another characteristic, equally visible though generally unnoticed. It was the unprinted, white parts of the page. Just as a sound is best heard against a background of silence, so the beauty of Renaissance printing relied on a neutral and uncluttered surround. The right amount of space between the lines of text, between the words in those lines, between the letters in the words, and even within the enclosed parts of the letters themselves, presented the reader with an inviting block of evenly textured lines. The printers of fine books had become more aware of the importance of the unprinted parts of the page when determining the best placement of printed matter. By making subtle differences in the widths of the margins they were able to hold the text within a balanced frame. Furthermore, their harmonious margins helped to express the pleasing proportions of their choice of format. In these ways, the unprinted parts of the Renaissance page were as eloquent of the book's style as any of the features that were made with ink.

In Italy, where an established craft tradition of paper making provided printers with some of the finest printing material, there was an incentive to exploit this resource. Some of the elegance of Aldus's series of octavo books comes from the large amount of unprinted paper. The effect of openness and lightness that could be created was further enhanced by the printers' restricted use of different sizes and styles of type. Cutting and casting a new style of type was expensive. Unlike today, where a single design can be scaled up or down automatically, printing with type required every character of every size of a particular style to be made piece by piece. The time and resources required to make a new size of type in the same style differed little from making a single size of a new style. In both cases a whole new set of types needed to be cut and cast. For this reason, the print in many Italian Renaissance books was restricted to just two sizes of a single style (usually one size for the heading and the other for the main text). Though this did not create any more white space, it did make the page look less cluttered.

The six so-called 'Italian' wars of the late fifteenth to mid-sixteenth centuries saw Rome sacked by an unpaid army of mercenaries, the collapse of Italy's system of city republics and eventually led to the Spanish domination of large parts of the peninsula. With Spanish support the Roman Church was able to centralize its power. It introduced a series of political and social reforms with a degree of control and devotional intensity that came to characterize the Counter-Reformation. The effect on printing was to make the publication of classical texts potentially heretical. An 'Index' or list of prohibited books was introduced in 1557 and regularly updated thereafter (it was only withdrawn in 1967). Italian publishers responded by selling cheap reprints of old best-sellers or traditional religious texts rather than fine editions of scholarly literature. The trend towards mass production that had been established by printing and the concomitant demand for cheap books furthered the decline in the standards of book production in Italy. Types were poorly designed, words were crammed onto the page, and the quality of illustration deteriorated.

It was during this same period, the first half of the sixteenth century, that the influence of the Italian Renaissance book took hold in France. It was an influence that was encouraged by an unparalleled degree of royal patronage from a succession of monarchs whose fondness for classicism was matched by a desire to harness the power of the printed word. The greatest royal patron was Francis I, who, through his appointment of Geoffroy Tory (*c.*1480–1533) as *imprimeur du roi*, or 'printer to the king', in 1531, established a centralizing trend that was to dominate printing in France forthe next 200 years. Tory, a scholar, teacher and

5.12: Roman and italic type, Claude Garamond, 1545

illustrator as well as a printer, brought the Italian book to the attention of Parisian printers. They and others, in Lyon especially, introduced a lightness and orderliness to the French Renaissance book. Such books became admired throughout Europe.

From around 1540, roman types began to replace the Gothic ones that printers in France had relied on since the first press was established in that country in 1470. The style of these new types was dominated by a version created by the Parisian punch-cutter Claude Garamont, or Garamond (*c*.1510–61) (as a French spelling reform had led him to spell it). Unlike other cutters, Garamond was rarely side-tracked into other aspects of printing. He devoted most of his time to refining his types, and in particular the version of roman he first cut in 1530, which had been based on the heavier Aldine roman. A notable accompaniment to the roman was his new italic type. Unlike the pages of earlier Italian books, the two appear side by side (*fig. 5.12*). French printers had begun to mix italic and roman in this way during the 1540s. They had been encouraged to do so by the appearance of a more fluent and legible italic which broke from the Chancery tradition in that it had sloped rather than upright capitals. This new form is thought to have first come from the hand of Garamond in about 1539, though it was closely followed by a similar but more legible version cut by his compatriot Robert Granjon (1513–90). The evenness of slope in Granjon's letters set it apart. Yet its slope and the general form of its letters was still not of a kind that allowed the type to sit comfortably within a line of roman text. Italics designed to accompany a specific roman only began to appear after 1600.

5.13: Geneva Bible, printed by Robert Estienne, 1553

Over a period of about 20 years, the brilliance of Garamond's types encouraged many imitators, so that by the time of his death in 1561 his style of type had appeared in all the main printing regions of Europe. Versions of it even ousted the Aldine roman from Italy. The fact that Latin was still the international language of scholarship is likely to have helped it become so popular. The pan-European trade of Latin books would have benefited from the existence of a universally accepted style of letter rather than a variety of regional styles.

The quality of these types was sometimes matched by the excellence of the printers who used them. Such printers created a graphic style that was more rigorously ordered and functional than any previous layout. A sign of this more ordered approach to text can be seen in a Bible produced by the Parisian printer Robert Estienne (1503–59) in 1553 (*fig.5.13*). It was printed in Geneva, to where Estienne had had to move in order to escape religious persecution. Though the design is undistinguished by the awkward spacing of the text, it is notable for being the first Bible to have its text divided into

Cy commence le Prologue de meſsire Iehan Froiſſart, ſur les Croniques de France & d'Angleterre, & autres lieux voiſins.

✳

A FIN que les honnorables empriſes & nobles auétures & faicts-d'armes, par les guerres de France & d'Angleterre, ſoyent notablement enregiſtrés & mis en memoire perpetuel, parquoy les preux ayent exemple d'eux encourager en bien faiſant, ie vueil traicter & recorder Hiſtoire de grand' louenge. Mais auant que ie la commence, ie requier au Sauueur de tout le monde, qui de neant crea toutes choſes, qu'il vueille creer & mettre en moy ſens & entendement ſi vertueux, que ie puiſſe continuer & perſeuerer en telle maniere que tous ceux & celles, qui le lirõt, verront, & orront, y puiſſent prendre ebatement & exemple, & moy encheoir en leur grâce.

On dit, & il eſt vray, que tous edifices ſont maſſonnés & ouurés de pluſieurs ſortes de pierres, & toutes groſſes riuieres ſont faictes & raſſemblees de pluſieurs ſurgeons. Auſſi les ſciences ſont extraictes & compilees de pluſieurs Clercs: & ce, que l'un ſceu, l'autre l'ignore. Non-pourtant rien n'eſt, qui ne ſoit ſceu, ou loing ou pres.

Donc, pour attaindre à la matiere que i'ay empriſe, ie vueil commencer premierement par la grâce de Dieu & de la benoiſte vierge Marie (dont tout confort & auancement viennent) & me vueil fonder & ordonner ſur les vrayes Croniques, iadis faictes par reuerend homme, diſcret & ſage, monſeigneur maiſtre Iehan le Bel, Chanoine de Sainct-Lambert du Liege: qui grand' cure & toute bonne diligéce meit en ceſte matiere, & la continua tout ſon viuant au plus iuſtement qu'il peut; & moult luy couſta à la querre & à l'auoir: mais, quelques fraiz qu'il fiſt, riens ne les plaingnit. *De qui Froiſ-* car il eſtoit riche & puiſſant (ſi les pouuoit bien porter) & eſtoit de ſoy-meſme large, *ſart a pris la pre-* honnorable, & courtois: & voulontiers voyoit le ſien deſpendre. Auſſi il fut en ſon vi- *ſente Hiſtoire.* uant moult aimé & ſecret à monſeigneur meſſire Iehan de Haynaut: qui bien eſt ramenteu, & de raiſon, en ce liure. car de moult belles & nobles aduenues fut il chef & †*De quel temps* cauſe, & des Roys moult prochain. parquoy le deſſuſdit meſſire Iehan le Bel peut *eſtoit Froiſſart.* delez luy veoir pluſieurs nobles beſongnes: leſquelles ſont contenues cy-apres. Vray *ſur quoy faut* eſt que ie, qui ay empris ce liure à ordonner, ay par plaiſance, qui à ce m'a touſiours *noter qu'il ne* encliné, frequenté pluſieurs nobles & grans Seigneurs, tant en Frãce qu'en Angleter- *porta que partie* re, en Eſcoce, & en pluſieurs autres païs: & en ay eu la congnoiſſance d'eux: & ay touſ- *de ce premier Vo-* iours, à mon pouuoir, iuſtement enquis & demandé du faict des guerres & des auen- *lume à la Roy-* tures, & par eſpecial depuis la groſſe bataille de Poitiers, ou le noble Roy Iehan de *ne Philippe. car* France fut pris.† car deuãt i'eſtoye encores moult ieune de ſens & d'aage. Nonobſtant *vous verrez* ſi empris ie aſſez hardiment, moy iſſu de l'eſcole, à dicter & à ordonner les guerres *qu'il racompte-* deſſuſdites, & porter en Angleterre le liure tout compilé: ſi-comme ie fei, & le pre- *ra la mort d'i-* ſentay adonc à Ma-dame Philippe de Haynaut, Royne d'Angleterre: qui liement & *celle, ſelon l'or-* doucement le receut de moy, & m'en fit grand profit. Et peut eſtre que ce liure n'eſt *dre des temps,* *en cedit premier* *& preſent Vo-* a mie *lume.*

5.14: *Jean Froissart's 'Chroniques', printed by Jean de Tournes, Lyons, 1559*

5.15: Euclid's 'Elements' printed by John Day, London, 1570

numbered verses. But the verses are not only numbered, they are also laid out as separate paragraphs with an exaggerated indent.

The functional nature of the book's typography gives an impression of stolid utility. The books of the Lyonnais scholar-printer Jean de Tournes (1504–64), though no less functional, demonstrate a light and polished harmony. In his edition of Jean Froissart's *Chroniques*, or 'Chronicles' *(<fig. 5.14)*, which he printed in 1559, the careful placement and weight of the printed forms makes them beautiful as well as useful. The large type at the top stands out as an introduction to the main text below. In doing so, it reveals the masterly shape of Garamond's letterforms. The thin column of Granjon's italic is a perfectly placed supplement to the block of roman text beside it. The column neither disrupts the block of main text by being too close to it, nor does it float in the margin. The italic's interline spacing, or 'leading' (so called because of the thin strips of lead that were used to separate the lines of type), is generous enough to allow the beauty of the vigorous flourishes to be expressed. In the floriated headband (the top bar of swirling floral patterns) and the wood-engraved decorative

initial, cut in the *manière criblée* style (characterized by white dots on a black background), form and function are again united: both are exquisite decorations, but equally they serve as typographic signposts to aid the reader when he or she scans the pages in search of the beginning of the book.

It is no small achievement to make typographic elements that are beautiful and useful, but what really distinguishes the art of the French Renaissance book are the waves of harmonic rhythms that are set in motion by the judicious placement of the beautiful and useful within the workaday setting of a page. In de Tournes' page, there is a harmony that comes from the match between the height of the white initial 'A' and the height of the white space above, on which the largest type sits. There is the same feeling of unity between the sequence of forms running down the page – decoration (headband), large text, small text – and the sequence that runs across it – decoration (initial), large text (main text), small text (italic). And there is a similar accord between the height of the headband and the width of the column of italic. There are many other subtle harmonies besides.

The precision and detail available to a printed design, as opposed to one set down by hand in a manuscript, made it possible to create more firmly and finely graded hierarchies of type and image. The printerly combination of precision and subtlety applied not only to the pages of books but also to the less literary, more diagrammatic discipline of cartography. Printing made it possible to describe the earth's land-masses more faithfully. What it could not do is resolve the difficulty that all world maps had to contend with, the problem of turning the spherical surface of the earth into an image on a flat page. The same sort of problem had been encountered by printers of books on the important mathematical discipline of three-dimensional geometry. There was no easy way of depicting the sorts of geometrical objects that had been discussed by ancient mathematicians – spheres, cones, pyramids and cylinders – on the two-dimensional surface of a printed page. A laborious but otherwise effective solution to this problem appeared in the first English translation of Euclid's *Elements (fig. 5.15)*, printed in London in 1570 by the British printer John Day (1522–1584). He used geometric shapes made out of pasted flaps of paper that could be folded up into three-dimensional models, as in a 'pop-up' book. It is one of the earliest known books of this kind.

An accurate depiction of the world was not always the aim of map makers. The first, printed, world map was a copy of a T-O (or O-T) map *(fig. 5.16)*, which had been the common form in manuscripts of the Middle Ages. Its schematic arrangement was never meant to show the extent of geographical knowledge at that time and certainly not at the time the T-O map was first printed in 1475. Like the scribes who had devised it, the readers who read it knew it to be a symbolic representation rather than a faithful depiction of the topographical features of the Earth's surface. The symbolism was Christian. It reminded the reader that God had created a world around His chosen land Jerusalem at the junction of Europe, Africa and Asia. The shape formed by the 'T' recalled the Christian symbol of the crucifix, which signified the sacrifice that Christ had made for the salvation of all mankind, hence its placement on an encircling, globe-like 'O'. The three continents of Europe, Africa and Asia are usually shown with Europe on the left, Africa on the right and Asia uppermost (a scheme that led us to derive the word 'orientation' from 'Orient'). This print shows no fine grading within a complex visual hierar-

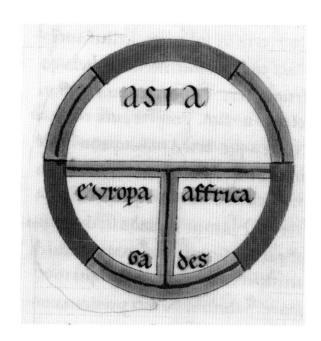

5.16: T-O map, manuscript, early thirteenth century

chy. That could only happen when maps had developed a more refined cartographic scheme. An important step in this direction was taken with the reintroduction into Europe of a second-century text called *Geographia* or 'Geography'. It had been written by the Greek astronomer and mathematician Ptolemy (AD 90–168), who had devised a method for preparing a world map using fixed co-ordinates plotted along lines of latitude and longitude. Though Ptolemy's text had been seen by some in the Near and Middle East, it was never widely known. In 1406, a Latin translation was made which allowed Europeans to follow his instructions. The resultant map was printed in book form first in Italy in 1477 – it was one of the first books to use engraved illustrations – and then subsequently, alongside the initial text, both in Italy *(>fig. 5.17)* and Germany. It was only through printing the map that the mathematical basis of Ptolemy's projection could be appreciated. While the extent of the knowledge of the world's land masses during the time of the Roman Empire was shown to be limited, Ptolemy's way of ordering space in two dimensions allowed others to start filling in the contours in ever greater detail.

Printing not only helped to make Ptolemy's projection more widely known, it also established a more mathematical approach to the whole field of cartography. The world map of 1507 by the German cartographer Martin Waldseemüller (*c.*1470–*c.*1518) *(>fig. 5.18)* shows the fruits of this new approach. Being the very

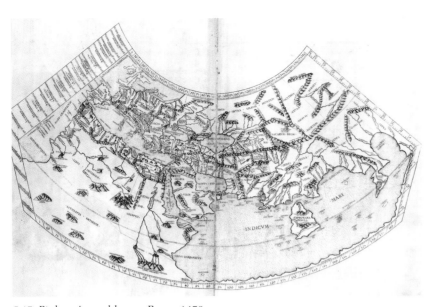

5.17: Ptolemaic world map, Rome, 1478

first to extend Ptolemy's projection of longitude to 360°
(though the north–south extent is incomplete), it
presented a whole new vision of the world. It also has
the distinction of being the first map to show the New
World with its current name: 'America'. Waldseemüller
added the name in honour of the Italian explorer
Amerigo Vespucci, who had travelled across the
Atlantic soon after Columbus. Whereas Columbus had
not realized what he had discovered – he thought the
islands he had arrived at were part of Asia, hence the
name the West Indies – Vespucci recognized the
continent as something new. (The contact made by
Vikings and others had never brought it to the attention
of Europeans as a whole.)

The quantity of detail in Waldseemüller's map was
printed from 12 separate woodblocks which when
printed amounted to an area almost 1.25 m (4ft 1in)
high and 2.5 m (8ft 2in) wide. It was thus one of the first
maps not to be bound in a book (no format could have
contained a map so large without it being extensively
folded). The detailed information in Waldseemüller's
map adds depth to the large expanse of flat paper. There
is a simple hierarchy between the important lines of
latitude – the equator and the two tropics – and the
lesser lines of latitude and longitude. There is a further
hierarchy in the extensive labelling and the panels of
descriptive text. Such descriptions of the topography,
customs and history of various regions were a common
feature of early printed maps. The map also contains
a miscellany of places, objects and events: continents
delineated by a fine shading, a legion of disparate place
names, regional and colonial flags, mountain ranges,
rivers, fish, an African elephant, and Vespucci sailing
the Atlantic while being buffeted by the puff-cheeked
Winds of classical mythology. In the top part of the map
and towards the right, Waldseemüller showed Vespucci

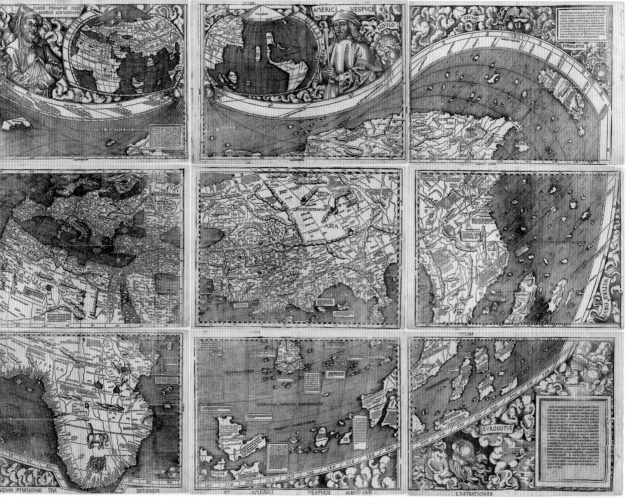

5.18: *World map, Martin Waldseemüller, Germany, 1507*

standing next to the New World, and had him looking across to Ptolemy, who stands next to the old one.

During the latter half of the sixteenth century, the centre of map publishing moved northwards to what is now the Netherlands. The seafaring prowess of this small north European republic, as it came to be in 1581, enabled the Dutch (for this time an inexact but convenient label) to seek out and successfully exploit new trading opportunities overseas. By establishing a vast trading empire in Asia, they were able to control the lucrative European spice trade. The unexpected levels of wealth that flowed into their young country throughout the seventeenth century resulted in a blossoming of culture known as the Dutch Golden Age. The republic became one of the world's most powerful nations and its coastal capital, Amsterdam, became the centre of international trade and finance. Untrammelled by monarchy or an

established state church, Dutch society enjoyed a relative degree of intellectual freedom (from which the philosophers Descartes and Spinoza both benefited). This form of liberty combined with the country's new-found wealth to stimulate a huge growth in printing and publishing. By the end of the seventeenth century, the Dutch could claim to have published more books in the previous 100 years than all the other countries put together.

27   CLEMENS VII PONT MAX IMP CAES CAROLVS V P F AVG   28   HENRIC COMES A NASSAV ARCII

6 POPULAR PUBLISHING
Dutch Renaissance & Popular Prints, c.1530 – c.1700

During the sixteenth century, the focus of the world's commercial power shifted northward from the Mediterranean towards the Atlantic. The coastal city of Antwerp, though only a relatively small regional capital, became both the centre of banking and trade as well as an important cultural hub. By the second half of the century, it had replaced Paris as the centre of the book trade. Among the foreigners who travelled to the city to find work in the burgeoning and, most importantly, more liberal publishing industry was the Frenchman, Christopher Plantin (c.1520–89). In spite of the waves of religious and political conflict that swept through the region throughout the century, Plantin succeeded in founding a printing and publishing dynasty unrivalled in size and scope. By remaining at the forefront of the industry for 200 years, his successors became the wealthiest family in the whole of the southern Netherlands.

Though the 'Officina Plantiniana' was hardly a typical printing office of the late sixteenth century, its influence makes it important. Its size and completeness also provides us with a view of how involved print production had become by that time. All the facilities required to turn a block of lead into a bound book came to be located within the walls of its rambling Renaissance buildings (now housing the Plantin-Moretus Museum). The Officina housed a type foundry (installed post-Christopher Plantin), a type store in which 22 tonnes of roman, italic and Gothic type as well as Greek, Hebrew and musical lead type were kept, a printing workshop where the printing itself took place, a corrector's room where the proofs were edited, a library for proofreaders to use when checking the text, a bookshop where some of the books were sold, various sundry offices as well as the family's living quarters. At its height, it employed over 20 presses and a workforce some 70 strong. Plantin and his successors turned what had been, and for many still was, a handcraft into a complete industry.

Plantin himself published an average of 55 works each year, a huge number at that time. But because his books were aimed at an international elite of scholars and students the number of copies of any work was never large. His bestsellers, mostly classical texts published for schools, sold around 2500 copies, while the steady sellers sold half as many, and a then more select range of scientific books between 600 and 800. About a third of his output was religious texts, but it was the humanist and science books within the larger section of secular texts that cemented his reputation as a progressive publisher.

The range of types needed to service this varied output is indicated by Plantin's type specimen of 1585 (>fig.6.2). Like other printers, or indeed typefounders, Plantin made a series of specimens to show potential clients the range of typefaces available. Though the example here was bound in book form, printers also produced specimens as leaflets or even on single sheets (>fig.7.7, p.116). Unlike many of his contemporaries, Plantin was keen to use the best types he could find. Rather than relying on those supplied by the handful of specialized type foundries throughout the southern Netherlands, he carefully sought out the finest punches and matrices from across Europe. In time, he was able to boast the largest collection of punches and matrices of any printer.

The sections of Latin text within his specimen are set in various kinds of roman type mostly based on the letterform made popular by Garamond. (Plantin had bought some of Garamond's punches, matrices and moulds from the sale of the deceased punch cutter's effects in 1563.) They are accompanied by some of Grandjean's italics, and both would have been used mainly in secular texts, while Gothic types would have mainly served religious texts.

Sometimes it was necessary for Plantin to combine a range of types within a single publication. One such was a large multi-language Bible known variously as the

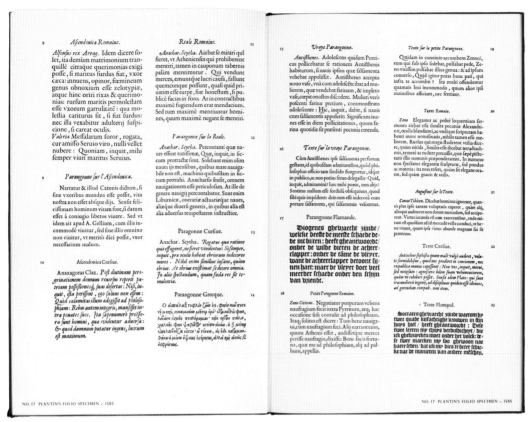

6.2: *Facsimile of 'Type Specimen', printed by Christopher Plantin, Antwerp, 1585*

'Antwerp Polyglot' *(fig. 6.3)* – 'polyglot' meaning 'many tongues' – or the *Biblia Regia* ('King's Bible') on account of its being issued under the auspices of the Spanish king, Philip II. Each of its eight volumes was published in a large folio format and together they contained text set in five different languages. The spread from the Old Testament shown here has a left-hand page with Hebrew text alongside a standard Latin translation (Vulgate), while the right-hand page had a standard Greek version (Septuagint) of the same text accompanied by its Latin translation. Running across the bottom is the text paraphrased in an ancient form of Aramaic (Chaldean), which clarified certain portions of the Hebrew text, followed by its Latin translation. (The fifth language, Syriac, was used instead of the Aramaic in the New Testament.) The order of languages – the Hebraic followed by the Greek then Latin – possibly reflects the special emphasis then being placed on the earliest sources of scripture. Plantin completed his Polyglot Bible in quick time between 1569 (the year in which the typesetting was started) and 1572/3, and though the process nearly left him bankrupt the book secured his reputation as the grandest printer of his age.

The orderly arrangement of such a complex layout, with its different languages, scripts and styles of type, each divided by the appropriate verse numbers and separated by simple unadorned rules, shows the new level of sophistication in layout that had been reached by the best printers at this time (a comparison with the first printing of Bible verses, *(<fig. 5.13, p. 94)*, makes this clear). Plantin's organized pages made it easier for scholars to make a detailed study of the text of the Bible. Such scrutiny went to the heart of the division between Protestants and Catholics, who each claimed to have a true understanding of the scriptures.

This kind of complex content and orderly layout gave an impetus to textual criticism and knowledge acquisition which extended far beyond the realm of biblical scholarship. Both activities were founded on an essential feature of the printed book: that of the edition. Because the printing process allowed texts to be duplicated identically – the same words appearing in the same order, size, style of lettering and position on a page – it conferred onto books a new authority. Readers were more inclined to look on a printed text as the unadulterated voice of the writer. The hand of the

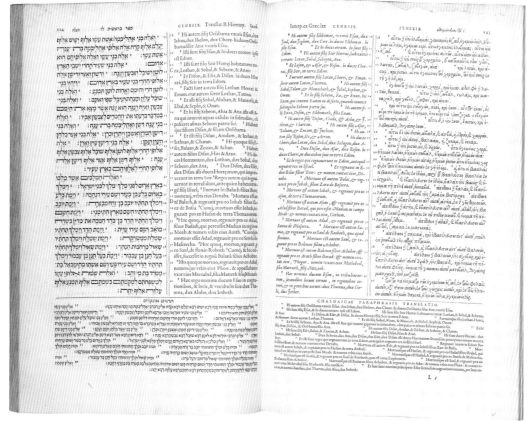

6.3: *Polyglot Bible, printed by Christopher Plantin, Antwerp, 1569–73*

scribe had not been allowed to come between the writer's voice and the reader's eye. Readers could make judgements about the merit of a text and know that copies of the same edition would present others with an identical text. There was therefore a common basis for future discussion and thought. Where a certain text existed in different editions, each of the editions could be compared, and the best picked out as the standard work. Where improvements were made in a later edition, this would then become the new standard. Much of the text in Tyndale's Bible, for example, was used as the basis for the later Authorized or King James Bible, first published in 1611, which in turn, was used as the basis for many of the modern Revised versions that are common today.

Of course, like the scribe before him, the compositor, who set the type before it was printed, was not infallible. However, unlike a scribe's handwritten text, his printed text provided readers with a more reliable point of reference. In a 1631 edition of the Authorized Bible, the so-called 'wicked Bible', the compositor had left out the word 'not' from the seventh commandment. Thus 'Thou shalt commit adultery' was its injunction. The error was obvious because the passage was so well known, but

with less familiar texts, printers were able to guard against similar errors becoming established by comparing their text with other editions. This process of standardization, comparison, revision and restandardization allowed knowledge to build up layer upon layer, and in this way the foundations of modern scholarship and science were laid. For a wide range of subjects, many of which were newly created, printing provided the means by which they could thrive and propagate.

The clarity that Plantin brought to a page of complex typography found an equivalent in many of his illustrations. His Polyglot Bible contained 22 illustrations, each of which were made from a process called copper engraving. This printing technique had been invented in Germany a few years before Gutenberg had first printed with movable type. It involved scratching lines with a sharp metal tool into a rectangular sheet of copperplate. After the engraved lines had been filled by rubbing a waxy ink into them, the surface of the plate, but not the engraved lines, was wiped clean. A sheet of dampened printing paper was then placed on top of the plate and both were put through a special rolling press that had two cylinders placed one above the other and a handle

6.4: Title page from Polyglot Bible, printed by Christopher Plantin, Antwerp, 1569–73

on the side, like an old-fashioned mangle (the English name given to such a press). As the paper and the plate passed through the rollers, the paper was forced into the engraved lines. The ink that it picked up tended to sit on top of the paper, rather than bleeding into it, leaving a darkly rich, raised imprint.

The arrival of copper engraving in Antwerp in the late 1540s led the city to become the printmaking centre of Europe throughout most of the next 100 years. The degree of detail, the range of textures and the size of print that could be produced with a copperplate surpassed anything that had been made with woodcuts at that time. A print made in Bruges during the early 1530s *(< fig. 6.1)* shows something of the appeal the medium must have held for artists and printers in Antwerp. The print shows the procession of Charles V into Bologna in 1529 prior to being crowned Holy Roman Emperor by Pope Clement VII. The king's extended retinue of noblemen, soldiers and servants was depicted with 40 large engravings which together appeared on a roll 18 in high and 34 ft long, before being bound in book form. Its greater detail and variety of textures were qualities that Plantin was keen to include in his Bible illustrations. They would allow him to show the skill of his artists and engravers, who had adopted the sophisticated late-Renaissance style of Mannerism/Baroque in which idealized forms of beauty rather than a truth to nature was emphasized. For them the overall effect of an image was more important than any particular subject within it.

Though fully engraved title pages had first appeared during the first decades of the century, they were still a rarity, especially in religious books, before the middle of the century. By including an engraved title page in his Polyglot Bible *(fig. 6.4)*, as well as in other books, Plantin helped to popularize the medium for such pages. Other printers adopted a similar style of illustration and similar motifs. The use of a classical arch as a device for carrying the book's title, here *Biblia Sacra* ('The Holy Bible'), and the printer's device or logo – Plantin's compass logo appears on the base of the right-hand column while the picture of Achilles on the other represents the biblical scholar who helped Plantin prepare the book – can also be seen in later engraved title pages. The animals allude to the different languages used in the book and behind them is shown the lands governed by Christian rulers. Together they represent the breadth of God's dominion.

Copper engraving was not without its disadvantages. It was more expensive than woodcut printing. The plate took longer to engrave, longer to ink and de-ink, and longer to pass through the rollers of the press. The pressure applied by the engraving press was such that the copperplate yielded fewer prints than a woodblock before becoming worn. The greatest disadvantage for publishers such as Plantin, who printed with type (as opposed to others who specialized in printing engravings), was that the copperplate and type could not be combined on the same press. Copper engraving belongs to a category of printing called intaglio (Italian for 'engravings') in which the printed image is formed by the recessed parts of the printing medium and not by the raised parts 'in relief,' as in a woodcut. So where an engraved illustration has to appear together with text, the printer either has to engrave both or to print each separately. For all the reasons mentioned above, when printing inexpensive books most printers still resorted to using woodcuts.

A popular and relatively cheap kind of picture book, which Plantin illustrated with woodcuts, was an emblem book. Such books could contain up to several hundred images, each one alluding cryptically to a moral contained in a motto and several lines of verse. The title page of *A Choice of Emblems* by Geffrey Whitney, which Plantin printed in 1586, describes the book as 'both fit for the vertuous, to their incoraging: and for the wicked, for their admonishing and amendment'. The example of one of its pages here *(fig. 6.5)* shows a woodcut illustration of a crying eye floating within a thick

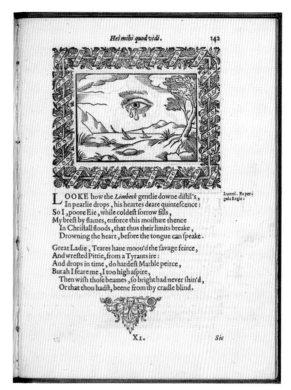

6.5: *Whitney's 'A Choice of Emblems', printed by Christopher Plantin, Antwerp, 1586*

decorative frame above 12 lines of English verse. Though Plantin printed most of his books in Latin, which then was still the language of scholarship, a few, such as his emblem books, used the language of everyday speech. The only piece of Latin on the page from Whitney's book is the motto at the top (*Hei mihi quod vidi*, 'Woe is me because I can see'). As the title of the book suggests, the text was taken from a previous emblem book, but so too were most of the pictures. Plantin had made a double economy by using second-hand woodblocks.

As the range of secular books increased during the sixteenth century so illustrations came to be used in new ways. While textbooks, grammar books, dictionaries and other aids to textual scholarship remained mostly typographic, other books such as science books dealing with the anatomy of the human body, say, or the classification of flora or fauna, required text and pictures to be united more closely. Each element could not be fully understood without the other.

This close unity of text and illustration was exemplified by a grand book of flowers (known as a *florilegium*) called *Hortus Eystettensis*, or 'The Garden at Eichstätt' *(>fig. 6.6)*, which was published in two editions in 1613.

6.6: Engraving of flora from 'Hortus Eystettensis', Nuremberg, 1613

The 'common' edition printed in black and white was intended as a reference book for herbalists, both medical and botanical, while the 'de luxe' edition was hand painted in a range of vivid and intricate colours. Its illustrations combined to form a catalogue of the different kinds of flowers contained in the garden at a Bishop's palace in the German diocese of Eichstätt in southern Germany. The garden boasted a series of eight terraces, each containing flowers from a different country, and a range of tulips in 500 colours. The garden's main designer, Basilius Besler (1561–1629) had over 1000 of the Bishop's favourite flowers and plants set down in detailed engravings based on drawings made from life and printed on the largest size of paper then available.

Besler's book predated the Linnean system of classification that was devised and adopted in the eighteenth century, but by showing many similar kinds of flowers it was necessary for him to distinguish them with a series of names in old German or Latin. By using a naming strategy based on the seasons Besler prompted others to adopt a more systematic approach later in the century.

However justified we might be in concentrating on some of the remarkable books that were printed during the first centuries after Gutenberg, we do so at the expense of a much larger group of printed items, one that was perhaps more representative of early printing as a whole. While books were the most prestigious kind of printed item and the main drivers of developments in graphic style, they were not the most common kind. The bulk of all printed matter comprised the fleeting, workaday items known as 'job-printing' or, in reference to their short-lived day-to-day use, 'printed ephemera' (from Greek *epi* meaning 'on, about or round', and *hemera* meaning 'day'). Printed indulgences (*< fig. 4.9, p.72*) are an example, as are the printed copies of Luther's theses they provoked. Unlike each of these though, most ephemera, at least from the sixteenth century onwards, was secular in content. Among the many different kinds of popular street literature, such as handbills, proclamations, advertisements, calendars, almanacs and chapbooks (*>fig. 8.12, p.131*), the most numerous were the printed ballads (*fig. 6.7*) or folk-songs. Since few people had enough money for non-essential items during the sixteenth and seventeenth centuries, most would have read broadside ballads that were pinned to the walls of buildings. The ballads themselves recounted the traditional tales known and sung by ordinary people. One of the most popular subjects, which continues to have currency today, was a person of uncertain origins, the hero of English folklore, Robin Hood.

A Robin Hood ballad printed in England in 1634 (*fig. 6.7*) tells of how he robbed the Sheriff of Nottingham by pretending to be a butcher. Below the ballad's title is a line of text giving the name of the tune to which the song should be sung. The woodcut corresponds to the story told in the song, though it may well have come, as in other ballads, from a previous edition. The style of type mixes italic and roman. Roman is used as a kind of emphasis: for the leading initial in the title, for subsequent mentions of Robin, for Nottingham and for the refrain of the chorus 'with a hey down down an a down', while Gothic is used for the rest of the text. A similar disregard for typographic purity and formal elegance was displayed in the way the text was positioned on the paper. It is bunched and cramped, with long broken lines having their remaining text placed either above or below the type line. But the very deliberate and consistent mixing of styles and positioning of broken lines show that the ballad's design was not wholly primitive. It was more that the printer had no

6.7: Broadside ballad, England, 1634

need to create great art. Cheapness and speed trumped the need for quality.

Since few of the early printers were supported by wealthy patrons or established institutions, as many scribes had been, they had to rely on their own ability to create and exploit local markets. For many, this meant large runs of circulars (leaflets and broadsides) and short texts in cheap editions set almost exclusively in vernacular languages. The need to communicate through the language of everyday speech helped to standardize regional and national languages. Printing fixed not just the spelling of words but also their meaning. This, in turn, made reading easier and increased the demand for printed items.

One response to this demand was the publication of topical and often local information. Summaries of court, church or government events had appeared in print almost as soon as printing arrived in a region, but from around 1500 a more formal presentation of single events appeared on broadsides, leaflets and pamphlets.

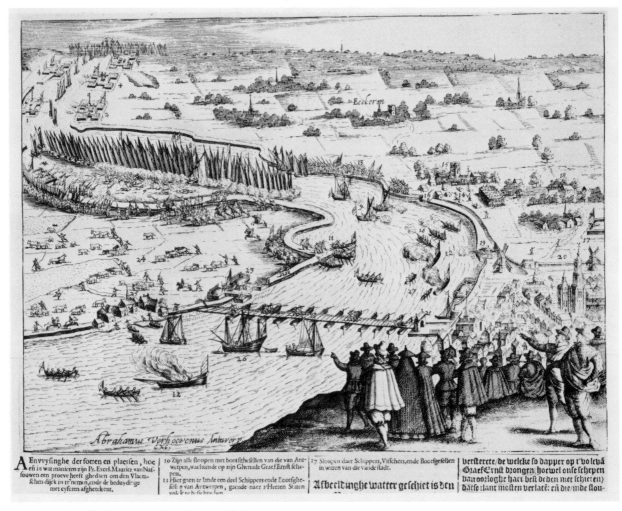

Within the engraving the following text is visible:

Abrahamus Verhoevenus Antwerp.

A Envvysinghe der forten en plaetsen, hoe en in wat manieren zijn Pr. Excel. Mauritz van Nat-souwen een proeve heeft ghedaen om den Vlaem-schen dijck in te nemen, ende de beduydinge met cyfren afgheteckent.

10 Zijn alle sloupen met bootsghefellen van die van Ant-werpen, wachtende op zijn Ghenade Graef Ernst sche-pen,

11 Hier gaen te lande een deel Schippers ende Bootsghe-fellen van Antwerpen, gaende naer s'Herren Staten vol- k te bichteben

27 Sloupen daer Schippers, Vischers, ende Bootsghefellen in waren van die vande stadt.

Afbeeldinghe watter geschiet is den

versterckte, de welcke so dapper op t'volcvā Graef Ernst drongen (hoewel onse schepen van oorloghe hart best orden met schieten) dorfse tlant mosten verlaté: en die/nde slou-

6.8: 'Nieuwe Tydinghe', printed by Abraham Verhoeven, Antwerp, 1605

Towards the end of the century broadsides were being used to describe a number of separate events that had occurred within a given period of time. The names given to this form of publication were varied, but the word 'coranto' (derived from the French *courir* 'to run') and its linguistic variants were common terms. The important distinction between many corantos and other forms of news printing was that they established a continuing relationship with the reader. By the 1620s corantos were appearing weekly and reporting on events in many different countries. While most corantos were crudely illustrated a few used copper engraving to give a detailed visual description of what was being reported in the text. It was in the Netherlands and Germany that this form of reporting and publishing developed most rapidly. The Antwerp printer Abraham Verhoeven (1575– 1652) used large engravings on the cover of his publication *Nieuwe Tydinghe (fig. 6.8)* to show 'all recent news,

victories, sieges and captures of cities' undertaken by the princes who had granted Verhoeven his licence to publish. The engraving showing the river battle in which Prince Maurice of Nassau captured Antwerp from the Spaniards in 1605 has numbers placed next to depictions of pivotal incidents in the battle, each of which are then described in the numbered text below.

The final stage in the development of the newspaper as we know it today was the appearance of news published in book form. Often named through the classical reference to the messenger of the gods Mercury, their bound and numbered pages included a title page and imprint. The more official looking versions took the name 'intelligencer' *(fig. 6.9)* to impress on the reader the accurate and exclusive nature of the information or 'intelligence' contained in its pages. Weekly editions described the newsworthy events that had taken place during each day of the previous

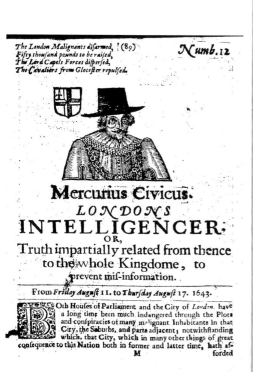

6.9: 'Londons Intelligencer', 1643

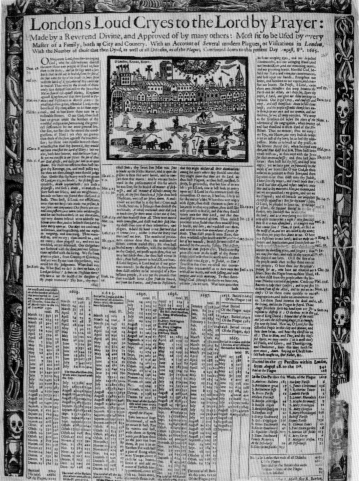

6.10: 'Londons Loud Cryes', broadside, 1665

week and the range of subject-matter broadened and accounts became more detailed. Rival papers allied to competing political factions sought to persuade readers of their greater claim to truthful reporting. On the cover of *Londons Intelligencer* the descriptive subtitle declared 'Truth impartially related from thence to the whole Kingdome, to prevent mis-information'. Above the title, in the top left corner, appeared a primitive form of news headline, while below, precise dates for the period covered by the paper was given.

Despite the rapid development of form and content that took place throughout the seventeenth century, it was only well into the eighteenth century that newspapers became commonplace items. Until then most people continued to rely on the vast array of broadsides for information. While the majority imparted information through prose there were also instances when statistical information was shown. The broadside 'Londons Loud

Cryes to the Lord by Prayer' *(fig. 6.10)*, printed in 1665, shows columns of data listing the number of Londoners that had died since 1591 during successive plagues. The sheet also includes appropriate biblical texts and a recipe for a herbal remedy. The woodcut surround and central illustration made the broadside's grim theme clear.

Data collected by observation and set down in print combined with new forms of secular literature to loosen the hold that religion had exerted on European society throughout the last millenia. The truth of divine revelation manifested in the Bible was forced to compete with the truth of nature as recorded and illustrated in an array of printed items. Through words and pictures Europeans became 'enlightened' to a new understanding of the natural world. It encouraged them to see the world more through their own eyes rather than the eyes of their priest or the text of the Bible.

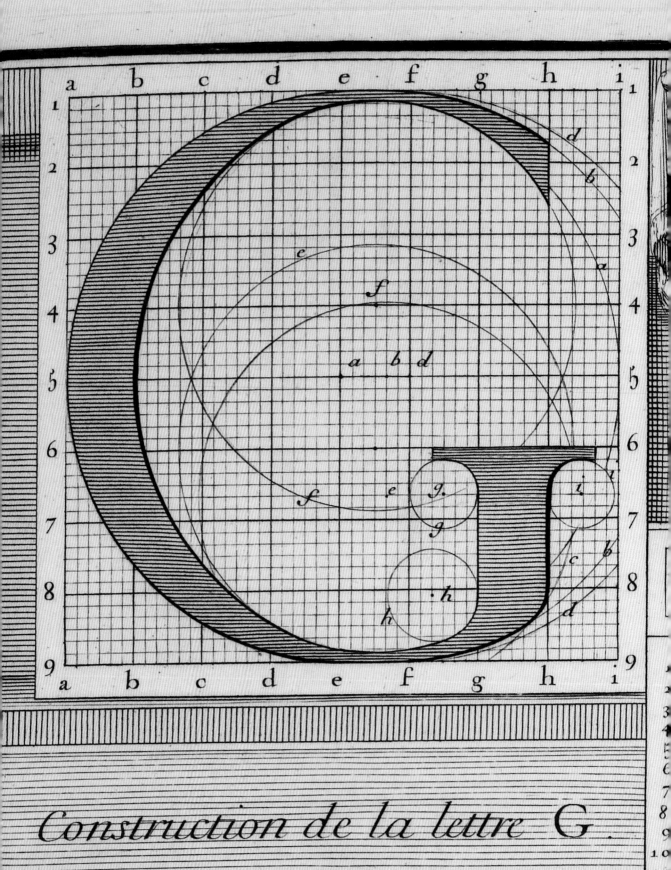

Construction de la lettre G.

7 PURITY IN PRINT

Rococo, Transitional & Modern, c.1700–c.1820

In 1692 a small group of French scientists, the 'little academy' as they came to be called, were brought together under the auspices of Louis XIV to organize the production of an encyclopaedia of French crafts. Their starting point was 'the art which preserved all others – namely printing'. A comprehensive analysis was undertaken in which the texts of 'all authors who had written on the subject' were studied, 'alphabets of every language both dead and living' were collected and 'the proportions of height to width, the outlines, the space between the different parts which make up the shape of each letter' were measured.

With this knowledge and the support of the Académie des Sciences, to which the little academy had been inducted, the scientists developed 'a new French Alphabet … chosen to please the eye as far as was possible'. Their roman letters were to serve as general models for future type designs. Between 1695 and 1718 the basic structure and proportion of their letters were illustrated through a series of copper engravings *(fig. 7.1, >7.2)*. These large and detailed engravings showed how the letters had satisfied the scientists' minds as well as their eyes. The shapes had been guided by circular and parallel lines and then set against a background grid (for the capital letters, shown here, 64 (8 x 8) main squares were subdivided into 2,304 (64 x 36) smaller squares). It produced shapes that showed a greater contrast between the thick and thin strokes. In this the letters broke from the kind of written forms that had guided previous type designs. The most notable break can be seen in a set of experimental italics. Unlike the normal cursive forms of italic (which in some instances were hardly sloped at all *(< fig. 5.7, p. 89)*, each letter was formed by shearing its roman counterpart *(>fig. 7.2)*. A more pertinent rejection of the usual written form's influence occurred in some of the lowercase letters. The 'b' had an unorthodox serif added to the foot of its stem so that it mirrored

the conventional serif at the foot of the 'd'; likewise, the form of the 'q' mirrored the 'p'.

At around the same time that the first engravings were being made the letters were tested to see how they would appear as type. The act of transposing the theoretical forms into effective pieces of type was carried out by the king's official punch-cutter Philippe Grandjean (1666–1714) in close consultation with the scientists. The process led to the creation of 21 sizes of capitals and lowercase, as well as sundry small capitals, figures and large titling capitals, which Grandjean and his two successors completed in about 1745. Though the letters of this *romain du roi* ('king's roman'), as it is generally called, were less rigidly geometric than their engraved counterparts, enough of the latter's novel geometry and contrast in stroke width was incorporated.

When the first sizes appeared in print in 1702 they were immediately popular. Even though the type had been created for the exclusive use of the king's own printing house, the Imprimerie Royale, copies used by other printers soon appeared. (Contrary to the common view, copying the royal type was only made illegal at the end of the century.) The effect of the type's appeal was to create a bridge between Old Style types (especially Garamond's type and its derivatives) and the style of later 'Modern' types that came to dominate printing in France at the end of the century. For this reason the *romain du roi* and others like it are sometimes called 'Transitional'.

The *romain du roi* first appeared in a luxurious book printed for the King, the *Médailles sur les principaux événements du règne de Louis le Grand (>fig. 7.3)*. As the title describes, the book showed the range of commemorative medals that had been issued (or in some instances newly designed in retrospect) to honour the principal events of his reign. Together they formed a collective monument to the King's achievements. By

7.2: *Engraved roman and italic capitals, Imprimerie Royale, Paris, 1716*

looking at the first, large capital 'M' on the title page and comparing it with the later engraved roman capital *(fig. 7.2)* one can see how the legs of the type form have been set wider, making it look less cramped in relation to the other capitals. The scientists, working closely with Grandjean, had stayed true to their initial aim by ensuring that the type satisfied their eye.

The title page is embellished by an engraved border and decorative centre-piece, devices that were continued on each right-hand page (the left-hand was left unprinted) in even more ornately expressive designs. Such ornate decoration became fashionable among the French aristocracy during the early eighteenth century. The name given to it in the nineteenth century, Rococo, is thought to combine the French word for shell, '*rocaille*' with the Portuguese word for Baroque, '*barocco*'. The style first appeared in French interior design, but by being reproduced in copper engravings it soon spread to other areas of the arts and to other parts of Europe.

The detailed grid that lay behind the little academy's engraved letters was used by printers at the Imprimerie Royale as a basic unit of measure for sizing type. At this time there was no exact, common standard governing the sizes of type. Neither were type sizes referred to by a number, as they are today. Instead they were given a sliding-scale of names coined by historical accident *(opposite)*. In France, the names of two common sizes, St Augustine and Cicéro, first appeared in the sixteenth century. It's likely they referred to specific editions of St Augustine and Cicéro that had used those sizes. Other kinds of names emphasized the type's diminutive charm, such as Paragon and Nonpareille ('without

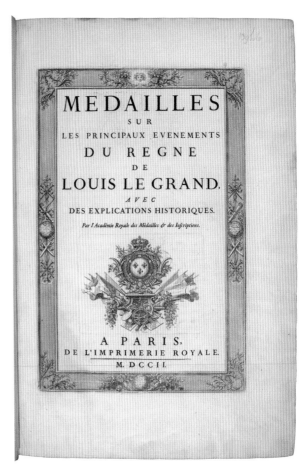

7.3: *Title page, 'Médailles', Imprimerie Royale, Paris, 1702*

parallel' or 'incomparable'), or they recorded the place where that size had first become common, as with Parisienne. In England, the three most common sizes, Pica, Brevier and Long Primer, referred to three kinds of ecclesiastical texts in which they were common ('Pica', Latin for magpie, had appeared in certain church books whose pages had a distinct black and white appearance; a breviary was a prayer book for the church service; and a primer was a small prayer book or an alternative name for a Book of Hours). Because these names denoted general sizes not specific ones, one person's Pica was unlikely to be exactly the same as another's.

The first published system of typographic measurement was that of the French typefounder Pierre-Simon Fournier le jeune (1712–68). Having studied engraving and having mastered punch-cutting and founding at a time when each had become separate disciplines, Fournier was able to appreciate the full requirements of such a system. In 1737 he drew up a 'Table of Proportions' in which 20 different sizes of type, from the smallest Parisienne to the largest Grosse-Nompareille,

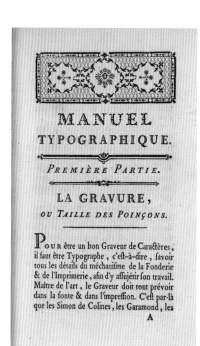
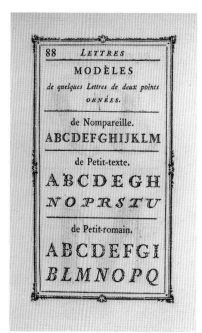
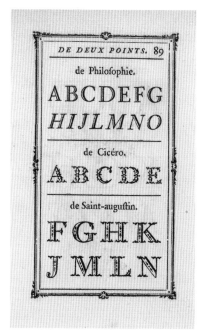

7.4 a,b,c: 'Manuel Typographique' written, designed and printed by Pierre-Simon Fournier le jeune, Paris, 1766

English (Caslon I) & French (P-S Fournier)
names for type body sizes*, 1766.

Pearl (4.70)	Parisienne (4.96)
Nonpareil (5.78)	Nompareille (5.89)
Minion (7.05)	Mignone (6.94)
Brevier (7.82)	Petit Texte (7.93)
Bourgeois (8.50)	Gaillarde (8.92)
Long Primer (9.60)	Petit Romain (9.83)
Small Pica (10.34)	Philosophie (10.93)
Pica (12.07)	Cicéro (11.81)
English (13.48)	St. Augustin (13.79)
–	Gros Texte (15.81)
Great Primer (16.94)	Gros Romain (17.82)
Paragon (18.78)	Petit Parangon (19.83)
Double Pica (20.93)	Gros Parangon (21.70)
2-line Pica (23.85)	Palestine (23.71)
2-line English (27.31)	Petit Canon (27.51)
2-line Gt. Primer (33.63)	Trismégiste (35.55)
2-line Dbl. Pica (41.10)	Gros Canon (43.12)
French Canon (46.94)	Dbl. Canon (54.93)†
	Trpl. Canon (71.10)†
	Gros Nompar. (94.81)†

* sizes in modern PostScript points (1pt = 0.353mm)
† approximate values

were related to each other 'in a regular gradation and general inter-relation … so that the large bodies are precisely the double, triple or quadruple of those under them'. Relating one size to the other in this way made the printer's task of setting blocks of type and varied ornaments easier. Though others had made similar attempts at a system of type sizes, none had also expressed the sizes as multiples of a single unit, the 'ligne' (subdivided into 'points'). Fournier had adopted the terms 'point', 'pouce' (the French 'inch') and 'ligne' (line) from the general system of measurement in France, though he later dropped the term 'ligne', preferring instead to make the diminutive 'point' his main unit of typographic measure. The size of his 'point' was equivalent to the sizes most printers were using.

Fournier displayed the perfected version of his point system in what was the crowning achievement of his working life, his *Manuel Typographique (fig. 7.4)*. The first volume was published in 1764 and the second in 1766. Within its pocket-book format were detailed descriptions and illustrations relating to the twin arts of punch-cutting and type founding. All the parts of the book – the words and their arrangement, the various samples of roman, italic, script and ornamental types – were combined in a remarkable stylistic unity. The decorative pages are examples of the Rococo style, not in the style's primary printing medium, copper engraving, but in letterpress-printed typographic ornaments.

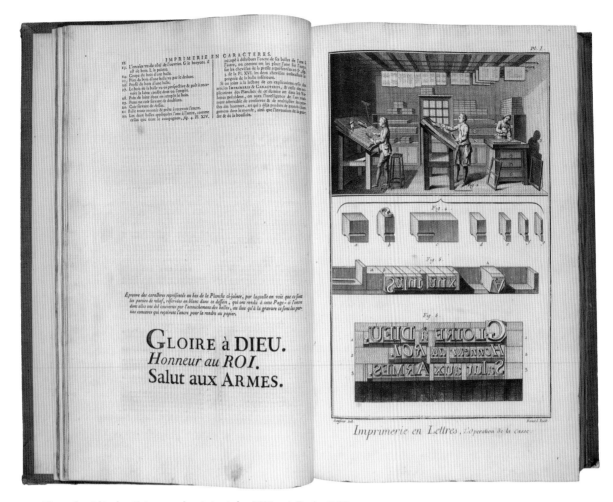

7.5: 'Encyclopédie des Sciences, des Arts et des Métiers', Paris, 1769

The hard and definite, impressed quality of type was softened by the perfumed elegance of Fournier's ornamental flourishes. The way he assembled units of ornament into greater wholes showed his mastery of this decorative art. They made the book more than an exemplar of an attractive style. Not only had Fournier written, designed and printed it himself, but almost all the elements within the design had been made by him too. It was a summation of all his type-related talents in printed form.

Fournier's *Manuel* shared its didactic aim with another book which in other ways was its opposite. The *Encyclopédie des Sciences, des Arts et des Métiers (fig.7.5)*, a 'systematic dictionary of the sciences, the arts and the crafts', was large and it combined the talents of many individuals. Though begun in a modest way, it soon grew into the biggest publishing venture ever undertaken. It was co-edited by two prominent Enlightenment figures, Jean le Rond d'Alembert (1717−83)

and, more extensively and importantly, Denis Diderot (1713−84). The first of its initial 28 volumes were published between 1751 and 1772 with later supplements and revisions being added over the following decade. Among the *Encyclopédie*'s 71,818 articles were contributions from writers such as Voltaire, Rousseau and Fournier. Aside from its vast scope and the quality of its text, what distinguished this encyclopedia from previous editions was its quantity of illustrations. Diderot believed that 'a glance at an object or its representation is more informative than a page of text'. He therefore commissioned some 3129 engravings, each of which were numbered and related to an accompanying footnote. On the right-hand page above, some of the processes involved in printing with type are illustrated. Underneath the drying pages that hang from the top of a workshop, a typesetter is shown picking out type from a type case while another returns used type and a third hammers the blocks level while they are bound in

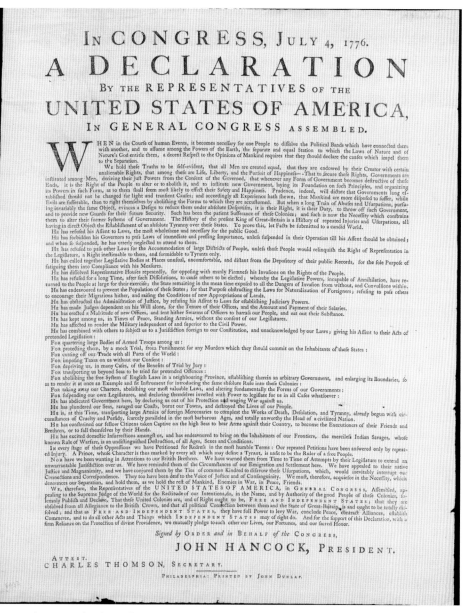

7.6: *Declaration of Independence printed by John Dunlap, Philadelphia, 1776*

a forme. Below this descriptive scene a series of more diagrammatic illustrations show different kinds of type at various stages of setting, all clearly delineated against an unprinted background. The fine detail accessed through copper engraving allowed each object to be clearly differentiated despite their similar shapes.

The *Encyclopédie*'s reasoned and orderly layout reflected the philosophy of rationality that had guided the book's creation. 'All things must be examined, all must be winnowed and sifted without exception and without sparing anyone's sensibilities' was Diderot's uncompromising creed. Following publication of the

first seven volumes, the book was officially banned. The French government had objected to its tone of religious intolerance in particular, though they turned a blind eye to the work that was carried out on the remaining volumes partly because the book had many prominent supporters and partly because by that time the whole enterprise had grown into a small industry employing an army of workers whose livelihoods depended on the book's completion.

By championing scientific freedom the *Encyclopédie* encouraged its readers to separate reasoned thought from religious belief. It also challenged the assumption

7.7: Type specimen sheet, William Caslon, London 1734

that political power had authority over intellectual and artistic matters. Both these challenges to religious and political authority helped to shape the social issues around which the French Revolution of 1789 turned.

The *Encyclopédie*'s spirit of rational self-determination also influenced the Founding Fathers of the United States. The document they wrote declaring independence from 'the State of Great-Britain' *(<fig. 7.6)* contains a famous second sentence which eloquently expresses some of the fundamental tenets of the Enlightenment: 'We hold these Truths to be self-evident, that all Men are created equal, that they are endowed by their Crea-

tor with certain unalienable Rights, that among these are Life, Liberty and the Pursuit of Happiness'.

Their 'Declaration of Independence' was printed on the night of 4th July 1776 only hours after the initial hand-written document (now lost) had been approved by Congress. The few hundred copies of this so-called Dunlap broadside – named after John Dunlap (1747–1812), the printer, whose name appears at the bottom of each copy – were distributed to the individual members of Congress and then throughout each of the 13 colonies that had united behind their rejection of British rule. By being printed the declaration could, as its text stated, let the relevant 'facts be submitted to a candid world'.

7.8: Reverse side of 13-star Fort Independence flag, 1781

7.9: Grand Union flag and East India Company flag

The concise and direct nature of the document's message was reflected in the clarity of its typography. The particular influence behind the form of its letters was a kind of type that had been made a generation earlier by the first English letter-engraver and type founder of note, William Caslon I (1692–1766). No previous type-founder had made types that British printers were prepared to buy in preference to the ubiquitous types from the Netherlands. Caslon's types were not only better cut and more legible than most of their foreign rivals, they were also cheaper. By the middle of the century his roman had become a common form in English newspapers and magazines and had spread throughout Britain's colonies. Though made in England, his type took on the dominant Dutch model of Old Style type, whose forms had derived ultimately from Garamond's roman. The roman capitals on Caslon's earliest surviving type specimen sheet *(fig. 7.7)*, printed in 1734, show a close similarity with those that appeared just over 40 years later on the Dunlap broadside. The 'A' is acutely slanted and has a concave hollow at its apex. The terminals of the 'C' are cut vertically. The arms of the 'E' have large diagonal serifs. And so on.

British influence can be seen in another important symbol of American independence: the Stars and Stripes. The flag's first form *(fig. 7.8)*, which appeared a year after the signing of the Declaration of Independence, contained 13 stars, one for each of the first states in the union, set 'in a blue field representing a new constellation'. The same numerical symbolism lay behind the 13 horizontal stripes of red (at top and bottom) and white, a symbolism that is preserved in the current flag.

The basic scheme of red and white stripes with a blue rectangle (or 'canton') in the upper left quarter had been used from 1775 in a flag flown by the Revolutionaries' small 'Continental' navy. Perversely, this Grand Union flag *(fig. 7.9)*, which is considered to be the first American flag – it was the unofficial national flag on 4th July 1776 – had its blue canton filled with the British Union flag. The same design had been used since 1707 by the East India Company, a British company that had traded in the Indian sub-continent and parts of the Far East since the early seventeenth century.

The earliest surviving 13-star flag is the Fort Independence flag of 1781, named after the fort in Boston harbour where it was flown. It has three rows of stars in a 4-5-4 formation, though a year later 13-star flags with columns of stars in a 3-2-3-2-3 formation appeared, as did others with circular or oval configurations. The shapes of the stars also varied. Six-, seven-, even eight-point stars were nearly as common as five-point ones. Such licence may have followed the example of early heraldic symbols, which had included a variety of pointed stars.

The potency of the Stars and Stripes as a symbol of nationhood was underlined in 1814 when the lyrics of the American national anthem, 'The Star-Spangled Banner', were written: 'Oh say can you see, by the dawn's early light, / What so proudly we hail'd at the twilight's last gleaming, / Whose broad stripes and bright stars through the perilous fight / O'er the ramparts we watch'd, were so gallantly streaming?', etc. (Here too a British influence prevailed in that the tune chosen was from a popular British drinking song.)

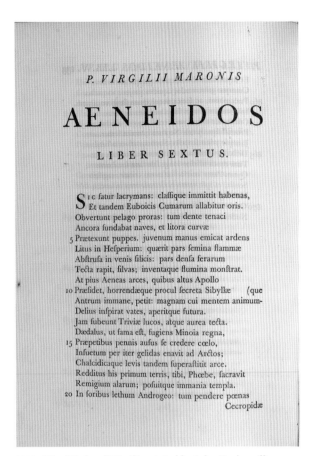

7.10: 'The Works of Virgil', printed by John Baskerville, Birmingham, 1751

The influence of European typography on British printing, which Caslon's types had demonstrated, began to be reversed with the publication in 1775 of the first book to be issued from the press of the British printer John Baskerville (1706–75). The pages of *The Works of Virgil* (*Publius Virgilius Maro* was Virgil's full Latin name) set a new standard in typographic elegance *(fig. 7.10)*. Though the type proved to be largely unsympathetic to British tastes, which had become wedded to the Caslon form, the book 'went forth to astonish all the librarians of Europe', as one historian put it. French tastes in particular had been primed to accept its sparseness despite the engraved ornaments that had enlivened their Rococo pages. Rococo decorations were often surrounded by a generous amount of white space and many of the decorative borders both framed and emphasized, through a formal contrast, the light and airy typography they surrounded *(<fig. 7.3)*. Baskerville's typography, with its widely spaced roman capitals and its set of thinner letter strokes, seemed to anticipate the greater appreciation that an exclusively typographic page would bring.

Baskerville's page is exclusively typographic. The only extraneous element, to our eyes at least, is the dutiful full-point that punctuates the book number *liber sextus*. The generous size and letter spacing of the story title's capitals allow us to fully appreciate the sturdy elegance of each individual letter. The spacing and the relative size of the four groupings of type are so well-balanced, even in this, his very first book, it makes one wonder whether all aspiring printers should not have done as Baskerville did when a much younger man and learn the art of design by carving tombstones and teaching others how to write a formal script.

Baskerville's skill as a designer was enhanced by the quality of his printing, which was thrown into brilliant relief by the innovations he brought to the ink, the paper and the printing-press. Coming to the craft from outside it and without any formal apprenticeship, Baskerville brought a greater objectivity to the printing process. Most printers had to serve a long apprenticeship, starting in their teenage years, which to some degree would have indoctrinated them in the established processes of printing. Being both unencumbered by its traditions and wealthy enough to pursue his interests, Baskerville was able to find new ways to make the ink richer and blacker, the paper a smoother 'wove' texture (as opposed to 'laid' where the paper was marked with faint ribbed lines), and the finish harder and crisper (by sealing the wet ink onto the paper with heated copper cylinders). Each innovation served to emphasize the beauty of his types and the stark grace of his layouts. The whole ensemble created a classical sense of order and simplicity.

The same aesthetic mood appeared elsewhere in the arts during the second half of the century. Within architecture, the decorative arts, and painting a reaction against the decorative excesses of Rococo combined with a new interest in the art of ancient Greece and Rome. This interest was assisted by several finely illustrated books detailing the range of artefacts unearthed from the recently rediscovered cities of Herculaneum (first excavated in 1738) and Pompeii (in 1748). This anti-Rococo pro-classical union resulted in a Neo-classicism. Unlike most arts though, and indeed unlike previous book-related revivals of classical ideals – the Carolingian and Italian Renaissances – printers of Neo-classical pages did not look to classical models for their type designs. Baskerville and others like him revived the idea of ordered simplicity rather than any previous representation of it.

7.11: 'The Universal Penman', George Bickham, London 1741

When Baskerville started making type he was already a wealthy man in his mid-forties. Despite his own assertion that Caslon's 'ingenuity has left a fairer copy for my emulation, than any other master', the types in his Virgil, with their contrasting thick and thin strokes, were more like the early 'Transitional' *romain du Roi*. Baskerville's previous employment as a letter-cutter and 'writing master' would have acquainted him with an even more highly contrasting letterform, a formal script known as English round hand (now better known as 'copperplate' or 'lettre anglaise'). The impetus behind the development of the round hand can be traced back to the middle of the previous century. With Britain having the highest rate of literacy in Europe at that time, its growing class of literates needed writing masters to teach them not only how to write but also to do so beautifully and appropriately. The demand for fine writing only increased in the eighteenth century with the rapid expansion of trade. An army of clerks had to be taught how to write a practical business script. By the first half of the eighteenth century, the various extravagant writing styles that had previously been developed were reduced in number and decorativeness. The new less elaborate round hand predominated. The popularity of this script spread overseas via the ubiquitous bills of lading and other items of business related ephemera. At home the large number of copy-books and writing manuals in circulation helped to make it the standard writing hand.

One of the largest and most splendid copy-books was *The Universal Penman* (fig. 7.11), which was compiled, engraved and published in numerous parts between 1733 and 1741 by the English writing master George Bickham (1684–1758). The book's 212 large folio pages showed engravings of lettering by 25 contemporary penmen (Bickham included), as well as various kinds of business-related writing such as letterheads, forms and receipts. Among the range of writing styles on display were numerous examples of the round hand. The title page above shows it in the three lines beginning 'Made Useful…'. In contrast with previous styles of script, where the calligraphic swelling of each letter was often formed around a diagonal axis as a result of a broad-nibbed pen held at an angle, the round hand was made with a special pointed but flexible nib which increased the weight of its line as its pointed ends splayed out when being pressed down. The ease with which thick and thin lines could be made regardless of the angle at which the pen was held encouraged a more looping style of script.

Like the manuals of the Renaissance writing masters *(<fig. 5.8, 5.9, p. 90-91)*, Bickham's book contained letters that were subtly altered by the translation of the original hand-written examples into engraved forms for printing. The medium of copper engraving allowed the engraver to produce a greater range of thicknesses – from a hairline scratch to a broad trench – and to make longer more elaborately curled lines since, unlike the penman, the engraver didn't have to think about running out of dipped ink. Both of these effects made their way into many of the engraved examples contained in copy-books, and naturally they reacted back on the writers who copied them. This led to the creation of a series of more elaborate scripts. It is also likely to have prompted Baskerville to include something of these features in his types. An example of the influence of looping can be seen in the rounded serifs of the italic 'N' which appears at the top of the title page of his Virgil *(<fig. 7.10)*.

The trend for a high contrast between thick and thin became most extreme in the types of the French printer Firmin Didot (1764–1836). By 1784, Firmin's father, Françoise Ambroise Didot (1730–1804) had printed what is considered to be the first 'Modern' type, which is to say the contrast between its thick and thin strokes was pronounced, the serifs were thin and unbracketed, not curved in any part but entirely flat, and the letters were shaded around a vertical axis, not a diagonal one. It is possible that his son may have cut the type, since he is known to have already mastered the skill even at that young age. Certainly Firmin went on to cut ever finer types, one of the most 'Modern' of which appeared in a copy of *The Works of Jean Racine* in 1801 *(fig. 7.12)*, three years after his elder brother Pierre Didot l'âiné (1761–1853) had taken over their father's business. The fine hairline strokes that appear on the title page look to be as thin as it is possible to print with type. The ability of the Didots to print these increasingly fine types so well was helped by their use of wove paper, which they recognized as being Baskerville's invention, and possibly also by using heated rollers to provide a clean finish. Also helpful were their own improvements to the printing press.

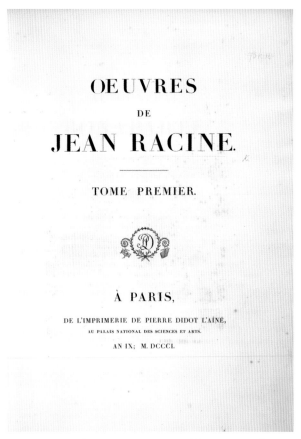

7.12: 'Oeuvres de Jean Racine' printed by Firmin Didot, Paris, 1801

By the beginning of the nineteenth century Modern types had disturbed the dominance that Old Style type had enjoyed since its introduction over 300 years earlier. In France, Italy and Britain, Modern type became popular for setting text and it remained fashionable in Europe throughout the nineteenth century. To this day it continues to have a certain prominence in French publishing, especially in setting works of fiction.

The most famous imitator of French Modern type was the Italian printer, Giambattista Bodoni (1740–1813). He had already developed a mature version of Modern type by 1787. The size of the capitals and the length of the ascenders and descenders in relation to the main body of the lowercase letters were especially pronounced. It forced him to add a generous amount of leading or line spacing to his lines of text *(fig. 7.13)*. More than any other printer, Bodoni used the unprinted parts of the page to create a clear visual hierarchy and a more refined sense of order. Where others, such as Baskerville and the Didots, had tended to place lines of capitals somewhat formulaically in the vertical centre of

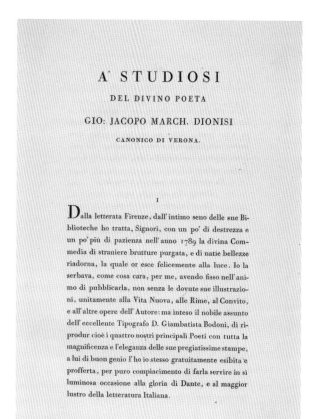

7.13: Dante's 'La Divina Commedia' printed by
Giambattista Bodoni, Parma, 1795

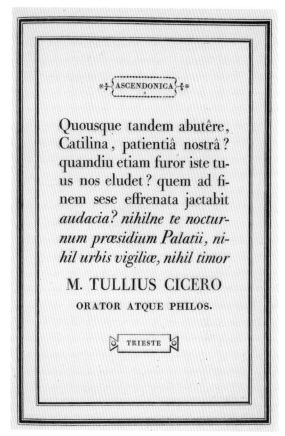

7.14: 'Manuale Tipografico', Giambattista Bodoni,
Parma, 1818

any available space, Bodoni dared to group the capitals,
creating a clear separation between them and the text.
He was also more judicious in sizing and spacing his
title type to better reflect the meaning of the title's
words.

The care he brought to every aspect of his books –
the quality of paper, printing and binding – made them
highly sought after and brought him a level of fame
that set him apart from his Neo-classical contemporaries and indeed any previous printer. The city of Parma,
where he worked, issued a medal in his honour, he
was praised by the pope and European monarchs alike,
and one of his three pensions was granted by Napoleon
Bonaparte.

Bodoni's most celebrated book was his *Manuale
Tipografico (fig. 7.14)*, which he had worked on for
nearly 45 years but was unable to finish assembling
before his death. His widow Margherita Dall'Aglio
(1758–1841) completed the assembly and in 1818
250 copies of the two-volume book were printed.
Though it lacks the breadth and explicative detail of

Fournier's *Manuel Typographique*, the small size and
the way Bodoni's types and ornaments were presented
within a commanding frame make it a Neo-classical
equivalent of Fournier's Rococo manual. The rigorous
precision with which the typographic matter was
positioned on the page and the fine, clean, solidity of
the letter shapes make each page look as though all its
contents have been locked into place. This sense of
fixity was reinforced by the subtle weighting and linear
austerity of his undecorated frames. The presentation of
his types as though they were typographic pictures was
accentuated by their being printed on the right-hand
page only. His subtler use of ornaments and his more
exact grouping of type elements combined with his
blacker ink and more precise printing to make each
page more emphatic than those in Fournier's manual.
Taken en masse, Bodoni's pages represented the calm of
classical quietude before the storm of commercial styles
that blew in with the Industrial Revolution.

8 THE TOOLS OF TRADE

Display Types & Victorian Design, c.1800 – c.1880

Before the nineteenth century, the use of capitals and lowercase, roman letters and italic, punctuation, decoration, margins and headings, was determined by conventions established in the design of books. To a large extent, the look of printing was book printing. Ever since the fourth century, when the Roman codex had replaced the scroll as the principal writing medium, the book had dominated the appearance of text. A thousand years of manuscript production and 400 years of book printing had established a standard form – a centred arrangement with a central block of horizontal lines of seriffed letters capitalized and punctuated according to certain accepted norms – and, with the exception of some specialist forms of engraving, this standard was taken to be the starting point for laying out most items of print, be it a broadsheet, newspaper or label. The onset of the Industrial Revolution challenged the dominance of book-related forms. The enormous growth in trade during the nineteenth century required a range of printed items that were dedicated to servicing and sustaining the production and distribution of goods. Price lists, order forms, invoices, banknotes and receipts were just some of the ephemeral but essential items required to oil the wheels of commerce.

Some of these had previously existed in written form, but many of them were entirely new. Recent inventions, such as the tin can and the matchbox, needed printed labels, as did familiar items such as bottles of beer and jars of medicine. Cotton and paper bags carried printed text for the first time and a whole range of new documents relating to travel, such as railway timetables, tickets and passports were introduced. Written correspondence was transformed by several new features: the postage stamp *(>fig. 8.13)*, the envelope – often with a printed design on it – and the first picture postcards. Even book printers experimented by placing text and sometimes advertisements onto the paper 'dust' jackets,

which had become a common form of protection for their cloth-bound books.

The development of printed ephemera can be traced back through the array of cheaply printed notices, picture prints and trade cards, to some of the earliest printed items, such as Gutenberg's indulgence of *c.*1454 *(<fig. 4.9, p.72)*, and then on further past the scribbled fragments of rock or ceramic *ostraca (<fig. 2.13, p.37)* used by ancient civilizations, to the birth of writing itself with the Sumerians' clay tablets *(<fig. 1.6, p.21)*. The quotidian nature of these texts carry some of the minutiae of the times in which they were made. The specificity and directness of their details can rarely be matched by any other kind of cultural artefact. The more established source materials of art history – sculptures, paintings, even books – seldom contain the same degree of specificity. The variety and depth of detail within so much ephemera combine with their aesthetic qualities to give graphic design an unparalleled cultural richness.

Many of the nineteenth century's new, commercially driven items of ephemera first appeared in Britain, home of the Industrial Revolution. The introduction of steam power into its cotton mills during the 1780s had led it towards full-scale industrialization by the 1850s. The consequent expansion in the growth of trade and the information explosion that followed quickly extended to other industrially advanced countries. Much of the ephemera related to this expansion was devoted to advertising *(fig. 8.1)*. Printers developed new kinds of advertisements with large, bold and increasingly decorative letters designed to capture and then hold the viewer's attention. These novel and fashionable forms were increasingly geared towards 'selling' the product, rather than merely announcing it.

In producing these kinds advertisements, printers were taking advantage of the new urban environment

8.2: Astley's playbill, 1877

that had been created by the rapid growth of cities during the nineteenth century. Workers and their families left the fields for factories in search of a more secure and prosperous living. At the start of the century, London was the largest city in Europe with a population of around 900,000. Paris followed with some 600,000 inhabitants. After a period of only 50 years, both populations had doubled. Over the next 50 years the rate of increase accelerated so that by the century's close, the populations had increased five- or sixfold. Other major cities across western Europe and America grew on a similar scale. Each were transformed by the commercial potential their growth had generated.

The cities' new buildings provided a broad, red-brick canvas on which a host of competing groups could paste their messages. New civic organizations, such as workers' unions and political parties, could communicate to their constituents out on the street, where the urban masses passed by in their hundreds daily. Such public notices were as much a part of the urban landscape as the buildings that supported them. These posters were known as 'bills' or, in some cases, more specifically by a combined term such as 'playbills' for theatre posters *(fig. 8.2)*, or 'handbills', in the case of smaller hand-held flyers and leaflets. Not only did they appear in ever-greater numbers, many also increased in size. Before 1800, broadside posters had seldom been larger than the largest book page, and consequently printers had been able to fill them with whatever book types they owned. With the advent of cheaper paper and larger presses, the size of the poster increased (by as much as a factor of six, i.e. a 40-fold increase in area). These larger posters required larger types. The very largest letters could be as much as 2 ft high and thus type made from wood was used rather than the much heavier metal. The cutting of wooden types was simplified during the second quarter of the century with the invention in America of the router, a mechanical cutter that could cut more quickly and precisely than a craftsman with his knives and gouges.

More significant than size though, was the letters' shape. By 1800, the Modern types developed in France by the Didots had become popular throughout Europe. Their highly contrasting thick and thin strokes had showed how the standard roman letter could be freed from the foundational Renaissance form, yet remain faithful to the utilitarian task of making lines of readable text. But as past scribes and writing masters, such as Paulus Franck *(<fig. 5.10, p. 91)* and George Bickham

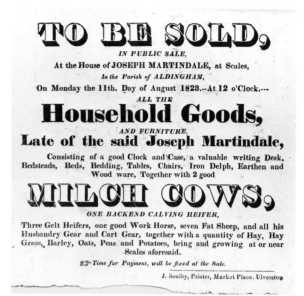

8.3: *Fat-face type specimen, Vincent Figgins, c.1835*

8.4: *Rural poster, printed by John Soulby, c.1824*

(< fig. 7.11, p. 119) had shown, letters need not always be restricted by the demands of text setting. Words did not have to be bound within a strait-jacket of legibility. Where the need to inform, as with the text in a book say, was equalled or exceeded by a need to excite or intrigue, as in an advertisement, it was necessary for key words, such as the name of the product, the company name or the name of the event, to stand out.

The first step towards a more attention-seeking type used for display had been taken in the 1690s when an ornamented type appeared on an English title page. Similar types appeared on some of the title pages printed in continental Europe during the following decades, though it was not until the 1760s, when Fournier's nine display types appeared in his *Manuel Typographique (< fig. 7.4, p. 113)* and when Old Style types began to be enlarged for use on posters that the display types became more prevalent and were codified (Fournier's manual included the first so-called 'shaded' or 'two-line' type, one which had a single white stripe running down the side of its thick strokes).

By the first quarter of the nineteenth century, display types had begun to appear in a series of forms that suggested they were part of an evolving trend. A turning point for this trend had been the appearance during the start of the century of an exaggerated version of Modern type known as fat-face *(fig. 8.3)*. It was a fashion forged in England, where the large and increasingly thicker Old Style types had developed. Fat-face letters possessed a very exaggerated contrast between their thick and thin strokes. The contrast was greater even than the extreme Modern types Firmin Didot had used on his later title pages *(< fig. 7.12, p. 120)*. Furthermore, unlike

the earlier Modern types, some of the features in fat-face letters suggested a certain roundness: the rounded termination of the upper arm of the 'a' and 'c', both of which were mirrored in many of the lower leading serifs of the italic capitals. The new kind of dark, dense words they made were applied to all kinds of posters. It mattered little if the product or event being advertised was a traditional one, as shown in this poster for a 'public sale' *(fig. 8.4)*, or indeed if the layout was the familiar, centred and stacked layout long favoured by book printers on their title pages. The type's solidity enabled it to stand out.

As an attention-seeking type with an almost comical geniality, fat-face succeeded in encouraging type-founders to explore its potential for emphasis. The range of fat-face types was soon extended. Outline forms appeared which were then given the illusion of three dimensions by a dropped shadow, as shown above. Though harder to read, they appear to almost jump off the page. Other types were shaded or made out of strokes patterned with stripes or dots, or a combination of these shaded and decorative features *(> fig. 8.7)*. The idea of a variant form in which a standard letter style, such as fat-face, could be decorated differently yet retain its basic shape proved that within the mechanized world of type printing a single style could be extended in an almost infinite variety of ways. Though it was only later that such types were described as a 'family', the notion of a family likeness had been established.

8.5: Slab-serif, type specimen,
Vincent Figgins, 1817

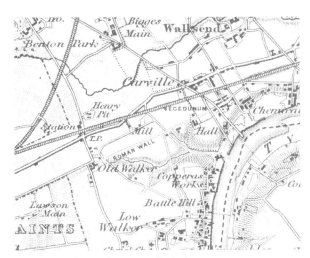

8.6: Sanserif, British 'One inch' Ordnance
Survey map, 1801

Having set the pace in the development of display types, fat-face was joined and then, gradually, replaced by two similarly emboldened styles of type: the slab-serif *(fig. 8.5)* and the sanserif *(fig. 8.7)*. The slab-serif was a logical progression in the evolution of an ever-more commanding and impressive letterform. It too had thick strokes and similarly proportioned letters, but, uniquely, the weight of the strokes was distributed more evenly throughout the letter, approaching a 'monoline' form, i.e. made from a single, uniformly thick line. In marked contrast to the hairline serifs of the fat-face, the serifs were thick. Each stroke was terminated by a large, rectangular black slab. The ascenders and descenders of the lowercase letters were kept short and the numerals large, as large as the capitals.

The earliest known example of the slab-serif are some letters printed in 1810 in a handbill for a London lottery. They were made from woodblocks, but the earliest known to be printed from metal type appear in a type specimen book for the British type-founder Vincent Figgins (1766–1844) (he called them 'Antique' though others in Britain called them 'Egyptian'). Within a decade, Figgins had produced the full range of capitals, lowercase letters and italics. The popularity of the style was such that, from the 1820s, having become the dominant type in posters, slab-serifs began to appear in smaller sizes as headings in books and other kinds of non-publicity text. It even went on to become a style within a style known in Britain as Clarendon. In the 1840s, this less monoline, somewhat condensed version of slab-serif was widely used for setting continuous lines of reading text. It went on to outlive the slab-serif

proper, which fell out of favour during the second half of the nineteenth century.

The second kind of emboldened type to rival the fat-face was the sanserif, a letter without (*sans* in French) serifs. Its secondary characteristic was, like the slab-serif, strokes that had a uniform thickness. Today, many designers assume the sanserif is a modern form; an industrial letter for an industrial age. Though it first appeared in print in the nineteenth century, its history is as old as the alphabet itself. Sanseriffed letters were the alphabet's foundational form. The letters of the first full alphabet, as written by the Greeks in the eighth century BC, were un-seriffed because they had been scratched or carved in simple lines with a rudimentary tool *(<fig. 2.2, p. 30)*. It was only at the end of the fourth century that serifs began to appear on some Greek letters and then, a century later, on Roman letters also.

The introduction of the sanserif as a type for printing grew out of a conscious revival of classical letterforms. The first Neo classical reincarnations of sanserif letters had appeared in the 1780s, though not in type form. They were hand-rendered initially in architectural drawings and then as carved letters on buildings and monuments. The vogue for such letters grew over the next three decades and the sanserif began to be seen painted onto signs, cast within bronze medals or copper engraved onto title pages. In 1816, the first series of British 'One inch' Ordnance Survey maps *(fig. 8.6)* used an engraved sanserif letter to mark sites of Roman antiquity, a function that is still performed by a sanserif today. The first sanserif to be printed from type is thought to have appeared in same year, in a type specimen for a

CANON ORNAMENTED.

TYPOGRAPHY.

TWO LINES ENGLISH EGYPTIAN.

W CASLON JUNR LETTERFOUNDER

TWO LINES ENGLISH OPEN.

SALISBURY SQUARE.

8.7: Sanserif type specimen, William Caslon IV, 1816

British type founder, William Caslon IV *(fig.8.7)*, great-grandson of the first William Caslon. His description of it as 'Two Lines English' refers to the size of the type (it was equivalent to two lines of standard 'English' type, about 20 points). Caslon's sanserif type is neither bold enough nor is it large enough to be used on a poster. It is also not small enough for text in a book. Its ill-fitting form offers some explanation as to why sanserif type did not start to appear in other printers' specimens until the early 1830s. Since it was Vincent Figgins's specimens that first showed the greatest range of sizes, it is he who is credited with launching the sanserif as a workable type.

For the early revivalists of the sanserif, both in Britain and elsewhere, its ancient origins were important. But the different associations each attached to it – for some it was a grand classical form, for others it was ruggedly primitive – were reflected in the variety of names they gave it. In Britain it was called, variously, Grotesque (i.e. primitive), Doric (classical) and Gothic (primitive). In Germany, the last term, or its equivalent, Grotesk, was used; while in the United States, the latter, Gothic, was preferred. French printers chose a different name, Antique (classical), which would have confused their British and American counterparts, who had used this term for the slab-serif. Compounding this confusion was yet another term, Egyptian, which some British printers had initially applied to the sanserif before using it as an alternative to Antique. The choice of the word Egyptian was connected to the swell of public interest

that surrounded Napoleon's discovery of ancient Egyptian remains, most notably the Rosetta Stone, which had been brought to England in 1802 *(<fig.i-1)*.

Not everyone welcomed the sanserif. Neither were any of the other new display types universally popular. 'Typographical monstrosities', '… folly of fat-faced preposterous disproportions', '… a disagreeable effect scarcely at a distance appearing to be writing', were some contemporary reactions. As a class of type, the status of the sanserif is now beyond question; except, perhaps, in relation to legibility, where it is still often cited as being less legible than a seriffed face (though legibility is determined by much more than the presence or lack of serifs). Its position is now such that, when describing a typeface, we often do so by first saying whether it is a serif or sanserif. Sanserif types can be seen carrying out every kind of typographic task, from listing names in telephone directories to the writing on street signs and roads. It is now the world's most visible letter form.

The desire to make types emphatic had encouraged a uniformity (of stroke-width) and simplicity (no serifs) in their design. The same desire also encouraged the opposite characteristics: variety and complexity. As bold simplicity became less of a novelty, some of its attention-grabbing power was lost. Its waning appeal left the way open for new kinds of more decorative letters. An inflationary pressure for ever more elaborate and unusual types built up throughout the 1830s, 1840s and 1850s. The constant demand for stimulation

8.9: Woodblock for letter Q shown opposite, c.1822

8.8: Ornamented type, Louis John Pouchée, c.1822

created a paradox: a tradition of novelty. It is a requirement that has guided the evolution of graphic style in the West ever since (and other arts besides), even leading it through periods when simpler and less emphatic types became fashionable because they countered a prevailing trend. These subsequent phases of complexity and simplicity in type design can trace their origins back to the explosion of variety that appeared on British posters in particular, during the second quarter of the nineteenth century. It was here that letters became condensed, serifs triangular or rounded ('Tuscan') and white letters appeared on a black or shaded background ('Cameo'). Others types were composed of wooden branches ('Rustic') or patterned with delicately intertwined garlands ('Floriated'). Whole sub-groups developed,

such as the range of heavily illustrated types on which various farm animals were depicted or else a sequence of rustic scenes. While many ornamented types were crudely drawn, there were some that were designed with such dexterity, balance and refinement they have become models of their form *(fig. 8.8)*. But irrespective of the artistic merit, both they and the other early nineteenth-century display types are a powerful testament to the flexibility of the Roman alphabet. Even when staying within the limits of legibility, the array of forms that they accommodated seems to be boundless.

Linked to the effect of commerce on graphic forms was the effect of the developments in printing that had taken place during the first half of the nineteenth century. The first significant development was a new way of making woodcuts, confusingly called wood engraving even though nothing was printed from ink-filled recesses as in a copper engraving. Like the earlier woodcut, a wood engraved print was made from the raised, uncut parts of a block. Where the new method differed was in the use a slow-growing and therefore hard wood which also was cut on the end-grain rather than the side-grain *(fig.8.9)*. It allowed the cutter to make a much more accurate and detailed image, one which approached the level of detail contained in a copper engraving. Not since Dürer, Rubens and Titian's celebrated woodcut prints 200 years earlier had the medium of wood been used to make such fine and lifelike images.

The popularity of wood engraving during the nineteenth century can be credited to a British engraver and artist, Thomas Bewick (1753–1828), who restored to the medium a level of skill and seriousness that had been denied it while cheaply printed broadsides and chapbooks had been its main mode of expression. Instead of using the traditional woodcutter's knife, Bewick worked with tools similar to the engraver's gouging tool or burin, which he had learnt how to use while training as a metal engraver. With these tools he deftly varied the width and shape of the white, unprinted parts of the print. He had also learnt how to cut back certain parts of the raised image to make the ink fainter or else he raised up other parts by inserting slips of paper under the block to make a sharper and darker impression. Both actions dramatically enhanced the sense of depth in the subsequent print. His mastery of the white line and spatial depth enabled him to render his favourite subject matter – the local animals, birds and landscapes – with a degree of realism not previously seen in print *(fig.8.10)*. His craft skills supplemented both his ability as a draughtsman and his deep knowledge of wildlife and livestock to reveal images that presented not just general examples of each species but seemingly individual instances of them.

Although Bewick did not invent wood engraving he developed and perfected it to such a degree that printers in Europe and America were also encouraged to exploit its potential. Their eagerness was increased by the cheapness of the medium – wood being less expensive, quicker to cut and longer lasting than copperplate – and by the important fact that a wood engraving could be printed alongside type. Both were made in relief, so they could be combined and then printed under the same impression.

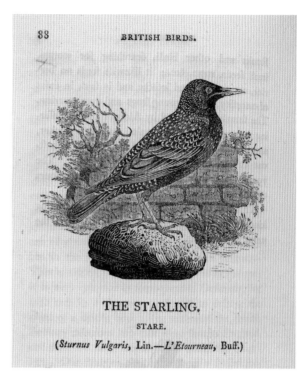

8.10: *Print from 'History of British Birds', written and engraved by Thomas Bewick, 1797*

By the 1830s, wood engraving had ceased to be the solitary craft of a skilled artisan. Whereas Bewick had, for the most part, drawn and engraved his illustrations himself, printers who were keen to meet the rising demand for illustrations from periodicals, newspapers and catalogues were now employing teams of engravers to work from drawings supplied by artists. As schedules in print journalism became more demanding, single images began to be divided into several separate blocks for a team of engravers to work on before being reassembled and printed. The woodblocks themselves began to be traded internationally, much as stock photographs are today, and the more so after improvements to a reproductive process known as stereotyping had become widespread. At the end of the previous century Firmin Didot (*< fig.7.12, p.120*) had helped to revive and develop the production of so called stereotype plates by casting them as sheets of metal from moulds made out of plaster-of-Paris. The mould contained a precise impression of the forme that needed to be printed, be it a woodblock, or type set as a block, or a combination of the two. This process not only allowed the original forme to be kept out of harm's way once the mould had been made, it also made it possible to print from a number of identical plates when long editions had to be

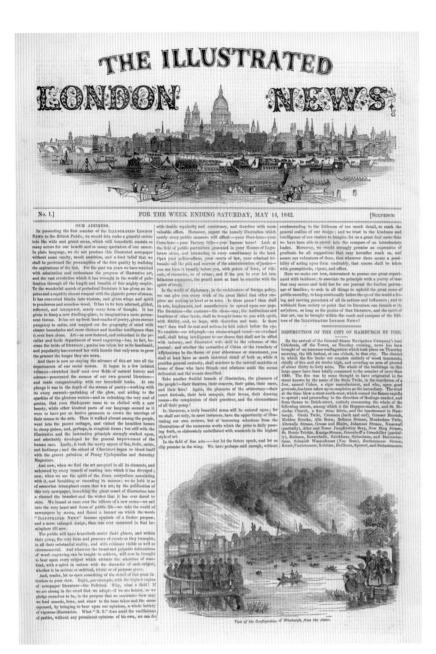

8.11: 'The Illustrated London News', 1842

printed quickly. (The word 'stereotype' which we now use in an extended, general sense was coined by Didot to describe these plates; and the related word 'cliché' is thought to have had similar origins in that it was derived from the sound made by the molten metal coming into contact with the cold mould.)

More important than stereotyping for its impact on printed illustration was the introduction of photography into commercial printing. When the French inventors of photography, Nicéphore Niépce (1765–1833) and Louis Daguerre (1787–1851), agreed to work together in

1829 it was to create 'a process for engraving on metal'. Their initial aim was to use their rudimentary form of photography to reproduce engravings. Fifty years later and the roles given to each process had been completely reversed. Wood engraving was being used to replicate photographic images. The whole process of engraving had changed from being a creative and expressive medium, as Bewick had used it, to being a cheap way of copying photographs for printing. By the 1860s it was possible to fix photographic images from negatives onto woodblocks coated with a light-sensitive substance. An

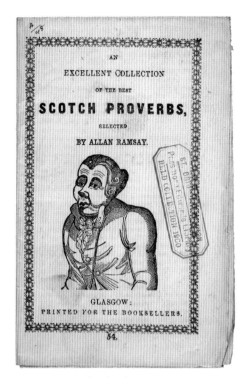

8.12: 24-page chapbook, 1820s

engraver would then cut into the resultant image either emphasizing its photographic range of tones with an array of carefully spaced and sized dots or translating the image in a purely linear fashion.

The main drivers behind this changed use of wood engraving were the series of illustrated magazines that started to appear from the 1840s onwards. The first weekly magazine to depict current events was *The Illustrated London News*, launched on 1 May 1842 *(fig. 8.11)*. Despite its claim to be a supplier of news, the magazine's first pictures were culled from second- or third-hand sources. The front page of the first issue included a report of a fire that had broken out in the city of Hamburg, which had left 20,000 people homeless. While the text contained facts and descriptions that can only have come from eye-witness accounts, the engraved illustration was made from an old topographical print of the city onto which flames and crowds of onlookers had been added. It looked to be an eye-witness depiction of the event, but by being a visual approximation it recalled some of the pictures that had been used in a similar way 400 years earlier in the *Nuremberg Chronicle* (<*fig. 4.16, p. 79*).

The Illustrated London News catered to a middle-class readership, who would have appreciated the aesthetic link of its wood engravings to book illustration

and fine art prints. For the mass of urban and rural poor the cheaper woodcut continued to be the standard fare. Though generally a much cruder and less sophisticated form of illustration, attempts were made to incorporate some of the finesse of the newer engraved form. In the figure that appeared on the front of a chapbook *(fig. 8.12)* from the 1820s (like others in the genre the chapbook was undated so that it wouldn't age so quickly) a series of fine lines were used to build up the shading that described the character's inexpertly drawn form.

Chapbooks were the cheapest kind of printed book. From as far back as the sixteenth century they had been hawked round hamlets, villages and towns by chapmen, or 'tradesmen' ('chap' is derived from *ceap*, the Anglo Saxon word for 'trade'). This late example here shows the basic way in which many such books were made: a single sheet was printed on both sides with the text positioned in such a way that when the sheet was folded into the appropriate number of pages (here a 24-page 'duodecimo' format is used (<*p. 88*) the text fell into the correct sequence. The dirty grey paper is thin and cheap, the alignment of the text slightly askew, but the content is clear and informative (though largely impenetrable to a modern English speaker). The 'Scotch Proverbs' are just one example of a whole profusion of subjects – stories, songs, riddles, biographies, speeches,

8.13: Penny Black and Two Pence Blue postage stamps
(actual size and detail), Britain, 1840

confessions, executions, hymns, religious tracts, and so on – that were selected from other books or supplied by anonymous authors in an attempt to meet the demand for cheap and accessible literature.

The sheer variety of printed items that came into existence during the nineteenth century made it harder for any single style to predominate. Graphic forms are rooted both in their uses and in the methods used to make them. The expansion of these at this time led to a vast range of styles. One new use which harnessed the precision of copper engraving was the postage stamp. The first pre-payment adhesive stamp, the Penny Black, was introduced in Britain in 1840 and was immediately followed by the Two Pence Blue *(fig. 8.13)*. The key to their design was the complex web of engraved patterning and varied initialling (in the bottom two corners) that had been employed to deter forgers. The fine, looped borders and spirals that were spun around the head of a young Queen Victoria did not only call for the expertise of a skilled engraver, they were also created by specially made machines for cutting part of the background pattern and for printing sheets of stamps. When attempting to create an exact match, forgers would have to contend with both man-made and machine-made forms.

Technical innovation during the nineteenth century touched every aspect of the printing industry, but nowhere more so than the workings of the press itself. Had Gutenberg walked onto the floor of a press room

in 1800 he would have had little difficulty recognizing the machine in front of him, still made of wood and with its central screw mechanism. Had he returned a few decades later, the press would have been unrecognizable. The most dramatic difference would have been the replacement of the man-powered screw with steam-powered or, in a few cases, electricity-powered rollers or cylinders. The first steam-powered press was secretly installed by *The Times* newspaper in 1814, in an attempt to steal a march on its rivals. 'Our paper today presents to the public the practical results of the greatest advance in printing since its invention … in one hour no less than 1100 sheets can be printed' (a four- or five-fold increase over the kind of press it had replaced). So wrote the paper's director in the first edition to be issued from the new press. By the 1860s, steam was being used to pass an unbroken roll of paper through the press, a considerable advance on the previous practice of cutting the roll into separate sheets and feeding them onto the press by hand. Other improvements followed, such as the ability to print on both sides of the paper in a single operation, so that by 1900 the hourly rate of newspaper printing had risen to 24,000 copies of a 12-page paper (including its cutting and folding).

By initiating these improvements, the newspaper industry was reflecting the growing importance of its product. Newspapers had been the most read item in Britain since the end of the eighteenth century and they achieved a similar status in other industrialized nations during the nineteenth century. As in much else that was technically and commercially progressive during the second half of the century, it was in the United States that developments in news reporting were most advanced. Generally, newspapers were not designed to be read quickly. There were no eye-catching illustrations and the articles tended to be written in reasoned and measured tones, and often at considerable length, sometimes continuing for several pages even. *The New York Herald* was more sensationalist than most. By the 1860s its more salacious editorial style and its novel use of bold headlines allowed it to claim to be 'the most largely circulated journal in the world'. Some stories merited the extra typographic emphasis it gave them. On the front page of an early edition for 15 April 1865 *(fig. 8.14)* a large, bold sanserif type was used to signal an 'important' announcement: the attempted assassination of Abraham Lincoln (which proved to be successful as the President died later that day). Half the left-hand column was set aside for headings of reports relating to

8.14: Front page, 'The New York Herald', 1865

the incident – 'Escape of the Assassin', 'Scene from the Deathbed of Mr. Lincoln', etc. – which had occurred little more than six hours earlier. A paper like this, printed in several editions each day, did not have time to create and incorporate illustrations or complex text setting. Its typographic emphasis was achievable and became an enduring mode of expression. Similar emphases continue to appear in papers today.

Among the most revolutionary changes in printing was one that had come from outside the industry and through the least modern of materials: the pre-industrial medium of stone. Large, rectangular half-ton slabs of it were the principal component in an entirely new reproductive process called lithography (*lithos* means 'stone' in Greek), which has since become the basis of nearly all commercial printing (though the stone has long since been replaced by rubber blankets).

Lithography was discovered almost by accident by an impoverished German playwright called Aloïs Senefelder (1771–1834). While searching for a cheap way of printing his own writing Senefelder was led to experiment with local Bavarian limestone as a medium for engraving text. Sometime between 1796 and 1799 (his own description makes it unclear) he scribbled a laundry list onto the stone with a wax crayon. This inspired him to exploit the antipathy between the oily wax and water for the purpose of printing. After wetting the porous stone he rolled a greasy ink over it and saw that while the ink had been repelled by the areas of damp it had stuck to the wax. The resultant inky image

could be printed, albeit crudely, by placing a piece of paper onto the stone and rubbing it. Senefelder had thus discovered the essential workings of an entirely new method of printing. It neither needed time-consuming cutting or gouging, nor did it have to rely on the ability of a woodcutter or engraver to faithfully interpret an artist's drawing. The artist could put his image down onto the stone directly, in his own hand, though he had to do so in reverse. For those images that contained text, printers turned to the section of skilled letter-engravers who, for generations, had practised the art of writing letters backwards.

Senefelder's 'planographic' or surface method of printing was met with interest from fine-artists and commercial printers alike. Artists of the stature of Delacroix, Géricault and Goya appreciated the ability it gave them to work on the stone directly. By the mid-nineteenth century, many commercial printers had been coaxed into adopting the process by the invention of transfer paper. By printing images onto a specially formulated paper with a greasy ink, it was possible to transfer them onto the stone by rubbing, much as children do with 'transfers' today. Images from woodblocks, printing type, engraved copperplates, even handwritten text could all be transferred in this way.

The flexibility provided by transfer paper led printers to see lithography as a way of reproducing a pre-existing image. But the three-step sequence of reproduction this involved – inked printing block to transfer paper, transfer paper to stone, stone to printed paper – resulted

8.15: Champollion 'Dictionnaire Égyptien en écriture hiéroglyphique', Paris, 1841–3

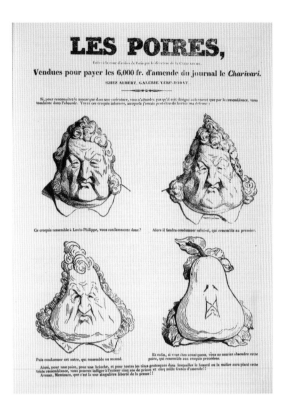

8.16: Les Poires from 'Le Charivari', Paris, 1834

in an appreciable blurring of the image. Accompanying this loss of quality was a loss of authority. Just as photocopied pages look or feel less credible or authentic compared to the pages they were copied from, so too did transferred lithographic prints, especially if they contained large amounts of text. For this reason most book printers avoided the process, though some included illustrations that had been drawn directly onto the stone.

For many kinds of commercial printing, lithography provided a quicker and cheaper alternative to engraving. Sheet music, maps, cartoon strips, military manuals, plans and technical drawings, diagrams, tables and charts, trade cards, postcards, letter-headed stationery, petitions, handwritten documents and facsimiles of texts were just some of the printed items that benefitted from the new process. For the French linguist and decipherer of the Egyptian hieroglyphs, Jean-François Champollion (<p.35), lithography enabled his life's work to be preserved in print. His dictionary of Egyptian hieroglyphs (fig. 8.15) could not be printed with the letterpress because no one had yet made a full set of hieroglyphic type. Only by writing out each of the 500-odd pages onto transfer paper could Champollion's dictionary be made available to a wider public. It established

lithographically printed handwritten text as the standard form for nearly all subsequent works on Egyptology throughout the next century.

In France especially, a more visible use of lithography appeared from the 1820s onwards in a succession of short-lived but popular satirical magazines. Their letterpress pages were often interspersed with lithographic prints lampooning the most prominent members of the political and social elite. The image of the increasingly illiberal and heavily jowled 'Citizen King', Louis-Philippe, turning by stages into a pear as though it were happening in slow motion (fig. 8.16), was drawn by the greatest caricaturist of the age, Honoré Daumier (1808–79). Daumier's illustration, which was based on another's earlier sketch, had first appeared in the journal La Caricature in 1831. The image's pun was a double one. It was verbal as well as visual since the French word for pear, poire, had the alternative slang meaning of 'fathead' or 'sucker'. The transformation was enhanced by the ability of the lithographic process to replicate Daumier's loose and mutable drawing. It helped to establish the pear as a general symbol applicable to anyone who was deemed to be ripe for satire. It also reinforced the symbol's association with

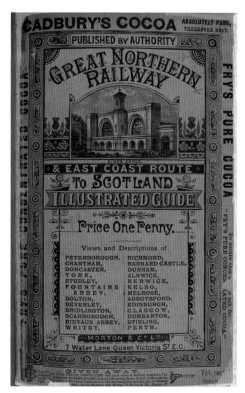

8.17: *Illustrated railway guide, London, 1891*

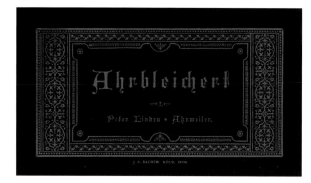

8.18: *German wine label, 1880s*

press-freedom, a link that the journal's editor, Charles Philipon (1800–61), had established weeks before when put on trial for 'outrages against the person of the king'. While in court Philipon had brought out his sketch of the image and asked cleverly at what point exactly it had broken the law.

The ability of lithography to reproduce almost any kind of image encouraged printers to include a range of different styles of type and decoration in their designs. From the 1820s a reaction to the unadorned and simple, geometric character of much Neo-classical design spread throughout the decorative arts. It lead to the revival of a series of more ornate styles, Neo-Renaissance and Neo-Rococo among others, which through the richness of their decoration seemed to express the new wealth and luxury that many Victorians came to enjoy during the nineteenth century. Even things that were linked to the most modern aspects of the new industrial age, such as the railway, did not escape from historical styles of decoration *(fig. 8.17)*. The cover of this illustrated railway guide shows a catholic mix of late-Renaissance ornamentation and varied styles of elaborate lettering, both of which contrast with the bold sanserif type in the surrounding advertisement.

In addition to historical styles lithography also

provided printers with an unrivalled range of new effects, such as crayon marks, various kinds of stippling and a whole range of mechanical tints and textures, though perhaps most novel of all was the ability to print broad areas of flat colour. Neither engraving nor relief printing could match the even transfer of ink that could be achieved from the stone's surface. The German printer of this wine label *(fig. 8.18)* harnessed this new facility to produce a flawlessly smooth deep-purple background, which helped to throw the intricate detail of the gold border into sharp relief. The label is just one example of a number of printed items that had begun to be printed in colour during the second half of the nineteenth century. Chromolithography's most important contribution was built on an earlier attempt to produce a range of colours out of a limited set of three or four base colours. By printing the base colours in small enough dots they created a spectrum of colours. The advances in printing technology that had made colour commercially viable were seized on and popularized by some of the members of a movement whose apparently contrary founding principle had been to revive the craft techniques of the Middle Ages. This aim was described in their name: the Arts and Crafts movement.

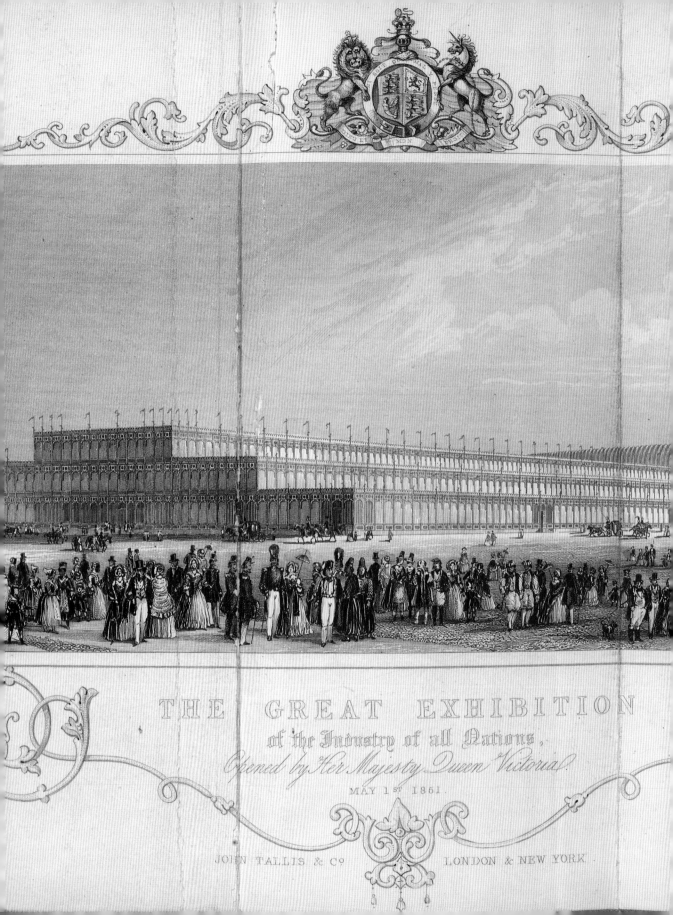

THE GREAT EXHIBITION

of the Industry of all Nations,

Opened by Her Majesty Queen Victoria

MAY 1ST 1851.

JOHN TALLIS & Cº   LONDON & NEW YORK.

9 MANUFACTURING THE MIDDLE AGES

Neo-Gothic & the Arts and Crafts, c.1840 – c.1910

A new word entered the world's dictionaries at the beginning of the second half of the nineteenth century: capitalism. Though the word had become common currency through the writings of the German philosopher Karl Marx, the founder of its ideological opposite, communism, it was the British novelist William Makepeace Thackeray who had coined it. The British had come to describe themselves as inhabiting 'the workshop of the world', and in celebration of their position as the prime exponents of capitalism, they organized an international trade fair in London's Hyde Park. The Great Exhibition of 1851 *(fig. 9.1)* was set out on an unprecedented scale. It attracted exhibitors and visitors from every continent. The event itself was housed in a symbolically long 1851ft 'blazing arch of lucid glass' (Thackeray again), especially designed for the occasion out of the most modern materials – steel rods and glass panels – and constructed according to the innovative principle of prefabrication.

Within the great gleaming 'Crystal Palace' – a space so large some old trees growing on the site were enclosed by it – eight miles of tables were erected, each of them displaying a profusion of artefacts. One contemporary account marvelled at the 'silks and shawls, lace and embroideries, jewellery and clocks and watches, behind them military arms and models, chemicals, naval architecture, philosophical instruments, civil engineering, musical instruments, anatomical models, glass chandeliers, cutlery, and animal and vegetable manufactures, china and pottery ... on the opposite side perfumery, toys, fishing materials, wax flowers, stained glass'. At a time when the total population of England was approaching 17 million, this vast and disparate array of artefacts managed to attract over six million visitors. Many of them, both native and foreign, travelled to and from the exhibition on specially commissioned trains along a network of rail track which, already

by the end of the 1840s, had spanned the length and breadth of the country. (The US transcontinental railroad, by comparison, albeit on a much larger scale, was not completed until some 50 years later.) The size of the exhibition and the wide range of goods on display, most of them machine-made, were evidence of how, within only half a century, from when the first steam-driven machinery had been introduced into the textile mills of northern England in the early 1790s, industrialization had transformed manufacturing in the West.

The Great Exhibition was one of the key cultural events of the nineteenth century, but its influence on design was driven as much by the criticism it provoked as by the praise it received. Some visitors came away appalled at the 'chamber of horrors', with its vulgar display of factory-made products. Exotic ornament and sensational effects could be seen applied to carpets, silverware, tables and chairs, with little regard for the object's use – whether, for example, a chair was comfortable to sit on – nor had there been an attempt to preserve the intrinsic or fundamental form of the object, for its own sake. Many artefacts were mawkishly or gaudily distorted by historical styles of decoration and naturalistic effects. An example that remains with us today, though usually in a less extreme form, is the wall-mounted light disguised as a profusion of flowering stems. It is an archetype of the kind of explicit and forced imitation of nature that the German word 'kitsch' was used to describe. Yet, the flowering light was positively restrained in comparison to other exhibits, which were so heavily disfigured it was difficult to know, just by looking at them, what they were for exactly.

The art of graphic design was caught up in the same syndrome of historical revivalism. In Britain especially, the sparse Neo-classical style of typography that Didot and Bodoni had mastered, and the varied

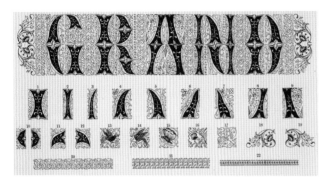

9.2: Gothic modular type, V&J Figgins, c.1850

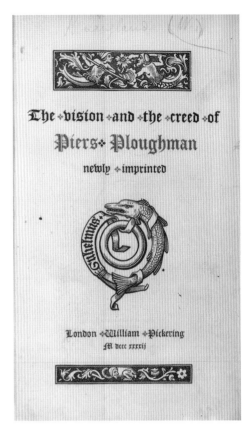

9.3: Title page printed by Charles Whittingham, 1842

styles of display type that had appeared on some of the new advertising hoardings, were joined, from the late 1840s and early 1850s, by a full-scale assault of pseudo-Gothic ornamentation. This Neo-Gothic style of design appealed to printers for much the same reason as it had first appealed to architects at the beginning of the century. Both considered the style to be a more indigenous and romantic alternative to the austere forms of Neo-classicism that had then become fashionable. Manuscripts, pattern-books *(<fig.3.16, p.63)* or medieval buildings were scoured for Gothic forms of lettering and decoration, but without any mechanical means of capturing these styles – the ability to make a visual record by photographic means was only just getting under way – copies of these forms had to be sketched by hand, and bundled into albums for reference. Designs produced during the Gothic Revival were often a medley of regional styles from widely differing sources and dates. Gothic art had never been a unified homogenous style. It had evolved within a number of distinct European cultures over a period of almost 1000 years. Several such influences can be seen in a set of modular type *(fig.9.2)* made in around 1850. The units cleverly combine to make letter shapes that hint at the illuminated letters of the Lindisfarne Gospels *(<fig.3.4, p.51)*, an eighth-century British manuscript, and yet the style of decoration that surrounds these modular forms is closer to a printed Renaissance decoration. The designer's passion for the overall ornamental effect had triumphed over any concern he might have had for historical accuracy.

Few printers managed to handle the range of Gothic forms with as much skill or sensitivity as the London printer Charles Whittingham (1795–1876), who worked in close co-operation with his publisher, William Pickering. Whittingham managed to temper the Gothic excesses in ornament and the angular types

by placing them within a spare, minimalist layout more characteristic of the Neo-classical page than of an illuminated manuscript *(fig.9.3)*. His 1847 edition of *Elements (fig.9.4)* by the Greek mathematician Euclid is an extraordinarily modern treatment of an ancient text *(c.*300 BC). The full title of this particular edition, 'The first six books of the Elements of Euclid, in which coloured diagrams and symbols are used instead of letters, for the greater ease of learners', indicates what is modern about it: the very functional use of colour. Its geometric symbols and text have been enlivened by Whittingham's careful registration of three primary colours, which prefigure by some 70 years the arch Modernist designs of the following century *(>fig.13.14, p.199)*. And yet, set within this very functional design are some small wood-engraved initials cut in the white dotted *manière criblée* style of the sixteenth century *(<fig.5.14, p.95)*.

In comparison with this modest excess, most other printers were much less restrained. By filling their designs with a profusion of decoration, they seemed to luxuriate in the ease with which modern methods

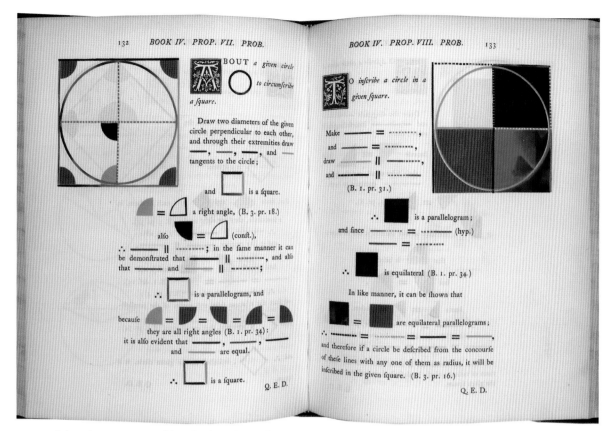

9.4: *Euclid's 'Elements' printed by Charles Whittingham, 1847*

of lithographic reproduction could replicate historical patterns and types. They may well have reasoned to themselves that, in an age of varied tastes, it made little sense to stick soberly to a single style. By casting their aesthetic net wider through the combined use of several styles, their designs might appeal to a greater audience.

Such blatant copying was anathema to an increasingly broad lobby of critics. Those artists and social reformers who had inherited the attitudes of the earlier Romantic movement, in which a love of nature and individual skill had been central, condemned historical revivalism chiefly for being a product of the machine. Few expressed their criticisms of the machine-made stylistic mêlée with as much eloquence and passion as the British art historian and critic John Ruskin (1819–1900). In his book *The Seven Lamps of Architecture*, written in 1849, a year after Marx's *Communist Manifesto*, Ruskin warned: 'All the stamped metals, and artificial stones, and imitation woods and bronzes, over the invention of which we hear daily exultation – all the short, and cheap, and easy ways of doing that whose difficulty is its honour – are just so many new obstacles in our already encumbered road. They will not make us happier or wiser – they will extend neither the pride of judgment nor the privilege of enjoyment. They will only make us shallower in our understanding, colder in our hearts, and feebler in our wits. And most justly. For we are not sent into this world to do any thing into which we cannot put our hearts.' For Ruskin, mechanical manufacture on an industrial scale had severed a vital link between the artisan and certain traditions of design that in some instances had sustained him and his kind for generations. As a consequence, modern manufacturers had been cast adrift on a sea of historical styles which they no longer understood, nor had the skills to execute faithfully.

While he and his fellow reformers agreed on the need for change, they were much less clear about the direction in which that change should take them. There was a small minority who wished to follow a clearly progressive route by engaging with modern methods of manufacture and materials, but the majority seemed to be unable or unwilling to see much aesthetic merit in mechanically made objects. In spite of being surrounded

9.5: *Illuminated gift book, 1848*

by many grand and innovative constructions – the bridges and stations built to service the new railways, for example – they remained blind to the potential of a machine aesthetic. From as far back as the 1770s, solid iron girders had been used to build bridges for roads, but not even a century of such building could awaken people to the beauty of the iron girder. We can all now admire the sturdy elegance of Paris's Eiffel Tower. For us it stands as an iconic piece of nineteenth-century design, but when it was erected in 1889 (a symbolic date, it being the centenary of the French Revolution) most Parisians disliked it. Having dismissed the Crystal Palace as a 'giant cucumber frame', it is unlikely that Ruskin would have had much praise for it. His contempt for the thoughtless copying of period styles was equalled by a disdain for the rigid order that he found in mechanical construction. Both attitudes prompted him to appeal to artists and designers to look more carefully at the art and craft of the pre-industrial era, and to observe how the imprint of a human hand could be detected on every object. Long-standing traditions had endowed medieval art with a 'living rhythm' through

which the essential nature of each object was revealed rather than disguised, and the link between the form of an object and its function was made more directly. It was among a like-minded section of reformers that the need to go back to school and learn the fundamental principles of decoration from these past traditions was both felt and acted upon.

Such a need was served by the publication in 1856 of a source-book of ornamental styles, printed in colour, called *The Grammar of Ornament (fig. 9.6),* which had been painstakingly put together by the British architect, teacher and book artist Owen Jones (1809–74). Earlier, Jones had provided decorations for 'illuminated' gift books, a genre that had been made popular in the 1840s through the richness of its illustrations. Its fashionable Gothic types appeared surrounded by medieval motifs set within brightly coloured borders, and all were reproduced in colour by the new process of chromolithography *(fig. 9.5).* Each colour was printed in flat blocks from its own lithographic stone and carefully aligned so as not to overlap with an adjacent colour. This kind of chromatic jigsaw puzzle produced some of the most

9.6: Owen Jones's 'The Grammar of Ornament', 1856

vivid and sumptuous books ever seen in London at that time. Through them, and others in the genre, chromo-lithography's potential became known.

The solidity, brilliance and variety of their litho-graphed inks emphasized just how monochrome books had been during the 350 years since the birth of printing. The hand-brushed washes and printed rubrica-tion of past books looked pallid and mean in compari-son with the full spectrum of colour that shone from the pages of Jones's *Grammar*. Jones's obituarist, indeed, described him as the 'most potent apostle of colour' in a land 'where colour was as much feared as the small-pox'. His *Grammar*, though, was much more than an advertisement for colour printing. It was also a monu-mental work of comparative research, unmatched in scope by any previous book on design. Jones had scav-enged hundreds of national and period patterns, from the Egyptians to the Elizabethans and beyond, from borders, columns, capitals and the like, and then sifted and studied each before setting them out in chronologi-cal order on large folio pages. His detailed analysis of these forms was acute – pointing out the centrality of geometry in pattern-making was especially helpful to later designers – but he also admitted in the preface that his efforts would come to little if his readers looked on these historical styles merely as a source for imitation rather than one of inspiration.

The influence of Ruskin and Jones led to a flour-ishing of craftsmanship across a wide spectrum of handicrafts in Britain, from calligraphy and weaving to furniture design and architecture. It grew into an artistic movement known in the English-speaking world as the Arts and Crafts movement. On the Continent, it was known by the French term, *Le Style Anglais*, which emphasized not only its English origins, but also the British character of many of its medieval motifs. Similar strains of the Arts and Crafts style appeared in Germany and America, but in both places, as across Europe more generally, the movement was more significant for the ideas it promoted than the forms it created.

Few artists put as much of their heart into reviv-ing ancient craft traditions than the movement's most prominent member, William Morris (1834–96). On his death bed at the age of 62 he was diagnosed as suffer-ing from an illness caused by 'simply being William Morris, and having done more work than most ten men'. When Ruskin called him 'the ablest man of his time' he was recognizing Morris's ability to combine the knowl-edge of the connoisseur with the practical skills of the maker. This enabled him to roam across the fields of art and design with a freedom that is no longer available to designers, required as they are to acquire a special-ism and stick with it. The range of Morris's activities is relevant because it describes the path that other design-ers were to follow during the following decades. In his own day, Morris was acknowledged as one of the finest Victorian poets, ranking alongside Tennyson and Browning, but, unlike them, he also wrote fiction (and early science fiction). He translated books from Greek, Latin, Old English and ancient Icelandic, and designed, printed and published some of the most beautiful books of the period. He painted and engraved, designed houses and the furniture to go in them, and he ran a successful interior design business from a prominent shop in central London. It is for his wallpaper and fabric that he is best known today.

As well as being an artist and a businessman, Morris was also a committed social reformer. He did much to develop the theory behind modern socialism in Britain. Some have even claimed him as a guiding light of the environmental movement, and others as a proto-feminist. In his passion, industriousness and self-reliance, he was the archetypical eminent Victorian, and yet, through his developed sense of social equality, he was a very modern man. His link to the subsequent Modernist movement can be over-emphasized, but he certainly had ideas in common with it, in spite of his preoccupation with the past.

All his ideas seemed to spring from the same primary, motivational source: that of 'unity', be it historical, social or artistic. In Morris's eyes, all parts of an artwork deserved equal attention because they all contributed to a single entity, the artwork as a whole. An artist should not therefore be concerned only with image making, i.e. the marks or colours he or she placed on a surface. Of equal importance was the surface material itself. The artist should choose the most appropriate material for the job in hand, and then work with that material, not against it. Something of this attitude was later contained in the Modernists' phrase 'truth to materials'. In Morris's work, the expression of this kind of truth is nowhere more apparent than in the books he designed and printed.

Morris came to book printing late in life. He set up his own printing office, the Kelmscott Press, during his late fifties, 'with the hope of producing some [books] which would have a definite aim of beauty, while at the same time they should be easy to read and should not dazzle the eye, or trouble the intellect of the reader by eccentricity of form in the letters.' Since he had 'always been a great admirer of the calligraphy of the Middle Ages and of the earlier printing which took its place', the books were printed with a hand press, and nearly all the other related methods of production were carried

9.7: Cover, 'The Works of Geoffrey Chaucer', William Morris, 1896

out according to fifteenth-century practice. (A significant exception was his use of photography to enlarge examples of early printing types so that he could study them better.)

His most celebrated book is *The Works of Geoffrey Chaucer (fig. 9.8)*, published in 1896 in the last months of his life. Many have considered it to rival the finest printed incunabula. It is fitting that this magnum opus, a folio edition of 556 pages and 87 illustrations, which took five years from conception to completion, was the last of Morris's great design projects. The unity of the whole book elevates it from a collection of fine pages into an object of beauty in its own right. No part of it was allowed to be sullied by the industrial practices then common among the publishing industry. The embossed pigskin cover of the finest edition *(fig. 9.7)* was not treated with chemical whitener as other covers had been. The hand-ground ink was similarly free of additives, and the type was designed and cut specially for the book. The style of type that Morris chose was determined by his desire 'to redeem the Gothic

HERE BEGINNETH THE TALES OF CANTERBURY AND FIRST THE PROLOGUE THEREOF

WHAN THAT Aprille with his shoures soote
The droghte of March hath perced to the roote,
And bathed every veyne in swich licour,
Of which vertu engendred is the flour;
Whan Zephirus eek with his swete breeth
Inspired hath in every holt and heeth

The tendre croppes, and the yonge sonne
Hath in the Ram his halfe cours yronne,
And smale foweles maken melodye,
That slepen al the nyght with open eye,
So priketh hem nature in hir corages;
Thanne longen folk to goon on pilgrimages,
And palmeres for to seken straunge strondes,
To ferne halwes, kowthe in sondry londes;
And specially, from every shires ende
Of Engelond, to Caunterbury they wende,
The hooly blisful martir for to seke,
That hem hath holpen whan that they were
seeke.

BIFIL that in that seson on a day,
In Southwerk at the Tabard as I lay,
Redy to wenden on my pilgrymage
To Caunterbury with ful devout corage,
At nyght were come into that hostelrye
Wel nyne and twenty in a compaignye,
Of sondry folk, by aventure yfalle
In felaweshipe, and pilgrimes were they alle,
That toward Caunterbury wolden ryde.

9.8: 'The Works of Geoffrey Chaucer', William Morris, 1896

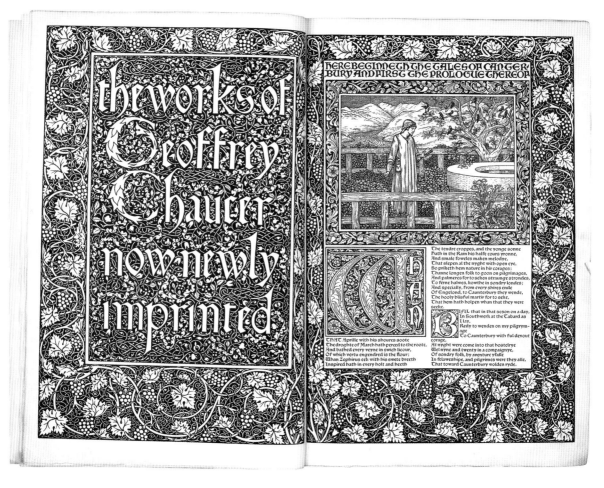

9.9: 'The Works of Geoffrey Chaucer', William Morris, 1896

character from the charge of unreadableness'. He decided to model the Chaucer type on some of the very earliest printing types, such as those used by the German printer Peter Schoeffer *(< p. 77)* in a Bible of 1462. Morris's resultant 12-point Gothic type does not completely escape the charge he sought to avoid – it is less legible than many early roman types for example – nevertheless, the letters are robust enough to hold their own alongside the densely engraved woodcut illustrations and highly ornamented borders and initials. The letters' slightly irregular outlines make them appear as though they too have been cut in wood, and the overall grey tone of the text closely matches the tone of the other printed parts of the page. The text's even tone was achieved in part by setting the individual letters and the words they make unusually tight, which avoided the obtrusive 'rivers' of white space that ran down the pages of so many contemporary books. It was also helped by spacing the lines of text

closer. Though richly patterned, the floral borders were evenly balanced and without fussiness, and the margins that surround them took on the basic ratio of medieval proportions with a thin inner width, a somewhat wider top, the outside edge wider still, and the bottom widest of all.

For Morris, the basic unit of his book was not the individual page, but the double-page spread *(fig. 9.9)*. In the introductory spread above, the text on each page is framed by highly decorated borders that have the same proportion and a similar design. Despite the different kinds of content that Morris set within each of the borders – large letters on the left, small letters, a framed illustration, decorated initials and lines of type on the right – the contents are united by a series of horizontal aligments. The top of the illustration's frame on the right aligns with the top of the letter 'f' in 'of' on the left; the top of the same illustration aligns with the 'x-height' of the same line of letters; the top bar of the

colour : built-up or heavy letters in black show extra *black* beside lighter writing, while the latter appears *grey* in comparison (see figs. 197, 186); in red writing the heavy letters appear *red*, the lighter letters, *pink* (see fig. 90).

Contrast of Size.—The simplest decorative contrast is that of LARGE¹ letters with SMALLER letters (fig. 185); the strokes being of equal, or

SIMPLE CONTRAST OF SIZE:HARMONY OF FORM,WEIGHT AND COLOUR

FIG. 185.

nearly equal, weight, there is an harmonious evenness of tone throughout. Where the large letters are very much larger, their parts are made somewhat heavier to keep their *apparent* "weight" approximately equal (see p. 486). This is one of the most effective treatments for inscriptions generally (see p. 299, and Plates V. and XXIV.).

Contrasts of "weight" and size.—In simple writing these are obtained by using two sizes of pen—the small, light letters being used for the bulk of the

¹ Where there is only a slight difference in size, the effect is improved by using a different *form* or *colour* (see pp. 130, 345).

328

text, the larger heavier letters being used for occasional words or lines (or *vice versâ*). This is a very effective simple treatment for MSS. (fig. 186).

a few lines of much larger
Writing gives an agreeable, simple contrast of size & colour. The larger writing is conveniently written between every other pair of writing-lines. It may be more decoratively treated. (a.)

FIG. 186.—(*See also fig.* 191.)

The occasional letters may be more decoratively treated (see *Responses and Rubrics*, p. 345) by introducing the further contrasts of *colour* (p. 144) or form (p. 336).

329

9.10: 'Writing & Illuminating & Lettering', Edward Johnston, 1906

wooden fences within the illustration align with the x-height of the subsequent two lines, and there are a similar series of aligments that fall down the page. Edward Burne-Jones, Morris's life-long friend, who drew the illustrations, predicted the Chaucer 'will be like a pocket cathedral'. The book was, indeed, filled with Gothic-inspired ornamentation, but even an inexpert eye can distinguish it from the kinds that decorated the incunabula of the late Middle Ages. Morris had too strong a sense of his own aesthetic taste to follow or imitate other models slavishly. None of the features in his Chaucer are actual copies of medieval forms. The borders, initials, illustrations and types, in accordance with Owen Jones's precept, were modern interpretations of them.

It was not just his work that established Morris as an important figure in the development of design. Many of the artists who came to work with him or his circle, though less versatile, were no less gifted in their chosen craft. Also, importantly, they were equally devoted to furthering the aims of the Arts and Crafts movement. Through their work, their writing and the various art societies they started, they inspired subsequent generations to carry the baton of the craft revival well

into the twentieth century. One such artist, sometimes referred to as 'the father of modern calligraphy', was Edward Johnston (1872–1944). On moving to London from Edinburgh, Johnston was brought into contact with members of Morris's circle and, through them, the scripts on display within the unique collection of ancient manuscripts in the British Museum. Johnston fell so completely under the medieval scribes' spell that he determined to devote the rest of his life to making 'living letters with a formal pen'. More importantly perhaps, he was committed to passing on his passion to several generations of students over a period of almost 40 years. Many of the best calligraphers and letter carvers of the twentieth century were taught by him or his pupils, or else first fell in love with letters while looking at his work.

Johnston's preparatory notes for his very first calligraphy class indicate the necessarily detailed, almost fetishistic attitude towards tools and techniques that was so characteristic of the members of the Arts and Crafts movement. The notes started: 'Writing and Illuminating – a practically lost art worth reviving; mss [manuscripts] the matter for illumination, therefore writing the main point; the qualities of good writing:

readableness, beauty, character; materials, parchment (skins), pens (quills), inks (Indian). Preparation: estimating, cutting, cleaning, 'pouncing' [preparing the writing surface]; cutting pen, form and manner. Ink (soln.), practice for copies (rough), ditto (careful).' Being a masterful calligrapher and a lucid teacher, it was apt that Johnston should combine both talents in a handbook. *Writing & Illuminating & Lettering (<fig. 9.10)* was first published in 1906, and it quickly became an indispensable guide to the craft of calligraphy, not just in England, but also overseas, in Germany and the United States especially. It soon became the calligrapher's 'bible' and was to remain in print, unchanged, throughout the last century. The clear and detailed instructions it gave were illustrated with examples in Johnston's own hand. The letters shown in this spread are written in his main, formal writing hand, one which he based on an English variant of the Carolingian minuscule, a tenth-century Winchester script *(<fig. 3.8, p. 54)* that appeared in a particular psalter. Johnston favoured this script because its rounded upright letter shapes were well suited to writing with a broad-nibbed pen, the best implement for beginners, and because its letter shapes approached those of a standard roman printing type.

One of the designers whose life as a maker of letters was guided by the examples in Johnston's book, as well as by Morris's Kelmscott books, was the German type designer Rudolf Koch (1876–1934). It is the first time that the word designer, as distinct from punch-cutter, type founder, printer or publisher, can be used with real authority. This is not to say that printing or typefaces in the past had not been designed. All the images seen thus far were the result of varying degrees of conscious planning and aesthetic judgement. But when, in 1906, the Klingspor type foundry asked Koch to join a select group of type designers, they did so not because they valued his skill as a craftsman necessarily, but because they recognized his abilities as a letter artist. Koch was employed to provide drawings of letter shapes which the foundry would convert into types for printing. The emergence of this new kind of artist, a 'designer', had two related impetuses: one was the example typified by Morris, of a recognized artist, who drew designs that others turned into a final material form. Some of the types in his books were made this way. The second was the invention of machines that could do the job of the craftsman. This left the way open for the designer, whose lack of craft skills (though not of knowledge of the craft) would not bar him from the task at hand. In

9.11: Kochschrift, 1910; Maximilian, 1914; Wilhelm-Klingspor Schrift, 1926; all designed by Rudolf Koch

the case of type design, a significant machine at this time was the punch-cutting pantograph *(>pp. 206–7)*, which allowed an operator to cut type by tracing over drawings supplied by a designer. In this way, the importance that had been placed on the craft of carving shifted onto the artist-designer's ability to imagine and specify letter shapes.

As an already accomplished calligrapher, Koch's ability as a designer of letters was not in doubt. Being both German and a devout Christian Koch was familiar with and had a deep affection for the Gothic letters favoured by some of the members of the Arts and Crafts. Gothic type had remained the standard form of letter for printing religious texts in Germany as elsewhere in Europe, but it had also remained a standard for more general printing too. Germany's pride in its printing heritage (being the birthplace both of printing and of the first printer) gave the Gothic letter an important role in the German national identity. The sense of pride was strengthened by the part it had played during the Protestant revolt of the Reformation, when it was seen as an indigenous alternative to the Catholic roman letters. In addition to these strong historical links, there

Richard WAGNERS Parſifal

Bismarcks Memoiren

Genf PARIS Ems

Sang an Aegir

Dante Heine

Niederland

Rudhard'ſche Gießerei in Offenbach·M

5

9.12: Type specimen of Eckmannschrift, designed by Otto Eckmann, 1900

were good linguistic reasons for their Gothic preference. The German language tends to have more long words than other European languages because it frequently combines words that others leave separated, e.g. *Kunstgewerbeschule* (School of Arts and Crafts), and even *Kleinkinderbeschäftigungsanstalt*, literally 'Young Child Activity Institute'; (to mark what was then believed to be the 400th anniversary of Gutenberg's invention, in June 1840, this word's inventor opened the first such institute, though he referred to it with the more manageable and recognizable word *Kindergarten*). Gothic types, with their narrower, more space-efficient letters, reduced the length of German words.

The first type that Koch designed for the foundry, the eponymously named 'Kochschrift' *(fig. 9.11 –* shown here as in all subsequent examples of type or typefaces, in a modern digital version), was completed in 1910 and it quickly became popular in printing not just works of literature, but also advertisements and even street signs. Its dynamic angularity combined elements of the textura form of Gothic script with the roughly cut characters that had appeared in block-books (<*fig. 4.6, p. 70*). Like Morris, Koch was not looking to

replicate the past graphically. 'We do not want to make letter books today so that they resemble old ones. We want to express ourselves in our own way, do what we think is attractive in our own style.' Many of his subsequent Gothic typefaces did incorporate a more modern, rounded letterform similar to Morris's Chaucer type. But compared to the type designs of some of his Klingspor colleagues they looked conservative. Otto Eckmann's (1865–1902) 'Eckmannschrift' *(fig. 9.12)*, designed in 1900, was a much bolder departure from the traditional German letter. The angular picket fence-like strokes of the medieval scribe's pen were warped, as though fashioned by the brush of an oriental scribe.

Despite its international exposure, the Arts and Crafts movement never gained the kind of popular appeal its founders had hoped for. The likes of Ruskin and Morris had wanted to see a revival of art in every craft, even the most common domestic trades: 'A true artist is only a beautiful development of tailor or carpenter.' But the movement failed to establish itself in more than a handful of esoteric or else inherently expensive crafts that, to Morris's dismay, involved 'ministering to the swinish luxury of the rich'. This complaint touched on the incompatibility between the movement's aims – to make art according to pre-industrial methods of manufacture – and the age in which the movement existed. Using highly skilled artisans to make things by hand out of the very best materials made those things expensive. However beautiful and whatever sense of satisfaction they gave their makers, few people could afford them. Moreover, the look and feel of them, their pattern and form, had to compete with more modern objects.

The decades either side of the turn of the century saw a series of industrial inventions which we recognize as the harbingers of mass communication: the telephone (1876), the gramophone (1888), the car (1893), the portable typewriter (1893), the public cinema (1895), the transatlantic wireless (1901), and the Wright brothers' first flight (1903). When graphic designers, such as Eckmann, began to embrace a more modern manner, it was with the help of an entirely foreign form. It was a turning point which hinged on the introduction of an aesthetic style that had been wholly absent from Jones's collection of exotic ornaments: the aesthetic of the art of Japan.

10 THE STYLE OF THE STREET
Art Nouveau, c.1880 – c.1914

Art Nouveau, as hinted at by its name, was made with the explicit intention to create a new kind of art. Despite competition from a range of rival styles, most of them historical revivals, it succeeded in becoming 'the style of the age'. It was adopted and adapted by artists in many countries and was applied to a vast range of items. By the turn of the century, Art Nouveau forms could be found on bill-posters, brooches, biscuit tins and buildings. In each instance, the main characteristic of decorativeness remained as a permanent reminder of the style's origins from within the decorative and commercial arts; and, in particular, the art of graphic design. It was within the confines of the printed page and the poster that many of Art Nouveau's signature features were developed.

Printing made for public display had first shown its potency at the beginning of the sixteenth century, with the circulation of Martin Luther's theses *(<p.65)*. The religious revolution that followed drew much of its energy from ideas that were brought to the public's attention by the printing press. But a similarly epoch-defining demonstration of printing's power also took place during the last decades of the nineteenth century, in what has been called 'the age of the poster'. In contrast to the religious and political tenor of much of the printing from the Reformation, the posters of the late nineteenth century served the more secular aims of commerce and entertainment. To many, posters came to symbolize a new era of 'conspicuous consumption': 'Nothing is really of a more violent modernity, nothing dates so insolently from today [as] the illustrated poster, with its combative colour, its mad drawing and fantastic character, announcing everywhere in thousands of papers that other thousands of papers will have covered over tomorrow, an oil, a bouillon, a fuel, a polish or a new chocolate.'

Improvements made to the printing technique of chromolithography throughout the second half of the nineteenth century allowed designers and artists to exploit the special graphic potential that lay within the poster format *(<p.11–12)*. Posters were able to be larger and more colourful than before. The attitude towards the public display of printing changed too. The previous ad hoc process of sticking posters to an available flat surface was replaced by a more organized and systematic approach, with special hoardings being erected by contractors who, in some instances, provided framed areas almost as though the posters were paintings. Whether the image presented was actually looked at rather than merely seen depended on the quality of the design, but if the public felt compelled to peruse it, they could do so with a fixity and intimacy that was only to be surpassed with arrival of the cinema screen.

The poster's power was most actively demonstrated on the streets of Paris. The city's boulevards and alleyways became lined with large and vibrantly colourful images. This new form of public art succeeded in making the previous Victorian posters, with their typographic bias and predominately monochrome palettes *(<fig.8.1, p.123)*, appear both timid and antiquated, especially when, as sometimes happened, the new posters had been pasted onto a wall in multiples of ten or more to form a kind of external wallpaper. Such images were often dominated by a single, large human figure, rather than the smaller detailed groupings that had previously been adopted from the style of illustration used in magazines and journals.

These changes brought in a number of artists, illustrators and designers who had the ability to exploit the new potential that had been given to the medium. An important inspiration for this group was provided by the large number of posters designed by Jules Chéret (1836–1932), the so-called 'king of the poster'. Chéret had both simplified the lithographic process and extended its range of colour effects. By combining simple outlines with subtle mixes of bright colour and various stippled effects he was able to change the view of colour lithography from that of a reproductive medium into an artistic one. Chéret allied his technique to the depiction of joyfully alluring young women *(<fig.10.1)*, whose carefree exuberance and thinly veiled sexuality were seen to represent the cult of pleasure then associated with *fin-de-siècle* Paris. In his sumptuous colours and hedonistic themes he was considered by some to be continuing a tradition established in the eighteenth century by the prints and paintings of some French Rococo artists (Debucourt, Watteau, Boucher and Fragonard). His posters' vibrant colour combinations, their female forms and their sense of gaiety were purposefully chosen by Chéret as the best means of attracting 'even the average man when the street-scene passes before his eyes as he walks along the pavement or drives past in his car'. By making the edges of his posters diffuse or bare, viewers were in no doubt as to where they should focus their attention. Even the lettering was peripheral. Chéret gave it only cursory consideration; when putting down the image, he left spaces as a rough indication of where the lettering should go. A specialist letter artist would then fill in these gaps, usually unsympathetically by stacking the letters in groups of roughly symmetrical lines.

The willingness of fine artists to turn their hand to commercial art was partly influenced by the possibility of a relatively reliable source of income. They were also influenced by a feeling of contempt for the traditional hierarchy that divided the arts. It was a division that graded them into three broad tiers: 'high' or 'fine art', such as painting (provided its style fell within an accepted academic school) and music (similarly, only classical, not folk); a middle tier of the decorative arts (such as ceramics, glassware, furniture, interior design and architecture); and at the bottom the popular or commercial arts (such as graphic design, advertising and popular forms of entertainment, such as music-hall theatre).

The dominance of these divisions at this time was shown by the hostile reaction that greeted the appearance of a poster known as *Bubbles (fig.10.2)*, which had been published in Britain in 1887 by the soap manufacturers A. & F. Pears. The poster showed a curly-haired boy gazing up at a soap bubble which he had just blown with a clay pipe. The image of the boy and his bubble

10.2: Pears' 'Bubbles' poster, 1887

was a reproduction of a contemporary painting by the artist Sir John Everett Millais (1829–96), then the most popular painter in Britain. The sense of innocence evoked by the subject matter would appear to be reinforced by the title Millais gave his painting, *A Child's World*, though it has been thought that this may have had a double-edged meaning. The bubble, which will soon burst, represented the transience of childhood and, perhaps, even of life itself.

Millais had been apprehensive that both the picture's sense of innocence and its darker undercurrent would be sullied, along with his reputation, if the painting were to appear in such an overtly commercial context. It did not help that the context would be made explicit by the company's name which appeared in large letters across the top of his picture, and the small bar of Pears' distinctive translucent amber soap which had been painted in next to the boy's foot as though it were part of the original. Having sold the painting's copyright to a third party the year before, Millais would have been unable to stop it being used in this way and, in the event, Millais is said to have become more accepting of the advert after seeing the quality of the printed proofs. When the poster did finally appear, he was forced to defend himself vigorously against a mass of hostile criticism. The matter continued to be debated in letters to *The Times* of London even after his death. The public as a whole appeared to be unmoved by such criticism; *Bubbles* was immediately popular. The image became so well known, indeed, that Pears was able to reduce the poster to a visual shorthand in which only the boy's head was shown. Today, despite the painting's obvious sentimentality, which seems to trump any deeper meaning about the sanctity or brevity of childhood, both it and the Pears poster are still widely appreciated, with the total number of individual reproductions made having run into the millions.

While Millais, the archetypal establishment figure, had to think twice about getting involved in advertising, a number of avant-garde artists welcomed the opportunity. (It was during this period that the military term *avant-garde*, literally 'advance guard', came to be used to describe those artists who were leading the developments in their respective fields of art.) Their antipathy towards the dominant nineteenth-century fashion for historical or narrative painting, as represented by Millais's picture, led them to seek influences from outside the European tradition. The most important exotic influence on the creation of Art Nouveau artists and designers was the art of Japan. One of the first and most active proponents of Art Nouveau, the Belgian artist Henri van der Velde (1863–1957), credited Japanese art thus: 'It took the power of the Japanese line, the force of its rhythm and its accents, to arouse and influence us'.

The prominence of Japanese influence during the last decades of the nineteenth century had a particular and peculiar cause. Europeans had first traded with the Japanese more than 300 years earlier, in the sixteenth century, but the exchange was cut short during the following century after Japan chose to close itself off almost entirely from the outside world. Two aspects of European civilization, the musket and Christianity, were thought to be exercising such a subversive influence on Japanese society that its rulers decided to cease trading with Europe (except for a few Dutch traders, who were said to have proven their willingness not to proselytize by trampling on a cross). And they tightly controlled the passage of people, foreign or native, entering or leaving the country. It was only in 1853, with the threat posed by the arrival of an American naval squadron into Tokyo Bay, that relations with the West were resumed. For the West, the renewal of trade with what was effectively an unknown country, led to a

10.3: 'The Actors', woodblock print, Toshusai Sharaku, 1794

flood of goods being imported from Japan. Exposure to such exotic ornaments and the novel attitudes they expressed initiated a craze for all things Japanese. The demand was so earnest and enduring it grew into a fully blown cultural phenomenon called *Japonisme*. Books and scholarly articles on the history and character of Japanese art were published. Great collections of artefacts were amassed and exhibited. Reproductions of Japanese woodblock prints proved to be especially popular and it was through these, both in the 'fine art' form of a single print *(fig. 10.3)*, and in the 'commercial art' form of book illustrations, that Western artists became familiar with the distinct characteristics of Japanese pictorial art. By the 1890s, fine artists had long incorporated these novel pictorial devices into their own pictures and prints.

One of the first artists to bring these characteristics into a poster was the Post-Impressionist painter Henri de Toulouse-Lautrec (1864–1901). Having first sought out Chéret for some preliminary instruction in the new poster art, Toulouse-Lautrec quickly adapted his own sketch-like style of painting to putting down a design on a lithographic stone. In a poster made for the opening of the nightclub 'Divan Japonais' in 1893

10.4: 'Divan Japonais' poster designed by Toulouse-Lautrec, 1893

(fig.10.4), he relied on a series of minimal, unbroken outlines to describe the general form of his subjects, and then on a similarly spare yet expressive set of marks to define their facial features. Both elements appear in the Japanese woodblock print overleaf. So too the lack of perspective or shadows, both of which Toulouse-Lautrec left out of his poster. An even more distinctive Japanese feature are the large areas of flat colour he used to divide up the poster's rectangular format. He dispensed entirely with the carefully coloured shading Chéret had used to describe form, and rejected the traditional method of shading or cross-hatching that generations of European artists had relied on to give their prints an illusion of three dimensions *(<fig.6.1, p.100)*. The resultant abstract quality of the flat shapes was enhanced by cutting off parts of the scene's principal characters – the woman's fan is severed by the left edge of the print and her feet by the bottom edge. This cutting device is applied most egregiously to the singer, whose decapitation followed a similar treatment to that his compatriot and contemporary Edgar Degas had applied to a number of earlier theatre paintings.

Trimming the contents of the image was not solely a Japanese device. It had also begun to appear during the late nineteenth century in pictures taken by a new generation of pioneering photographers. They had turned away from the conventions inherited from painting, which had demanded that the principal characters in a picture be shown in their entirety within a formal pose and, often, a carefully staged set. The new photographers welcomed the camera's ability to capture a slice of life as it moved across the lens. They wanted to fix a particular moment in time set within a 'real' space rather than a contrived one.

Toulouse-Lautrec's poster contained another Japanese feature that had a counterpart in European picture-making: the use of asymmetry. The invention of lithography had removed many of the technical difficulties of printing asymmetrically, and like previous designers or printers he readily exploited the flexibility that an asymmetrical layout could provide. He positioned the lettering according to what best suited the overall design, which was frequently towards one or other side of a more or less central figure. In doing so he was able to create a total design in which all parts of the poster were fully balanced and integrated. In contrast with Chéret's more cursory concern for the overall form, every mark that appeared on Toulouse-Lautrec's poster, be it a sinuous outline or a sequence of letters, was made by his own hand.

10.5: *Title page, 'Wren's City Churches', Arthur H. Mackmurdo, 1883*

Though he accentuated the abstract shapes in his posters, Toulouse-Lautrec never let them obscure his subject or setting. The woman with her fan is clearly sitting with her monocled companion in the stalls of a theatre, and looking out over an orchestra to a singer on a stage. In order for Toulouse-Lautrec to bring the cast of colourful characters that populated his posters to life, it was necessary for him to retain a degree of realism. But both his dedication to realism and the urbanity of his settings were out of step with the developing trend of Art Nouveau. This self-consciously modern style rapidly moved towards a greater degree of abstraction, one which was promoted by the unlikeliest of influences: forms rooted in nature. Plant-like shapes, with their stems, petals and leaves, became the principal, most characteristic element of the style. Though nearly always recognizable, these botanical motifs were frequently stylized into extensively and rhythmically curved shapes.

The botanical forms followed on from the Arts and Crafts movement's use of floral decoration which itself

10.6: Coca-Cola logo on signage, c.1910

c.1906-11

1890s

1927

1900

c.1960

2004

10.7: Ford logo   10.8: General Electric logo

had been inspired by the illuminated pages of medieval manuscripts and the printed pages of Renaissance books. The difference though between the Arts and Crafts' form of decoration and Art Nouveau's motifs was first defined visually by the British architect and designer Arthur H. Mackmurdo (1851–1942) in 1883. His cover and title page (<fig. 10.5) of *Wren's City Churches* (the group of late seventeenth- and early eighteenth-century London churches that were designed by the architect Sir Christopher Wren) anticipated by nearly a decade the full expression of the Art Nouveau style. The novel features in Mackmurdo's design were threefold: its asymmetry, its flat picture plane and its rhythmic dynamism. His dramatic black and white bands can be seen to stem from the lower centre right of the design, and then turn sharply upwards before traversing back across the page in a rhythmical motion and terminating in three seeded flower heads or flame-like tendrils. Unlike the floriated borders in Morris's *Chaucer* (<fig. 9.8, p.143), where the contrast between the larger vine leaves and grape bunches and the smaller, more intricate stems and branches suggests a certain depth and richness, Mackmurdo's flatter and broader leaves present a shallower picture plane. Most distinct of all though is the design's general sense of movement. Whereas Morris's decoration is made from a series of static units loosely repeated, Mackmurdo's entire plant form looks as though it is being acted on by some external force, such as water or wind. Its undulating waves of motion are carried over into the rippling banner and even, to some extent, the letters of the title. The only static elements are the elongated peacocks flanking the floral motif and then the letters and numbers at the bottom of the page.

By appearing on a banner, the title's letters avoided the full force of Art Nouveau's rhythmic energy. An example of lettering that came closer to the spirit of the style is a set of letters that have since become the most recognizable grouping of any kind in whatever style. They are the letters that appear in the Coca-Cola logo *(fig. 10.6)*, which was first registered as a trademark in 1887 though possibly displayed shortly before. The letters' rhythmical curves make it easy to categorize them as relatives of the Art Nouveau family, but this ease can lead us into error if we are to assume that they were made with that style in mind. Their early date means they were almost certainly not, though they may have benefited from the style's popularity in the United States a few years later. Far from being the creation of an avant-garde artist riding the crest of the new wave in art and design, the shapes of the letters were determined by the company's bookkeeper, Frank Robinson (1845–1923). He had suggested the company's name, by way of reference to the coca leaves and kola nuts used in the initial blend of 'medicinal' syrup that predated the fizzy cola drink we are familiar with today. It was also Robinson who proposed that the name should be written out in the style of formal handwriting he used for his bookkeeping. This carefully looped style of script, known as Spencerian, was prominent in the United States between c.1850 and c.1925. The commonality between the Art Nouveau style and a formal script was a feature of several later logos that also remain with us today, albeit in modified forms. One is the Ford logo, which appeared as a formal signature in 1904 *(fig. 10.7)* and was used on the Model T between 1908 and 1927, before the car was replaced by the Model A, which then

10.9: Coca-Cola logos

10.10: 'Manuel français de typographie moderne' compiled and published by François Thibaudeau, 1924

sported the script framed within an oval. Another similar script-based logo is the monogrammatic form used by General Electric *(fig. 10.8)*, whose elaborate initials were encircled and first placed on various electrical appliances in 1907.

The particular combination of Coca-Cola's letters lent itself to being rendered in a curvilinear design. All but one of the letters from the two near-identical four-letter groupings have a circular shape: 'c-o-c-a' and 'c-o-l-a' (and even the normally straight 'l' takes on an elliptical form, '*ℓ*', when written in a script). Within the logo's flowing form there is a simple correspondence between the sound of the letters and their shape. The childlike rhyming of the two groups – 'co-ca' and 'co-la' – is emphasized by a similar graphic treatment: both have large initial 'c's with extended flourishes. The slight difference in sound has a visual parallel: the two 'c's in the first group are topped off with rounded, disc-shaped terminals, while the equivalent 'c' and 'l' in the second group have flowing, looped terminals. None of these characteristics is consciously registered when we read the logo, not least because it is now so familiar it no longer has to be read; not in the same way that we read a regular piece of text. (To those coming across the logo for the first time, deciphering the letters of such a comparatively 'busy' logo is not easy.) Instead, we recognize the word at a glance by the 'global' impression of its internal patterns and their relationship to the external word shape; and then also, of course, by the now well-established colour of a standardized red. Our speed of recognition and recall is further increased by the fact that there are so few other logos like it, and that the seductively simple sounds it represents are easily

remembered. It is this last attribute, the simple sounds, which have helped it to be adapted into several of the world's scripts *(fig. 10.9)*.

The play of Japanese and Art Nouveau influences also spread to printed letters and their accompanying decoration. Perhaps the best-known example of type of this kind is an extensive range of pseudo-Japanese calligraphic letterforms which the French writer, illustrator and type designer Jean-Georges Huyot (1863–1938) – better known by his adopted name of Georges Auriol – designed between 1901 and 1911 for a Parisian type foundry run by Georges Peignot (1872–1915). They played a prominent part in the design of the first two French books on Art Nouveau typography *(fig. 10.10)*, which the printer François Thibaudeau (1860–1925) compiled and published in 1921 and 1924. The latter of the two books, his *Manuel français de typographie moderne* ('French Manual of Modern Typography'), was the one of the earliest manuals to feature specially made examples to guide the designer in laying out a page. Auriol's most popular and enduring type design (it's

10.11: Cover, 'The Chap Book', Will Bradley, 1895

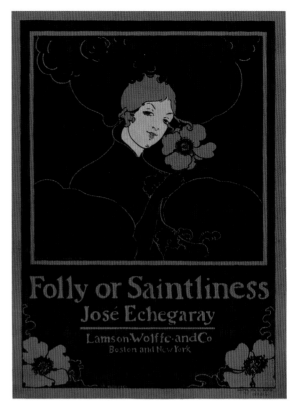

10.12: 'Folly or Saintliness' poster, Ethel Reed, 1895

still possible to find examples of these letters on some of the signs for staircases leading down to the Paris Métro), which had broken, brush-like forms, was used by Thibaudeau for the chapter titles. Despite its being so clearly contrived – they were inspired by the Japanese calligrapher's brush, but not made with it – the letters remain remarkably legible.

After an initial period of development in Paris, London and Brussels, the Art Nouveau style spread to other major European cities – most notably Glasgow, Munich, Barcelona, Turin, Budapest, Prague and Helsinki – as well as the east coast of the United States. During the last decade of the nineteenth century, Americans were exposed to developments in European design through exhibitions and special American editions or imported copies of European art magazines. The audience for progressive foreign design had been developed through the work of the Arts and Crafts movement, but Art Nouveau stimulated a new level of interest. By the middle of the 1890s, European posters, particularly those designed by French avant-garde artists, became fashionable. Prints were collected and discussed with a seriousness that had previously been the preserve of paintings, and this

elevated status was carried over to posters created by home-grown designers. While the majority of clients continued to prefer posters with straightforwardly realistic images, the more daring Art Nouveau posters were praised for providing the public, as one magazine had it, with 'a liberal education in Art and [being] a stimulator of good taste'.

The most proficient American Art Nouveau designer, Will Bradley (1868–1964), taught himself the salient features of the style and how best to replicate them by copying out illustrations from magazines. His poster for *The Chap Book* magazine *(fig.10.11)* shows how he applied the stylistic trait of rhythmical curves not through the depiction of natural, plant-like forms but in the billowing folds of cloaks or dresses. One of his contemporaries, by contrast, the designer and illustrator Ethel Reed (1868– after 1898), frequently supplemented her fine, minimal outlines and large abstract areas of flat colour with clusters of flowers, usually poppies or lilies *(fig.10.12)*. It is notable that Reed is the first female designer to be mentioned in these pages. Three historical factors account for this: the barring of women from positions of prominence within the printing and design industry; the failure to record the contribution made by women on the few occasions that they were able to make one; and the general lack of research into the role that women have played in the past. Though the number of women allowed to work in the industry grew from the second half of the nineteenth century, few of them were given a position of any real power or independence. As Bradley wrote in his own art and literary magazine: 'The so-called "poster movement" has brought into first prominence but one woman designer ... Miss Ethel Reed of Boston.' Despite the overt male chauvinism within the industry and the fact that Reed's career as a designer lasted only four years (1894–98), she managed to establish a reputation both at home and abroad. There were those in her home town of Boston who were said to be captivated by the face of the beautiful young girl that had often appeared in her posters, as shown here, partly because they believed it to be a self-portrait. Their fascination is likely to have become more intense after Reed's disappearance at the age of only 24. Though she is known to have travelled from England, where she had briefly settled, to Ireland in order to recuperate from an illness, no mention can be found of her after 1898.

The importance of the personality behind the design of a poster was confirmed by the frequent appearance of a signature in the design. Posters were signed by their designers for the same reason that a painting was marked by the artist, not just to show who made them, but also to increase the picture's appeal and thus its commercial value. The fact of being a 'Chéret' or a 'Toulouse-Lautrec' rubbed off onto the product or event being promoted. Few other items of graphic design were marked in this way since for the most part they were collaborative works. Their creation sometimes involved four or five different individuals, be they photographers, engravers, typesetters or printers. Moreover, such works were essentially industrial products manufactured by mechanical means and therefore they often carried no trace of a human hand. The Art Nouveau poster by contrast was clearly 'handmade'. Its outlines and coloured forms had all the irregularities indicative of a tool held in the hand. The potential this gave designers to construct a highly personal and idiosyncratic style allowed some of the very best of them to acquire a level of fame and recognition that exceeded that of even the best-known painters. The gallery of the street provided the former with an audience that was denied to the latter.

10.13: 'Gismonda' poster, Alphonse Mucha, 1894

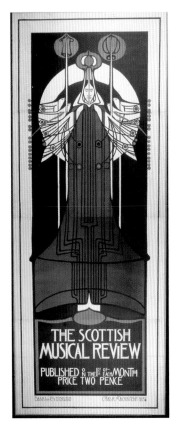

10.14: 'Scottish Musical Review' poster designed by Charles Rennie Mackintosh, 1896

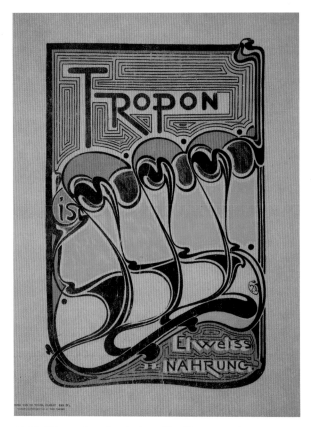

10.15: 'Tropon' poster designed by Henry van de Velde, 1906

Chéret was one of the earliest design celebrities – as 'the creator of an art industry' he was the first designer to be awarded France's prestigious *Légion d'honneur* – but the most celebrated internationally was the Czech designer Alphonse Mucha (1860–1939). On his first trip to America in 1904, he was heralded by the New York *Daily News* in a special colour supplement as 'the world's greatest decorative artist'. Mucha's fame had first come to him a decade earlier and almost overnight after he designed a poster for the celebrated Parisian actress Sarah Bernhardt *(< fig. 10.13)*. Such a prestigious commission had come to him by default. On Christmas Eve in 1894 the regular designers in the studio where her posters were produced were all on holiday. Mucha, who had come to the studio to do some work as a favour for a friend, was given the job and he succeeded in creating a design that made a greater impact than any previous Bernhardt poster. His poster became so popular indeed that collectors were reported to have bribed the bill-stickers for a copy or else removed it from the hoardings late at night. Bernhardt herself was pleased enough with it to offer Mucha a five-year contract which

involved designing not only posters but costumes, jewellery and the backdrops of her stage sets. Her tours across the continent and in America introduced his artistry to a wide audience and brought him an international following.

Being over 2m (6ft 6in) high, the poster presented Bernhardt at nearly life-size, and thus when displayed at ground level her face appeared directly in view of the passing public. He fixed her in an enigmatic pose which had all the insistent stillness of a monument. While the poster included some of the features that had dominated others of the period – Chéret's emphasis on female beauty, the integrated lettering of Toulouse-Lautrec and some of the simple outlines seen in Reed's posters – each of these elements was displayed within a visually richer and more decorative whole. The simple phrases of the main shapes were elaborated with a hitherto unseen quality of draughtsmanship. The colours were also new; more muted and sophisticated, with soft browns, rich mauves and turquoise, and decorative touches of gold and silver, all of which replaced the bright reds, yellows and blues that had enlivened Chéret's posters. Mucha's

10.16: Cover, 'Ver Sacrum' magazine designed by Koloman Moser, 1899

10.17: 'Ver Sacrum', poster designed by Koloman Moser, 1902

display of artistry gave the historical drama *Gismonda* a compellingly strange and exotic allure.

Despite his posters' exoticism the intricacy and brilliance of the decoration made them very accessible. Similar kinds of simple, angular patterning became prominent features in other Art Nouveau designs. Some early examples of this variant appeared in the graphic work *(fig.10.14)* of the architect and designer Charles Rennie Mackintosh (1868–1928), then the most acclaimed member of the Scottish Arts and Crafts movement. His brand of symmetrical decoration became an important influence on the work of a group of Austrian architects, artists and designers. Known as the Vienna Secession, the group was formed in 1897 as a challenge to the city's governing arts organization, which was wedded to the traditional hierarchy of high and low art, and hostile to modern styles of art. In seceding from the local art establishment, the Vienna Secession followed in the footsteps of a similar group based in Munich, which had promoted a brand of Art Nouveau known as *Jugendstil* ('Youth Style'), a name connected with their magazine *Die Jugend* which had promoted the style.

A mid-point between the more rounded forms of the Munich group and the more angular forms of the Viennese was struck by a poster designed in 1898 by the Dutch designer van der Velde for the food manufacturer Tropon *(fig.10.15)*. It is an exercise in pattern-making for its own sake as much as for the sake of the product it promotes. By this time, the motif of swirling naturalistic forms had become well enough established for their abstract beauty to take precedence over any obvious realism.

Initially, the Vienna Secession's brand of Art Nouveau differed little from that of their Munich colleagues. In their own magazine, *Ver Sacrum* ('Sacred Spring'), they too displayed designs with a swirling, dreamlike quality, as shown here on a cover *(fig.10.16)* from 1899, but with the change of century came a change in tack. A hint of the direction of this change could be found in their magazine's unusual square format. Its designer, Koloman Moser (1868–1918), was also responsible for the design of several of the group's exhibition posters, and it is in one of them that the new direction became more apparent. Moser's Secessionist

10.18: Wiener Werkstätte symbols, 1903

10.19: AEG logos

1896

1908

1908

1912

poster *(< fig.10.17)* of 1902 is strikingly similar to Mackintosh's earlier poster: the elongated format, the central symmetry, the stylized female figure, and the white circle at the top and lettering at the bottom. For all these parallels, the design of Moser's poster is more abstracted, more decorative and, in the bottom third especially, more rectilinear. It looked as much to the square for its foundational form as earlier Art Nouveau had looked to the circle, or the curve.

The dominance of the square became complete in designs for a new Secessionist project, the Wiener Werkstätte (Vienna Workshops), which Moser set up in 1903 with the Austrian designer Josef Hoffmann (1870–1956). This project was part of a larger workshop movement that had started in Germany a few years earlier with the aim of revitalizing craft traditions in the design and manufacture of household goods especially. Furniture, tableware, carpets, clothes and jewellery were produced for the emerging market of middle-class customers, but in contrast to the earlier attempt made

by William Morris and the English Arts and Crafts movement, who had tried to revive pre-industrial traditions of handcraft, the new Austro-Germanic workshop movement used machines and standardized units within an overall process of semi-mass production. In the Wiener Werkstätte standardization was applied to the design of its own stationery as well as the production of household items. By using the basic graphic elements of a solid black line delimited by a simple square shape, Hoffmann devised a set of symbols, which appeared on the workshop's letterheads, invoices, cards, and supplementary items of publicity. His logo for the workshop was a rectangular rose *(fig.10.18)*, which, except for its leaf and stem, was made out of an accumulation of squares. It was used in combination with a special monogram for the workshop, which had both initials, the two 'W's, placed within a square box. Hoffmann and Moser also designed their own personal monograms by fusing their initials within a square format. A combination of these

10.20: AEG turbine factory, Peter Behrens, 1908–09

symbols, the rose, the Werkstätte monogram, the designer's monogram, and that of the product's maker, were marked onto each of the workshop's products. By applying a concertedly unified graphic style in this way Hoffmann created one of the very earliest examples of corporate identity design or branding.

Hoffmann's emphasis on geometry, simplicity and a systematic approach to design was mirrored in the designs made for a large electrics company called AEG (*Allgemeine Elektrizitäts-Gesellschaft*), then based in Berlin *(fig. 10.19)*. The work was carried out between 1907 and 1913 by a self-taught architect and designer, Peter Behrens (1868–1940), and it is this work, rather than Hoffmann's, that is usually credited with being the first corporate identity programme. The size of the company and the broader application of its identity gave it a greater prominence. AEG had asked Behrens initially to design 'artistic shapes for arc lamps and all accessories', but his remit was soon extended to include the design of its factory buildings *(fig. 10.20)*, its workers' housing, various electrical appliances and all the company's graphic communication. It was not just the greater scope and complexity of Behrens's task that distinguished it from Hoffmann's earlier corporate design, but also the whole nature of Behrens's involvement with AEG was new. As someone from outside the company charged with creating a coherent visual identity, Behrens established the role of the design consultant. Prior to his involvement with AEG, Behrens had designed several typefaces with clear Art Nouveau features but, by the

time of his appointment with AEG, he had shed this influence in favour of a more neutral and classical style of letter. It is this idiom that characterized the set of capital letters he created for the company's exclusive use and which appeared in his ultimate design for the company's logo and in various other pieces of publicity material.

Art Nouveau's emphasis on abstraction and decoration had allowed different regional influences to create different versions of the style. Some had emphasized curvilinear complexity, others rectilinear simplicity, and both extremes had proved themselves to be effective methods of communication. The power of the former to excite and surprise was matched by the power of the latter to inform through a rationalized sense of order; but, ultimately, both of these opposing trends served to pull the style apart. The unifying force of decorativeness could no longer contain them, especially when strikingly new developments began to range across the spectrum of the visual arts. The first of these occurred in painting. In 1907 Picasso and Braque began their 'logical destruction of matter', known as Cubism. By choosing to display successive facets of an object rather than any single view of it, Cubist artists made Art Nouveau and other contemporary forms of realism seem like the end of a tradition rather than the start of something new. The Cubists' destruction of conventional form appeared to presage the more widespread destruction that was caused by the First World War. An important weapon in this more modern and lethal warfare was the ancient art of propaganda.

PUBLIC WARNING

The public are advised to familiarise themselves with the appearance of British and German Airships and Aeroplanes, so that they may not be alarmed by British aircraft, and may take shelter if German aircraft appear. **Should hostile aircraft be seen,** take shelter **immediately** in the nearest available house, preferably in the basement, and remain there until the aircraft have left the vicinity: do not stand about in crowds **and do not touch unexploded bombs.**

In the event of **HOSTILE** aircraft being seen in country districts, the nearest Naval, Military or Police Authorities should, if possible, be advised immediately by Telephone of the TIME OF APPEARANCE, the DIRECTION OF FLIGHT, **and whether the aircraft is an Airship or an Aeroplane.**

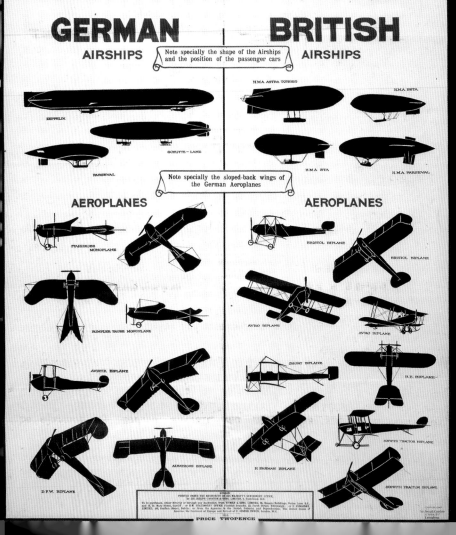

GERMAN

AIRSHIPS

Note specially the shape of the Airships and the position of the passenger cars

ZEPPELIN

SCHÜTTE – LANZ

PARSEVAL

AEROPLANES

Note specially the sloped-back wings of the German Aeroplanes

STAHLTAUBE MONOPLANE

RUMPLER TAUBE MONOPLANE

AVIATIK BIPLANE

ALBATROSS BIPLANE

D.F.W. BIPLANE

BRITISH

AIRSHIPS

H.M.A. ASTRA TORRES

H.M.A. BETA

H.M.A. ETA

H.M.A. PARSEVAL

AEROPLANES

BRISTOL BIPLANE

BRISTOL BIPLANE

AVRO BIPLANE

AVRO BIPLANE

SHORT BIPLANE

B.E. BIPLANE

SOPWITH TRACTOR BIPLANE

H. FARMAN BIPLANE

SOPWITH TRACTOR BIPLANE

LONDON
PRINTED UNDER THE AUTHORITY OF HIS MAJESTY'S STATIONERY OFFICE.
By SIR JOSEPH CAUSTON & SONS, LIMITED, 9, Eastcheap, E.C.

To be purchased, either directly or through any Bookseller, from WYMAN & SONS, LIMITED, 29, Breams Buildings, Fetter Lane, E.C., and 54, St. Mary Street, Cardiff; or H.M. STATIONERY OFFICE (Scottish Branch), 23, Forth Street, Edinburgh; or E. PONSONBY, LIMITED, 116, Grafton Street, Dublin; or from the Agencies in the British Colonies and Dependencies. The United States of America, the Continent of Europe and Abroad of T. FISHER UNWIN, London, W.C.

PRICE TWOPENCE

11 THE SIMPLE ART OF WAR
Sachplakat & First World War Graphics, c.1880 – c.1920

Two important but opposing new developments in the style of graphic design emerged during the first decades of the twentieth century. One was an unbridled gallop of experimentation, led by several small groups of radical artists and designers – the pioneers of Modernism *(>ch.12, p.175)* – who wanted to make art that would challenge and change society. The distance between their unconventional style of art and the public's understanding of it was frequently worn as a badge of honour. By acting as much in a spirit of negative protest as in a spirit of positive transformation, they often appeared to turn convention on its head for its own sake. Indeed, scandal seemed to be the cement that bound them.

The second development, by contrast, was led by a quieter, more amorphous group of artists and designers. They tried to keep a closer distance between their own tastes and those of the public. If any of them were motivated to use their art to change society, they sought to do so from the inside. But by developing a simplified graphic language, one that allowed their clients' messages to be relayed clearly and memorably, they were no less inventive than their more provocative contemporaries. They had to tread a narrow path between working within the limits of conventional form, so as not to alienate their audience, and offering enough visual surprise to ensure their work was engaging. Initially their simplified designs were directed to commercial advertising, but with the onset of war and revolution their focus turned away from matters of corporate gain and towards the more momentous issue of personal survival. The life of an individual could sometimes hang on the successful communication of a graphic message *(fig. 11.1)*.

The first steps along this new road of a more simplified and direct form of communication were taken with the design of posters. Such posters developed alongside the Art Nouveau poster, and, though they were less praised as works of art, their formal properties proved

to be more enduring. Instead of using swirling and decorative patterns to surprise and delight the viewer, the posters displayed stark arrangements of simple graphic images and minimal typography. In an era when mechanized, street-bound forms of transport were becoming popular – the bicycle, the tram and the car – a less elaborate poster could be decoded more quickly. It was possible for the more mobile masses to 'read' the pictures and texts at a glance.

An early demonstration of this minimalizing trend was revealed in an initial series of posters designed by the Italian caricaturist, illustrator and graphic designer Leonetto Cappiello (1875–1924). After moving from his home town in Italy to Paris in his early twenties, Cappiello started a 40-year career in poster design that resulted in more than 500 different designs. His simple style and his prolific output led to his being known as 'the father of modern advertising'. Almost immediately on starting work as a poster designer he developed a stark arrangement in which a central figure and minimal lettering were set against a solid black background *(>fig.11.2)*. In what has become perhaps his best-known poster, a devilish green imp sneakily uncorking a bottle of the popular apéritif Quina (made from the bitter-tasting and medicinal substance quinine), is thrown into sharp relief by an expanse of surrounding black space. In choosing this character to advertise this popular product for the company Maurin, Cappiello was possibly evoking the nickname *la fée verte* (the green fairy) used for a similarly potent beverage, absinthe, which derived its natural green colour from its distinct herbal ingredient, anise.

Before designing posters Cappiello had worked as a caricaturist, and it was the graphic idiom of caricature that defined the impish cartoon-like quality of his poster illustrations. Caricature had dominated many kinds of publicity printing throughout the nineteenth

11.2: 'Maurin Quina' poster designed by Leonetto Cappiello, 1906

11.3: 'Simplicissimus' magazine poster, designed by Thomas Theodor Heine, 1897

century, so by using it in his poster, albeit in an ar-restingly sparse way, Cappiello may be seen partly as continuing a tradition rather than creating a new one. In any case, the black background, simple lettering and cartoon-like figure had appeared several years earlier in a poster *(fig.11.3)* advertising the German magazine *Simplicissimus* (the name was taken from a comic character in a seventeenth-century German novel). The magazine was a mouthpiece for liberal and literate members of German society, and it spoke in sceptical and mocking tones through a medley of aphorisms, fables, literary sketches and anecdotes. The contributors (who includ-ed the novelist Thomas Mann and the poet Rainer Maria Rilke) were all young writers who, when not lampoon-ing the authority figures of the day, were poking fun at the social pretensions of the magazine's own middle-class readership. The title's root word 'simple' may have influenced the poster's designer, Thomas Theodor Heine

(1867–1948), to produce his starkly graphic image: an aggressive-looking, red bull-dog, which stared out menacingly from a simple black background. The title and the emblematic bull-dog alluded to the magazine's content; beware of the unfettered, biting, red-blooded satire, they seemed to say.

Both these instances of the simple poster then were linked to the established tradition of caricature. A much more definitive break with the past was provided by a unique partnership of two British designers who went by the name of the Beggarstaffs (though they came to be known as the Beggarstaff Brothers). James Pryde (1866–1941) and William Nicholson (1872–1949) were actually brothers-in-law, but the level of mutual understanding demanded by their close working relationship bordered on the frater-nal. In a singular spirit of collaboration both men designed each poster together, without any division of

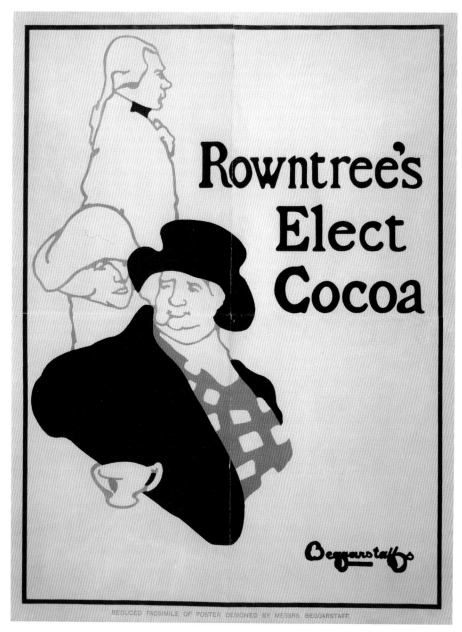

REDUCED FACSIMILE OF POSTER DESIGNED BY MESSRS. BEGGARSTAFF.

11.4: 'Rowntree's Elect Cocoa' poster designed by the Beggarstaff Brothers, 1897

labour. They would agree on the contents and then flesh it out together with a method of mark making that was also unusual. Instead of working directly onto a lithographic stone, as some of their Art Nouveau contemporaries were doing, the Beggarstaffs cut up and stuck down pieces of coloured paper onto enormous sheets of background paper (some as large as 3 x 2.5 m (10 x 8 ft)). This operation involved the only action that seemed to separate them. While one chose to cut the paper with scissors, the other preferred to use a pen-knife.

In contrast with the two previous examples of simple posters, and with the Art Nouveau poster indeed, the forms they created were not linked to satire, nor did they show the overt decoration of Art Nouveau. With a measured use of outlines and flat, boldly contrasting, abutting shapes the Beggarstaffs created a poster for Rowntree's Elect Cocoa *(fig. 11.4)* in 1897. Of the three 'elect' figures (the description was a literal one in the case of the top and bottom figures, modelled as they were on prominent British politicians), the top two were delineated by delicately cut strips of grey paper, whereas parts of the head and body of the bottom figure were described by the edges of his black hat and coat, and by a mauve waistcoat. The Beggarstaffs' unusual but compelling images were praised by artists and designers in France, Germany and the US especially, who were able to see reproductions of the work in prominent design magazines. Unfortunately, the esteem in which they were held by their peers was matched by the rejection they experienced from potential clients. As Pryde recalled of one their designs: 'We took it to the office of the firm in question and pinned it up on the wall of the very small room into which we were shown. After a while, the art editor or manager or whatever he called himself, a dear old gentleman rather like Father Christmas in appearance, came into the room; he gave the poster one glance and went out of the room without saying anything. Later, it was offered to Sir George Alexander ... but he did not find it suitable ....' Because only two of their posters ever received widespread showing on the hoardings, their partnership broke up after a couple of years.

The Beggarstaffs' lack of commercial success contrasted with the immediate impact made by a later, ardent admirer of theirs, the German designer Emil Kahn (1883–1972), who was also better known by an adopted name, that of Lucian Bernhard. Though the details of Bernhard's early career have been confused by his own conflicting accounts, it appears that sometime around the age of 19 he made his first poster design for a competition sponsored by the Priester Match Company *(fig. 11.5)*. His entry won first prize and appeared on the hoardings in 1906. On the back of this early success, Bernhard established a career lasting some 30 years, during which he became identified with a loose-knit school of designers known as the Berliner Plakat (Berlin Poster). His Priester poster encapsulates the simplicity of their style, yet it seems that he had not been wholly aware of the poster's merits while designing it. His initial arrangement was much busier, but as the competition's deadline drew near a colleague advised him to remove all the non-essential and confusing elements. What remained was the object being advertised, matches, and the name of the company, Priester. In following this advice Bernhard had enacted, albeit circuitously, a curious principle of design: that a maximum effect can often be achieved by an economy of means. In Bernhard's case this applied as much to the form of his poster as it did to the content. He used the same method of describing

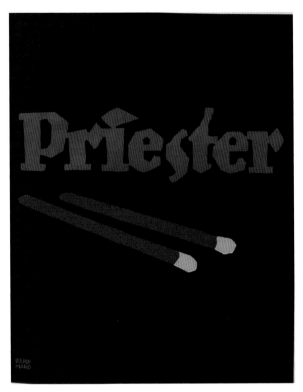

11.5: 'Priester' poster designed by Lucian Bernhard, c.1906

form as the Beggarstaffs had – abutting shapes of flat colour – but whereas they had combined this method with outlines, Bernhard relied on it exclusively. This dual economy, of form and content, was accentuated by his choice of distinctly vivid colours, the most unusual and commanding of which was the deep, dark red background. A similar awareness of the power of simple graphic shapes can be seen in the way he marked his name. Instead of using a conventional signature, as the Beggarstaffs had done, he created a personal logotype made from two tiers of capitals, 'BERN' above and 'HARD' below.

The poster style developed by Bernhard and his colleagues became known as Sachplakat (object poster) or, sometimes, Plakatstil (poster style). A supreme example of the primacy of the object within this style is the advert designed and illustrated in 1923 by the Swiss artist Otto Baumberger (1889–1961) for the Zürich clothing store PKZ *(fig. 11.6)*. By illustrating the part of an overcoat that showed the manufacturer's label, Baumberger cleverly fused the object and client's name into a single entity. The thing being sold promoted the company that was selling it. The effect he created would have appeared at that time to be almost surreally sparse, shorn as it was of any formal typography.

11.6: 'PKZ' poster designed by Otto Baumberger, 1923

The image looked more like a work of art or a photograph even than a piece of advertising. The high degree of realism with which he depicted the fine golden lining and the coat's thick herringbone pattern, a realism which was reinforced by the apparently natural way that the label had been exposed, expressed an important secondary characteristic of the object poster: its sense of objectivity or neutrality. The style of illustration in such posters was often devoid not only of ambiguity but also of exhibitionism. As in a story told without embellishment, the message they communicated seemed all the more believable for being so matter-of-fact. This preference for plain speaking in typography and illustration would have contrasted with the explicitly subjective and emotive style of Expressionist illustration that had been common in central Europe during the first two decades of the century (>fig. 13.3, p.190). It would also have allied itself to the supposed objectivity of the photograph, which was then becoming a common form of illustration. Indeed, it was a colour photograph that Baumberger had used as a model for his image rather than the coat itself.

11.7: 'Automobile Opel' poster designed by Hans Rudi Erdt, 1911

One of Bernhard's colleagues from the Berlin school, who also pioneered the Sachplakat style, was Hans Rudi Erdt (1883–1918). Much of Erdt's work showed how simple designs didn't always have to rely on a more or less realistically depicted object. In his poster for the car manufacturer Opel *(fig. 11.7)*, Erdt used a dark striped band at the base of the driver's collar to link the driver's head with the text below, and thus, paradoxically, create a sense of depth that set the head back behind the lettering, rather than leave it hovering in the surrounding flat background. This sense of depth was provided with a context, albeit a suggestive rather than concrete one, by a large, entirely circular 'O'. The different size and lettering style of the O in comparison to the letters in the rest of the word allowed it to be seen as somewhat separate, and this slight separation helped it to be interpreted as a steering-wheel. Both graphic tricks – the sense of space and the O's separation – allow us to interpret the poster as showing the dapper driver peering round at us over the side of his car. By making the O suggestive in this way, Erdt produced the kind of visual pun or metaphor that caricaturists had long exploited (Daumier's king's head for a pear, <*fig.8.16, p.134*) and which was to become a stock-in-trade for subsequent graphic designers. Its merits are two-fold. The first is the initial surprise and delight that comes as soon one 'gets' it, while the second has a longer-lasting appeal, as an *aide-mémoire*. The word 'Opel' is more easily remembered as the name of a car manufacturer once the visual association with a steering-wheel has been planted in our minds. This trick of using pictures to remember words stretches back to the manuscripts of the Middle Ages. It shows how the mnemonic power of a graphic image has been exploited by illustrators and designers of many ages.

Following Germany's entry into the First World War in 1914, designers were drawn towards more serious and patriotic forms of print. On each side of the conflict the move to war had initially received broad support, but as the fighting quickly developed into a punishing stalemate between heavily defended forces, governments needed to shore up this early support. They did so partly through barefaced propaganda, but also through messages of a more practical and informative kind. In Britain, the heavy losses sustained by its small regular army created an urgent need for new recruits, not in their hundreds but in their hundreds of thousands. To meet this need an image that had first appeared on the cover of a magazine late in 1914 was quickly converted into a recruitment poster *(fig. 11.8)*. It showed Britain's secretary of state for war, Lord Kitchener, with his distinctive walrus moustache, pointing at the viewer more in a spirit of instruction than entreaty. The moustache had made Kitchener recognizable enough that, rather than spell out his name in the text, it was possible to present his portrait as part of a rebus *(< p. 22–3)* to be read thus: 'Britons, Lord Kitchener wants you'. An appeal to patriotism was explicitly stated with the addition of 'Join Your Country's Army!' and 'God Save The King'.

The poster's designer, Alfred Leete (1882–1933), had appreciated the importance of simplicity in getting this crucial message across, but unlike Erdt with his artfully stylized and simplified portrait in the Opel poster, Leete was concerned to make his portrait of Kitchener true to life. The more the poster was seen to be a direct appeal from the man himself, the better its chance of success. Such an appeal was harder to ignore after Leete had endowed his depiction of Kitchener with a resolute jawline below an unwavering gaze. When combined with the gloved hand and military bearing, the portrait seemed to present a retrospective personification of the Victorian authority figure. By the end of 1915, two-and-a-half million men had answered the poster's call. Its success is said to have led the daughter of Britain's prime minister to say of Kitchener, 'If not a great soldier, he is at least a great poster.'

A further, clear demonstration of the influence of Leete's image occurred in 1917 with the appearance of an American recruitment poster *(fig.11.9)* following America's entry into the war in support of the Allies. Their version of the pointing poster had also been

11.8: Lord Kitchener recruitment poster illustrated by Alfred Leete, 1914

11.9: Uncle Sam recruitment poster illustrated by James Montgomery Flagg, 1917

adapted from a magazine cover but, unlike its British predecessor, the person pointing was not a contemporary figure, nor even a real one. It was Uncle Sam, a personification of the United States (whose initials he shares), which had become a popular caricature during the previous century. The poster's version of Uncle Sam was painted by James Montgomery Flagg (1877–1960), who modelled the character's face on his own less aged and less hirsute features. The character's wizened and bearded countenance and his particular style of antiquated clothing were of a kind then associated with the popular nineteenth-century president Abraham Lincoln, whose whiskered chin had frequently been shown in illustrations nestling on a broad-lapelled overcoat and crowned by a tall top hat. The success of the poster – over four million copies were printed during the First World War – caused it to be reissued during the Second World War, and enabled Flagg to claim it to be 'the most famous poster in the world'.

Both these recruitment posters show how caricatures need not always be satirical. Reputations can be bolstered as effectively as they can be tarnished by

the portrayal of a person, be he real, as in the case of Kitchener, or imaginary, like Uncle Sam, with positive and often idealized attributes. Yet, if these qualities are to be accepted as genuine, they usually have to be set within a portrait that looks realistic. If the portrait is lifelike, the qualities emanating from it will be taken to be true to life. Many extreme examples of this principle have been provided by dictators – Mao Zedong, Saddam Hussein and Kim Jong Il are prominent recent examples – who in an attempt to entrench their position of power, have used such pictures (and sculpture) to establish and perpetuate a personality cult.

For both sides of the war, the need to raise recruits was matched by a need to raise funds. After three years of hard fighting and the mobilization of millions of men, the conflict was proving to be as costly to the public purse as it was to soldiers' lives. The simple image (>fig.11.10) created in 1917 by the German poster designer Louis Oppenheim (1879–1936) enabled the commander of the German army, Paul von Hindenburg, to make a direct appeal for funds, though in this instance the appeal was made partly through the use

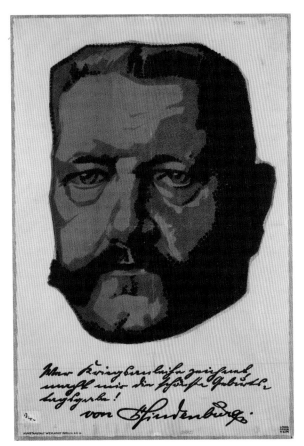

11.10: Paul von Hindenburg poster designed by Louis Oppenheim, 1917

Union Jack (UK)   Iron Cross (German)

French   British   American

11.11: Flags and roundels

of handwriting rather than a pointing finger. Below the commander's monumental head is the line, in what is meant to be von Hindenburg's own writing hand: 'Whoever subscribes to the War Loan is giving [me] the best birthday present!', followed by his signature. By taking advantage of von Hindenburg's popularity the poster was able to use his gratification as a foil for this demeaning plea for funds.

As important as propaganda, recruitment and the raising of funds undoubtedly were, they were generally less life threatening than the set of more neutral instructions or warnings that necessarily accompany all forms of warfare. For the Allies and the Axis powers alike, there was a clear need to impart information that was unmodified by any appeal to patriotism. In 1915, when British towns and cities began to fall victim to German air raids, the British government issued a poster which it hoped would help its citizens take evasive action by allowing them to differentiate between enemy and friendly aircraft (<fig.11.1). Though visually much more involved than the previous Sachplakat-inspired war

posters, this poster was, nevertheless, admirably direct and graphically effective. The three main parts of the poster – its heading, the block of descriptive text and the series of simple silhouettes – are clearly separated. But more importantly, the illustrations manage to show each aircraft at its most distinct, be it in the length of an airship or the forked nature of a plane's tail. The silhouettes would have corresponded to what would have been seen when an aircraft was flying overhead.

Simple graphic symbols were as important in saving the lives of soldiers as they were the lives of civilians. The ability to read the military insignia on planes, tanks and transport was vital in avoiding 'friendly fire', as British forces had found out to their cost during the first months of the war. The Union Jack insignia that had appeared on the underside of their aircraft looked blurred when seen from far away or when partially obscured by cloud. This blurring caused the cross-shaped aspect of the symbol to dominate over its diagonal aspect, and thus the symbol was sometimes mistaken for the black cross of the German Luftwaffe (Airforce). As soon as the cause of this effect was discovered, the British air force adopted a symbol that could only be confused with that of their allies. They took the insignia that appeared on French planes, a roundel in red, white and blue, and reversed the sequence of colours to blue, white and red (fig. 11.11). It was a happy coincidence that the colours of the French flag, the tricolour, on which their roundel had been based, were the same as those that appeared in the Union Jack. Since the Americans' Stars and Stripes also had the same colours, when the United States Air Force began to fly alongside the Allies in 1917, this same device was adopted, though in a new configuration of red, blue and white.

What applied to military hardware also applied to men on the ground. They too needed to be clearly identified, and not just to avoid attack from their own

11.12: 'Dazzle' camouflage on a British gunboat, 1918

guns. Within each army the hierarchy of ranks had to be visible, but not in a way that would be easily apparent to the enemy. If the ranks could be identified from any great distance, officers would become targets for snipers, as happened to a number of British officers while firing from the trenches during the early years of the First World War. Only by removing the insignia from the cuffs of their jackets and thereby looking more like their subordinates were they able to avoid being targeted. At the end of the war, cuff badges were abolished and shoulder badges became standard issue.

Another example of how graphic forms were used to reduce the threat of attack came from a kind of camouflage, which from 1915 was adopted by the Allies for certain kinds of naval vessel *(fig. 11.12)*. It was called 'dazzle' and, as the name suggests, the role it played was rather different to what is normally expected from a system of camouflage. Far from making a ship blend in with its surroundings, dazzle made it stand out, albeit by default. The thinking behind this counter-intuitive approach rested on the difficulty of hiding a ship at sea. The fluctuations of light, visibility and sea state caused by the ever-changing weather and the perpetual movement of the sun make it impossible for a vessel to blend into a seascape at all times and to all angles of view, especially from above as well as the side. The patterns of disturbed water that trail behind a moving vessel and the visible plumes of smoke emitted by many warships at that time only increased the difficulty. Rather than attempt the impossible, a new tack was taken. The shades of neutral grey with which all naval ships were painted at the start of the war were changed to a series of patterns that disrupted the appearance of the vessel's shape. Stripes and other forms of patterning were set at strange angles and in highly contrasting tones in order to produce an illusion of distortion. The most effective markings were those that affected the sense

of perspective or otherwise altered the sense of form. By doing so they might impede or delay recognition, or else cause confusion as to the course and speed of a vessel. It was a form of defence that was dedicated to reducing the chance of a successful attack rather than avoiding attack altogether. Despite the excited praise of the popular press on both sides of the Atlantic – 'The original idea was ingenious and affords one more proof of the practical possibilities dormant in art when it is exploited' – the wisdom of the scheme was questionable. It seems to have favoured only certain vessels in particular situations rather than all ships equally.

Though the First World War began as an essentially European conflict, by the time of its official end in 1918, more than 100 countries from Africa, America, Asia, Australasia and Europe had played some part in it (albeit, for many, a part defined by their colonial links). Thus, naming the conflict a 'world war' was not a European conceit. No previous large-scale warfare had involved so many nations. Casualties were suffered by all countries, but of the ten million or so people estimated to have died in direct conflict, nearly two million were Russian; this despite Russia's early cessation from war with Germany in 1917.

This unprecedented loss of life was accompanied by, and contributed to, Russia suffering economically. The extent of her troubles brought the state to the brink of collapse. The inability of a provisional government to improve on the tsar's defunct regime – the former failed to provide the Russian people with what they wanted above all else, peace and bread – led in October 1917 to a coup, the so-called 'October Revolution' (it followed an earlier revolution, in February, which had led to the tsar's deposition). It was carried out by the Bolshevik party which, though its name means 'one of the majority' in Russian, was then made up of a small group of professional revolutionaries who mainly represented the industrial working class. The Bolsheviks' revolutionary aims extended far beyond their national borders. The writings of the German philosopher and founder of modern Communism, Karl Marx, had presented the destruction of Europe's prewar capitalist order by a mass revolution of the working class as not merely desirable but as a historical inevitability. Though time has proved this to be unfounded, it can still be claimed that Marx's ideas spread further and faster than those of any other thinker. By 1953, only 70 years after his death, a third of the world was governed by regimes that defined themselves as Marxist.

For the Bolsheviks' brand of Marxism to be established overseas, it was first necessary for them to root it more firmly at home. During the turmoil of the civil war that followed the coup, the Bolsheviks' hold on power became reliant on the political acumen and personal charisma, and ruthlessness indeed, of their leader, Vladimir Ilyich Lenin. In order to garner support for his party, Lenin relied heavily on the promotion of a new 'revolutionary art' which, he declared, 'should be understood and loved by these masses. It must unite and elevate their feelings, thoughts and will. It must awaken and develop the artistic instinct within them. Must we serve sweet cakes to a small minority while the workers and peasants are in need of black bread?' The prescriptive tone of this ostensibly high-minded declamation was a consequence of Lenin's cynically calculating attitude towards the political potential of art. Not only did he, as his statement indicated, seek to deny workers a choice of fare – like most people workers would prefer 'sweet cakes' to 'black bread' – he also made sure that the ingredients in their 'bread' were carefully vetted. In 1918 he initiated a programme of propaganda on a vast scale. The new revolutionary art appeared on posters, in films, as monumental sculpture, in parades and re-enactments, and was carried across the country on specially commissioned 'agit-trains', brightly painted and decked out with flags and bunting.

Whereas today the word 'propaganda' has negative connotations, for Lenin it was a commendable and entirely necessary political tool. He made a distinction between 'propaganda', which he defined as the reasoned use of historical and scientific arguments to win over the educated, and its baser twin, 'agitation', defined as the use of slogans, parables, and half-truths to exploit the emotions of the uneducated. Both terms were combined within the over-arching term *agitprop*, which amounted to a barrage of visual and verbal messages to 'educate' all sections of society about the past glories of the October Revolution and Communism's bright future.

For Lenin, the new, mechanical medium of film was ultimate, partly because it best symbolized the revolutionary and industrial basis of Bolshevism. Throughout the years of the civil war, it proved to be much less conspicuous than the more traditional medium of the poster however. Between 1918 and 1922 (an interval sometimes referred to as Russia's 'poster period'), some 3600 different posters were created, an average of more than 20 a week. Many were entirely conventional in their design: a short statement put across by a single

11.13: *'Did You Volunteer?' poster, Dimitri Moor, 1920*

realistic image – there was even a Bolshevik version of the pointing recruitment poster *(fig. 11.13)* – but such posters were unable to communicate many of the more involved messages of revolutionary propaganda. Topics such as the history and success of the October Revolution, or which factions should be fought in the civil war, or the nature of new food taxes, all these kinds of issues needed to be explained in such a way that even the large number of illiterates could understand them. The combination of an ill-educated audience and a set of more complex narratives inspired a new form of poster art. Simple, brightly coloured, hand-painted images, pieced together as in a comic strip *(fig. 11.14)*, began to be produced by the newly created state news agency, known by its acronym ROSTA, which displayed them in the numerous empty shop windows that lined the streets first in Moscow and then in other cities too. The very earliest examples of these so-called 'ROSTA Windows' were made in single editions, as one-offs, though before long print runs of up to 150 were being produced through a cheap, manual process of hand stencilling. With each poster possessing eight individual frames on average, the Moscow ROSTA

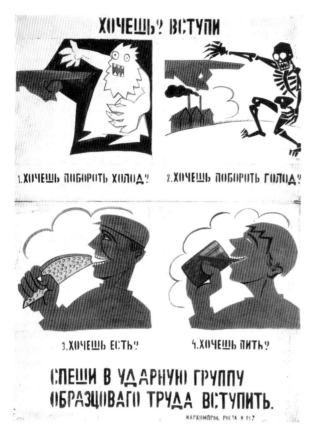

11.14: 'ROSTA Window', Vladimir Mayakovsky, 1920

commune alone produced over two million individual frames. Other cities – chiefly St Petersburg (then Petrograd), Vitebsk, and Odessa – followed Moscow's example and started to produce their own version of ROSTA Windows.

Both the text and the pictures in this example were made by a young revolutionary poet, Vladimir Mayakovsky (1894–1930), who produced nearly all the text for Moscow's ROSTA Windows. For the poster's title, Mayakovsky chose a line from a polemical verse, 'DO YOU WANT TO JOIN UP?', and then added four questions '1. Do you want to conquer cold?', '2. Do you want to conquer hunger?', '3. Do you want to eat?', '4. Do you want to drink?'; and, finally, at the bottom, 'Hurry up to join the strike team of exemplary labour' ('strike' having the meaning here of 'advanced' or 'expert'). For this text, as for all others, Mayakovsky used the colloquial speech of the working class into which he wove simple puns and rhyming slang to form a sort of agitational street poetry (lost in translation here). It was a process that, as he himself acknowledged, demanded as much poetic skill as writing conventional verse. The particular difficulty of having to make slogans that were short,

informative and memorable was made somewhat easier by the inclusion of pictures that could flesh out the text's context and meaning.

Like the text, the cartoon-like figures and simple, graphic shapes also had local roots. Their style was derived from three main sources: the style of icon painting associated with the Russian Orthodox Church; a popular primitive style of Russian woodcut, known as *lubok*; and a native form of satirical caricature (Mayakovsky was known to have been an admirer of the satirical magazine *Simplicissimus, <fig.11.3*). Each influence helped to make the ROSTA posters seem familiar, though with the development of a simple colour coding and various other symbolic conventions, the posters quickly established their own graphic language. In the example here, the two pointing fingers, the factory, and the two happy workers appear in the Bolsheviks' signature colour of red, a colour that was said to symbolize the blood shed in the struggle against capitalism (black was reserved for capitalists and white often for the 'White Russian' tsarist supporting forces). The factory, with its chimneys, was included as a symbol of economic progress, whose attainment was central to the workers' revolution.

From the early 1920s, Russia's revolutionary propaganda began to feature a new, home-grown style of design called Constructivism. It was one of a cluster of experimental styles that developed out of an ever closer union of artists, architects and designers. They had been brought together, in part, by a common artistic language, the Modernist language of abstraction. Art Nouveau graphic design and the Sachplakat style had both included an element of abstraction, but in almost all cases it had been combined with, and made supplementary to, some form of realism, be it swirling flowers, geometric female forms or even a couple of matches. In the few instances where abstraction was not dominated by, or clearly derived from, real forms, it appeared as a combination of repeated elements within a decorative pattern. The more experimental pioneers of Modernism, by contrast, rejected realism and decoration as outdated and restrictive. They wanted to find a new kind of visual language, one that would liberate them from the revivalist urges of the nineteenth century and represent the ideas and sensations of the new machine age. It was this rejection of the past in search of something new that launched them on a headlong flight into experiment and innovation.

F. T. MARINETTI FUTURISTA

ZANG

TUMB TUMB

ADRIANOPOLI   OTTOBRE 1912

TUUUMB

IN LIBERTÀ

PAROLE

TUUUUM TUUUUM TUUUUM TUUUUM

EDIZIONI FUTURISTE
DI "POESIA"
Corso Venezia, 61 - MILANO
1914

12 THE ISMS OF ART
Futurism, Dada, De Stijl & Constructivism, c.1900 – c.1930

'Courage, audacity, and revolt will be essential elements of our poetry ... We will destroy the museums, libraries, academies of every kind ... We affirm that the world's magnificence has been enriched by a new beauty: the beauty of speed.' With these declamatory statements, the Italian journalist and poet, Filippo Tommaso Marinetti (1876–1944), heralded the birth of Futurism. His statements were contained in the movement's first manifesto, which he wrote in 1909 and then had published in various newspapers and journals, most notably the French newspaper *Le Figaro*. Though the aim of the text was to promote a new kind of poetry, it ranged widely, and wildly, giving vent to his thoughts and feelings towards society in general. His contempt for the past was matched by a reverence for the future: specifically, an electrically powered, machine-age future of neon lights, planes and automobiles, each of which had begun to make a mark on the new century. Attitudes of both contempt and reverence, and the strident manner in which such attitudes were expressed, were to become standard features in the many avant-garde manifestos that appeared over the following two decades.

The rash of avant-garde groups that wrote them also marked themselves out with a name. Most were encouraged to use the suffix '-ism' following the success of its earlier use in Impressionism (a name derived from a criticism of the style as one that merely offered an 'impression' of its subject) and in its several progeny, Pointillism (also known as Divisionism) and Fauvism. Each of the subsequent early twentieth-century avant-garde styles – Cubism, Expressionism, Futurism *(fig. 12.1)*, Vorticism, Dada(ism), Neo-Plasticism/De Stijl, Rayonism, Constructivism, Suprematism and Surrealism – fell under a wider and more commanding '-ism', that of Modernism. What brought them all under Modernism's broad canopy, apart from a shared love of the new and a rejection of the past – a rejection that was to receive

even greater impetus after the shockingly destructive effects of the First World War – was their emphasis on abstraction. Even Expressionism and Surrealism, the two Modernist styles that continued to include more or less recognizable or lifelike forms, were touched by a sense of abstraction. In Expressionism, forms were abstracted so as to convey the psychological or emotional response of the artist and/or his subject, while in Surrealism they were abstracted out of a familiar, everyday context into a dream world mediated by the subconscious.

Futurism was the first Modernist movement to make a significant impact on graphic design, but the forms it latched onto and developed had been founded decades earlier by the French poet Stéphane Mallarmé (1842–98). Mallarmé was a leading figure in the literary Symbolist movement, a mainly French group of writers who, during the last decades of the nineteenth century, had attempted to create a pure form of literature; a way of writing that would be free of the linguistic clichés that had been handed down through common usage and literary tradition. The influence of his writing style was considerable. By emphasizing the abstract, aural qualities of verse, he helped to establish modern European poetry. His verse was more a poetry of suggestion than description, more of the spirit than the flesh, and this aversion to the concrete and quotidian he carried over onto the printed page. When supervising the setting of his poem 'Un coup de dés jamais n'abolira le hasard' ('A throw of the dice will never abolish chance') in 1897, Mallarmé asked for the rectangular text block of a conventional setting to be dispensed with. 'Let us have no more of those successive, incessant, back and forth motions of our eyes, tracking from one line to the next and beginning all over again – otherwise we will miss that ecstasy in which we have become immortal for a brief hour, free of all reality.' It was an attitude that was central to the more refined reprinting of the poem that

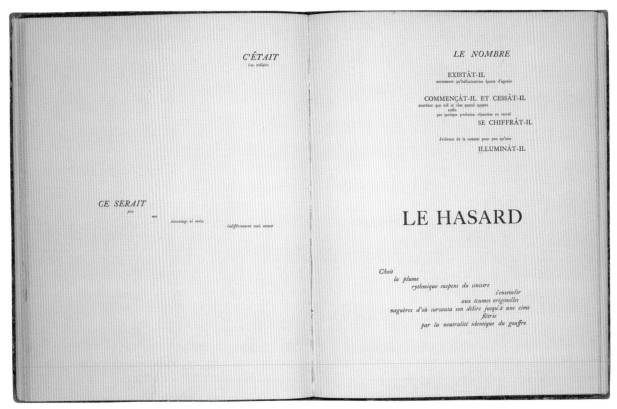

12.2: 'Un coup de dés', Stéphane Mallarmé, 1914

took place in 1914 *(fig. 12.2)*, 16 years after Mallarmé's death. The layout followed the specifications that Mallarmé had written down but not managed to pass on to a printer. It liberated the text from the rigid frame of four uniform margins by allowing words of differing sizes, styles (roman and italic, capitals and lowercase) and weights of type to be spread diffusely across a series of double-page spreads. This typographic freedom was held in check though by the strict horizontalism of the text and the use of a single typeface: a conventional literary Dutch/Transitional style of type *(<fig. 7.7, p.116)*.

The spaciousness and sobriety of Mallarmé's design gave the text an ethereal, contemplative quality. It was a visual impression that was reinforced by the way the text had to be read. For Mallarmé the act of reading was itself an integral part of an overall poetic experience. It was an experience that he wished to heighten by using the graphic spaces between words to create new poetic rhythms and new verbal associations. Space was 'the significant silence that is no less beautiful to compose than verses'. The reader would be guided in how to phrase a poem by the position of the text on the page, and new kinds of emphases could be established in partnership with varied styles and sizes of type. In the example above, the three groups of words 'c'était' (it was), 'le nombre' (the number) and 'ce serait' (this would be), which each begin a separate poetic phrase, have been brought into an equal relation by the equal size of italic capitals. They are though subordinate to the larger 'le hasard' (chance), which was one of four themes introduced by the title ('a throw of the dice', 'never' and 'will abolish' being the others) which, according to Mallarmé, are equivalent to the four movements in a symphony. (The same number had a symbolic resonance with other phases of time: the four divisions of a day, the four seasons, etc.) This kind of use of type, the creation of visual hierarchies in an effort to reflect the meaning and influence the rhythm of reading, had long been exploited for more prosaic purposes on title pages *(<fig. 7.3, p. 112)* and then, more fully during the nineteenth century especially, on posters and other forms of advertising *(<fig. 8.2, p.124)*. But it was in Mallarmé's poems that the same kind of expressive typography was first used within the main body of a literary text.

This escape from the dominance of the rectangular text block in book and literary typography was highly significant for subsequent avant-garde designers.

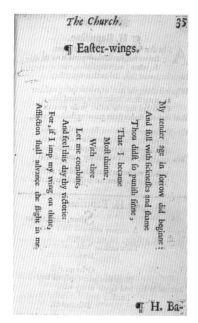

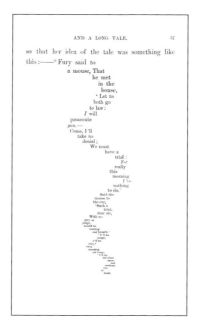

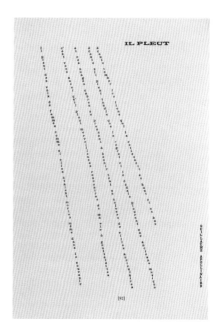

12.3: 'Easter-wings', George Herbert, 1633

12.4: The mouse's tail, Lewis Carroll's 'Alice in Wonderland', 1865

12.5: Apollinaire's 'Il Pleut', 1916

Mallarmé's examples introduced them to a new way of expressing a text's meaning, but they were not the first instance of unorthodox typography in book pages. Some of the earliest printed books made at the beginning of the sixteenth century had contained examples of unusual text layouts, but in them the effect had been decorative, not expressive (of the text's meaning). Another kind of unorthodox arrangement, which had also appeared centuries earlier, sought to depict a simple object with the text's silhouette, such as (to pick two of the best-known examples) an angel's wings *(fig. 12.3)* or, more recently, a mouse's tail *(fig. 12.4)*. This kind of straightforwardly illustrative poetry is sometimes known as 'figure poetry' or 'shaped' or 'emblematic' verse, and each term comes under the more general label of 'pattern' or 'concrete' poetry. Though concrete poetry is known to be very old – the earliest records date it to the third and second centuries BC in Greece – none of these very early examples has survived. Of the many existing examples of twentieth-century figure poetry, one of the most vivid is the 1916 print of the poem *Il Pleut* ('It is Raining') *(fig. 12.5)*, written by the avant-garde poet Guillaume Apollinaire (1880–1918). The poem's cascade of letters do not form a silhouette as such but, in accordance with the manuscript Apollinaire presented to the printer, the five lines of type artfully mimic streaks of rain. Like Mallarmé, Apollinaire rejected punctuation, though not

in order to enhance the rhythm or the poetic quality of the words. His aim was less semantically sophisticated. He wanted to be illustrative, to position the letters in such a way that they captured the sensation of falling raindrops. The need to make a convincing illustration was even more important than the need to make the poem legible. Without any recognizable word shapes, the reader is forced to look at each letter individually, raindrop by raindrop so to speak, which makes for a much slower, albeit more evocative, shower of comprehension.

The Futurist, Marinetti, proceeded in a similar vein to Mallarmé. He too wanted to enhance the expressive power of his writing by the way the words were laid out. In his poetic novel, *Zang Tumb Tuuumb* (< *fig. 12.1*), published piecemeal in journals from 1912 before being collected into book form in 1914, Marinetti attempted to convey something of the emotional tone or sensation of war, which he himself had experienced as a reporter in the Balkans conflict of 1912–13. Much of his text was onomatopoeic – the 'zang, tumb, tuuumb' of the title seems to suggest a volley of shell-fire – and the associations it conjured were ripe for visual interpretation. Bold contrasts and dynamic lines of typography were arranged in whatever way best encapsulated the words' clamorous timbre. What helped Marinetti to treat his typography so freely – as, indeed, it had Mallarmé before him – was the loose construction of the writing.

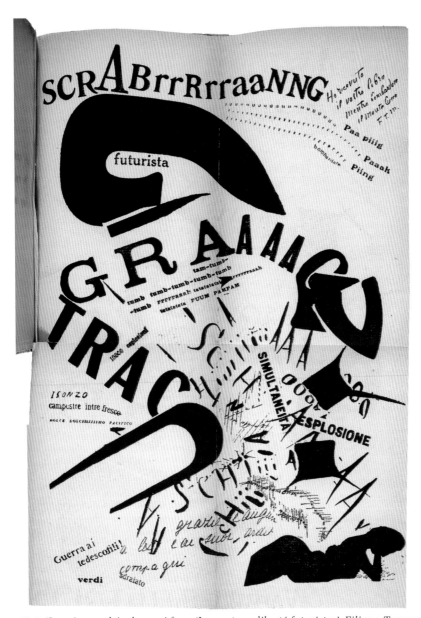

12.6: 'Le soir, couchée dans …' from 'Les mots en liberté futuristes', Filippo Tommaso Marinetti, 1919

His *tipografia in libertà* ('free typography') was linked directly to the *parole in libertà* (in French, *les mots en liberté*) or 'words in liberty'. Since Marinetti and Mallarmé had abandoned any standard form of sentence structure in their poetry, they had no need to include standard capitalization or provide pauses or other semantic instructions through the standard set of punctuation marks. Their looser language gave them greater freedom to use type to express the poetic sense of the words. Furthermore, and no less significantly, it provided the whole page with a sense of space and movement. A definite illusion of depth was created by pieces of large, bold type which seemed to leap out in front of the smaller, quieter lines of text. It was an illusion that Marinetti sometimes enhanced by mixing different typefaces within a single line of text or even within a single word. This new, three-dimensional space was then set in motion by abandoning lines of horizontal type vertically aligned and uniformly set within inviolable margins. Marinetti's text was pointedly unaligned so that the reader's eye was forced to move across the page as it searched for the beginning of each new piece of text. He enhanced this sense of space and movement by varying the direction of the lines of text with vertical, diagonal or even circular settings, as shown on the cover of *Zang Tumb Tuuumb*.

It is this, the layout's greater dynamism, that most clearly distinguishes Marinetti's designs and those of his Futurist colleagues from the formative designs of Mallarmé. Whereas the latter had attempted to tease out a holistic, poetic essence, Marinetti's aims were much more concrete and, in a sense, combative. His attempt at expressing the emotions or feelings of war were part of a broader effort to express the feelings he associated with the world more generally; feelings of destruction, speed, primitivism and immediacy. 'The Futurist will begin by brutally destroying the syntax of speech. He wastes no time in building sentences. Punctuation and the right adjectives mean nothing to him. He will despise subtleties and nuances of language. Breathlessly he will assault your nerves with visual, auditory, olfactory sensations, just as they come to him.'

The contrast between this aim and Mallarmé's search for an ethereal, literary essence is heightened in Marinetti's later work. By 1919, Marinetti had broken free from the constraints imposed by the typesetting process, with its reliance on rectangular blocks of type set in straight or circular lines. Instead, he had taken up the more flexible technique of collage (French for 'pasting'). It was a method of image making that had been developed seven years earlier by the painters Braque and Picasso in their Cubist pictures. Before then, both painters had occasionally brushed stencilled or free-hand letters onto their pictures, but in 1912 they also began to stick objects, including scraps of newspaper headlines and other kinds of printed text onto the painted surface. Marinetti adopted a similar approach in some of his printed work by combining cut-out pieces of printed text with hand-drawn lettering and other expressive marks. In one of a series of fold-outs that appeared in his book *Les Mots en liberté futuristes (fig. 12.6)*, he applied this wider repertoire of forms to a scene described by its caption: 'At night, lying in bed, she rereads the letter from her gunner at the front.' By attempting to represent visually the explosive story behind the words, Marinetti lent this wartime vignette an almost comic-book quality. A cartoonist's thought bubble would not have looked out of place.

Marinetti's public persona appeared to match the scatter-gun energy of his printed work. Like other members of the Modernist avant-garde, he took full advantage of the increasing ease of travel and communication within Europe by touring the continent's capital cities in order to promote his version of Futurism. Many Modernist artists were keen that their movement should

12.7: 'Worldbackwards' by Aleksei Kruchenykh and Velimir Khlebnikov, 1912

have an international identity. Partly they wanted to reflect the strong streak of anti-nationalism among their ranks – though Marinetti's Fascist sympathies proved an exception to this rule – but they were also responding to the understandable sense of solidarity engendered by the scorn or ridicule they frequently encountered from society at large. Both of these reactions were commonplace at the talks and poetry recitals that Marinetti gave during the years leading up to the First World War. The role of provocateur rather than poet or painter caused him to punctuate his readings with howls in imitation of the motor car, and the zest with which he performed his revolutionary rhetoric and loose verse supported the description he gave of himself as 'the caffeine of Europe'.

Such an idiosyncratic form of Futurism could not be taken up and developed in the same way by all avant-garde artists. In pre-revolutionary Russia, from 1912 to 1916, a group of artists who wrote, illustrated and published books of Futurist poetry *(fig. 12.7)* rendered most of their texts and pictures by hand using the direct reproductive technique of transfer lithography *(< p. 133–4)*. It allowed the squat and sometimes fractured character of their Cubist-inspired illustrations to cohere with their

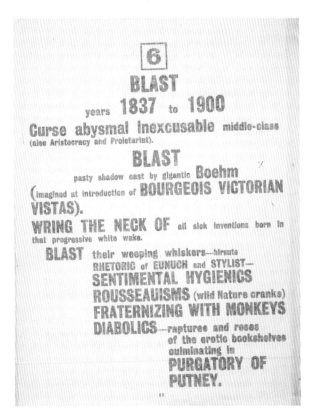

6

BLAST
years 1837 to 1900
Curse abysmal inexcusable middle-class
(also Aristocracy and Proletariat).

BLAST
pasty shadow cast by gigantic Boehm
(imagined at introduction of BOURGEOIS VICTORIAN
VISTAS).
WRING THE NECK OF all sick inventions born in
that progressive white wake.
BLAST their weeping whiskers—hirsute
RHETORIC of EUNUCH and STYLIST—
SENTIMENTAL HYGIENICS
ROUSSEAUISMS (wild Nature cranks)
FRATERNIZING WITH MONKEYS
DIABOLICS—raptures and roses
of the erotic bookshelves
culminating in
PURGATORY OF
PUTNEY.

12.8: 'Blast' magazine cover and inside designed by Wyndham Lewis, 1914

broken, handwritten verse into a seemingly impromptu and expressive whole. By contrast, in London, British Futurists or 'Vorticists' as they called themselves, filled each of the two editions of their short-lived magazine *Blast* with woodcut illustrations, also rendered in a Cubist style, alongside poetry and prose, which they printed, for the most part, in the kind of bold sanserif type *(fig. 12.8)* more commonly associated with newspaper or poster headlines *(< fig. 11.8, p.169)* than literary texts. Though the strict horizontalism of the inside text more closely resembled Mallarmé's pages, the design of the magazine's first cover in all its bold, diagonal directness, though not in its minimalism, matched Marinetti's use of type.

By 1916 Switzerland's largest city, Zürich, had become a refuge for various opponents of the war. Protected by Swiss neutrality, they were allowed to associate freely, and it was there that an international though nihilistic relative of Futurism called 'Dada' was founded. According to one account, the word Dada – which is French baby talk for a hobbyhorse – had been chosen by randomly pointing a knife into a dictionary. Whether true or not, the story contains the combination of chance

and mocking infantilism that characterized many of the movement's subsequent attacks on bourgeois society. One especially potent strike was made at an exhibition in New York in 1917 with the submission of a urinal as an example of 'ready-made' art. It was entered with the ironic title 'Fountain' by the fictitious 'R. Mutt' (and signed as such), a pseudonym which the French artist Marcel Duchamp (1887–1968), who was then a director of the exhibition, chose to hide behind (and never officially owned up to). His urinal contributed to the subsequent artistic trend of the ready-made and its media-related companion, the *succès de scandale*. After being refused entry, his work received a degree of notoriety that was unlikely to have come its way had it been accepted.

In keeping with its anti-art credo, Dadaism never developed an overarching style of its own, though a greater degree of consistency was shown in its graphic design than in any other area of expression. A novel and dominant feature of Dadaist graphics was a powerful brand of photomontage, which was derived from a Futurist style of collage. Though the Dadaists were the first to establish photomontage as a form of avant-garde art, they did not invent the technique. Cutting out and reassembling photographs or their negatives had been relatively common throughout the nineteenth century – humorous and commemorative postcards, compositional studies for painting, and various kinds of compound photographic prints made by combining negatives had begun to appear almost immediately after the invention of photography early in the nineteenth century – but in each case, the resultant image was defined by the then dominant pictorial tradition of realism. The Dadaists took photomontage out of that tradition and put it into the Modernist idiom of a more or less fractured form of surrealism.

In its method and its symbolism, photomontage was a natural medium for Dadaist artists. Alongside printed text in newspapers and journals, which their Futurist cousins had gleaned to make collages, there appeared a bountiful supply of pictures. Most of these pictures had illustrated news stories or advertisements, so they tended to depict the incidental scenes or objects of everyday, modern living. The fact that such images were second-hand, ready-made items rather than specific artistic creations, and the fact that they were the product of an industrial and commercial process rather than an artistic one, fitted the movement's wider (anti-)artistic aims. Moreover, because these various printed scraps had been made for the newsstand, rather than the exhibition hall or salon, their content had not been censored by any art establishment or mediated by an artistic tradition. Compared to the paintings and fine-art prints of conventional art, they were a much more 'modern' and egalitarian kind of representation. Among the most identifiable items to appear on the cover of the third edition of the journal, *Der Dada* ('The Dada', *fig. 12.9*), which was published in 1920 by a group of Dadaists based in Berlin (and different to the Zürich group's journal *Dada*), are a car tyre, a row of bicycles, an iron and even a toothbrush. That this kind of series of incidental images was the principal feature of an artistic magazine was startlingly novel. Their appearance challenged the tastes of the time just as much as the fractured way in which they had been combined.

The cover's designer, John Heartfield (1891–1968), who had anglicized his name from the German Helmut Herzfeld in protest at the rise of German nationalism and anti-British sentiment during the First World War, was one of the magazine's three editors (the others being George Grosz and Raoul Hausmann, though all three playfully assumed the swapped and spliced names 'Groszfield', 'Georgemann' and 'Hearthaus' in the

12.9: 'Der Dada' cover designed by John Heartfield, 1920

magazine). The rudimentary, collage form of photomontage that appeared on the cover of their magazine was used inside it and on other forms of publicity material – leaflets, posters and journals. It was ideally suited to the task of promoting the Dadaist movement, since it was itself an example of what it was promoting: the overthrow of conventional form. It was Dada in action. The technique, as Heartfield and his colleagues applied it, in all its iconoclastic disorder, encapsulated the anti-establishment message at the heart of the movement. The medium was very much the message.

Each of the Berlin Dadaists had their individual strengths, but none managed to rival Heartfield in harnessing the concentrated graphic power of montage. It was a power generated by two forces: the freedom and speed given to the designer in creating almost whatever image came into his or her head, and the impression of reality it passed on to the viewer. An object cut out from a photograph, though removed from its surrounding context, usually remains highly recognizable. The photographic process imbues it with a degree of detail that makes it recognizably real. During the German elections of May 1928 Heartfield used a cut-out picture of a raised hand on an election poster for the German

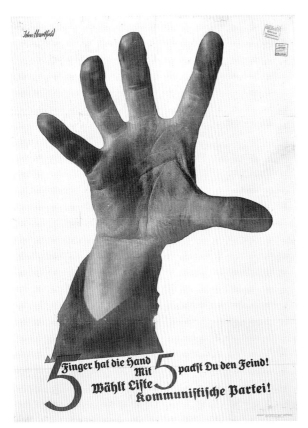

12.10: 'Die Rote Fahne' poster designed by John Heartfield, 1928

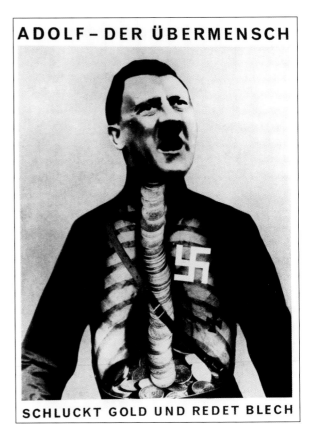

12.11: 'Adolf the Superman' poster designed by John Heartfield, 1932

Communist Party *(fig.12.10)*. The hand is raised with fingers splayed as though it and the whole arm were being pushed upwards and out of the page in an attempt to grab the viewer. This primal gesture certainly succeeded in grabbing the viewer's attention. But had the hand looked less realistic, the power of the design would have been diminished. The fact that the image looks like, and is known to have derived from, a real hand gives it more power and significance than the printed dots of ink really deserve. Even today, when we know how publishers like to alter or 'touch up' photographs to fulfil some, usually commercial, agenda – the lengthening of a model's legs or the smoothing of a face – our tendency is to assume that the image represents reality merely because it is photographic. The impact of Heartfield's image was enhanced by the starkness of the design – the hand almost silhouetted against an unprinted background – and also the subtle illusion of depth he created by having the arm rising up behind the large number 5 and block of text at the bottom. It may also be that some of the poster's emotional power came from an atavistic reaction to the perceived threat of a

splayed hand. But each of these contributory factors was supplementary to the impression of realism provided by the photograph.

Throughout the 1920s and into the 1930s, Heartfield developed the technique away from the group's initial, collage style and towards a more realistic, or surrealistic, form of imagery. He cut, combined and airbrushed his photographs so as to remove any trace of the joins between them. This more seamless and apparently simplified style of photomontage was usually placed in the service of political satire, a mode of expression he and his Dadaist colleges had pursued as soon as they had realized that they could 'say, in pictures, what would have been banned by the censors if we had said it in words'. Heartfield's most biting satire was fuelled by a twin loathing for Fascism and capitalism. Both targets were the subject of a poster he made in 1932 titled *Adolf the Superman: Swallows Gold and Spouts Junk (fig.12.11)*. The image exposed the hollowness of Hitler's rhetoric and the corruption that lay behind it. Far from being, as Nazi propaganda had it, an incorruptible idealist wedded to the purity of his convictions, Hitler is shown to be little more than a capitalist mouthpiece, willing to say whatever his fee demands of him. The slew of gold coins cascading down his gullet immediately fuses the concept of Hitler with corruption, and though the montage is clearly not a 'real' image, the element of 'truthfulness' generated by the photographic medium brings home Heartfield's criticism of Hitler more forcefully than, say, a caricaturist's sketch might have done. In line with the tradition of the political cartoon, the caption helps to pin down the meaning of the image, which, in turn, through its sheer surrealistic oddness, reacts back on the text to make the words more memorable.

The revolutionary periods of Dada and Futurism were brought to an end by the combined effects of the First World War and the Russian Revolution. The realization that war and the machine, both of which had been exalted by the early Futurists, could bring about such an unprecedented level of destruction, made each appear less worthy of veneration. As within Europe's population as a whole, many among the avant-garde blamed the war on a bungling and backward-looking ruling class. The inability of this latter group to deliver a secure and equitable society only intensified the desire among the former to break free from the constraints of tradition. But rather than follow the negative responses of Futurist destruction or Dadaist derision, there were some who sought a more positive approach. It was through two kinds of positive approaches that they succeeded in advancing the Modernist movement.

The first of these was developed by a movement known as De Stijl (The Style), which was formed in Holland in 1917 around a magazine of the same name. The magazine's editor and designer, Theo van Doesburg (1883–1931), had chosen the name because he had intended the magazine to promote a single style of design applicable to all forms of art, be it fine art, architecture or graphic design. Within this broad remit, however, there was to be no room for realism, decoration or individual expression. Such tendencies were considered to be dangerously divisive. An art that aimed for a universal application could only be served by a pure, non-figurative form of abstraction; one made out of the simplest abstract shapes, such as lines, circles or triangles. Such shapes, he and his colleagues believed, were the foundation of all pictorial art, and possessed a significance that transcended any particular culture or class. In the opening line of the first issue of the magazine, the Dutch

12.12: 'De Stijl' magazine cover designed by Theo van Doesburg and Vilmos Huszár, 1917

painter Piet Mondrian (1872–1944) stated, 'The life of contemporary cultivated man is turning gradually away form nature; it becomes more and more an a-b-s-t-r-a-c-t life.' By choosing to separate the letters through the use of hyphens, Mondrian was emphasizing the letters' elemental nature. It was through the discovery and representation of the elemental building blocks of art that the artists of De Stijl hoped to reveal an ultimate reality behind all appearances, be they the appearances of the natural world or those of the world made by man. In so doing, they believed they might reveal the objective laws by which all things were governed and 'establish an international unity in life, art [and] culture'. For Mondrian, if not for all members of De Stijl, the movement was as much a spiritual quest as it was an artistic one.

Guided by this kind of idealism, the members of De Stijl restricted themselves to using only the straight line, the right angle, the point and the three primary colours, red, blue and yellow, in combination with black (or grey) on a white background. All such elements were to be locked into a rectilinear arrangement, curves being 'too personal'. On the magazine's first cover (fig. 12.12),

12.13: 'Beat the Whites with the Red Wedge' poster designed by El Lissitzky, 1919

van Doesburg placed his title lettering above an abstract composition, which itself sat on top of a few lines of descriptive text. Each one of the title's letters was made out of black rectangular blocks set either vertically or horizontally within an invisible square frame; their abstract nature blended with the abstract composition below. In order to avoid any obvious realism, the subject of the composition was kept intentionally vague. Its weighty black blocks suggest some sort of architectural form, but exactly which of them represent the foreground and which the background is ambiguous.

The number of examples of pure De Stijl graphic design was never large. The medium of print, with its vast range of formats and tasks – a countless variety of posters, labels, magazines, newspapers, packages, etc. – could never thrive on such a stringent diet of rectangular abstraction. Most printed matter needs to say something specific. If images that accompany text are to be easily 'read', they have to have a degree of realism. The German poster for Opel (<fig. 11.7, p.168) and the British recruitment poster of Lord Kitchener, (<fig. 11.8, p.169) for example, were both able to plant a straightforward proposition into the mind of the viewer because the illustrations were unambiguous. They combined with their respective texts to create a clearly formed central concept, be it the need for recruits or the desirability of a certain kind of car.

This is not to say that abstract forms have no place in graphic design. The cover of De Stijl's magazine is an exemplary demonstration of the new style of art, but if the picture were to be removed from this context it would become essentially decorative. In this way, in its general decorative effect, pure abstraction is similar to music. The main quality of each is sensory rather than verbal or conceptual. They can speak eloquently about their own, inner relations, but without some other contextualizing element, they can say little about the external world, the specific events or objects that exist outside of themselves. For De Stijl, the interplay of the inner relations of colour, shape and tone could be exploited by its architects, furniture designers and painters – Mondrian spent the remaining 25 years of his life exploring the nuances of rectangular abstraction – but it was difficult for graphic designers to do so to any great degree. They required a fuller, more flexible and informative mode of expression.

12.14: 'Third International' spread from 'For the Voice' designed by El Lissitzky, 1923

As early as 1920, van Doesburg was forced into using diagonal lines – an act Mondrian roundly denounced, so intent was he on preserving the movement's purity – and thereafter he rapidly took up fully representative forms. In spite of this eagerness to escape the confines of orthodox De Stijl, van Doesburg remained a keen advocate of the movement's core concepts. Through his writing and through personal contacts, he encouraged others to address the themes of universalism, objectivity and the basic building blocks of form.

The second positive approach towards the creation of a new style had its character built into its name: Constructivism. The political aims of this almost exclusively Russian movement were tied to the aims of the Russian Revolution: the defeat of the tsarist regime and support for the founding of Communism. The forms it developed were derived from a Russian style of abstract painting, similar to De Stijl, called Suprematism. The abstract elements of Suprematism – hard-edged lines and flat shapes of primary colours – appeared in the paintings and posters of one of Constructivism's foremost designers, El Lissitzky (1890–1941). In his

rallying poster of 1919, 'Beat the Whites with the Red Wedge' *(fig. 12.13)*, abstract symbols were used to depict the forces of Bolshevik power united within a sharp pointed red triangle as it pierced the soft circular heart of the White Russian enemy. Unlike the proponents of De Stijl, the Constructivists preferred the dynamism of the diagonal line to the 'passive' horizontal and the 'authoritarian' vertical. Dynamism and action were the attributes valued by this more overtly political and practical movement. A political transformation was necessary before the new kind of society it championed had the space to create any kind of spiritual transformation.

Constructivism's development was not carried out entirely within Russia. The revolution and Russia's subsequent civil war forced many Russian artists to seek refuge in Berlin, then the eastern capital of the European avant-garde (Paris remained their capital in the west). In Berlin they were exposed to a range of foreign influences, but equally the free association of Russian émigrés with other Europeans who had come to Berlin from various parts of the continent brought a greater awareness of Constructivism to the European avant-garde. El Lissitzky, who used the city as a base for several years, was a key figure in this process of cultural exchange. Following his arrival there at the end of 1921, he received a commission from the Russian state publishing house to design a collection of poetry in collaboration with the pre-eminent Russian revolutionary poet, Vladimir Mayakovsky, who then travelled to Berlin specifically to work on the book. Their partnership continued a tradition of collaboration between artist and poet that had existed within the Russian avant-garde since the earliest years of the century. This tradition played a part in determining the book's pocket-book size format, though not in its novel Constructivist design, nor in the features from other avant-garde styles that were woven into that design.

In recognition of the book's content (ie. poems that were meant to be read aloud), the collection was called *For The Voice (<fig. 12.14)*. It comprised 13 of Mayakovsky's poems, each of which were laid out and illustrated using the common Constructivist elements of diagonal lines and blocks, and then printed in the movement's signature colours of red and black. Unlike the Futurist books of the previous generation of Russian avant-garde artists *(<fig. 12.7)*, little in *For the Voice* was hand-drawn. The text was set with type and the illustrations were, for the most part, constructed out of the kind of simple, geometrical units commonly found in all printers' type cases.

In the dynamic opening spread of the third poem, 'Third International', El Lissitzky layered the forms he had created with these abstract components, one on top of the other, as in a Futurist or Dadaist design. On the spread's left-hand page, El Lissitzky laid a black hammer shape over the handle of a red sickle to form the emblem of the Soviet state. The hammer also sat on top of two instances of the roman numeral 'III', one black, the other red, which alluded to the poem's title. On the opposite, right-hand page, El Lissitzky used two features that were to become common Constructivist motifs. One was a single, large letter dominating the design, and the other was the intersecting of two words at a common letter, in the style of a crossword (though the format of this only remotely popular word game would not have been known to him). Both features were combined within a single form. The large, red vertical bar stands both as a dominating capital T in the Russian word meaning 'THIRD', and in the word meaning 'INTERNATIONAL', which runs diagonally across the page (and parallel to the black hammer's handle opposite). A final, singular feature of the book was the outer edges of the

pages, which had been cut to make a thumb-index, as in an address book. Instead of following the convention of a contents page and page numbers, the book displayed a series of small titles and graphic symbols on each of the index's tabs, which allowed the reader to see at a glance both the entire range of poems and where each could be found. By cutting a thumb-index into a book that also had letters formed out of layers of geometric shapes and words fused by common letters, El Lissitzky created the graphic equivalent of a work of Modernist architecture. The book's format and design visibly expressed the movement's guiding concept: construction.

Support for the avant-garde from the Soviet state declined during the latter half of the 1920s. The state's initial acceptance of and periodic praise for revolutionary forms of art turned into a period of grudging tolerance before descending, during the early 1930s, into complete antipathy. The Constructivists' tendency towards experimentation was incompatible with the state's increasing control of the arts, and the movement's strong links with other Western and non-Communist Modernist movements provided the state with the opportunity to condemn it as bourgeois and decadent. The state's anti-internationalism was encouraged by its de facto leader, Joseph Stalin, whose rise to power had followed Lenin's death in 1924. Soviet Russia's increasing political and economic isolation during this period was turned by Stalin into a powerful ideological weapon through the introduction of a policy of national self-reliance and solidarity, which he promoted through the slogan 'Socialism in one country'. This antipathy towards international influences culminated in a formal denunciation of avant-garde art in 1932 and in the explicit promotion of traditional forms of Russian art. For the visual arts, this meant a return to a form of realism, though not one that was geared to showing life as it was experienced by most Russians. It was an idealistic or heroic realism – muscular workers with tools held aloft as they looked out over a glistening industrial landscape.

The Soviet state's rejection of avant-garde abstraction was reinforced by the rise of a medium whose origins owed nothing to the avant-garde nor indeed to any tradition of Russian picture making: the new medium of film. Its popularity in Russia during the first decades of the twentieth century led Lenin to champion it as 'the most effective method for propaganda'. From the mid-1920s, the state-run cinema combined with the

НОВЫЙ

леф

12.15: 'New LEF' magazine cover designed by Alexander Rodchenko, 1927

invention of the compact portable camera to create an appetite among the public and designers alike for life-like, photographic images. One of the few Modernist Russian designers to successfully straddle this transition from abstraction to realism was Alexander Rodchenko (1891–1956), who in 1925 acquired one of the first portable Leica cameras ('small negatives – large images' was the camera designer's motto), and he used it to take specific shots for particular pieces of design. The cover for an edition of the avant-garde's *New LEF* magazine *(fig. 12.15)*, designed in 1927, shows a photograph which, in its scale and contrast, perfectly fitted the magazine's format. Its careful and unusual placement created a startlingly bold design. The large, cut-out profile of a smiling head sporting a worker's red-starred hat, created simple and harmonious divisions within the magazine's rectangular format. The novelty of the contrast between the more peripheral, background shapes and the tilted photographic one in the centre

was matched by the contrast between the irregular and naturalistic silhouette of the black and white photograph and the geometric, black, red and white abstract forms within and around the magazine's title.

By the early 1930s, Russian Constructivism ceased to exist as a movement. The imposition of a realistic style of art devoted to a specifically Russian form of socialism – or 'Socialist Realism', as Stalin himself is said to have named it – had removed any lingering hope among the avant-garde that they might create a forward-looking, cosmopolitan society. Russia, though, was not the only country in which an internationally minded avant-garde was at work. The most active advocates of a progressive aesthetic, certainly during the 1920s, were to be found in Germany. There, the most significant centre of avant-garde activity was not in a state-run publishing house, nor in the more self-determining environment of an artist's studio, but within the spartan classrooms of a fledgling art school called the Bauhaus.

13 FORM AND FUNCTION

Bauhaus & the New Typography, c.1919 – c.1933

Of the many varied styles of graphic design to emerge during the twentieth century, none was as influential as the Bauhaus. Nearly all subsequent styles were built on the foundations it laid or else developed in direct opposition to it. Few could ignore it. The dominant Modernist graphic designers of the twentieth century incorporated its main characteristics into their work, and many designers today continue to do so, whether they are conscious of it or not. But given its origins, the fact that the Bauhaus had any kind of influence, let alone one so enduring, is remarkable.

   The word 'Bauhaus' comes from the name of the German art school, the Staatliches Bauhaus *(fig. 13.1)*, where, between 1919 and 1933, the style first developed. The school's life was short and peripatetic. By being forced to move twice in 14 years, it was only really able to function fully for ten of them. Its first incarnation was not located in one of the busy industrial cities that had managed to transform the region's principalities into the economically powerful German state, but in the provincial town of Weimar which, at that time, was a well-established but conservative cultural centre.

   During the early 1920s the town suffered, as did all others in Germany, following the humiliating defeat in the First World War. A severe economic depression caused by hyper-inflation crippled the German economy. The fall in the value of the mark and the consequent rise in the cost of goods was so rapid that new notes could not be printed quickly enough. The two-million-mark note, commissioned in 1923 from the Bauhaus student Herbert Bayer (1900–85), was put into circulation before the ink had had time to dry *(>fig. 13.2)*. By November of that year, a German citizen would have needed 12,000 such notes to buy a newspaper. Into the gulf that separated the country's pre-war aspirations of wealth and empire from the post-war realities of poverty and national humiliation, extreme political groups

from both the left and the right gathered. Both sides advocated revolution and each frequently met dissent with violence. During the 15 years that separated the end of the war in 1918 and the rise to power of the most nationalistic of these groups, the National Socialists (or Nazis), 17 different governments came and went. In the middle of such a volatile economic, social and political climate, the existence of the Bauhaus as a newly created and functioning entity was perhaps as great an act of creation as any of the designs that came out of its classrooms.

   No one contributed more to the school's survival than its founding director and lifetime proselytizer, Walter Gropius (1883–1969). Gropius had made a name for himself as an avant-garde architect in Berlin, but it was through his work for several arts and crafts organizations that he came to be considered as a candidate for the directorship of the Bauhaus. In 1919, after being put in charge of the newly constituted school (a merger between Weimar's fine art academy and a local school of art and craft), Gropius wrote a manifesto and programme outlining the curriculum, which he published in a four-page leaflet. The cover of this leaflet *(>fig. 13.3)* was illustrated with a woodcut by the school's first member of staff, Lyonel Feininger (1871–1956), an American-born member of a group of avant-garde painters who initially formed the core of the Bauhaus staff. In this, the Bauhaus's very first graphic work, there is no trace of the minimal, geometric forms that were to characterize the Bauhaus style proper. The style of the illustration is Expressionistic, then the dominant idiom among artists of the German avant-garde. For all its explosively luminous expressiveness, Feininger's central image of a cathedral was not a standard Expressionist motif. It had been purposefully chosen by Gropius to symbolize the unity of craftsmanship he hoped to recreate within the school. To him the cathedral represented

13.2: Banknote designed by Herbert Bayer, 1923

the essence of Gothic art: a house made by mankind for a common worship, and in whose creation all the arts were brought together to forge a fellowship of artisans. The three spires depicted in the woodcut represented the three principal arts involved in a cathedral's construction: painting, sculpture and architecture. Alongside the painters, sculptors and architects, were carpenters, welders, weavers, and many other specialist craftsmen whose task it was to decorate the massed walls of stone that had been erected by an army of stonemasons. Each of these groups had been organized into a cluster of formal societies known as cathedral guilds or *Bauhütten*, literally 'building huts' (so named after the stone masons' on-site huts where the stone was prepared and assembled), and from which the school's name was derived. *Bauhaus* was thus literally a 'Building House' or 'House of Building'.

Gropius's manifesto, like others published by the artistic avant-garde, was both political and declamatory. Its first line read 'The ultimate aim of all the visual arts is the complete building!', and the text that followed continued in a similar vein: 'The artist is an exalted craftsman ... let us create a new guild of craftsmen without the class distinctions that raise an arrogant barrier between craftsman and artist!' It was a tone and content that worried an already anxious local government, who had not been comforted by the progressive Expressionism of the leaflet's illustration and the leftist allusion of its three shining stars, the star having recently been adopted as an emblem of Communism. In spite of their worries, Gropius was given approval to proceed because his accompanying programme was, largely, orthodox. The description of it differed little from that of any other school of art and craft. Moreover, there was a welcome range of subjects on offer and a strong vocational bias in the way that each would be taught. Within the six basic areas of craft, training would be provided in: i) sculpture – for stonemasons,

13.3: 'Bauhaus manifesto' cover, Lyonel Feininger, 1919

wood carvers, ceramicists and plaster casters, ii) metalwork – for blacksmiths, locksmiths, founders and metal turners, iii) cabinetmaking, iv) decorative painting – for glass painters, mosaic workers, enamellers, v) printing – for etchers, wood-engravers, lithographers, art printers, and vi) weaving. In addition, there was drawing and painting, which included murals, lettering design, exteriors, gardens and interiors, and furniture design; and then also science and theory, that is, art history (not 'a history of styles, but rather to further an understanding of historical working methods and techniques'), the science of materials, anatomy, colour theory, and even basic business studies.

What had been planned by Gropius in the abstract changed as soon as the teachers began to teach. The programme had not included what was to become the cornerstone of the Bauhaus's teaching method and one of its most potent legacies, the Preliminary Course (or *Vorkurs*). The idea of providing a general introductory course to teach the fundamental aspects of art was not new, but it was through the Bauhaus that such a course became the standard feature of art education in Europe and the United States during the second half of the twentieth century. With only few exceptions, the Bauhaus students, or *Bauhäusler,* were obliged to attend the Preliminary Course for the first six months, which meant that during the first few years it was this course that set the tone for the school as a whole, and thus, by extension, so did its enigmatic head, Johannes Itten (1888–1967). Itten was the only qualified teacher to be appointed by Gropius, but the teaching methods he employed were far from orthodox. He saw the main purpose of the 'Basic Course', as he preferred to call it, as being to free the students from any prior learning so that their own individual nature could emerge. By incorporating ideas from the kindergarten movement as well as others from Eastern philosophy and the developing discipline of modern psychoanalysis – this at a time when each of the latter were entirely esoteric – Itten hoped to develop a level of 'self-awareness' within each student that would allow them to discover the medium in which they could best express themselves. Personal experience was held to be the key to unlocking this expressive potential. It meant that, for example, before a student could draw a circle, they had to experience one by walking it or else tracing it with their arms. In addition to conventional lessons on colour theory and 'Old Masters', Itten gave classes in breathing and concentration. His methods and his manner proved to be so persuasive that some students decided to bring what they had learnt in the classroom into their daily lives. They took up what, at that time and in that place, were highly unusual practices, such as fasting, acupuncture, or frequent gargling and garlic eating. In imitation of their teacher, some even adopted the appearance of Buddhist monks by shaving their heads and sporting an assortment of colourful, baggy clothes, which they had garnered from Russian prisoners-of-war.

Interest in the activities of the Bauhaus extended beyond the surprised residents of Weimar. By 1921 the Dutch De Stijl painter Theo van Doesburg *(<p. 183–5)* had moved to the city and it was there, during the following year, that he convened a meeting of Dadaists and Constructivists, which included such prominent figures as Tristan Tzara, Hans Arp and El Lissitzky. Van Doesburg also began to give lectures, which some of the Bauhaus pupils attended. Those students who had felt lost among the whirl of free spirits and competing

13.4: 'Staatliches Bauhaus in Weimar 1919–23' exhibition catalogue cover, 1923

ideologies fostered by Itten found a clear and definite point of reference in Van Doesburg's almost fanatical adherence to the principles of De Stijl. His theories on the use of colour in defining space, the importance of a restricted colour palette (white, grey, black and the three primary colours), and the objective analysis of the best methods of construction had a visible effect on the students' work.

Van Doesburg's influence was felt by teachers too. He was quick to bring to Gropius's attention the disparity between Bauhaus theory as expressed in the school's manifesto and Bauhaus practice within the classrooms, dominated as it was by Itten's Preliminary Course. The multitude of individual forms that had resulted appeared to Van Doesburg as so much 'Expressionist jam'. The initial aim of uniting art and craft by teaching students how to design practical and usable artefacts for the home or the workplace had little chance of success while students were being encouraged to focus on self-expression. Indeed, there was a danger that the school was turning into 'an island of recluses' for whom meditation and ritual were more important than practical craft skills. Gropius's socialist belief in community and the role of art in binding communities together required his students to engage with the world around them, not retreat from it.

An additional and more pressing concern was the issue of the school's finances. The Bauhaus's pointedly experimental work and its perceived mismanagement had prompted the conservative local government to threaten to withdraw funding. This forced Gropius to make a shift in emphasis away from experimental craft and towards the design of prototypes for industrial production. Put simply, students would need to be taught how to both design and make items that could be sold. For Itten, such a move constituted a betrayal of the grossest and most flagrant kind. To neglect the personal development of individual students for the sake of making money was wholly unacceptable. He would rather 'cling to his romantic island' than make such a compromise and thus, in 1923, he left with a coterie of his most devoted pupils to start his own school in Berlin.

The man chosen to replace Itten was a young, energetic Hungarian painter called László Moholy-Nagy (1895–1946). Moholy-Nagy had been one of the artists who had attended Van Doesburg's earlier meeting of the avant-garde, and on his return to Weimar he came 'bursting into the Bauhaus circle like a strong, eager dog', as one fellow teacher put it. It was at a time when just such an attitude was most needed. In order to prove to the local government that the school was worth funding, Gropius had agreed to mount an exhibition of the school's work but, having done so, he had been effectively forced to declare a state of emergency. All teaching had to be suspended so that the exhibits could be prepared. The centrepiece of the exhibition was to be a fully furnished house with the foundations, the furniture and all the fixtures and fittings designed and made by the school using some of the very latest materials. The house was to demonstrate a new kind of living. Many of its features, such as the widespread use of concrete, inner and outer walls filled with insulation, floors without corridors, and a fitted kitchen made from standardized units have now become commonplace items of domestic design and architecture, but at that time they were almost entirely new. In addition to the house, there were to be displays of the students' pictures and workshop products, and also concerts of avant-garde music and jazz.

At the opening of the exhibition in August 1923 Gropius delivered a lecture whose title encapsulated the school's new direction. The once-sacred slogan of 'art and craft' had now given way to the more modern mantra of *Art and Industry – a New Unity*. A visible sign of this change could be seen in the exhibition's publicity material, which the school had produced in its own printing workshop. The range of items included a newspaper advertisement, posters and a catalogue

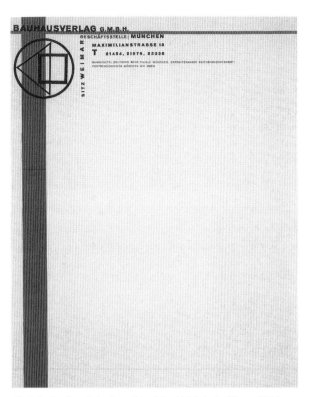

13.5: Letterhead designed by László Moholy-Nagy, 1923

in book form titled *Staatliches Bauhaus in Weimar 1919–1923* (< fig. 13.4). Inside the catalogue, Moholy-Nagy set out visually what he referred to in the text as 'the new typography'. The primary aim for this new kind of design was for it to be functional, or, as he put it, to find 'the right form for the stated function'. His formulation can be seen as the graphic design equivalent of the Modernist architects' dictum 'form follows function', which the American architect Louis Sullivan had helped bring into common usage at the turn of the century. Moholy-Nagy conceded that some books in the past had possessed a certain aesthetic purity, particularly in the smooth and even grey tone of their text, but their purity had come at a price. Such books lacked the ability to guide the reader through the text as the best illuminated manuscripts and incunabula had managed to do through their arresting use of colour and their decorative and illustrative illumination. He considered this ability to be central: 'Defining the content pictorially by the organisation of visual effects ... is the essential task of visual typogra-phic design.' What he meant was that, as well as using type in its various ranks of weight, the designer should marshal all the other forces at his disposal, such as rules, dots, arrows and even a secondary, invariably red, colour in order to clearly emphasize, separate or connect the various kinds of information that appeared on the page.

In addition to the exhibition's publicity material, Moholy-Nagy designed a logo, some stationery *(fig. 13.5)* and a prospectus for the school's new in-house publishing company. The logo was made out of a square, circle and triangle, three forms which, in line with the teachings of De Stijl, were held by some Bauhaus teachers to be the elementary building blocks of all graphic form: an irreducible core with a universal significance. The illusory sense of depth created by the layered forms of the logo and, on the letterhead, by some of the overlapping, line-hugging bold type, constituted a new and arresting graphic style. Many of the reporting press were critical of it, though of greater significance was the local government's assessment of the exhibition as a whole. It was thoroughly negative. Not even the inclusion of Albert Einstein's name in a list of prominent national figures that Gropius had invited to form a 'Circle of Friends' could change the government's opinion, and they withdrew their funding. By the end of 1924, after Gropius had had his house searched and the students condemned as political activists, the teachers voted to dissolve the school and start the search for a new home.

Not all local governments were as culturally conservative as Weimar's. In Dessau, only a short distance from Berlin, the mayor personally expressed his support for the school in the hope that it might help tackle the town's lack of housing and its poor urban planning. The lure of a less hostile government, and the twin promises of help in establishing closer links with industry and of new architectural commissions, starting with a new set of buildings for the school itself, could not be resisted. Over the next six months, Gropius eagerly set about designing a new school and supervising the various phases of building. The result was a gleaming white construction clearly conceived as the epitome of Modern architecture *(< fig. 13.1)*. Such was its novelty that hundreds of visitors came each month to glimpse the singular structure. Though each of the asymmetrical, rectangular spaces was built out of brick, Gropius had covered and combined them with the more modern materials of concrete, steel and glass. He set these last two within a trademark feature of his, a hanging curtain-wall of glass, which wrapped around the corners of the building, causing the interior to be flooded with natural light. Within the rectangular structure were spaces for workshops, an administration unit, a lecture theatre and

13.6: 'Malerei, Photographie, Film', László Moholy-Nagy, 1925

stage, work rooms, a canteen and, something that had not existed in Weimar, a dedicated department of architecture. Housing for the masters was built nearby in a similarly modern manner (though for some of the inhabitants it was a little too modern; one master painted his glass wall white to stop people looking in, while another insisted on replacing the Bauhaus furniture with his own antiques).

In its new home, the Bauhaus established a more settled form of pedagogy and a more homogenous set of students. A sign of this greater cohesion was reflected both in the day-to-day activities and in the students' work. Partnerships with industry were pursued in earnest, particularly by those within the metal and weaving workshops. The union bore fruits that have since become synonymous with the school: Marcel Breuer's tubular chairs, Marianne Brandt's lights, and Gunta Stölzl's tapestries. Each of the workshops benefited from having new equipment, but none more so than the printing workshop. Not only did it receive two new presses, but it was also provided with new equipment for composing type, and a new set of type – a range of weights and sizes of a late nineteenth-century sanserif commonly used in advertising of the time. Its application to literary (books and journals) and administrative

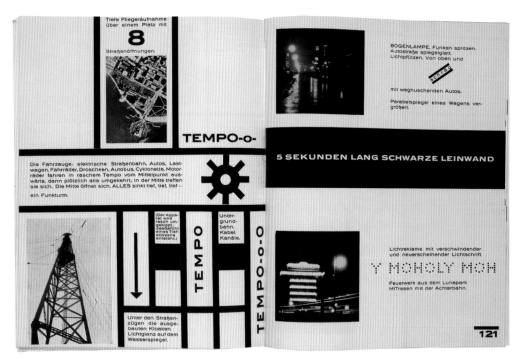

13.7: 'Malerei, Photographie, Film', written and designed by László Moholy-Nagy, 1925

(stationery, banknotes, etc.) items became a hallmark of the school's emerging graphic style. A new emphasis on commercial art and advertising, rather than fine-art printing, brought the workshop a new status, which was reflected in its new name: 'The Printing and Advertising Workshop'.

Even in Dessau, however, the school found it necessary to seek extra financial and political support. An attempt at raising funds and generating publicity was made through the use of the new facilities in the printing workshop to produce a series of *Bauhausbücher* ('Bauhaus books') on 'artistic, scientific and technical aspects of various specialist fields'. From 1924 to 1930, a total of 14 volumes were made, each of which had been conceived and commissioned – six from various Bauhaus masters – and also edited by Gropius and Moholy-Nagy. The insides of all except two were also designed by Moholy-Nagy, as were nine of the covers. But it was in the eighth in the series that Moholy-Nagy made his most complete contribution. Not only did he design it cover to cover, but he also wrote the text, and this text was to form the basis of a later, influential publication, *The New Vision*, in which he set out more fully the potential of the new mechanical and kinetic art of Modernist photography and film. The title of his Bauhaus book, *Malerei, Photographie, Film* (*Painting, Photography, Film*), was partly a misnomer because the

pages contained only short references to painting; there were no paintings in the hundred-odd illustrations. Instead, experimental photographs were shown – ones that had been made without a camera by exposing light directly onto film *(<fig. 13.6)* – alongside photomontages, abstract compositions and images of unusual subjects. These images were followed by a series of spreads in which type and photographs were used in combination, each vying for prominence with the other, though separated by Moholy-Nagy's characteristic use of thick rules to form a sketch of the storyline of an as-yet-unmade experimental film *(fig. 13.7)*. Moholy-Nagy called this arrangement an example of 'typophoto', a form of design he considered to be 'the most visually exact rendering of communication'. By using photographs in the place of some words, the meaning of any communication could be pinned down with more precision and concision than with words alone. But it was not just the ability of a picture to paint a thousand words that made it valuable. Equally important was the way they and the words were combined. Conventionally, when text and photographs appeared together, as in a magazine say, they were more or less clearly separated. In this orthodox form of 'linear typography', as Moholy-Nagy called it, both were passive vehicles of meaning. Like virtuous children, they were to be seen but not heard. In typophoto, however, they should be seen, heard and listened

13.8: 'Kandinsky zum 60 Geburtstag' exhibition poster designed by Herbert Bayer, 1926

to. By appearing within a more creative and dynamic arrangement, like the one he employed for his film sketch, they were active participants in the provision of meaning.

In placing so much emphasis on the creative potential of photography, Moholy-Nagy was reflecting a common view among the Constructivist avant-garde. For them painting, whether it be representational or expressive, had become an outmoded method of image making. As Moholy-Nagy explained in his text, his preference for the mechanical over the handmade was not just the knee-jerk response of a neophyte. It was more positive than that. It was born out of the twin recognition that the cold, hard purity of mechanical reproduction could have a special form of beauty of its own, and more than that, that by breaking free of the human prejudice and artfulness that plagued the painter's hand, these new methods of image making could come closer to revealing the world as it really was. Put simply, a photographic print was more truthful than a painted picture. It was in keeping with this preference for the impersonal that, at this time, Moholy-Nagy marked the back of his images with a date and a number, as though they were industrial products, rather than signing the front with his signature.

Since all Moholy-Nagy's designing had to be done outside of the hours spent running the Preliminary

Course and the metal workshop, the organization of the remaining graphic work was assigned to the new head of the printing workshop, a talented 25-year-old ex-pupil, Herbert Bayer. As his design of a poster for an exhibition of watercolours by the Bauhaus teacher Kandinsky shows, Bayer had quickly absorbed the principles of De Stijl and Constructivism, with their respective emphases on geometrical alignment and diagonal dynamism *(fig. 13.8)* – in this case both were cleverly achieved by rotating the paper or printed matter by 7° before printing – but he was equally quick to then synthesize his learning into a new, more rational and orderly style. The facility provided by the new workshop to design and print under the one roof allowed him to experiment and refine his designs. It led him to develop the Bauhaus's style of graphic design into its most distinct and coherent form.

One of Bayer's earliest tasks was to design a new school letterhead *(> fig. 13.9)*. The difference between it and Moholy-Nagy's Weimar version *(< fig. 13.5)* for the school's publishing company shows how Bayer's greater attention to the principle of functionalism produced a more considered and minimal arrangement. He stripped away the heavy red bands and the symbolic logo which had so dominated Moholy-Nagy's design, and replaced them with a simple new logo: the school's name, 'Bauhaus Dessau', in bold lowercase letters, which was

13.9: Bauhaus letterhead designed by Herbert Bayer, 1927

given extra emphasis by being set within a red rectangular box. The remaining text on the letterhead was broken into small, readable chunks and then aligned down the page in such a way that the reader would be led from one to the next in order of relevance. This concern for the practical workings of the design even extended to how the letter would be sent. By printing two thin lines on the left edge of the letterhead, he provided a guide to double folding the page so that the address, which had its position marked similarly with four thin corner marks, could be read through the window of an envelope.

This example of Bayer's letterhead shows another kind of text too: text that has been hammered onto the page with the keys of a typewriter. This, now almost extinct, but previously ubiquitous form of print had first appeared in a practicable form as early as the 1860s, though it took several more decades before the machine that made it, the typewriter, had acquired the features that would allow its letters to become an essential tool for office work. Such features included the ability to see what was written as one typed; a shift key, which allowed capitals and lowercase letters to be typed from a single set of alphabetic keys rather than two separate sets, as was initially the case; and a replaceable inked ribbon. The legibility and immediacy of typing, and, at the hands of a skilled typist, its astonishing speed (a proficient touch-typist can type considerably faster – 60 words per minute (wpm) – than he or she can write – 20 wpm) heralded the slow death of a tradition of fine handwriting which had continued in an unbroken series of evolving styles for over a thousand years. The art of habitually writing Latin letters in an elegant, joined up or cursive script had been passed down by monks to a larger group of professional scribes, before being taken up by the even more numerous members of the educated class, for whom this kind of writing became the first measure of gentility. Throughout this protracted period, it survived the threat posed by the invention of printing; indeed, it thrived on the exposure that printing provided partly through writing manuals but also copies of handwritten documents. Such items gave the art of penmanship a greater prominence than it had ever achieved in the era of the manuscript. Schools taught it and commercial clerics soon made it their own; until, that is, the typewriter became commonplace. By the middle of the twentieth century, penmanship both as an ideal, as something valuable in itself, and as a discipline, had been almost completely usurped by this very efficient form of mechanical writing. Today, most adult handwriting is so unpractised it looks primitive, almost childlike. Even on the rare occasion when it has flowed from the pen of an expert calligrapher, its very mannered and self-consciously beautiful flourishes seem only to emphasize the loss of any common kind of truly living, workaday script.

Today, the typewriter's letters have become victims of their protean progeny, which we now tap out through a computer keyboard. Though we might exult in being able to clothe our writing in any number of aesthetic guises through the simple click of a mouse, it is likely that Bayer and his fellow Modernists were perfectly accepting, or approving even, of the single, mechanical-looking typeface that had been moulded onto their typewriters' keys. The very uncalligraphic and impersonal nature of these monospaced letters (each of the keys took up an equal amount of space regardless of whether the letter was a narrow one, like an 'l', or wide, like an 'm') and the way they were set onto the paper, in a subtle grid of evenly spaced columns as well as rows, would surely have appealed to Bayer's preference for order and simplicity.

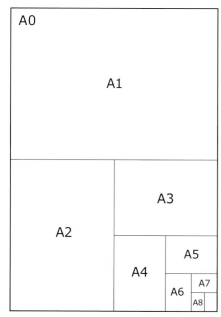

13.10: A-size proportions

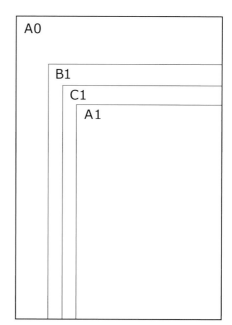

13.11: A, B and C sizes

Confirmation of this preference was provided by the change he made to the size of letterhead paper. He chose to use a new kind of format, the A4 size, which was one of a series that had been formulated by a German organization only a few years earlier, in 1922. In their attempt to rationalize the multitude of more or less haphazard paper sizes then in use, they had devised a whole system of sizes comprising four groups, the A, B, C and D series, all of which had the same proportion of height to width. The proportion was defined by the ratio of 1:√2 (1: 1.414) which, by a quirk of mathematical magic, replicated itself each time a sheet was cut or folded in half parallel with its short edge *(fig. 13.10)*. The resultant half size was always the same proportion as the previous full size, and no matter how many times the paper was folded it continued to be so. Being the only ratio of a rectangle that self-replicates in this way, each series acquired a standard set of sizes from a sequence of successive halvings.

The master series was the A series, and its large poster size, called A0, the foundational size from which all others were derived. The surface area of the large A0 size was one square metre, and thus it linked the entire scheme to the metric system of measurement. By halving the A0 size, the second size in the series, A1, was arrived at. By halving A1, the third size, A2, was made, and so on and so forth. While the A series was to be used for most printing, alternative sizes were provided by the B, C and D series. Each size in the B

series sat in between two successive A sizes (because each B size was the geometric mean between two A sizes, meaning that the same factor of magnification used to scale, say, A0 down to B1 also scaled B1 down to A1, *fig. 13.11*). Similarly, sizes in the C series were the geometric mean between the A and B series; thus the C1 size sat between A1 and the larger B1 size, C2 between A2 and B2, etc. Later, the C series was adopted as the standard size for envelopes, because it fitted the A series so well. The names for these new standard sizes were usually prefixed by the acronym DIN (*Deutsche Institut für Normung*), though today, after the worldwide adoption of the first three series – North American countries being notable exceptions – they are usually referred to as 'ISO' sizes (not originally, as is often presumed, an acronym of the International Organization for Standardization, the body that has promoted them, but rather an abbreviation of the Greek *isos* meaning 'equal').

The size of Bayer's letterhead was novel, but it was not offensively so; its merits were clear and rational. The same could not be said for Bayer's controversial use of type, made up as it was entirely out of lowercase letters. Bayer banished capitals from all his designs during this period. The results would have looked particularly striking to German readers, who, from the early sixteenth century, had been used to seeing capital letters not only as other Europeans had, at the beginning of sentences and names, but also at the beginning of all nouns. Bayer's rejection of such an established convention only increased

abcdefghi jklmnopqr stuvwxyz

HERBERT BAYER: Abb. 1. Alfabet
„g" und „k" sind noch als
unfertig zu betrachten

Beispiel eines Zeichens
in größerem Maßstab
Präzise optische Wirkung

sturm blond

13.13: Stencil lettering, Josef Albers, 1926

13.12: Universal lettering designed by Herbert Bayer, 1926

the provocation that he and others at the Bauhaus had caused by their complete reliance on sanserif type. Though sanserifs had become common enough for headings on posters, it was rare in small sizes on stationery and text for all kinds of continuous reading. For many Germans, the long-standing preference for Gothic letters, in newspapers and books especially, was linked to their national identity, not least since two of their most cherished historical figures, Johannes Gutenberg and Martin Luther *(<p. 65)*, had themselves favoured Gothic type. Thus, the Bauhaus's rejection of two distinctively German characteristics of print, Gothic type and capital letters, was considered by many within the printing industry to be a perversion bordering on the offensive. They were not persuaded to think otherwise by the explanation Bayer printed at the bottom of an early version of the letterhead: 'Text loses nothing when composed only of lowercase letters, but becomes easier to read, easier to learn, essentially more economic. Why is there for one sound, for example 'a', two signs 'A' and 'a'? One sound, one sign. Why two alphabets for one word, why double the number of signs when half would achieve the same?'

For Bayer, as for his colleague Moholy-Nagy, the preservation of a national identity was among the worst reasons for choosing a particular style of design. Both men had seen how, within the wider political context, the claims of nationalism had led Germany into a horrific war and the protracted difficulties that followed

defeat. If the future were to be peaceful and prosperous, Germans would have to exchange their divisive nationalism for a broader and more inclusive identity. Such a change would depend, in part, on a more universal form of communication, one that emphasized the common bond between nations, not the differences. The use of lowercase sanserif letters was one small step in the direction of this kind of international solidarity. By representing type at its most basic, Bayer hoped to reveal the common form that lay behind all the varied national styles of printed letters.

Bayer's dedication to the idea of universal forms led him to look more closely at the shape of each sanserif letter. In 1925 he began to experiment with the construction of a new kind of sanserif *(fig. 13.12)*, one that was made out of the simplest geometric shapes rather than those inherited from any historical model. He wanted to construct his new letters out of the most elementary building blocks of geometric form, more elemental even than the square and the triangle, both of which could be made out of smaller units of straight lines. All his lowercase letters – again, he ignored the capitals – consisted of either straight lines, circles or segments of a circle arranged in ways that made only the most minimal shape necessary to identify each letter (the lowercase 'f' had a cross-bar on the right side only, and the long vertical stroke in letters such as 'b' and 'd', or 'p' and 'q', did not extend downwards or upwards respectively beyond the curve of the circular bowl). He described his letters as a

13.14: Product catalogue, Herbert Bayer, 1925

13.15: Bauhaus brochure, Herbert Bayer, 1927

'new machine alphabet', one that was designed to suit all methods of reproduction: handwriting, stencilling, printing and typing. But though his sanserif was made out of apparently 'universal' and easily reproducible parts, its usefulness was limited. The very uneven visual weight of the letters – the dense, cramped 'm' compared to the overtly open 'n' – meant that the type could only really be effective in large sizes.

A similar kind of experiment was carried out in the same year by another ex-student-come-teacher, Josef Albers (1888–1976), who designed a 'stencil' lettering out of squares, triangles and quarter circles fitted onto a grid *(fig. 13.13)*. As with Bayer, Albers' strict adherence to a modular scheme restricted the letters' legibility and, hence, their versatility. However, they did have an emphatic quality which designers at the Bauhaus were able to exploit by using them on items of industrial design as well as in print.

Bayer also applied his rational method of design to more complex items, such as the school's new curriculum and a new product catalogue *(fig. 13.14)*. The contents of each were laid out within a simple grid system, which allocated a specific style and position for each of the different kinds of information that repeatedly appeared on each page. Not only did this approach make the task of designing each page easier, it also enabled the reader to gather information more quickly. The basic, repeated structure sparked a set of expectations in the reader's mind as to where each common kind of

information might be found. In using this method to exploit the readers' perceptual habits – how the mind understands what the eyes see – Bayer hoped to relay the contents of his design more directly and cogently. It was an approach that ran counter to all previous Modernist designers, from the Futurists to the Constructivists, who had exulted in breaking free from the restrictions of the traditional form of the printed page. But this did not mean that Bayer was any less Modernist. He accepted restrictions when they were necessary for the job in hand rather than imposed by the weight of tradition. The spartan alignment of type and image that made up the cover of the Bauhaus's brochure of 1927 *(fig.13.15)* is a succinct example. But equally, he was content to reject the grid when the situation allowed, as it did on the cover of the Bauhaus's journal *(>fig. 13.16)* a year later. Its surreal cover montage indicated the direction in which his interest in the perceptual process was to lead him. His later experiments with photography and montage continued this Surrealist bent.

Towards the end of 1927, Gropius suddenly announced he would be leaving. Years of dealing with the school's complex administration and negotiating with local governments had dulled his enthusiasm for the directorship. It had also robbed him of the time he needed to practise his architecture, an activity he intended to pursue full-time. For a number of teachers, Bayer and Moholy-Nagy included, a Bauhaus without Gropius

*13.16: Bauhaus journal cover designed by
Herbert Bayer, 1928*

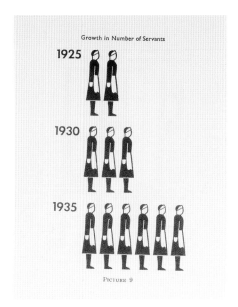

*13.17: Human chart from 'International Picture
Language' by Otto Neurath, 1936*

would not be a Bauhaus at all, and they too left. Their fear for the school's future was well founded. The new director, Hannes Meyer (1889–1954), though more politically motivated than Gropius, was a less gifted politician, and he was sacked by the local government after only two years. His tenure, though short, was not unproductive. Meyer gave architecture more prominence, emphasizing in particular its collaborative nature. 'Building is nothing but organization: social, technical, economical, psychological organization.' Accordingly, students were encouraged to conduct more objective and systematic research before beginning their designs. They were helped in this direction by a number of visiting teachers, among them an Austrian philosopher, economist and social scientist called Otto Neurath (1882–1945). While a member of the so-called 'logical positivist' group of philosophers that had formed in Vienna, Neurath had begun to devise a sign system in collaboration with a designer and illustrator, Gerd Arntz (1900–88). Neurath's initial objective had been to develop a form of pictorial statistics that could convey complicated social and economic facts to a largely

uneducated Viennese public, but this not unambitious aim was soon trumped by the even more challenging goal of developing a comprehensive picture language for an international audience, which he called the 'International System of Typographic Picture Education' or Isotype. Neurath saw that a system of simple symbols had the potential to cross the language barrier in a way that words on their own could not. It was a view he simplified into the slogan 'Words divide, pictures unite', which is not to say that he thought pictures had the power to communicate all things to all people. His system of charts and diagrams relied on a combination of words and pictures, not least to clarify those symbols that carried specific cultural meanings.

The human chart above *(fig. 13.17)*, which appeared in 1936 in his book *International Picture Language*, shows the increase in the number of household servants employed over a given period. To readers who were familiar with the European dress code, the diagram was almost self-explanatory, but to those who weren't the inclusion of the diagram's title was essential. Both groups, however, benefited from the care taken by Neurath and Arntz to exclude from their symbols any 'details which do not improve the [symbols'] narrative character'. In this they pointed the way forward for the creation of the many simple symbols that we depend on today, be they in the communal space of an international airport or the more private domain of our computer screens or the screens of our mobile phones.

Following Meyer's departure from the Bauhaus in 1930, the German Modernist architect Ludwig Mies van der Rohe (1886–1969) was appointed director. During his stewardship the Bauhaus became more like a normal school of architecture – printing and advertising were all but eliminated – but outside events prevented Van der Rohe from developing the school fully in the way he would have liked. In 1932 the Bauhaus was forced to move out of its beloved buildings into a temporary home. Three months later restrictions imposed on the school by the Nazi government led the staff and students, in a characteristic spirit of self-determination, to dissolve the school rather than have their aims compromised.

It is telling in its ignorance and hypocracy that long before the Nazis banned nearly all Modern art for being 'un-German', 'Jewish' and 'Bolshevist' – examples were famously hung up for ridicule in 1937 in an exhibition titled *Degenerate Art* – the symbol they chose to represent their nationalist cause was a black geometric shape, the swastika (whose origins are ancient and multicultural), set on a white circle in a red rectangle. They are a combination of elements that would not have looked out of place on an early Bauhaus letterhead.

Even before the school closed a number of German designers had begun to adopt the Bauhaus's new, more functional style of design. None did so with as much rigour or finesse as the young designer Jan Tschichold (1902–74), who seemed to combine Bayer's sense of order with Moholy-Nagy's dynamism. But by filtering both through his own highly developed sense of spatial balance he created a very refined form of asymmetrical design. Born in Leipzig, then the centre of the printing and publishing trade in Germany, Tschichold took an informal apprenticeship with his father, a sign-painter, before studying at Leipzig's reputable graphic arts college. He subsequently spent some time working as a typographic designer in a large printing firm, where he acquired the practical knowledge that was to become one his great strengths. But it was his visit to the Bauhaus's exhibition of 1923 that had the greatest effect on his development. There and then he felt his young life change course. He left the exhibition 'in turmoil'. The calligraphic forms that had dominated his previous designs were gradually eclipsed (though, contrary to belief, never completely so) by the full repertoire of Bauhaus effects: the signature colours of black and red, sanserif lettering arranged asymmetrically in dynamic contrast with thick rules and photographs, and each of these elements cohering with

13.18: Prospectus for 'Die neue Typographie', Jan Tschichold, 1928

the negative space, the white parts of the page, to form an orderly, balanced whole.

Tschichold's commitment to Bauhaus design inspired him to write what was the first truly Modernist typographic manual. Simply called *Die neue Typographie* or 'The New Typography' – taking Moholy-Nagy's phrase *(<p.192)* – it was published in 1928 when Tschichold was only 25 years old. Though others had written about the technical aspects of printing, or touched on such aspects as the classification of letterforms or the systems of measurement, none had produced such a comprehensive and practical guide to the art of modern graphic design. Using the strident and sometimes haughty language common to many Modernist texts, Tschichold began the first half of the book with a provocative philosophical justification of the new method, before delivering a brief but learned description of printing's history and a systematic outline of Modern art's development. In the more practical second half, he showed how the New Typography should be applied, be it to a periodical, poster or logo. The examples he chose to illustrate the style formed a collection of work from

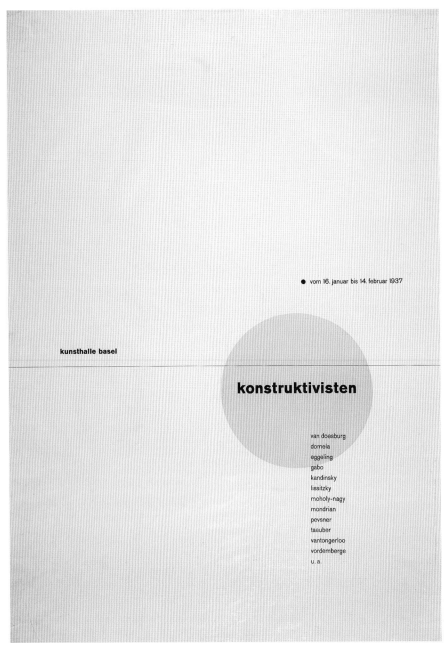

13.19: 'Konstruktivisten' exhibition poster designed by Jan Tschichold, 1937

the avant-garde's brightest typographic luminaries. Since Tschichold was a true craftsman, thoroughly trained and widely informed, neither shying from details, nor losing sight of the broad principles, he was able to communicate the method that lay behind these examples in a way that could be understood by the trade.

His own design work was equally illuminating. At first glance, the design of his book's prospectus *(fig. 13.18)* appears to conform to the rigid rules that had guided much of Bayer's work: sanserif type, with a clear contrast between its bold and regular weights, is laid out asymmetrically in neat columns. And yet the short, thick vertical bar and the bottom column of text both sit outside the two-column grid established by the main text above. By subtly breaking out of a clear vertical alignment, Tschichold breathed life into an otherwise entirely formulaic design.

Over time he was to hone his mastery of this kind of dynamic, balanced asymmetry to such an extent that even the most free-form and minimal arrangements

ABCDEFGHIJKLMNOPQRST
UVWXYZ
abcdefghijklmnopqrstuvwxyz
0123456789

ABCDEFGHIJKLMNOPQRST
UVWXYZ
abcdefghijklmnopqrstuvwxyz
0123456789

13.20: Futura roman and italic, Paul Renner, 1927–30

were suffused with a sense of harmonious equilibrium. His poster for an exhibition of Constructivism is the supreme example *(fig. 13.19)*. It is a study in contrasting pairs: the pair of rectangles, large and small, created by a thin bisecting horizontal line; the pair of circles, large grey and tiny black above; the pair of arrangements of small light text, a single line above and a thin column below; and, lastly, the pair of lines of bold text in contrasting sizes. None of them derived their character from any overarching rationale, there is no apparent formula guiding their placement, and yet the tension generated between them and, also, between them and the edges of the poster, creates a dynamic harmony that reverberates throughout.

In addition to his writing and designing, Tschichold promoted the Bauhaus style through teaching. From 1926 to 1933 he taught typography at the *Meisterschule für Deutschlands Buchdrucker* (Advanced College for German Printers) in Munich to classes of 25 students or more, many of whom had come from outside Germany. Where much of the work at the Bauhaus was conducted in a spirit of experimentation, the attitude in Munich was one of consolidation. Each student was given individual instruction in how to create clear and functional design through the careful placement of judiciously weighted and spaced type. This more considered and practical approach was reflected in the design of a new, geometric sanserif typeface *(fig. 13.20)*, which the school's director, Paul Renner (1878–1956), had created for a local publisher. In 1924, the year before becoming director, Renner began the task of making, as the publisher's brief put it, the 'typeface of our time'.

But, rather than base his design exclusively on abstract geometric forms, as those at the Bauhaus had done, Renner referred back to the Romans' inscribed square capital letter: 'I did not want to glorify the compass as a tool, instead I wanted to lead [typographic] form out of the wilderness and back to its origins.' Roman letterers had also designed their square capitals around the simple proportions of the square, circle and triangle, but never fixedly so. They made fine adjustments to each letter – e.g. the 'O' was not perfectly circular but slightly narrowed, and the vertical strokes of the 'M' were splayed *(<fig. 2.19, p. 42)* – so that together they would cohere into a unified set of shapes. The same sort of adjustments led Renner to make his lowercase letters blend with the capitals. Their shape 'followed from the desire to carry the strict geometric structure of the capitals into the small letters' and to avoid 'all those small qualities that creep in … when the form is developed from writing'; thus, his 'a', 'l', 't' and 'u' had their tails docked.

The resultant typeface, which he called Futura in spite of its historical basis, was released by the Bauer type foundry in 1927 and proved to be immediately popular. It was praised both for its versatility and its legibility. The type could be used as a text face in books as readily as a display type on posters. While the simple forms of its letters were valued for the contribution they made to the legibility of a text, they were also appreciated for their own sake. Otto Neurath saw them as the perfect complement to his own pared-down diagrams and used them in many of his publications *(<fig. 13.17)*. As the demand for this new typeface spread across Europe to the United States (where it was known as 'Twentieth Century' or 'Spartan') so its range of weights and condensed forms was expanded. By the end of the 1930s, Futura had become one of the most extensively used types of its time.

Running parallel to the Bauhaus and other proponents of New Typography was an entirely opposite view of printing and letterform design. It was held by a small but influential section of the publishing industry, connected to or existing within the so-called private presses, which aimed to produce small numbers of expensive books with techniques and equipment that differed little from those used by Gutenberg nearly 500 years earlier.

THE CENTAUR. WRITTEN BY MAURICE DE GUÉRIN AND NOW TRANSLATED FROM THE FRENCH BY GEORGE B. IVES.

I Was born in a cavern of these mountains. Like the river in yonder valley, whose first drops flow from some cliff that weeps in a deep grotto, the first moments of my life sped amidst the shadows of a secluded retreat, nor vexed its silence. As our mothers draw near their term, they retire to the caverns, and in the innermost recesses of the wildest of them all, where the darkness is most dense, they bring forth, uncomplaining, offspring as silent as themselves. Their strength-giving milk enables us to endure without weakness or dubious struggles the first difficulties of life; yet we leave our caverns later than you your cradles. The reason is that there is a tradition amongst us that the early days of life must be secluded and guarded, as days engrossed by the gods.

My growth ran almost its entire course in the darkness where I was born. The innermost depths of my home were so far within the bowels of the mountain, that I should not have known in which direction the opening lay, had it not been that the winds at times blew in and caused a sudden coolness and confusion. Sometimes, too, my mother returned, bringing with her the perfume of the valleys, or dripping wet from the streams to which she resorted. Now, these her home-comings, although they told me naught of the valleys or the streams, yet, being attended by emanations therefrom, disturbed my thoughts, and I wandered about, all agitated, amidst my darkness. 'What,' I would say to myself, 'are these places to which my mother goes and what power reigns there which summons her so frequently? To what influences is one there exposed,

14 THE WEIGHT OF TRADITION
Traditional Typography, c.1910 – c.1947

The tragedy for early Modernist art was that it was rejected by the people for whom it had been created. Each of the movements that made up the first wave of Modernism, from the Cubists to the Bauhaus, had the welfare of ordinary people at heart, and each had hoped their art might play a part in creating a more just and equitable society. The majority of the public, however, looked on the varied forms of newfangled art with incomprehension and even hostility. One of the earliest exhibitions of Modernist art in America, the infamous Armory Show (so named after the regimental armoury in New York City where the show had opened), which toured three eastern states in 1913, is remembered as much for the reaction it provoked as for the art it displayed. On the final night in Chicago, students from the city's most prestigious art school staged a mock trial in which a dummy of the French painter Henri Matisse, which they labelled 'Henri Hairmattress', was condemned to a bout of ritual stabbing before being set on fire. Ex-president 'Teddy' Roosevelt, in what was generally a laudatory review of the exhibition, nevertheless described the work by Matisse and other Post-Impressionists as belonging to a 'lunatic fringe'.

On the other side of the Atlantic, Modernist art was subject to a similar strain of bemused and mocking rejection. Political leaders from both the right and the left, some of whom had initially promoted the new art, came to reject it in favour of more traditional forms. This lack of appreciation was not only felt in the fine arts; Futurist, Dadaist and Constructivist styles of graphic design never enjoyed the level of popularity that, say, the Art and Crafts or Art Nouveau design had achieved decades earlier. During the first decades of the twentieth century, most designers and printers were content to rely on the various, standard historical styles of design they had inherited from their predecessors. And those, such as the designers of the Plakatstil posters, who had been willing to try something new but not in the service of avant-garde politics, tended to stay within the bounds of realism *(<fig. 11.5, p.166)*.

In most book and newspaper design, where type predominated and where the force of historical styles was especially strong, a thoroughgoing revival of traditional typography took place. The revival was most visible in western Europe, where social and artistic values had been threatened but not destroyed, as they had been in eastern Europe through the combination of war and revolution. The threat to the traditional form of the printed page, which had been posed first by industrialization and then by the avant-garde's shockingly modern abstract asymmetry and sanserif text, also reached across the Atlantic to the United States. In an attempt to repel these attacks, groups of influential designers and printers on both continents were led to look more closely at some of the very earliest styles of printing. Letterforms and layouts from the first German, Italian and Dutch books were scoured and copied *(fig. 14.1)*. For this combined group of transatlantic traditionalists, the refined, classical grandeur of the best early books seemed to encapsulate all that was worth preserving in print.

Many had been pointed in this direction at the end of the nineteenth century by the proponents of the Arts and Crafts *(<ch. 9, p. 137)*. The English artist and designer William Morris, in particular, had shown what could be achieved when book printers were prepared to approach their work with a sound historical and practical knowledge *(<fig. 9.8, p. 143)*. He had printed books in much the same way as Gutenberg had nearly 450 years earlier: hand-cut punches, cast, composed and inked by hand, were printed on handmade paper with a traditional screw press. But while Morris's successors shared his love of Renaissance typography, they were less wedded through the force of ideology to traditional methods of printing. The new century had provided them with a

< 14.1: 'The Centaur' designed by Bruce Rogers, 1915

radically new technology, one that, with the exception of a few purists, they were happy to exploit.

The technology in question was a method of casting and composing type by mechanical means rather than by hand. The amount of time and manpower required to cast type mechanically was much less than doing so by hand, and the speed of setting text with a machine was three to four times faster. The first composing machine to be developed sufficiently for commercial use was invented in the United States by a young German émigré, Ottmar Mergenthaler (1854−99), during the 1890s. Mergenthaler's initial aim had been to find an efficient way of reproducing typewritten documents. It had led him to devise a keyboard through which a series of letter moulds, known as matrices, could be brought together in a line corresponding to the sequence of letters in a line of text. The machine filled the combined matrices with molten metal (hence this method of composing being referred to as 'hot-metal') to produce a single, horizontal block (known as a 'slug'). In this way, by simultaneously casting and composing a line of text into a single piece of metal, and doing so for each line of text, one after the other, it was possible for a single operator to prepare an entire page for printing. Mergenthaler's descriptively named Linotype (line-of-type) machine was patented in 1884 and first used commercially in 1886 by the New York *Tribune* which, being a newspaper, placed a premium on preparing each edition quickly. The less time required to prepare the text, the greater the chance of being able to include the latest news stories 'hot off the press'.

Mergenthaler's invention was closely followed by the invention of a rival machine (made up of two separate units rather than the single Linotype unit) called the Monotype, which also cast and composed type using hot metal, though, significantly, it cast single pieces of type (mono-type), rather than type in lines. It too was invented in the United States, by a civil servant and part-time inventor called Tolbert Lanston (1844−1914), who received a patent for his machine in 1887. While the faster Linotype machine managed to establish itself in the newspaper industry, Lanston's Monotype became the machine of choice for printers working at the higher end of book production. Its type, being harder than Linotype metal, produced printed letters that approached the quality achieved by traditionally made type; the control for positioning the type on the page was superior to that of the Linotype, which was important when setting text with mathematical symbols for example;

by using individual pieces of type, corrections could be made more easily (the Linotype needed the whole line replacing, though this was less of a disadvantage when lines were short, as in a newspaper column); and each individual piece of type could be retained for use in hand-setting or, indeed, be specially made for that purpose (clearly, Linotype's slugs could not be reused, other than being thrown back into the mix of molten metal for recasting).

Both kinds of composing machine provided the revival of traditional typography, which the Arts and Crafts had started, with a new impetus. The Linotype and the Monotype machines required their own, specially made matrices, and a complete set of matrices needed to be made for each separate size of type. Thus, as composing machines grew in popularity, a vast number of new matrices for a whole range of fonts, in all their various sizes, had to be produced. The range of type designs required by printers during the first decades of the twentieth century was limited to the standard set of historical models that catered for most forms of printing. The most common kind was the late eighteenth- and early nineteenth-century style of letter called Modern, whose letter shapes were characterized by a strong contrast between the thick and thin strokes (<*fig. 7.12, p.120*). The next most popular model was the rounder and uniformly weighted Old Style letter, whose shapes were based on some of the Venetian types made during the latter part of the fifteenth century. Complementing both were other styles, such as Gothic and, to a lesser degree, sanserif, a popular style for publicity printing, and then again various national scripts, such as Gaelic, Cyrillic and Greek. All were made available for the new machines, and in being so, they helped popularize this new method of setting in markets old and new in various parts of the world.

The process of making such a large number of matrices quickly and consistently could not have been achieved without the recent adaptation of a mechanical type-cutting tool, which had first been created for making large, wooden poster types, back in the middle of the nineteenth century. By 1885, an American type founder called Linn Boyd Benton (1844−1932) had modified and extended the use of this type cutter so that it could cut small sizes of type out of metal. By exploiting the pantographic principle (the Greek *panto* means 'all' or 'universal') on which the earlier cutter had been based, Benton made it possible for the outline of a large drawing of a letter to be traced with a sharp point and

14.2: 'The Compleat Angler', title page designed by Bruce Rogers, 1909

ABCDEFGHIJKLMNOPQRST
UVWXYZ
abcdefghijklmnopqrstuvwxyz
0123456789

*ABCDEFGHIJKLMNOPQRST
UVWXYZ*
abcdefghijklmnopqrstuvwxyz
0123456789

14.3: Centaur, roman designed by Bruce Rogers, 1912

then, through a series of pivoted levers, for the movement of the tracing point to be replicated on a reduced scale by a cutting tool that was sharp enough to cut through type-metal. The increased accuracy of his pantographic cutter and the subsequent improvements made to it by the Linotype and Monotype companies during the first decades of the twentieth century convinced each that it would be commercially viable to extend the range of typefaces they offered. But, rather than create entirely novel letter shapes, as the De Stijl or Bauhaus designers were beginning to do, they took a more conservative approach and for the most part focused on expanding their range of historical styles. In doing so, unlike their Modernist contemporaries, they were responding to a commercial market which would have rejected too much experimentation. They were also taking advantage of the particular expertise of those people most able to design type, many of whom had had their interest in letterforms kindled by the Arts and

Crafts movement. These designers had acquired a working knowledge of types by joining or setting up small-scale, private presses dedicated to producing limited editions of high-quality books. In this way, paradoxically, the transformation of printing into an almost wholly mechanical process during the first decades of the twentieth century led to a further emphasis on historical type styles and a concomitant revival of traditional page design.

Examples of this tendency can be seen in the work of the American type and book designer Bruce Rogers (1870–1957). His title page for a 1909 edition of *The Compleat Angler (fig. 14.2)* follows the pre-Modernist convention of a centred typography placed within traditionally proportioned margins, and each of the printed parts reflects historical styles: the title type is a version of Caslon, which Rogers himself designed *(fig. 14.3)*, while the lower italic incorporates some of the swash capitals of Italian Renaissance scribes. Though the illustration is not an etching, its drawing style and subject matter look almost like something the Dutch seventeenth-century artist Rembrandt might have done. Perhaps only the inventive mix of line and leaf in the angular border shows a hint of modernity.

Rogers produced a more fully antiquated design in 1915 for an English translation of a French novel called *Le Centaure (< fig. 14.1)*. The book was published in 1915 in a limited edition of only 135 copies, but the faithfulness with which it mimicked the typographic style of the Renaissance, and the precision with which its pages were laid out – his wife Anna had set the whole thing by hand – have made it one of the most highly prized books of any era. The type had been designed by Rogers the year before for the Metropolitan Museum of Art in New York, who had used it in various kinds of publicity material, but this was its first appearance in a book. The shape of its letters had been based on the Venetian type of the fifteenth-century printer Nicolas Jenson, whose foundational form Rogers had seen in the 1470 edition of the writings of Eusebius (<*fig. 5.4, p. 86*). In order to gain a better appreciation of the features that produced such a balanced, even tone of text, Rogers took a photograph of a page of the book and then practised writing the letters out with a broad pen over some enlarged copies of the photograph. In response to requests from the printing trade, Rogers arranged to make it available for machine composition by approaching the Lanston Monotype's sister company in Britain, the Monotype Corporation. The version he made with them was released in 1929 with an accompanying italic (not designed by Rogers) which was based on the script of the sixteenth-century calligrapher and writing master, Ludovico Arrighi (<*p. 90–1*). The skill and faithfulness with which Rogers used this and other types to replicate a range of late Renaissance and Baroque book styles earned him the backhanded compliment of 'the greatest artificer of the book who ever lived', and led bibliophiles to seek his books out for the archaic beauty of their design rather than the content of the writing.

Of all the American traditionalists from the early twentieth century, Rogers may well have been the most accomplished book designer, but as a designer of type he was much less prolific and less broadly influential than his friend and compatriot Frederic Goudy (1865–1947). Goudy only started to design types in his mid-thirties, yet by the time of his death, at the age of 82, he had created around 120 different typefaces. Such unstinting application is even more remarkable when one learns that he twice lost his working drawings and printing equipment as a result of fire, and also that he was at his most prolific in his sixties, even though this period was marked by the loss of sight in one eye. Like Rogers, Goudy also came to learn the subtleties of type design through the hand-craft traditions of the private press. His early love of hand-lettering led him, in the first phase of his working life, to find work as a letter artist, a commercial printer and a teacher, though eventually it developed into a passion for type design. In order to pursue this passion he started his own press and foundry in 1903. It was there, within the freedom of his own commercial practice, that he was able to bolster his theoretical and historical knowledge of type with a thorough understanding of the craft of type design. The craft proved to be so compelling it sometimes led him to create a whole new type for a particular item of print.

Almost half his designs were regular book types (the other half included types for advertising or display and more specialized uses, such as Gothic, Greek and Hebrew text), and the majority of his book types were variations on a theme: the seriffed Old Style or Venetian types of the fifteenth century (<*fig. 5.6, p. 87*). He wrote disparagingly of the sanserif form and had no affection for hard-edged or geometrically regular types. His role as 'art adviser' to Lanston Monotype, which lasted for 27 years, would have given him licence to broaden his repertoire considerably had he been so inclined. But he rarely was. He retained his affection for this early style throughout.

Goudy asserted that 'the perfect type would be completely invisible'. By this he meant that the shapes of its letters would be free of any idiosyncrasies that take the reader's attention away from the text and onto the type itself. His own artistic temperament, however, made it a difficult ideal to live up to. In one of his descriptions of designing type, he confirmed what is evident to the eye; that if a type has been designed by Goudy, it will tend to look like a Goudy design: 'Once in a while a type face by some other designer seems to present an interesting movement or quality that I like. I take an early opportunity to make it mine, frankly and openly, in the same way that a writer might use exactly the same words as another, but by a new arrangement of them present a new thought, a new idea, or a new subtlety of expression … By copying carefully a few characters of the type that appeals to me drawn by another hand, I try to secure in my own drawings some certain movement or rhythm this may present. I soon discard my model and proceed from there, as it were, under my own steam.' Nearly all his designs carry traces of his own hand and eye.

The personal style within any type design is revealed by the individual features of the letters – the shape of the serifs or the swelling and tapering of the letter strokes – but putting into words precisely which features are most salient and why they are so is never easy. In this respect, the tongue is less subtle than the eye. Recognition of a distinct personal style usually relies on how the features work in combination rather than on any of the features individually. This fact explains why descriptions of personal styles tend to be couched in

ABCDEFGHIJKLMNOPQRS
TUVWXYZ
abcdefghijklmnopqrstuvwxyz
0123456789

ABCDEFGHIJKLMNOPQRS
TUVWXYZ
abcdefghijklmnopqrstuvwxyz
0123456789

ABCDEFGHIJKLMNOPQRS
TUVWXYZ
abcdefghijklmnopqrstuvwxyz
0123456789

14.4: Examples of typefaces designed by Frederic Goudy: Kennerley, 1911; Goudy Old Style, 1915; Deepdene, 1927

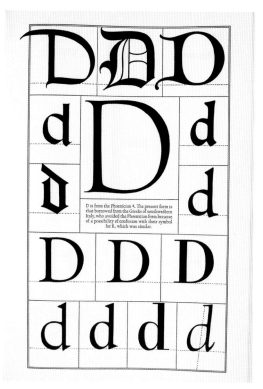

14.5: 'The Alphabet', Frederic Goudy, 1914

the impressionistic language of metaphor, more than in direct statements about specific shapes. Thus, the qualities that emanate from a Goudy type are usually those of quaintness or a slightly quirky homeliness. Such characteristics are prominent in one of his most popular types, an Old Style book type called Kennerley *(fig. 14.4)*, first designed in 1911 and reproduced by the type founders Lanston Monotype in 1920. Generally its letters have a softness which is reinforced by the irregular curves of the serifs, and some of the type's characters look self-consciously antiquated (the high horizontal bar of the 'A', for example). But a similar feeling of cosy antiquity is contained in other types of his, even when they lack those specific features *(fig. 14.5)*.

Bruce Rogers alluded to Goudy's conspicuous personal style in a short description he made of a Goudy type, 'even with occasional modifications this type, much as I admire it, was too striking in effect and had too strong an appeal as "typography"'. It can be argued, though, that by habitually putting something of his own personality into his types, Goudy was merely carrying out the task that had been assigned to him. The new composing machines required their own purpose-made matrices, and if no punches or types of a particular

historical typeface existed, both would have to be made from a set of drawings of each of the type's characters. Such drawings needed to be provided by someone with an eye for a compelling letter shape and a sound technical knowledge of how to construct a complete typeface: in other words, a designer. This overt separation of design from manufacture placed a greater emphasis on the importance of design as a discrete activity, which in turn conferred on the designer a greater status and authority (often at the expense of the more technically minded matrix makers, whose considerable skill at turning the designer's drawings into a workable product frequently went unrecognized). In this way, the composing machine helped to establish a new role within the print industry: that of the freelance type designer or typographer.

The growing prominence of the designer within the field of type production was recognized by the Linotype and Monotype companies. Each had chosen to equip their machines with historical typefaces, and such types had to be given a name. As mentioned above, their first series of typefaces was adapted from existing handmade punches and types, and so generally, they were given simple generic names such as 'Modern' or 'Antique Old

14.6: Cast of carved alphabet, Eric Gill, 1909

ABCDEFGHIJKLMNOPQRST
UVWXYZ
abcdefghijklmnopqrstuvwxyz
0123456789

ABCDEFGHIJKLMNOPQRST
UVWXYZ

14.7: Perpetua roman and titling

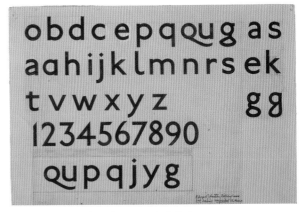

14.8: Drawing of Underground alphabet,
Edward Johnston, 1916

ABCDEFGHIJKLMNOPQRST
UVWXYZ
abcdefghijklmnopqrst
uvwxyz

14.9: New Johnston, 1979

Style'. But, as soon as it was realized that printers were more willing to take up the new technology if they were given a greater variety of type styles, the range was extended. Copies of other historical types were made and they were given the names of the original 'designer', that is the printer or punch-cutter. Thus, the series of typefaces released by the Monotype Corporation during the 1920s and 1930s pay tribute to some of the greatest names in Western printing: Plantin, Caslon, Baskerville and Bodoni. Lanston Monotype gave the same kind of recognition to Goudy, though because he designed so many types for them his name was combined with the generic style of the type, thus: Goudy Old Style, Goudy Modern, etc. (*<fig. 14.4).*

Neither Rogers nor Goudy had attempted to make entirely original designs. Their typefaces were conceived as either straight copies or, more loosely, interpretations of pre-existing types. One of the first typefaces to be designed without any direct reference to a specific pre-existing type or, indeed, any established typographic style was a seriffed type called Perpetua *(fig. 14.7)*, which was made for the Monotype Corporation by the English stone-carver and wood-engraver Eric Gill (1882–1940). In 1924, Gill had been asked by the company's influential typographic adviser, Stanley

Morison (1889–1967), to provide drawings for an 'original' seriffed face. Thus, it was not to be a specific revival, like Roger's Centaur, nor a general style, like Goudy Old Style, but neither was it an entirely modern form. Instead Gill turned to the letterform he had inherited from the craft tradition of stone-carving, which he had begun to imbue with his own particular style *(fig. 14.6)*. The influence of these stone-carved letters was honoured most explicitly in the design of a special set of capitals, called Perpetua Titling *(fig. 14.7)*, which retain, even in their digital form, as here, some of the grandeur of a classical inscription.

A similar genesis lay behind Gill's next and most popular typeface, the eponymous Gill Sans *(fig. 14.11)* which, though begun sometime after Perpetua, was released several years before it in 1929. (The success of its first incarnations, Gill Sans roman and an accompanying italic, led to the creation of other weights and display versions throughout the early 1930s.) This new sanserif was also unrelated to any previous type, but then it was not wholly related to his carving hand either. For this less traditional form of letter, Gill turned to the sanserif letters that his one-time teacher, Edward Johnston *(<p. 145–6)* had created for the London Underground (or London Electric Railways as it was called

14.10: Marble Arch Underground station, 1930s

ABCDEFGHIJKLMNOPQRST
UVWXYZ
abcdefghijklmnopqrstuvwxyz
0123456789

14.11: Gill Sans

14.12: 'St John's, Cambridge' poster designed by
Fred Taylor, 1927–30

then). Johnston had become a significant member of the
Arts and Crafts on account of the success he had had in
helping revive the art of calligraphy in Britain, and to
some degree, in Germany, during the first decade of the
century. It was surprising then that he should have been
commissioned to replace the Underground's various
Victorian 'grotesques' with a sanserif that would 'belong
unmistakably to the times in which we lived' *(fig. 14.8)*.
Johnston's sanserif was designed between 1915 and
1916, with some assistance from Gill. The proportions
of his 'block' (i.e. monoline) letters, as he called them,
with the thin, double-square 'E' and the almost circular
'O', were based on the ancient Roman square capital,
particularly the form that had been carved on the base
of the Trajan Column *(<fig. 2.19, p. 42)*. The lettering was
also distinguished by a calligraphic diamond-shaped
dot for the 'i' and 'j'. Thus the brave new world of
electric subterranean travel that London's Underground
must have represented *(fig. 14.10)* was allied to letters
whose 'essentially Roman forms link them with classical culture'.

Johnston's lettering, like its Roman model, was
made to be used in large sizes for display purposes,
initially on posters and then later as the names of stations. It became an important part of the Underground's

corporate identity (alongside the 'bull's-eye' logo – redrawn by Johnston from its previous solid disc shape
into its present circular one – and then later its map
>fig. 16.22, p. 255). Following the addition of new
weights and widths, it quickly became the most comprehensive lettering of its kind, and was later looked on as
a model not only for other subway systems but for transport lettering in general. (Eventually, it was redrawn
as New Johnston, and this new version continues to be
used in the London Underground today, *fig. 14.9*).

Gill's version of sanserif lettering also started out as
signage. He had first used a Johnston-based sanserif for
some of his own hand-painted signs and then on a shop
front for a bookseller friend. But when the Monotype
Corporation asked him to adapt his letters into a new
typeface, perhaps in the hope that it might repeat the
success of the recently released German sanserif Futura
(<p. 13.20, p. 203), Gill had to make sure his letters
would work in a wide range of applications. Since the
London & North-Eastern Railway company (LNER)
had expressed an interest in using such letters as their
corporate typeface, it was necessary to make sure
that they would be legible in the demanding realm of
printed menus and railway timetables as well as station
signs and posters *(fig. 14.12)*. In order to give the letters

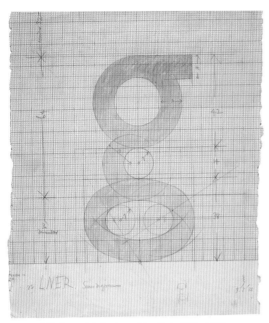

14.13: Gill Sans 'g' designed by Eric Gill, 1933

this versatility, Gill tapered some of the letters' strokes, at their joins especially, in order to avoid them looking excessively heavy when printed in small sizes (ink tends to 'fill in' around the join). Because he was less wedded to Roman classical proportions than Johnston, Gill adjusted the proportion of his letters away from the Roman model and more in the direction of his Perpetua type; indeed, the lowercase especially can be thought of as a sanserif version of it.

Perpetua seems to have influenced the form of his sanserif in other ways too. The protracted difficulties he and Monotype's technicians were having in converting the drawings of his letters into a satisfactory form for hot-metal composition made him aware of just how hard it was 'for a set of more or less tame employees … to know what a letter enlarged a hundred times [as they were in his own drawings] will look like when reduced to the size of the intended type'. Thus, when it came to the drawing out of his Gill Sans letters, he tried to make shapes that were mathematically measurable. A drawing of the lowercase 'g' from a special poster version of his sanserif, which he made on a sheet of tightly gridded graph paper *(fig. 14.13)*, shows how the classical proportions of Johnston's prototype had given way to a geometrically curved and straight-lined letter. Such a letter would have been easier for the matrix makers to reproduce.

In spite of its classical links Gill Sans became the typeface of choice for those British designers who

wished to give their designs a sense of modernity. However, their idea of what 'modernity' looked like was rather less progressive than some of their European counterparts. Generally, British designers with Modernist leanings – few can be called Modernists – appeared to be less willing to reject traditional influences completely. As a consequence their designs looked less experimental and less unified stylistically. An indication of this more tentative, mixed approach is shown in the LNER poster above, but a more extensive and typographically orientated example can be seen on the first covers produced by the British publisher Penguin *(fig. 14.14)*, which was founded in 1935. Penguin's initial covers were designed by an untrained 21-year old, Edward Young (1913–2005). He created a distinctive striped design in which the new, modern-looking Gill Sans was used alongside historical types and realistic imagery within a centred layout. In spite of the traditional features, the public considered them to be strikingly modern nevertheless. In part it helped that the books themselves were an unusual form of publication: printed as paperbacks in a handy pocket size and sold, from vending machines in some instances, for the price of a packet of cigarettes. Likewise, the books' being colour-coded according to their subject matter and having an avian company name were features generally new to the British public, though not so in Germany where a series of colour-coded paperbacks had been published four years earlier under the Albatross imprint. The influence of Albatross on Penguin's design and name was acknowledged by Penguin. By choosing the name of an animal and by representing this name with a pictorial logo, rather than a logotype made from the founder's name, as was then conventional, Penguin and Albatross stood out from the established publishers. Most significantly for Penguin, though, was that all these novelties were wedded to texts that people wanted to read. Three million books were sold in the company's first year. Such success helped Penguin become synonymous with the new paperback format (to the displeasure of the company's founder, who doubtless feared it might inhibit future growth). It was a link that proved stronger than that established by the pioneering German paperback publishers, the first of which had published paperbacks as far back as 1845.

Britain's aesthetically conservative attitude to graphic design during the 1930s and 1940s was supported partly by a Goudy-like respect for 'invisibility'. The attitude was especially marked in book design,

14.14: Penguin paperback cover designed by Edward Young, 1935

of the words. It was a stance she described as Modernist because, she said, it responded to the question, 'What must it [a piece of design] do?' rather than 'How should it look?'. But the 'doing' she referred to (i.e. preserve legibility) was such a sedentary kind of doing, especially compared to the doing that was being done within Modernist designs from the European mainland *(fig. 13.8, p. 195)*. There, legible but nevertheless aggressively bold headings, novel sanserif types and asymmetric layouts were forcibly commanding the viewers' attention and then actively directing it throughout the various parts of the design. By comparison Warde's version of 'less is more', as suggested by her Crystal Goblet metaphor, was so passive it verged on the anti-Modernist.

There is always a place for passive clarity in printed communication, and nowhere more so perhaps than in the grey columns of text that filled the daily broadsheet newspapers. Such papers sought to tread a narrow path between the dispassionate dissemination of information on one side and the compelling eye-witness account of an event, or the polemical championing of a cause, on the other. For both sides, though, the need to appear authoritative and reliable was considered paramount. The requisite sense of authority would best be conveyed by a quiet and sober form of design. Moreover this was still the age when many newspapers, such as *The Times* of London *(fig. 14.15, 14.16)*, gave the front page over to personal adverts, be it a £40 reward for finding a diamond bracelet 'in or near the Palace Theatre' or the sale of Lt. Col Richardson's Airedale dogs ('world-known for protective purposes'). An editor today would not be willing to relinquish so much prime print real-estate to such an assortment of parochial titbits, but since it was there it was fitting that the listable nature of the text be served by a clear, legible and formulaic layout. Other more practical considerations also came into play. The speed at which the papers had to be put together would have allowed little time for constructing anything but the most straightforward layout.

Clarity and practical utility were the guiding principles behind *The Times*'s greatest contribution to design: the twentieth-century's most used text face, Times Roman. With its first appearance in October 1932, Times New Roman, as it was called in its early incarnations (and the recent digital ones provided by Microsoft and Linotype), had an immediate impact. It made the paper's previous 'modern' style of type, which had adorned the paper's pages for more than a century, looked small and ill-formed. On the day of the change,

where for many designers and printers the more passive and unobtrusive a piece of typography the better. Such an approach is now sometimes referred to by the expression 'The Crystal Goblet', a phrase that is derived from a speech given in 1930 by the Monotype Corporation's publicity manager, Beatrice Warde (1900–69). The term gained currency after Warde added it to the title of subsequent printed versions of her speech: 'The Crystal Goblet, Or Printing Should Be Invisible'.

To help carry her argument for the primacy of clarity in typography, Warde had constructed her talk around an elaborate metaphor of wine in a crystal goblet. 'You have two goblets before you. One is of solid gold wrought in the most exquisite patterns. The other is of crystal-clear glass, thin as a bubble, and as transparent … if you are a member of that vanishing tribe, the amateurs of fine vintages, you will choose the crystal, because everything about it is calculated to reveal rather than hide the beautiful thing which it was meant to contain.' Here 'the beautiful thing' refers to the meaning

14.15: Front page, 'The Times', Friday 30th September 1932

14.16: Front page, 'The Times', Monday 3rd October 1932

the paper's editor described reading the old type as 'an act of heroic endeavour, a Spartan trudge for the eye, obliged to plough endless unbroken furrows of dense print'. The success of Times New Roman was the product of a close collaboration between the paper and the Monotype Corporation. Central to this partnership was Stanley Morison (1889–1967), who was at that time typographic advisor to both organizations. *The Times* had commissioned Morison to redesign the paper and provide it with a new typeface, but being principally a historian of book design and typography, not a draughtsman or type designer even, he turned to one of the artists working at *The Times*'s publicity department, Victor Lardent (1905–68), to draw the letters. Lardent's hand-rendered lettering for a number of the paper's advertisers had proved that he possessed a sufficiently detailed understanding of letterforms and the requisite set of skills to set them down in a unified design. The established account has it that Lardent based his drawings on two sources: one provided by Morison in the form of some instructional sketches and a photograph of a sixteenth-century type from the Plantin-Moretus Museum *(<p. 101)*; and the other from Monotype's recent design of its own version of Plantin type. From this combination Lardent was able to create a

single sturdy roman. Recently, however, the centrality of these influences has been questioned. It has been suggested that a printed sample of a type designed decades earlier, in 1904, by a young American polymath, Starling Burgess (1878–1947), was the true source of Monotype's design. The resemblance between that purported to be Burgess's earlier design and Times New Roman is so close, it is hard to believe they could have been made independently of each other. They must have either shared a common model, or one must have been based on the other. The Burgess theory has created enough doubt for *The Times* newspaper itself to describe its earlier type as being designed by Stanley Morison, Victor Lardent 'and possibly Starling Burgess'.

Whatever the case, the resultant type generally fitted its purpose. Times New Roman's slightly condensed characters, with their unusually large x-height and short pointed serifs, created a space-efficient type that was sturdy enough to remain legible when printed on the newspaper's high-grade newsprint with thin ink at high speed. Despite the New Roman's greater legibility, Morison believed its usefulness would be limited: 'It is a newspaper type – and hardly a book type – for it is strictly appointed for use in short lines ....' He was mistaken. On its release the following year designers and printers

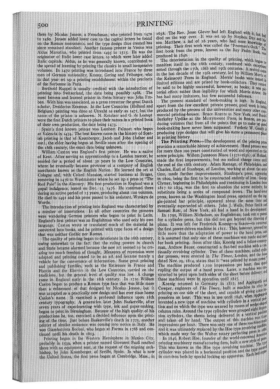

14.17: 'Encyclopedia Britannica', 1936

were quick to use it for setting books and magazines, and in designs for advertising. Numerous variants were subsequently developed to fit different printing conditions and new technologies, though in every instance the somewhat impersonal, almost bland, sense of efficiency that lay at the heart of the design was preserved. It appears that as a type for text, Times's very neutrality and lack of character actually contributed to its popularity. Goudy and Warde were not alone in valuing 'invisibility' in a typeface: both the Encyclopedia Britannica (fig. 14.17) and Penguin adopted it, and more recently Microsoft and Apple Computers chose an updated digital version of it as one of their default fonts for their operating systems and several key programmes. Even now it remains popular both for private and commercial use. This sustained period of popularity has allowed it to become the predominant typeface for the setting of continuous text.

Typography was not the only aspect of graphic design in which traditional styles were revived during the first part of the twentieth century. Private presses, commercial printers, publishers and advertisers also began to use a historical method of illustration, the handmade wood-engraving, to sit alongside their traditional types. Though wood-engraving had been introduced in the seventeenth century, it only really became prominent after the British artist Thomas Bewick (<p. 129) had revealed its potential in the late eighteenth century. Bewick's influence was gradually eroded during the second half of the nineteenth century by advances in lithographic and photo-mechanical printing. But just when it looked as though it might lapse into obscurity, the Arts and Crafts movement revived the technique. The engraved block could be cut in a style that harmonized visually with old-fashioned styles of type, and by needing to be printed in relief, it was well suited to being printed alongside type.

The impetus provided by the Arts and Crafts to the fading art of wood-engraving drew a number of British artists into what Eric Gill described as 'this adventure in discovery'. In so doing they helped to reinvent wood-engraving as an autonomous medium as well as a form of illustration to accompany text. Among the group of early twentieth-century engravers who continued Bewick's brand of rustic realism (there were other contemporary engravers who explored more modern styles of illustration) was the British artist Reynolds Stone (1900–79). Stone was rare in that his skill as a draughtsman was combined with a strong sense of design and a keen appreciation of letterforms, the last of which he had developed through an apprenticeship in printing. With this combination of skills, he was able to branch out beyond the confines of fine book illustration and explore more public areas of design. During his later life when he could have claimed that more people in Britain knew his work than that of any other designer, or artist even. Not only had he designed the heraldic masthead for Morison's redesign of The Times (fig.14.15, 14.16), he had also produced a series of postage stamps and several banknotes. Most of these items, as with his bookplates and book covers, benefited from his skilful rendering of wild flowers, weeds and woods and his mastery of the engraved letter; in particular, the italic form of letter as it had first been developed by some of the late-Renaissance writing masters (<fig. 5.8, p. 90). He used their exuberant flourishes to fill out the available space, thereby creating a series of balanced yet explicitly decorative designs (>fig. 14.18). Many of his overtly beautiful and rustic engravings could be criticized for being old-fashioned or escapist, but for a lover of nature living in an increasingly industrialized world, and for an artist whose work was interrupted by war, Stone had had much to escape from.

14.18: Title page design by Reynolds Stone, 1938

1935

1938

1938

1949

14.19: Penguin logos

The need to escape was an important influence on traditional typography's most controversial exponent, Jan Tschichold *(<p.201–3)*. In 1933, a systematic purge of left-wing sympathizers by Germany's newly elected, Nazi-led government saw Tschichold arrested and imprisoned. Though he had not been politically active, his captors viewed his practice of and support for Modernist art as evidence of 'cultural Bolshevism'. Following his release after four weeks of incarceration, Tschichold was effectively forced to flee with his wife and young son to Switzerland. It was in the relative calm of his adopted country that he first began to question both his previous dogmatic attitude to design and the validity of the style he had promoted so passionately: 'to my astonishment I detected most shocking parallels between the teachings of *Die neue Typographie* ['The New Typography'] and National Socialism and Fascism. Obvious similarities consist in the ruthless restriction of type-faces, a parallel to Goebbels' infamous *Gleichschaltung* [bringing into line], and the more or less military arrangement of lines.' Moreover, he came to appreciate the practicality and legibility of much traditional typography, with its easily implemented centred typography, its readable seriffed types and attractively engraved decoration. By 1939, Tschichold had largely turned his back on the New Typography and on the one area of design in which he considered it to be still valid, advertising. He focused instead on designing books in an essentially traditional style.

Despite his renewed devotion to traditional forms of design, Tschichold could still not escape censure. While some designers responded to his apparent *volte-face* by hailing him as a prodigal son, others, among the avantgarde especially, condemned him as a Judas *(>p.245)*. (In fact, he had never been as exclusively Modernistic as his early writing made him out to be. Even in his most polemical phase, either side of writing *The New Typography*, Tschichold continued to design a number of typographically traditional book covers and bindings.) Many of the traditional designs that were to characterize the final phase of his career were created in the role of design consultant to various European publishers; notably, the British publisher Penguin, who between 1947 and 1949 commissioned him to redesign some of their most prominent series of books, and whose well-known logo he adjusted *(fig.14.19)* (though it differed little to the one that had been drawn more than a decade earlier by Edward Young, the logo's real designer).

The style of Tschichold's later work is sometimes referred to as New Traditionalism. While each of the graphic elements – the seriffed types and old-style decoration – had traditional origins or associations, they were artfully arranged with a modern sense of space. The negative or white parts of the page were given an almost equal prominence with the positive, printed parts. The design he created for the cover of a prospectus for Penguin's Pelican imprint *(fig.14.20)*, with its integrated lines of black and subtle terracotta type, immaculately

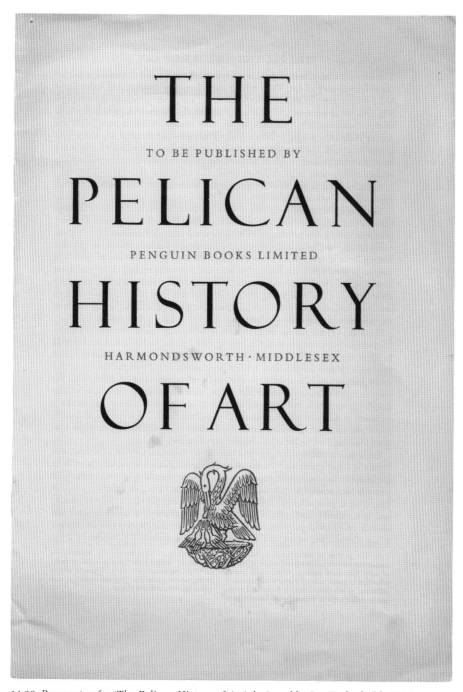

THE
TO BE PUBLISHED BY

PELICAN
PENGUIN BOOKS LIMITED

HISTORY
HARMONDSWORTH · MIDDLESEX

OF ART

14.20: Prospectus for 'The Pelican History of Art' designed by Jan Tschichold, 1947

sized, spaced and weighted, leave one in no doubt that it was a twentieth-century design. Such an arrangement would not look out of place on the title page of a book today. Throughout this later phase, Tschichold was able to bring the same acute sense of spacial balance that had guided him through his Modernist phase. Such was his skill that, however faithfully publishers attempted to implement the various 'house styles' he designed for them, they were rarely able to match the finesse and sensitivity of the examples he set before them.

The wealth of typographic and pictorial effects thrown up by Modernist designers began to spread throughout mainstream graphic design during the middle of the twentieth century. Designers took it out of its initial ideological context and applied it to more straightforwardly commercial ends.

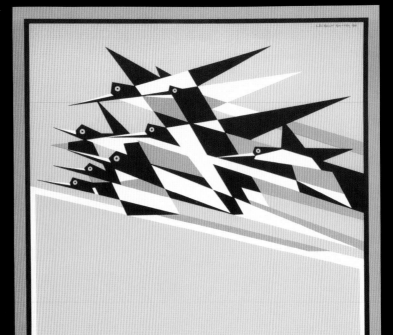

Soaring to Success !

DAILY HERALD

— the Early Bird.

15 GOOD DESIGN IS GOOD BUSINESS
Commercial Modernism, c.1920 – c.1960

Flat-roofed buildings made out of glass and concrete, open-plan interiors and fitted kitchens, steel-framed chairs and stackable cups, sundry photographic images on postcards, magazines and newspapers, all these are now such very ordinary features in the landscape of a modern life. We walk in and out of them, work, sit and talk in them or look at them and read them without ever being aware of the often intensely political or, in some cases, spiritual aims that prompted their creation. Today, taken as a whole, such objects carry no special significance. And yet it was through them and other similarly practical items that Modernism managed to enter the lives of ordinary people. The things that the post-war public considered to be 'art' – the 'high' arts, such as painting and classical music – were even more peripheral to most people's lives than they are today. It was through the predominantly utilitarian arts of architecture and graphic, industrial or interior design, the so-called 'applied arts', that Modernism came to reshape, in quite a literal sense, the way people lived. Thus the effective carriers of Modernism were commercial items, things bought and sold; and also the various ways these things were marketed, be it through posters and brochures or the advertisements in magazines and newspapers.

An early example of Modernist graphic design within a clearly commercial context is the poster produced in 1919 for a new, left-wing British newspaper, the *Daily Herald (fig.15.1)*. The dynamic, Futurist forms used to depict birds in flight were made by Edward McKnight Kauffer (1890–1956), an American artist then living in England. Kauffer did not make the design specifically for the newspaper. He had first worked out how to combine the direction of the birds' flight with the contrary movement of the birds' wings in his own black-and-white woodcut illustration. He then adapted this illustration to fit into a simple, colour design, shorn of any text, for a non-specific and speculative poster. It was only after

the *Daily Herald* bought his design that the stylistically ill-suited text was added (most inharmonious was the traditional style of calligraphic letters that defined the paper's masthead). In this way the bird motif was linked metaphorically with the paper's own aspiration for success and the more general aspirations of its readers. The organizer of the newspaper's poster campaign described Kauffer's birds as 'a symbol, in those days of hope, of the unity of useful invention and natural things', a unity the British were forced to rely on during the period of reconstruction that followed the end of the First World War.

What makes the birds' arrangement so compelling, even to us with our own rather different aspirations, is the tension between the flock's two opposing formal qualities. The sense of movement generated both by the diagonal lines of the birds' flight as they burst into the picture frame, and by their triangular beaks and wings, is set in competition with the static, mosaic-like pattern of sharply defined light and dark shapes that Kauffer had carried over from his initial woodcut. This dynamic sense of movement does not lead us to a fixed focal point, but neither can we pass over the angular patterns without letting our eyes pause; the resultant cycle of flitting and stopping, of movement and repose, contributes to our continued engagement with the image.

Kauffer's subject matter and the style in which he rendered it are thought to have had two direct influences. One was a nineteenth-century Japanese print of birds in flight, similarly grouped though realistically drawn, which suggested to him how his own close scrutiny of flying birds might best be expressed. But the style in which Kauffer chose to render his subject was inspired by the various woodcut illustrations that had appeared in editions of the magazine *Blast*, which had been published recently to promote Vorticism *(<p.180)*, the British brand of Futurism.

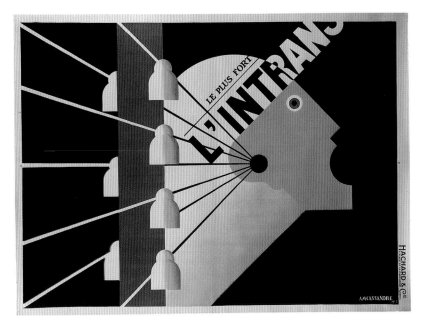

15.2: 'L'Intransigeant' poster designed by Cassandre, 1925

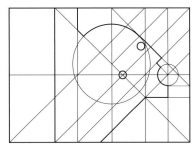

15.3: 'L'intransigeant' design scheme, based on a sketch by Cassandre, 1925

As well as adapting Modernist styles of illustration for commercial designs, graphic designers worked with forms from Modernist styles of painting. An arch-exponent of the Cubist-inspired Modernist poster was the Ukraine-born Parisian designer, Adolphe Mouron (1901–68), better known as Cassandre (like other designers before him, he chose a pseudonym for his design work so that his reputation as a painter would not be compromised; in the event, his success at and passion for design supplanted his desire to become a painter). It was while studying painting in Paris that Cassandre had become familiar both with the formal developments within Cubism and with the subsequent stylistic reactions it provoked (Le Corbusier's plainer, more mechanical 'Purism' especially). He made no secret of the influence that this brand of Modernist painting had on his early posters: 'Some people have called my posters Cubistic. They are right in the sense that my method is essentially geometric and monumental.'

The geometry behind his poster for the Parisian newspaper *L'Intransigeant (fig.15.2)*, which he designed in 1925 when still a young man of 24, was revealed in a diagrammatic preliminary sketch *(fig.15.3)*. The four circles that guided the form and placement of the ear, eye, mouth and head were set within a grid that was defined by two squares and various related diagonal and vertical lines. Cassandre was careful, though, not to let the complexity of his underlying scheme intrude on the simplicity of his starkly graphic final image.

The finished design showed the most modern medium of journalistic communication, the telegraph, bringing information directly to the ear, and then had it being delivered forcefully out of the mouth. The shouting head – some say it is the head of Marianne, France's national emblem, others that it is simply a newspaper boy – is made with a powerfully simple and geometrically angular profile, though this central feature was softened, as were other hard-edged forms in the poster, by Cassandre's skilful use of an air-brush. The flat, angular shapes and the smooth gradations of air-brushed colour mimic some of the painterly effects displayed by several Cubist artists; and the poster's collage-like text, the newspaper's masthead, is clearly a Cubist motif.

The close integration of text and image was a primary aim for Cassandre when designing his posters. Being aware of how effectively verbal puns could add meaning to the image, he would frequently adapt or alter the text of his posters. In *L'Intransigeant*, he shortened the newspaper's name – the two syllables of 'L'Intrans' were less of a mouthful and, indeed, an eyeful – and he also reduced the paper's byline from *'Le plus fort tirage des journaux de soir'* ('The best-selling evening paper') to *'Le plus fort'*, which not only emphasized 'best-selling' but also created an alternative, literal meaning: 'the strongest'.

Elements from other Modernist styles, such as De Stijl and Constructivism, began to be exploited for commercial ends from the second half of the 1920s and

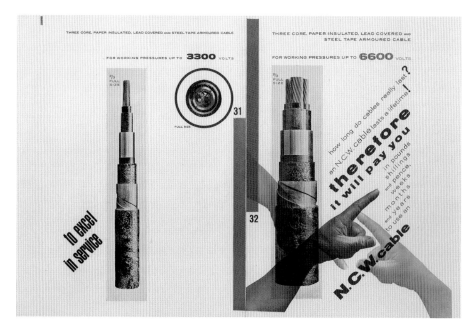

15.5: *Monogram designed by Piet Zwart, 1920s*

15.4: *Dutch Cable Factory catalogue designed by Piet Zwart, 1928*

into the 1930s. The Dutch designer Piet Zwart (1885–1977) was a pioneer in this regard. He used dynamic, diagonal typography and arrestingly cropped and cut-out photographs, though not in a way that was merely attention-seeking or slavishly subservient to these styles. His arrangements were carefully considered so that they might impart information with clarity as well as interest. In a catalogue for the Nederlandsche Kabel Fabriek (Dutch Cable Company) in Delft published in 1928 *(fig. 15.4)*, Zwart used a series of highly detailed cut-out photographs, as opposed to the then more established form of explanatory illustration, the technical drawing, to illustrate the various kinds of high-tension and telephone cables being sold. The close-up photographs provided a degree of detail which an illustrator could only have matched with great skill and patience. By showing cross-sections of cables and by exposing the cables' many layers, Zwart was able to convey the quality and combination of materials used to make them. Each kind of cable was set out across its own double page and shown at two-thirds its actual size so that the reader could make an easy comparison. Though the photographs were essentially static, Zwart was able to set them within a dynamic design by carefully considering the size, position and direction of the type so as to create an illusion of spacial depth and movement.

Even Zwart's most apparently unstructured and decorative designs were informative. The page from a booklet *(> fig. 15.6)* printed in 1931 showing a swarm of layered letters in a multitude of type styles and sizes, and coloured with the primary colours of De Stijl, looks like a purely artistic experiment – and no doubt it was, partly, experimental – but the design was also instructive. The booklet had been designed for a Dutch printing company called Trio – hence the page's emphasis of the numeral '3' – who had wanted to publicize the variety of typefaces they offered. The design's only line of text reads *'een kleine keuze uit onze lettercellectie'* ('a small sample of our collection of type'). However, through Zwart's startling array they were also able to show the skill with which they could print, in colour, a layered and visually complex page. Another similar, though much more succinct demonstration of Zwart's informative yet playful use of Modernist forms was contained in the design of his own monogram *(fig. 15.5)*. The combination of a bold sanserif 'P', for Piet, and a black square is to be read somewhat like a rebus, since the Dutch word for black (derived from the German) is *zwart*.

Zwart's use of photography as a form of illustration reflected a trend among designers and printers, both in Europe and the United States, that had grown steadily throughout the first quarter of the twentieth century. The stimulus for it was chiefly technological: the advance of a printing process that could convert the smooth, greyish tones of a photographic negative into an array of black dots of varying sizes. Provided the dots were small enough (when used for a magazine or

15.6: Trio booklet designed by Piet Zwart, 1931

15.7: 'Life' magazine, 1937

newspaper) or looked at from far enough away (when for a poster), they could mimic the appearance of the original photograph. This dotted or 'half-tone' image could be made for printing in relief and thus could be placed alongside the type in a letterpress (also in relief) and printed together in the same run through the press. Though the 'half-tone' process had in fact been invented in the middle of the nineteenth century, it was only during the last decade of that century that the technique, and the paper and ink it required, had been refined sufficiently for commercial use. Even then the prestige accorded to established forms of engraved illustration had delayed its eventual dominance. When the half-tone did take over, it was not just because the method was quicker and cheaper. The half-tone was also considered to be a more neutral and truthful form of reproduction. Its more or less imperceptible array of dots appeared to replicate the photograph exactly and thus it helped to sustain the belief common among the new readers of the mass media that 'the camera cannot lie'. By comparison, the hand-crafted lines and stippling of the average etching or engraving looked more like an artist's impression of the real world, rather than a faithful reflection of it.

The popularity of the photograph in printing was also linked to another technological innovation, the invention of a relatively inexpensive and portable, small-format (35mm) camera, which not long after its

invention became equipped with roll film and detachable high-speed lenses. These new machines turned the protracted ritual required by older, slower and larger cameras into an almost point-and-press reflex, and consequently allowed photographers to garner eye-witness accounts of newsworthy events as they unfolded. In this way a new vitality and prominence were given to the fledgling profession of photo-journalism, which brought it into a closer relationship with its more established literary cousin, reportage. A definitive demonstration of this development was the appearance in several magazines of a now famous photograph taken by the celebrated Hungarian war photographer, Robert Capa (1913–54). It showed a soldier at the very moment of being shot while fighting in the Spanish Civil War (fig. 15.7). The editor of the American magazine Life had initially rejected the image because it was blurred in parts and awkwardly cropped, but when it was finally included it had an immediate impact (which in the magazine was heightened by the contrast between the picture's subject matter and the magazine's title). Capa's photograph proved that such imperfections could actually enhance the dramatic effect of an image.

The combination of the half-tone process and the miniature camera freed photography from its previously limited set of specialized uses in military reconnaissance, basic forms of news reporting, formal portraiture,

15.8: 'Pontresina' poster designed by Herbert Matter, 1936

head, the small downhill skier and the glimpse of an alpine range are clearly derived from separate sources. Yet, they still lead us to presume that each is a faithful representation of the resort. Realizing that the images are a composite, we might well doubt that any of them were photographed at the resort itself, but because they are photographic and, therefore, true to life, we assume that they were also true to Pontresina.

Proof of the photograph's newfound popularity appeared with the relaunch in 1936 of the previously mentioned magazine, *Life*. Formerly an ailing humour magazine, *Life* was reinvented as a picture magazine and its design and content were altered accordingly. The new version sought to open a window on the world by filling its pages with photographs. As suggested by the magazine's title, the new *Life* would enable its readers, in the words of its editor: 'To see life; to see the world; to eyewitness great events; to watch the faces of the poor and the gestures of the proud; to see strange things – machines, armies, multitudes, shadows in the jungle and on the moon; to see man's work – his paintings, towers and discoveries; to see things thousands of miles away, things hidden behind walls and within rooms.' Being published in the era before television and mass travel, *Life* magazine allowed Americans to see what their country – its places and people – looked like. It allowed them to get to know the face of their own president or, indeed, that of his wife, and more broadly, how their fellow countrymen lived and worked. The very first picture inside the first edition showed a doctor in a delivery room, and this image was followed by a full-page photograph of the doctor's gloved hand holding a newborn baby. Introducing this image was the punning title 'Life begins here…'.

Life was the first fully fledged, photographic picture magazine to appear in the United States, but in Europe similar kinds of magazines had been available for a decade. They first became prominent in Germany where, significantly, the first miniature cameras were made. Throughout the 1920s and 1930s the photographic picture magazine established itself as a popular way of getting news and reflecting on current affairs. Where previous magazines had used pictures as a supplement to the text, the new picture magazines reversed these roles. They set the relationship between picture and text explicitly in favour of the picture. As well as showing, as in the case of Capa's image, single shots of specific events accompanied by a short caption or text, they also showed sequences of photographs of a single subject,

family albums, postcards and pornography, and helped it to become the main vehicle for imparting pictorial information across a wide range of printed media. The half-tone and the miniature camera turned the photograph from being a single, often private and treasured object into a mass-produced, public and largely disposable artefact, and thus made it ripe for commercial exploitation. The allure of the photograph among the advertising industry was further increased by the promise, or belief, that this kind of image presented the world as it really was. Such a belief was then, as now, both widespread and persistent. It endured even when the photograph in question was clearly contrived. Between 1933 and 1936, the Swiss-born Modernist, Herbert Matter (1907–84), designed posters for the Swiss National Tourist Office in which Dada-like photomontages were placed alongside a Constructivist-influenced typography. In the montage for his poster for the ski resort of Pontresina *(fig.15.8)*, the oddly goggled yet handsome

15.9: 'The Weekly Illustrated' magazine, 1934

in a manner analogous to, and influenced by, the stills of cinematic film. In effect they created a kind of photo-essay. Some designers referred to this method of developing a pictorial narrative as the 'third effect'. By showing two or more pictures next to each other, often in contrasting scales, a more complete impression of the subject could be given. The spread *(fig. 15.9)* of the Italian Fascist leader, Mussolini, while at work in his so-called study, leaves us with an impression of the man that is more than the sum of its photographic parts. It is possible to feel that one knows *Il Duce* ('The Leader') a little better and more intimately than if one had come across each image separately. The way we acquire this knowledge has been carefully choreographed by the designer. He has sized and positioned the pictures in such a way that the eye is led first to the largest image, on the right, glimpsing what a visitor would have seen on entering the study, and then directed down and across to the bottom left, looking at how Mussolini worked 'like an animal, poring over his papers', before being taken along the bottom, to the right, where the leader's own particular gestures and mannerisms are revealed.

Photographic illustration was not alone in being transformed by the camera. The camera's unposed, snap-shot effect and its potential for a penetrating degree of detail reacted back onto traditional forms of illustration. Realistically painted illustrations had remained popular in America, as elsewhere, despite the compelling novelty of the photograph and the exotic glamour associated with Modernist forms of abstraction. Magazines and posters were frequently illustrated with the same kind of allegorical themes that easel painters had developed during the nineteenth century. They showed idealized and sentimental scenes, completely without irony or cynicism, similar to the representation of innocence that Millais had conjured in his painting of the boy and the soap bubble *(<fig. 10.2, p.150).* The most popular twentieth-century examples of this genre in America belonged to the illustrator Norman Rockwell (1894–1978), who endeared himself to a vast national public over a period of nearly half a century, primarily through the 321 cover illustrations he made for the *Saturday Evening Post* magazine. Among his most celebrated images, however, were those made for a

OURS...to fight for

![Freedom From Want poster]

FREEDOM FROM WANT

15.10: 'Freedom From Want' poster, illustrated by Norman Rockwell, 1943

15.11: Magazine covers, c.1950s

series called 'The Four Freedoms', painted in 1943 and which, like all his work (and indeed most art today), became familiar through their reproduction on posters or in magazines, rather than as original artworks hung on the walls of a gallery. As with most of Rockwell's illustrations, this series captured and reasserted a popular American self-image; the small-town, familial world of a God-blessed America free of greed, violence or suburban alienation. It included simple domestic scenes, such as two parents tucking their child into bed at night, as a representation of freedom from fear, or the extended family gathered round a lavishly laid dining table for the traditional Thanksgiving meal *(fig. 15.10)*, which represented freedom from want.

Though printed as a poster, the Thanksgiving illustration is clearly the work of a painter. What is also evident is that the hand of the painter has been guided by the eye of the camera. The whole ensemble, the reflections in the salt and pepper pots, the creased smiles of the dinner guests, even the expression of concentrated strain that grips the face of grandma as she lowers the gigantic turkey onto the table, has been

painted with an almost hyper-real degree of detail equivalent to a well-focused photograph shot through a pristine lens. The framing of the image, too, with the half-heads of the guests and with the near end of the table chopped off, looks just as it might have, had we, the viewer-guest, stood up from the table and snapped the scene ourselves with a pocket camera.

By presenting new pictorial descriptions of the world, be it through photographs or photographically influenced illustrations, the picture magazine heralded the start of a new visual age, one that we continue to inhabit. Clearly, no era can ever be encapsulated by a single slogan. There are too many influences competing for dominance over the way we live our lives. But, it is also true that different historical periods have distinct characteristics. Our current reliance on and enchantment with a superabundance of pictorial images – which through film, television, the internet and mobile phone cameras are now set in motion and combined with sound – can be traced back to the rapid increase in the use of printed photographs during the 1920s and 1930s. It was the beginning of our current pictorial era, what can be thought of as 'the age of the image'.

The editors of picture magazines understood the importance of an 'image' in the wider sense of the word. An important element in defining the image of the magazine to the potential buyer was the photograph that appeared on the cover. Initially, picture magazines showed a variety of subjects. The covers of the early editions of *Life* magazine for example ranged from an abstract picture of America's new Fort Pick dam to a pastoral vision of grazing sheep, but quite soon it (like others) began to favour close-up shots of individuals, especially those made famous by Hollywood *(<fig.15.11)* or politics. Their editors had realized the pulling-power of a recognizable or attractive face, or ideally one in which both characteristics were combined. Gradually a pecking order for the preferred cover image established itself, with female beauty and youth at the top of the list. A recent description of the pecking order for magazine covers today shows how, with the exception of political power and the new medium of television, the priorities have remained more or less constant: 'Young is better than old. Pretty is better than ugly. Rich is better than poor. TV is better than music. Music is better than movies. Movies are better than sports. Anything is better than politics. And nothing is better than the celebrity dead.' Whether the last item on this finally macabre list really is the best (the fate of Michael Jackson and Princess Diana among others suggests it might be), the presumption behind each item is that it refers to a picture of a face. One only needs to see the crowd of printed faces that stare out at us from the racks of magazines in our newsagents to accept the truth behind this presumption.

The feature that makes the face so compelling is the eyes. Proof of their importance can be found in the prevalence of eyes and related concepts, such as vision or blindness, in everyday speech. English-speakers say 'he is lacking vision' yet, in spite of his faults, he may be 'the apple of her eye', and who are we to question her judgement, for though 'love is blind', 'beauty is in the eye of the beholder'. We can 'see eye-to-eye' unless we want 'an eye for an eye'; we have eyes of needles and of storms; we 'keep an eye out' and may even have them peeled or skinned, unless, that is, we are looking at the things in our 'mind's eye'. Eyes are important because, in comparison with other parts of the face, they seem to reveal most about the intentions or the psychological and physical condition of their owner. Age and gender, fear or hostility, fatigue or excitement – these and other characteristics can all be gauged by the look in someone's eyes. And here the plural, 'eyes', is important. A single eye seen in profile is less expressive than two eyes seen head-on. We are less able to read a person's emotions from their profile, and sometimes can even struggle to identify who the profile belongs to. Again, a newsagent's shelves will confirm how much more expressive and, therefore, more popular with designers and editors, a full or three-quarter view of the face is compared to a face seen in profile.

The rise in the use of photographs in magazines and newspapers during the second quarter of the twentieth century led the eye of the camera to be focused more intently on celebrities, whether in the formal setting of a public engagement or in the act of committing some private indiscretion. The dramatic, photographic exposé of a celebrity's misdemeanours was just one example of how publishers exploited photographic reproduction; another, twinned with scandal in its close relation to celebrity, was the display of *haute couture* fashion. By the 1930s and 1940s, a new generation of photographers had brought fashion photography to the level of high art. The gallery that provided them with the largest audiences was that made with ink and paper rather than bricks and mortar: the printed pages of the American fashion magazines – *Vogue* and *Harper's Bazaar* especially.

Harper's eminence during this period was due in large part to the magazine's designer, a Russian émigré called Alexei Brodovitch (1898–1971), whose influence helped to spread commercial Modernism across the medium of magazines more generally. Brodovitch was employed by *Harper's* within the newly defined role of 'art director', a position he held for 24 years and one which allowed him to be involved in deciding what the contents should be as well as how they should appear. This greater control enabled him to fill each issue with a related series of dramatically simple designs in which the text and pictures were fully integrated and often so across a double-page spread. The form he gave to the text was unbounded by any dominant 'house-style'. No single grid guided its placement. Often, in an evocation of the typographic effects displayed by the Symbolist or concrete poets *(<fig.12.2, p.176)*, floating chunks or shapes made from the text's outline were fitted into the spaces suggested by the accompanying photographs. In their placement and cropping, the photographs were treated with a similar degree of artistic licence. They too displayed Modernist influences, either through some dramatic contrast in scale or through strong, often diagonal, divisions of space. In this late example *(fig.15.12)*, a diagonal division appears in duplicate. It also makes a Surrealistic contrast between the coiffed and elegantly dressed model and her prosaic props, the ladders. Such Modernist devices succeeded in grabbing readers' attention, an attention which Brodovitch then directed skilfully onto the clothes, for he had realized that one way of drawing attention to something was to contrast it with a similar but not identical thing – here

Mainbocher: His long, slender, fluid evening line—
as simple as it is portentous—in pink and white
dotted chiffon, bound at the waist with pink
grosgrain streamers. Diamond eardrops, Harry Winston.

Mainbocher: His sleeveless, double-breasted blue
and white silk dinner suit, its jacket carved
to the waist and shaped out over a floating skirt.
Diamonds from Cartier. Gloria Vanderbilt poses.

15.12: 'Harper's Bazaar' magazine designed by Alexei Brodovitch, 1955

the two sets of clothes – and then to further enhance this contrast he made all other parts of the images the same. The sameness of the text, the model, the ladders and the nebulous grey backgrounds help to accentuate the differences between the two sets of clothes. We are led to flit automatically from one set to the other as though playing a grown-up version of spot-the-difference.

Brodovitch was significant to the development of commercial Modernism both as an individual, through his design work, and as a member of an influential group. He was one of a large number of European designers who, having fled political or ethnic persecution at home, managed to make their way across the Atlantic by steamship with their knowledge of Modernist design in tow. The list of European designers who came to America as exiles or émigrés leading up to and during the second quarter of the twentieth century includes prominent figures from almost every Modernist movement: Fortunato Depero (Futurism); George Grosz (Dada); Naum Gabo (Constructivism); Marcel

Duchamp (Surrealism); Piet Mondrian (De Stijl); and Walter Gropius, Herbert Bayer, László Moholy-Nagy, Marcel Breuer, Mies van der Rohe (Bauhaus). Their arrival had been preceded during the nineteenth century by successive waves of large-scale immigration which, by creating a stream of cheap labour and a continuously expanding domestic market, had helped to make America the world's leading industrial power by the time the First World War broke out in 1914. The consequences of that war helped it become the world's financial power too. Though immigration was curtailed in the 1920s and had almost ceased by the late 1930s, and despite America being laid low by the Great Depression – an economic downturn that affected all industrialized nations during the 1930s – the lure of a large, politically stable, ethnically diverse and culturally modern country remained strong, especially among those Europeans who could find none of these attributes at home.

A symptom and symbol of America's economic strength was the export not just of new raw materials

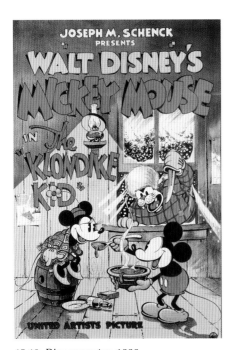

15.13: Disney poster, 1933

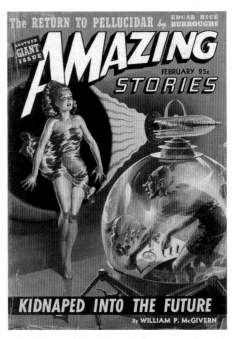

15.14: Cover, 'Amazing Stories' magazine, 1942

and manufactured goods (the icon of early mass production being the Ford Model T), but also the export of its culture. Historically Americans had been willing recipients and active imitators of European culture, its visual and plastic (three-dimensional) arts especially. American painters had pursued Romanticism and French Impressionism, and its architects had adopted the Neo-classical style for the nation's grandest buildings (the White House, the Capitol building). But during the 1920s this direction of influence began to be reversed as new, identifiably American forms of popular culture spread overseas. The pioneering movies made in Hollywood (Chaplin and Disney) and the melding of several American musical traditions into a new form of era-defining music, jazz – which could be brought to millions through new mechanical means, either at the time of the listener's choosing via the gramophone or else to many simultaneously via the radio – exposed Europeans to the sights and sounds of a modern America. These forms of cultural Americana inspired Europeans to recreate their own similar forms of art, for example the films of Jacques Tati and the music of Django Reinhardt in France. Both art forms, cinema and jazz, were publicized by posters which, in the case of the early animated films, incorporated new styles of imagery derived from the films themselves *(fig. 15.13)*. Cartoon lettering in particular became absorbed into the expanding repertoire of modern graphic styles.

A similar kind of hand-drawn lettering was brought to a mass audience through the popularity of science fiction writing. The American magazine *Amazing Stories (fig. 15.14)*, launched in 1926, was the first to devote itself solely to this genre of literature. By giving the public works of fiction at the price of a magazine it helped to establish the 'pulp fiction' genre or 'the pulps', a term which referred to the cheap paper (made from wood 'pulp') used in printing them. By the 1950s pulp fiction was available in paperback form. Part of the appeal of 'the pulps' lay not just in the stories themselves but in their sensationalized hand-drawn covers. A common scenario involved an endangered semi-clad woman waiting for the story's hero to free her from the clutches of some terrifying alien or monster. The cover art was considered to be so important to sales that it was frequently used to define the story inside. The cover would be designed first and then shown to the authors (though many were themselves the illustrators) who would then write the story around the cover image. The covers and the stories they illustrated had an international appeal. Most successful of all was the story of Tarzan, created by the American writer Edgar Rice Burroughs (whose science fiction appears in the example above), which increased its international appeal by being adapted into a comic-strip form and published in newspapers all over the world.

This same shift in cultural influence between the United States and Europe began to take place in graphic

15.15: 'Rural Electrification Administration' poster designed by Lester Beall, 1939

design during the 1930s and 1940s. Those Europeans who had brought their knowledge of Modernist graphic design to America helped to educate a new generation of American designers, as much through formal teaching as through their work. Together, master and pupil continued the transformation of Modernist design into a diverse commercial style. What they created was a more flexible and less narrowly focused style of design – Brodovitch for example mixed a version of the eighteenth-century typeface Bodoni with his Modernist photographs *(<fig. 15.12)*. Paradoxically, though, the variety of forms they used tended to be placed within a more unified, less fractured layout. Because the early European Modernists had wanted to break out of the

conventional, seriffed and centred straitjacket they had inherited from past styles of design, they had proceeded to break up the page or poster. The new generation of more commercially minded Modernists picked up the pieces, so to speak, and put them back together, but in a new way and without any loss of surprise or graphic power. It was in America that this process of reassembly was most vigorous and therefore to America that others began to look for the latest developments in graphic style.

A definite inspiration for those who wished to take up this more eclectic yet spatially unified approach to Modernism was the work of America's first great home-grown Modernist, Lester Beall (1903–69). In one of his posters *(< fig. 15.15)* from a celebrated series designed between 1937 and 1941 for the Rural Electrification Administration (a division of the US Government's Department of Agriculture), Beall unified two contrasting elements: a black and white, half-tone cut-out of two children leaning on a wooden fence, and then a series of solid, abstract coloured rectangles, which plainly evoked the American flag, in spite of the fact that the red stripes appeared above, not below or to the right of, a blue rectangle, which was itself starless. The glue with which Beall fused these two different kinds of images was a simple formal device: the succession of white bands that appeared between the red stripes which were then continued by the bars of the gate. Their unifying, venetian-blind effect fulfilled an important guiding principle Beall later described thus: 'To insure the workability of a design one must take care that no one of the established planes becomes completely disassociated from the others.' By using the bands and bars to associate the background plane of stripes with the foreground plane of the half-tone, he was also able to fuse the poster's two broader pictorial concepts: the patriotic appeal of nationhood espoused by the flag and the happy rural youngsters. Added to these, through the poster's partly stencilled lettering, was a third concept, the electrification of America's rural heartlands. The message presented by this threefold fusion of concepts could be summed up as 'electricity will benefit the next generation of rural Americans'. Such a graphically simple but conceptually sophisticated image was very original, certainly when compared with what had previously been presented to the public, and yet the viewer required no special knowledge in order to interpret it. It did not try to speak a coded language known only to a select number of initiates, as novel art often seems to do. The attributes of accessibility and boldness were recognized early in Beall's career by the Museum of Modern Art in New York which, in 1937, offered him a one-man exhibition. It was the first time a graphic designer had been honoured in this way.

The museum continued to recognize the commercial application of Modernist design when, in 1952, it mounted an exhibition of the advertising, industrial design and architecture of the European typewriter manufacturers Olivetti. Never before had America's foremost modern art museum given such prominence to a single corporation. The exhibition was a celebration of the company's early acceptance of Modernism, a position that had first been encouraged in the mid-1930s by the

15.16: Olivetti poster designed by Giovanni Pintori, 1952

founder's son, Antonio Olivetti, and pursued so comprehensively thereafter that the company soon became a byword for the style. 'The Olivetti style' became common currency in discussions on design during the 1940s and 1950s. Its meaning was minted as much through the progressive design of the company's posters as by the sleek curves of its typewriters' casing. Its graphic style during this period was dominated by the designs of Giovanni Pintori (1912–99), who over three decades produced a varied range of Modernist-inspired posters. One of his most prominent series showed a simple photograph of the latest model set within colourful patterns of abstract shapes *(fig. 15.16)*. In the example here, the company's iconic 'Lettera 22' model (which was to become part of the museum's permanent collection), is accompanied by an array of dots and lines. They pick up on the tapping of the typewriter keys much as a child might had he or she been asked to write out the musical score of some grand typewriter symphony. This element of playfulness was fundamental to the success of much commercial Modernist design. It helped to humanize the new range of unfamiliar consumer products that became available during the 1950s. Those who had never owned a typewriter before, for example, might have thought that such a complex-looking machine was

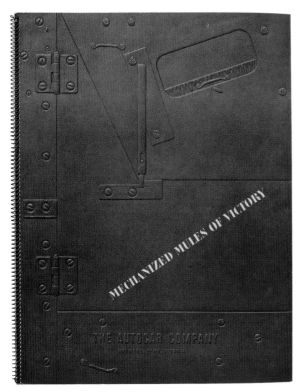
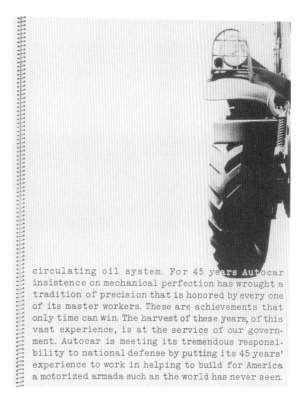

15.17 & 15.18: 'Mechanized Mules of Victory' brochure cover and inside page designed by Paul Rand, 1942

only for the most mechanically minded. Part of the success of commercial Modernist designers, both graphic and industrial, was that they convinced the public that such products were suitable for everyone. They helped to make the newfangled more approachable.

Pintori was employed as a permanent member of staff, but Olivetti also commissioned some of Europe's and America's most progressive designers on a freelance basis. Among them was a young designer from Brooklyn called Paul Rand (1914–96). Rand became one of the few American Modernist designers to achieve a greater respect and wider renown than his more senior contemporary, Beall. His success came early and remained more or less constant throughout his 60-odd-year career. Few, if any, designers have managed to stay relevant for so long. The covers he designed in his twenties for the arts magazine *Direction* (work he did for free in exchange for complete creative control), his work as an art director for magazines and for an advertising agency, the various books on design he wrote (and designed), the corporate identity designs he devised for some of America's most familiar corporations (e.g. IBM, Enron and ABC television), and in his latter years, his teaching at Yale and elsewhere, all turned him into America's best-known graphic designer. Moreover, and importantly,

his work helped to make the world of business take the profession of design more seriously. In knowing his own mind and articulating his knowledge with an assuring degree of certainty (though it would slide over into dogmatism in his later years), Rand was given full licence to express his artistically inspired brand of Modernist design within a commercial context.

One of his earliest exercises in corporate identity, in its most literal sense, was the creation of his own name. As a young designer, just starting out on his career, he felt that the Jewish nature of his birth name, Peretz Rosenbaum, might hinder his professional prospects, so he changed it to a more English-sounding combination of four-letter words. This awareness of people's pre-conceptions, and the preference for simplicity and unity suggested by his choice of name, proved to be the defining characteristics of his graphic style. Like Beall he reassembled the forms created by Modernist artists and designers into a variety of more unified designs. The cover of a brochure he designed in 1942 *(fig. 15.17)* for the Autocar Company, then a supplier of heavy-duty trucks to the US military, shows how this sense of unity did not always have to depend on a single formal device, like the white stripes in Beall's poster. Here the unity of Rand's design was determined by the dominance of a clear, central concept; that of the no-nonsense, practical utility commonly associated with the military. It was a kind of design-by-association in which every aspect of the design was devoted to expressing the concept. The cover was made to look as though it were made out of armour plating, with embossed rivets and edges of metal panels. Even some of the lettering was embossed, rather than printed. Although the title *Mechanized Mules of Victory* was formed out of the surrounding print, it appeared in a functional style of stencilled lettering easily associated with the military or else, as in Beall's poster, the practical kind of labelling common to agricultural products. On the brochure's inside pages (< *fig. 15.18*), the same sense of military utility was expressed by the use of typewriter lettering, which he extended to the very edges of the page, rather than have it surrounded artfully with generous margins. Rand even expressed his concept through the brochure's binding. The perforated ring-binding was a material expression of mechanical utility. While most of these component parts were not themselves Modernist, their arrangement was. Asymmetry, strong diagonal forces, abstract shapes and even cut-out half-tone photographs, all contributed to the kind of stark graphic surprise that characterized Modernist design.

Rand's best-known piece of design, the IBM logo, was, paradoxically, one in which his creative input was rather limited. The International Business Machine Corporation, or IBM, had first begun to use its initials as a logo in 1947 (perhaps after the initials had become the common way of referring to the company). For their sequence of widening letters – 'I' (narrow), 'B' (medium) and 'M' (wide) – they chose a moderately bold, slab-serif typeface *(fig. 15.19)*. In 1956, Rand was hired as a design consultant by the company's new president, Thomas J. Watson Jr., the eldest son of the founder and, importantly, a corporate leader with a rare appreciation of the importance and potential of good design – he is credited with having coined the mantra 'Good design is good business'. Rather than radically change the logo, as a new consultant seeking to make an impact might have been tempted to do, Rand, who had sensed a degree of conservatism among his employers, proposed that it be set in a slightly wider, bolder and more angular kind of slab-serif *(fig. 15.19)* called City, which had been released in Germany in 1930. The square counters (the negative spaces enclosed in the letters) in the 'B' and the pointed trough of the 'M'

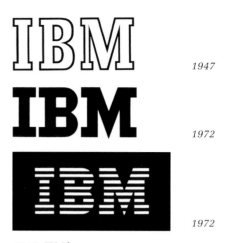

1947

1972

1972

15.19: IBM logos

certainly made it look more distinctive and, in combination with the heavier weight, more assertive, but essentially it was similar.

Logos, however, like people, can have their characteristics interpreted in several different ways. What at one time comes across as assertiveness may at other times be seen as inflexibility or stodginess. Rand appears to have recognized this in the logo. He had also noticed that the geometric serifs and counters would perfectly accommodate regular horizontal stripes, and so proposed a new version of the logo made out of 11 stripes. This alteration removed any hint of stodginess, and also produced a counter-intuitive effect in which the broken letters coalesced into a more unified and memorable design. By disrupting the letters' individual identity, Rand forced them to cohere into a single logographic entity. It was this relatively modest intervention that marked his main contribution to the logo's design, a contribution the company itself recognized and appreciated, for in 1972 they adopted the definitive and still current 'Eightstriper' logo. It was in the varied ways that Rand applied the logo, rather than in the design of the logo itself, that the full extent of his creativity was expressed. He was able to exploit the logo's decorative potential in a range of colourful designs *(fig. 15.20)*, though in every instance, he relied on simple graphic shapes to express a single unifying concept, be it the abstract one of the logo's stripes on packaging, or the linguistic one that lay behind his design of a rebus *(fig. 15.21)*.

Rand certainly had to earn the freedom he enjoyed at IBM – the trusting relationship he developed with his client ensured he remained a consultant there until 1991 – but equally the licence to pursue a Modernist style of design had to be granted to him. The company

15.20: IBM package design by Paul Rand, 1979

15.21: IBM rebus designed by Paul Rand, 1981

had to be open to a Modernist idiom in order for him to apply it. Before the 1950s, most corporate clients appear to have had only a passive engagement with design, Modernist or otherwise. Few of them considered graphic design to be anything more than a perfunctory means of conveying information. When any other role was assigned to it, it was usually as a more or less elaborate form of decoration: something pretty, but not unconventionally so. What made the likes of Thomas Watson Jr. – and indeed Antonio Olivetti before him – so unusual was their ability to see the commercial and social potential of innovative design. Watson, moreover, combined this vision with the resolve to pursue it even in the face of opposition from his own business colleagues.

The fact that Watson and Olivetti pursued these similar paths was not coincidental. The former was influenced, indirectly, by the latter. In his autobiography, Watson described how 'during a stroll down Fifth Avenue in the early 1950s … I found myself attracted to a shop that had typewriters on sidewalk stands for passersby to try. The machines were done in different colors and had a sleek design. I went inside and saw modern furniture and bright colors. The name over the door was Olivetti.' When he later compared some of Olivetti's graphics with a selection of IBM's, he saw that 'the Olivetti material was filled with color and

excitement and fit together like a beautiful picture puzzle. Ours looked like directions on how to make bicarbonate of soda'. The contribution made by enlightened clients to the creation of good design has often been ignored, in part perhaps because historically such clients have been scarce. Nevertheless, there is no doubting the effect of Watson's attitude on IBM's design and, by extension, on design in the corporate sector generally. It is thought not to be a coincidence that IBM's adoption of Modernist design coincided with its transformation into the world's largest company and an icon of American corporate power. Yet it would be wrong to overstate the importance of a client in the creation of good design. Watson did not dictate what the design should look like, let alone do the design himself. He wisely entrusted that to Rand.

From the mid-1940s to the mid-1960s, the fields in which Rand first established his reputation, that is, magazine publishing and advertising, were at their most fertile and frenzied in New York, then as now the world's business capital. Nearly all of America's leading art directors were concentrated within the few blocks that lined Manhattan's Madison Avenue – Rand, Beall and Brodovitch all spent time there – and the so-called 'New York School' that developed there was seen to be

15.22: 'Woman's Day' magazine advertisement designed by Gene Federico, 1954

15.23: Anti-war poster designed by Herb Lubalin, 1972

MARRIAGE

MOTHER

Families

A READER'S DIGEST PUBLICATION

15.24: Typographic designs, Herb Lubalin, 1962–5

ero	9ine	subtrcting	cl°wn
1ne	10en	multimultiplying	dea
2we	11even	div id ing	f⌐oor
3hree			nO!se
4our	+dd	?uestion	eaning
5ive	–tract	!xclamation	incomplet
6ix	xultiply	advertisiNg	o
7even	div÷de	togethemess	ver
8ight	addding	aut₀m₀bile	fallin g

15.25: Typographic designs, Brownjohn, Chermayeff & Geismar Associates, 1962

at the forefront of the 'New Advertising', a product of what was later referred to as the 'Creative Revolution'. Each of these phrases was coined in recognition of the increased sophistication of American advertising and editorial design. Rather than rely on the tried and tested hard sell, with its direct appeal to the viewer to buy such and such because it was the biggest or the best, or else on the simple sell of the Sachplakat, with its single picture and product name *(<fig. 11.5, p.166)*, this new brand of communication frequently relied on the smart sell, an approach that demanded a little more from the viewer. Where each of the former methods required the viewer to be passive, this latter kind required them to be active. The viewer had to engage with the design in order to decode its more thoughtful and sometimes pointedly unorthodox messages. The main tool used to elicit this more active engagement was wit. By delighting the viewer with verbal and visual puns, not only were the products more likely to be remembered, they might also become associated in the viewer's mind with the positive responses the humour provoked.

The special emphasis on a witty interplay between image and text demanded a close working relationship between the art director and the copywriter. This necessary unity of type and image was exemplified by an advertisement *(fig. 15.22)* for *Woman's Day* magazine which first appeared in *The New Yorker* in 1954. It was

created by the art director, Gene Federico (1918–99), and the copywriter, Bill Bernbach (1911–82), both of whom were leading figures in their respective disciplines. Federico helped to turn the 'o's in 'Go Out' into bicycle wheels through his careful choice of typeface, Futura Light. The unusually circular 'o's of Futura and the thinness of its light weight perfectly resembled bicycle tyres. It formed a visual pun that was similar to the one used by the Sachplakat designer Hans Erdt in his Opel poster *(<fig. 11.7, p.168)*, but was also different to it in that the punning concept was less oblique. Where Erdt's example was suggestive, here it was explicit. It was both more central to the design and more fully integrated with the text. But it was not just the pursuit of a visual pun that had led Federico and Bernbach to emphasize the words 'go out'. These words expressed the core of the advert's message. Its purpose was to persuade other advertisers to place their own ads in *Woman's Day*, not an unattractive proposition when the magazine could boast a female readership of nearly four million, and even less unattractive when such numbers would, as the last line of text explained, go 'out shopping where your products are sold'. By going out to get a copy of *Woman's Day*, its readers might also go out to get the things that *Woman's Day* advertised.

This mutual support between type and image did not always mean that each had to be given equal status.

Another of the New York School's art directors, Herb Lubalin (1918–81), specialized in creating designs out of a commanding and active typography. The full effect of his anti-(nuclear) war poster (<fig. 15.23) may have relied on the support of an image, but it was the emphatic white letters rather than the carefully illustrated insects that carried the burden of his cautionary message. Lubalin produced many other examples of witty typography, often without any pictorial element at all. He used the type to be its own illustration. Each of these three examples (<fig. 15.24) deliver their meaning with an economy and immediacy that comes from an exclusive reliance on typography. They are such succinct and definitive expressions of their concepts, it's hard to think how an image could have improved them; it surely would only have got in the way. However, the style of type, though not incidental, was not essential to their picture-making ability. The idea that letters can be used to illustrate the meaning of the words they make, independently of the typeface they appear in, was demonstrated most emphatically, and playfully, in the pages of a booklet designed by the New York agency Brownjohn, Chermayeff and Geismar Associates. The agency recognized that it was possible to take the essence of concrete poetry (<p.177) and distil it into a single word, and that each of these punning type-pictures (fig. 15.25) could be formed out of the same, simple sanserif typeface, Helvetica.

By the 1960s, a single dominating concept had become such a significant part of the new advertising that it began to be referred to by a name. That name was the 'Big Idea'. The majority of Big Idea designs were made to promote the various unexceptional but nevertheless desirable goods and services then available in the United States. Yet on occasion designs appeared that were devoted to other truly big ideas. In 1962 CBS television placed an advertisement (fig. 15.26) in the *New York Times* to publicize the next day's broadcast of the first attempt by an American to orbit the earth. The attempt was successful. Lt Col. John Glenn completed a triple orbit in just under five hours, and joined an exclusive club, which the Russian, Yuri Gagarin, had initiated the year before when he had become not just the first person to orbit the earth, but also the first man in space. The art director Lou Dorfsman (1918–2008) and his colleague Al Amato were able to reflect the patriotic pride and anticipated drama generated by Glenn's attempt with a design that hinged on the simple equivalence of stars in the American flag with stars in space. They placed their

central visual pun into a dramatic arrangement in which the vertical thrust of the three white stripes, some filled with text, vied for dominance with a surrounding solid black background that was penetrated by a rocket climbing starward. The contrast between the small, diffuse half-tone image of the rocket and the impenetrable array of hard-edged, angular stars seemed to reflect the contrast between the potentially hubristic ambition of mankind to escape earth's gravity and the vast, immutable forces that govern all objects in space.

The broadcast itself was watched by millions of Americans. For the first time, they had been able to witness a defining moment in their nation's history almost as it unfolded. As the programme's commentator was to say sometime after the event, 'it was a story that television was born to tell'. The compelling nature of television, with its cinematic combination of picture, movement and sound, and the fact that this combination was brought directly into people's homes, was to have a huge and largely negative impact on print advertising. As the number of households with televisions increased throughout the 1960s, money that had previously been lavished on magazines and posters began to be transferred to the production of advertisements and programmes on TV. The medium of print, which had been the primary form of visual communication for 500 years (and survived 60 years of competition from the cinema), could not compete with television's greater immediacy and accessibility. The status that print had once wrested from the manuscript passed over on to the small screen.

The dominance of screen-based information has only increased with the arrival of the PC, the internet and related technologies. They have made such information permanently accessible and have hugely expanded its global reach. The desire and ability of large corporations to address a global audience had already become strong by the middle of the twentieth century. It was partly in order to service this need, to communicate to people of differing cultures and languages, that many graphic designers chose to reject the stylistically varied forms of commercial Modernism. Instead, they turned to a new, single style based on the largely abstract and functional form of Modernism that had originated with the Bauhaus and other proponents of the New Typography. This new style was referred to variously as Swiss Design, in reference to the country where its development was initially most active, or else as the International Typographical Style, in recognition of the transnational and largely typographic character of the style.

THE ROCKET'S RED GLARE...

Early tomorrow morning – if all goes well – the eyes of a nation, and its hopes and prayers, will be focused on the first attempt of an American to orbit the earth.

As the rocket propelling Lt. Col. John H. Glenn, Jr. soars into space, the magic of television will enable millions of his fellow Americans to share in one of the great moments of their history.

Starting at 7:00 a.m., the CBS Television Network will stand ready to transmit continuous pooled reports of Colonel Glenn's three-orbit flight starting with the advance preparations for the lift-off to his recovery some six to eight hours later in the waters off the Bahamas.

REPORT ON RECOVERY

The CBS Television Network will interrupt its program schedule to present the video-tape report of Colonel Glenn's recovery the moment it becomes available. Should the flight be postponed, the network will, of course, broadcast the event whenever it is scheduled.

For its own special coverage and supplementing the pooled reports of the event, CBS News has assembled the largest complement of reporters, technical personnel, and facilities ever concentrated on a single news event with the exception of the national conventions and elections. Stationed at the CBS News control center adjacent to the launching site at Cape Canaveral, CBS News "anchor man" Walter Cronkite, assisted by Charles von Fremd and Richard Bate, will provide a running commentary at the missile area. The event will also be broadcast by the CBS Radio Network with CBS News correspondent Dallas Townsend as "anchor man" and Arthur Godfrey providing commentary.

To picture the course of the flight, a model of the capsule will be moved by magnets on a flat projection map showing the astronaut's location at any given moment. In addition, two animated globes will also reveal the orbital course.

HOW TO FLY A CAPSULE

CBS News will also present a striking demonstration of how to "fly" a capsule in a special 20-minute filmed report showing an engineer manipulating the controls of a capsule identical to the space craft carrying Colonel Glenn on his journey.

From London, Paris, and Moscow CBS News correspondents will report foreign reactions to the flight; while in Washington CBS News reporters Roger Mudd and Neil Strawser will describe Congressional reactions and the United States Information Agency's broadcasts throughout the world. From New York CBS News Moscow correspondent Marvin Kalb and UN correspondent Richard C. Hottelet will describe the Soviet man-in-space program and contrast the relative secrecy of the Russian experience with the full publicity surrounding the American effort.

FAMILY REACTIONS

In New Concord, Ohio, Colonel Glenn's home town, CBS News correspondents Harry Reasoner and Hughes Rudd will interview the astronaut's parents and report the mass gathering of the town's 2100 citizens at Muskingum College to watch the broadcast. In Arlington, Virginia, CBS News correspondent Nancy Hanschman will report the reactions of Mrs. Glenn, her children, and her parents at their home.

For the benefit of the thousands of daily commuters and other travelers in Grand Central Station, a giant screen will report the flight, as CBS News correspondent Doug Edwards moves through the crowds to pick up the reactions of the public.

Finally, if all goes according to schedule, CBS News will present a special report tomorrow night at 7:30 p.m. reviewing the highlights of the day's events and including the press conference with top NASA officials following the completion of the flight.

Tomorrow will be a day to remember as television once again demonstrates its unique power to enlarge and deepen the range of human experience. From the dawn's early light to the twilight's last gleaming, you can see it all.

CBS⊙2

15.26: 'Rocket's Red Glare', CBS advertisement designed by Lou Dorfsman, 1962

16 SYSTEMS AND SIGNS
Swiss Typography, c.1945–c.1972

'The epitome of ugliness' – Wolfgang Weingart; 'The ... lowercase "a" in the original foundry and linotype is the most beautiful two-dimensional form ever designed' – Katherine McCoy *(fig.16.1)*; 'Never liked it, never used it' – Willi Kunz; 'It is a modern type. It is a clear type. It is good for everything' – Massimo Vignelli; 'It also says bland, unadventurous, unambitious' – Neville Brody; '[It] is the "blue jeans" of typefaces' – Adrian Frutiger.

Logos, traffic and shop signs, posters, brochures, magazines and newspapers, business letters and labels – all such items have been set in the typeface referred to in the quotations above. Its letters are as likely to be seen on a train station's signage as in a logo spread across the side of a carriage, or the minute columns that make up a booklet of train times. Through the addition of new characters and accents, its letterforms have been adapted to serve non-Latin alphabets such as Greek, Cyrillic and Hebrew. Sanserif characters matching its style of letter strokes have even been developed for wholly different writing systems, such as Chinese, Japanese and Korean. The typeface has also been among the first to be adapted to new forms of printing technology. It quickly made the leap from lead type to photosetting during the early 1960s, and it was widely copied throughout the 1970s by new photo-typesetting companies especially, each of whom wanted to ensure that their particular machines could set it or at least some version of it. With the rise of digital typesetting in the 1980s, it was again considered essential and thus was among the first few fonts to be pre-installed on PCs: Macs began to include it in 1985, and from 1992 to 2007 Microsoft's operating system included what was essentially a copy of it. Governments (Canadian and Swiss) have adopted it as their standard typeface, as have national and international organizations (New York's subway signage system, the European Union) and

innumerable businesses. No other typeface has received such wide-ranging and frequent use (if in this we are able to include its many imitations) and it can fairly claim to be the world's most popular typeface.

The typeface in question is the simple and unassuming sanserif font, Helvetica *(>fig.16.2)*. A clear indication of Helvetica's popularity lies in the broad range of weights and widths that have been developed for it following its first appearance in 1957 in the basic pairing of roman and bold weights. The desire to extend Helvetica's range ever wider is the result of the enormous variety of tasks it has been asked to perform. Such was the importance attached to these variants and indeed to the typeface as a whole that the entire range was re-released in 1983 under the name Neue Helvetica, in which all the weights and widths, from Ultra Light Condensed to Black Expanded *(>fig.16.3)*, were redrawn and related to each other in a wholly systematic way. Helvetica's extraordinary popularity was founded on more than its range of variants however. A contributing factor was the associations it forged, first through its name and then through the style of design that first claimed it for its own.

Helvetica derived its name from its country of origin, Switzerland; the word 'Helvetica' means 'Swiss' in Latin. Helvetica was chosen in preference to Helvetia, Latin for Switzerland (both words are derived from *Helvetii*, a Roman word for the Celtic tribe who inhabited what is now a part of modern Switzerland).

This symbolic name was not the first one the typeface was given. When it was initially released, it carried the more workaday title of Neue Haas Grotesk (*neue* is German for 'new', Haas the name of the Swiss typefounders who created it, and *grotesk* the German word for 'sanserif'). A couple of years later, in 1960, Haas's new parent company, Stempel, developed the face for use with the Linotype machine *(<p.206)*, and supported

< 16.1: Neue Haas Grotesk publicity leaflet, Stempel foundry, 1958

ABCDEFGHIJKLMNOP
QRSTUVWXYZ
abcdefghijklmnop
qrstuvwxyz

АБВГДЕЖЗИЙКЛМН
ОПРСТУФХЦЧШЩЪ
ЫЬЭЮЯ
абвгдежзийклмнопр
стуфхцчшщъыьэюя

ΑΒΓΔΕΖΗΘΙΚΛΜΝΞΟ
ΠΡΣΤΥΦΧΨΩ
αβγδεζηθικλμνξο
πρσςτυφχψω

16.2: Latin, Cyrillic and Greek alphabets in Helvetica

16.3: Neue Helvetica, 1983 (*black weight)

	Condensed	Normal	Expanded
Ultra Light / Ultra Light Oblique	Helvetica / Helvetica	Helvetica / Helvetica	Helvetica / Helvetica
Thin / Thin Oblique	Helvetica / Helvetica	Helvetica / Helvetica	Helvetica / Helvetica
Light / Light Oblique	Helvetica / Helvetica	Helvetica / Helvetica	Helvetica / Helvetica
Normal / Normal Oblique	Helvetica / Helvetica	Helvetica / Helvetica	Helvetica / Helvetica
Medium / Medium Oblique	Helvetica / Helvetica	Helvetica / Helvetica	Helvetica / Helvetica
Bold / Bold Oblique	Helvetica / Helvetica	Helvetica / Helvetica	Helvetica / Helvetica
Heavy / Heavy Oblique	Helvetica / Helvetica	Helvetica / Helvetica	Helvetica / Helvetica
Black / Black Oblique	Helvetica / Helvetica	Helvetica / Helvetica	Helvetica / Helvetica
Extra Black / Extra Black Oblique	Helvetica / Helvetica	Helvetica* / Helvetica	

the release of a Linotype version with a new and, as it turned out, highly successful marketing strategy. The strategy involved replacing Haas's name – at the time Haas was as much Stempel's competitor as its affiliate – with one that was more pronounceable for English speakers. Tapping into the popularity of Swiss design among designers in Europe and America, the name Helvetica was chosen, and thereafter the typeface rose to become one of the most prominent of its time.

For all the benefits that an attractive and resonant name or, indeed, a fashionable style of design can bring to a typeface, it is the shapes of its letters that will really determine its success. In Helvetica's case, clearly, its letter shapes made it very popular, but not because they were especially novel or striking. Unlike previous twentieth-century sanserifs, such as the experimental Bauhaus designs (*< fig. 13.12 & fig. 13.13, p. 198*) or the commercially successful Futura (*< fig. 13.20, p. 203*) and Johnston/Gill Sans (*< fig. 14.8 & fig. 14.11, pp. 210-11*), all of which had broken new ground for the sanserif through their geometric and/or classically proportioned forms, the inspiration for Helvetica's design was not as theoretical or historical. Haas's sales rep, Max Miedinger, who drew each of Helvetica's characters, and Eduard Hoffmann, who as Haas's manager had

both commissioned and advised Miedinger, looked to the existing range of German sanserif types, the 'grotesques'. (The German name *grotesk* is likely to have derived from this non-American English and French form, though in American English, confusingly, the name used was 'Gothic'.) Among the range of grotesques that informed Miedinger and Hoffmann's new design, the dominant influence was a version called Akzidenz Grotesk (Akzidenz means 'jobbing', i.e. advertising), while a secondary influence was Schelter Grotesk (Schelter being one of the first German founders known to have produced a sanserif/grotesque).

The origins of sanserif type can be traced back to the first half of the nineteenth century, but it was only in the last two decades of the century that it became relatively common in Germany. It appeared in scientific texts and, in its condensed form especially, it became a staple of German advertising. During the second quarter of the twentieth century, it was taken up by Modernist designers such as Bayer, Matter and Tschichold (the last-named wrote in his book *Die neue Typographie*, 'Among all the types that are available, the so-called "Grotesque" [this being an English translation]… is the only one in spiritual accordance with our time,' though he did later recant this view). By the 1950s

ABCDEFGHIJKLMNOPQRST
UVWXYZ
abcdefghijklmnopqrstuvwxyz

ABCDEFGHIJKLMNOPQRST
UVWXYZ
abcdefghijklmnopqrstuvwxyz

ABCDEFGHIJKLMNOPQRST
UVWXYZ
abcdefghijklmnopqrstuvwxyz

16.4: Comparison of Akzidenz, Helvetica and Univers

CJQRcgst

CJQRcgst

CJQRcgst

16.5: Comparison of Akzidenz, Helvetica and Univers

the grotesque, particularly in its Akzidenz form, had become the type of choice for Modernist designers in Switzerland. They appreciated its commercial pedigree and its modern, yet rounded more human-looking letters, as compared to the more literary, irregular and complex letters of the traditional German gothic or roman type, or, indeed, the new more mechanical-looking geometric sanserifs (e.g. Futura).

Haas's aim for the design of Helvetica was to make, as Stempel's publicity material later put it, 'a carefully and judiciously considered refinement of the grotesque [ibid] letterform'. What this amounted to was the removal of some of Akzidenz's peculiarities, though not to the extent that the basic character of the letters changed. The most conspicuous refinement was the replacement of the diagonal terminals that had appeared in the Akzidenz form – particularly evident in the 'c' and 's' *(fig. 16.5)* – with new horizontal or vertical terminals. Each of the letters so changed seemed to acquire a new sense of self-containment. The dynamism or energy within the letters' strokes, which had previously been directed outwards onto the page, was now fed back into the letters, lending them a feeling of security, or inviolability even. Miedinger also looked carefully at the weight and spacing of each letter, and made sure that when strung together in a line of text they presented the eye with an even, grey tone. Related to these two refinements, though more subtle and perhaps more significant than each, was the Escher-like balance Miedinger achieved between the letters' positive, black shapes and the surrounding negative, white background. The white

shapes he created within and/or around each letter – in the 'a' *(<fig. 16.1)* and 's' for example – possessed such beauty and balance, they were as pleasing a point of focus as the black shapes of the letters themselves. These surrounding background shapes are a part of Helvetica's mysterious charm; always looked at but seldom seen. They seem to hold the black parts within an invisible vice, binding them into a configuration that possesses a look of inevitability, as though even the most marginal thinning or refinement would mar them. (Perhaps it is this feature that prompted McCoy's praise in the opening quotations?)

Helvetica's popularity was shared by other new members of the grotesque family; in particular, by what can be thought of as Helvetica's twin, a similar kind of neo-grotesque, called Univers *(fig. 16.4)*. This typeface was also released in 1957 and its letters were also influenced by Akzidenz Grotesk. But while it can be said that both faces have a similar typographic voice, each speak it with a slightly different accent. For instance, whereas in Helvetica the tail of the 'Q' was diagonal, in Univers it was horizontal; while the top of Helvetica's lowercase 't' was horizontal, the top of the 't' in Univers was slanted; and generally, throughout Univers's letters, the strokes were a little less monoline. This slightly greater contrast between the letters' thick and thin parts made Univers more like a normal seriffed roman typeface, which have led some to claim that it was better suited to setting long texts.

Univers's designer, Adrian Frutiger (1928–), who went on to become one of the century's most prominent type designers, was also Swiss, and, therefore, had grown up under the influence of the grotesque. It

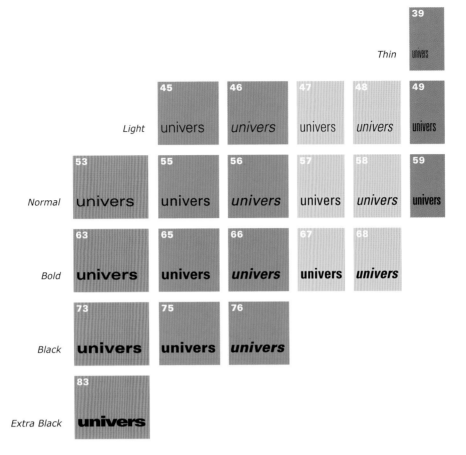

16.6: Univers numbering scheme, 1957

was while working in Paris for the pioneering French foundry, Deberny & Peignot, however, that he designed his new version of sanserif. The company had asked him to design it for a new kind of setting machine, the Lumitype, which, as its name hints at, set text using light, within a photographic process. The technique of composing text by shining light through a negative onto a light-sensitive surface had been developing since the 1940s, and although direct-photography photocomposition, to give it its full name, was to have a relatively short life, it was, nevertheless, a highly significant technology. It made clear the direction of an evolving trend: the dematerialization of printing. Photocomposition signalled a decisive break with the tactile, object-orientated printing process that Gutenberg had established 500 years earlier. Away went the sculpted punches and moulded lead matrices that had exerted such a dominating influence on printing since its inception, and in came letters on film made from shadows cast by electric light. No longer was a printed image the inky mirror of a solid object and, by extension, no longer was it

necessary to invest large sums of money in the manufacture of metal punches and matrices.

Frutiger took full advantage of this new economy. He was able to make a typeface with 21 variants, comprising six different weights and widths *(fig. 16.6)*. The early availability of so many variants contrasted with the much slower pace of development that had typified the design of metal types. Because this earlier method had required a varied range of tools and materials and a number of skilled hands, only the two standard weights, regular and bold, and their accompanying italics, would usually be released. More would follow if the demand for the initial pair had been high enough. Frutiger was unburdened by such restrictions and so could plan and design his entire Univers family as a single, integrated system. He could make sure, for example, that a strong family resemblance was carried throughout the entire range, even in the italics. Historically, many italics had looked wholly unrelated to their roman counterparts *(<fig. 5.12, p. 94)*. Because the italic had been derived from a cursive form of handwriting rather than directly

from roman letters, it had developed some distinct shapes of its own. Frutiger, however, chose to ignore these conventional differences and instead made his italics from the roman by shearing his roman letters along a central, horizontal axis half-way up their x-height. Thus, his italics were really a form of sloped roman, or, as he called it, 'oblique' roman, rather than a traditional italic. The advantage of this method was not just that the letters required less designing, it also helped to produce a smoother, more even tone when they were set alongside roman letters, as they inevitably would be in continuous text.

Designing each of the variants in one go also allowed Frutiger to make sure that they contained the right degree of variation designers were looking for, be it a subtle contrast between the italic and roman within a piece of continuous text, or a distinct one between a bold heading and the continuous text below it. No matter how complex a job was typographically, designers were provided with enough variety for them to rely on Univers alone if they so wished (and the more so when Frutiger helped to make a new digital version of Univers, released in 1997, which carried a total of 63 variants).

A related feature of Frutiger's Univers was the rational system he invented for naming its variants. As implied by its name, Univers was made with an international audience in mind. But, perhaps because Frutiger had grown up in Switzerland, with its four national languages, he was aware of the problem that a linguistically diverse market would pose such an extensive typeface. The names of weights in various languages were not directly equivalent. The English terms 'bold' and 'semibold', for example, did not always match the German *fett* and *halbfett* or the French *gras* and *semi-gras* (meaning literally, in both languages, 'fat' and 'half-fat'). In order to avoid any confusion, Frutiger decided to name the various weights and widths with numbers instead of words. He devised a logical two-digit system in which the first numeral referred to the variant's weight (e.g. thin or bold) and the second to its width (e.g. condensed or wide) or else its angle (e.g. roman or italic). The starting point for his numbering system was the roman variant of normal weight and normal width. He gave this the mid-range, decimal value of 5 for its weight and, similarly, 5 for its width and roman form, thus establishing a base number of 55. All other variants then extended upwards or downwards from this mid-point. Despite the logic of the system, printers and designers found it hard to use.

By relying so heavily on just two numerals, either one of which could be easily misread or misheard, Frutiger's system suffered more from human error than the conventional system of names ever had, and so it was later altered and used in combination with the normal way of naming.

The words used to describe Univers, Helvetica and the other neo-grotesque typefaces are similar to those used to describe the style of design in which they first featured. This style is known generally as 'Swiss Typography' or else, sometimes, 'Swiss Graphic Design' (in German it is Neue Schweizer Grafik), though in Switzerland itself the style was called Konstruktive Grafik or Neue Grafik. Both it and the typefaces associated with it are usually described by words such as 'rational', 'functional' or 'plain' (as in undecorated) and 'impersonal' (as in emotionally neutral). The style became one of the most dominant graphic styles of the latter part of the twentieth century, and even today it continues to have a certain prominence.

Why this set of characteristics should find expression in Swiss graphic design at the beginning of the second half of the twentieth century can be partly explained by geography. Switzerland shares its northern border, as well as its dominant language, with its large and culturally influential neighbour, Germany. During the first half of the twentieth century, the force of this influence exposed Swiss printers and designers to the various strands of functionalist Modernist design then being developed beyond their northern border. The Berlin brand of Constructivism and the New Typography from Munich and the Bauhaus (which latterly had had a Swiss director, Meyer, as well as two prominent Swiss teachers, Itten and Klee, and several Swiss students, Ballmer, Bill and Schawinsky, each of whom went on to become prominent Modernist designers) were certainly known, if not initially praised, in Switzerland.

During the 1920s, most Swiss printers and designers dismissed Modernist graphic design as a fad, but as the style became more entrenched during the 1930s, they were forced to engage with it. The Bauhausian ideas associated with it were as relevant to traditionalists as to Modernists: the importance of a rational and economical basis for design within an increasingly complex industrialized society, the need for an objective analysis of communication in a more international marketplace, the significance of egalitarian forms of design in the face of Fascist governments beyond Switzerland's borders.

16.7: 'Die gute Form' exhibition panels by Max Bill, 1947

These sorts of issues and the graphic styles they influenced were discussed and displayed in a number of prominent Swiss magazines. They were also promoted by individual designers through direct contact. Many foreign designers came to Switzerland either as visitors to give lectures or put on exhibitions, or else as refugees seeking asylum in one of the few European countries that had remained neutral during the Second World War. Most refugees stayed only temporarily, but some influential Modernist artists – such as van de Velde, van Doesburg and Tschichold – settled there permanently.

Two features particular to Swiss society are also thought to have contributed to its development of a rational Modernism. One was Switzerland's political system, which, since the middle of the nineteenth century, had developed a unique form of direct democracy (though before 1971, it could only be accessed by the male population). It allowed citizens to challenge and vote to amend laws in their country's constitution, and it gave the regional states, or cantons, that made up the Confederation an unprecedented degree of autonomy. Today no other federal democracy is so decentralized politically. Prior to voting, Swiss citizens had to receive

concise political and legal information from their canton or from the federal government (some of which appeared in four different languages). This placed an onus on designers and printers to present information clearly and impartially. It caused a civic, as opposed to a capitalist, bias to develop within Switzerland's information culture.

The second feature of Swiss society to nurture the Swiss style of graphic design was the strong tradition of craftsmanship that existed within the printing trade. This tradition had grown out of the early establishment of book printing in many of Switzerland's major cities. Basel (in 1466) and Geneva (in 1478) were among the first cities anywhere to follow the lead set by Mainz, the German city in which Gutenberg had first printed c.1450–54. The continuation of this tradition could be seen, during the middle of the twentieth century, in the high standard of tuition that existed within Switzerland's technical colleges. It was also apparent in the actions taken by the Swiss government to help the ailing economy, which, like all others in the West, had been hit hard by a worldwide recession during the 1930s and the world war that followed in 1939. In spite of being surrounded by warring nations Switzerland managed to remain sovereign and neutral, but it could not protect itself from the effects of such a close conflict. Political unrest and rationing were constant preoccupations for Swiss citizens, as they were for others elsewhere. To support the economy during the war and the decades that followed, the Swiss government and some of the larger regional cantons sponsored a series of international and domestic trade exhibitions in which Modernist design was sometimes not only tolerated but actively encouraged. Display panels showing examples of Modernist design were themselves laid out in a Modernist style (fig. 16.7). The government also established annual design competitions, most notably a poster competition, which also served to promote the style.

Following the end of the war in 1945, Swiss artists and designers began to transform the functional Modernist design they had inherited from Germany into a more distinctively rational and sparse style. One of the most ardent and influential champions of this new form of design was the Swiss artist and ex-Bauhaus student, Max Bill (1908–94). In 1946 Bill was provoked into outlining the style's principles during a dispute with fellow designer Jan Tschichold. Each laid out their competing views in the pages of several Swiss design and typography magazines. Bill had been stirred into publishing his support for Modernist graphic design after hearing reports of a lecture Tschichold had given at the end of 1945, in which he, Tschichold, had argued that the New Typography was ill-suited to book design. In his opinion, the style was too ephemeral. Because of the enduring nature of books, they required a more conventional treatment, one that had withstood the test of time. This contradicted the position he had promoted so passionately throughout the 1920s, and the one that Bill continued to stand by. Indeed, Bill saw the New Typography as the first step in a progressive march towards an ever more functional form of design. Many of the graphic elements that had marked the New Typography out as progressive – the thick rules and varied blocks of type – were, in fact, essentially decorative. In so far as they attracted the viewer's attention, such decorations could be said to have performed a certain function, but in Bill's eyes they usually did so at the expense of a more important function: legibility. They had rarely made the text any easier to read. Bill wanted to strip away these decorative, attention-seeking devices so that every part of the design could be justified by the contribution it made to a clear understanding of the content: 'the requirements of language and legibility must be fulfilled before purely aesthetic considerations can be introduced ... when this typography is also directed towards designing text such that it becomes a living text organism, void of decorative trimmings and convolutions, then we would call it "functional" or "organic" typography.'

The increasing emphasis on clarity and functionalism within Swiss graphic design was exemplified by a poster made at the end of the decade *(fig. 16.8)* by the Swiss Modernist Carlo Vivarelli (1919–86). With three simple elements – two lines of tightly spaced white text, both set in Akzidenz Grotesk, and a small half-tone photograph – Vivarelli delivered a message in a manner that was both immediate and compelling. Nothing was superfluous. Everything in the design was dedicated to imparting the poster's message. Its success as an appeal for 'voluntary donations' (*Freiwillige Spende*) on behalf of the charity 'Help the Aged' (*Für das Alter*) was formally recognized by the Swiss government when it awarded the poster first prize in its aforementioned poster competition. Part of the poster's power comes from the aged head, with its elephantine skin and penetrating gaze, dramatically lit as though by candlelight. But another part of its power comes from the placement of the head within a daring but wholly fitting asym-

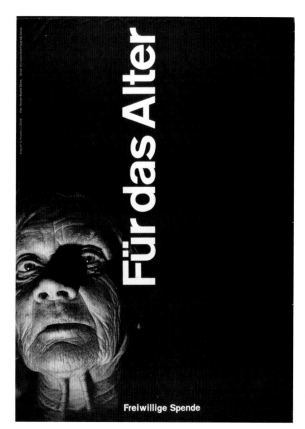

16.8: 'Für das Alter' poster designed by Carlo Vivarelli, 1959

metry. The large vertical text, whose baseline runs up the centre of the poster, has been placed in front of the woman's head, which is cropped on the other side by the poster's left-hand edge, giving the impression that she is peering through a half-opened door, or perhaps, even, the metaphorical bars of a cell, behind which she has been imprisoned by her age. The carefully crafted drama in the photograph is just one example of a tendency among many Modernist designers to use the supposedly neutral medium of photography very subjectively. While praising photography for being emotionally neutral and objective, they often took or chose images that were highly charged and partial.

A purer attempt at an impersonal form of design was made by the Swiss designer Josef Müller-Brockmann (1914–96), a pioneer of the new style and, subsequently, its most widely known practitioner. Over a period of almost 50 years, Müller-Brockmann developed a rational, simple and at times wholly abstract style in his perennial pursuit of graphic clarity. His series of concert posters for Zürich's Tonhalle (Concert Hall), in particular, became archetypes of the Swiss style at its most minimal, abstract and impersonal. One of the best known of the

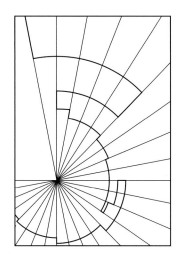

16.10: 'Beethoven' poster
design scheme, 1955

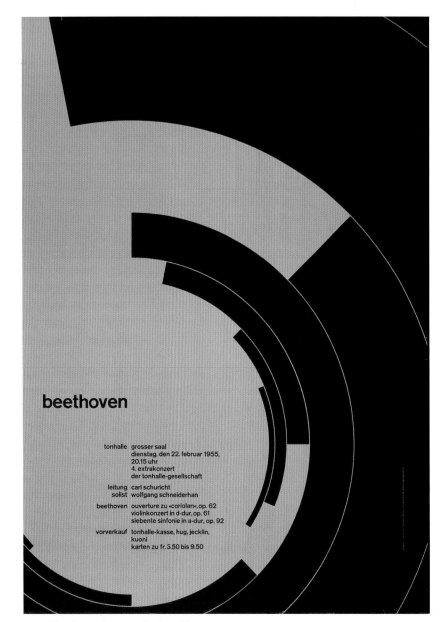

16.9: 'Beethoven' poster designed by
Josef Müller-Brockmann, 1955

series was his 1955 'Beethoven' poster *(fig. 16.9)*, with its lowercase sanserif text set in the familiar Akzidenz Grotesk and surrounded by a concentric maze of black arcing shapes, whose purpose, as his wife later described it, was 'to express the world of Beethoven, this storm … the movement between the heavens and the earth'. At first glance, the black type and black shapes look like they are floating freely in space, but quite soon a sense of order asserts itself. Vertical and diagonal alignments become apparent. In fact the size and placement of almost every element is determined by an

overarching geometry or a series of spatial relationships. For example, the lengths of the black arcs – where they start and end – are determined by a number of invisible segments formed from 32 equal divisions of a circle *(fig. 16.10)*, which itself is centred on the top left corner of the main text block, that is the 'g' of *grosser*. This centre point is positioned at the intersection of an imaginary diagonal connecting the top right-hand corner with the bottom left, and a horizontal line forming the base of the upper square section of the poster's rectangle. The radiating black arcs double in width as they

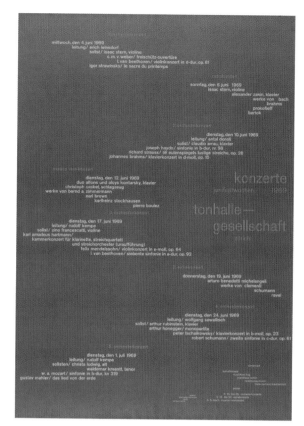

16.11: 'June Festival' poster designed by
Josef Müller-Brockmann, 1969

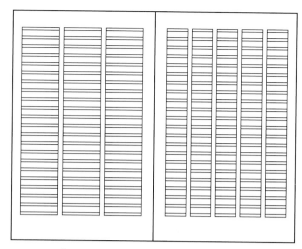

16.12: 3-column and 5-column grids

spread outwards so that the largest, outer arc is 32 times the width of the smallest, inner arc. In the middle of the arcs, Beethoven's name is placed half-way between the bottom of the text block and the inner edge of the black arc directly above the text, and the size of the name, or at least its x-height, is the same as the distance between the top x-height and lower baseline of two lines of small text. These are just some of the spatial relationships that suffused Müller-Brockmann's design with a subtle sense of order.

The creation of an objective style of design was not his only reason for relying on abstract shapes. Müller-Brockmann thought the subject matter of his Ton-halle posters – music – would be best represented by forms that reflected music's essentially abstract nature (< p. 184). By arranging abstract forms into a series of structured rhythms, they would be able to express the structured rhythms contained in Beethoven's music. But for his compatriot, colleague and friend, Vivarelli, such an approach was not objective enough. As Müller-Brockmann later recalled, Vivarelli advised him that his 'use of geometrical elements was too subjective. This is

what led to my making concert posters exclusively typographic. I now tried, using a dynamic organization of words and lines [of text], to achieve a floating, transparent typography which would be able to give the effect of musical poetry' (fig. 16.11). Why, indeed, add abstract shapes when they already existed in the form of letters within the text?

Müller-Brockmann created a musical poetry with a free-floating quality not dissimilar to the airy Symbolist compositions Mallarmé had produced nearly a century earlier (< fig. 12.2, p. 176). Falling rhythmically from side to side as it made its way down the poster, Müller-Brockmann's text looked like the visual equivalent of free verse; and yet, as in his Beethoven poster, its apparent looseness was underpinned by a very definite spatial metre. On close inspection one can see that each line of text is carefully aligned with word-breaks in the lines above or below them. Such a scheme successfully evoked the structured rhythms of music, while also managing to limit the degree of Müller-Brockmann's self-expression. Moreover, and more importantly, such minimal means – the positioning and colouring of a single style of lowercase text (set in Helvetica this time rather than the usual Akzidenz) – still allowed readers to find the information they needed. For such a fluid design, it is surprisingly easy to navigate through the text to find out information about the Tonhalle's concerts, which after all was the poster's main purpose.

The rational underpinning of a layout was of prime importance to the post-war Swiss Modernists. For them, a design could only be truly objective, truly free from the whims of an individual designer, if it were laid out according to a set of rational or mathematical principles. The main tool used for applying these principles was the grid *(< fig. 16.12)*: an invisible series of lines that divided the surface into uniformly sized rectangles so as to guide the laying out of a design. Whether on posters or in books or magazines, a grid would ensure the text and pictures were positioned in a rational and orderly manner. Perhaps the most influential example of the grid in action was the magazine *Neue Grafik* or 'New Graphic Design' *(fig. 16.13)*, 18 issues of which were published between 1958 and 1965. This quarterly magazine was edited and, for the most part, written and designed by Vivarelli and Müller-Brockmann in partnership with two other Swiss designers, Richard Paul Lohse (1902–88) and Hans Neuburg (1903–83). Their broad aim, as expressed at the beginning of the first issue in a statement which they signed with the collective, lowercase initials 'lmnv', was 'to create an international platform for the discussion of modern graphic and applied art. Contrary to that of existing publications, the attitude of *Neue Grafik* is characterized by exclusiveness, consistency and lack of compromise [i.e. a strict adherence to the principles of Swiss design].' In reality, though, rather than create a platform for modern graphic and applied art as they were generally practised, the magazine was largely filled with examples of art and design from Switzerland. In spite of this national bias, the magazine succeeded in capturing an international audience, not least because the text appeared in the three languages of German, English and French. Because it was clearly written and because it gained such a wide readership, *Neue Grafik* became perhaps the single most effective means of promoting the Swiss style.

Part of its effectiveness was due also to its own exemplary style of design, which expressed visually what was discussed verbally in the text *(fig. 16.14)*. The magazine's near-square format seemed to emphasize the geometric principle on which the grid was based: the

16.13: 'Neue Grafik' magazine cover, 1958

force of the right angle. The cover was entirely typographic and, in serving as a contents page, overtly functional (listing the contents so comprehensively on the cover was as unusual then as it is common now). It was designed, as were the inside pages, with a four-column grid, which particularly suited the trilingual text. Where appropriate, each of the three languages could be placed in separate columns of text, while the titles, headings or captions, being short, could be kept in trilingual units within a single column. A single typeface, Akzidenz Grotesk, was used throughout and almost everywhere it appeared in a single size and weight. This very restricted typography not only fulfilled the designers' aesthetic aim, but also supported their democratic beliefs. All the individuals mentioned in the text, be they artists of international renown or an assistant designer fresh from college, were treated as equals typographically. The arrangement of the text was only one aspect of the magazine's graphic clarity; the pictures were similarly organized. Most, but not all, were printed in black and white, and sized to fit within a single column. A simple numbering system then linked them to the relevant captions or main text.

As the pages of *Neue Grafik* demonstrated, as much through the designs they illustrated as through the style of their layout, the grid had become an integral part of the new Swiss style. While it established the grid as

16.14: 'Neue Grafik' magazine spread, 1959

an important tool of design, it did not invent it. Early in the era of manuscript production, long before books were printed, simple grids had been used to mark out where the lines of handwritten text should appear. Many parchment pages still show the faint rules that scribes had used to guide them in writing out their script. Some of the first printed books also had a visible grid, and in later liturgical books especially, the grid was not incidental but emphatic. It was printed, often in red, in order to help readers follow the text of a shared book during a service. In both forms of the book, manuscript and printed, the primary purpose of a grid, whether visible or invisible, simple or complex, was to facilitate a systematic process of production. The scribe or the printer could work more quickly if his text was to appear in the same place on every page.

During the second half of the twentieth century, the purpose of the grid changed. It developed more in the direction of the reader than the producer. Modernist designers such as Bayer and Tschichold had shown how a grid could be used to lead the reader through the contents of a layout in a systematic way, but as printed pages began to incorporate more varied kinds of information – headings, main text, captions, illustrations, diagrams and the like – the grid had to become more complex and, therefore, be considered more carefully. Guided by the example of their German colleagues, the Swiss Modernists developed the grid into a detailed and comprehensive design system in which every kind of arrangement could be catered for. The benefits to the reader became more apparent. The organizing unit on which they based their grids was the line space and column width of the main text. Every element on the page was fitted into a series of rectangular sections or 'fields', as they were called, whose height matched the standard line space and whose width either matched or was a simple division of the width of a standard column. In this way, all parts of the page could be aligned or related to each other spatially. Within these more orderly layouts, it was believed that designs could reap the triple benefit of being read more quickly, understood better and therefore remembered more easily. It also, importantly, lent the contents a greater sense of authority. What appeared visually to be rational and well considered, was taken to be so conceptually too.

The three decades that followed the end of the Second World War were a golden period for the industrialized economies of the 'developed' world. Record levels of employment and productivity were sustained by and, in turn, helped to maintain, a rapid expansion in the building of roads – in particular, long, multi-lane highways linking major cities – and the development of new high-speed rail links. A huge increase in the production of cars, trucks and buses, powered by cheap fuel, contributed to a greater movement of people and goods within and across continents. The transport of freight across the oceans was revolutionized by the container ship, while commercial air travel made mass international tourism both feasible and fashionable, and allowed for a new breed of globe-trotting business-men and women. These advances in transport were combined from the 1960s with a revolution in commu-nication, caused in part by new technologies, such as magnetic tape recording (allowing radio and television programmes to be pre-recorded rather than having to be broadcast live) and digital computing (a beneficiary, like all subsequent electronic devices, of the microchip or transistor). The effect of these trends was reinforced by the more widespread ownership of existing technolo-gies, such as telephones and televisions. In combina-tion, modern modes of transport and communication allowed goods to be manufactured transnationally; that is, for a single product to be assembled in several countries. They also enabled large businesses, based in one country but operating in several (the so-called 'multinationals'), to increase their influence on how life was lived in what began to be referred to as the 'global village'.

These three pillars of globalization – transport, com-munication and business – needed to be supported by an effective exchange of information. The movement of goods and people within and across national borders depended on a clear and consistent mode of commu-nication among a more culturally diverse workforce, and then also between them and their customers. The rational, minimal and apparently impersonal, or corporate, character of Swiss design provided just such a mode of communication. Multinational corporations and the audiences they courted appreciated the style's sense of simple efficiency. Each accepted it as being representative of a new more modern and international age. Moreover, the set of rules inherent in its grid sys-tem and its uniform typography could be understood and implemented even by designers who had grown up outside the Swiss tradition. The dominance of its typography, which the grid had thrown into relief, and the uptake of the style outside Switzerland, led Swiss design to be referred to as the International Typographic Style.

The powerhouse behind the post-war economic boom was the American economy, which was itself driven by what was then the world's most populous and

16.15: 'Think Small', VW Beetle poster designed by Helmut Krone, 1959

culturally diverse city, New York. 'The Big Apple' (a name promoted in the early 1970s by the organization in charge of the city's marketing and tourism) was the world's commercial capital, and the capital of adver-tising too. The potential benefits brought by the use of the grid – speed of reading, understanding, memorabil-ity, authority and modernity – were especially valu-able to advertisers, and they often adopted the Swiss style in campaigns for their new multinational clients. The grid was used as a sober counterpoint to the witty concepts behind many of their Big Idea advertisements (< p. 236). In 1959, Helmut Krone (1925–96), the art director of the New York agency Doyle Dane Bernbach, used a simple, three-column grid to advertise the new Volkswagen Beetle (fig. 16.15). Though the bold, cen-tred sanserif by-line 'Think small' did not conform to the asymmetric alignment of the grid, but by being fit-ted precisely into the central column it did not disturb the advertisement's overall sense of order. The cool logic of its layout contrasted with the ad's playfully unorthodox message. The message was an early exam-ple of the subtle 'soft sell' with which the agency was to become closely identified. The contrast between the advertisement's layout and its message was in keep-

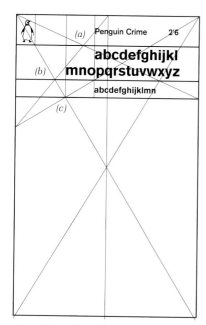

16.16: *Romek Marber's Penguin grid, 1961*

16.17: *Penguin paperback cover designed by Romek Marber, 1961*

ing with Krone's conviction that 'the page ought to be a package for the product'. The car's famously well-functioning engine contrasted with the playfully unorthodox design of its body shape.

The international use of Swiss design also spread to more indirect forms of advertising. In 1962, the British publisher Penguin chose a Swiss style of design for the bulk of its book covers. So successfully had the company pursued its founding aim of publishing paperback books for a mass market that after 25 years it could boast a monthly publication schedule of around 70 titles. But with this success came new challenges. Even by the mid-1950s, the largely typographic cover designs (< *fig. 14.14, p. 213*), which had distinguished the books during the company's first few decades, had begun to look out of date. The tendency towards a greater use of pictures, photographic ones especially, across most forms of graphic media had encouraged rival publishers to produce much livelier, pictorial covers. Penguin decided that it too should follow the trend. It experimented with full-colour and full-cover pictures, but with its expanding number of titles, the introduction of more varied and complex designs led to a weakening of its corporate style. The main fiction series had begun to use a different design scheme to the main non-fiction series, for example, though neither scheme was adhered to with much rigour. One solution to this problem was to adopt a single scheme based on a standard grid. A set

of consistent and practical, yet potentially eye-catching, designs would help to promote Penguin in the crowded and competitive book-publishing market.

The grid's Polish-born, UK-based designer, Romek Marber (1925–), created a simple scheme from a set of geometrical intersections (three of which (*fig. 16.16, a, b, c*) determined the position of the cover's three horizontal black rules). Initially it was only to be applied to Penguin's green crime series, though, as soon as its merits were recognized, the grid was applied more widely. An important feature of Marber's arrangement was the corralling of the text into the top third of the cover, which left the bottom two-thirds free for the illustration (*fig. 16.17*). Never before had Penguin's various picture designers and illustrators (of whom Marber himself was one) been given so much text-free space to work with. It was a luxury which they exploited by producing a series of arresting and starkly graphic images in a decidedly modern idiom. Different kinds of illustration were combined on the same cover: photographs mixed with hand-drawn symbols and more conventional kinds of illustration. And a variety of reproductive techniques were applied – cut-outs and overprinting – which lent an allure of contemporaneity even to republished novels that in some cases were decades old.

This modern style of illustration was matched by a modern style of typography. The three horizontal bands contained three kinds of text: at the top the series name (flanked by the logo and the price), in the middle the book's title, and then below it the author's name. Within each band the text was left-aligned, just to the left of centre, though a secondary position was also provided for long lines of text (proving that extremes can be accommodated in a grid system). While Penguin's first cover design had looked like a historical hybrid, with the contemporary typeface Gill Sans set in a traditional, centred layout, Marber's covers displayed a more resolutely Modern manner. They followed the standard Swiss formula of a left-aligning, asymmetric typography set in Standard, the name given to Akzidenz Grotesk within the English-speaking market. Full capitalization, which had dominated the company's earlier book covers, was dropped, and so too the capitalization of nouns within the book's title, which had also been common. Instead Marber relied on a more minimal mix of upper and lowercase, as found in normal text. The contrast between the ordered simplicity of the typography and the loose, complex style of illustration made each more noticeable than they would have been without the other. An indication of the covers' impact can be gauged by the behaviour of several retailers who, after receiving the first batch of new designs, gathered up the remaining copies of the old design and returned them to the publisher with the request that they be replaced by the new ones.

Penguin's move to promote itself through a set of more consistent cover designs was indicative of a new, more active interest in graphic design among the business community during the early 1960s. Businesses – large ones especially – began to take graphic design more seriously. The commercial success of corporations such as Olivetti and IBM seemed to put beyond doubt the importance of placing modern graphic design at the heart a corporate business strategy *(< pp. 230 & 232–3)*. For multinationals wanting to break into new regional markets, graphic design could be especially effective at establishing the company's profile, provided it were not limited to a series of printed advertisements. Every aspect of corporate communications, the logo, the company's annual reports, even its job advertisements, influenced the perception of the company among its potential customers. A company's stationery, its packaging and the design that appeared on its cars and trucks, if carefully considered and co-ordinated, could help to create a distinct, memorable and attractive identity.

Graphic design was not alone in forging this identity. The architecture and the interior design of a business's

16.18: *Corporate identity manual for Mobil designed by Chermayeff & Geismar, early 1970s*

offices or stores also affected how the company was perceived, and thus, such elements were often considered alongside graphic design within an overarching design programme. For some of the larger companies, co-ordinating such a program was important enough for it to be placed under the control of a dedicated in-house design team, rather than farmed out to various freelance designers. By internalizing design in this way, it was hoped that the organization would reap greater benefits from within as well as from without. The employees themselves would benefit. They would better understand the company's aims and feel a greater affinity for them; especially those who worked in a regional office that was otherwise estranged from the more active corporate culture within a head office. By having a work environment that was clean, comfortable and laid out specifically for the job in hand, they might also work better and be happier. The importance given to the social role of design during this period was summed up by one of America's foremost Modernist industrial designers in a comment he made about a new range of designs: 'These are not desks and file cabinets. This is a way of life.'

16.19: Mobil service station, 1966

16.20: Woolmark logo designed by Francesco Saroglia, 1964

None of these benefits would accrue, however, if a corporation's design programme was not implemented consistently. Consistency is especially important for the graphic component of a corporate identity, not just because an image is made more memorable by repetition but also, and less positively, because a business's reputation can be damaged by a lack of consistency. It can give the impression that the business is badly organized or unfocused. The main way of achieving a consistent graphic identity was through a printed manual. This so-called corporate identity manual described verbally and visually what the principal graphic elements of the identity were – what the logo looked like and what the company's main typeface was – and how these graphic elements should be applied to the company's various items of print – its stationery and packaging – as well as, where necessary, to such things as signage or the fabric design for interiors. By referring to the manual, all such items could be made in a uniform manner, even when being produced, say, in different countries by the international branches of a multinational company.

The Swiss style was ideally suited to meet this need for consistency. The simplicity and the structure that lay at the heart of the style lent itself to the role of exemplar within a design manual. The ranged-left, grid-based, sanserif typography neither needed, nor allowed, much interpretation from designers and it could be easily described with visual examples and minimal annotation. As Rand, who came to appreciate the virtues of the style after initially holding it in contempt, had commented, '… there is no counterpart to Swiss design in terms of something that you can describe, that you can follow, that you can systematically understand'.

Rand's comments seemingly described the design

behind a brief set of guidelines that formed one part of a much larger corporate identity programme that was begun in 1964 for the oil company Mobil *(fig. 16.18)*. The graphic design part of the identity was carried out by an American company, Chermayeff & Geismar. Though they quickly developed strict rules for signs, packaging and vehicle markings, Chermayeff & Geismar allowed a good deal of latitude when it came to implementing the graphic identity in advertising and promotional material – 'its effectiveness often depends on its newness. Change of pace, idea, content and look are essential…'. In being made as a guide for outside suppliers, however, the later set of guidelines referred to above were a picture of graphic clarity. All the requisite attributes of the Swiss style were brought to bear: the Helvetica (and Futura) inspired sanserif typeface, designed exclusively for the company's use; the short columns of legible, ranged-left text set alongside explanatory illustrations within an orderly grid; and the simple use of bold primary colours.

Part of the guidelines contained a clear description of the correct form and use of the logo that Chermayeff & Geismar had designed for the company. The logo's letters were derived from the corporate typeface, which was itself used for all titles and headlines. This consistent use of bold sanserif letters proved to be one of keys to the success of the programme. An important part of the logo's effectiveness was the dominant red circular 'o' (or concentric double 'o' for monochrome printing). Its simple geometry expressed the Swiss style's preference for abstract, universally applicable, geometric forms. The initial spur for highlighting the 'o' came from an idea that had guided the design of the company's service stations *(fig. 16.19)*. A special

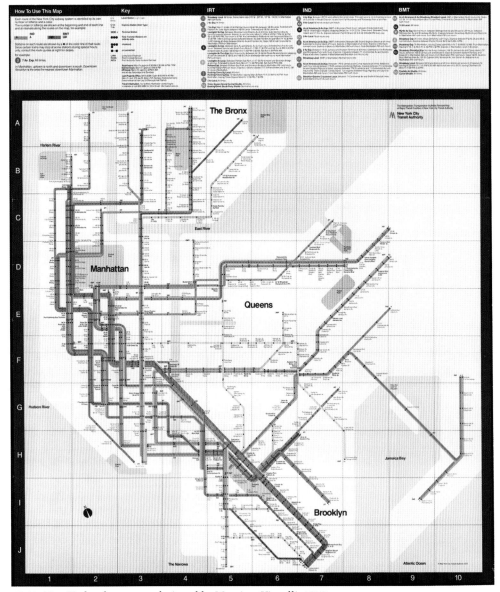

16.21: New York subway map designed by Massimo Vignelli, 1972

emphasis had been placed on the circle. It was used to determine the shape of the stations' canopies, pumps and equipment. Such items seemed to echo the apt associations that were made by the logo's dominant 'o': the company's core product, oil, as well as the wheels of a car.

Not all abstract logos had to be reduced to a simple geometry, nor did they have to be combined with type. The Woolmark logo, which was designed to signify the quality of a woollen product *(< fig. 16.20)*, needed no accompanying typography. The simple symmetry of its undulating curves, which also carried associations with the product it represented – the soft threads of spun

wool and a ball of wool – had a graphic purity that reflected the logo's purpose.

Another area of graphic design to be dominated, or, at least, heavily influenced, by the Swiss style was the increasingly technical realm of information graphics. Rather than appealing to people's emotions, as advertisements did, or presenting an image for a business through a corporate identity programme, the primary task for information graphics was to relay directions or instructions unambiguously. Signs directing road traffic or the increasing number of travellers through stations and airports; diagrams showing how to assem-

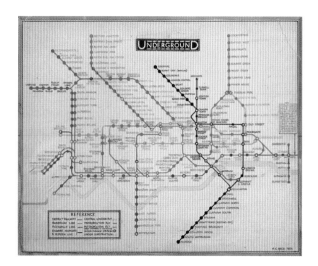

16.22: London Underground map designed by
Harry Beck, 1933

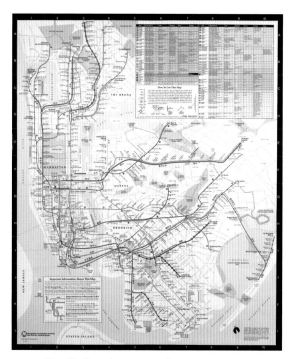

16.23: New York replacement subway map, c.1979

ble or operate the plethora of new electrical goods that had begun to fill people's homes; maps describing the layout of city centres and subway systems or national parks; all such items had to impart information to a linguistically varied audience, many of whom carried with them their own, quite different set of culturally determined sign conventions.

Nowhere, perhaps, was the ability to communicate complex information to a culturally and linguistically diverse audience more keenly tested than in the subway map of New York. By the early 1970s, New York city, with its large, widely dispersed population, had developed an intricate subway system of 476 stations linked by 26 different train lines, along which more than three million passengers would pass each day. To help these mobile masses navigate their way through the labyrinthine network of rail track and tunnels, a map was published in 1972 *(fig. 16.21)* which concentrated more intently on the lines and stations, rather than the range of supplementary information above the ground – landmark buildings, prominent streets, local districts and the like – as most previous maps had. The set of forms used to make this new, more focused subway map was founded on the strictures of the Swiss style. The map's designer, Massimo Vignelli (1931–), had come to New York from Italy, where he had studied

Swiss typography. Every aspect of his map design was dedicated to creating an image that was logically ordered and visually clear: Helvetica type appeared throughout; the explanatory notes in the upper section were set within a five-column grid; and the map itself, clearly framed within a thick, black square, was made up of brightly colour-coded lines set within a very simplified outline of the main land masses and surrounding waterways; and all were overlaid with a visible grid. The contrast between it and its predecessors was distinct.

What also set it apart was the very schematic arrangement of its train lines and stations. Such a scheme had first appeared in a map of New York's subway in 1958, though the inspiration for that and by extension Vignelli's map had appeared nearly three decades earlier in a map of the 'Underground' in London *(fig. 16.22).* Though the designer of this foundational London map, Harry Beck (1903–74), had spent 27 years refining the details of his design, it was the two innovations he had worked out in his earliest sketches, in 1931, that proved to be most significant. The first innovation was to restrict the direction of the train lines to either verticals, horizontals or diagonals. Such a configuration would have been familiar to Beck through the electric circuit diagrams that he had had to draw when employed earlier as an engineering draughtsman. His second innovation was to enlarge the central area of the network in relation to the outlying areas, so that the more concentrated connections in the heart of the city could be seen more clearly. Both innovations, however, forced him to abandon any strict geographical accuracy in relation to the world above ground.

Most of the time this lack of accuracy mattered little, but in some instances it was unhelpfully misleading. For example, according to the map, the best way to get from Regent's Park station, in the heart of London's West End, to Great Portland Street nearby, is to head up to Baker Street and change. In reality, though, this sends you out in the opposite direction before bringing you back only a couple of hundred metres (650ft approx.) from where you started. Local knowledge would have suggested the alternative of a pleasant, two-minute stroll along a single road with views of some of London's finest Regency buildings. In creating a scheme that contained these sorts of distortions, Beck had not really designed a map, but more of a diagram. Not that the British public minded. Whatever was lost to them in geographical, or even verbal, accuracy was more than made up for in clarity. They appreciated the greater ease with which they were able to plan their journeys and the supplementary benefit brought to them by the map's almost logo-like distinctiveness. By reducing London's layout to such a simple scheme – fittingly accompanied by London Transport's simple sanserif lettering (< fig.14.8, p.210) – the map enabled people to build a better general awareness of the various parts of their city, despite misleading them on occasion through the inaccuracy of its details.

On the other side of the Atlantic the reaction to Vignelli's map was generally less positive. It should be said that, with more than twice the number of lines and stations, Vignelli's task was harder than Beck's. It led Vignelli to set the station names in a size of type that proved difficult to read over the shoulder of a fellow passenger. More fundamentally and generally, though, his map did not meet the expectations of the people using it. Partly, this was a matter of old-fashioned neophobia: the reaction that accompanies any attempt at changing an established way of doing something. In spite of the existence of the schematic 1958 version, New Yorkers had become accustomed to seeing geographically correct maps in which the position of the train lines and stations corresponded to the features they were familiar with above ground. However, to some extent such

16.24: Munich Olympics logo designed by Otl Aicher, 1972

expectations were also induced by the way Vignelli had adapted the earlier schematic examples. Few New Yorkers could fail to notice the mismatch between the Central Park they knew, which is more than five times longer than it is wide, and the map's depiction of it as being wider than it is long (neither of the earlier examples included any parks). The stations too suffered from similar disparities, much as the stations in London had. Yet New Yorkers were more sensitive to these disparities than Londoners. The gridded pattern of their streets had given them a better understanding of the distances within their city. Telling someone 'It's a couple of blocks away' is a meaningful indication of distance in New York, but in London, with its web of variegated streets and alleyways, it could mean it's a stone's throw away or else a half-mile hike.

Another expectation not met, which this time would have been shared by New Yorkers and Londoners alike, was the natural and conventional one that maps should show parks in green and water in blue. Whereas Beck had fulfilled this expectation by using a series of blue lines for the river Thames, which snakes its way right across London, Vignelli it may be assumed had to give priority to colouring the numerous train lines. And he had to make sure that the lines he coloured with greens and blues would not get lost when they passed over parks or waterways. Thus, he marked these natural features with the graphically legible but counterintuitive colour combination of light grey and beige.

In a sense, Vignelli's design was a victim of its willingness to be helpful. As he later admitted, he should perhaps have been even more narrowly focused on the subway system and excluded any representation of the world above ground. By leaving out the depictions of land masses, waterways and parks, he would have

16.25: Munich Olympics poster designed by Otl Aicher, 1972

reduced the expectation for geographical accuracy and removed any expectation for intuitive colouring. Such a map might have avoided the fate that befell his actual map, which after only seven years was replaced by a less schematic and more geographically correct but, also, much busier version *(<fig. 16.23)*, the progenitor of the current map. Perhaps in time, as people in New York are more able to access detailed maps on their own portable, hand-held devices, they will welcome a clear diagrammatic map dedicated to showing how to get from one subway station to another (much indeed like the new

speculative version that Vignelli has recently designed).

In the same year that Vignelli's map was released, 1972, one of the most wide-ranging applications of the Swiss style appeared in Europe. The Olympic Games in Munich, though lasting only 16 days, presented its designers with a task equal in size and scope to any ad campaign or corporate identity they might have undertaken for a large multinational corporation. The games needed a complete design programme involving the creation of advertisements, a corporate identity and a whole range of information graphics. The number of

16.26: Munich Olympic pictograms designed by Otl Aicher, 1972

separate items to be designed was vast, and each design needed to appeal to a global audience based around the 121 participating nations.

Because the Munich Olympics was the first international event to be held in Germany since the war, the Olympic committee was keen for it to be seen as a festive occasion. They wanted 'The Happy Games', as they officially called it, to stand in direct contrast to the previous German Olympics, the so-called 'Nazi Games', which had been held in Berlin in 1936. For the Munich Olympics's principal designer, Otl Aicher (1922–91), showing the new games in a more positive light was not merely a matter of good PR. Having grown up in Ulm in southern Germany, Aicher had spent many of his formative years living under a Nazi regime he grew to loathe and had actively resisted, at some personal cost. Designing the Munich Games would allow him to express visually what he had learnt through experience about the value of individual liberty and inclusivity.

His first piece of design, the games' logo, boldly stated his positive intentions. Aicher presented a sun symbol, abstracted into a circular 'wreath of rays' and then, at the behest of a design committee, orientated it around a spiral shape (<fig.16.24). Unlike almost every other Olympic logo before or since, the design contained no symbolic reference to the host nation. For Aicher any appeal to nationalism, however well intentioned, would contravene the essence of the games as a globally unifying event (a unity which the Olympics' own interlinked five-ring logo symbolized, one ring representing each of the participating continents). By leaving out any nationalistic reference, Aicher was also pointedly contrasting these games with the very overt nationalism that had dominated the Berlin Olympics. The colour chosen for the logo was a mid-blue, the principal colour within a spectrum of seven bright and vibrant colours specially selected by Aicher. None of them was red or black.

The feeling of lightness and freshness that steered Aicher in his choice of colours also guided him in his choice of type. He selected the clean lines of Frutiger's neo-grotesque Univers, and applied them alone to all items; though rather than take advantage of the typeface's wide range of variants, Aicher tended to rely on a single weight and width of it, Univers 55. No aggressive contrasts of varying weights or slant were allowed to disturb an overall sense of cleanliness and typographic quietude. He applied this minimal style of typography, together with the logo and his standard set of colours, to a series of 21 sports posters, each of which was dominated by a single, dynamic but universally recognizable photographic image (<fig.16.25). The posters were able to convey something of the essence of the games to their culturally and linguistically mixed audience because each image captured the relevant sport at its most characteristic. Athletes were shown in the most identifiable poses – a gymnast leaping or sprinters dipping as they crossed the finishing line. Moreover, the symbolic character of each pose was enhanced by their being abstracted into a limited set of tonal blocks. Such a process both removed any superfluous or distracting detail and helped imbue what might otherwise have been a rather hackneyed image with a compelling sense of novelty. At least one part of each photographic image was cropped by the edges of the poster so as to give the impression that the athletes had been caught in a single moment of action as they burst, usually from left to right, across the viewer's field of vision. Finally and more subtly, Aicher made sure that many of the fragmented tonal photographs included strong horizontal bands of colour, which helped to connect them to the otherwise disparate horizontal band of neat, linear type and five-ringed Olympic logo.

Aicher's very integrated approach to design, which his earlier experience of Nazi propaganda and censorship had encouraged in him, could only achieve the openness and inclusivity he sought if his designs were clear and informative. Clarity of information was an important requisite for the games too. A mass of

information was needed to guide the thousands of competitors and spectators to each of the numerous venues that were spread out across the city of Munich. Maps, timetables, guidebooks and brochures had to be designed with the same graphic clarity and simplicity as the posters. Of all the examples of the Munich Olympics' information graphics, none displayed these characteristics so starkly as the set of pictograms Aicher made for various individual sports *(fig. 16.26)*. The benefit of having a set of symbols generally intelligible to a multilingual audience – 34 different languages were spoken in Europe alone – had first been realized at the Berlin Olympics and then, more fully and systematically, in the 1964 Olympics in Tokyo. But what made Aicher's symbols so powerful was their success in marrying two important but opposing tasks. Like the posters, the symbols had to represent specific sports unambiguously, which, again, as in the posters, they did by showing athletes in poses and with props that most characterized their respective sports: diving swimmers, ball-dunking basketball players and paddling canoeists. And yet the symbols also had to be simple and schematic enough to be understood or 'read' at a glance. Aicher resolved this dichotomy by reducing the figures to a limited set of geometric shapes and then combined and positioned the shapes according to a geometric grid *(fig. 16.26, last)*. Heads, arms, bodies and legs were all aligned vertically, horizontally or diagonally. Whatever these regular shapes lacked in dynamism (and certainly a greater sense of movement was contained in subsequent Olympic pictograms), they made up for in recognizability. Their bold, regular and simple forms lent them a strong family likeness, which made them easier to pick out from the visual noise of a busy street or a dense page of printed information. The earlier pictograms designed in the 1930s by Neurath and Arntz *(< fig. 13.17, p. 200)* had not maintained such a distinct family likeness. Indeed Aicher's pictograms were considered to be so successful that they and the larger

set of more general pictograms he also designed for the games went on to be used at sports complexes and schools throughout Germany as well as at the next Olympics in Montreal.

The vibrant and festive rainbow colours that Aicher used in his Olympic designs approached the palette of colours that characterized a contemporary style of graphic design; although which, in all other ways, was the very antithesis of the Swiss style. Psychedelic art, the style with which the counterculture movement of the 1960s was most closely identified, was one of several counter-styles of the 1960s and 1970s to set themselves in direct opposition to the clinical, corporate and overtly mechanized design of the International Typographic Style. What linked them was their emphasis on illustration, or, at least, on an impression of being handmade or home-made. They appeared to place the individual over the corporate, the subjective over the objective, and the manual over the mechanical. They expressed the more liberal and individualistic attitudes of the post-war generation by deriving their character from the freedom that lay within a designer's hand.

17 HANDMADE AND HOMESPUN
Illustrated Modernism & Psychedelia, c.1950 – c.1970

The freedoms fought for by the war generation were defined by questions of nationhood, empire and trade. For the following generation – the populous, post-war generation of so-called 'baby-boomers' – such freedoms were no longer threatened in quite the same way. Growing up behind secure national borders and during a period of unprecedented economic growth (by contrast with their Depression-torn parents), it was only natural that their attention should focus on a rather different set of freedoms: those that centred more closely on the individual. From the mid-1950s, they began to campaign for individual liberties under various banners such as 'civil rights', 'the peace movement', 'women's liberation' or 'free speech'; phrases which today are more commonly couched within the social '-isms' of anti-racism, pacifism and feminism, or, with respect to free speech, within a phrase that befits our media-orientated age: freedom of information. Each of these campaigns grew into a fully fledged mass movement and accumulated all the requisite graphic paraphernalia: placards, banners and posters, which helped to promote the movements' symbols and slogans *(fig. 17.1)*, and then pamphlets and magazines, which allowed each to flesh out its aims more fully.

Much of the support for these movements was provided by a hugely expanded student population, at university level especially. Mass rallies, strikes and sit-ins attracted protesting students in their thousands. During the late 1960s college campuses became battlegrounds, sometimes quite literally and very publicly, with a number of violent clashes between protesters and the police forcing their way onto the evening's news bulletin. The sheer number of students and the sense of solidarity that was forged through the pursuit of a common cause changed the relationship between various social groups – the sexes and races began to interact in new ways – and also gave a new prominence and autonomy

to the young. Young people no longer viewed their place in society as an interim phase leading to adulthood, as their parents had done. They had their own way of living, which they expressed most evidently through new forms of music and fashion. A guiding principle behind both forms of expression and, indeed, youth behaviour more generally, was the mantra of 'personal expression'. However, despite being encouraged to 'do their own thing', peer pressure and a desire to be 'with it' meant that many people's own things turned out to be similar. In this way various subcultures became established, the most popular and widespread of which was a countercultural movement of second-generation 'hipsters', or hippies, whose style of dress and anti-materialist, sexually liberal attitudes influenced groups of mainly urban, middle-class young people in countries around the world.

Like other professionals from within the arts, graphic designers were both subject to these influences and generators of them. As a growing number of designers and design students became aware of countercultural attitudes during the 1960s, so many of them began to turn away from the clean, orderly, corporate style of Swiss typography. In fact they came to view Swiss design as one of the cultural forms that ought to be countered. While Swiss design embraced abstraction, countercultural design tended to be figurative; where the former sought simplicity, the latter welcomed complexity; minimalism was replaced with decoration, universal forms with personal expression, rationality with mysticism, and on a more technological level photography was frequently replaced with illustration. This last difference, the prevalence of hand-rendered illustration in countercultural graphic design, also owed a debt to two other influences: the fine arts and printing technology.

By the mid-1950s the close relationship between graphic design and fine art was almost a hundred years old. The two had first come together in earnest during the late 1860s, when developments in colour lithography had coincided with a democratic impulse to break down the traditional hierarchy that separated the fine and applied arts. These twin influences encouraged artists to turn their hand to poster design and thereby supplant the existing illustrative influence of the newspaper caricature with a range of more painterly effects and new, oriental influences. This initial link between fine art and graphic design was strengthened in the late nineteenth century by a number of celebrated poster artists – Chéret, Toulouse-Lautrec and Mucha – and then reinforced in the twentieth by successive generations of Modernist artists, whose theories on abstract and mechanically produced art encompassed all facets of art and design.

Shadowing this fine-art influence, however, was the rise of the photograph, which began to compete more and more with hand-rendered forms of illustration. By the middle of the twentieth century, the photograph had established itself as the standard kind of image across most printed media. In posters, books, magazines and newspapers the, usually, black-and-white photograph had forced its way into becoming the principal form of illustration. Its prominence had been made possible by successive improvements in printing technology, especially regarding the dot-bearing half-tone and the speed at which half-tone photographs could be combined with type on the same press. But the full range of photo-reproductive possibilities only came to fruition in the mid-1950s with the invention of a new kind of photographic film that made it much more economical to print colour photographs. Paradoxically, though, this development, which was refined over the next decade, led to an increase in the reproduction of all forms of colour media, hand-rendered ones as well as photographic ones. The true chromatic richness of a series of hand-rendered poster designs, say, or illustrated magazine covers could be reproduced in a magazine and appreciated just as much as any photograph of a sunset or photographic portrait. In this way book, magazine and poster designs became better known and it was with this spread of knowledge that a canon of works and a more considered appraisal of designers began to take place.

The same process influenced and popularized works of fine art too. The ability to print pictures in full colour allowed artworks to be better known and appreciated. Their value became less dependent on the judgement of an expert and more on the opinion of the layman. This

17.2: 'Vallauris' poster designed by Pablo Picasso, 1951

democratizing force was sometimes powerful enough to elevate the status of an artwork into the category of a masterpiece. It goes without saying that most of the people who recognize Leonardo's *Mona Lisa* will never have stood in front of it; they know what it looks like, largely because they have seen it reproduced in print. Before the twentieth century, however, this picture was much less familiar. It was considered to be one among many of Leonardo's great paintings, but not as highly regarded as a number of pictures by other Renaissance artists. The *Mona Lisa*'s popularity increased during the first half of the twentieth century (partly as a result of being stolen), and as the prevalence of colour reproduction grew during the 1950s and 1960s its status continued to rise. Today no other painting is better known. Its current pre-eminence is attested by, and partly due to, its popularity with the advertising industry, which has embraced it more than any other picture. Its almost continual appearance in printed and televised advertisements somewhere in the world (thought to be at a rate of at least once a week as far back as the 1980s) is mirrored by the range and quantity of printed *Mona Lisa* merchandise that is now available. Clearly many factors affect the status of an artwork, but familiarity is one of the more important ones. Many aesthetic objects benefited from the familiarity that colour reproduction brought about. By being more frequently reproduced in colour, practitioners in the fields of fine art and graphic design gained a greater awareness of each

17.3: 'Sgt. Pepper's Lonely Hearts Club Band' album cover designed by Peter Blake and Jann Haworth, 1967

other's work. With this increased awareness came a new period of exchange.

During the late 1950s a number of artists did as their predecessors had done and crossed over into graphic design by designing posters. None of them did so with as much commitment as the Spanish painter Pablo Picasso (1881–1973), who designed more than 70 posters over a period of 25 years. Though most of the posters were made to advertise exhibitions of his own work, some were made for others' too. This early example *(fig. 17.2)* is from a series of posters he designed for the potters of Vallauris, a region in the south of France that had sparked in him a belated but intense interest in the artistic potential of clay. As in all the posters he designed, every mark on this Vallauris poster was the product of his own hand. What is perhaps more striking about these marks though is that, despite coming from the hand of one of the most technically proficient artists of his or, indeed, any era, they are so childlike. Each leaf or petal shape, each line or dot, looks as though it

could have been made by the boy in the poster, though, clearly, he could not have positioned them with the same degree of decorative balance and illustrative skill. What is also striking, especially in comparison with the established conventions of poster design, is that this apparent simplicity and immediacy applies to all the marks, regardless of whether they appear as lettering or as flowers or parts of the face. The product of this shared simplicity is a unity, which Picasso took advantage of by setting the facial features, and the eyes especially, somewhat away from the other marks so that they can exercise their arresting power more freely and fully.

Forty years of fruitful experimentation across all kinds of media had made Picasso the most famous artist of his era, and yet none of his graphic designs became especially well known. The most celebrated piece of graphic design to have been made by an artist from this time was, by contrast, by a young British artist who, though identified as one of the most talented of a new generation of post-war artists, was far from being a household name. It was after talking to the singer Paul McCartney (1942–) that the young Peter Blake (1932–) conceived the collage effect that appears on the cover of the Beatles' 1967 album *Sgt. Pepper's Lonely Hearts Club Band* (<*fig. 17.3*).

Blake took the photomontage style of the Dada designers (<*fig. 12.9, p. 181*) and adapted it in a surreal and novel way. Though the cover looked like a genuine montage, it was in fact a photograph of a carefully staged set. Central to this surreal adaptation was Blake's then wife and fellow artist, Jann Haworth (1942–), who helped bring the conception to life with a series of life-sized, hand-coloured photographic cut-outs, which she and Blake arranged into unruly rows, as in a joke school photograph. Standing in front of the cut-outs and several sundry waxworks were the real 'fab four' dressed in a garish military-band uniform, pretending to be members of the fictitious Sgt. Pepper's Lonely Hearts Club Band. McCartney later commented that by this time the band 'were getting a little fed up of being the Beatles. It was all getting so bloody predictable'. Their appearance and that of the waxworks at the front of the group helped to fuse the two-dimensional characters behind them with the three-dimensional scene in front, with its shrine-like or grave-like mound of flowers, which had been planted, as in a municipal park, in the form of words or objects, the most predominant being the name of the real band, the 'Beatles', and a guitar.

Along with the photomontage effect, the DayGlo colours and the clash of cultural references made this funereal or shrine-like scene ironical. The figure of Bob Dylan (at the right-hand end of the back row) was shown rubbing shoulders with Sigmund Freud, an Indian guru and one of the wax dummies. This diverse cast of characters had been chosen partly by the Beatles as the people they would most like to have in an imaginary audience, but mostly by the designers. The richness, variety, playfulness and ambiguity of the whole scene mirrored the music it promoted. As Blake was to say later, 'I wanted to make art that was the visual equivalent to pop music.'

This statement strikes at the heart of what was different about the new relationship between fine art and graphic design during the 1950s and 1960s. The direction of influence was now two-way; it was less dominated by the effect of fine art on graphic design. Though some painters (the American, Stuart Davis, for example) had started to focus on aspects of mass culture as early

First Things First 2000 - A design manifesto

We, the undersigned, are graphic designers, art directors and visual communicators who have been raised in a world in which the techniques and apparatus of advertising have persistently been presented to us as the most lucrative, effective and desirable use of our talents. Many design teachers and mentors promote this belief; the market rewards it; a tide of books and publications reinforces it.

Encouraged in this direction, designers then apply their skill and imagination to sell dog biscuits, designer coffee, diamonds, detergents, hair gel, cigarettes, credit cards, sneakers, butt toners, light beer and heavy-duty recreational vehicles. Commercial work has always paid the bills, but many graphic designers have now let it become, in large measure, what graphic designers do. This, in turn, is how the world perceives design. The profession's time and energy is used up manufacturing demand for things that are inessential at best.

Many of us have grown increasingly uncomfortable with this view of design. Designers who devote their efforts primarily to advertising, marketing and brand development are supporting, and implicitly endorsing, a mental environment so saturated with commercial messages that it is changing the very way citizen-consumers speak, think, feel, respond and interact. To some extent we are all helping draft a reductive and immeasurably harmful code of public discourse.

There are pursuits more worthy of our problem-solving skills. Unprecedented environmental, social and cultural crises demand our attention. Many cultural interventions, social marketing campaigns, books, magazines, exhibitions, educational tools, television programs, films, charitable causes and other information design projects urgently require our expertise and help.

17.4: First Things First manifesto, updated version, 1999

as the 1920s, it was only in the 1950s and 1960s that a large enough group of artists had dedicated themselves to this aspect of modern life for their efforts to be accepted as part of a *bone fide* movement. Popular culture had become too much a part of everyday living for artists not to take note of it and bring it into their work, especially the form of popular culture that was most equivalent to fine art: graphic design. Not only was graphic design a legitimate subject for fine artists, but its motifs became accepted as part of the visual language of art.

as a graphic designer and illustrator. Indeed, the name of Andy Warhol (1928–87) is now synonymous with repeated brand images, such as Campbell's soup or Brillo soap pads, or even the face of Marilyn Monroe, who by the late 1950s had become a sort of human brand image. The enlarged reproductions of comic book graphics by the American Pop artist Roy Lichtenstein (1923–99) were similarly equivocal yet iconic.

Scepticism about the more commercial aspects of graphic design existed within the industry as well as outside it. During the early 1960s a number of British graphic designers became increasingly unhappy about the commercial direction of their profession. In January 1964 they were joined by several photographers and students in expressing their dissatisfaction in a manifesto called *First Things First*. The text of the document had been inspired by, and based on, a short impromptu speech delivered by one of the 22 named supporters months earlier at a Design Society meeting in London. The designer in question, Ken Garland (1929–), had scribbled his thoughts down during the meeting and then read them out to a packed audience at the end of it. His passionate declamation was greeted with applause and he received immediate expressions of support.

What had prompted Garland, a man of strong left-wing convictions, to speak out was, as he saw it, an imbalance in the profession towards commercial or corporate ends rather than social or political ones. By publishing his thoughts in a manifesto, he and his supporters had hoped 'to encourage students, designers and photographers to think about the opportunities for graphic design and photography outside advertising'. The signatories did 'not advocate the abolition of high pressure consumer advertising', nor were they asking designers to become impoverished saints by dedicating themselves to good causes free of charge. Their challenge was more realistic than that, and also more fundamental and personal. They wanted designers to stop and think before offering their services to clients. As implied by the manifesto's title, they wanted designers to look to their priorities, and to do so from the point of view of citizens within a society rather than business people in search of a profit.

Though *First Things First* didn't stop the graphic design industry from becoming increasingly corporate in character, it did resonate with a significant number of individuals over a long period of time. The manifesto was taken up and printed in some of the most prestigious design magazines and translated into several

This new reciprocity between fine art and graphic design was explicit in the title 'Pop art'. The name was quickly adopted by the relevant group of artists, but in doing so they were not expressing their unqualified approval of popular culture. In fact, like most people, they were ambivalent about it. As well as celebrating it they frequently parodied the banality or kitschness attendant on its more consumerist side. It is no surprise that the most iconic examples of this parodic form were provided by an artist who had initially trained and worked

17.5: 'The Man with the Golden Arm' poster designed by Saul Bass, 1955

languages. It also appeared more than three decades later in a revised form with a new, more international list of signatories (< fig. 17.4).

The commercial forces that shaped the design industry during this period were not entirely malign. As had been the case from as far back as the early nineteenth century, commercial pressures put a premium on creating novel forms. During the period of post-war prosperity, an intense competition for the public's attention both within the medium of print, and between print and its rival, television, led graphic designers to seek out new ways of engaging their audience. Many looked to the fine arts, which continued, as before the Second World War, to provided graphic designers with an array of motifs. A number of the early film posters of the American designer Saul Bass (1920–96) showed fine-art influences, though it is his poster for the 1955 film *The Man with the Golden Arm (fig. 17.5)* that is especially celebrated. As with Picasso's poster, every mark in it is

handmade: the lettering was drawn by hand by a specialist lettering artist in a style that matched the jagged, hand-cut silhouette of the arm and the large, irregularly cut blocks of paper.

The technique of cutting out and arranging simple shapes of coloured paper into a more or less abstract composition had been given a degree of prominence during the previous decade by the works of the French painter Henri Matisse (1869–1954). Though Matisse is known to have used cut paper to test how a particular colour or shape might look in his paintings as early as the 1930s, it was only in the final decade or so of his life, while in his late sixties and seventies, that he began to use cut paper as a medium in its own right. Having all but abandoned painting owing to ill health, Matisse developed the cut-out into a fully fledged method of picture making. It sustained him during his convalescence to the extent that he could say: 'Only what I created after the illness constitutes my real self: free, liberated.' His liberation was secured by a small pair of scissors and some specially coloured paper. The paper had been painted by his assistants in carefully chosen hues and tones using a special brand of gouache paint. The act of slicing through this paper gave him the sensation of sculpting in pure colour; of creating shape and colour in a single gesture. It encouraged him to carve out, mostly in freehand, a huge variety of brilliantly vibrant silhouettes and patterns, some of which he combined into pictures for hanging on the wall, while others were made as designs for books, magazines, tapestries or even, as in one of his last works, the stained-glass windows of a church.

The earliest published example of his *découpages* or 'cut-outs' was the cover of the 1940 edition of the French art magazine *Verve*, but both this and his other subsequent designs for the magazine were eclipsed by the publication in 1947 of his limited-edition book, *Jazz (fig. 17.6)*. Though only 250 copies were printed, its 20 cut-out illustrations combined with the large looping swirls of his handwritten text – 'the exceptional size of the writing seems necessary to me in order to be in a decorative relationship with the character of the colour prints', explained Matisse – to create one of the most celebrated examples of a relatively new literary genre: the *livre d'artiste* or 'artist's book'. (Its equivalent in graphic design has come to be referred to by the inelegant title of 'graphic authorship'.) It was a form of literature in which at least as much importance was attached to the illustration as to the writing. As a work

17.6: 'Jazz' livre d'artiste by Henri Matisse, 1947

of art in book form, its value, like that of other works of art, derived as much from the reputation of the artist and the exclusivity of the work (i.e. how many or, more pertinently, how few copies were published) as from the merits of the work itself.

For Matisse, an old man brimming with a lifetime of experiences, the title *Jazz* seemed an appropriate metaphor for the apparently spontaneous workings of his memory and imagination, which brought forth scenes from the circus and French music-hall, moments from popular tales and myths, and events from his life and the places he had visited. None of the scenes related to the title directly, but the cut-out techniques reinforced the appropriateness of the book's title. When making his cut-outs Matisse allowed an element of chance to help create shapes that were arrived at fortuitously as well as others that had been consciously looked for. It was a process suggested in the words he had once used to describe jazz, the music: 'chromatic and rhythmic improvisation'.

It is not known whether Bass ever cited Matisse as an influence, but it is hard to think that he could have used such a similar method of picture making so soon after it had been established without having been influenced by Matisse in some way, if only subliminally. Just as the technique had suited Matisse's circumstances, so it also fitted the particular needs Bass had for his *Golden*

Arm poster. Bass chose the arm to be the film's symbol because of the reference it made first, and most obviously, to the film's title, which itself was an allusion to the central character's skill as the dealer within an illicit card game; and then second, and more obliquely, to the film's central and controversial theme of heroin addiction, in which the arm is of course a favoured adjunct. It was in order to express this latter theme better that Bass gave the arm a fractured and grasping quality.

The arm's simple logo-like shape proved to be as effective on the poster as it had been in the medium for which it was first designed, the film's title sequence. Part of its effectiveness in the sequence was due to its very novelty. Designing a title sequence with animated graphic shapes had never been done before. Usually the perfunctory list of names that appears at the start of each film would be displayed against a black background or a still of some kind. But for Bass, this functional chunk of time offered the opportunity to do something more. It allowed him 'to set [the] mood and the prime underlying core of the film's story, to express the story in some metaphorical way. I saw the title as a way of conditioning the audience so that when the film actually began, viewers would already have an emotional resonance with it.' By animating his title sequences so arrestingly, Bass elevated them to an art form almost single-handedly. His legacy is not confined to the

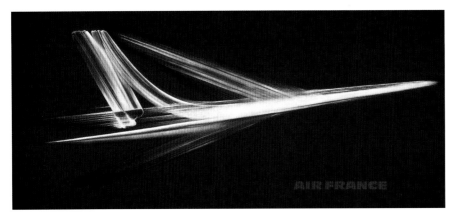

17.7: Air France poster designed by Roger Excoffon, 1965

many different kinds of title sequence that most feature films begin with today, but also ultimately to the obligatory sequence of graphics that start almost all programmes on TV.

The boldly graphic, cut-out arm helped to establish the right mood among the *Golden Arm*'s audience, but it also importantly fitted in with the other shapes in the title sequence while remaining a commanding element on the screen. The same duality applied to the poster. The jagged arm fitted in with the other cut-out shapes without being swamped by the surrounding text and imagery. Naturally Bass was keen to preserve the prominence of the film's symbol on his poster, so he took the unusual step of excluding any photographs of its leading stars. Not even Frank Sinatra, one of Hollywood's biggest stars at the time, was allowed to make an appearance. The film studio considered this excessively precious, and subsequent versions of the poster conformed to type with the inclusion of stills of all the leading actors.

At around the same time that Bass created this new kind of filmic art, a new form of abstract painting had begun to receive mainstream recognition. Though the roots of Abstract Expressionism can be traced back to the early European avant-garde, the style was seen nevertheless as a fundamentally American form of art. 'The new American painting' was a popular tag. Its dominance during the 1950s was not determined solely by the paintings themselves. Interest was also generated by the bohemian lives and tragic deaths of the artists involved (Jackson Pollock's car crash, Mark Rothko's suicide), and by their unusual methods of making paintings (Pollock dripped paint on a canvas laid flat on the floor, while some of Rothko's canvases were larger than most people's living rooms). The qualities that united

the style's very divergent set of paintings were, reasonably enough, those described in the style's name: abstraction and expressionism. The American artist Franz Kline, who was one of the style's many New York-based artists, projected both qualities in a way that related very specifically to the style's main medium: paint on canvas. In his early, best-known, abstract period, he reduced the colour of his paintings to a monochrome palatte, which heightened the very particular visual and textural quality of paint pushed and slid with a brush across a lightly mottled canvas surface. A similar focus on the expressive quality of monochrome brushstrokes also defined a simple, almost child-like, poster created in 1965, not long after Kline's painting, for Air France *(fig. 17.7)*. With only a handful of almost fluorescently brilliant strokes, its French designer, Roger Excoffon (1910–83), captured the rush and thrust of a plane in flight. Its shape prefigured Air France's first supersonic plane, Concorde, with its distinctively pointed nose; and, indeed, the image was used more than a decade later on a promotional poster leading up to Concorde's first commercial flight in 1976. It was Excoffon's appreciation of the expressive potential of sliding brushstrokes, which the Abstract Expressionist painters had first seized on, that enabled him to fuse the aeroplane's shape with the sensation of speed in such a minimal sequence of strokes.

Not all fine art-influenced graphic design took its aesthetic cue from contemporary styles of art. The influences that guided the style of animation and posters of the so-called 'father of Polish poster design', Jan Lenica (1928–2001), were the late nineteenth- and early twentieth-century movements of Expressionism and Surrealism. In a freakish theatre poster he designed in 1964 for the avant-garde opera *Wozzeck (fig. 17.8)* –

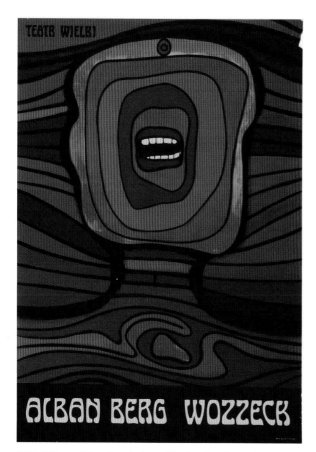

17.8: 'Wozzeck' poster designed by Jan Lenica, 1964

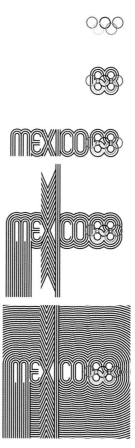

17.9: Olympics logos designed by Lance Wyman, 1968

Alban Berg was the opera's Austrian composer – the Expressionist influence is very specific. The poster takes its basic motif from a painting that has come to define the movement, *The Scream*, by the Norwegian artist Edvard Munch, who first painted it in 1893. In order to convey the opera's drama, or psycho-drama even, Lenica gave Munch's motif a surreal twist by depicting a square-shaped screaming mouth in the middle of a square-shaped cycloptic head. The poster's lettering looks back to an earlier period still, that of Art Nouveau. The curved letterforms mirror the undulating waves of sound that appeared to reverberate around the screaming figure. In its Art Nouveau lettering, rhythmical lines and intensely vibrant colours, the poster prefigured the counterculture's signature form, the psychedelic poster, which was also prey to several fine-art influences rather than a single influence. Where the psychedelic poster differed from Lenica's, however, was that its strongest fine-art influence was a contemporary one.

Though the origins of Op art can be traced back to some of the Constructivist-orientated teachings of the Bauhaus, it was in the 1960s that it became a fully fledged movement. The characteristic that united this very varied yet predominantly geometric form of abstract art was the arrangement of hard-edged linear shapes into patterns that created various kinds of optical illusions. By producing ambiguities between which parts of the picture represented the foreground and which the background or which were receding or advancing, the eyes of the beholder were forced to flit between each possibility to find a correct reading. In moving to and fro over such highly contrasting patterns, an after-image or shadow appeared on the retina, which added to the impression of a fluctuating or shimmering picture surface.

It was a kind of sensation the designers of the psychedelic posters were looking for. Unlike many Op artists though, and in contrast with some other high-profile, Op art-influenced graphic design – most notably the logo design for the 1968 Mexico Olympics *(fig. 17.9)* – this group of designers was not content to restrict its range of colours to a monochrome black and white. Indeed, the reverse was true. In order to heighten the shimmering effect of their designs, they sought out the

17.10: 'The Association' poster designed by Wes Wilson, 1966

most vibrant colour combinations. Through their use of colour-combined and optically illusionistic forms the designers were able to replicate the visual sensations of a hallucinogenic trip (as produced by LSD in particular). San Francisco was the counterculture's creative capital and it was there that the psychedelic poster first came into being, coaxed by a hedonistic triumvirate of sex, drugs and rock-'n'-roll. While the posters of this style were dedicated to reproducing the sensory effects of hallucinogenic drugs, content was frequently suffused with sexual overtones and function dedicated to promoting folk or psychedelic rock bands. The same set of aims and influences dominated the fliers handed out for gigs, and the bands' album covers. It was while studying colour theory under the ex-Bauhaus teacher, Josef Albers (1888–1976) that one of the 'Big Five' San Francisco-based designers, Victor Moscoso (1936–), had first learnt how to create a chromatic shimmering effect by matching the tones of contrasting colours. But what first inspired him to apply this knowledge to posters

17.11: 'Youngbloods' poster designed by Victor Moscoso, 1967

was the work of his compatriot Wes Wilson (1937–), one of the pioneers of the psychedelic style. The vibrancy of Wilson's own colour combinations and the skill with which he fashioned his sculptural, hand-wrought letterforms are exemplified in the fist-like ball of flame *(fig. 17.10)* that blazed on one of a range of posters he designed for San Francisco's Fillmore dance-hall. At first glance the flames yield little that is intelligible to the viewer, but then quite quickly a number of letter shapes reveal themselves, and before long whole words can be read. By seeing the graphic potential that lay within the protean nature of fire, Wilson cleverly made every flickering flame into a letter, and thereby allowed an easy association to be made between the ball of flame and the level of energy created each night on the Fillmore's dance floor.

By warping his hand-drawn letters into irregular shapes and spaces, Wilson helped to establish what became a signature feature of much psychedelic lettering. The fact that the resultant distortion of the letters made them somewhat illegible or, as in some cases, positively difficult to read, was taken by fans of the music to be a positive endorsement. It was evidence of what had attracted them to the countercultural scene in

the first place. The whole movement had been created in opposition to the mainstream; it was necessarily underground and mysterious, or subversive even. Like the quote about an earlier, twentieth-century countercultural genre, jazz – 'Man, if you gotta ask what it is, you'll never know' – so too with psychedelic lettering: if you minded that the letters were almost illegible, you shouldn't be bothering yourself with them. Most of Wilson's clients understood this and, in the spirit of much design that is poorly paid and forced into an unfeasibly tight deadline, they gave him and others like him latitude to do as they saw fit. Wilson was often able to deliver his artwork to the printer without its having to be approved first. Some clients were a little less insouciant, and as an insurance policy they had the text reprinted in small capitals at the bottom of the poster.

Op art was not the only artistic form to influence the psychedelic style. The decorative richness that could be found in Victorian styles of lettering and traditional forms of exotic patterns was also prized. Each became common components of the style. Examples of both appear in Moscoso's 'Youngbloods' poster *(fig. 17.11)*, which has a 'playbill' kind of slab-serif that sits above and below a traditional Japanese pattern of concentrically circular fish-scale shapes. Their appeal lies in the almost psychotic richness they give to the overall patterning, a richness that is heightened by the way they have been bastardized.

Two other very particular and unusual sources lay behind one of the era's most popular posters, the silhouetted portrait of the counterculture's most poetic musical chronicler, Bob Dylan *(> fig. 17.12)*. The poster was not made to inform the public about an upcoming gig or the release of a new album. It was a keepsake that came with one of Dylan's records. Its lack of information or of anything that identified it as a clearly commercial item indicates how the status of the poster had changed during the second half of the twentieth century. It went from being an object of purely public value to one that had a potentially private importance. Posters didn't only have to live their lives out on the street, they could also be welcomed inside and accepted as part of an interior design. When stuck on the wall of a student's bedroom, the sometimes passionate identification of its owner with the subject matter and, by extension, the graphic style of the poster lent it an almost totemic status.

The American designer of the Dylan poster, Milton Glaser (1929–), was less involved in the countercultural scene than either Moscoso or Wilson had been. With this

17.12: 'Dylan' poster designed by Milton Glaser, 1966

unlike the psychedelic poster proper with its suffusion of hallucinogenic colours and forms, the concentrated colours around Dylan's head were geared to serving a compelling concept rather than a specific sensation. Instead of the sensation of an hallucinogenic trip, Glaser sought to convey the idea of artistic inspiration. The inspiration that fed Dylan's very original song-writing was shown surging round his temples. This bright, metaphorical form is such a dominant part of the poster that it is easy to pass over the poster's third, lesser element: the letters that form Dylan's name. These letters are twinned visually as well as semantically with the profile, not only through their muted hue but also through their shape, which had been adjusted into a sort of lettering equivalent of the silhouette. Like the profile of the face, they have had most of their internal features removed so that they can be read in outline.

In spite of the portrait's popularity, it remained wedded to its role as a poster image. The design was too dependent on its rectangular format for it to be easily applied elsewhere. This single state stood in contrast to another popular graphic portrait of the era; one which differed from Dylan's in several respects, but especially in its independence from any particular design format or even a precisely defined graphic form. This paradoxical position, of being immensely popular yet not identified with any particular object or exact version of itself, belonged to the iconic portrait of the Argentinian-born Marxist revolutionary, Dr Ernesto 'Che' Guevara *(fig. 17.13)*. Walk through any of the world's major cities and it is likely you will, at least, catch a glimpse of it somewhere, whether printed on a passing T-shirt, stencilled on a brick wall or parodied on the cover of a magazine or poster. Although the portrait is now over 40 years old, Guevara's concentrated, far-away gaze and his roughly bearded and tousled head, incongruously crowned with a starred military beret, stares out at you with a force of recognition that is almost unique in the history of portraiture. The status of the image is now such that it is known in nearly every corner of the world, and this in spite of the inevitable and gradual decline in Guevara's political significance since his heyday in the late 1960s. Currently the portrait can claim to be better known than almost any other picture of a face. Even the world's most popular religion, Christianity, which has a history of portraiture that stretches back to the first centuries of the common era, has not produced anything that has become so familiar to so many. If any real rival to Guevara's portrait does exist, it

greater distance came a more varied range of influences. The main source for his Dylan poster was a simple self-portrait in silhouette by the ex-Dadaist Marcel Duchamp which the artist had made late in life, in 1958, several decades after abandoning art as a profession in favour of playing and writing about chess. Glaser followed Duchamp's lead by keeping the amount of detail in his Dylan profile to a minimum, and yet it remained an effective carrier of information all the same. By 1966, when the poster came out, Dylan's distinctive features were well enough known to his fans for the silhouette to be recognized. This is not to suggest, though, that the poster's popularity rested solely on the representation of a famous face. Its success had as much to do with how the face was rendered as with whom it depicted.

Crucial to its effectiveness was the contrast between the single, meandering black-and-white edge of the silhouette's profile, and the multiple, flowing lines of brightly coloured, cartoon-like hair. The source of these swirls of colour was both less specific and more exotic than that of the profile. It came from the range of bright colours Glaser had observed in Islamic painting. But,

17.13: Che Guevara graffiti, Havana

is more likely to come from the secular side of art. The *Mona Lisa* is an obvious contender and maybe now the giant head of Mao Zedong, which hangs over the main entrance to Tiananmen Square in Beijing, is another.

For the Che portrait, why this sort of rendition of this particular head should have acquired its logo-like status cannot be explained by any single fact or reason. Its success has relied on a host of influences, some of which are historical and have little to do with the image *per se* – the longevity of Fidel Castro as Cuba's leader, or the periodic vogue for countercultural styles of design, say, or perhaps even the intervening periods of anti-Americanism – while other influences relate to the image very directly. As important as any of this more direct kind are the set of influences connected to the semantics of the image: what the particular portrait meant to people when it first appeared and how its meaning has changed over time. The fact that this image has been able to absorb multiple meanings has been essential to its success. For those who knew Che Guevara the man, or the myth of him at least, it has been able to stand both as a particular representation of him, and also as a general representation of 'the guerrilla' or else, more generally still, as a symbol of rebellion. Today these more general meanings predominate since most people who know of the portrait could neither say whom it depicts nor why he is celebrated.

Che Guevara first launched himself onto the world stage during the late 1950s after he had helped Fidel Castro overthrow a corrupt and unpopular Cuban dictatorship with only a small guerrilla force. Though the insurrection was modest in size, certainly when compared to some of the other guerrilla rebellions of the time, it received widespread international attention. The victory of this small band of social revolutionaries was welcomed not only by most Cubans, but also by many from beyond the shores of the Carribbean island, especially those on the left of the political spectrum in the West. Having endured a decade of conservatism in their own countries, they could hardly have imagined a more glamorous or inspirational political coup. The leaders of the new Cuban government were deemed to be especially heroic. For one, they were astonishingly young. Few of them, including the principal figures of Castro and Guevara, were much over 30 years old. But also many of them were ex-students, principled young men from the middle classes, who had chosen to reject the privilege and ease that their upbringing had brought them in order to help improve the lives of the poor and the oppressed. Guevara, himself a medical graduate from Buenos Aires University and from a wealthy upper-class family, seemed to speak for his comrades when he described himself as 'one who risks his skin to prove his truth'.

Of all the various leaders of 'third-world' guerrilla groups from the 1950s and 1960s, Guevara was especially venerated. It helped that he regularly supplemented his deeds with words. In addition to writing several books on the art of guerrilla warfare, he also published his own diaries, which described his travels within and beyond South America, and thereby gave greater definition to the varied impressions then being sketched of him by the international press. As well as being young, brave and articulate, Guevara was also photogenic or, as some accounts had it, positively beautiful. The rugged features captured on camera succeeded in fluttering the hearts of even the most non-political observers. A more sombre but none the less powerful influence on his public persona was the manner and timing of his death. While leading another guerrilla-style insurrection, this time in the South American country of Bolivia, Guevara was captured, held prisoner and then executed. By paying the ultimate price for proving his truth at the relatively young age of 39, Guevara's persona became imbued with a macabre form of glamour twice over: that accorded to the martyr and that of the young dead.

All these facets of Guevara's life and character made him, in the era of a picture-based mass media, an ideal candidate for the role of the Left's poster boy; if, that is, one can accept, as his many admirers seemed to

17.14: Che Guevara contact print by Korda, 1960

17.15: Contact print (detail)

(peace-loving hippies included), the essentially violent manner in which he prosecuted his political aims. In spite of his numerous murderous actions, his attractive qualities remained. For a graphic image to dominate in quite the way it did, it had to encapsulate or, at least, suggest these more positive qualities, and clearly, this particular portrait did so successfully. But it also did so variously. As well as symbolizing Guevara's compelling history, his long hair and beard, which was emblematic of the guerilla the world over, also aligned him with contemporary youth fashions inside and outside Cuba, while at the same time setting him against the clean-cut look of the American establishment. His beret, not the peaked cap one might expect of a military leader, aligned him with the common man. Its star denoted his high rank and signalled the socialist orientation of his revolutionary aims. Other positive associations linked to the symbol (a celestial object, a divine signal, a light shining out of the darkness) and to the word 'star' (a celebrity, a person of great ability) also accrued.

Just as important as each of these associative qualities was the very practical quality of the image's reproducibility. The flat, ink-blot-like shapes which made up the portrait's features could be sprayed through a stencil onto a wall, or squeezed through the gauze of a silk-screen, without any loss of emotional intensity or symbolic power. They contributed greatly to the wide take-up of the image and its appearance on almost any kind of material that was capable of holding its painted or printed form. It was this that contributed to its paradoxical position of being enormously popular yet not identified with any particular object or exact version of itself.

This defining aspect of the image, its mutable graphic simplicity, had not always been a feature of the portrait.

The origins of the image lay in a photograph taken in 1960 *(fig. 17.14 & fig. 17.15)* by a Cuban photographer, Alberto Díaz Gutiérrez, or Korda as he was known professionally. Korda had been asked by a newspaper to cover a mass funeral which was to take place the day after a violent explosion had ripped through the side of a munitions ship that had been moored in the harbour of Cuba's capital, Havana. The blast succeeded in killing more than 80 people. Castro, who was goaded by the belief that an American invasion was not just inevitable but imminent, blamed the CIA, and said as much during the funeral address he gave to a vast crowd that had gathered in Havana's central Revolution Square. Throughout the sombre ranks of mourners that had come to honour the dead, a latent sense of indignation and solidarity grew and spread until all were transformed into the kind of passionately partisan throng more usually associated with a mass rally. The funereal tone had mutated into a spontaneous expression of national unity. It was within this highly charged atmosphere, during a part of Castro's speech, that Korda 'panned the podium and suddenly Che moved forward into my camera. I made a picture, and immediately thinking of a cover for our newspaper, turned the camera vertical, made another – and the moment had gone.'

In the all-important first, horizontal picture, Korda captured an almost messianic intensity in Guevara's expression. It appeared to stem from some inner conflict: from an impassioned commitment yet also an ethereal sense of detachment. The set of his eyes, staring out over the sea of mourners into the middle distance, and the resolute cast of his other facial features, the upward tilt of the head and the slightly opposing slant of his beret, all combined to give the impression that in that very

DIA DEL GUERRILLERO HEROICO 8 DE OCTUBRE
JOURNEE DU GUERILLERO HEROIQUE 8 OCTOBRE
DAY OF THE HEROIC GUERRILLA OCTOBER 8
يوم المقاوم الباسل ٨ تشرين اول

17.16: 'Day of the Heroic Guerilla 8th October 1968' poster designed by Elena Serrano

moment, within the sliding click of the camera's shutter frame, Guevara had determined to avenge the indiscriminate loss of life and redouble his efforts in furthering the spread of his revolutionary brand of Marxism. The eloquence of his expression was also informed by some important formal properties. The photograph's angle of view, being from below, exposed the whites of his eyes which in turn helped to define the dark intensity of his gaze, while the auspicious fall of shadow that surrounded his face emphasized his bone structure beautifully. Both properties contributed to the power of the subsequent ink-blot image.

For all its strengths as a portrait, the newspaper that had commissioned Korda didn't use the picture. In fairness, it was only when Korda returned to the studio and cropped the picture tightly around the head (as indicated by the red crayon mark he made on the contact print), focusing on the intensity of Guevara's expression, that its true power became apparent. Subsequent prints of this cropped version, which Korda gave out to various visitors, soon found their way into some early posters and other kinds of printed material, but even then the image had to wait until Guevara's death in 1967 before achieving its iconic status.

One of the posters made in direct response to his passing was the official commemorative poster produced on the first anniversary of his death *(fig. 17.16)*. The 'Day of the Heroic Guerrilla', on 8th October, is still honoured in Cuba. The poster's Cuban designer, Elena Serrano, centred Guevara's portrait on the country of Bolivia at the heart of South America, where Guevara had died, and then had his image radiate out across the whole continent and beyond. The international emphasis of the poster's message reflected the international nature of the socialist ideology that had guided Cuban poster design during the first decades of the revolution. The name of the government agency that had commissioned the poster, OSPAAAL (the Organization in Solidarity with the People of Asia, Africa and Latin America), made this global emphasis explicit, as indeed did the poster's title, by being printed in four languages: Spanish, French, English and Arabic. By limiting the amount of text on the poster to the title only – in other words, by relying on an image to carry its core message – Serrano made sure that the international appeal of the poster would not be hindered by any language barrier. A similar awareness of the poster's international audience lay behind the style of its design, which like other Cuban posters of the time contained the kind of vibrant

17.17: *Magnum 'Cherry Guevara' ice-cream wrapper, date unknown*

colours and strong Op art contrasts that had made the psychedelic posters of its continental neighbour so popular.

By the late 1960s, the portrait of Guevara had spread outside Latin America. It had been adopted by anti-Vietnam War protesters in the United States who, by adhering to the logic of the ancient political maxim 'the enemy of my enemy is my friend', expressed support not only for the guerrilla leader they were being asked to fight, Ho-Chi-Minh ('*Ho Ho Ho-Chi-Minh*' was the popular chant), but for other guerilla leaders too. Placards showing the portrait of Guevara were held aloft by anti-war protesters inside and outside the United States. For student demonstrators in Paris, Prague and Tokyo, Guevara was adopted as an icon of rebellion as well as a symbol of protest against the war in Vietnam.

The left-wing orientation of many of these groups chimed with Korda's own political sympathies. It was because he was only too keen to see Guevara's socialist message spread that Korda refused to accept payment for the use of his photograph. Such a principled stance certainly contributed to the image's popularity, but, in so doing, it established a paradox. By rejecting the capitalistic notion of intellectual property, Korda opened the way for others to exploit the commercial potential of his image, especially after the idea of 'the guerrilla' had become established as a romantic symbol of rebellion (due in no small part to the effectiveness of his own photograph). Quite unintentionally then, what had begun as an inspiration for a whole generation of socialists was in time transformed into a marketing tool for some of capitalism's most quintessential goods: cigarettes, bikinis, cars, ice cream *(fig. 17.17)* and the like. In this way it seemed that the more Guevara's image spread, the further it strayed from the man. Or as one commentator described the process more generally, 'Capitalism devours everything … even its enemies.'

The rapacity of capitalism was a common concern among the Guevara-toting demonstrators of the late 1960s. It was certainly central to the wave of student demonstrations and strikes that surged through France during the month of May 1968, which through their scale and intensity stimulated similar expressions of student dissent in other countries throughout the remaining months of the year. The origin of the unrest in France was an apparently minor, internal dispute at one of Paris's new, suburban universities – the dispute centred on the restriction of male students to female dormitories – but as ripples of protest flowed through other sections of France's student population, so the scope of the protest widened to include the restrictive nature of French society as a whole, and the capitalist foundation on which that society was based. When university buildings began to be occupied, streets barracaded, and running battles between young people and the police broke out, sections of the wider society were drawn into the fray. The occupation of factories by low-paid workers in protest at their working conditions was followed by a nationwide general strike, which then culminated, a little more than a week later, in half of France's workforce coming out in sympathy and the French government teetering on the brink of collapse.

Success in galvanizing the workers and students into supporting the protest was partly due to the mass of simple street posters that had been plastered onto the walls of Paris *(fig. 17.18)* and other French cities. The main centres of production for the posters were Paris's two main art schools, the École des Beaux-Arts (School of Fine Arts) and the École des Arts-Décoratifs (School of Decorative Arts), both of which had been requisitioned by groups of politically active professional artists, who set up what they called *ateliers populaires* or 'people's workshops', a series of makeshift printing studios. Some of the artists were alumni (in fact, each

17.18: *Atélier Populaire posters, Paris, 1968*

was an alumnus, a male, as opposed to an alumna, a female), while others were night-class students, but this latter group represented the extent of any actual student influence within the heart of Paris's main ateliers. Some full-time students did get involved with aspects of the production process, such as finding materials or distributing posters, but the main executive function, including the design of the posters, appears to have been carried out by non-students.

The methods used in the ateliers were necessarily basic. In order to make what limited resources they had to hand go as far as possible, the artists printed most of the posters in a single colour and on newsprint, a low-grade newspaper paper. Much of this was donated by sympathetic commercial printers, though when stocks were depleted it was necessary on occasion for butcher's packing paper to be used. As well as a lack of basic materials, there was a pressing need for speed. The very first posters were made in order to raise money for the demonstrators, but as soon as it was realized what a galvanizing effect was being had out on the street their purpose changed. Subsequent posters were devoted entirely to the twin tasks of bolstering support for the demonstrations and countering the hostile propaganda being put out by the government and other antagonistic groups.

With many of the usual sources of public information, such as state television and daily newspapers, affected by the strike, the ateliers' posters received more attention than they might have otherwise. If they were to capitalize on this situation, they would have to be able to react to the day's events, and the only way an under-resourced and untrained staff were going to produce posters quickly enough, and in sufficient quantities, was by using the simple but little-used technique of screen printing. In the United States, screen printing had been popularized in the early 1960s by Andy Warhol's use of it for his repeated prints, but in France it was almost entirely unknown. At its most basic the process required little specialist equipment. Each of the printing units could be more or less home-made and no external power source would be needed to work them. The technique was also simple enough for a novice to pick up the essentials quickly and, provided the design was restricted to a set of simple shapes rather than intricate layers of detail, it could be designed and printed in a matter of minutes. By limiting the designs to flat areas of solid colour rather than any more complex and time-consuming tonal or photographic effects, it was possible to meet the demand for speed.

Far from making the posters less effective, such restrictions brought definite benefits. Perhaps as many as 400 different designs were produced in Paris's two main ateliers, yet they and the many other designs produced elsewhere were united by a loose style linked to the reduced circumstances in which they were made. The style marked each poster out as belonging to a group of images with common themes and origins. People on the street could tell what they were from their general appearance alone, and their graphic simplicity made them stand out against the more elaborate, conventional commercial posters that usually dominated the wall space. What also marked them out, in a very literal sense, was a simple stamp, which was pressed by hand onto each poster after the printer's ink had dried. By stamping the name *atelier populaire* and also, in many instances, the name of the specific atelier that had made the poster – *ex-Beaux Arts* was one example – the makers often

17.19: 'Oui Usines Occupées' poster, Atélier Populaire, 1968

distinguished their work from a rival atelier's. In the case of the two art schools, it was a fierce rivalry, almost violently so. Their identifying marks spoke more of an extreme competitiveness than of any solidarity with their brothers in arms.

If any rivalry between artists within a single atelier existed, it was less explicit. No poster was marked with any form of personal identification, be it a signature or a monogram. The communal nature of the posters' creation and, indeed, of the movement's aims made the notion of personal credit a redundant one. This concept of a work of art as a collaborative anonymous creation was already well established within the particular group of art activists who had set up the first and most influential atelier at the Beaux-Arts in Paris. Before the occupation they had worked under the name of the *Salon de la Jeune Peinture* (Salon of the Young Painters), but their activities had involved more than painting. They had also written, often working with existing texts rather than creating their own original compositions, and they debated and discussed the content of their work in formal meetings. Both practices became integral to the ateliers' method. Most posters were planned and vetted during daily meetings, or 'general assemblies' as they were commonly known. The meetings were open to all and anyone could voice their opinion on what political idea should be put across that day and how that idea could be best expressed. After the meetings and late into the night teams would print the posters for others to surreptitiously post up or deliver to the factory gates for workers to distribute.

The posters themselves nearly always combined short phrases with simple, diagrammatic or cartoon-like images *(fig. 17.19)*. As well as being pictographically simple, the images were also stereotypical. Pointing fingers, clenched fists, smoke-stacked factory symbols and other hackneyed icons of revolution were used to communicate general concepts to the passing public. Whatever the poster's content, it had to be easily understood, and yet the best posters were more than a collection of visual clichés. Some of the symbols were combined in witty and surreal ways: a factory's chimney that stood for the 'i' in 'oui' say, or a safety-pin that hinted at the gagged mouth in a bandaged head *(<fig. 17.18)*. Such images were capable of stepping out beyond the threshold of familiarity and planting resonant pictures in people's minds. The fact they were made out of easily understandable parts ensured that their cleverness or oddness could be gauged at a glance; and once appreciated, their strangeness or wit made them hard to forget.

In its handmade simplicity the posters' imagery was similar to other countercultural graphics, such as those made for the anti-Vietnam war movement *(>fig. 17.23)*, but equally it recalled the style of a similar set of items produced for a real revolution, the Russian revolution of 1917 *(<fig. 11.14, p. 173)*. Both the ateliers' posters and the Russian ROSTA windows used simple cartoon-like forms, partly because of the similarly reduced circumstances in which both were made, and yet there were also marked differences. The ROSTA windows had to impart specific political messages to a largely illiterate audience, whereas the ateliers' audience was decidedly literate and their messages political only in the broadest sense. Rather than articulating specific demands, they touched on the kind of general political themes that might be found in any left-wing protest: the power of the common man ('It's our turn to speak'), solidarity with the workers ('Support for the occupied factories for the victory of the people'), state oppression ('De Gaulle responds to our legitimate grievances with Fascism') and individual liberty ('Kill your inner cop!').

The source of the posters' text was varied. Most came from outside the ateliers, either via workers with their own specific suggestions or with slogans they had heard chanted on marches, or they came from the rash of graffiti that appeared on city walls across France. Dominating this ancient mode of protest were many of the more quotable phrases of philosophy that cropped up in the student debates of the time. Competing for influence with the more established Maoist and Trotskyist texts were the writings of a small, post-war artistic and political group, the Situationists, or the Situationist International (SI), as they called themselves. Their particular brand of Dadaist- and Marxist-influenced politics found a uniquely receptive audience during 1968. Underpinning each of the SI's core concepts was the idea of subversion. Not just the subversion of the traditional forms of authority, such as the government, the police or parents, but of almost any established figure or accepted way of doing something. Fashionable intellectuals – the philosopher Jean-Paul Sartre and the film-maker Jean-Luc Godard – were lampooned, as were orthodox forms of art. The conceptual weapon they used to attack art and the capitalist system that sustained it was the idea of *détournement*, a word whose common meaning in French is similar to the English word detour, but which for the SI described the act of taking a work of art, or some part of it, out of its normal context and placing it into a new one specifically in order to undermine its authority or purpose. In this respect, the SI may be seen as the inheritors of a tradition of iconoclasm, which Duchamp had defined so eloquently with his Dadaist submission of a urinal as a work of art *(<p. 180)* more than 50 years earlier.

The importance of the SI to the demonstrators was not restricted to philosophical writing. The members of the SI took an active part in the demonstrations, especially the occupation of Paris's universities. They also produced a handful of posters, though in contrast to those from the ateliers, theirs were produced at a local print-shop. Their posters were entirely typographic and set, somewhat conservatively, in a single typographic style that was dominated by large, white sanserif letters centred on a black background. The text of the posters was concise and unambiguous, but also banal ('Abolition of the class society', 'Power to the Workers' Councils', etc.), in comparison with the range of SI-inspired graffiti, which through its wit ('Humanity will not be happy until the last bureaucrat is hanged with the guts of the last capitalist'), aphoristic concision ('It is forbidden to forbid') and mocking provocation ('Be cruel!') made a more telling and memorable contribution to the events of Paris '68.

Despite the formal differences between the two sets of posters, both of the groups who produced them were similarly uncompromising about how their images should be used. They considered their posters to be gifts or tools, not commodities or works of art, and any appreciation of them outside the events they had been made for (as here, in this book for example) was condemned without reservation: 'Their rightful place is in the centres of conflict, that is to say, in the streets and on the walls of the factories. To use them for decorative purposes, to display them in bourgeois places of culture or to consider them as objects of aesthetic interest is to impair both their function and their effect. ... Even to keep them as historical evidence of a certain stage in the struggle is a betrayal, ... these works should not be taken as the final outcome of an experience, but as an inducement for finding, through contact with the masses, new levers of action ...'.

This extreme position, and the utopian dream of global revolution that had underpinned it, was not shared by all. Most workers were not revolutionaries. They just wanted better pay and improved working conditions. The same sort of ambivalence towards extreme political ideologies existed throughout the counterculture movement. Many of its adherents appreciated the movement's aesthetic forms – its fashion or music and the lifestyle that each promoted – but they paid lip-service to its politics. The fashion potential of the psychedelic style, in particular, was evident almost from the outset. Its formal properties were exploited by commercial organizations in cities across America and Europe, though nowhere more so perhaps than in London, which in 1966, in a well-known cover story from *Time* magazine, was voted 'city of the decade' (somewhat prematurely, surely). The text went on to describe, in the language of the time, how in 'the swinging city', 'the most "In" shop for gear is Biba's boutique in Kensington, which is a must scene for the switched-on dolly-bird at least twice a week'. Biba was unusual in that its owners created much more than a shop. They understood that what often motivated people to buy things or shop somewhere was a sense of identification with the ambiance or style of the shop itself. For many, the desire to have a particular aesthetic experience while shopping was

17.20: Biba stationery designed by John McConnell, 1967

at least as strong as the desire to acquire an object for some practical purpose or for its own aesthetic quality. This understanding led Biba's owners to create an all-embracing 'Biba experience' within the shop's dark, decorated interior. Through its café, and its occasional gigs and fancy-dress parties, people came to view Biba as more of a social club than a boutique. 'A private members' club for the general public' was one description.

The same all-encompassing outlook guided Biba's graphic image. Shopping bags, clothes labels, packaging and stationery *(fig. 17.20)* all carried the same set of swirling Art Nouveau-inspired forms. Though Biba's logo underwent several stages of evolution, it is the gold-on-black version from 1966, designed by the British designer John McConnell (1939–), with which the store is most commonly identified now. McConnell managed to capture the Art Nouveau idiom so completely that his logo almost went beyond the point of parody. Indeed it is hard to tell, just by looking at the logo's shape (as opposed to the object it appeared on), whether the logo is a 1960s revival or an authentic design from the 1890s. This adoption of Art Nouveau forms into the family of decorative elements that made up the psychedelic style was a natural and rational union. The rhythmically linear shapes commonly found in nineteenth-century Art Nouveau *(<fig. 10.15, p. 158)* had a dreamlike quality that tallied with the psychedelic style's hallucinogenic agenda, and the preponderance of plant-like forms in Art Nouveau struck a chord with the strong environmental or anti-industrial bias within the counterculture (which alongside its commitment to non-violent protest was recognized in the movement's slogan of 'flower power').

The psychedelic poster and its related graphic style may have been the counterculture's most emblematic form, but the movement was also closely associated with a *bona fide* logo: the still-current peace logo. The origins of this simple circular sign lay somewhat outside the counterculture, and even today it remains the official logo of the British organization CND (the Campaign for Nuclear Disarmament), which adopted it soon after the logo was created in 1958. Though the symbol was quick to be associated with CND, it was not created for an organization per se, but more for an event. The occasion in question was Britain's first large-scale anti-nuclear protest march, which took place over the Easter weekend (4–7 April) of 1958. This march, the first in a series of large 'Aldermaston marches' (Britain's atomic weapons research centre is still sited close to the town of Aldermaston), had been organized by the 'Direct Action Committee Against Nuclear War' (DAC), a pioneering though short-lived organization in the non-violent protest against nuclear weapons. Within CND, a less radical organization than DAC, there were mixed views about the merits of the march; though, in the event, many of CND's leaders, as well as its rank and file supporters, took part in the protest. It was a few months after the march that CND first adopted the 'ND symbol' as its own (though neither they nor DAC ever patented it).

Like the anti-nuclear movement as a whole, CND has a much lower profile today than it did during the late 1950s and early 1960s when the Cold War was at its height. For as long as the two post-war superpowers, the United States and the Soviet Union, were engaged in a frenetic arms race, centred as it was on the stockpiling of nuclear weapons, CND could rely on tens of thousands of supporters to come out onto the streets for rallies or protest marches *(<fig. 17.1)*. The seeds of their support had been sown over a decade earlier, during the first week of August 1945, when the US Air

17.21: Sketch of 'ND' symbol by Gerald Holtom, 1958

Force dropped an atomic bomb first on the Japanese city of Hiroshima and then, three days later, on Nagasaki. Both events provided mankind with a new, powerfully haunting graphic image, the mushroom cloud, which became identified generally as a symbol of nuclear weapons' destructive potential. And how much greater the potential had become a decade or so later when the Iron Curtain was hemmed in on either side by a considerably more destructive arsenal. It was a situation that led many to believe a nuclear exchange was not just likely but inevitable. The only point of uncertainty indeed concerned the extent of the imminent destruction. 'There … is in the use of the atom bomb and the hydrogen bomb a new danger, a danger which is not only new in kind but greater in degree than any that has existed in previous wars. We do not quite know what may be the effects of letting loose great floods of radioactivity. There are those – among them Einstein – who think that the result may be the extinction of all life on our planet.' These were the words of Bertrand Russell, the British philosopher and one of the founding members of CND. It was only a few months after he and the organization's co-founders first met in 1957 that a British designer, Gerald Holtom (*c.*1914–85), eagerly set about designing a symbol for the Aldermaston march.

Holtom based his design *(fig. 17.21)* on the signs for the letters 'N' and 'D' (for Nuclear Disarmament) from the international system of communication called semaphore which, before the invention of radio, had been used by the military (the navy in particular). The system required hand-held flags to be set in certain configurations in order to spell out the letters of the alphabet or the range of numerals *(>fig. 17.22)*. As well as drawing on this rather obscure, antiquated and inappropriate reference, Holtom was guided by a more personal

17.22: Semaphore alphabet

motivation. He also wanted to symbolize the despondency he felt towards a world that had only relatively recently come through a second, hugely destructive world war and yet, with its creation of the nuclear threat, had apparently learnt little from the experience. 'I drew myself: the representative of an individual in despair, with hands palm outstretched outwards and downwards in the manner of Goya's peasant before the firing squad.' In fact, the figure he referred to, from the Spanish painter Francisco Goya's famous painting *The Third of May 1808*, had his arms thrust upwards, not downwards, and more in a spirit of defiance, or entreaty at least, than despair. But then, by coincidence, Holtom came to prefer this same upward configuration too. It has been said that he changed his mind about the design after a member of the public suggested that the drooping arms looked a bit depressing whereas peace was something that should be celebrated. From then on, Holtom drew the symbol with the diagonals pointing upwards, and he even asked (in vain) for this upward version to be carved on his gravestone.

Once out in public, the symbol was quickly taken up by various international movements. It was adopted by peace groups in the United States and it appeared at civil rights marches, where its connotation of peace acted as confirmation of the movement's strong commitment to non-violent protest. As early as 1963 the symbol was taken on by anti-Vietnam War protesters inside the United States initially and then later outside it too. It was during this period of appropriation that the symbol's core meaning shifted away from CND towards a broader concept of peace. It was a shift that was made all the more complete after the counterculture took on the symbol as a visual complement to their mantra of 'peace and love' and the palm-outward 'V' sign. Confirmation of the logo's effectiveness as a sign of peace was provided by the attacks it received from the pro-Vietnam War lobby who, in reference to the central bird's-foot shape, mocked the sign as being 'the footprint of the American Chicken'.

Today the peace symbol occupies a privileged position as one of the few graphic signs that can communicate its meaning across a range of languages, faiths and cultural conventions. It has become an almost obligatory counterpoint to many conflicts over the decades, appearing on both sides of the Berlin Wall, for example, or worn on T-shirts by citizens in Sarajevo during the Bosnian War of the 1990s, and even on the helmets of American soldiers in Baghdad during the recent war in Iraq. One reason for its ubiquity is that, like the portrait of Che Guevara, it has never been protected by copyright. In a spirit of freedom and anti-materialism, which was driven by a genuine desire to see the logo's message spread, Holtom and the DAC allowed the logo to be used without charge. This, again mirroring the fate of Guevara's portrait, has left the way open for commercial organizations to exploit the symbol's associations of youthful rebellion and personal liberty.

As well as its free access, the success of the logo was also related to its simple form. Being composed of only four lines, it was both easy to remember and easy to draw. Such attributes are significant for a symbol that sometimes, in a spirit of protest or defiance, had to be scrawled onto a wall hurriedly and furtively. It is significant too that, like most examples of graffiti, Holtom's original version was clearly handmade. He did not imagine it as a neat, mechanically produced, mathematically precise work of geometry, as almost all printed versions are today. The unsymmetrically splayed, radial arms identify Holtom's original as an irregular, hand-rendered, human mark, qualities that coincided with the graphic ethos of the counterculture.

For a shape of such simple symmetry, it is perhaps not surprising that the essential, central part of it, the bird's-foot shape, has a history of its own. Between the fifth and eleventh centuries AD it appeared as a letter in an Anglo-Saxon runic alphabet, which was used by several different languages in various parts of northern Europe. During the Middle Ages, the same shape was seen as a quasi-religious death symbol because of its perceived resemblance to an upturned crucifix. This supposedly anti-Christian symbol earned it the name of 'Nero's cross', in reference to the Roman emperor Nero, who is reputed to have been the first persecutor of the Christians. Each of these earlier instances, however, shows the bird's-foot shape on its own, unbounded by a circle. It is a difference that sets it apart from the peace symbol proper. Whether the circle was just a simple framing device or whether, as some have claimed, it had particular meanings, such as representing the earth or the unity of mankind, it is an essential component of the peace sign.

At the beginning of this chapter, the phrase 'the post-war generation' was used to describe the baby-boomers, that populous group in the West and in parts of Asia and Australasia who were born between the end of the Second World War and the mid- to late 1950s. While the tag 'post-war' is generally appropriate, it is not ap-plicable to all Western nations equally and least of all perhaps to the United States. For those Americans who grew up during the 1950s and 1960s, the description fails to register the seriousness of the conflicts in which their country was involved after the Second World War: first, from 1950 to 1953, the 'Korean conflict' (as it was euphemistically called, though it was a proper war); and then the Vietnam War, the major part of which oc-curred between 1965 and 1975. The 'post-war' tag also ignores the effects that these conflicts had on the rest of American society. As one prominent American senator remarked mid-way through the Vietnam War, 'This war has already stretched the generation gap so wide that it threatens to pull the country apart.'

The rightness or wrongness of the war itself was the central point of contention between the generations, but equally emotive was the draft policy. Many of the older generation, who had put their own lives on the line during the Second World War, were duly outraged at those young people who refused military service. On the other hand, many of the refuseniks were from poor families, and they bitterly resented the draft system, at least as it was initially formulated, because it systemati-cally favoured the wealthy. Exemptions and deferments were handed out to college and graduate students, whose families were generally wealthy enough to afford college fees.

The fear that her 16-year-old son would be drafted one day led Lorraine Schneider (1925–72), an American printmaker and artist, to enter a small protest image *(fig. 17.23)* – what she called her own 'personal picket

17.23: 'War is Not Healthy' card designed by Lorraine Schneider, 1967

sign' – into a local print competition in 1967. The almost elementary simplicity of Schneider's bright, floral design was partly determined by the rules of the competition, which required that each print be no more than four square inches (10cm²) in size, smaller than the size of a postcard. A more complex design in such a small space would have been both hard to make and difficult to read. For the child-like text that surrounded the flower, Schneider had wanted to say something incontrovertible; something that was self-evidently true; something, indeed, that a child itself might say: 'War is not healthy for children and other living things.' Though her design did not win the competition – it was considered too simplistic – its very directness and lack of complexity suited the needs of a small, local women's group that had been set up by a close friend of hers. The group chose to use the image on a special Mother's Day card which they planned to send to the president and every member of Congress. The card's message read: 'For my Mother's Day gift this year, I don't want candy or flowers. I want an end to killing. We who have given life must be dedicated to preserving it. Please talk peace.' The effect of their small-scale campaign was dramatic. The image became so popular that the initial print run of 1,000 cards had to be increased to 200,000,

17.24: 'I Want Out' poster designed by the Committee to Help Unsell the War, 1971

and it began to be taken up by the anti-war movement generally. Before long the design could be seen on posters, bumper stickers and note cards, as well as the prized gold medallions that had been made specially for members of the new anti-war organization, 'Another Mother for Peace', which had been founded on the back of the card's success.

The success of the design led Schneider to campaign on behalf of all dissenting voices: '… it is up to us, the artists, the people who work in media, to prepare the emotional soil for the last step out of the cave. We can create symbols of the new day, and light the world with our hope. And the Neanderthals that attempt to restrict our freedom of expression, that attempt to frighten us into silence, that give you only four square inches with which to cry out your anger? Use it.' Similar sentiments were held by many within the arts and media industries, particularly after December 1969, when the findings from an American senator's investigation into the government's spending on propaganda were first made public. It exposed the lengths to which the government had gone in its attempt to 'sell' the war to the nation. Carefully packaged news items on TV, radio and in

print; Hollywood-produced feature films vetted by the Pentagon; regular tours of military installations laid on for VIPs; aerial demonstrations and military-band parades; and speeches promoting the war given by a select group of colonels around the country. All such efforts were made to shore up popular support for the war. By 1971, after a highly controversial documentary based on this earlier investigation had been broadcast on prime-time television, a combined group of students and people from within the advertising industry decided to set up the 'Committee to Help Unsell the War', which, as its name suggests, attempted to counter the slew of state-run propaganda with its own anti-war campaign. Advertisements for print, radio and TV were made free of charge by some of the leading figures from New York's advertising community. The tenor of the campaign was encapsulated by a poster *(fig. 17.24)* that parodied the famous pointing Uncle Sam recruitment poster from the previous two world wars *(< fig. 11.9, p. 169)*. In this new version the loose realism of the original's illustration was replaced with a photograph of a model dressed as a battered and bandaged Uncle Sam holding his crumpled hat under one arm and a hand held out in supplication rather than pointing provocatively as before. The text appeared in the same graphic treatment, but instead of there being two lines of text beginning 'I Want You', a simple, succinct line appeared: 'I Want Out'. In a further contrast with the original, the new version was unsigned, suggesting perhaps that taking on the government in this way was best done with a degree of anonymity.

The Vietnam War is sometimes described as the first television war. Certainly the conflict coincided with a new era of mass ownership of and programming for television, which led it to be more scrutinized and reported than any previous conflict. As the Canadian communication theorist Marshall McLuhan (1911–89) said in May 1975, soon after the withdrawal of US troops, 'Television brought the brutality of war into the comfort of the living room. Vietnam was lost in the living rooms of America – not on the battlefields of Vietnam.' Though this view has been countered strongly, it is certainly the case that the public were exposed to a view of war they had never seen before. The pictures presented to them were not necessarily bloodier – censorship was carefully maintained – but the quantity and closeness of the film footage drew people into the 'narrative' of war as never before. This closer public engagement contributed, no doubt, to the sense of stalemate and of the war

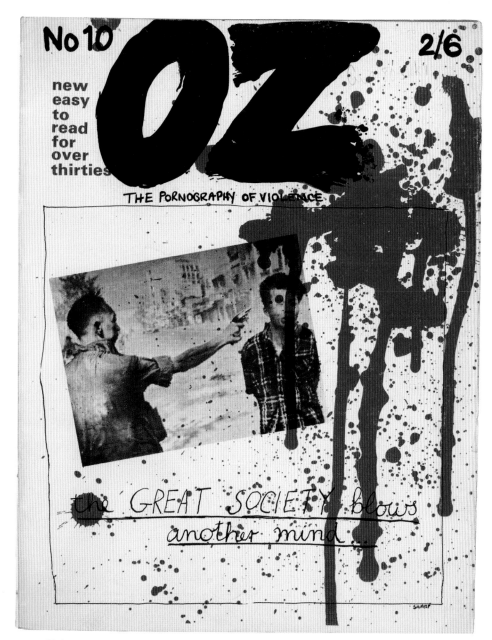

17.25: 'Oz' magazine cover, 1968

being unwinnable, which turned American opinion against the war during the end of the 1960s.

The influence of documentary media on public attitudes towards the war was not limited to the medium of television. More established forms of communication technology, such as radio and print – in newspapers and magazines especially – also made their mark. Indeed some printed images had a more lasting effect than their televisual equivalents. The famous photograph of a naked, napalm-covered girl running towards the camera with her arms out from her sides, or the street execution of a bound prisoner by a police chief with a pistol held only inches from the victim's head *(fig. 17.25)*, both proved how a photograph can crystallize the drama of a moment in a way that moving pictures never quite can. The still image captures a certain concentrated brutality of fact – this particular thing happened at a particular moment in time – which makes it a potentially more memorable medium. The after-image of a photograph seems to burn more brightly in the memory, which is to say that its details are more easily stored and then recalled. Sometimes the ability of

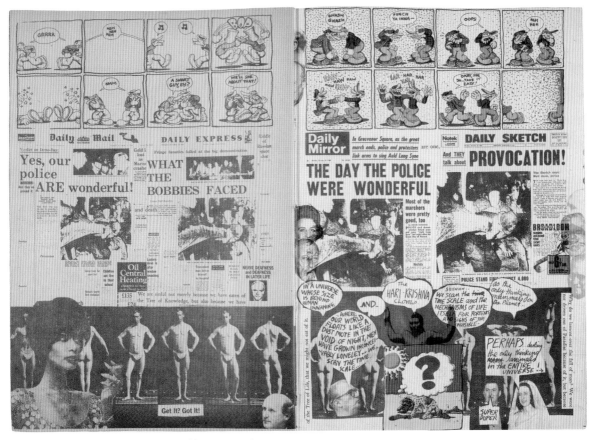

17.26: 'Oz' magazine spread designed by Martin Sharp, 1968

a still image to impress itself is so great that it becomes representative of the broader situation. If the moment has been well chosen, the drama in a photograph will resonate outwards until it stands metaphorically for the whole event, though it may actually be only a very small part of it. Such was the fate of the first of the images mentioned above. For many it still stands as an iconic reprover of the Vietnam war, and for some, by extension, of all war.

These images made an immediate impact when they were first published in newspapers, but it was through the longer-term media of magazines and books that their impact was sustained over the following months and years. Magazines, a medium for the medium term, and books, a long-term medium, extended the lives of these pictures beyond the capability of the more ephemeral newspaper. The general acceptance of the magazine as a flexible, medium-term format – one that could be topical or superficial even, yet also enduring and substantial – was exploited by the counterculture movement. Several of its publications packed a greater range of expression into a single edition

than other magazines managed to do in a whole year, and this sometimes very eclectic form of compression was reflected in the publication's design. Printed text, illustration and photography were sat side by side, or in some instances, as on the cover of the counterculture's most graphically diverse magazine, *Oz*, quite literally on top of one another. Though the magazine's title referred to its country of origin, Australia, it was in Britain, to which its founders moved in 1966, that the magazine's graphic range flourished.

One of *Oz*'s principal designers, Martin Sharp (1944–), saved his most multifarious concoction for one of his last editions, the highly illustrated 'Magic Theatre' issue of November 1968 *(fig. 17.26)*. It was largely a theatre of the absurd; a surrealist's scrapbook of mild profanity, social satire and crazed whimsy, as the cover alluded to with its declaration: 'price of admittance – your mind ... and 3 shillings' (a shilling was then a British unit of currency). On the inside the layout made no concession to orthodoxy. Instead of columns of text crowned with a hierarchy of headings and enlivened with neatly captioned illustrations, each page was dominated by a variety of pictorial effects. The main mode of expression was the photographic montage in which images from various kinds of printed ephemera – newspapers, other magazines and comic books – were taken (ignoring whatever claims of copyright existed) and combined with frames from comic-book cartoons and handwritten texts. Across each spread several stories ran alongside each other, which then continued on subsequent spreads. In the example here, cartoon strips by one of the counterculture's foremost comic-book artists, the American cartoonist Robert Crumb (1943–), appear alongside some adulterated front pages of British newspapers, including an advert for oil central heating, quotes by Franz Kafka and Rainer Maria Rilke, an assortment of disembodied heads, and one of the issue's most prominent features: a rolling sequence of stills by the British Victorian photographer Eadweard Muybridge (1830–1904), whose mute characters Sharp endowed with the gift of speech through some hand-drawn speech-bubbles and lettering. Supporting this rampant profusion of psychedelia were broad washes of colour half-tone and, on the cover, clear blocks of more intense colour. Each was an indication of the novel approach taken towards the magazine's production, which in other issues included gold, silver and fluorescent inks and a variety of formats: portrait or landscape, fold-out or perforated. Even the masthead was never allowed to appear in the same form twice.

The variety of Oz's design was indicative of the casually experimental attitude that defined the genre of counterculture publications more generally, and, indeed, the movement as a whole. But in order for this spirit of experimentation to be given full rein on the pages of a magazine like Oz, it had to rely on the recent combination of two kinds of printing technology: the graphically versatile process of offset-lithography and the paper-handling capability of high-volume letterpress printing. Since the middle of the nineteenth century, letterpress machines had been adapted to deal with the long and fast print runs required by newspapers and magazines through their use of a 'web' of paper fed from a roll, rather than individual sheets, as before. Printing on a roll of paper was much quicker because it removed the need to position each new individual sheet carefully on the press. By the late 1960s this roll-method of paper feeding had also been applied to offset-lithography machines, creating what is known as 'web-offset' which, because it could quickly print almost any kind of mark, in colour, went on to establish itself as the dominant

method of printing for all kinds of publications; books such as this one included. Indeed it is the digital version of web-offset that predominates today.

By being so very varied in their design, the magazines of the counterculture were less emblematic visually than the psychedelic posters or album covers. And yet it was this variety that succeeded in capturing the tenor of the movement. It gave a better indication of the movement's influences and interests. In this way it was the magazines of the counterculture that were the movement's mouthpiece. They allowed a set of subjective voices from within both to mirror and define the movement's identity, in contrast to the more objective, mainstream voices that so frequently miscomprehended the movement from without. Adherence to this principle of authenticity was exemplified by the editors of Oz, who went so far as to hand over control of several single editions to specific countercultural groups. One of its issues was given over to a group dedicated to women's liberation, another to gay liberation and another, notoriously, to a group of 14- to 18-year-old 'school kids' (whose sexually provocative product resulted in the editors receiving deportation orders and prison sentences, though the verdict was later quashed on appeal). There was even an issue given over to a truly countercultural constituency of 'alien enthusiasts'.

For over a ten-year period, from the mid-1960s to the mid-1970s, the movement's magazines were thrown together by groups of like-minded individuals, who printed them cheaply and sold them at news-stands or hawked them on the streets and in clubs. It was a process and product that came to be referred to as the Underground Press, a term which had previously been used to describe the set of secret publications made by resistance groups in the occupied Netherlands and France during the Second World War. While the postwar Underground Press was clearly not clandestine in the same way – the offices of some were regularly raided by the police – their content was often marginal and subversive. It voiced concerns that had previously been denied a public platform – issues such as homosexuality or pornography had only really been discussed publicly within a medical or criminal context – and it criticized or lampooned the common values and petty prohibitions of the day.

This form of self-publishing was to become even more rudimentary during the mid-1970s. Music was the motivating force behind a DIY graphic style, which thrived in cheaply produced home-made magazines.

18 TEARING IT UP
Punk, c.1975 – c.1985

By the mid-1970s, many of the more socially conservative members of Western society began to rail against the cultural, moral and social revolution of the post-war decades. 'The permissive society', which they felt had been foisted on them, was held responsible for a host of social ills. It had damaged the foundational social unit, the family, through a rising divorce rate and an increase in teenage pregnancy, and it had strained relations outside the family by engendering a lack of deference to authority and by encouraging a disturbing change in people's appearance. Not only were the sexes becoming confused, with women looking like men by wearing trousers, but so too the classes, with all classes adopting the fashion, or what they thought was the fashion, of the urban lower classes. Such changes in the manners and customs of Western society were taken by social conservatives to be a sign of social decay, a deterioration that was compounded by a worsening economic climate. The oil-price shock of 1973 and the stock market crash that followed it – the first crash since the Great Depression and one that set a permanent seal on the golden years of the post-war economic boom – were not seen as temporary inconveniences, but confirmation of the seemingly unstoppable decline of Western civilization.

During the previous period of growth the world had changed greatly, but not necessarily in ways that matched the desires, or promises, of the counter-culture. Much of the change had been more in the direction of mass consumerism, high-rise building and suburban sprawl than any kind of bucolically spiritual turning on, tuning in and dropping out. Evidence of the progressively commercial orientation of Western society could even be found in what had been the counterculture's most dominant mode of expression, rock music, the one area perhaps where an anti-materialist ethos might have been expected to survive. By the early 1970s, rock had become part of a maturing 'music industry'. The huge market for music that had opened up during the 1960s had been exploited by a small number of multinational companies, who placed as much emphasis on promotion as they did on production. The commercial competition between them encouraged each to view music as a commodity and, as such, it was manufactured and marketed according to principles dedicated to identifying, exploiting and developing popular trends. In this way, the promise of rebellion that had been presented by the birth of rock-'n'-roll in the mid-1950s – first with Bill Haley and The Comets, but more with Little Richard, the real king of rock-'n'-roll, and then his less worryingly effeminate or black compatriots, Elvis Presley and Jerry Lee Lewis – had faded into a formulaic kind of corporate 'prog(ressive) rock'.

Against this background of economic recession, generational friction and commercialism a new social movement developed, in the US and Britain in particular: the essentially suburban subculture of Punk. On the one hand Punk seemed to be motivated by a destructive negativity, or nihilism, while on the other, it exhibited an inspiring strain of self-reliance, and provided its followers with the apparent sense of freedom that comes from living outside social norms. As a movement, it was fundamentally iconoclastic. At its core was a reflex desire to knock whatever figures and values were most cherished by the mainstream. The Punk sense of alienation from common values was expressed most vividly through music and fashion, and then also the range of related graphics that appeared on posters *(fig. 18.1)*, album covers and fanzines.

This last item, the fanzine or 'zine', was, as its name indicates, a magazine made for fans by fans *(> fig. 18.2)*. Its origins as a necessarily limited and rudimentary publication may be traced back to some of the literary groups of the nineteenth century, but it was only in the

< 18.1: 'Sex Pistols' poster artwork designed by Jamie Reid, 1977

18.2: 'Ripped and Torn' punk fanzine poster (detail), 1977

1930s that the form became at all common. New genres of literature and art, such as science fiction and horror movies, had yet to be given space in the more established commercial magazines, so the followers of these novel genres were forced to rely on fanzines to share information with fellow enthusiasts, in much the same way as equivalent groups do today on blogs or social networking sites.

Central to the existence of the Punk fanzine were two mechanical devices, the typewriter and the photocopier. Together they succeeded in revolutionizing the process and culture of printing. The ability to create multiple copies of a legible text almost immediately on comparatively cheap equipment and with no formal training was to have its most profound impact in the world of work. Every office in effect acquired its own in-house printing department or, increasingly, several of them on a single floor. Both technologies also had an impact outside the work environment. For the very first time it was possible for ordinary people to make cheap notices and publications without any expertise or any outside agency. At the tap of the keys of the

typewriter and the touch of the copier button printing was made available to all.

Neither device could match the quality of print and layout produced by more established methods of printing, but then for the creators and readers of the Punk fanzines such limitations were part of the magazines' appeal. Far from compromising the final design, they gave it a sense of immediacy, authenticity and egalitarianism even; qualities that chimed with Punk's strong do-it-yourself credo. It mattered little if the photocopied artwork was skewed or if the quality of reproduction was poor. And if a page needed a style and size of type not offered by a typewriter, it could be rubbed down in a more or less regular fashion from a sheet of dry-transfer lettering. If that were not available then a marker pen or biro would do. The sense of urgency that inspired this blithe and frantic approach was expressed both graphically and verbally in a spread from one British magazine thus: 'SOMETHING BETTER CHANGE – Punk never was just about music – it's about doing something and saying something – not gas – and getting off your ass and seeing what a

18.3: Cover, 'Sniffin' Glue' fanzine, Mark Perry, 1976

chord shapes for the guitar and the caption 'This is a chord. This is another. This is a third. Now form a band.' The magazine's creator, Mark Perry (1957–), wanted to reflect the kind of attitudes that were central to the movement and crucially he did so from the point of view of an insider, as someone who was himself going out to gigs and playing in a Punk band. He described his attitude to the magazine thus: 'Most of the things in the *Glue* were written straight down, no looking at it later, which is why you get all the crossing out ... I didn't really care about the magazine. It was the ideas that were important.' And, strange as it may seem now, there was nowhere else for people like him to explore or express these ideas. Not only were there no digital media – the internet, MP3 players and so on – and no cable or satellite TV, there were next to no music videos, no MTV, barely any music programmes on TV at all, and very few places on the radio or in print that were prepared to discuss any kind of rock music, let alone something that was genuinely underground. The only way for Punk to spread was by word of mouth or self-generated print, or by grabbing the attention of the very thing it was reacting against, the mainstream media. In order to take this last option without compromising its integrity, it had to subvert the media while simultaneously courting it. Or, to adapt one definition of a diplomat, Punk had to tell the media to go to hell in such a way that it looked forward to the trip.

Where an equivalence between the graphic design of Punk and Dada did exist was in the work of Punk's more knowing section of professional designers, the most celebrated of whom was the British designer Jamie Reid (1947–). Reid gained prominence as the designer for the archetypal punk band, the Sex Pistols, who themselves successfully performed the difficult task of media subversion and courtship, though in a way that was ultimately self-destructive. Their ironically titled single *God Save the Queen* (the title of Britain's national anthem) became the archetypal statement of the Punk aesthetic, aurally, verbally and visually. The cover of the single *(<fig. 18.1)*, which Reid designed in 1977, showed a bastardized image and text. The image was made out of a second-hand print of the portrait of the British monarch, Queen Elizabeth II, which Reid had found in a newspaper. No attempt was made to disguise this fact. The coarseness of his photocopied newspaper print seemed almost to mock the polished, even tones of the

shitty place this is and what a jam place it could be – it's about being fucked off with the non-stop lecture from the last generation – what do they know, WHAT DO THEY KNOW – DO SOMETHING DIFFERENT!'

The home-made quality of Punk fanzines distinguished the movement from the earlier, similarly iconoclastic movement of Dadaism *(<p. 180–183)*, with which it has often been compared. In contrast with most Punk graphics, Dada's brand of anti-art had remained unmistakably artistic all the same. It had been created by trained artists who, though they challenged the limitations that had been placed on their profession, were committed to exploring the aesthetic potential of their art. Punk fanzines, by contrast, were put together by enthusiastic amateurs who had little interest in making art, or anti-art for that matter. Mostly, they just wanted to put things down on the page with passion and honesty, and a bit of wry humour.

Something of each contributed to a second-hand illustration that appeared in one of British Punk's earliest and most influential fanzines, *Sniffin' Glue (fig. 18.3)*. The illustration in question showed three

18.4: Billboard, Times Square, New York, 2007

official royal portrait that the British society-photographer Sir Cecil Beaton (1904–80) had carefully crafted earlier in the year. More provocative though than the portrait's coarseness was the fact that Reid had ripped out the Queen's eyes and mouth, and filled the gaps with a ransom-note style of cut-out lettering. The eyes were replaced with cut-out words, and the mouth contained separate tooth-like letters. Clearly the symbolism of this adulterated head was provocative, but the nature of the provocation was ambiguous. Either it suggested that the Sex Pistols had taken the Queen, or what she represented, as a hostage and were keeping her blindfolded and gagged, or else that she (or again, what she represented) was the offending party and, as in a poster for an international criminal, her identity was being kept secret by masking out her most salient features. What made the design more controversial was the timing of the single's release. It intentionally coincided with the lead-up to a nationwide celebration for the 25th anniversary of Elizabeth's accession to the throne, her 'Silver Jubilee'. To ram the provocation home, Reid had his design printed in the official jubilee colours of blue and silver. In this way the Sex Pistols stuck out as a solitary beacon of dissent amid the wave of patriotism that had seemed to wash over the nation.

To appreciate the impact that Reid's designs had at the time, it is important to recognize not only the greater respect and reverence then accorded to the British monarchy, but also how much more conservative public attitudes towards visual imagery were then than now. The degree of nakedness, say, which we now take for granted in fashion adverts on billboards *(fig. 18.4)* would have been very shocking to most people in the mid-1970s. This conservatism was expressed in a common dress code, which only

a decade before had defined the standard dress for a man as a suit and tie, and for a woman a skirt or dress *(< fig. 17.1, p. 260)*. Though the force of this code had weakened considerably by the mid-1970s, Punk's signature look of dyed and spiked hair, and faces pierced with rings, studs and safety pins, was shockingly novel. As a provocation it was all of a piece with the movement's graphic image.

One of the effects on the Sex Pistols of having courted so much public hostility was that their graphic image assumed a greater importance than perhaps even they would have liked. TV companies and radio stations had rejected the band's promotional advertisements; the British broadcasting authorities had banned their single on the grounds that it was 'against good taste or decency, likely to encourage or incite to crime, or lead to disorder'; and some of the major retailers had refused to sell it. The printing was not without difficulties, too, with some printers refusing to handle the job. And yet, when the design did appear, the single and the promotional items that accompanied it succeeded in establishing a graphic identity not only for the band, but for the Punk movement as a whole.

Reid was aware of public sensibilities, but he did not set out to challenge them for its own sake or to simply make money. The main motivation behind his design was political, especially the actively artistic politics defined by the Situationists *(< p. 279-80)*. While studying at art college, he had designed the cover of a British Situationist magazine, and during the summer vacation of 1968 he made a trip to Paris, where, though the riots had ended, many of the atéliers' posters and Situationist graffiti could still be seen. On leaving college Reid set up a small-scale community printing press, the Suburban Press, with a group of friends. As well as supporting various social causes, it was also used to publish Situationist writings and Reid's own Situationist graphics (fluorescent stickers saying 'Save Petrol, Burn Cars', 'Special Offer – This Store Welcomes Shoplifters' or 'A Brick Will Do The Trick' were printed and stuck onto local shop windows). It was partly through a lack of time and money that some of the Suburban Press's leaflets, magazines and other graphic items were set with the kind of cut-out or dry-transfer letters that were to appear in his later Punk graphics. But alongside these practical factors was an important conceptual or philosophical one. The cut-out letters were a kind of Situationist *détournement*, a way of subverting an established

18.5: 'This Year's Model' album cover designed by Barney Bubbles, 1978

medium by appropriating it. A similarly plagiarizing tendency may also have contributed to one of Reid's Queen's-head images, which instead of having the eyes and mouth ripped out had a safety pin through the lip and swastikas in the eyes (the Nazi symbolism was considered a step too far even by the record company and they refused to use it). Both features had parallels with an earlier poster from one of Paris's ateliers, which showed a bandaged head *(<fig. 17.18, p. 277)* tied with a mouth shaped safety pin (though its eyes had concentric circles rather than swastikas).

Like the graffiti from May '68, Reid's designs succeeded in dragging some of the Situationist's ideas out of the esoteric world of left-wing philosophy and into the more exoteric arena of popular culture. Yet despite the fact that album covers and other forms of rock-related graphics were making large numbers of people interested in graphic design, often for the very first time, the design industry in general considered this kind of work to be unimportant. Whereas writing about rock music had begun to bring young writers a degree of recognition, album cover design was generally regarded as the perfunctory product of an anonymous layout designer or illustrator. The status of music-related graphics only began to rise once designers such Reid and the British graphic designer and

18.6: 'Hard Werken' magazine spread designed by Hard Werken, 1980

illustrator Colin Fulcher (1942–1983) had shown its potential for expression and wit.

Fulcher, who was better known by his adopted name of Barney Bubbles (Bubbles seems to have been a reference to the multi-coloured bubbling effects he had created in some of the rock concert lighting shows he had made early in his career), was too wide-ranging and too reliant on his own illustrative skill for his work to be categorized strictly as punk. Some of his earliest work had involved making illustrations for the British underground magazine *Oz*, and the eclectic mix of graphic forms that crowded its pages were also to be a feature of Bubbles's work. What he did share with punk though was some of its subversive wit. His cover design for Elvis Costello and The Attractions's album *This Year's Model* (<fig.18.5), first released in 1978, looked as though it had been misprinted. The photograph of the singer posing behind a camera – itself a play on the album's title – and the type that ran across the top and bottom of the photograph were all shifted to the left. While the band's

name remained intelligible ('Lvis Costello'), the album's title made a new (non)sense ('His years Model'). More dominant than each of these though was the printer's swatch of proofing colours that appeared to have been mistakenly exposed down the right-hand side of the cover. Bubbles's wit even extended to a sticker that appeared on the cover to publicized the album's eponymous single. Its text read 'Free Album With This Single'. Similarly mischievous was the bogus information printed on the space between the holding spirals on one side of the record: *'Special pressing No.003. Ring 434 32 32. Ask for Moira for your prize'*. The album's design so confounded the American record company that they had the cover reprinted, shifting the image back to the right (a position it continued to occupy in subsequent printings).

Music and culture more broadly were the focus of an influential Dutch magazine, *Hard Werken* ('Hard Working'), which also contained a more knowing form of punk-related graphic design. It was written, edited, designed and published between 1978 and 1982 by a design collective based in the industrial city of Rotterdam in the Netherlands. Being self-published (though funded by the city's authorities), the magazine gave its designers the same kind of freedom to experiment that designers of the Underground magazines of the 1960s had enjoyed. Both the nature of the city itself and the collective nature of its design contributed to the magazine's very unorthodox and varied range of design.

Hard Werken's designers had aimed to 'shed more light on Rotterdam's social and artistic climate' which, like other Dutch cities, had struggled to escape from the shadow cast by the country's two established cultural centres, The Hague and, in particular, Amsterdam. In its architecture and the nature of its commerce Rotterdam was much younger, more modern and industrial than those two cities. The destruction that had seen the city centre almost entirely flattened during the Second World War had allowed the city to be substantially rebuilt, and from the 1950s onwards it became a focus for all kinds of architectural innovation. By the late 1960s it had grown into the world's busiest port (a title it has only recently relinquished). The city's new industrial bias and its lack of established forms of culture provided an open environment in which new forms of cultural activity – theatre, dance, music and film – could develop.

The designers of *Hard Werken* played a prominent part in this development. The initial success of the magazine encouraged them to adopt its title as a name under which they could branch out into other areas of graphic design and design more generally. They produced posters, brochures, books and more for a variety of cultural organizations – museums, publishers, architects and the like – and made corporate identity designs and interior design for a host of commercial clients. By not wanting to adhere to the established conventions that guided most graphic design, and by allowing each member in the collective to pursue their own modes of graphic expression, they produced a stylistic variety that appeared to be united only by its novelty and apparent lack of structure. Hand drawn lettering was as likely to be appear next to typewriter or photocopied lettering as it was to historical styles of type. Pictures were sometimes written over and framed with painted outlines, or they were cut into varied, irregular shapes rather than being rectangular. Some appeared with visible cut marks and were cropped by the edges of a page in an apparently casual fashion *(fig. 18.6)*. Within the pages of the magazine,

such characteristics combined to form a loose medley of expression, which the magazine's large A3 format only seemed to encourage.

One of the justifications given by the group in defence of their stylistic variety was that every piece of communication amounted to a unique exchange. It had its own particular message which needed to be delivered through a particular medium to a certain audience in a particular social context. Both the symmetrical seriffed design of traditional typography and the asymmetrical sanserif design of Modernism seemed not to reflect this degree of uniqueness. With this in mind, the *Hard Werken* designers did not set out to be provocative necessarily, though others were provoked by them, particularly when designs for cultural of commercial clients started to appear. Such work was criticized for being self-indulgent and for celebrating ugliness. Certainly, *Hard Werken*'s designs were rarely neat or precious, but many of them had a simple kind of robustness or were knowingly 'undesigned' at least. Punk fanzines had also been 'undesigned' *(< fig. 18.2 & fig. 18.3)* but not in the same way. They had never set out to be experimental or to explore stylistic contrasts. They were simply rudimentary. *Hard Werken*'s designs were not. Their more knowing approach was evident not just in the design but in the production processes used. The quality of printing and the variety of different media used told of the knowledge *Hard Werken*'s designers had acquired since first being brought together in a state funded 'graphics workshop' with its own printing press.

Subsequent designers took up the fractured mix of forms and symbolism that Punk graphics and, indeed, the Underground Press before them had exhibited. Like *Hard Werken* these designers applied it to a more commercial context. The pioneers of this more formal and self-conscious kind of eclecticism felt they were surfing a new wave of design. It was to act as a prelude to and an influence on the larger digital wave that crashed over the profession during the coming decades.

19 LESS IS A BORE
New Wave & Postmodernism, c.1970 – c.1990

One way of signalling the passing of something is to attach the prefix 'post-' to it. Post-Impressionism, post-industrial, post-colonial, post-Gutenberg; each of these terms is used to mark the passing of a particular situation or a particular way of doing something. But in adding the 'post-' prefix to a word, a choice is being made to define the present in relation to the past rather than to the future. As in a funeral address, attention is focused on past events rather than any potential afterlife. The same kind of uncertainty or lack of clarity about the future lay behind the term 'Postmodernism', which featured prominently in discussions about style and culture during the last decades of the previous century. Within the arts, where the term first became commonplace, Postmodernism acquired many meanings, most of which were defined by an opposition to the style that had preceded it: Modernism.

It was in architecture that the term first became prominent. During the late 1970s, a number of architects and architecture critics had begun to use it to describe buildings whose design playfully incorporated an overt surface decoration as well as explicit references to period styles and local architectural features – 'wit, ornament and reference' is one summary of Postmodern architecture. Such characteristics were partly a reaction to the plainness and seriousness of Modernism and to the impersonality of its internationalism ('less is a bore' was a parodic jibe of one prominent Postmodernist architect). Some of the playfulness and eclecticism apparent in Postmodern architecture could be seen in other arts too. In music, the word 'Postmodern' was sometimes used to describe a minimalist form of modern classical music that began to be made mainly in the United States (John Adams, Steve Reich and Philip Glass). The music's varied influences and references, freely expressed within textured layers of sound, were developed as a reaction to the austerity and atonality

of some mid-twentieth-century classical music. But it was in the field of literature that the term carried most weight. It was used here to describe certain kinds of prose writing and poetry, but its main place of reference was within literary theory and criticism. Abetted by the writings of various French post-structuralist philosophers (Jacques Derrida, Michel Foucault and Roland Barthes), the concept of Postmodernism was used to outline new and complex ideas about language, and during the 1980s some of these ideas spilled over into graphic design.

The term 'Postmodernism' was, however, used sparingly and only very generally within graphic design. A more common term, especially for designers and writers in the United States, was 'New Wave'. Some of the roots of New Wave may be traced not only to Postmodern language theory, but also to Punk. However, the primary root of New Wave design came out of a reaction to the orderliness of Swiss typography *(<ch.16, p.239)*, which first took hold in Switzerland itself and then elsewhere, particularly the United States. The person most identified with this reaction is Wolfgang Weingart (1941–), a German teacher of typography and graphic design, who conducted a series of influential experiments in his commercial work, though more notably in the courses he taught at the Basel School of Design (*Kunstgewerbe schule*) in Switzerland.

As a young man Weingart had trained as a compositor, learning to set blocks of metal type by hand. This introduction to the practical side of typography gave him a technical knowledge that he later supplemented with an aesthetic appreciation of Swiss typography in particular, which he had studied at the school in Basel under two of the style's leading practitioners, Emil Ruder (1914–70) and Armin Hofmann (1920–). After being elevated from the position of student to teacher in 1968, Weingart soon applied his technical and aesthetic

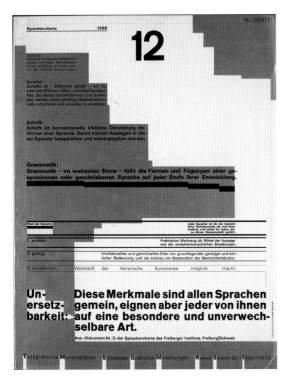

19.2: 'Typografische Monatsblätter' magazine, designed by Wolfgang Weingart, 1968

knowledge to the task of extending Swiss typography's idiom. '[Its] conservative design dogma and strict limitations stifled my playful, inquisitive, experimental temperament … Yet at the same time I recognized too many good qualities in Swiss typography to renounce it altogether.' By taking the fundamental elements of the style – the typographic grid and its prominent sanserif typeface, Akzidenz-Grotesk – out of its functional and minimal straitjacket, he was able to create a set of more visually complex designs. Letterforms were broken up in order to test the limits of legibility and the grid was used more flexibly to create various kinds of unorthodox and decorative typographical arrangements.

In one of a series of 14 covers Weingart designed for the prominent Swiss trade magazine *Typografische Monatsblätter* ('Typographical Monthly', or 'TM') during the early 1970s *(fig. 19.2)*, various rules and blocks of solid tone were used to partition portions of text. The rectilinearity of the stepped blocks of line and tone that dominate the cover mimics the aesthetic of a grid-based design. The cover's rectilinear bias was partly due to Weingart's use of letterpress for proofing the covers. But, though almost every part of the design is set at right angles, little of it is actually aligned or evenly spaced, as with a true grid. Instead, the different parts of the cover

take their cue from the varied sections of text, which in their fractured order allude to the analytical thrust of the contents. Weingart referred to this series of covers as his 'Seeing, Reading and Learning' covers, and each element in this description is touched on by the cover's content: *Sprachen* (languages), *Sprache* (speech), *Schrift* (writing), *Grammatik* (grammar) and so on. Despite the irregular blocking and the backwards hierarchy of type, which had the dominant text at the bottom of the cover and the subservient text at the top, the text remained both legible and intelligible.

Weingart's initial experiments were almost exclusively typographic, but by the mid-1970s he started to include various kinds of non-typographic imagery. Sheets of clear film with various dot-screen textures, some of which he had worked on by hand, were combined with parts of photographs to produce a series of multi-layered and multi-textured arrangements *(fig. 19.3)*. His use of textured film in this way was novel; 'I'd discovered the intrinsic aesthetic of a new process', he wrote. The novelty was made possible by the twin processes of photocomposition and offset-lithography, which allowed Weingart to make his artwork entirely out of film and then expose it directly onto the printing plate. A stabilizing element for the posters' shifting imagery was the exclusively horizontal text, though in some instances this was disturbed by being blurred at the edges or subtly textured. Weingart's multi-layered and softened forms became the dominant features in a series of large-format, monochrome posters he designed for several cultural organizations, such as the Basel Art Gallery (*Kunsthalle*) shown here, during the late 1970s. The obliqueness of their shifting planes and subtle textures prevented any one piece of the poster from becoming a focal point. No clear hierarchy between the text and image was established, nor was there one between the different parts of the text. In fact all that stopped his designs from being seen as photomechanical Cubist collages was the text, whose meaning remained clear and informative.

Weingart's experiments provoked considerable interest among other designers and design critics. Some praised their novelty, others condemned what they considered to be self-indulgence. What enabled the coursework of a young teacher from an art school in a relatively small European city to gain such widespread attention was its threefold means of transmission: it appeared in *TM* magazine and various trilingual supplements, which brought it to the attention of the

19.3: 'Kunstkredit' poster designed by Wolfgang Weingart, 1977

magazine's international readership; it also became the subject of a series of lecture tours that Weingart conducted in Europe and the United States; and then a succession of foreign students that attended Weingart's courses (some of whom went on to become well-known designers) took what they had learnt away with them and incorporated it into their own work back home or taught it to a new group of design students.

One of the consequences of Weingart's transcontinental reach is that other designers who had also begun to extend Swiss typography's idiom received less attention than they deserved. The fact that their work inhabited a more local commercial sphere also contributed to this lack of recognition. An especially vivid example of the abstract and decorative potential that lay within one of the building blocks of Swiss typography, its sanserif letters, appeared in 1981 on the back cover of a brochure for a firm of Zürich printers *(> fig. 19.4)*. The brochure had been designed by the Swiss graphic designer Rosemarie Tissi (1928–), then a partner in one

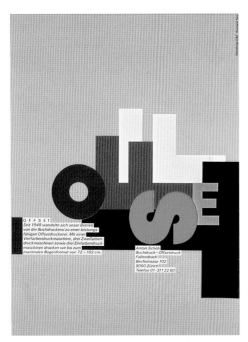

19.4: Printer's brochure, back cover designed by Rosemarie Tissi, 1981

it well enough. When stressing the importance of a high degree of legibility, what many of the advocates of Swiss typography were really valuing was the idea of legibility, or clarity perhaps, rather than the reality of it. It was an aesthetic of clarity, what clarity looked and felt like emotionally, rather than the practical effect of it that was their real passion. By contrast, Tissi, and others like her, recognized that most readers could decode even quite complex typographical arrangements. She also appeared to appreciate the importance of being able to grab and hold the reader's attention. (As Weingart once put it when discussing a design, 'What's the use of being legible, when nothing inspires you to take notice of it?'). By creating a design with a playfully sculptural quality, she made sure that this important function was fulfilled, but also that the text could be read.

Many of the subsequent developments in New Wave design can be seen as a series of similar challenges to the conception of clarity and order. In Italy and the United States in particular, these challenges became increasingly explicit. One of the most striking was a new acceptance, or indeed promotion, of ornament and decoration. The almost complete rejection of ornament by Modernists, which had been encapsulated in the mantra 'less is more', was itself rejected. The case in favour of decoration had been made over the course of the previous decade by movements such as Op and Pop art as well as by the psychedelic poster. They had revealed the aesthetic potential of a series of repeated shapes or a richly wrought pattern *(<fig. 17.11, p.271)*. They had also contested the grounds on which ornament had been rejected. The very early Modernist claim that decoration was uncivilized because it had predominated in uncivilized societies counted for less and less as notions of what it was to be 'civilized' were challenged and changed.

This new openness to the artistic potential of decoration was made visible during the early 1980s by an influential Italian design collective known as Memphis. The name was chosen in an impromptu, Dada-like fashion from a song by Bob Dylan. By also recalling the birthplace of Elvis and an ancient Egyptian capital city, the title seemed to emphasize the group's whimsical, eclectic and pop-oriented nature. At the centre of this group of young artists and designers was an older Austrian-born architect and industrial designer, Ettore Sottsass (1917–2007), who had spent

of Switzerland's most reputable practices, Odermatt & Tissi. The tight, rectilinear bordering of the text and the layering of the large letters that made up the word 'Offset' may have offended the functionalist credo of Swiss typography, but these features did not have the effect of making the letters illegible. Certainly the letters are of different sizes and colours, and some are tipped onto their back while others are turned onto their front, but still the word can be read.

It was designs such as this, as well as those by Weingart, that exposed the fallacy behind some of the arguments that had been made in support of Swiss typography. In simple terms, Swiss typography's quest for maximum legibility was at best overly precious and at worst intellectually dishonest. Any increase in legibility over a certain, often quite low, point makes little difference to our ability to read. It is an ability that rests on a powerful need, which we all share, to make sense of the world around us. Each of us is predisposed to scan our environment in search of meaning, and the strength of this predisposition enables us to read text even under quite challenging conditions. A lot of lettering that we are presented with is quite small, crudely rendered (especially if it's on a computer screen or from a computer printer) and is often looked at under low levels of ambient light (as is the case in many offices), yet most of us can read

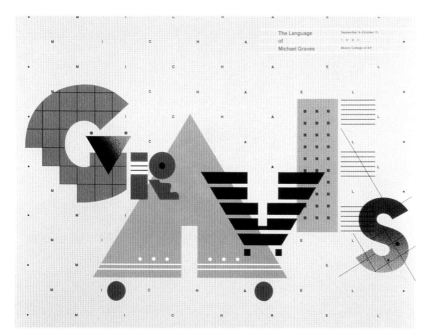

19.5: 'Michael Graves' exhibition poster designed by William Longhauser, 1983

the previous decade experimenting with new kinds of patterns, colours and materials as part of an earlier 'counterdesign' movement. Under Sottsass's influence the Memphis group designed a range of domestic items – furniture, lighting, tableware and ceramics – that rejected the established Modernist conventions of beauty and 'good taste'. As well as making chairs that had differently shaped legs, Memphis produced multi-coloured bookcases and sideboards whose shape half-resembled totemic figures and whose surfaces were covered with sheets of highly decorated plastic laminate. The decorations were not revivals of past styles, but new textures often spotted or lined in seemingly random markings. The same aesthetic irreverence was applied to other measures of artistic value: 'I don't understand why enduring design is better than disappearing design …' Sottsass was once heard to remark.

Memphis had a particular appeal and influence in the United States and it was here that a similar attitude towards patterning and simple suggestive forms began to be seen in graphic design. In 1983, the American designer William Longhauser (1947–) created a poster *(fig. 19.5)* for an exhibition of the work of perhaps the best known Postmodern architect of the time, the American architect and industrial designer Michael Graves. Longhauser designed his poster around Graves's name. He spelt out the surname with a series of architectural motifs mostly made out of decorated or modular forms.

The grid and stepped shape in the 'G', for example, made an allusion to an architect's plan and a stairway, while other letters made references to specific shapes in Graves's buildings. Graves's best-known structure, the Portland Building, in Portland, Oregon *(< fig. 19.1)*, was credited on its completion in 1980 with marking the arrival of Postmodernist architecture. Longhauser represented it through two of the building's signature features: its dominant keystone-like shape, mirrored in the 'V'; and its regular rows of small square windows, which formed the vertical stroke of the 'E' and were also picked up on by a background pattern of capital letters that repeatedly spelt out Graves's first name, Michael. The specific references in Longhauser's playful, almost childlike, patterning and shape making would not have been recognized by most people perhaps, but nevertheless they were an arresting departure from the more sober and apparently rational design of the Swiss style.

The specific architectural symbolism in Longhauser's poster contrasted with the much more general architectural symbolism that dominated a unique series of posters created over a 20-year period by the Swiss-born American designer, Willi Kunz (1943–). Between 1984 and 2003 Kunz designed several posters each year for the Graduate School of Architecture at New York city's Columbia University. His marathon sequence of posters demonstrated the graphic potential that lurks within even a quite restricted set of conditions. Kunz's

19.6: Columbia University Graduate School of Architecture and Planning poster designed by Willi Kunz, 1985

tions were imposed during the first decade of designing the posters by the production method then available to him which, with computers not yet common in design studios, required him to make the artwork by hand using transfer lettering, and then paste it together with the other graphic elements. The whole process was not made any easier by frequent last-minute changes to the text, which sometimes forced Kunz to redesign the poster completely.

In light of the above, Kunz's decision to use just the one typeface, Frutiger's Univers *(<fig.16.6, p.242)*, for each poster throughout the entire series might suggest a degree of masochism – indeed, he has stood by this self-imposed restriction for most of his life (on occasion he has combined this sanserif with the seriffed face Bodoni) – but, in fact, this act of parsimony was less punishing than it appeared. By using the same typeface over and over again, Kunz would have acquired an intimate knowledge of its particular characteristics. Every typeface has them: the sculptural essence that is enshrined in each letter shape, which of course differs between its uppercase and lowercase forms; the tonal colour of words set in specific sizes and weights; the particular degree of emphasis created when used as a heading; and the kind of texture produced when set as a chunk of text. Just as concert pianists are able to express themselves more fully if they have learnt their repertoire by heart, so Kunz would have been more able to achieve the effects he was looking for because he knew the typeface so well. If he had used it less, he would not have been able to express himself so freely.

The general effect aimed for by Kunz was to 'simulate structural form'. Knowing that the posters' main audience would be architects or architectural students, he had wanted to create designs that would act as 'a metaphor for architectural space'. In a poster he designed in 1986 to announce Columbia University's programme for a 'Master of Science' in 'Historic Preservation' *(fig.19.6)*, the text is accompanied by an abstract photograph relating to the subject of study, and then also by a collection of loosely symbolic shapes. The way the text and the shapes are fitted together evokes something of an architectural plan: the columns of text suggest an elevation, as though we are looking at the side of a building, while the coloured shape and the bold headings give the sense that we are looking down on a plan. There is architectural symbolism too in the very structured way each of these elements has been related to the photograph. But rather than relating

nearly 50 variations on a single architecturally orientated theme were made not only in the face of pressure to be repetitive, which came from having to use very similar kinds of information each year, but they were also made with a limited budget. This forced Kunz to restrict himself to using two colours only, usually black and one other (which in some instances was a special metallic ink). The need for economy also prompted him to design his posters in such a way that they could be folded up and used as a leaflet. It led him to restrict their size to two formats: 61cm (24in) high and either 46cm (18in) wide or 30.5cm (12in) wide. Further limita-

them in a formulaic way according to the dictates of a typographic grid, as others might have done, Kunz established a series of alignments and spatial rhythms that came out of the particular forms and arrangements as he created them. Rather than imposing the alignments and rhythms on the design from without, he allowed them to suggest themselves from within, particularly in relation to the various abstract features within the photograph. The wave shape that runs through the bottom half of the poster picks up on similar curves in the top-right portion of the photograph. It also makes an effective linear contrast with the rectangular shapes of the columns of text below it. Similarly, the two circular, rivet-like shapes on the left of the poster echo the photograph's circular stone studs. Even the photograph's thick stepped shadow is alluded to by the stepped part of the central coloured shape and then, in a smaller way, by the black bar at the bottom.

The same kind of links are made with the type. The two horizontal lines at the bottom of the photograph are picked up by a pair of thin triple white lines, one below the photograph and the other in the top-left black bar. Each pair is also positioned and spaced to fall along the baselines of each set of large type. On the left side of the poster the two circles are positioned like remote bullet points, the white one for the title 'Columbia University' above it and the coloured one for the three columns of text to its right. And the width of each of these columns fits with the vertical forces suggested by the left edge of the photograph and other divisions within it. It is not possible to grasp all these subtle contrasts and connections at a single glance, yet they give the design an immediate albeit subtle sense of order.

Another challenge to Swiss typographic order was made by overlapping and layered forms. Whereas Kunz's layering produced a relatively clear sense of spatial depth, other New Wave designs made it intentionally ambiguous. This ambiguity was central to the work produced by the Dutch designer Gert Dumbar (1940–) during the 1980s. He and his associates in their studio in The Hague developed a particular method of design, for arts posters in particular, in which two-dimensional typographic forms were printed onto photographs of carefully staged sets *(fig. 19.7)*. The marrying of these different spatial dimensions was done in such a way that they created a shifting, ambiguous and arresting virtual space. In one of a series of posters designed for the Holland Festival, an annual festival for the performing arts, the space was made even more ambiguous by the

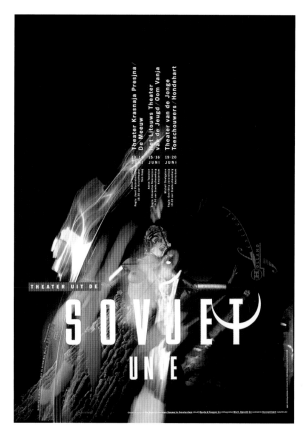

19.7: 'Holland Festival' poster designed by Studio Dumbar, 1989

inclusion of coloured whirls of light which illuminated the space around the poster's central dancing figure. The fluctuating and almost explosive sense of depth they created were intended to reflect the dynamism and richness of the festival's programme. While the poster's typography stabilized the design in much the same way as Weingart's typography had in his exhibition poster (<fig. 19.3), it also injected an element of playfulness: the turning of the top of the 'E' and the adjacent 'T' into the Soviet Union's (*Sovjet Unie*) hammer and sickle symbol; and then, also, and more egregiously, the exuberant festival logo, which broke several typographic norms partly through its lack of compactness and its mix of letter styles, but mostly through being made in three slightly different versions. Part of their shape was based on the treble-clef symbol used in musical notation, but beyond that element of consistency Dumbar was able to ignore an apparently fundamental tenet of logo design: faithfulness to a single definitive form. Because the overall character of the logo was so unusual, none of the three were likely to be confused with anything else. The slight differences between them were

19.8: Musée d'Orsay poster, 1986

19.9: Musée d'Orsay brochures, 1987

19.10: PTT corporate identity manual
designed by Studio Dumbar, 1989

less than the difference between them and any other logo; for example, the more conventional blue logo of the festival's sponsor, KLM (the Royal Dutch Airways).

An interesting comparison can be made between Dumbar's logo and an earlier logo *(fig. 19.8)*, which also broke an accepted rule of logo design. The logo was made in 1984 for the Musée d'Orsay in Paris by two Swiss émigrés, Jean Widmer (1921–) and Bruno Monguzzi (1941–). Unlike Studio Dumbar's triple logo, Widmer and Monguzzi's logo existed as a single form, but it was not one that made a complete visual statement. It was purposefully partial. The museum's name was abbreviated down to its initial letters, and then the initials were sliced in half before being set either side of a thin dividing line and combined with a graphically eloquent apostrophe. The logo's partial form also dictated how it could be used. Its state of incompleteness gave the designers licence to intrude on its form further. They frequently used it as a large background element, cropped in various ways by the edges of the posters or brochures it adorned *(fig. 19.9)*. Instead of being an isolated and inviolable brand mark, it was allowed to

move freely into whatever portion of the printed surface its designers thought best.

This run of rule breaking was continued by Studio Dumbar in a number of subsequent corporate identity designs. For them, a decoratively expressive and playful graphic design was not only appropriate for arts organizations. Some of the institutions of state, such as the Dutch police force and the Netherlands' newly privatized telecommunications company, PTT, could also benefit from the positive associations triggered by a more playful graphic image. Both organizations became the recipients of Dumbar's exuberant brand of New Wave design. The main graphic component of PTT's corporate identity design of 1989 was the logo *(fig. 19.10)*. There was a playfulness in its having lowercase letters, rather than the capital form usually used in the acronymic logos of large corporations (e.g. IBM <*fig. 15.19, p. 232*). But there was an additional playfulness in the decorative geometric shapes that accompanied the logo. The way these elements, the coloured squares and dots, were taken and applied, or in the Studio's words, 'deconstructed', onto various two- and three-dimensional items such as vehicles, telephone boxes and electrical equipment, created a lively and novel mode of design.

An even more direct challenge to the seriousness expected of an organization's design was made by Dumbar's compatriot, R.D.E. 'Ootje' Oxenaar (1929–) in the design of six new Dutch banknotes *(fig. 19.11)*. Between 1964 and 1977 Oxenaar updated three existing banknotes, using a series of strong colours and an almost children's-book style of illustration for each of the notes' portraits. But it was during a second phase of

19.11: Dutch banknotes designed by R.D.E. 'Ootje' Oxenaar, 1964–85

design, between 1977 and 1985, that he incorporated a more extreme form of playfulness into three new notes. The 50-guilder note, introduced in 1982, is indicative of this second phase. What is immediately apparent is that Oxenaar has avoided the muted colouring that dominated most other currencies. Moreover, instead of using a single dominant colour, he spread the range of dominance between a vibrant orange and yellow; orange being the Netherlands' national colour, and yellow the colour of the note's principal motif, the sunflower, which was an indirect reference to the nation's best-known artist, Van Gogh. Both colours complemented the intense browns and pinky purples that distinguished the other notes in this latter series. More unconventional still was Oxenaar's choice of the kind of motif mentioned above. Instead of continuing the ubiquitous theme of portraits of more or less unrecognized historical figures, Oxenaar introduced an animal, a vegetable and a mineral – specifically, a snipe (a species of wading bird), a sunflower and a lighthouse.

But behind his bright colours and informal imagery lay a deeply considered and rational design. Banknotes are the ultimate industrial product. They have to be mass-produced in their billions as a series of exact replicas that can withstand constant daily use in all kinds of weather and lighting conditions. Central to their function is the need to distinguish each denomination but through a series of related designs. Oxenaar's strong colours and unconventional imagery met this need, as did his use of large sizes of the familiar sanserif, Helvetica, which he positioned in a clear part of the design on a specially white and, therefore, highly contrasting paper. The print quality of the three printing processes used gave crisp definition to the intricate layers of detail that, as in all notes, are added in an attempt to deter forgers. All these features allowed the denominations to be identified by young and old, native and foreign, well-sighted and poor-sighted. Consideration was also given to those whose eyesight was very poor – surprisingly, it was the first banknote design to do so – through the inclusion of a series of specially raised marks in the bottom left corner of the note's front face, which allowed each to be distinguished by touch (the inverted triangle on the 50-guilder note, for example).

When the notes were released the response was mostly very positive. The more negative reactions were dominated by the common complaint that the notes looked like toy money. Some people didn't even believe they were genuine. This criticism of them as looking like the kind of money one would find in a board game was apt though hollow because toy money had indeed influenced Oxenaar's designs. Moreover, the element of play in his notes was actually much greater than it appeared to be. The position of the bee on the 50-guilder's sunflower only came about by getting stuck there after coming loose from an early piece of artwork. Oxenaar liked the new position and so kept it. This instance of serendipity represents the kind of accident that often plays a part in all artistic activity, however well organized the process of creation is. Most designs incorporate some chance element in their final form, in spite of any later claims or assumptions that everything was wholly intentional.

A more deliberate element of playfulness was Oxenaar's inclusion of a number of entirely alien features; things such as one of his own fingerprints, which formed a wave of hair on the portrait of the philosopher Spinoza; a picture of his girlfriend's rabbit; and then three names, his girlfriend's, his mother's, and that of a secret friend, each of which were small enough or disguised so as to go largely unnoticed. Indeed, the names were revealed to his client only after the notes concerned had been printed.

The point about the notes being playful, though, was not restricted to the private thrill that can be derived from a secret act of subversion. Oxenaar wanted to show that this quotidian and essentially administrative artefact, a banknote, was a product of work done by individuals, and that it was to be held by and exchanged between individual human beings, one to the other, sometimes in an act of kindness, and not just during some perfunctory commercial transaction. It was an emphasis that bolstered the designs' Postmodern identity. Where Modernism had stressed the importance of objectivity and the collective, Postmodernism embraced subjectivity and the individual. Emphasizing what was unique about people was seen to be as important as emphasizing what people had in common.

The contribution that individuals made in realizing Oxenaar's designs was also reflected in the relationship he developed with his client. During the second design phase, Oxenaar was given a remarkable degree

of responsibility, especially in being allowed to propose the contents of each banknote. Had this responsibility been retained by a committee of bankers, it is hard to imagine that they would have proposed such a radical change. As with Pintori's work for Olivetti, and Rand's for IBM *(< p. 232-3)*, the freedom that Oxenaar received had to be granted to him, and here again individuals were involved. Oxenaar describes how the president of the Bank of the Netherlands, after having discussed the proposed designs, said to him 'it's awful what you make. But your arguments are sound. It's your profession and my things are in it [i.e. criteria are met], and if it's safe [i.e. unforgeable], OK. Your arguments are very intelligent and very reasonable, so I accept them.' The president's willingness to accept Oxenaar as a capable individual with a knowledge and a training that the president himself lacked was essential to the design's creation.

The complexity in Oxenaar's design, though clearly related to his aim of individual expression, was mainly the result of having to make banknotes that were hard to forge. The complexity within New Wave graphic design as a whole was rarely tied to such a specific task. Individual expression was certainly a contributing factor, but another significant influence was design theory, in particular a series of theories derived from linguistics and literary analysis. When Studio Dumbar used the term 'deconstructed' to describe PTT's logo design, they were using a word that had come out of recent writings on the philosophy of language, a philosophy called post-structuralism. The set of meanings these writings gave to the word was rather specific, but most cultural commentators and graphic designers used the term loosely to mean 'broken apart' or 'disassembled', and they applied it specifically to form, to what something looked like, rather than to a process of analysis, as the originators of the term had.

As befits an academic theory, the place that first showed how deconstruction and its related concepts could be applied to graphic design was an art college, the Cranbrook Academy of Art, part of a complex of colleges located in a suburb of Detroit. The person responsible for steering the academy's design department in this direction was Katherine McCoy (1945–), who from 1971 to 1995 co-chaired the design department with her partner Mike McCoy. While he was in charge of three-dimensional design, she looked after the two-dimensional programme. During the late

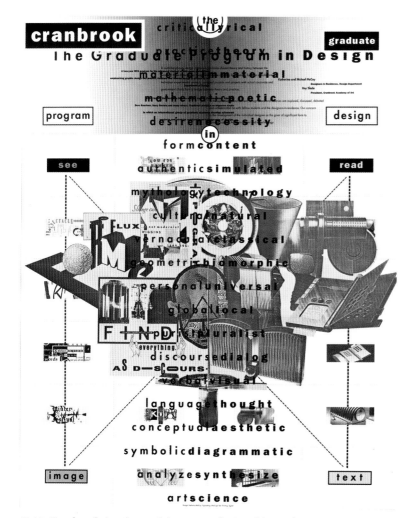

19.12: Cranbrook Academy of Art poster designed by Katherine McCoy, 1989

1970s Katherine McCoy introduced 'semiotics', the study of signs (which in the study of linguistics also includes words) into the graphic design programme. Then, as now, Cranbrook was unusual in that it offered no courses as such, but instead required students to self-direct their learning while the tutors acted as guides. Within a few years the students were discovering and experimenting with a raft of related theories: 'structuralism, post-structuralism, deconstruction, phenomenology, critical theory, reception theory, hermeneutics, letterism, Venturi vernacularism, postmodern art theory'.

It was during this theory-laden phase, between the mid-1980s and the early 1990s, that many of the department's designs became more visually complex. Their complexity was partly a result of experimentation, but it also had a basis in particular ideas. One important idea was an emphasis on relevance. Stu-

dents were encouraged to hold a mirror up to the modern world in all its media-related complexity. But this did not mean that complexity should only be applied to form. McCoy was keen to have complexity of meaning in the design too. In a poster she herself designed in 1989 to publicize the department's graduate programme *(fig. 19.12)*, this idea is made explicit. The first layer of meaning, the headings 'Cranbrook' and 'Graduate Design Program', is immediately apparent, while the second layer of more practical information, in small lines of type, appears around the headings. Below these is a range of layered typography and imagery that stands both as an illustration of the involved nature of the coursework and the complexity inherent in the subject itself. Its verbal profusion sets out some of the current key concepts and presents them as opposites, such as 'form' and 'content', or 'image' and 'text', which was then a favoured form of analysis within deconstructivist philosophy.

The same oppositional contrast was applied to the pictures. The left side of the poster shows examples of the students' two-dimensional designs, coloured in pinkish tints, while on the right side, in opposing green tints, are examples of their three-dimensional designs. The images and some of the text are displayed through the use of two opposing Modernist idioms: rectangles evenly spaced down the sides of the poster, as in a Swiss-typographic grid, or else as a cluttered Dadaist photographic montage in the centre. What shows a Postmodern mixing of styles most emphatically though is the adoption of an essentially pre-Modernist device: a centred layout. Because it was able to emphasize the oppositional basis of the text, it was an entirely appropriate idiom, but it is not a device that a Swiss typographer, or even someone like Weingart, would have chosen. This overt mixing of styles became a key component of Postmodern graphic design.

Not all mixing of styles had to be so explicit. An earlier design created in 1983 by the British designer Peter Saville (1955–) relied on a more subtle contrast. His cover for an album by the band New Order *(fig. 19.13)* was dominated by the central part of a late nineteenth-century painting by the French artist Henri Fantin-Latour. The artist's careful study of a basket of roses was one of a whole series of similar still-lifes painted between 1860 and 1900. The picture's age, the traditional artistic medium of oil paint, its classical style of realism and the conventional subject matter contrasted with the small strip of coloured blocks that hugged the top edge of the right side of Saville's cover, as though they were part of a printer's colour-proof swatch which had mistakenly strayed onto the final image.

Saville had been guided towards this kind of eclecticism by the climate of retro-chic and rediscovery that had influenced much of the music, fashion and Pop art graphics he had grown up with during the early 1970s. His own recycling or appropriation of past images allowed him to create not just a graphic contrast, but also a contrast between what was expected from such a design and what he actually delivered. The classicism of the artwork confounded the expectations that were held for any kind of contemporary design, let alone an album of technology-driven synthesizer music.

One of the key qualities of Saville's design was the compelling sense of quietude produced by the difference in size and position of the cover's two graphic elements. The subtlety of this approach had its roots in a book of early Modernist graphic design, and in

19.13: 'Power, Corruption & Lies' album cover designed by Peter Saville, 1983

particular its chapter on Jan Tschichold. Tschichold's graphic quietude, as demonstrated in his exhibition poster of 1937 *(<fig.13.19, p.202)*, struck a chord with Saville. Unlike Tschichold, though, Saville used this cool, understated approach to introduce a degree of ambiguity and irony. The ambiguity of the design became ironic once anyone who was familiar with the band's music had realized that it was the cover of a New Order album. And of course, its ambiguity was reinforced by the fact that there was no text on it, nor any picture of the band. The only clue given to the name of the band or the title of the album was contained in the strip of coloured rectangles. They were actually an alphabetic code, which could be deciphered through a colour key printed on the back. In this way, Saville tapped into the same sort of feeling of knowingness and exclusivity among the band's fans that designers of the psychedelic poster had earlier exploited with their barely legible lettering *(<p.271)*. Saville described this approach as creating 'a mass-produced secret'. The way the secret was hidden made it all the more alluring.

The Postmodern use of ambiguity didn't always need to involve secrecy. A more open form of ambiguity has long been a defining quality of the art produced by the American artist and writer Barbara Kruger (1945–). As well as making sculpture, video and film, Kruger has also drawn on her training and earlier work experience as a graphic designer to create images out of the building blocks of graphic design – printed words and pictures – as well as some of its visual language – here, the half-tone screen and an advertising style of typography *(fig. 19.14)*. In contrast to the poster by McCoy *(<fig. 19.12)*, Kruger's omplex meanings had simple forms. Their most common and distinctive form was a black-and-white photograph overlain with a short piece of often aphoristic text laid out in a distinctive bold italic version of Renner's Futura typeface *(<fig. 13.20, p.203)*, which was itself often reversed out of one or several bright red rectangles. With their low-grade photography and simple black, white and red colouring, they were suggestive of populist tabloid newspapers or cheaply printed advertisements. Kruger blurred the distinction between art and graphic design further by producing some of her images as things that were more likely to be found in a gallery's gift shop than in an exhibition space. By having them printed onto things such as postcards, mugs, T-shirts and even umbrellas, she gave them a life beyond the confines of a gallery, and brought them into people's homes.

While they may have looked like genuine works of graphic design, such items were clearly not pieces of advertising. They were not trying to sell or promote a product. Behind their graphic simplicity was a pointed and yet multi-layered concept. Their uncommercial concepts marked them out as an anti-propaganda form of conceptual art. The 'panorama of social relations' that Kruger homed in on frequently centred on the linked themes of consumerism and sexual politics. The former was the target of one of her best-known pieces made in 1987, which showed a hand holding a card with the words 'I shop therefore I am' on it. This parody of the seventeenth-century French philosopher René Descartes' phrase 'I think therefore I am' invites an initial reading as a straightforward critique of the power that is exerted over our identity by our consumerist society. The clothes we wear, what car we drive, the furniture we choose to fill our homes with, all these things help to buttress and project a sense of self. What is clever about Kruger's design, though, is that this message is reinforced by the way it is presented. The card is being held and purposefully displayed as an act of self-promotion, as though the holder were themselves a consumer product.

But what we latch on to at first glance is soon called into question if we are taken to consider the image further. Kruger presents the text as a personal statement, governed by the personal pronoun 'I', but exactly who is supposed to be making the statement is not quite clear.

19.14: 'I Shop Therefore I Am' image designed by Barbara Kruger, 1987

Is it the person depicted, or is it really the artist (though the hand looks like a man's hand)? Or perhaps it represents a group of people? The kind of people who bought and wore the T-shirt while out shopping, in light-hearted acceptance or celebration even of their predilection for buying things. Or perhaps they might have worn it in a more knowing and critical way, as an ironic gesture, showing that they were aware of the power of consumerism and therefore to some extent beyond its reach. The range of possibilities within Kruger's ambiguous graphic images are thought-provoking and manifold. While they appear to be both verbally and visually direct, the themes they contend with are never pinned down. Kruger preferred instead to be provocatively suggestive.

What is remarkable about the build-up of complexity, particularly of visual complexity, in New Wave design is that, quite unwittingly, it anticipated the arrival of a technology that not only made it easier to create complex forms, but also put complexity at the heart of a new graphic aesthetic: the aesthetic of the digital image. Where previously designers had had to create complex forms by hand, they were now able to make them within the virtual space of a screen. In so doing, the process of dematerialization that had previously impacted on type now made an impression on graphic design as a whole. It was possible for the entire process of design, from how it was made to how it was displayed, to be a digital one.

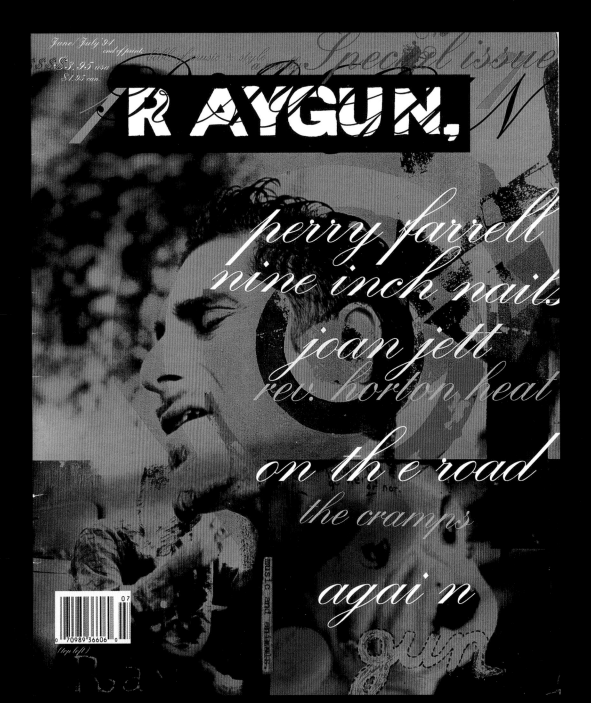

June/July '94
end of print
$3.95 usa
$4.95 can.
music + style
Special issue

RAYGUN.

perry farrell

nine inch nails

joan jett

rev. horton heat

on th e road

the cramps

agai n

20 PRINTING WITH PIXELS

Digital Expressionism & Postscript: The Digital Future, c.1984 –

The final chapter in the story of Western graphic design is dominated by a single unifying technology: the personal computer or PC. It was in January 1984 that a now famous commercial first announced the coming of the ground-breaking Apple Macintosh computer to millions of American viewers during that year's Super Bowl (the final game in America's top American Football league). The commercial's cinematic, 60-second storyline was based on a scene from a book that had been written almost four decades earlier, in 1948: George Orwell's dystopian novel *Nineteen Eighty-four*. The novel was haunted by a malign dictator, 'Big Brother', who was the dominant persona behind an all-pervasive system of surveillance and propaganda set up by a governing elite to subjugate the citizens of a totalitarian state. Big Brother dominated the commercial too, and many within the computer industry took him to be a thinly veiled reference to what was the largest computer company at that time, IBM, or 'Big Blue' as it was nicknamed within the industry (blue was the company's corporate colour). The coming of Apple's new Macintosh computer, by contrast, was represented by a solitary heroic dissenter who ran up to a large televised image of Big Brother and smashed it with a sledge hammer.

Had Orwell written his novel at a time when computers were commonplace, he surely would have made them an integral part of Big Brother's system of surveillance. Yet, Apple's presentation of itself as a modern-day iconoclast had some truth to it. No other company did more to make the personal computer personal. Apple invented or helped to establish many of the key features that made its computers the standard tool for modern graphic designers. The mouse, a PostScript laser printer (made in partnership with the digital typeface and software company Adobe) and the first desktop publishing software (made by the Aldus corporation, which later merged with Adobe) helped to turn the computer into a more intuitive technology, as well as one that could be used for 'Desktop Publishing' (DTP). The innovation that contributed most to its ease of use however, was its graphical user interface (GUI), a phrase which refers to the way graphic information on the screen allows computers to be used. Most previous computers had presented users with a largely blank, dark screen on which only monospaced characters could be typed. Only by knowing the appropriate programming language could the computer be made to do something. Apple's innovations removed this layer of learning. By exploiting some of the pioneering research into GUI design that had been carried out by the Xerox Corporation during the 1970s, Apple was able to establish the essential features of the modern computer desktop: icons, drop-down commands and 'windows'. Crucially, the windows allowed a white, page-like background to be created, onto which a selection of seven digital typefaces could be typed. Both the page-like windows and typefaces were fundamental to the Macintosh's most important design-related feature, that of WYSIWYG (What You See Is What You Get); that is, what was shown on the screen more of less corresponded with what would be printed. Today we expect nothing less so the acronym is rarely used, but at the time this was a revolutionary feature. The close correspondence between the screen-based design and the final output, coupled with the ability to manipulate the design through the Macintosh's point and press technology, encouraged designers to create entirely new graphic forms.

The digital forms they developed were not the very first examples of a computerized aesthetic in print. Since the 1950s computer technology had exerted a small but significant influence on typeface design. During the middle of the decade, banks in the United States were having to employ scores of clerks to handle and

1234567890 ⑆⑉⑆⑈

20.2: E13-B, 1958

ABCDEFGHIJKLMNOPQRS
TUVWXYZ
abcdefghijklmnopqrs
tuvwxyz
1234567890

20.3: OCR A, 1966

ABCDEFGHIJKLMNOPQRS
TUVWXYZ
abcdefghijklmnopqrs
tuvwxyz
1234567890

20.4: OCR B, 1968

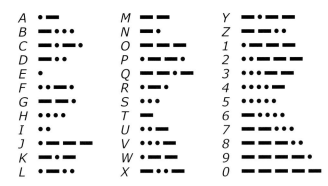

20.5: Morse code alphabet

20.6: Barcode

sort the billions of cheques being cashed each year. Each cheque contained information that had to be typed up and filed individually. It was in an effort to reduce this administrative burden that an engineer from Stanford University in conjunction with General Electric created and then refined, under the auspices of Bank of America, the first set of machine-readable characters. By using a special magnetic ink he and his colleagues settled on a set of 14 characters – the so called E13-B character set made out of 10 numerals and 4 supplementary banking symbols ('transit', 'amount', 'on-us' and 'dash', *fig.20.2*). In 1958 the American Bankers Association adopted them as the standard set of machine-readable characters. The characters' shapes were determined by the need to distribute the magnetised ink in distinct configurations across a uniform grid (made from 63 (7 x 9) 0.013in squares, hence the 13 in the name of the set; E stood for the fifth design tested and B the second version of this successful fifth design). These distinct distributions allowed each character to be scanned and read at speeds of 1,100 characters per second. Today the characters continue to be used as the standard form of machine-recognizable numbering on cheques in territories such as the United States, Canada and Britain.

The need for a fuller set of machine-readable characters inspired a series of similar designs, though not ones that needed to be used with magnetised ink. These new characters were identified by their optical

properties alone. The ability to do so had been developed during the previous 40 years through a process known as Optical Character Recognition (OCR). It led to the design of a typeface called OCR-A (*fig.20.3*) whose characters could be read by scanning them with a beam of light. In contrast to E13-B's characters, the much larger set of characters in OCR-A, which included letters and punctuation marks as well as numerals, were given the same stroke width (they were monoline as well as being monospaced, like typewriter letters) and yet their shapes were dictated by the same design principle: to be visually distinct. In this fuller set letters such as 'C' had to be distinct from 'G', 'O' from 'Q', etc. As in E13-B, the resultant distortions made them easy for machines to read but difficult for humans. It was a disparity that arose from the difference between the way the machines and humans read. Each time we fix our gaze on the letters in a line of text, our eyes register the overall internal and external shape of several words, before moving on to the following group of letters. The machines, by contrast, scanned each letter shape individually. OCR-A, released in 1966, had been commissioned by the American National Standards Institute (ANSI), but its relatively poor legibility for humans prompted the European Computer Manufacturers' Association (ECMA) to approach the eminent type-designer Adrian Frutiger *(<p.241–3)* to come up with an alternative design. By harnessing improvements in character

recognition technology, Frutiger was able to close the gap between the needs of humans and machines. His finer grid (18 x 25) resulted in the more legible OCR-B *(fig. 20.4)*, which was released in 1968 and adopted as an international standard in 1973.

This international standard has since become one of the most used, though seldom noticed, of all modern typefaces. For nearly half a century it has been the ubiquitous accompaniment to another similarly common graphic form: the lowly barcode *(fig. 20.6)*. Few of the items we buy are unmarked by this distinctive box of black stripes. Before its invention, large grocery stores had had to close periodically in order to carry out an inventory of their stock. Every packet, can, bag and bottle on its shelves had to be counted to find out how many items had been sold. With the appearance of the first barcoded item – a packet of chewing gum sold in a store in Ohio in 1974 – the process of making an inventory became an automatic consequence of selling an item.

The conceptual spur to the creation of the barcode's vertical bars was an earlier and previously unrelated graphic form, the alphanumeric symbols of Morse code *(fig. 20.5)*. The system of communication that was served by the code's distinctive dots and dashes (or 'dits' and 'dahs') was the electric telegraph (from the Greek *tele* meaning 'far' and *graphē* 'writing'), which had been invented during the first decade of the nineteenth century. By sending pulses of electric charges along highly conductive cables and then deciphering the sound of the pulses with a code, it was possible for words to be communicated, in contrast to printing, almost instantaneously, and then across distances that were no longer limited by what was immediately visible, in contrast to all previous, more rudimentary forms of visible communication, such as the ancient practices of smoke signals, beacons, reflected light or even the more modern semaphore *(< fig. 17.22, p.282)*. The telegraph and its subsequent graphic code were the first steps along the now crowded road of electronic communication. (The biblical line 'What hath God wrought' was the first official message to be sent by Samuel Morse in May 1844. The second, which was of a more practical value, was: 'Have you any news' – there was no question mark in Morse's initial code.)

The graphic representation of Morse code acted like a musical score for a monotone composition. The dots and dashes signified only the rhythm of the short bursts of sound, not the pitch, timbre or loudness, as

20.7: 'Vormgevers' poster designed by Wim Crouwel, 1968

true musical notation does. Two aspects of the code's graphic form contributed to the barcode's development. First was the different lengths of the marks which, when grouped and then extended downwards, enabled the resultant sequence of bars to be easily scanned and 'read'. Second was the space that separated the dots and dashes, which was as meaningful as the black marks themselves in that it signified a fixed span of time. Accordingly, the spaces between the lines in a barcode were also used to encode information. Thus both the bars and the spaces were entirely utilitarian. Nevertheless, they and their accompanying OCR lettering were representative of a computerized aesthetic.

Letterforms with a more intentional digital aesthetic were created during the second half of the 1960s by the Dutch designer, Wim Crouwel (1928–). As an avowed Modernist, Crouwel had become familiar with the design potential of grid systems and he had also developed an interest in the advances being made in digital type generation. Both interests were provoked and combined in 1966 by a series of printouts produced by one of the earliest digital typesetters. The machine's

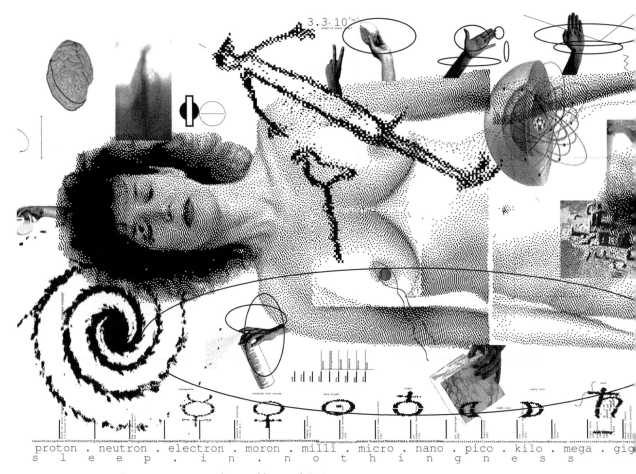

proton . neutron . electron . moron . milli . micro . nano . pico . kilo . mega . gig
s l e e p . i n . n o t h i n g n e s s

20.8: 'Design Quarterly' magazine poster designed by April Greiman, 1985–6

poor resolution had distorted a digital version of
Garamond's type in such a way that the letters looked
different in various sizes. In the smallest sizes they were
grossly ragged and broken. Their jagged edges led
Crouwel to experiment with several new designs that
would work with the limitations of the machine. In
1968 he designed a typeface for Amsterdam's Stedelijk
Museum *(<fig. 20.7)*, which not only made a feature of
the jagged edges, it was also impervious to the kind of
breaking up that had afflicted the earlier version of
Garamond. Each of his new letters was made out of a
series of rectangular forms pieced together in a grid
formation. The way Crouwel applied the typeface to the
Stedelijk's *Vormgevers* ('Designers') exhibition poster
shows how the letters' design as well as their placement
on the poster fitted into a grid. His decision to make the
letters in lowercase only reinforced the strong allegiance
he felt to the earlier experiments in type design that
had been carried out by designers at the Bauhaus
(<fig.13.12, p.198).

One of the first designers to exploit the aesthetic
potential of new digital forms more fully was the
American designer April Greiman (1948–). It is surely
no coincidence that Greiman was living and working
in California, then as now the centre of the computer
industry. Before computers had been developed as a
tool for graphic design, she had spent a short period, in
the early 1970s, studying at the Basel School of Design
in Switzerland, where she was taught by Wolfgang
Weingart *(<p.297–9)* among others. The complexity and
visual richness of Weingart's experimental designs was
picked up by Greiman, but whereas Weingart continued to make his investigations free of digital forms, she
fused her designs with the image-making potential of
the early Apple computers.

An early example was a design she made between
1985-6 for a special edition of the American magazine
Design Quarterly (fig. 20.8). Its publisher, the Walker Art
Center, in Minneapolis, had invited her to use the entire
magazine as a showcase for her work. But 'rather than

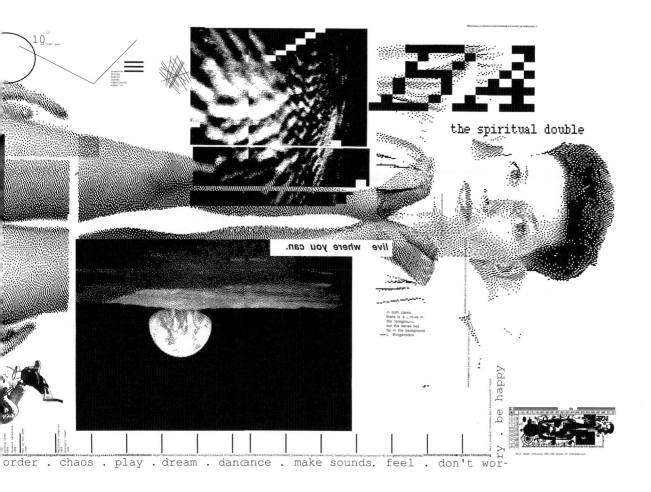

© 1988 MIT Center for Advanced Visual Studies at Massachusetts Institute of Technology

the spiritual double

live where you can.

in both cases
there is a picture in
the foreground,
but the sense lies
far in the background.
— L. Wittgenstein

. be happy

This image contains 289,322 bytes of information.

order . chaos . play . dream . dancance . make sounds. feel . don't wor-ry

do yet another retrospective, I wanted to make it a personal piece,' she explained. Greiman concertinaed the pages into a two-foot by six-foot double-sided poster, the front of which was dominated by a cosmological self-portrait showing a life-sized digital image of herself followed by the head of her 'spiritual double' (distinguished by a recent haircut). 'I decided there could be nothing more personal than a nude, digitized portrait of myself.' Along the bottom of the portrait was a timeline of technological innovations, starting with the birth of the solar system and ending with the birth of the Apple Macintosh. On the back were colourful video-images interspersed with detailed notes outlining the arduous technical process involved in creating and printing the image. The poster was notable for being printed from a single computer file rather than from a conventional piece of artwork.

The nature of the varied and layered, collage-like forms, with their rich symbolism of video stills, hand-drawn symbols and short texts, were related to the profound influence that the writings of the twentieth-century Swiss psychiatrist, Carl Jung, had had on Greiman since she first studied design in the late 1960s. (Jung's connection with Basel, a city in which he had both studied and taught, had encouraged her to study there 'to be closer to the source'.) Central to Jung's writing was his concept of the unconscious, which he believed to be as 'real' a part of life as the conscious. He believed that the unconscious communicated through symbols, which included words, names or even pictures. Some of the symbols or images were archetypes, universal themes common to all people of all eras, though they like the others carried other connotations besides their conventional meanings. It is these other associations that inform our dreams and enable our unconscious to connect with the rational mind. According to Jung, it is only by accepting and integrating the unconscious and rational parts of ourselves that we can harmonize the various aspects of our personality.

This openness to associations seemed to guide Greiman's working method as well as the form of her work. 'The thing that I think is most interesting abut technology is not having a result in mind; to suspend making judgements about things … To drift and float is the profound aspect of the dialogue between you and that tool'. To a certain extent, like all pioneers, Greiman was able to drift and float in an open and uncharted territory because it was free of tradition or any established aesthetic. In this way she was able to treat the computer as just another tool, in the same way as she would a pencil.

What was especially challenging about Greiman's design was its very personal nature – her naked body of course, though also the personal interests and attitudes she revealed through various texts and symbols – which was rendered with the new supposedly impersonal medium of the computer. In this, it combined the personal and the technological twice over, first through the content and the production method, and then, importantly, through the content and its form. Using the broken, dotted imagery (in her portrait) and bit-mapped type (the large BA) then common to early computer displays and printouts was entirely unconventional. Such forms were generally considered to be the base expression of an imperfect or even corrupting technology. Greiman however, far from avoiding these forms, embraced them wholeheartedly. She presented them as an intrinsic part of the work. Their presence stood as a visual response to the question she posed on the magazine's slipcase 'Does it make sense?', which she also replied to verbally, on the inside with a quote by the Viennese philosopher of language, Ludwig Wittgenstein, 'If you give it a sense, it makes sense'. Because she gave the various digital forms a 'sense', or a place in which to exist, then they made 'sense', that is, they became entirely valid components within the broadening repertoire of graphic forms.

A more consistent and ultimately more influential demonstration of digitally orientated graphics appeared in *Emigre,* a magazine started in 1983 by three Dutch émigrés based, for the most part, in Berkeley, California. Though the publication began as a general arts magazine with an international emphasis (as reflected by its title), by 1987 its focus had shifted almost entirely to graphic design. This change in course had been steered by one of the founders, Rudy VanderLans (1955–), who after the poor sales of the first few issues had been left in total control of the magazine. He had become its sole editor,

20.9: 'Emigre' magazine cover, 1988

its art director and its publisher. The freedom this gave him was reinforced by the magazine's source of funding, which derived mostly from selling typefaces. The digital foundry he established with Zuzana Licko (1961–), his wife, built on the popularity of the initial Mac-generated typefaces she designed for the magazine. This internal source of funding meant that VanderLans was untrammelled by the need to make the magazine attractive to advertisers or accord with the dictates of a proprietor.

Between the late 1980s and mid-1990s *Emigre* became a forum for new experimental design, particularly design that was exploring the graphic potential of the new digital technology. The entire 11th issue, published in 1988, was given over to discussing the role of the Macintosh in graphic design *(fig. 20.9)*. On the cover the names of fifteen prominent graphic designers, who had been interviewed on this subject, were displayed in a typeface that had an explicitly digital character. The rectangular blocks that make up its letter shapes echoed the bitmapping effect that had been a singular feature of the early Macintosh computers (as shown in Greiman's poster).

20.10: 'Emigre' magazine spread, 1988

For VanderLans it was important that these novel forms were used in a way that related to the contents. Inside the Macintosh issue, each of the interviews was set in a different typeface, each designed by Licko. The different 'voice' behind each one was thus represented graphically. This simple typographic expression was then added to by the way the text was positioned. Rather than keep each interview separate, as an unbroken sequence of text, as is conventional, columns from different interviews were run alongside one other. The resultant mixing of fonts and columns of text expressed something of the clamorous sense of urgency and excitement that the Macintosh had generated for a number of graphic designers *(fig.20.10)*. The layout made the content look as though the magazine itself was part of a much larger conversation of competing thoughts and opinions. This variety was also expressed by Vander-Lans's decision to let each of the designers design a page on the theme 'Keep on Reading' (one of which is shown above).

VanderLans was also keen to promote the work of young or less well-known designers. The page numbers in this issue were designed by graduate students from the California Institute of Arts (commonly referred to as 'CalArts') – the example here shows an undigital, non-numeral, line-counting-method number six – but in other instances an entire issue, the editing, design and production of it, was given over to students. It provided them with the kind of space that the established design magazines were not willing to offer. There was a logic behind *Emigre's* very catholic approach to its design. Since the subject matter changed from one issue to the next – different designer's work or different themes were concentrated on – it made sense to VanderLans that the layout should change too.

The varied expressionism in *Emigre's* design also came from its method of production. The design of its pages was an expression of the tools that had been used to make it. The mouse, keyboard and screen, when used in conjunction with new computer software, allowed designers to do things with type in particular that previously, if not actually impossible, would have taken a lot of time and money to produce. Mixing sizes of type within a line (for emphasis), or closely abutting

20.11: Nike advertisement by Neville Brody, 1992

columns of text, or layering complex combinations of letters and boxes, all of which appear, would have required the designer to give complex instructions to a (now redundant) typesetter. The Macintosh, however, enabled the designer to do this on his own. It could be as complex and as difficult to describe as he or she liked. Most significant of all though, was that the Macintosh allowed designs to be looked at, compared and changed there and then on screen. This degree of control and the ability to make fine adjustments and see the results immediately allowed *Emigre* to strike a balance between visual impact and legibility. In spite of the comparative busyness of the pages, the text was still legible.

For all its digital expressionism, *Emigre's* typography remained rooted in some long-standing conventions. The most dominant was the convention that text should be set in a sequence of horizontal rows. Sticking to this arrangement was perhaps as much a practical decision as an aesthetic one. For all the computer's ability to create complex typographic arrangements, it was still easier to set large quantities of continuous text in a conventional way. In other instances, though, when a design had less text to set, this convention could be let go of more easily. In a press advertisement for Nike *(fig. 20.11)* designed in 1988 by the British graphic designer Neville Brody (1957–), a set of five short phrases were set in a series of vertical and horizontal arrangements. Though the letters all appear in the same typeface, their varied sizes and careful positioning, and the positioning of the shoes they advertise, were made possible by the immediacy and control that came from designing with a computer. A comparison with a design from the 1930s, Piet Zwart's much more loosely designed yet fuller booklet cover *(<fig.15.6, p.222)*, indicates just

how much more precisely Brody had been able to size and align the letters in his computer-made design. From the 'b' in bounce – which has its left edge aligned with the edge of the eye of the face behind it, while its right edge is visually aligned with the vertical centre of the photograph, and its bottom edge with the shadow that falls across the lower lip – all the way to the last 't' of the grey 'just do it' in the bottom-right corner, which is aligned on the right with the much larger 't' above it, while its baseline aligns with the edge of the vertical blue 't' to its left. Nearly every letter picks up on some kind of similar alignment.

One of the intentions behind Brody's expressionism was to arrange each of the phrases in a way that illustrated or alluded to its meaning, much like the French symbolist Apollinaire and others had done with their figure poetry *(<fig.12.5, p.177)*. 'Just zap it' was zapped in red; 'bounce' went up and down, as well as near and far through varied sizing; 'slam' went up, like a basket-ball's slam dunk, and then slammed into the 'it' with such force that the latter was knocked out of the former's final 'm'; 'smash' was smashed into two parts, large and small; and 'just do it', in grey, was just done, quietly, without any fanfare. The ability to nudge and shift each letter and then assess each change immediately on screen had also allowed Brody to combine each of these expressive units into a dynamic and rule-flaunting whole. The style of the expression was distinct enough to be applied to a range of merchandise – baseball caps, beach towels, T-shirts and the like – as well as to a TV commercial. In each instance, the novelty of his typographic expression came not from some digital quality within the shapes of the letters – they were made with the most common of all typefaces, Helvetica – but from the way the letters were sized and combined.

Brody's choice of Helvetica was part of an attempt to discourage the kind of copying that had plagued (and flattered?) him throughout most of the 1980s. By the late eighties, the level of attention his work had received exceeded anything that any other British designer had experienced before or since. Brody's early record cover designs and the design of two culture magazines, *The Face* (1981-86) and *Arena* (1987-90), in particular, had brought him a degree of notoriety that comes only to a small handful of graphic designers in each generation. In 1988, having just entered his thirties, a retrospective exhibition of his work was held in Britain's principal art and design museum, and he also became the subject of a best-selling monograph. Such exposure served to

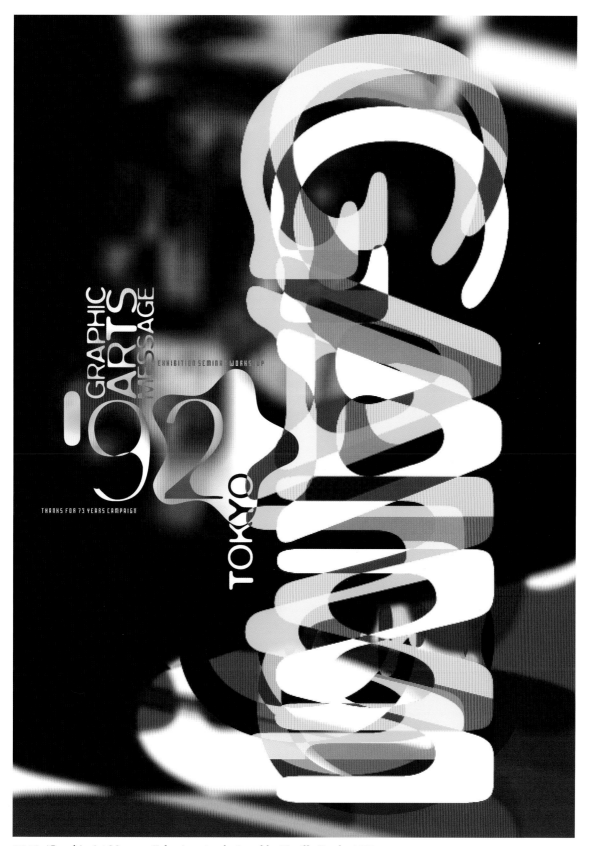

20.12: 'Graphic Art Message Tokyo' poster designed by Neville Brody, 1992

ABCDEFGHIJKLMNOPQRSTU
VWXYZ
abcdefghijklmnopqrstu
vwxyz

ABCDEFGHIJKLMNOPQRS
TUVWXYZ
abcdefghijklmnopqrs
tuvwxyz

ABCDEFGHIJKLMNOPQ
RSTUVWXYZ
abcdefghijklmnopq
rstuvwxyz

ABCDEFGHIJKLMNOPQRSTUV
WXYZ
abcdefghijklmnopqrstuv
wxyz

ABCDEFGHIJKLMNOP
QRSTUVWXYZ
abcdefghijklmnopq
rstuvwxyz

abcdefghijklmnopqrstu
vwxyz

abcdefghijklmnopqrs
tuvwxyz

20.13: Modern digital fonts

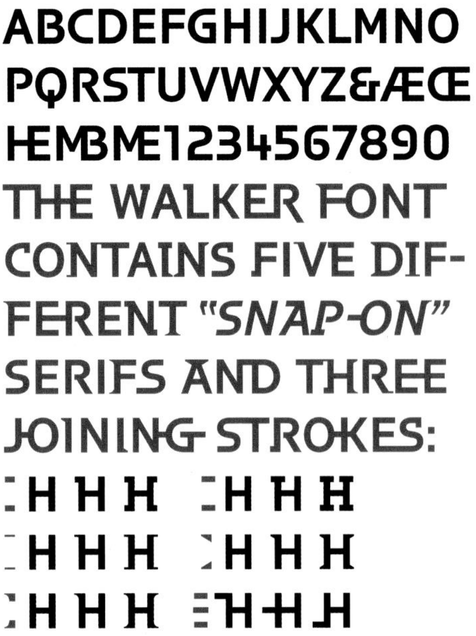

ABCDEFGHIJKLMNO
PQRSTUVWXYZ&ÆŒ
HEMBME1234567890
THE WALKER FONT
CONTAINS FIVE DIF-
FERENT "SNAP-ON"
SERIFS AND THREE
JOINING STROKES:
HH H H HH H H
HH H H HH H H
HH H H HH H H

*20.14: Walker Art Gallery, Corporate typeface,
designed by Matthew Carter, 1994*

fuel the cycle of compelling innovation and artistry on
his part and sham imitation on the part of others: 'There
were times when I felt that my work had been ripped
off so much that I didn't want to make any new statement on the page whatsoever. I had initially developed
hand-drawn lettering because it couldn't be so easily
reproduced.' But after that had been copied many times
over, Brody had taken to using the impersonally familiar
Helvetica. Though even this failed to halt the numerous
attempts to copy his style.

  During the early 1990s Brody began to explore the

computer's potential for image creation and manipulation. A poster he designed for the 'Graphic Arts Message'
conference *(fig. 20.12)* in Tokyo in 1992, shows how even
a simple set of shapes, such as the three initials, GAM,
could be endowed by the computer with an entirely novel digital richness. The overlapping, blending and colour
manipulation functions within a standard computer
software allowed Brody to create a vibrantly expressive
design. There is no grid involved, nor any conventional
kind of typographic hierarchy. The type seems to float
for the most part on a foreground plane, though its edges
are softened by some of the blurred background shapes
and some subtle blending of colours. This sumptuous
melding of shifting pattern and colour was the product
of the supposedly rigid, mathematical, conformist and
corrupting computer. Like Greiman before him, Brody
had turned this apparently impersonal tool into a highly
personal and expressive medium. His curiosity towards
the range of digital effects that could be coaxed out of a
computer, and his search for the beauty that lay hidden
within its digital code, was as much the expression of
an artistic desire, the need to give vent to a particular
aesthetic sensibility, as it was a commercial one, the
willingness to provide a fitting design for a paying client. It was the digital character of the medium itself that
guided him. The shapes he created were not imposed
on the machine from a blueprint held in his mind's
eye. It was impossible for any artist/designer to hold

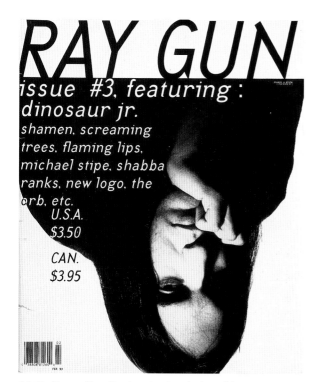

20.15: Cover, 'Ray Gun' magazine designed by
David Carson, 1993

20.16: 'Ray Gun' magazine page designed by
David Carson

that amount of visual complexity, richness and detail. He may have set out with a general plan to produce something typographic and colourful, but the essential character of the design was derived from the shapes he saw on the screen. Through a process of trial and error he was able to build and refine his design, much as a painter would through the marks made on a canvas, though of course Brody was painting with pixels.

The explorations that Brody made across a wide range of digital graphics included the design of typefaces. He produced a range of forms, some of them considered and comparatively orthodox, others more experimental. The ability to turn a set of shapes into a digital type-face was made possible by the creation of dedicated type-design software, which could be operated without any detailed knowledge or long training. It opened up the previously closed world of type design, which had been inhabited by only a small number of highly skilled (and almost exclusively male) individuals, to anyone who had a basic understanding of computers and the patience to apply a particular set of shapes to the range of characters required in a typeface. Any kind of visual effect or form could be assigned to the letters of a key-board (fig.20.13). Letter shapes could be converted into

3-dimensional objects each with their own recessive perspective; they could be built out of a rough outline that also became an in-line; they could be vaporized into conglomerations of small particles, or made to look like rough, slightly smudged woodblock prints; they could even be made out of a quirkily, illustrative style of handwriting.

This new access to or 'democratization' of the mak-ing of typefaces had a paradoxical effect on the individ-ual style of a type-designer. Because the range of forms that could be created by any individual was so wide, it was harder for an individual's style to assert itself. Unlike the designs by Goudy, say, from the first half of the twentieth century, many of which were variations on the same kind of roman letter (<fig.14.4, p.209), there was now too much variety for a telling comparison to be made between the designs from any one individual.

Digital software did not only influence the shape of typefaces, it even called the very notion of a typeface into question. In the early 1990s, the Walker Art Center commissioned a British type designer, Matthew Carter (1937–), to design a new typeface for the Gallery's identity. It had been decided that the Gallery's previous monolithic, modernist designs should be replaced with a typeface whose letter shapes ought not have a fixed form. Each of the typeface's letters could exist in several variant forms defined by the addition of serifs or special joining strokes *(fig. 20.14)*. Use of the typeface was not to be restricted to spelling out the Gallery's name in varying combinations of letter shapes, it was also to appear in the headlines and titles within the Gallery's literature. Carter therefore made the letters' basic form a bold sanserif capital or so-called 'titling' face. Added to this sanserif superstructure were five different kinds of 'snap-on' serifs, which could be selected or removed through various keyboard combinations. Carter also gave each letter a set of horizontal strokes which could be placed below, above or in the middle of a letter to underline, overscore or join one letter with the next. The technological know-how that allowed him to take this very unorthodox approach had been acquired while designing a typeface for setting an Asian alphabet called Devanagari, the main script used to write Hindi. Like many alphabets of South and South East Asia, Devana-gari needed various vowel strokes to be added to its letters. The Gallery's decision to adopt a similar graphic approach was intended to reflect its commitment to experimental art and to work of an international nature.

No designer's experiments received as much attention during the late-1980s and 1990s as those made by the American graphic designer, David Carson (1952–). The designs he created for two magazines in particular, *Beach Culture* and *Ray Gun* (mainly a music magazine), gave him an international profile that was (and continues to be) greater than any previous designer. The unconventional way in which he combined text and pictures, as well as other kinds of graphic marks, was rooted in his lack of formal training. Not having been schooled in the conventions of graphic design, it was easier for him to ignore them. (They were known to him, as they are to all people who can read, but only, like them, in a general, cursory way.) The kind of direction in which his disregard for convention and his appetite for experimentation took him can be seen in a cover of *Ray Gun* from 1993 *(< fig. 20.15)*. The cover's portrait is shown upside-down. In presenting it this way, Carson was being playful and somewhat subversive, but as with so much of his exuberantly expressive design there was thought and judgement behind it too. Because a face is such a recognizable image *(<p.226)*, it can survive being turned upside-down. It can still be 'read' instantly, which many other kinds of image would struggle to be. In order to draw attention to this orientation, a dark image with a strong silhouette was chosen and then set

20.17: *Carl Cox album cover designed by Me Company, 1995*

against a light grey background. The gently meandering curve of the inverted head and shoulders also threw the image into sharper relief through its contrast with the strong horizontal line that separated the portrait from the magazine's title. Both these contrasts gave the cover a greater impact (in the same way that similar contrasts had in Rodchenko's Constructivist magazine cover, *<fig.12.15, p.187)*. Carson's cover did not only express his playfulness and skill as a designer, it also expressed something about the person in the portrait or, more particularly, their reaction to the situation in which they had been placed. The singer had had a strong mistrust or dislike of journalism and self-promotion. Setting him in a grumpy pose, with his head resting sulkily on his crooked hand, and then inverting him was Carson's way of expressing this attitude. There was playfulness too in the typography. Inserted into the list of artists featured in the magazine was an oblique prompt to the appearance of a 'new logo'.

Neither the form or the type nor the way it had been combined with the picture looked overtly digital, although some of the letter shapes and the loose layering of forms seemed to indicate that a computer had been involved at some point in the design process. Reflecting the technology used to make a design was less important to Carson than the immediate visual statement that a design made. Much modern graphic design has to compete in a visually crowded environment so it has to engage with or communicate something to its

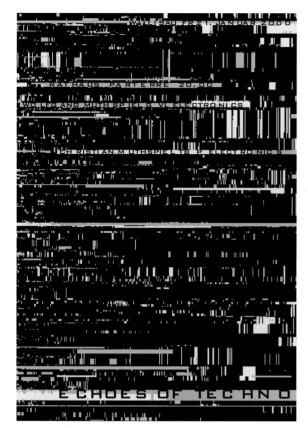

20.18: 'Echoes of Techno' poster designed by Niklaus Troxler, 2000

expected audience instantly. It has to appeal to their first instincts by sending an immediate message about its general nature – who it is for and what kind of subject matter it might contend with – before engaging them in a more discursive way. Creating these forms was clearly a considered act but it was also one that relied heavily on Carson's intuition; his own instinct or gut reaction. Thus, part of his approach to design can be seen as a communication between instincts; his in the creation and the audience's in their initial response.

The range of visual effects that could be conjured from the new digital medium grew as various new kinds of software were developed. Both type and image were the recipients of a specifically kitsch digital aesthetic that grew out of new digital modelling capabilities. One of the pioneers of this form was the British design company, Me Company. The company's founder had been inspired by the example of Peter Saville *(< p.308)*, whose initial design work had been devoted to contemporary music. But the particular way that Me Company pursued this direction was through pushing pixels into sculptural forms that had a particular appeal to its

increasingly computer-literate audience. The 1995 album cover for the British techno and house DJ, Carl Cox *(fig. 20.17)*, mixed elements of science fiction and high fantasy alongside a technological aesthetic appropriate to both the drug-induced aesthetic of rave culture and the album's style of music. With the ability to apply a range of lighting and surface effects to a 3-D wire frame, it was possible to cast the shape of a head or a sequence of letters into fluid, shimmering, glass like forms. The quality of shading, the electric colouring and intricate reflected lighting enabled these forms to be converted into more complete 3-D objects on TV or in web graphics.

As a digital aesthetic became more established and familiar, so it became more possible to create it through non-digital means. The Swiss graphic designer Niklaus Troxler (1947-) has been designing posters for the jazz festival he founded in his home town of Willisau since 1975. For Troxler, graphic design and jazz are both parallel and complementary pursuits. 'Everything that fascinates me about jazz music, is also what interests me in design: rhythm, sound, contrast, interaction, experiment, improvisation, composition, individuality.' Like the majority of his posters, his 'Echoes of Techno' poster *(fig.20.18)*, from 2000, was sketched by hand. The idea of using coloured abstract shapes to express the music's technological character came before Troxler used the computer to give the poster its final form. The forms in the poster were twin graphic metaphors. The way the varied blocks of colour seem to float in space recalled the shifting layers of sound that fill the album promoted in the poster. But they also represented the pixelation that can sometimes be seen on digital screens. In this way Troxler's digital-like abstraction was able to illustrate the echoes of techno.

The novelty and surface beauty of these sorts of digital images were quickly exploited by large corporations. The British design company Blue Source harnessed the positive associations that such forms could create in a poster it designed for the multinational sportswear company Adidas *(fig. 20.19)*. Within the highly competitive area of sportswear fashion, the apparently progressive, technology orientated set of forms could be used to highlight a novel aspect of some new design. The clean precision of the poster's intricate linear forms helped to unite the ideas of design and 'technology' which were suggested by use of 'Rubber Outsole Technology' in making the 'Water Moccasin' (a shoe that was purported to hug the feet and maintain its grip in wet conditions).

20.19: Adidas poster designed by Blue Source, 2001

The idea of technology was even subtly promoted by the inclusion of a series of decimal-pointed numerals.

As a reaction to the lack of human mark making in digitally expressive design and the inability of many such designs to reflect the extent of the designer's labour, the Austrian-born US-based designer Stefan Sagmeister (1962–) began to make designs in which the human endeavour was explicit. As well as the aesthetic merits of such an approach, such evidence could also have commercial benefits. Clients could see what they were paying for. If a long process of experimentation led to a busy and involved design, it would be easier for the designer's fee to be accepted than if the process led to a sparse and minimal one.

The design that most forcibly expressed Sagmeister's preference for visible human endeavour was a poster for a lecture he had been asked to give by the Detroit division of the American Institute of Graphic Arts (AIGA) and the Cranbrook Academy of Art (fig. 20.20). Sagmeister later identified the lecture poster as a genre of poster with a special significance in the United States. It was often able to receive a larger and more attentive audience than other kinds of poster. Generally, the centres of American cities are geared towards travel by car. The streets therefore tend to be dominated by large billboards advertising commercial products (whose makers can

afford to pay the requisite fee). In European cities, where cars are less dominant, smaller, cultural posters can thrive because they have a walking audience. One of the few areas in the United States that also has a walking audience is the grounds of its large college campuses. The legion of walking students have allowed the American lecture poster to thrive.

In wanting to reveal the process involved in the design of his AIGA poster, Sagmeister created what was as much a record of a piece of performance art as a straightforward work of graphic design. The performance itself had been far from straightforward. After trying and failing to cut the relevant text with a scalpel blade himself, Sagmeister had had to ask an assistant to carefully and legibly etch each letter. A band-aid (or 'plaster') was needed to cover up a 'typo' under his right nipple (as we look at it), and it is the box of band-aids that appears in his hand (its white lettering contains a simple pun: 'strips', as Sagmeister does for the poster). The effort and endurance required to make the design is painfully apparent. Sagmeister's scratched torso and arms look like an act of martyrdom made in service to the religion of graphic design. The nakedness of his blood-scored body gives this act a biblical quality. The unsettling nature of the poster was not unintentional. Sagmeister had wanted the poster to redress an imbalance he had observed between the difficulties that existed in the profession and

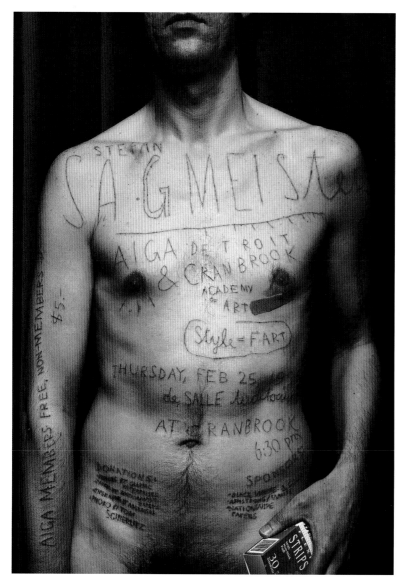

20.20: AIGA lecture poster designed by Stefan Sagmeister, 1999

the happy, colourful images that had tended to represent the profession in previous lecture posters.

An indication of the importance that Sagmeister placed on the individual designer was given by the poster's 'Style = FART' equation. This light-hearted, punning dictum (a play on 'style = art') had appeared above the door of his studio for a number of years. It was intended as a warning against falling into 'stylistic traps'; that is, anything that could be identified with another period of design or designer or, indeed, any formulaic expression of beauty.

But style is a more complex riddle than this phrase makes it out to be (as Sagmeister himself was/is aware). The French filmmaker Jean-Luc Godard described style as 'the outside of content, and content the inside of style, like the outside and inside of the human body – both go together, they can't be separated'. We consistently view our external and internal bodies in separate ways, just as we do style and content, yet there is a simple truth to Godard's description. What it doesn't touch on though is another relevant distinction, that between the designer(s)/maker(s) and the viewer. The meaning of the content and style of a particular work for the former will never be exactly the same for the latter. It is by looking more closely at the designer's aims and influences that we might be able to close this gap a little.

Science fiction often says more about the period in which it was made than the one it seeks to describe. Whenever we try to predict the future we are restricted by both the limits of our knowledge and the preferences and prejudices that help us interpret that knowledge. The cover of the *Amazing Stories* issue *(<fig.15.14, p.228)* reveals some of the assumptions that played on the author and his readership during the time in which it was made (the early 1940s). The design of the alien's spacecraft is wholly mechanical; its dashboard is all levers and dials rather than the blinking lights and computer-driven digital displays we would expect today. But our current expectations are just one stage in an evolving set of human tastes, values and insights. It is no more likely that an egg-headed kidnapper from Pellucidar would have had digital technology at his disposal than mechanical levers and dials. By the same token, the alien's humanoid form underlines the self-reflective, mirror-like property of science fiction.

Any attempt at predicting the future of graphic design will suffer from the same sort of limitations. Furthermore, we are living in a period when the introduction of new technologies is occurring so rapidly that new ways of applying graphic design are arising over increasingly shorter periods; matters of years rather than decades or centuries. When this book was started a mobile phone was something you used if you wanted to speak to somebody. Now you can also surf the web, send and receive e-mails, find your location with GPS, read books, play games, listen to music, take photographs, make videos and much more. And yet digital technology is still in a relatively early phase of development. Changes will continue to be made, and some of them will affect graphic design dramatically.

In spite of the limits to our knowledge, and irrespective of how quickly technology changes, there are people whose livelihoods depend on their ability to predict the future correctly. Professionals in all forms of media publishing, be it print or on-line, music or movies, are straining to work out the direction in which their industries are headed. The focus for these people is to develop a commercial model that will best take advantage of the evolving technologies. The focus here, by contrast, in this brief postscript, is on the general direction of technological development. Some of the current trends in the way graphic design is delivered will provide us with clues as to its future form.

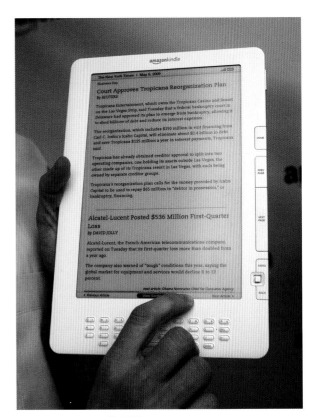

p.1: Amazon's Kindle DX, 2009

The most significant trend is the accelerating move of established graphic formats, such as the book, magazine or newspaper, from the medium of print to the now ubiquitous screen. This move has combined with the trend in computer electronics towards miniaturization to produce a series of pocket-sized devices, such as the mobile phone, that have a wide range of communication abilities. While these devices vary in size and functionality, those designed with reading in mind, the so called 'e-book (electronic book) readers' or e-readers *(fig.p.1)*, have screens that are roughly the same size as the text area of a small paperback. This seems to be the lower limit for any dedicated reading device, that is to say, one that is comfortable for reading quantities of continuous text, as in a novel (though there are indications that some people are happy to read books on their phones). The main attraction of the e-reader is not its portability. Most printed material is easily carried. The e-reader's great gift is that it massively increases the amount of reading material that can be made available by a single object. Like MP3 players, which allow us to carry an entire CD collection in our pockets, so the e-reader can connect us wirelessly to an ever-increasing portion of the world's available reading material. The

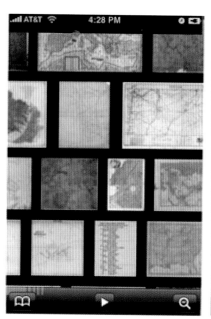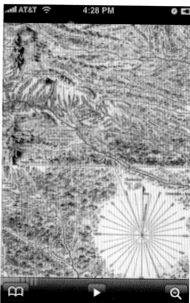

p.2: Maps on Apple iPhone, 2008

inclusion of a keyboard or a touch-sensitive screen and even handwriting recognition software have made them not just receptive devices but also generative ones. Information can be sent as well as received.

An important corollary to this is that they are interactive. This is significant because it changes not just what we read but how we read. The standard print-based paradigm is defined by the page, an individual unit of information that can be strung together in a fixed sequence. In this way, text and pictures are presented in a linear fashion, flowing from one page to another. Any information that is supplementary to the main text – a glossary or list of sources, say – usually has to be placed at the beginning or the end of the main text so that it doesn't break the linear sequence. While the same linear approach can be adopted by screen-based displays – scrolling from top to bottom or clicking for the next 'page' – a new kind of zonal access is also available to it. Words can be clicked on or touched and a definition will appear. Words or phrases can be searched for and an index of results are displayed. As all internet users know, this way of reading can spiral upwards into any number of related texts. While this might inhibit us from tackling a particular text, or 'book', from beginning

to end, there are some definite benefits to being able to read in this way. For a class of students, for example, it can allow information to be accessed according to each of the student's individual needs. Within a group of students studying Shakespeare, say, there will be different levels of comprehension. Those that understand a certain passage can pass on to the next, while those who don't can click on the text and be presented with a translation in modern English. A further click could provide them with detailed notes or a reminder of the main characters and the relation of the characters to each other. This kind of facility would allow each student to study at a speed that matched their level of understanding or interest.

All of us engage in this sort of reading when browsing the web. Currently, the established way of accessing supplementary information on web-pages is by clicking or touching text that has been underlined or coloured. A somewhat different method of accessing information is what could be called the 'Google Earth' approach. Instead of clicking or touching text to get new 'pages', the displayed image is enlarged or reduced and at every level of zooming, a new degree of detail is presented. Apple's iPhone pioneered the intuitive method of zooming by stroking the screen with two fingers. The fingers were moved either in a pinching motion, to zoom out, or in a slow flicking motion to zoom in. Each of the displays of maps shown here *(< fig.p.2)* can be accessed in this way. But what is most significant about this facility is not the method of zooming or that something can be enlarged or reduced. The important point is the presentation of an essentially new image as one zooms or enlarges. The circular shape that appears in the last image is hardly visible in the first one (fourth row down and fifth from the right), but the impression that this first one contains all its subsequent detail is misleading. Different data is being brought to the screen with each level of enlargement. There is potential then to embed really quite separate bits of information with each successive zooming. In theory this process could go on and on, zooming and zooming into more and more embedded information. Architects, say, could use this facility to show the picture of a building, and then zoom in to perhaps reveal the precise fit of a window within a wall, and then closer still to show the compound used to make the window frame. And then maybe closer again to read the contact details of the supplier or manufacturer of the window frame.

In spite of the enormous graphic potential within e-readers and similar devices, it is likely we will continue to read words on paper for some decades or perhaps centuries to come. Just as now, the kind of medium we choose to read from will depend on the kind of reading we do and, in particular, where we do it: on the beach, in a boat, at a desk or in a bed. The range of situations is so wide and the kinds of reading matter so varied that while we can be sure the use of screens for reading will continue to grow, 'the end of print' is still some way off.

One obvious limitation of electronic reading devices is their size: reading material that is made to be looked at in large sizes – an architect's plan say – becomes unintelligible when reduced down to the size of a small screen. It is no surprise that, thus far, the most popular kind of e-reader material has been the novel and other forms of unillustrated continuous text. The problem of size is significant when it comes to displaying pictures. Presenting pictures in small sizes goes against a current trend for larger pictures both in print and on screens. Pictures in newspapers are becoming larger; illustrated 'coffee-table' books have increased in size and number; computer and TV screens are getting bigger; and large projected images are much more common than before.

In thinking how future product designers and electrical engineers might solve the dilemma of size, it will be worth dipping a toe into the murky pool of science fiction. What we are trying catch a glimpse of is a likely way of combining portability and flexibility within a digital image technology. How can large images (perhaps even the size of a movie screen) be displayed by a device that is also easy to carry? One current area of development is that of image projection. If this is to prove successful, it will need to exploit the abiding trend in the computing industry towards miniaturization. In 1965 Gordon E. Moore, the co-founder of the computer chip manufacturer, Intel, made a prediction to the effect that the processing power of computer chips would double every year over the following decade, just as it had done since their invention in 1958. His claim became known as Moore's Law, and though he later revised it to a doubling every two years, its continued fulfilment decades later is a telling indicator of the rate of technological development in the late twentieth and early twenty-first centuries. The practical implication of Moore's Law, of course, was that electronic devices would become smaller and smaller, as they have done.

This relentless pursuit of miniaturization has led scientists to explore the potential of certain atomic structures to perform some of the basic tasks required by computers. It is work that has come out of the silent revolution in nanotechnology, which has had a transformative effect on electronic engineering over the last decade. The scale encompassed by this kind of technology is 100 nanometres or smaller; one nanometre being one billionth of a metre (10^{-9} metre), which makes the head of a pin a million nanometres wide. The application of this technology to the design and manufacture of supercapacitors and microchips has now endowed them with features that are invisible to the naked eye. By making parts of chips this small, savings have been made in speed and cost as well as size.

As this technology develops, so computers will start to appear in unexpected places. One such place is in contact lenses. Scientists have already applied nanotechnology to the design of computerized contact lenses that will be able project a bifocal, virtual display. The aim is to partially power the lenses through small solar cells fixed to the edge of each lens. Information will be received through a wireless connection and then displayed through microlenses that appear to project an image a short distance in front of the eyes. Potentially, the size of the image could be equivalent to a movie screen or the page of a book. The gamut of visual information presented would thus be freed from the size constraints that limit the current range of electronic reading devices. Though this technology still inhabits the realms of science fiction, were it to become science fact some of the other issues that plague the current range of e-readers, such as a constant power source and durability, would also be resolved.

There are many other ways in which scientific knowledge is likely to impact on graphic design. A number of them are likely to come through our understanding of human perception, which has been increased by recent advances in neuroscience, the study of the nervous system and the brain. Since the 1990s, improvements in scanning and brain imaging technology have provided scientists with remarkably detailed pictures of the brain in action. These pictures, in conjunction with other forms of evidence, have improved our understanding of the different functions carried out by particular parts of the brain; though, equally, they have confirmed just how interconnected the different parts of our brain are. Some experiments carried out in the early 1970s created an exaggerated impression of the biases that exist between the left side and the right side of the brain. The idea that the left side deals with logic and facts while the right side is more intuitive and interpretive is too simple a dichotomy; but it is not so simple as to be dismissed entirely. Though each side works in tandem, there are a number of subtle left/right differences. It has been established that the two sides process certain kinds of visual information in slightly different ways: the left side of the brain (which is connected to your right eye) appears to have a bias towards detail, while the right side (connected to your left eye) has a more general outlook. One area where this difference is expressed is in face recognition. When people look at a face, most use their right cerebral hemisphere, fed by their left eye, more than their left hemisphere, fed by their right, to recognize the face's gender and expression. Because our left eye reads the left side of the face (as we look at it) more than the right side, most of us end up reading more into the left side of a face than the right.

A simple test of this phenomenon can be done by looking at the following two faces *(fig.p.3)*. Which of them appears to be happier? Is it the bottom one? They are each a mirror image of the other, so they contain exactly the same visual information. Each one is made from the same half pictures, one half taken from a

neutral expression and the other from a smiling face. Because most of us have a bias towards the left side when reading the emotion in a face, we see the bottom example as the happier of the two.

The relevance of this kind of knowledge to graphic designers is clear. If a designer wants to maximize the expressiveness of a lopsided smile (as all smiles are, to a greater or lesser extent) he or she would make sure that it dominates the left side. It may be that a designer would do this intuitively by comparing a number of smiling faces and picking the one with the right kind of expression, but one imagines that this is just one example of a whole range of other graphic design related neurological quirks that are waiting to be discovered. By looking in some detail at graphic design's history, we will be more informed about the kind of problems that designers have to contend with and, therefore, be better able to search for these new discoveries.

p.3: Face in half repose, half smiling

ENDNOTES

INTRODUCTION

p.10: *'Advertising design is'* – W. A. Dwiggins, 'New kinds of printing calls for new design', Graphic Arts section, part 3, *The Boston Evening Transcript,* 29 August 1922, p.6.

p.10: *'a dictionary definition'* – the Merriam-Webster on-line dictionary (2009) defines graphic design as *'the art or profession of using design elements (as typography and images) to convey information or create an effect; also: a product of this art'.*

p.13: *'such as Cicero'* – see *Cicero's Brutus, or History of Famous Orators (c.46BC)*, and Anton Daniel Leeman, *Orationis Ratio: The Stylistic Theories and Practice of the Roman Orators, Historians and Philosophers*, 2 vols (1963).

p.13: *'of period styles'* – see Johann Joachim Winckelmann, *History of Ancient Art* (1764), and later, Heinrich Wölfflin, *Principles of Art History* (1915).

CHAPTER 1

p.17: *'He would not admit "civilization"'* – record of conversation from Monday, 23 March 1772 while Johnson was preparing the fourth edition of his dictionary; James Boswell, *The Life of Samuel Johnson* (1791), Oxford University Press 1970, p.466.

p.17: *'harmless drudge'* – *'who bullies himself to find the original … words'* is how Johnson completed his definition of 'lexicographer' in the first edition of his dictionary; Samuel Johnson, *Dictionary of the English Language*, vol.2, London 1755.

p.17: *'the painting of the voice'* – Voltaire, *A Philosophical Dictionary: From the French* (1791); trans. J. and H. L. Hunt, University of Wisconsin 1824, p.170.

p.18: *'language instinct'* – see Steven Pinker, *The Language Instinct,* Harper Collins, London 1995.

p.18: *'grammar'* – see Mark C. Baker, *The Atoms of Language: The Mind's Hidden Rules of Grammar*, Oxford University Press 2003, in which a theory associated with the American linguist Noam Chomsky, that of 'Universal Grammar', is described.

p.18: *'We have learnt nothing …'* – possibly apocryphal quotation, see Paul Bahn, *A Lot of Bull? Pablo Picasso and Ice Age Cave Art,* San Sebastian 2005.

p.18: *'only 200,000 years ago'* – see Dan

Jones, 'A Window on the Past', *The New Scientist*, vol.202 (2705), 25 April 2009, pp.30-1.

p.20: *'there is speculation'* – see Denise Schmandt-Besserat, *How Writing Came About,* University of Texas Press, 2006, p.72.

p.23: *'fully formed around 3400BC'* – Steven Roger Fischer, *The History of Writing,* Reaktion Books, London 2001, p.36.

CHAPTER 2

p.29: *'Hear ye, Cretans and Danaans'* – Steven Roger Fischer, *The History of Reading*, Reaktion Books, London 2003, p.77.

p.30: *'whoever of the dancers now dances most lightly'* – translation given by the Louvre Museum, Paris.

p.45: *'on the command of God'* – Arnold H. M. Jones, *Constantine and the Conversion of Europe*, University of Toronto Press 1978, p.191.

CHAPTER 3

p.47: *'In the beginning was the Word'* – St John's Gospel 1:1, translated in this form in the Authorized King James Bible of 1611, closely following Tyndale's earlier translation of *'In the beginning was that Word'.*

p.47: *'the end of print'* – title of a monograph on David Carson by Lewis Blackwell; Laurence King Publishing, London 1995.

p.48: *The Iliad and All the Adventures'* – Martial (Marcus Valerius Martialis), *Epigrammata*, 1st century, ch.14.

p.50: *'… when he read'* – translated from *The Confessions of St Augustine* (397–8), VI, iii; Mary Carruthers, *The Book of Memory*, 2nd ed., Cambridge University Press, 2008, p.213.

p.51: *'You will make out intricacies'* – Gerald of Wales (Giraldus Cambrensis), *Topographia Hiberniae* (1185).

p.55: *'Now it came to pass in the thirtieth year … that the heavens were opened, and I saw visions of God'* – Ezekiel 1:1, Authorized King James Bible.

p.56: *'Judge not, that ye be not judged'* – St Matthew's Gospel 7:1, Authorized King James Bible.

CHAPTER 4

p.69: *'I made the world, I redeemed the*

world, and I bear the sins of the world' – Alfred Carl Hottes, *1001 Christmas Facts and Fancies*, Kessinger Publishing 2004, p.45.

p.72: *'as the inventor of printing'* – until the late nineteenth century a Dutch printer, Laurens Janszoon Coster, had been considered a rival to Gutenberg as the inventor of printing with moveable type in the West.

p.73: *'various early items'* – Gutenberg's copy of the most widespread book for teaching Latin at the time, *Ars minor*, by the mid-fourth-century Roman grammarian Aelius Donatus, had previously been thought to be the earliest printed book, but recent dating has thrown its early date into doubt (see www.bl.uk/treasures/gutenberg/donatus).

p.73: *'And lightly as it comth, so wol we spende'* – Geoffrey Chaucer, *The Canterbury Tales* (1387-1400).

p.74: *'All that has been written'* – Cardinal Juan de Carvajal in a letter sent to the future pope, Pius II, in 1455.

p.81: *'How I shall shiver for the sun'* – in a letter sent by Albrecht Dürer in 1506; Andrews Norton and Charles Folsom, *Select Journal of Foreign Periodical Literature*, vol.2, Charles Bowen, Boston 1833, p.42.

CHAPTER 5

p.88: *'prayer books of a lay culture'* – Brian Richardson, *Printing, Writing and Readers in Renaissance Italy,* Cambridge University Press 1999, p.128.

p.90: *'every sort of ancient and modern letters of all nations'* – Giambattista Palatino, *Libro nuovo d'Imparare a Scrivere,* Rome 1540.

p.92: *'the Bible'* – according to Colonal Isaac Coles in a letter written on 23 February 1816 to John Hartwell Cocke.

p.93: *'aware that units of measurement'* – Andrea Palladio, *The Four Books on Architecture*, trans. Robert Tavernor and Richard Schofield, The MIT Press, MA 2002, p.19.

CHAPTER 6

p.103: *'Thou shalt commit adultery'* – Exodus 20:14, *The Wicked Bible*, printed by Robert Barker and Martin Lucas, London 1631.

CHAPTER 7

p.111: *'the art which preserved all others'* – Allen Hutt, *Fournier: The Compleat*

Typographer, Rowman and Littlefield, Totowa 1972, p.6.

p.111: *'alphabets of every'*, *'the proportions of height to width'* – ibid., p.6.

p.113: *English (Caslon I) & French'* – adapted from table shown in James Mosley's blog, typefoundry.blogspot.com.

p.113: *'in a regular gradation and general inter-relation … so that the large bodies are precisely the double, triple or quadruple of those under them'* – op cit., Hutt. p.19.

p.114: *'perfumed elegance'* – James Mosley's fragrant phrase; 'Editor's Introduction' from *Fournier on Typefounding*, vol.3, Darmstadt 1995, p.13.

p.114: *'systematic dictionary of the sciences'* – part of the title of Diderot's *Encyclopédie*, 1751.

p.114: *'a glance at an object or its representation is more informative than a page of text'* – Michel Wlassikoff, *The Story of Graphic Design;* trans. Lisa Davidson and Sally Laruelle, Gingko Press, California 2005, p.17.

p.115: *'All things must be examined'* – Denis Diderot, *Rameau's Nephew and other Works;* trans. Jacques Barzun and Ralph H. Bowen, Hackett Publishing, London 2001, p.297.

p.116: *'the State of Great-Britain'* – contained in *The Declaration of Independence*, 1776.

p.117: *'in a blue field representing a new constellation'* – The Continental Congress, *Journal*, Saturday, 14 June 1777.

p.117: *'Oh say can you see'* – from the poem 'Defence of Fort McHenry' penned by Francis Scott Key on 16 September 1814.

p.118: *'went forth to astonish'* – Lord (Thomas) Macaulay, *The History of England*, vol.1, ch.3, Longman, Brown, Green & Longmans, London 1848.

p.119: *'ingenuity has left'* – Alexander S. Lawson, *Anatomy of a Typeface*, David R. Godine, New Hampshire 1990, p.187.

CHAPTER 8

p.127: *'typographic monstrosities'* – T. C. Hansard, *Typographia*, Baldwin, Cradock and Joy, London 1825, p.618.

p.127: *'folly of fat-faced, preposterous disproportions'* – ibid., p.360.

p.132: *'Our paper today'* – Lucien Febvre and Henri-Jean Martin, *The Coming of the Book*, trans. David Gerard, NLB London 1976, p.68.

p.132: *'the most largely circulated'* – by-line introduced April 9, 1861; Carl

Sandburg, *Abraham Lincoln*, Houghton Mifflin Harcourt, New York, 2002, p.266.

p.135: *'outrages against the person'* – Sandy Petrey, *In the Court of the Pear King*, Cornell University Press 2005, p.10.

CHAPTER 9

p.137: *'blazing arch of lucid glass'* – William Makepeace Thackeray, 'A May Day Ode' published in *The Times*, 1 May 1851.

p.137: *'silks and shawls, lace and'* – 'The Industry of All Nations 1851', *The Art Journal* exhibition catalogue, George Virtue, London 1851.

p.138: *'The first six books of the Elements of Euclid, in which coloured diagrams and symbols are used instead of letters, for the greater ease of learners'* – the book's full title.

p.139: *'All the stamped metals'* – John Ruskin, *The Seven Lamps of Architecture* (London 1849); Dover Publications, New York 1989, p.174.

p.141: *'most potent apostle of colour'* – Anon; obituary in *The Art Journal*, London 1874, p.211.

p.141: *'simply being William Morris'* – Fiona MacCarthy, *William Morris*, Faber and Faber, London 1994, p.vii.

p.142: *'with the hope of producing'* – H. Halliday Sparling, 'A note on his aims in founding the Kelmscott Press, by William Morris', 11 November 1895; *The Kelmscott Press and William Morris Master-Craftsman*, Macmillan, London 1924, p.135.

p.142: *'always been a great admirer'* – ibid., p.135.

p.142: *'to redeem the Gothic'* – ibid., p.136.

p.145: *'will be like a pocket cathedral'* – Martin Harrison and Bill Waters, *Burne-Jones*, Barrie and Jenkins, London, 1989, p.164.

p.145: *'Writing and Illuminating'* – Fiona MacCarthy, *Eric Gill*, Faber and Faber, London, 1989, p.44.

p.147: *'We do not want to letter'* – Gerald Cinamon, *Rudolf Koch: Letterer, Type Designer, Teacher*, The British Library, London 2000, p.77.

p.147: *'A true artist is only'* – John Ruskin, *Fors Clavigera*, George Allen, Orpington 1871; (27:186).

p.147: *'ministering to the swinish'* – W. R. Lethaby, *Philip Webb and his Work*, Oxford University Press 1935, p.94.

CHAPTER 10

p.149: *'Nothing is really'* – Ghislaine Wood, 'The Age of Paper'; *Art Nouveau 1890-1914*, V&A Publications, London 2000, p.149.

p.151: *'It took the power of'* – Anna Jackson, 'Orient and Occident'; *Art Nouveau 1890-1914*, V&A Publications, London 2000, p.107.

p.157: *'The so-called "poster movement"* – Will Bradley, *Bradley: His Book*, vol.1, no.3, Wayside Press, Springfield, MA, July 1896, p.74.

p.158: *'the creator of an art industry'* – citation on receipt of Légion d'honneur, 1890.

p.158: *'the world's greatest decorative artist'* – description used in a billboard poster produced by *The New York Sunday News* on Mucha's first visit to America in 1904; *Alphonse Mucha*, Ed. Sarah Mucha, Intro. Ronald F. Lipp, Mucha Ltd, Prague 2000, p.10.

p.161: *'artistic shapes for arc lamps and all accessories'* – Alan Windsor, *Peter Behrens: Architect and Designer*, The Architectural Press, London 1981, p.79.

p.161: *'logical destruction of matter'* – Wassily Kandinsky, *Concerning the Spiritual in Art* (1911); trans. M. T. H. Sadler, Dover Publishing, 2004, p.18.

CHAPTER 11

p.166: *'we took it to the office'* – Colin Campbell, *The Beggarstaff Posters*, Barrie & Jenkins, London 1990, p.111.

p.165: *'three 'elect' figures'* – Charles James Fox (1749-1806), Lord Nelson (1758-1505), William Pitt (1759-1806); ibid., p.111.

p.168: *'If not a great soldier'* – Margot Asquith, *More Memories*, Cassell, London 1933, ch.6.

p.171: *'The original idea was ingenious'* – *The Illustrated London News*, 4 January 1919.

p.172: *'should be understood and loved by these masses'* – Clara Zetkin, *Reminiscences of Lenin*, Modern Books Ltd, London 1929, p.13.

CHAPTER 12

p.175: *'Courage, audacity, and revolt will be essential elements of our poetry'* – *Art in Theory: 1900–1990*, Eds. Charles Harrison and Paul Wood, Blackwell, Oxford 1992, p.147.

p.175: *'Let us have no more of'* – Johanna Drucker, *The Visible Word: Experimental Typography and Modern Art, 1909–1923*, University of Chicago Press, Chicago 1996, p.56.

p.176: 'the significant silent' – Stéphane Mallarmé, *Un Coup de Dés;* trans. Daisy Aldan, Tiber Press, London 1956.

p.179: 'The Futurist will begin' – Alan Bartram, *Futurist Typography and the Liberated Page,* The British Library, London 2005, p.20.

p.179: 'At night, lying in bed' – ibid., p.30.

p.182: 'say, in pictures, what would' – Hans Richter, *Dada: Art and Anti-art,* Thames and Hudson, London 1965, p.117.

p.183: 'establish an international unity' – *Art in Theory: 1900–1990,* Eds. Charles Harrison and Paul Wood, Blackwell, Oxford 1992, p.279.

CHAPTER 13

p.190: 'The ultimate aim' – Hans M. Wingler, *The Bauhaus,* The MIT Press, MA 1980, p.31.

p.190: 'The artist is an exalted' – ibid., p.31.

p.190: 'a history of styles' – ibid., p.32.

p.191: 'Expressionist jam' – Magdalena Droste, *Bauhaus,* Taschen, Köln 1993, p.45.

p.191: 'an island of recluses' – ibid., p.46.

p.192: 'bursting into the Bauhaus circle' – Gillian Naylor, *The Bauhaus Reassed,* The Herbert Press, London 1985, p.100.

p.194: 'artistic, scientific and technical' – description from the prospectus for '8 Bauhaus Books', Hans M. Wingler, *The Bauhaus,* The MIT Press, MA 1980, p.130.

p.198: 'text loses nothing' – Bayer used the same text that appeared in Tschichold's 'Elementare Typographie' originally published in *Typographische Mitteilungen,* no.10, 1925.

p.199: 'new machine alphabet' – Gillian Naylor, *The Bauhaus Reassessed,* The Herbert Press, London 1985, p.159.

p.200: 'Building is nothing but' – ibid., p.167.

p.200: 'Words divide, pictures unite' – Otto Neurath, *Empricism and Sociology,* D. Reidel Publishing, Dordrecht 1973, p.217.

p.200: 'details which do not improve' – ibid., p.240.

p.201: 'a white circle in a red rectangle' – in *Mein Kampf* ('My Struggle'), published in 1925/26 Adolf Hitler (the one-time artist) claimed: 'I myself, meanwhile, after innumerable attempts, had laid down a final form; a flag with a red background, a white disk, and a black swastika in the middle. After long trials I also found a definite proportion between the size of the flag and the size of the white disk, as well as the shape and thickness of the swastika.' Trans. Ralph Manheim, Houghton Mifflin Harcourt, New York (1943) 1999, p.496.

p.201: 'in turmoil' – Christopher Burke, *Active Literature: Jan Tschichold and New Typography,* Hyphen Press, London 2007, p.25.

p.201: 'first truly Modernist' – Thibaudeau's *Manuel Français de Typographie Moderne,* published in 1924, showed contemporary examples of design but none could be described as Modernist, not as we now understand the term. The same applies to *Graphic Design* by W. G. Raffe, published in 1927, and Dwiggins's *Layout In Advertising,* published in 1928.

p.203: 'the typeface of our time' – Christopher Burke, *Paul Renner: The Art of Typography,* Hyphen Press, London 1998, p.81.

p.203: 'I did not want to' – ibid., p.96.

p.203: 'followed from the desire' – ibid., p.97.

CHAPTER 14

p.205: 'Henri Hairmattress' – Richard W. Bulliet, *The Columbia History of the 20th Century,* Columbia University Press, New York 1998, p.8.

p.205: 'lunatic fringe' – Theodore Roosevelt, 'A Layman's View of an Art Exhibition', *Outlook* magazine, no.103, 29 March 1913, pp.718-720.

p.208: 'the greatest artificer' – Sir Francis Meynell's carefully ambiguous description; Alexander S. Lawson, *Anatomy of a Typeface,* David R. Godine, New Hampshire 1990, p.62

p.208: 'the perfect type would' – Andrew R. Boone, 'Type by Goudy', *Popular Science,* vol.140, no.4, April 1942, p.114.

p.208: 'Once in a while a type' – Walter Tracy, *Letters of Credit,* Gordon Fraser, London 1986, p.121.

p.209: 'even with occasional' – ibid., p.144.

p.211: 'belong unmistakably to' – Peter Holliday, *Edward Johnston: Master Calligrapher,* The British Library, London 2007, p.155.

p.211: 'essentially Roman forms' – ibid., p.155.

p.212: 'for a set of more or less' – Eric Gill, *An Essay on Typography* (1931); Lund Humphries, London, 1988, p.79.

p.214: 'an act of heroic endeavour' – The *Times: Past, Present, Future*; The Times, London 1984; p.50.

p.214: 'and possibly Starling Burgess' – Joel Alas, 'The History of the Times New Roman Typeface', *The Financial Times,* London, 1 August 2009.

p.214: 'It is a newspaper type' – Walter Tracy, *Letters of Credit,* Gordon Fraser, London 1986, p.194.

p.215: 'adventure in discovery' – Eric Gill; foreword to catalogue, *An Exhibition of Woodcuts by the Society of Wood Engravers and Other Artists,* Basnett Gallery, Bon Marché, Liverpool, February 1927.

p.216: 'the logo's real designer' – see Phil Baines, *Penguin by Design,* Penguin Books, London 2005, pp.250–51.

CHAPTER 15

p.219: 'a symbol, in those days' – Mark Haworth-Booth, *E. McKnight Kauffer: A Designer and His Public,* V&A Publications, London 2005, p.18.

p.220: 'Some people have called' – www.cassandre.fr, the official web-site created by his grandson Roland Mouron; retrieved 16 May 2009

p.223: 'To see life' – Henry Luce; prospectus for *Life* magazine: New York 1935.

p.223: 'Life begins here' – *Life* magazine, vol.1 no.1, Henry Luce, New York 23 November 1936, p.2.

p.224: 'like an animal' – contained in the article illustrated.

p.226: 'Young is better than' – 'Stolley's Law of Covers', mid- 1970s and after 1980, by Richard Stolley, the first editor of *People* magazine. See Bob Colacello, *Holy Terror: Andy Warhol Close Up,* Cooper Square, New York 1999.

p.233: 'during a stroll down' – Thomas J. Watson and Peter Petre, *Father, Son & Co.,* Bantam Books, New York 1994.

p.233: 'the Olivetti material' – ibid., p.258.

p.236: 'it was a story' – from an interview with Walter Cronkite, the celebrated American news anchorman, on American National Public Radio, 20 February 2002.

CHAPTER 16

p.239: 'The epitome of' to 'of typefaces' – *Helvetica: Homage to a Typeface,* Lars Müller, Baden 2007.

p.240: 'Among all the types' – Jan Tschichold, *The New Typography;* trans. Ruari McLean, University of California Press 1995, p.73.

p.241: 'a carefully and judiciously' –
D. Stempel A. G. Typefoundry specimen
sheet, c.1958.

p.245: 'the requirements of language' –
Richard Hollis, Swiss Graphic Design:
the Origins and Growth of an International Style, Laurence King, London
2006, p.145.

p.246: 'to express the world' – Kerry
William Purcell, Josef Müller-Brockmann, Phaidon, London 2006, p.163.

p.247: 'use of geometrical elements' –
Richard Hollis, Swiss Graphic Design:
the Origins and Growth of an International Style, Laurence King Publishing,
London 2006, p.156.

p.252: 'These are not desks' – Stanley
Abercrombie, George Nelson: The Design
of Modern Design, The MIT Press, MA
1995, p.213.

p.253: 'there is no counterpart to' – Steven Heller, Paul Rand, Phaidon, London
1999, p.158.

p.253: 'its effectiveness often' – Mobil
design guidelines created by Chermayeff
& Geismar during the early 1970s which
Tom Geismar outlined to the author.

p.256: 'schematic 1958 version' –
www.aiga.org; Paul Shaw, 'The (Mostly)
True Story of Helvetica and the New York
City Subway', retrieved 30 June 2009.

p.257: 'Vignelli has recently designed' –
Men's Vogue, May 2008.

p.258: 'behest of a design committee' –
see The Official Report of the Organizing
Committee for the Games of the XXth
Olympiad Munich 1972, vol.1, pro Sport,
Munich 1974, p.270.

CHAPTER 17

p.264: 'were getting a little fed up' – see
Bill Harry, The Paul McCartney Encyclopedia, Virgin Books, London 2003.

p.264: 'First Things First 2000' – first
published in Adbusters magazine, no.27,
Autumn 1999, p.57.

p.264: 'I wanted to make art' – Nicholas
Wroe, 'The Bigger Picture', The Saturday
Guardian, review section, 21 January,
2006, p.11.

p.265: 'not advocate the abolition' – Ken
Garland, 'First Things First: A Manifesto', A Word in your Eye, Department
of Typography and Graphic Communication, University of Reading 1996, p.30.

p.266: 'Only what I created after' – Henri
Matisse, Jack Flam, Matisse On Art, University of California Press, 1995, p.6.

p.266: 'the exceptional size of' – www.
henri-matisse.net; retrieved 7 September 2009.

267: 'chromatic and rhythmic improvisation' – www.henri-matisse.net; retrieved
7 September 2009.

p.267: 'to set [the] mood' – Pamela
Haskins; 'Saul, Can You Make Me a
Title?', interview with Saul Bass, Film
Quarterly, Autumn 1996, pp.12-13.

p.268: 'The new American painting' –
from the title of an international exhibi-
tion of the first generation of Abstract
Expressionists, organized by New York's
Museum of Modern Art between April
1958 and May 1959; the title followed
Geoffrey Wagner's article in The Antioch
Review, spring 1954.

p.271: 'Man, if you gotta ask' – attrib-
uted to the American jazz trumpeter and
singer, Louis Armstrong.

p.273: 'one who risks his' – contained in
Che Guevara's last letter to his parents,
1965.

p.274: 'panned the podium' – anon.,
obituary for Korda in The Times of London, 28 May 2001.

p.277: 'bikinis, cars, ice cream' – the text
in the illustration of Magnum's 'Cherry
Guevara' wrapper reads: 'The revolutionary struggle of the cherries was
squashed as they were trapped between
two layers of choclotate. May their
memory live on in your mouth!'.

p.277: 'Capitalism devours everything' –
quoted by Iván de la Nuez, artistic director of the Palau de la Virreina, Barcelona,
in the 2008 documentary Chevolution
directed by Trisha Ziff and Luis Lopez.
'Capitalism devours everything' is also
the title of a poster c.1920 by the Russian
Constructivist designer Dmitri Moor.

280: 'Their rightful place' – from an un-
paginated statement issued by the Atelier
Populaire in 1969.

p.280: 'the swinging city' – 'Great Britain:
you can walk across it on the grass', Time
magazine, US edition, vol.87, no.15,
Friday 15 April 1966.

p.281: 'powerfully haunting graphic
image' – see F. H. K. Henrion's 1963
Stop Nuclear Suicide poster for CND,
and Brownjohn, Chermayeff & Geismar
Associates' cover for Bertrand Russell's
Common Sense and Nuclear Warfare, by
Simon & Schuster, New York 1959 (see
www.designarchives.aiga.org).

p.282: 'I drew myself' – from a letter written in 1973 by Gerald Holtom to Hugh
Brock, the editor of Peace News, now contained in 'The Hugh Brock Papers' which
are part of the Commonwealth Collection
held at the University of Bradford, UK.

p.281: 'created in 1958' – some have
claimed the peace logo was first created
in the 1930s by Bertrand Russell for
Britain's anti-fascist movement. There is
no suggestion of this in the explanation
that Russell himself gave in a reply of
15 April 1962 to a letter from the editor,
H. Pickles, of the publishers, Lichthort
Verlag, who had complained that the
downward pointing arms made the logo
a death symbol. Russell replied thus:
'I am afraid that I cannot follow your
argument that the ND [Nuclear Disarma-
ment] badge is a death-symbol. It was
invented by a member of our movement
as the badge of the Direct Action Committee against Nuclear War, for the first
Aldermaston March. It was designed
from the naval code of semaphore, and
the symbol represents the code letters
for ND. To the best of my knowledge, the
Navy does not employ signallers who
work upside down.'

p.281: 'There … is in the use' – Bertrand
Russell, The Basic Writings of Bertrand
Russell, Simon & Schuster, New York
1961, p.700.

p.283: 'this war has already' – statement
given by Senator Frank Church before
the Senate Foreign Relations Committee, 11 May 1970.

p.284: 'it is up to us' – www.aiga.org; Steven Heller, 'War Is Not Healthy: The True
Story', retrieved 20 October 2009.

p.284: 'American senator's investigation'
– the report was delivered in a series
of speeches to the US Senate by a then
junior senator from Arkansas, J. William
Fulbright, between 1–5 December 1969.
They later formed the basis of Fulbright's
book The Pentagon Propaganda Machine, 1970.

p.284: 'prime-time television' – 'The
Selling of the Pentagon' was broadcast by
CBS on 23 February 1971.

p.284: 'Television brought' – Marshal
McLulan, quoted in the Montreal Ga-
zette, 16 May 1975.

p.285: 'the end of the 1960s' – on the
evening of 27 February 1968 the popular
CBS news anchorman Walter Cronkite
closed his 'Report from Vietnam: Who,
What, When, Where, Why?' with the
view that the war was unwinnable.
Some aides of President Lyndon Johnson
later remarked that it was after watch-
ing Cronkite that the president realized
public-support for the war had declined
decisively.

CHAPTER 18

p.290: 'SOMETHING BETTER CHANGE'
– see Ken Garland, A Word in your Eye,
Department of Typography and Graphic
Communication, University of Reading
1996, pp.136–7.

p.291: *'second-hand illustration'* – it first appeared in the British Punk fanzine *Sideburns* in December 1976.

p.291: *'Most of the things'* – Jon Savage, *England's Dreaming,* Faber & Faber, London 1991, p.202.

p.291: *'aesthetic, aurally, verbally'* – first two verses and chorus: *God save the Queen / Her facist regime / They made you a moron / Potential h-bomb; God save the Queen / She ain't no human being / There's no future / In England's dreaming; Don't be told what you want / Don't be told what you need / There's no future, no future / No future for you.*

p.291: *'found in a newspaper'* – a British tabloid newspaper *The Sunday People,* 6th February, 1977.

p.292: *'against good taste or decency'* – Section 4 (10) (A) of the IBA (Independent Broadcasting Authority) Act.

p.295: *'shed more light on'* – Kees Broos and Paul Hefting, *Dutch Graphic Design,* Phaidon, London 1993, p.202.

CHAPTER 19

p.297: *'the term first became'* – the term Postmodernism was first used at the end of the nineteenth century in reference to painting, and then variously throughout the twentieth century in writings on religion, philosophy, art, literature, music and history. *The Language of Post-Modern Architcture* (1977) by the American writer and historian Charles Jencks is regarded as having established the term in architecture; *The Postmodern Condition: A Report on Knowledge* (1979) by the French philosopher Jean-François Lyotard, is cited as having established it in philosophy.

p.297: *'wit, ornament and reference'* – commonly used but of unknown provenance.

p.297: *'less is a bore'* – Robert Venturi, *Complexity and Contradiction in Architecture* (The Museum of Modern Art, New York, 1966), 2nd ed. Architectural Press, London 1977, p.17.

p.298: *'conservative design dogma'* – Wolfgang Weingart, 'My Typography Instruction at the Basle School of Design/Switzerland, 1968 to 1985', *Design Quarterly,* no.130, Walker Art Center, Minneapolis 1985, p.1.

p.298: *'I'd discovered the intrinsic'* – Wolfgang Weingart, *Typography: My Way To Typography,* Lars Müller Publishers, Basle 2000, p.73.

p.300: *'What's the use'* – www.keithtam.net; 'Wolfgang Weingart's Typographic Landscape', retrieved 6 November 2009.

p.300: *'song by Bob Dylan'* – 'Stuck Inside of Mobile with the Memphis Blues again', which first appeared on Dylan's 1966 album *Blonde On Blonde.*

p.301: *'I don't understand why'* – Ettore Sottsass, 'I Don't Understand why the President's Speeches are better than Love Whispering in a Room at Night'; *Quotations and Sources on Design and the Decorative Arts*, Ed. Paul Greenhaulgh, The Manchester University Press, 1993.

p.302: *'simulate structural form'* – Kenneth Frampton, 'Architectural Typography: Willi Kunz at Columbia', *Octavo* magazine 87.3, London 1987, p.10.

p.302: *'a metaphor for architectural space'* – *NewWork* magazine, no.3, 2009.

p.306: *'it's awful what you make'* – from a speech given by Oxenaar at the ICOGRADA congress in Amsterdam in 1987 (www.rgaros.nl).

p.307: *'structuralism, post-structuralism, deconstruction, phenomenology'* – from an interview with Katherine McCoy by Rick Poynor, 'After Cranbrook: Katherine McCoy on the Way Ahead', *Eye* magazine, vol.4, no.16, 1995.

p.308: *'a book of early Modernist'* – Herbert Spencer, *Pioneers of Modern Typography*, Lund Humphries, London 1969.

p.308: *'a mass-produced secret'* – quoted in the documentary *New Order Story*, Warner Bros 2005.

p.309: *'panorama of social relations'* – Kate Linker, *Love for Sale: The Art and Words of Barbara Kruger,* Abrams, New York 1990, p.29.

CHAPTER 20

p.312: *'created and then refined'* – Dr. Kenneth R. Eldredge of the Stanford Research Institute was granted a US patent in September 1961 for an 'Automatic Reading System' using magnetic character recognition technology.

p.313: *'What hath God wrought'* – Numbers 23:23, Authorized King James Bible.

p.313: *'the lowly barcode'* – see Tony Seideman, 'The history of the barcode', *Inside Out: The Wonders of Modern Technology*, ed. Carol J. Amato, Smithmark Publishing, New York 1993.

p.313: *'a series of printouts'* – the printout was made by the German company Hell's new electronic typesetter, the Digiset, which was being exhibited at RUPA, an annual print and paper exhibition in Düsseldorf.

p.315: *'I decided there could be nothing'* – mkgraphic.com; retrieved 20 December 2009.

p.315: *'to be closer'* – Liz Farrelly, *April Greiman: Floating Ideas into Time and Space,* Thames and Hudson, London 1998, p.10.

p.316: *'The thing that I think'* – Rick Poynor, 'Drift and Float: April Greiman', *Design Without Boundaries,* Booth-Clibborn, London 1998, p.43.

p.320: *'There were times when'* – Jon Wozencroft, *The Graphic Language of Neville Brody,* Thames and Hudson, London 1988, p.102.

p.323: *'Everything that fascinates me'* – www.artyfactory.com, retrieved 10 November 2009.

p.325: *'the outside of content'* – Richard Roud, *Godard*, Thames and Hudson, London 1970.

POSTSCRIPT

p.328: *'silent revolution in nanotechnology'* – John Pickrell, 'Instant Expert: Nanotechnology', *The New Scientist*, 4 September 2006.

p.328: *'computerized contact lenses'* – currently researched by Prof. Babak Parviz, University of Washington, US.

Abercrombie, Stanley, *George Nelson: The Design of Modern Design*, The MIT Press, Cambridge, Massachusetts and London, 1995

Ades, Dawn, *Photomontage*, Thames and Hudson, London, 1986

Alexander, Jonathan J.G., *Medieval Illuminators and their Methods of Work*, Yale University Press, New Haven and London, 1992

Anikst, Mikhail, *Soviet Commercial Design of the Twenties*, Thames and Hudson in association with Alexandria Press, 1989

Avrin, Leila, *Scribes, Script and Books: The Book Arts from Antiquity to the Renaissance*, The British Library and the American Library Association, London and Chicago, 1991

Backhouse, Janet, *The Illuminated Manuscript*, Phaidon Press, London, 1979

Backhouse, Janet, *The Lindisfarne Gospels*, Phaidon Press in association with the British Library, London, 1987

Bain, Iain, *Celtic Knotwork*, Constable and Co., London, 1986

Bain, Peter and Shaw, Paul (Eds), *Blackletter: Type and National Identity*, Princeton Architectural Press and the Cooper Union for the Advancement of Science and Art, New York, 1998

Baines, Phil and Dixon, Catherine, *Signs: Lettering in the Environment*, Laurence King Publishing in association with Harper Design International, London, 2003

Baines, Phil and Haslam, Andrew, *Type and Typography*, 2nd Edition, Laurence King Publishing, London, 2005

Ball, Johnson, *William Caslon: Master of Letters*, The Roundwood Press, Kineton, 1973

Banham, Reyner, *Theory and Design in the First Machine Age*, The Architectural Press, London, 1983

Barnicoat, John, *Posters: A Concise History*, Thames and Hudson, London, 1988

Barr, John, *The Officina Bodoni: Books Printed by Giovanni Mardersteig on the Hand Press 1923-1977*, British Museum Publications, London, 1978

Barrow, John D., *Cosmic Imagery: Key Images in the History of Science*, The Bodley Head, London, 2008

Bartram, Alan, *Bauhaus, Modernism and the Illustrated Book*, The British Library, London, 2004

Bartram, Alan, *Futurist Typography and the Liberated Text*, The British Library, London, 2005

Barzun, Jacques, *From Dawn to Decadence, 1500 to the Present: 500 Years of Western Cultural Life*, HarperCollins Publishers, London, 2001

Becker, Lutz and Hollis, Richard, *Avant-Garde Graphics 1918-1934: From the Merrill C. Berman Collection*, Hayward Gallery Publishing, London, 2004

Beegan, Gerry, *The Mass Image: A Social History of Photomechanical Reproduction in Victorian London*, Palgrave Macmillan, Basingstoke, Hampshire and New York, 2008

Benson, Richard, *The Printed Picture*, The Museum of Modern Art, New York, 2008

Berger, John, *About Looking*, Writers and Readers Publishing Cooperative, London, 1980

Berger, John, *Ways of Seeing*, BBC and Penguin Books, London, 1981

Bernstein, David, *Advertising Outdoors: Watch this Space!,* Phaidon Press, London, 1997

Bierut, Michael, Drenttel, William, Heller, Steven and Holland, D.K. (Eds), *Looking Closer: Critical Writings on Graphic Design*, Allworth Press, New York, 1994

Bierut, Michael, Drenttel, William and Holland, D.K. (Eds), *Looking Closer Two: Critical Writings on Graphic Design*, Allworth Press, New York, 1997

Bierut, Michael, Drenttel, William and Heller, Steven (Eds), *Looking Closer Four: Critical Writings on Graphic Design*, Allworth Press and The American Institute of Graphic Arts, New York, 2002

Blackwell, Lewis, *Twentieth-Century Type*, Laurence King Publishing, London, 1992

Bland, David, *A History of Book Illustration*, Faber and Faber, London,1958

Bloomer, Carolyn M., *Principles of Visual Perception*, Litton Educational Publishing, New York, 1976

Bringhurst, Robert, *The Elements of Typographic Style*, 2nd Edition, Hartley and Marks, Washington, 1996

Broos, Kees and Hefting, Paul, *Dutch Graphic Design*, Phaidon Press, London, 1993

Brown, Michelle P., *A Guide to Western Historical Scripts from Antiquity to 1600*, 2nd Edition, The British Library, London, 1993

Brown, Michelle P., *Understanding Illuminated Manuscripts: A Guide to Technical Terms*, The British Library and J. Paul Getty Museum, London and Los Angeles, 1994

Brown, Michelle P., *The British Library Guide to Writing and Scripts: History and Techniques*, The British Library, London, 1998

Brown, Michelle P., *The Painted Labyrinth: The World of the Lindisfarne Gospels*, The British Library, London, 2004

Brown, Michelle P., and Lovett, Patricia, *The Historical Source Book for Scribes*, The British Library, London, 1999

Brown, Peter, *The Book of Kells*, Thames and Hudson, London, 1980

Burke, Christopher, *Paul Renner: The Art of Typography*, Hyphen Press, London, 1998

Burke, Christopher, *Active Literature: Jan Tschichold and New Typography*, Hyphen Press, London, 2007

Bury, Stephen (Ed.), *Breaking the Rules: The Printed Face of the European Avant Garde 1900-1937*, The British Library, London, 2007

Campbell, Colin, *The Beggarstaff Posters: The Work of James Pryde and William Nicholson*, Barrie and Jenkins, London, 1990

Campbell, Colin, *William Nicholson: The Graphic Work*, Barrie and Jenkins, London, 1992

Carruthers, Mary, *The Book of Memory: A Study of Memory in Medieval Culture*, 2nd Edition, Cambridge University Press, Cambridge and New York, 2008

Carter, Harry, *A View of Early Typography up to about 1600*, 2nd Edition, Hyphen Press by arrangement with Oxford University Press, London, 2002

Catich, Edward M., *The Origin of the Serif: Brush Writing and Roman Letters*, 2nd Edition, Catich Gallery, Davenport, 1991

Challis, Clive, *Helmut Krone. The Book: Graphic Design and Art Direction*

(Concept, Form and Meaning) after Advertising's Creative Revolution, The Cambridge Enchorial Press, Cambridge, 2005

Chappell, Warren, *A Short History of the Printed Word*, Nonpareil Books, Boston, 1980

Cinamon, Gerald, *Rudolf Koch: Letterer, Type Designer, Teacher*, Oak Knoll Press and The British Library, Delaware and London, 2000

Clair, Colin, *Christopher Plantin*, Cassell & Co, London, 1960

Compton, Susan P., *The World Backwards: Russian Futurist Books 1912-16*, The British Library, London, 1978

Compton, Susan P., *Russian Avant-Garde Books 1917-34*, The British Library, London, 1992

Cook, B. F., *Greek Inscriptions*, British Museum Publications, London, 1987

Crossley, Heather and Young, Anne, *The British Library Souvenir Guide*, The British Library, London, 1998

Crow, David, *Visible Signs: An Introduction to Semiotics*, Ava Publishing SA, Crans-pres-Céligny, 2003

Czwiklitzer, Christopher, *Picasso's Posters*, Random House, New York and Toronto, 1971

Davies, Martin, *Aldus Manutius: Printer and Publisher of Renaissance Venice*, The British Library, London,1995

Davies, Martin, *The Gutenberg Bible*, The British Library, London, 1996

De Hamel, Christopher, *A History of Illuminated Manuscripts*, Phaidon Press, London, 1994

De Hamel, Christopher, *The Book: A History of the Bible*, Phaidon Press, London and New York, 2001

De Hamel, Christopher, *The British Library Guide to Manuscript Illumination: History and Techniques*, The British Library, London, 2001

De Nave, Francine and Voet, Leon, *Plantin-Moretus Museum Antwerp*, Ludion-Culture Nostra, Amsterdam, 1989

Dilke, O.A.W., *Mathematics and Measurement*, British Museum Publications, London, 1987

Diringer, David, *The Alphabet: A Key to the History of Mankind*, Munshiram Manoharlal Publishers, New Delhi, 1996

Donoughue, Carol, *The Story of Writing*, The British Museum Press, London, 2007

Doordan, Dennis P. (Ed.), *Design History: An Anthology*, The MIT Press, Massachusetts and London, 1995

Dormer, Peter, *Design Since 1945*, Thames and Hudson, London, 1993

Dowding, Geoffrey, *An Introduction to the History of Printing Types: An Illustrated Summary of the Main Stages in the Development of Type Design from 1440 up to the Present Day; An Aid to Type Face Identification*, The British Library and Oak Knoll Press, London and Delaware, 1998

Dreyfus, John, *Into Print: Selected Writings on Printing History, Typography and Book Production*, The British Library, London, 1994

Driver, Martha W., *The Image in Print: Book Illustration in Late Medieval England and its Sources*, The British Library, London, 2004

Droste, Magdalena, *Bauhaus: Bauhaus Archiv 1919-1933*, Benedikt Taschen Verlag, Berlin, 1993

Drucker, Johanna, *The Visible Word: Experimental Typography and Modern Art, 1909-1923*, The University of Chicago Press, Chicago, 1994

Drucker, Johanna, *The Alphabetic Labyrinth: The Letters in History and Imagination*, Thames and Hudson, London, 1999

Drucker, Johanna and McVarish, Emily, *Graphic Design History: A Critical Guide*, Pearson Education, Upper Saddle River, New Jersey, 2009

Edson, Evelyn, *Mapping Time and Space: How Medieval Mapmakers Viewed their World*, The British Library, London, 1999

Eisenstein, Elizabeth L., *The Printing Revolution in Early Modern Europe*, 2nd Edition, Cambridge University Press, Cambridge and New York, 1993

Eskilson, Stephen J., *Graphic Design: A New History*, Laurence King Publishing, London, 2007

Essays on Design 1: AGI's Designers of Influence, Booth-Clibborn Editions, London, 1997

Evans, Harold, *Printing and Design: A Five-volume Manual of English, Typography and Layout*, 3rd Edition, William Heinemann, London, 1984

Evans, Harold, *Pictures on a Page: Photo-journalism, Graphics and Picture Editing*, Pimlico, London, 1997

Fahr-Becker, Gabriele, *Wiener Werkstaette 1903-1932*, Taschen, Cologne, 2003

Farrelly, Liz, *April Greiman: Floating Ideas into Time and Space*, Thames and Hudson, London, 1998

Febvre, Lucien and Martin, Henri-Jean, *The Coming of the Book: The Impact of Printing 1450-1800*, NLB, London, 1979

Fiedler, Jeannine and Feierabend, Peter (Eds), *Bauhaus*, Könemann, Cologne, 1999

Firmage, Richard A., *The Alphabet Abecedarium: Some Notes on Letters*, Bloomsbury Publishing, London, 2000

Fischer, Steven Roger, *A History of Language*, Reaktion Books, London, 1999

Fischer, Steven Roger, *A History of Writing*, Reaktion Books, London, 2001

Fischer, Steven Roger, *A History of Reading*, Reaktion Books, London, 2003

Fletcher, Alan, *The Art of Looking Sideways*, Phaidon Press, London, 2001

Frantz Kery, Patricia, *Art Deco Graphics*, Thames and Hudson, London and New York, 2002

Friedl, Friedrich, Ott, Nicolaus and Stein, Bernard, *Typography: When Who How*, Könemann, Cologne, 1998

Gage, John, *Colour and Meaning: Art, Science and Symbolism*, Thames and Hudson, London, 1999

Garland, Ken, *Illustrated Graphics Glossary*, Barrie and Jenkins, London, 1980

Garland, Ken, *Mr Beck's Underground Map: A History*, Capital Transport Publishing, London, 2008

Gaur, Albertine, *A History of Writing*, 2nd Edition, The British Library, London, 1992

Gaur, Albertine, *A History of Calligraphy*, The British Library, London, 1994

Glasier, Milton, *Graphic Design*, The Overlook Press, New York, 1973

Golding, John, *Cubism: A History and an Analysis 1907-1914*, 3rd Edition, Faber and Faber, London, 1988

Gombrich, E. H., *The Sense of Order: A Study in the Psychology of Decorative Art*, 2nd Edition, Phaidon Press, London, 1992

Gombrich, E. H., *The Preference for the Primitive: Episodes in the History of Western Taste and Art*, Phaidon Press, London and New York, 2002

Gorman, Paul, *Reasons to be Cheerful: The Life and Work of Barney Bubbles*, Adelita, London, 2008

Gottschall, Edward M., *Typographic Communications Today*, International Typeface Corporation and The MIT Press,

New York, Cambridge, Massachusetts and London, 1989

Gray, Nicolette, *XIXth Century Ornamented Types and Title Pages*, Faber and Faber, London, 1951

Gray, Nicolette, *A History of Lettering: Creative Experiment and Letter Identity*, Phaidon Press, Oxford, 1986

Greenhalgh, Paul (Ed.), *Art Nouveau 1890-1914*, V&A Publications, London, 2000

Griffiths, Antony, *Prints and Printmaking: An Introduction to the History and Techniques*, 2nd Edition, British Museum Press, London, 1996

Guedj, Denis, *Numbers: The Universal Language*, Thames and Hudson, London, 1998

Harling, Robert, *The Letter Forms and Type Designs of Eric Gill*, 2nd Edition, Eva Svensson and Westerham Press, London, 1978

Harrison, Charles and Wood, Paul (Eds), *Art in Theory 1900-1990: An Anthology of Changing Ideas*, Blackwell Publishers, Oxford and Massachusetts, 1994

Harrison, Charles and Wood, Paul (Eds) with Gaiger, Jason, *Art in Theory 1815-1900: An Anthology of Changing Ideas*, Blackwell Publishers, Oxford and Massachusetts, 1998

Hart, Horace, *Hart's Rules for Compositors and Readers at the University Press Oxford*, 38th Edition, Oxford University Press, Oxford, 1978

Harthan, John, *The History of the Illustrated Book: The Western Tradition*, Thames and Hudson, London, 1997

Harvey, P.D.A. and McGuinness, Andrew, *A Guide to British Medieval Seals*, The British Library and Public Record Office, London, 1996

Heller, Steven, *Design Literacy: Understanding Graphic Design*, Allworth Press, New York, 1999

Heller, Steven, *Merz to Emigre and Beyond: Avant-Garde Magazine Design of the Twentieth Century*, Phaidon Press, London and New York, 2003

Heller, Steven and Ballance, Georgette, *Graphic Design History*, Allworth Press, New York, 2001

Heller, Steven and Chast, Seymour, *Graphic Styles: From Victorian to Post-modern*, Thames and Hudson, London, 1988

Heller, Steven and Fili, Louise, *Typology: Type Design from the Victorian Era to the Digital Age*, Chronicle Books, San Francisco, 1999

Heller, Steven and Finamore, Marie, *Design Culture: An Anthology of Writing from the AIGA Journal of Graphic Design*, Allworth Press and The American Institute of Graphic Arts, New York, 1997

Hellinga, Lotte, *Caxton in Focus: The Beginning of Printing in England*, The British Library and Oak Knoll Press, London, 1982

Hellinga, Wytze G., *Copy and Print in the Netherlands: An Atlas of Historical Biography*, North-Holland Publishing Company, Amsterdam, 1962

Hewitt, Graily, *Lettering: For Students and Craftsmen*, Seeley, Service & Co., London, 1976

Hill, Rosemary, *God's Architect: Pugin and the Building of Romantic Britain*, Allen Lane, London, 2007

Hillier, Bevis and Escritt, Stephen, *Art Deco Style*, Phaidon Press, London and New York, 2003

Hind, Arthur M., *An Introduction to a History of Woodcut, Volume One: With a Detailed Survey of Work Done in the Fifteenth Century*, Dover Publications, New York, 1963

Hobsbawm, Eric, *Age of Extremes: The Short Twentieth Century 1914-1991*, Michael Joseph, London, 1962

Hobsbawm, Eric, *The Age of Revolution, 1789-1848*, Weidenfeld and Nicolson, London, 1975

Hobsbawm, Eric, *The Age of Capital, 1848-1875*, Weidenfeld and Nicolson, London, 1987

Hobsbawm, Eric, *The Age Of Empire, 1875-1914*, Weidenfeld and Nicolson, London, 1996

Holliday, Peter, *Edward Johnston: Master Calligrapher*, The British Library and Oak Knoll Press, London and Delaware, 2007

Hollis, Richard, *Graphic Design: A Concise History*, Thames and Hudson, London, 1994

Hollis, Richard, *Swiss Graphic Design: The Origins and Growth of an International Style 1920-1965*, Laurence King Publishing, London, 2006

Howard, Philip, *We Thundered Out: 200 Years of The Times 1785-1985*, Times Books, London, 1985

Howard, Philip, *The British Library: A Treasure House of Knowledge*, Scala Publishers in association with The British Library, London, 2008

Hughes, Robert, *Nothing If Not Critical: Selected Essays on Art and Artists*, Harvill, London, 1991

Hutt, Allen, *Fournier: The Compleat Typographer*, Rowman and Littlefield, Totowa, 1972

Ing, Janet, *Johann Gutenberg and His Bible: A Historical Study*, 2nd Edition, The Typophiles, New York, 1990

Jaspert, W. Pincus, Berry, Turner, W. and Johnson, A.F., *Encyclopaedia of Type Faces*, 4th Edition, Cassell & Co, London, 2003

Jobling, Paul and Crowley, David, *Graphic Design: Reproduction and Representation since 1800*, Manchester University Press, Manchester and New York, 1996

Johnson, A.P., *Type Designs: Their History and Development*, 2nd Edition, Grafton & Co, London, 1959

Johnston, Edward, *Writing & Illuminating & Lettering*, 2nd Edition, Sir Isaac Pitman & Sons, London, 1939

Jubert, Roxane, *Typography and Graphic Design: From Antiquity to the Present*, Flammarion, Paris, 2006

The Kemsley Manual of Journalism, Cassell & Co, London, 1950

King, Emily, *Richard Brownjohn: Sex and Typography*, Laurence King Publishing, London, 2005

Kinross, Robin, *Modern Typography: An Essay in Critical History*, Hyphen Press, London, 1992

Koch, Rudolf, *The Book of Signs: 493 Symbols Used from Earliest Times to the Middle Ages by Primitive Peoples and Early Christians*, Dover Publications, New York, 1955

Lewis, John, *Anatomy of Printing: The Influences of Art and History on its Design*, Faber and Faber, London, 1970

Lissitzky, El and Arp, Hans, *The Isms of Art*, Verlag Lars Müller, Baden, 1990

Livingston, Alan and Isabella, *The Thames and Hudson Encyclopaedia of Graphic Design and Designers*, Thames and Hudson, London, 1992

Lovett, Patricia, *The British Library Companion to Calligraphy Illumination and Heraldry: A History and Practical Guide*, The British Library and Harry N. Abrams, London and New York, 2000

Lupton, Ellen and Abbott Miller, J. (Eds), *The ABCs of the Bauhaus: The Bauhaus and Design Theory*, Thames and Hudson, London, 1993

MacCarthy, Fiona, *Eric Gill*, Faber and Faber, London, 1989

Marks, P.J.M., *The British Library Guide to Bookbinding: History and Techniques*,

The British Library, London, 1998

Mayakovsky, Vladimir, *For the Voice*, The British Library, London, 2000

Mazur Thomson, Ellen, *The Origins of Graphic Design in America 1870-1920*, Yale University Press, New Haven and London, 1997

McKendrick, Scot, *In a Monastery Library: Preserving Codex Sinaiticus and the Greek Written Heritage*, The British Library, London, 2006

McKendrick, Scot and Doyle, Kathleen, *Bible Manuscripts: 1400 Years of Scribes and Scripture*, The British Library, London, 2007

McLean, Ruari, *The Thames and Hudson Manual of Typography*, Thames and Hudson, London, 1992

McLean, Ruari (Ed.), *Typographers on Type*, Lund Humphries Publishers, London, 1995

McLean, Ruari, *Jan Tschichold: A Life in Typography*, Lund Humphries Publishers, London, 1997

McLean, Ruari, *How Typography Happens*, The British Library and Oak Knoll Press, London and Delaware, 2000

McLuhan, Marshall and Fiore, Quentin, *The Medium is the Massage: An Inventory of Effects*, Penguin Books, London, 1969

Meehan, Bernard, *The Book of Kells: An Illustrated Introduction to the Manuscript in Trinity College Dublin*, Thames and Hudson, London, 1994

Meggs, Philip B., *A History of Graphic Design*, 3rd Edition, John Wiley and Sons, New York, 1998

Moholy-Nagy, László and Seligman, Janet (trans.), *Painting, Photography, Film*, Lund Humphries, London, 1969

Mollerup, Per, *Marks of Excellence: The History and Taxonomy of Trademarks*, 2nd Edition, Phaidon, London and New York, 1998

Morison, Stanley, *Four Centuries of Fine Printing: Two Hundred and Seventy-two Specimens of the Work of Presses Established between 1465 and 1924*, 2nd Edition, Ernest Benn, London, 1949

Morison, Stanley, *Tally of Types: One of the Major Statements of Typographical Practice of our Time*, David R. Godine, Boston, 1999

Mosley, James, *The Nymph and the Grot: The Revival of the Sanserif Letter*, Friends of the St Bride Printing Library, London, 1999

Mucha, Sarah (Ed.), *Alfonse Mucha*,

Mucha Ltd in association with Malcolm Saunders Publishing, Prague, 2000

Müller, Lars (Ed.), *Josef Müller-Brockmann: Pioneer of Swiss Graphic Design*, Lars Müller Publishers, Baden, 1995

Müller, Lars, *Helvetica: Homage to a Typeface*, 3rd Edition, Lars Müller Publishers, Baden, 2007

Müller-Brockmann, Josef, *Grid Systems in Graphic Design: A Visual Communication Manual for Graphic Designers, Typographers and Three-dimensional Designers*, 5th Edition, Niggli, Zurich, 2007

Munder, Heike (Ed.), *Peter Saville Estate 1-127*, JRP-Ringier with Migros Museum fur gegenwartskunst Zurich, Zurich, 2007

Musatti, R., Bigiaretti, L., Soavi, G. and Gendel, M. (trans.), *Olivetti 1908-1958*, Olivetti & Co, Ivrea, 1958

Naylor, Gillian, *The Bauhaus Reassessed: Sources and Design Theory*, The Herbert Press, London, 1985

Neurath, Marie and Kinross, Robin, *The Transformer: Principles of Making Isotype Charts*, Hyphen Press, London, 2009

Newark, Quentin, *What is Graphic Design?*, Rotovision SA, Mies, 2007

O'Connell, Sheila, *The Popular Print in England*, British Museum Press, London, 1999

Otis Thompson, Susan, *American Book Design and William Morris*, 2nd Edition, The British Library and Oak Knoll Press, London and Delaware, 1996

Pachnicke, Peter and Honnef, Klaus, *John Heartfield*, Harry N. Abrams, New York, 1992

Parkes, M. B., *Pause and Effect: An Introduction to the History of Punctuation in the West*, Scolar Press, Aldershot, 1992

Parkinson, Richard, *Cracking Codes: The Rosetta Stone and Decipherment*, University of California Press, Berkeley and Los Angeles, 1999

Percy Bliss, Douglas, *A History of Wood-Engraving: 120 Reproductions of Woodcuts from Dürer to Paul Nash*, J.M. Dent and Sons, London, 1928

Pevsner, Nikolaus, *Pioneers of Modern Design: From William Morris to Walter Gropius*, 3rd Edition, Penguin Books, London, 1984

Pevsner, Nikolaus, *An Outline of European Architecture*, 7th Edition, Penguin Books, London, 1985

Pollard, Michael, *Johann Gutenberg: The*

Story of the Invention of Movable Type and How Printing Led to a Knowledge Explosion, Exley Publications, Watford, 1992

Porter, Norman, *What is a Designer: Things. Places. Messages.*, 4th Edition, Hyphen Press, New York, 2003

Postrel, Virginia, *The Substance of Style: How the Rise of Aesthetic Value Is Remaking Commerce, Culture and Consciousness*, HarperCollins Publishers, New York, 2003

Poynor, Rick, *Design without Boundaries: Visual Communication in Transition*, Booth-Clibborn Editions, London, 1998

Poynor, Rick (Ed.), *Designed by Peter Saville*, Frieze, London, 2003

Poynor, Rick (Ed.), *Communicate: Independent British Graphic Design since the Sixties*, Laurence King Publishing in association with Barbican Art Gallery, London, 2004

Radice, Barbara, *Ettore Sottsass: A Critical Biography*, Thames and Hudson, London, 1993

Railing, Patricia (Ed.), *Voices of Revolution: Collected Essays*, The British Library, London, 2000

Rand, Paul, *Design, Form and Chaos*, Yale University Press, New Haven and London, 1993

Rand, Paul, *From Lascaux to Brooklyn*, Yale University Press, New Haven and London, 1996

Reeve, John (Ed.), *Sacred: Books of the Three Faiths: Judaism, Christianity, Islam*, The British Library, London, 2007

Rothschild, Deborah, Lupton, Ellen and Goldstein, Darra, *Graphic Design in the Mechanical Age: Selections from the Merrill C. Berman Collection*, Yale University Press, New Haven and London, 1998

Ruskin, John, *The Lamp of Beauty: Writings on Art*, 3rd Edition, Phaidon Press, London, 1995

Russell, John, *Matisse: Father and Son*, Harry N. Abrams, New York, 1999

Sassoon, Donald, *The Culture of the Europeans: From 1800 to the Present*, HarperCollins Publishers, London, 2006

Savage, Jon, *England's Dreaming: Sex Pistols and Punk Rock*, Faber and Faber, London, 1992

Scharf, Aaron, *Art and Photography*, Penguin Books, London, 1979

Schmandt-Besserat, Denise, *How Writing Came About*, 2nd Edition, University of Texas Press, Austin, 2006

Scholderer, Victor, *Johann Gutenberg: Inventor of Printing*, 2nd Edition, The British Museum, London, 1970

Scott, Kathleen L., *Tradition and Innovation in Later Medieval English Manuscripts*, The British Library, London, 2007

Selborne, Joanna, *British Wood-Engraved Book Illustration 1904-1940: A Break with Tradition*, The British Library and Oak Knoll Press, London and Delaware, 2001

Seligman, Patricia and Noad, Timothy, *The Art of Illuminated Letters: A Practical Guide for Calligraphers*, Headline Book Publishing, London, 1994

Shaughnessy, Adrian, *How to Be a Graphic Designer without Losing your Soul*, Laurence King Publishing, London, 2005

Silverman, Debora L., *Art Nouveau in Fin-de-Siècle France: Politics, Psychology and Style*, University of California Press, Berkeley and Los Angeles, 1989

Simon, Oliver, *Introduction to Typography*, 2nd Edition, Penguin Books in association with Faber and Faber, London, 1954

Smeijers, Fred, *Counter Punch: Making Type in the Sixteenth Century; Designing Typefaces Now*, Hyphen Press, London, 1996

Smith, Anthony, *The Newspaper: An International History*, Thames and Hudson, London, 1979

Smith, Margaret M., *The Title Page: Its Early Development 1460-1510*, The British Library and Oak Knoll Press, London and Delaware, 2000

Sontag, Susan, *On Photography*, Penguin Books, London, 1979

Southall, Richard, *Printer's Type in the Twentieth Century: Manufacturing and Design Methods*, The British Library and Oak Knoll Press, London and Delaware, 2005

Spencer, Herbert, *Pioneers of Modern Typography*, 2nd Edition, Lund Humphries Publishers, London, 1990

Spencer, Herbert (Ed.), *The Liberated Page: An Anthology of Major Typographic Experiments of this Century as Recorded in 'Typographica' Magazine*, Lund Humphries Publishers, London, 1990

Spurling, Hilary, *Matisse the Master: A Life of Henri Matisse: Volume Two, 1909-1954*, Penguin Books, London, 2005

Standard, Paul, *Arrighi's Running Hand:*

A Study of Chancery Cursive and an Explanatory Supplement, Taplinger Publishing Co., New York, 1979

Steinberg, S.H., *Five Hundred Years of Printing*, 2nd Edition, Penguin Books, London, 1961

Stone, Reynolds, *Engravings*, John Murray, London, 1977

Swanson, Gunnar, *Graphic Design and Reading: Explorations of an Uneasy Relationship*, Allworth Press, New York, 2000

Sylvester, David, *About Modern Art: Critical Essays 1948-96*, Chatto & Windus, London, 1996

Thau Heyman, Therese, *Posters: American Style*, Harry N. Abrams in association with the National Museum of American Art, Smithsonian Institution, New York and Washington, 1998

Thornton, Peter, *Form and Decoration: Innovation in the Decorative Arts 1470-1870*, Weidenfeld and Nicolson, London, 1998

The Times: Past, Present, Future; To Celebrate Two Hundred Years of Publication, Times Newspapers, 1985

Tracy, Walter, *Letters of Credit: A View of Type Design*, The Gordon Fraser Gallery, London and Bedford, 1986

Tschichold, Jan and McLean, Ruari (trans.), *The New Typography: The First English Translation of the Revolutionary 1928 Document*, University of California Press, Berkeley and Los Angeles, 1995

Twyman, Michael, *The British Library Guide to Printing: History and Techniques*, The British Library, London, 1998

Twyman, Michael, *Printing 1770-1970: An Illustrated History of its Development and Uses in England*, 2nd Edition, The British Library in association with Reading University Press, and Oak Knoll Press, London and Delaware, 1998

Twyman, Michael, *Breaking the Mould: The First Hundred Years of Lithography*, The British Library, London, 2001

Uglow, Jenny, *Nature's Engraver: A Life of Thomas Bewick*, Faber and Faber, London, 2006

Van Kampen, Kimberly and Saenger, Paul (Eds), *The Bible as Book: The First Printed Editions*, The British Library and Oak Knoll Press in association with The Scriptorium: Center for Christian Antiquities, London and Delaware, 1999

VanderLans, Rudy (Ed.), *Rant*, Emigre no. 64, Emigre and Princeton Architectural Press, Berkeley, 2003

VanderLans, Rudy (Ed.), *Graphic Design vs. Style: Globalism, Criticism, Science, Authenticity and Humanism*, Emigre no. 67, Emigre and Princeton Architectural Press, Berkeley, 2004

VanderLans, Rudy (Ed.), *Nudging Graphic Design*, Emigre no. 66, Emigre and Princeton Architectural Press, Berkeley, 2004

Venturi, Robert, *Complexity and Contradiction in Architecture*, 2nd Edition, The Architectural Press, London, 1990

Walker, C.B.F., *Cuneiform*, The British Museum Press, London, 1987

Wallis, Lawrence W., *Modern Encyclopaedia of Typefaces, 1960-90*, Lund Humphries Publishers, London, 1990

Whitfield, Peter, *The Image of the World: 20 Centuries of World Maps*, The British Library and Pomegranate Artbooks, London and Rohnert Park, 1994

Whitfield, Peter, *Mapping the World: A History of Exploration*, The British Library, London, 2000

William Purcell, Kerry, *Josef Müller-Brockmann*, Phaidon Press, London and New York, 2006

Williams, David, *Naval Camouflage 1914-1945: A Complete Visual Reference*, Chatham Publishing, Rochester, Kent, 2001

Williamson, Hugh, *Methods of Book Design: The Practice of an Industrial Craft*, 2nd Edition, Oxford University Press, Oxford, 1966

Wingler, Hans M., *Bauhaus: Weimar, Dessau, Berlin, Chicago*, The MIT Press, Cambridge, Massachusetts and London, 1980

Wolfe, Tom, *From Bauhaus to Our House*, Picador, London, 1993

Wolpe, Berthold (ed.), *Vincent Figgins Type Specimens, 1801 and 1815*, Printing Historical Society, London, 1967

Wozencroft, Jon, *Brody: The Graphic Language of Neville Brody*, Thames and Hudson, London, 1997

Ziff, Trisha (Ed.), *Che Guevara: Revolutionary and Icon*, V&A Publications, London, 2006

i.1 The Rosetta Stone, Egypt, 196BC. British Museum, EA24.

i.2 Variations on the theme of a match, Pentagram, 1967. Courtesy Pentagram.

1.1 Cave painting of a horse, Lascaux, France, c.18,000–10,000BC. Photo: akg-images.

1.2 Decorated antler bone pin (or spatula), Dordogne, France, Aurignacian period. British Museum, Palart.151.

1.3 Incised cup, wheel-made, Ninevite 5, Iraq, 2750–2500BC. British Museum, 1953,1010.18 (AN581812).

1.4 Clay token, Susa, Iran, Protohistoric era, c.3800BC. Musée du Louvre, Paris. Inv. SB2520. Photo: © RMN/Franck Raux.

1.5 Clay bullae, Susa, Iran, Uruk period, c.3300BC. Musée du Louvre, Paris. Inv. SB1927. Photo: © RMN/Gerard Blot.

1.6 Clay tablet (cuneiform) recording the allocation of beer, Uruk period, 3300–3100BC. British Museum, ANE 140855.

1.7 Clay cuneiform tablet recording barley rations, Girsu, Early Dynastic III, 2351–2342BC. British Museum, ANE 102081.

1.8 Limestone relief slab from the tomb of Rehotep, Meidum, Egypt, 4th dynasty. British Museum, EA 1242.

1.9 Egyptian letters.

1.10 Red sandstone sphinx with inscription of Proto-Sinaitic alphabet, Serabit el-Khadim, c.1800BC. British Museum, EA41748.

1.11 Arrowhead with Phoenician alphabetic inscription giving the owner's name; 'Arrowhead of Ada', Iron Age, 11th century BC. British Museum, ANE136753.

2.1 Phaistos disc, Crete, second millennium BC. Heraklion Archaeological Museum, Crete. Photo: Herve Champollion/akg-images.

2.2 Dipylon jug, wine jug (oenochoe) with incised inscription, Geometric period, Archaic Greek, 735–730BC. National Museum, Athens. Photo: The Art Archive/National Archaeological Museum Athens/Gianni Dagli Orti.

2.3 Faience scarab with cartouche of Amenhotep III, Egypt, 18th dynasty, 1390–1352BC. British Museum, EA71870,1008.130.

2.4 Book of the Dead of Hunefer, papyrus, 19th dynasty. British Museum, EA 9901.

2.5 Greenstone seal of Adda, Akkadian, c.2300BC. British Museum, ANE 89115.

2.6 Scribal palette and brush, Thebes, 18th dynasty. British Museum, EA 12784.

2.7 Quartzite statue of Peshuper, Karnak, 25th dynasty. British Museum, EA1514.

2.8 The Rosetta Stone, Egypt, 196BC. British Museum, EA24.

2.9 'The Teachings of Amenemhat', sheet 2 showing hieratic script, papyrus, hieratic script from Memphis, Egypt, 19th dynasty, 1200–1194BC. British Museum, EA10182/2.

2.10 Demotic script on papyrus, Thebes, Ptolomaic, 194BC. British Museum, EA10831.

2.11 Greek inscription, Athenian decree of constitution of Ionic city of Erythrae, Athenian marble, 450BC. British Museum, 1816,0610.346.

2.12 Book of Didymus, son of Aspasius, farm bailiff to Epimachus, in the neighborhood of Hermopolis, giving his receipts and expenditures for the 11th year of the Emperor Vespasian, semi-cursive script, AD78–79. BL, Papyrus 131 frame 3, col.12.

2.13 Pottery ostrakon containing 18 lines of different psalms written in Coptic, Egypt, 7th–8th century. British Museum, EA 14030.

2.14 Wax writing tablet from Greece, AD2. BL, Add.Ms.E3934186, f.1.

2.15 Etruscan alphabetic inscription, terracotta vase in shape of cockerel, Italian peninsula, c.650–600BC. Metropolitan Museum of Art, New York, Fletcher Fund, 1924. Acc.no. 24.97.21a,b. © 2007. Image copyright The Metropolitan Museum of Art/Art Resource/Scala.

2.16 The base of Trajan's Column, Rome, c.AD113. Photo: akg-images.

2.17 Vergilius Augusteus, manuscript of the works of Virgil showing square capitals, 4th century. Vatican Library, Cod.Vat.lat.3256, f.3v.

2.18 Rustic capitals, Vespasian Psalter, 8th century. BL, Cotton Vespasian Ms. A.1. f.3v.

2.19 Trajan's Column, detail of the inscription, c.AD113. Photo: akg-images.

2.20 Roman graffiti, Pompeii, AD79. Courtesy James Mosley.

2.21 Letter from Octavius, Old Roman cursive, Vindolanda, 1st–2nd century AD. British Museum, P&EE 1989.0602.74.

2.22 Harley Latin Gospel, showing uncial script, 6th century AD. BL, Harley Ms. 1775, ff.390-391.

2.23 Papyrus showing New Roman cursive, Egypt, c.AD345. BL, Papyrus 447r.

2.24 Eugippius, *Excerpta ex operibus Augustini*, showing New Roman half-uncial script, end of the 5th century. Vatican Library, Vat.Lat.3375, f.29v.

3.1 Jewelled treasure binding, Christ in Majesty, gospel manuscript, Tours, c.820. BL, Add.ms.11848.

3.2 (& 3.3) St John's Gospel, Codex Sinaiticus, mid-4th century. BL, Add.Ms. 43725.

3.4 Carpet and incipit page from St John's Gospel, Lindisfarne Gospels, c. AD715–720. BL, Cotton Nero Ms. D.IV, ff.210v-211r.

3.5 St John's Gospel, Lindisfarne Gospels, showing Irish half-uncial, c. AD715–720. BL, Cotton Nero Ms. D.IV, f.208.

3.6 Carpet page from St John's Gospel, Lindisfarne Gospels, c. AD715–720. BL, Cotton Nero Ms. D.IV, f.210v.

3.7 St Matthew's Gospel, showing Carolingian miniscule script, Central Loire, France, 9th century. BL, Harley MS 2795 f.13v.

3.8 The Ramsey Psalter, Winchester or Ramsey, last quarter of 10th century. BL, Harley Ms. 2904, f.36.

3.9 Basic set of character shapes for reading English.

3.10 Beginning of Ezekiel, Worms Bible, Germany (Frankenthal near Worms, Middle Rhineland), 2nd or 3rd quarter of 12th century. BL, Harley Ms. 2803 f.229.

3.11 Magna Carta, 1215. BL, Cotton Augustus Ms. II.106.

3.12 (& 3.13) Glossed Bible text page, France, 13th century. BL, Add.Ms.15253, f.247v.

3.14 The Hours of Joanna of Castile, Bruges, c.1490–1500. BL, Add.Ms. 18852, ff.287v-288.

3.15 *Roman de la Rose*, showing bâtarde script, Bruges, c.1490–1500. BL, Harley Ms. 4425, f.14v.

3.16 Pattern book, France, 15th century. BL, Sloane Ms. 1448A.

3.17 The Sforza Hours, showing rotunda script, Milan, 1490–1504. BL, Add. MS. 34294, f.255.

4.1 Type setting for first page of the Mainz Psalter, 1463. Gutenberg Museum.

4.2 Ox head watermark, Gutenberg Bible, Mainz, c.1455. BL, c.9.d.4.

4.3 The Diamond Sutra, China, 868. BL, Or.8210/P2.

4.4 The 'Sittener Tapete' with scenes of the life of Oedipus, Italy, 14th century. Historisches Museum, Basel. Photo: HMB M.Babey.

4.5 Colour woodcut print of Buxheim St Christopher, 1423. Reproduced by courtesy of the University Librarian and Director, The John Rylands University Library, The University of Manchester.

4.6 *Biblia Pauperum*, Netherlands, 1470. BL, c.9.d.2.

4.7 Collected commentaries on the Spring and Autumn Annals, Korea, 1434. BL, c.16015.c.3.

4.8 Four gold ducats of Sforza Dukes of Milan. British Museum, CM 1849-11-21-562/844, CM 1853-7-29-1, CM 1847-11-8-694.

4.9 31-line papal indulgence printed by Johannes Gutenberg, 1454. BL, IA.E8762.

4.10 (& 4.11) First page of Genesis, Gutenberg Bible, Mainz, c.1455. BL, c.9.d.4.

4.12 Colophon and printing device (2 shields), Mainz Psalter, printed by Fust & Schoeffer, Mainz, 1457, facsimile edition. BL, c.180.f.3.

4.13 The Mainz Psalter, printed by Fust & Schoeffer, Mainz, 1457. BL, G.12216.

4.14 Papal bull for Pope Pius II, printed by Fust & Schoeffer, Mainz, 1463. John Rylands University, Manchester, 16122, f.1r. Reproduced by courtesy of the University Librarian and Director, The John Rylands University Library, The University of Manchester.

4.15 Boccaccio, *De mulieribus claris*, printed by Johan Zainer, Ulm, 1473. BL, IB.9113.

4.16 Illustrations of Mainz and Lyon, The Nuremberg Chronicle, printed by Anton Koberger, 1493. BL, IC.7452.

4.17 *The Recuyell of the Histories of Troye*, printed by William Caxton, Bruges, c.1473/4. BL, c.11.c.1.

4.18 Bible translated into English by William Tyndale, beginning of Gospel of St John, Worms, 1526. BL, c.188.a.17.

5.1 Galeazzo Capella, *Commentarii*, Venice, 1539. BL, Davis 766.

5.2 *Sforziada di Giovanni Simoneta*, Milan, 1490. BL, G.7251.

5.3 Felice Feliciano, *Alphabetum Romanum*, Verona, 1463. BL, cup.510.ee.58.

5.4 Eusebius, *De Evangelica Praeparatione*, Venice, 1470. BL, c.14.c.2.

5.5 *Calendarium*, printed by Erhard Ratdolt, Venice, 1476. BL, IB.20482.

5.6 Francesco Colonna, *Hypnerotomachia Poliphili*, printed by Aldus Manutius, Venice, 1499. BL, 86.k.9.

5.7 Virgil, *Opera*, printed by Aldus Manutius, Venice, 1501. BL, c.19.f.7.

5.8 Ludovico Arrighi, *La Operina da'Imparare di scriuere littera Cancellarescha*, Rome, 1522. BL, c.31.f.8(1).

5.9 Giovanni Battista Palatino, *Libro Nuovo d'imparare*, Rome, 1561. BL, c.31.h.13.

5.10 Paulus Franck, *Schatzkammer Allerhand Versalien*, Nuremberg, 1601. The Getty Research Institute Library, Los Angeles (1384-072).

5.11 Andrea Palladio, *I Quattro Libri dell'Architettura*, Venice, 1570. BL, 686.h.3.

5.12 *L'Histoire De Thucydides*, printed by Claude Garamond, Paris, 1545. BL, c.104.dd.82.

5.13 Opening of St John, French New Testament, printed by Robert Estienne, Geneva, 1553. BL, 691.a.4.

5.14 Jean Froissart, *Chroniques...*, Lyons, 1559. BL, 674.l.9.

5.15 Euclid, *Elements of Geometry*, translated by H. Billingsley, printed by John Day, London, 1570. BL, c.40.l.7.

5.16 Diagrammatic T-O map, early 13th century. BL, Add. Ms. 22797, f.99v.

5.17 Ptolemaic world map, Rome, 1478. BL, c.3.d.6.

5.18 *Universalis Cosmographia Secundum Ptholomaei Traditionem et Americi Vespucii Alioru[m]que Lustrationes* (world map), Martin Waldseemüller, St. Die, 1507. Library of Congress, Washington, D.C.

6.1 Nicolaus Hogenberg, *The Coronation Procession of the Emperor Charles V at Bologna in 1530*, Antwerp, 1532. BL, 1899.p.21.

6.2 Facsimile of *Type Specimen*, printed by Christopher Plantin, Antwerp, 1585. St Bride Printing Library, London.

6.3 Polyglot Bible, printed by Christopher Plantin, Antwerp, 1569–73. BL, 691.k.1.

6.4 Polyglot Bible, printed by Christopher Plantin, Antwerp, 1569–73. BL, 691.k.1.

6.5 Geffrey Whitney, *A Choice of Emblems*, Leiden, 1586. BL, G.11572.

6.6 Basilius Besler, *Hortus Eystettensis*, Nuremberg, 1613. BL, 10.Tab.29.

6.7 *Robin Hood and the Butcher*, Roxburghe Ballads, 1634. BL, c.20.f.7 (Rox.I.356).

6.8 Front page of Verhoeven's *Nieuwe Tydinghe*, showing the capture of Antwerp in 1605, Antwerp, 1605.

6.9 *Londons Intelligencer*, 1643. BL, Burney 14-24.

6.10 *Londons Loud Cryes* (1665). BL, 816.m.9/26.

7.1 (& 7.2) Engraving of capital 'G' from *Romain du Roi*, Imprimerie Royale, Louis Simmoneau, 1702. BL, c.160.d.1.

7.3 *Médailles sur les principaux événements du règne de Louis le Grand*, Paris, 1702. BL, 139.h.6.

7.4 Pierre-Simon Fournier, *Manuel Typographique*, Paris, 1766. BL, 680.b.25.

7.5 Denis Diderot, *Encyclopédie des Sciences, des Arts et des Métiers*, Paris, 1769. BL, 65.g.12.

7.6 The Dunlap broadside, the first printed version of the 'Declaration of Independence', Philadelphia, 1776. The Beinecke Rare Book and Manuscript Library, Yale University.

7.7 Type specimen sheet, William Caslon, London, 1734. BL, c.180, f.4(2).

7.8 National, 13 stars 'Jonathan Fowle' flag (Castle Island flag, Fort Independence flag), Massachusetts,1781. Massachusetts State House, Boston. 1989.29. Courtesy Commonwealth of Massachusetts Art Commission.

7.9 Grand Union and East India Company flag.

7.10 Virgil, *Bucolica, Georgica, et Aeneis*, printed by John Baskerville, Birmingham, 1751. BL, 687.k.1.

7.11 George Bickham, *The Universal Penman*, London, 1741. BL, L.1.c.2.

7.12 *Oeuvres de Jean Racine*, printed by Firmin Didot, Paris, 1801. BL, c.3.e.6-8.

7.13 Dante, *La Divina Commedia*, printed by Giambattista Bodoni, Parma, 1795. BL, 75.i.12.

7.14 Giambattista Bodoni, *Manuale Tipografico*, Parma, 1818. BL, 59.c.19.

8.1 A group of boys stand in front of a wall plastered with bill posters from Barnum's museum, theatre, and minstrel show, New York, c.1860s. © The Mariners' Museum/CORBIS.

8.2 Playbill for 'The Courier of Saint Petersburg', Astley's Amphitheatre, London, 1877. Victoria & Albert Museum, London. © V&A Images.

8.3 Vincent Figgins, Specimen of Printing Types, London, 1835. BL, RB.23.b.3588.

8.4 Rural poster, printed by John Soulby, c.1824. Museum of English Rural Life, University of Reading.

8.5 Vincent Figgins, Specimen of Printing Types, London, c.1817, facsimile. St Bride Printing Library, London.

8.6 First one-inch-to-a-mile Ordnance Survey map, engraved by Thomas Foot, originally published by W. Faden, 1801. BL, Maps 64.a.22.

8.7 William Caslon IV, Specimen of Printing Types, London, 1816. St. Bride's Printing Library, London.

8.8 Ornamented type, Louis John Pouchée, c.1822. Courtesy of Ian Mortimer.

8.9 Woodblock for letter 'Q', c.1822. St Bride printing Library, London.

8.10 Thomas Bewick, *History of British Birds*, Newcastle, 1797. BL, 672.g.17.

8.11 *The Illustrated London News*, first edition, Saturday 14 May 1842. Mary Evans Picture Library.

8.12 Allan Ramsay, *Scotch Proverbs*, Glasgow, 1820s. St Bride Printing Library, London.

8.13 Penny Black and Two Pence Blue stamps, 1st editions, Britain, 1840. BL, Philatelic Collection.

8.14 *The New York Herald*, 2nd edition reporting Lincoln's assassination, Saturday 15 April 1865. Library of Congress, Washington, D.C.

8.15 Jean-François Champollion, *Dictionnaire Égyptien en écriture hiéroglyphique*, Paris, 1841–3. BL, 1487.h.10, f.130.

8.16 Honoré Daumier, 'Les Poires', *Le Charivari*, Paris, 1834. BL, X.415/654.

8.17 *Great Northern Railway and East Coast Route to Scotland Illustrated Guide*, London, 1891. BL, 010360.k.3 (4).

8.18 German wine label, 1880s. St Bride Printing Library, London.

9.1 William Gaspey, *The Great Exhibition of the World's Industry held in London in 1851: described and illustrated by … engravings, from daguerrotypes by Beard, Mayall, etc.*, London, 1852. BL, 10348.b.17.

9.2 *Epitome of Specimens*, V& J Figgins, London, c.1850. BL, 7950.dd.1.

9.3 *The Vision & the Creed of Piers Ploughman*, London, 1842. BL, 1162.d.28/29.

9.4 Oliver Byrne, *The first six books of the Elements of Euclid, in which coloured diagrams and symbols are used instead of letters, for the greater ease of learners*, printed by Charles Whittingham, London, 1847. BL, c.117.e.2.

9.5 Henry Noel Humphreys, *The Miracles of Our Lord*, London, 1848. BL, c.30.b.3.

9.6 Owen Jones, *The Grammar of Ornament*, London, 1856. BL, Afl/336 DSC.

9.7 Pigskin cover, *The Works of Geoffrey Chaucer*, by Edward Burne-Jones, printed by William Morris, Kelmscott Press, 1896. BL, c.42.l.12.

9.8 *The Works of Geoffrey Chaucer*, illustrated by Edward Burne-Jones, printed by William Morris, Kelmscott Press, 1896. BL, c.43.h.19.

9.9 *The Works of Geoffrey Chaucer*, illustrated by Edward Burne-Jones, printed by William Morris, Kelmscott Press, 1896. BL, c.43.h.19.

9.10 Edward Johnston, *Writing & Illuminating & Lettering*, 1906. BL, 07942.e.1/5.

9.11 Digital versions of Kochschrift,

1910; Maximilian, 1914; Wilhelm-Klingspor Schrift, 1926; all designed by Rudolf Koch.

9.12 Otto Eckmann, *Schriften und Ornamente*, Offenbach, 1900. Klingspor Museum, Offenbach.

10.1 'Olympia' poster, designed by Jules Chéret, 1894. Photo: akg-images.

10.2 Pears's *Bubbles* poster, original artwork by John Everett Millais, 1886. Photo: Advertising archives

10.3 'The Actors', woodblock print by Toshusai Sharaku, 1794. British Museum AC 1090,0618,0.53.

10.4 'Divan Japonais' poster, Toulouse-Lautrec, 1893. Photo: akg-images.

10.5 Arthur H. Mackmurdo, *Wren's City Churches*, London, 1883. BL, c.102.i.10.

10.6 The first outdoor advertisement for Coca-Cola, a 1910 oilcloth sign hung from the awning of Jacobs Pharmacy in Atlanta. Courtesy of the Coca-Cola Company.

10.7 Ford logos. Ford Motor Company.

10.8 General Electric logos. General Electric Corp.

10.9 Coca-Cola logo in various scripts, 1980s.

10.10 François Thibaudeau, *Manuel français de typographie moderne*, Paris, 1924. BL, 011908.e.30.

10.11 *The Chap Book* cover, designed by Will Bradley, 1895. Photo: akg-images.

10.12 Ethel Reed, *Folly or Saintliness* by Jose Echegarry, 1895. New York Museum of Modern Art (MoMA). Gift of H.H. Corning 889.1979. © 2009. Digital Image, The Museum of Modern Art, New York/ Scala.

10.13 *Gismonda* starring Sarah Bernhardt, poster by Alphonse Mucha, for the play by Victorien Sardou at the Théâtre de la Renaissance, Paris, 1894. Photo: The Art Archive/Kharbine-Tapabor/Collection Grob.

10.14 *The Scottish Musical Review* (colour lithograph) poster, designed by Charles Rennie Mackintosh, 1896. Hunterian Museum & Art Gallery, University of Glasgow.

10.15 'Tropon' poster, designed by Henry van der Velde, 1897. Photo: akg-images.

10.16 *Ver Sacrum* vol.2 no.4 cover, designed by Kolomon Moser, 1899. Photo: akg-images/Erich Lessing.

10.17 *Ver Sacrum* poster, designed by Kolomon Moser for the 13th Secession exhibition, 1902. Austrian Museum of Applied Arts / Contemporary Art, Vienna (MAK). Photo: © MAK/Georg Mayer.

10.18 Wiener Werkstätte symbols, 1903. Austrian Museum of Applied Arts / Contemporary Art, Vienna (MAK). Photo: © MAK/Georg Mayer.

10.19 Behrens AEG logos, 1907–14.

10.20 AEG turbine factory, Berlin, designed by Peter Behrens, 1909. Photo: akg-images.

11.1 'Public Warning' poster, H.M. Stationery Office, 1915. The National Archives, TNA MEPO 2/1621.

11.2 'Maurin Quina' poster, designed by Leonetto Cappiello, 1906. Photo: akg-images. © ADAGP, Paris and DACS, London, 2010.

11.3 *Simplicissimus* poster, designed by Thomas Theodor Heine, 1897. Photo: akg-images/ullstein bild. © DACS 2010.

11.4 'Rowntree's Elect Cocoa' poster, designed by the Beggarstaffs (William Nicholson and James Pryde), 1896. Photo: akg-images.

11.5 'Priester' poster, designed by Lucien Bernhard, c.1906. Private Collection. © DACS 2010.

11.6 'PKZ' poster, designed by Otto Baumberger, 1923. Merrill C. Berman Collection. © DACS 2010.

11.7 'Automobile Opel' poster, designed by Hans Rudi Erdt, 1911. Merrill C. Berman Collection.

11.8 'Britons. Join Your Country's Army!' poster, illustration by Alfred Leete, 1914. Imperial War Museum, PST 2734.

11.9 Uncle Sam recruitment poster, illustration by James Montgomery Flagg, 1917. Photo: akg-images/Jean-Pierre Verney.

11.10 'Wer Kriegsanleihe Zeichnet Wunscht Mir die Hochste Geburtstagsgabe - von Hindenburg' [Anyone Who Subscribes to the War Loan is Giving Me the Supreme Birthday Present - von Hindenburg], poster designed by Louis Oppenheim, 1917. Imperial War Museum, PST 0435.

11.11 Flags and roundels.

11.12 Gunboat HMS Kildangan in dazzle camouflage, 1918. Imperial War Museum, Q.43387.

11.13 'Did You Volunteer?' poster, designed by Dimitri Moor, 1920. Photo: akg-images/Erich Lessing.

11.14 'ROSTA Window', designed by Vladimir Mayakovsky, 1920. David King Collection.

12.1 *Zang Tumb Tuuum*, cover designed by Filippo Marinetti, Milan, 1914. BL, 12331.f.57. © DACS 2010.

12.2 Stéphane Mallarmé, *Un coup de dés jamais n'abolira le hasard: poème*, Paris, 1914. BL, 11482.m.10.

12.3 George Herbert, 'Easter Wings' from *The Temple. Sacred poems and private ejaculations*, Cambridge, 1633. BL, c.58.a.26.

12.4 Lewis Carroll, 'The Mouse's Tail' from *Alice in Wonderland*, London,

1865. BL, c.59.g.32.

12.5 Guillaume Apollinaire, 'Il Pleut', Paris, 1916. BL, P.903/188.

12.6 Filippo Marinetti, 'Le soir, couchée dans…' from *Les mots en liberté futuristes*, Milan, 1919. BL, c.127.c.16. © DACS 2010.

12.7 *Worldbackwards* written, illustrated and published by Aleksei Kruchenykh and Velimir Khlebnikov, Moscow, 1912. BL, c.114.mm.42.

12.8 *Blast* no.1, designed by Wyndham Lewis, 1914. Inside page: BL, cup.410.g.186, f.18; Cover: Tate Archives. © The Wyndham Lewis Memorial Trust.

12.9 *Der Dada* 3, photomontage by John Heartfield, 1920. Bildarchiv Preussischer Kulturbesitz. © The Heartfield Community of Heirs/VG Bild-Kunst, Bonn and DACS, London 2010.

12.10 Communist election poster, designed by John Heartfield, 1928. Merrill C. Berman Collection. © The Heartfield Community of Heirs/VG Bild-Kunst, Bonn and DACS, London 2010.

12.11 *Adolf the Superman* poster, designed by John Heartfield, 1932. Photo: akg-images. © The Heartfield Community of Heirs/VG Bild-Kunst, Bonn and DACS, London 2010.

12.12 *De Stijl* vol.1, no.1 cover, designed by Theo van Doesburg and illustation by Vilmos Huszár, 1917. BL, LR.411.a/7a.

12.13 'Beat the Whites with the Red Wedge' poster, designed by El Lissitzky, 1919–20. Photo: akg-images. © DACS 2010.

12.14 Third International spread from *For the Voice*, designed by El Lissitzky, 1923. BL, YC.2000.a.13608. © DACS 2010.

12.15 *New LEF* no.6 magazine cover, designed by Alexander Rodchenko, 1927. BL, c.104.dd.51. © Rodchenko & Stepanova Archive, DACS 2010.

13.1 Bauhaus Dessau building, designed by Walter Gropius. Photo: akg-images/Florian Profitlich. © DACS 2010.

13.2 Banknote, designed by Herbert Bayer, 1923. Merrill C. Berman Collection. © DACS 2010.

13.3 Cover of Bauhaus Manifesto, illustration by Lyonel Feininger, 1919. Bauhaus-Archiv Berlin, Inv. Nr.8676/1. © DACS 2010.

13.4 *Staatliches Bauhaus in Weimar 1919–23* exhibition catalogue cover, 1923. Photo: akg-images. © DACS 2010.

13.5 Letterhead designed by László Moholy-Nagy, 1923. Bauhaus-Archiv Berlin, Inv. Nr.8710/1. © Hattula Moholy-Nagy/DACS 2010.

13.6 *Malerei, Photographie, Film*, written and designed by László Moholy-Nagy,

1925. BL, X.410/1411. © Hattula Moholy-Nagy/DACS 2010.

13.7 *Malerei, Photographie, Film*, written and designed by László Moholy-Nagy, 1925. BL, X.410/1411. © Hattula Moholy-Nagy/DACS 2010.

13.8 Herbert Bayer, 'Kandinsky zum 60 Geburtstag' (exhibition celebrating the 60th birthday of Kandinsky), 1926. New York, Museum of Modern Art (MoMA). Gift of Mr and Mrs Alfred H. Barr, Jr. 109.1968. Photo: © 2008. Digitial image, The Museum of Modern Art, New York/Scala, Florence. © DACS 2010.

13.9 Letterhead designed by Herbert Bayer, 1927. Bauhaus-Archiv Berlin, Inv. Nr. 9471. © DACS 2010.

13.10 A-size paper proportions.

13.11 A, B and C size paper proportions.

13.12 Herbert Bayer, 'Universal Lettering', from *Offset Book & Advertising Art*, 1926. Bauhaus-Archiv Berlin, Inv. Nr. 2006/127.1. © DACS 2010.

13.13 Stencil alphabet, designed by Josef Albers, 1926. Merrill C. Berman Collection. © The Josef and Anni Albers Foundtion/VG Bild-Kunst, Bonn and DACS, London, 2010.

13.14 Table lamp page, from 'Catalogue of Designs', designed by Herbert Bayer,1925. Bauhaus-Archiv Berlin, Inv. Nr.2005/42. © DACS 2010.

13.15 Brochure cover, designed by Herbert Bayer, 1927. Bauhaus-Archiv Berlin, Inv. Nr. 2435. © DACS 2010.

13.16 Bauhaus journal cover, designed by Herbert Bayer, 1928. BL, c.142.e.5. © DACS 2010.

13.17 Human chart from *International Picture Language*, written by Otto Neurath, 1936. BL, X.955/570.

13.18 Prospectus for *Die neue Typographie*, designed by Jan Tschichold, 1928. Private collection.

13.19 Constructivism exhibition poster, designed by Jan Tschichold, 1937. Merrill C. Berman Collection.

13.20 Digital version of Futura typeface, designed Paul Renner, 1927–30.

14.1 Opening page of *The Centaur* by Maurice Guerin, translated by George B. Ives, designed by Bruce Rogers and printed at the Montague Press, 1915. The Beinecke Rare Book and Manuscript Library, Yale University.

14.2 Izaak Walton, *The Compleat Angler*, designed by Bruce Rogers, printed at the Riverside Press, Cambridge (Mass), 1909. BL, c.100.h.22.

14.3 Digital version of Centaur typeface, roman designed by Bruce Rogers, 1912.

14.4 Digital version of Kennerley, 1911;

Goudy Old Style, 1915; Deepdene, 1927; typefaces, all designed by Frederic Goudy.

14.5 Frederic W. Goudy, *The Alphabet and Elements of Lettering*, revised edition, Los Angeles, 1942. BL, L.R.274.d.17.

14.6 Upper and lowercase inscription by Eric Gill, plaster cast of stone relief, 1909. Museum & Study Collection at Central St Martins College of Art and Design, London.

14.7 Digital version of Perpetua typeface designed by Eric Gill.

14.8 Drawing of Underground alphabet, Edward Johnston, 1916. Victoria & Albert Museum, London, E18-1936. © V&A Images.

14.9 New Johnston typeface, designed by Eiichi Kono, 1979.

14.10 The entrance to Marble Arch Underground Station, 1930s. London Transport Museum.

14.11 Gill Sans typeface.

14.12 'St John's Cambridge' poster, designed by Fred Taylor for LNER, 1927–30. Photo: Science & Society Picture Library.

14.13 Lowercase 'g' on graph paper by Eric Gill, 1933. St Bride Printing Library, London.

14.14 E. M. Forster, *A Passage to India*, Penguin paperback, designed by Edward Young, c.1936. Patrick Cramsie.

14.15 Masthead of *The Times*, London, 30 September 1932. BL, Newspaper Library.

14.16 Masthead of *The Times*, London, 3 October 1932. BL, Newspaper Library.

14.17 *Encyclopedia Britannica*, 14th edition, 1936. BL, 012224.c.2.

14.18 Title-page wood-engraving by Reynolds Stone, 1938. Patrick Cramsie.

14.19 Penguin logos. Penguin Archive, University of Bristol Library, Special Collections.

14.20 Prospectus for *The Pelican History of Art*, designed by Jan Tschichold, 1947. Penguin Archive, University of Bristol Library, Special Collections.

15.1 'Soaring to Success' poster, designed by Edward McKnight Kauffer, 1919. Victoria & Albert Museum, London. © V&A Images.

15.2 *L'Intransigeant* poster, designed by Cassandre, 1925. Merrill C. Berman Collection. © Estate of A.M. Cassandre.

15.3 *L'Intransigeant* design scheme, based on a sketch by Cassandre, 1925.

15.4 Dutch Cable Factory catalogue, designed by Piet Zwart, Delft, 1928. Merrill C. Berman Collection. © DACS 2010.

15.5 Monogram, Piet Zwart, 1920s.

15.6 Trio booklet, designed by Piet Zwart, 1931. Merrill C. Berman Collection. © DACS 2010.

15.7 'Death in Spain', photograph taken by Robert Capa, *Life* magazine, July 12, 1937. BL, PP.6383.cke.

15.8 Pontresina poster, designed by Herbert Matter, 1936. Museum of Design, Zurich, Poster Collection. Photographer Franz Xaver Jaggy.

15.9 The *Weekly Illustrated*, August 4th 1934. BL, Newspaper Library.

15.10 'Freedom from Want' poster, illustration by Norman Rockwell for the *Saturday Evening Post* Thanksgiving edition, 1943. Library of Congress, Washington D.C., LC-USZC4-1606.

15.11 Selection of magazine covers from the 1950s featuring Marilyn Monroe. Getty Images.

15.12 Spread designed by Alexei Brodovitch for *Harper's Bazaar* magazine, June 1955. Photographs by Richard Avedon.

15.13 Mickey Mouse in *The Klondike Kid*, poster, 1933. Photo: akg-images.

15.14 *Amazing Stories*, February issue, 1942. Mary Evans Picture Library.

15.15 Rural Electrification Administration poster, designed by Lester Beall, 1939. Merrill C. Berman Collection. © Estate of Lester Sr. Beall. DACS, London/VAGA, New York 2010.

15.16 'Olivetti Lettera 22' poster, designed by Giovanni Pintori, 1952. Museum of Design, Zurich, Poster Collection. Photographer Franz Xaver Jaggy.

15.17 (& 15.18) *Mechanized Mules of Victory* brochure, designed by Paul Rand, 1942.

15.19 IBM logo (old), 1947; IBM logo solid black, designed by Paul Rand, 1972; IBM logo, 8-stripper designed by Paul Rand, 1972. IBM.

15.20 IBM package designs, Paul Rand, 1979. IBM

15.21 IBM logo rebus, Paul Rand, 1982. New York, Museum of Modern Art (MoMA). Gift of the Designer. Acc. n.: 520.1983. © 2008. Digital image, The Museum of Modern Art, New York / Scala.

15.22 'She's Got to Go Out to Get Woman's Day', advertisement designed by Gene Federico, 1954. Gene Federico Papers, Duke University Library, North Carolina.

15.23 'The Next War Will Determine Not What is Right, But What is Left' poster, Herb Lubalin, 1972. The Herb Lubalin Study Center of Design and Typography at the Cooper Union School of Art, New York.

15.24 'Mother and Child', 'Marriage', and 'Families', typographic designs by Herb Lubalin. The Herb Lubalin Study Center of Design and Typography at the Cooper Union School of Art, New York.

15.25 Typographic designs, Brownjohn, Chermayeff & Geismar Associates, 1962.

15.26 'Rocket's Red Glare' CBS advertisement, designed by Lou Dorfsman, 1962. Reproduced with the permission of Elise Dorfsman.

16.1 'Neue Haas Grotesk' publicity leaflet in Helvetica typeface, Stempel Foundry, 1958. St Bride Printing Library, London.

16.2 Latin, Cyrillic and Greek alphabets in digital versions of Helvetica.

16.3 Digital version of Neue Helvetica, 1983.

16.4 Comparison of digital versions of Akzidenz, Helvetica and Univers.

16.5 Comparison of digital versions of Akzidenz, Helvetica and Univers.

16.6 Facsimile of Univers numbering scheme, designed by Adrian Frutiger, 1957.

16.7 Photograph showing panels from 'Die Gute Form' exhibition, Zurich, 1947. Museum of Design, Zurich, Design Collection. © DACS 2010.

16.8 'Für das Alter' poster, designed by Carlo Vivarelli, 1959. Museum of Design, Zurich, Poster Collection. Photographer Franz Xaver Jaggy.

16.9 'Beethoven' poster, designed by Josef Müller-Brockmann, 1955. Museum of Design, Zurich, Poster Collection. Photographer Franz Xaver Jaggy.

16.10 'Beethoven' poster design scheme, 1955.

16.11 'June Festival' poster, designed by Josef Müller-Brockmann, 1969. Museum of Design, Zurich, Poster Collection. Phtographer Franz Xaver Jaggy.

16.12 3-column and 5-column grids.

16.13 *Neue Grafik* no.1, cover, 1958. Museum of Design, Zurich.

16.14 *Neue Grafik* no.2, 1959. Museum of Design, Zurich.

16.15 VW Beetle 'Think Small' advertisement, designed by Helmut Krone, 1959. Photo: Advertising archives.

16.16 Penguin grid, Romek Marber, 1961.

16.17 *Boiled Alive*, Penguin paperback cover, designed by Romek Marber, 1961. Penguin Archive, University of Bristol Library, Special Collections.

16.18 Mobil corporate identity guidelines, designed by Chermayeff & Geismar, early 1970s. Courtesy Chermayeff & Geismar Inc.

16.19 Mobil service station, 1966.

Courtesy Chermayeff & Geismar Inc.

16.20 Woolmark logo, designed by Francesco Saroglia, 1964. Australian Wool Innovation Ltd / The Woolmark Company.

16.21 New York subway map, designed by Massimo Vignelli, 1972. New York City Subway Map © Metropolitan Transport Authority, New York. Used with permission.

16.22 London Underground map, card folder edition, designed by Harry Beck, 1933. London Transport Museum.

16.23 New York subway map, designed by Michael Hertz, c.1979. New York City Subway Map © Metropolitan Transport Authority, New York. Used with permission.

16.24 Munich Olympics logo, designed by Otl Aicher, 1972. IOC/Olympic Museum Collections.

16.25 'Gymnast' Munich Olympics poster, designed by Otl Aicher, 1972. Otl Aicher Archive.

16.26 Munich Olympic pictograms, designed by Otl Aicher, 1972. © 1976 by ERCO GmbH.

17.1 Aldermaston marchers in Trafalgar Square, London, 1958. © Topfoto.

17.2 'Vallauris 1951 Exposition' poster, designed by Pablo Picasso. New York, Museum of Modern Art (MoMA). Given anonymously 172.1968. © 2008. Museum of Modern Art, New York / Scala. © Succession Picasso/DACS 2010.

17.3 *Sgt. Pepper's Lonely Hearts Club Band* album cover, designed by Peter Blake and Jann Haworth, 1967. © Peter Blake. All rights reserved, DACS 2010.

17.4 *First Things First* manifesto, updated version, 2000.

17.5 *The Man with the Golden Arm* poster, designed by Saul Bass, 1955. New York, Museum of Modern Art (MoMA). Gift of Otto Preminger Productions, United Artists 202.1956. © 2008. Museum of Modern Art, New York / Scala.

17.6 Frontispiece and titlepage of livre d'artiste book *Jazz*, Henri Matisse, c.1947. BL, f85/0086. © Succession H. Matisse/DACS 2010.

17.7 Air France poster, designed by Roger Excoffon, 1965. Photo: Les Arts Decoratifs, Paris / Laurent Sully Jaulmes.

17.8 *Wozzeck* poster, designed by Jan Lenica, 1964. New York, Museum of Modern Art (MoMA). Gift of the designer 485.1987. © 2008. Museum of Modern Art, New York / Scala. © ADAGP, Paris and DACS, London 2010.

17.9 Mexico Olympics logos designed by Lance Wyman, et al 1968. Courtesy Lance Wyman.

17.10 'The Association' poster, designed by Wes Wilson, 1966. Collection of Paul Olsen, www.olsenart.com. Reproduced with permission, © Wes Wilson.

17.11 'Youngbloods' poster, designed by Victor Moscoso, 1967. Museum of Design, Zurich, Poster Collection. Photographer Franz Xaver Jaggy.

17.12 'Dylan' poster, designed by Milton Glaser, 1966. Courtesy Milton Glaser.

17.13 Che Guevara graffiti, Havana, Cuba. Getty Images.

17.14 (& 17.15) Che Guevara contact print, Korda (Alberto Díaz Gutiérrez), 1960. © 2008. ADAGP, Paris / Scala, Florence. © ADAGP, Paris and DACS, London 2010.

17.16 'Day of the Heroic Guerilla, 8th October, 1968' poster designed by Elena Serrano. New York, Museum of Modern Art (MoMA). Gift of OSPAAAL Accn.: 503.1987. © 2008. Museum of Modern Art, New York / Scala.

17.17 Cherry Guevara, Magnum ice-cream wrapper, Magnum ice-cream. David Kunzle/Centre for the Study of Political Graphics, and Trisha Ziff.

17.18 Posters during the Paris riots of May 1968. Topfoto/Chapman.

17.19 'Oui Usines Occupées' poster, Atélier Populaire, 1968. Photo: akg-images.

17.20 Range of Biba stationery, designed by John McConnell. Courtesy Pentagram.

17.21 Sketch of Nuclear Disarmament symbol by Gerald Holtom, 1958. Commonwealth Collection, University of Bradford.

17.22 Semaphore alphabet.

17.23 'War is not Healthy…', Lorraine Schneider, 1968. Sunflower design and words by Lorraine Art Schneider, image and text © 1968, 2003 by Another Mother for Peace, Inc. (AMP) (www.anothermother.org).

17.24 'I Want Out' poster, designed by the Committee to Help Unsell the War, 1971. Library of Congress, Washington, D.C.

17.25 Oz magazine, no.10, 1968. BL, cup.805.k.

17.26 Oz magazine no.16, designed by Martin Sharp, November 1968. BL, cup.805.k.1.

18.1 God Save the Queen artwork, designed by Jamie Reid and John Marchant. Courtesy Jamie Reid.

18.2 Page on Patti Smith from Ripped and Torn, 1977. BL, ZD.9.b.296.

18.3 Sniffin' Glue fanzine, November 1976. BL, YD.2006.b.102.

18.4 Eva Mendes billboard in Times Square for 'Secret Obsession', 2007. Getty Images.

18.5 This Year's Model album cover, designed by Barney Bubbles, 1978. © Riviera Global.

18.6 Hard Werken magazine, issue no.6, designed by Hard Werken, March/April 1980. Courtesy Rick Vermuelen.

19.1 The Portland Building, Oregon, designed by Michael Graves, 1980. Courtesy of Michael Graves and Associates.

19.2 Typografische Monatsblätter magazine cover, designed by Wolfgang Weingart, 1968. Courtesy Wolfgang Weingart.

19.3 'Kunstkredit' poster, designed by Wolfgang Weingart, 1977. Courtesy Wolfgang Weingart.

19.4 'Offset' brochure, designed by Rosemarie Tissi, 1981. Courtesy Odermatt und Tissi.

19.5 Michael Graves exhibition poster, designed by William Longhauser, 1983. Courtesy Bill Longhauser.

19.6 'Masters in Historic Preservation', Columbia University poster, designed by Willi Kunz, 1985. Courtesy Willi Kunz.

19.7 Poster for Holland Festival, 'Theater Uit De Sovjet Unie', by Studio Dumbar, 1989. Courtesy Studio Dumbar, photography Lex van Pieterson.

19.8 Musée d'Orsay poster, 1986. Musée d'Orsay, Paris.

19.9 Musée d'Orsay brochures, 1987. Musée d'Orsay, Paris.

19.10 PTT corporate identity manual, designed by Studio Dumbar, 1989. Courtesy Studio Dumbar, photography Gerrit Schreurs.

19.11 Banknotes of the Netherlands, designed by Ootje Oxenaar: 5-guilder note, 1973; 10-guilder note, 1968; 25-guilder note, 1971; 50-guilder note, 1982; 100-guilder note, 1977; 250-guilder note, 1985. Bank of the Netherlands and the Utrecht Geldmuseum.

19.12 Cranbrook Academy of Art poster designed by Katherine McCoy, 1989. Courtesy Katherine McCoy.

19.13 Power, Corruption & Lies album cover, designed by Peter Saville, 1983. A Basket of Roses, Henri Fantin-Latour, 1890, National Gallery, London.

19.14 'Untitled' (I shop therefore I am), photographic silk screen/vinyl, designed by Barbara Kruger, 1987. Copyright Barbara Kruger, Courtesy Mary Boone Gallery, New York.

20.1 Raygun cover issue 17, three images combined in Photoshop and Collage, designed by David Carson, 1994. Courtesy Chris Ashworth.

20.2 E13-B, 1958.

20.3 OCR A, 1966.

20.4 OCR B, designed by Adrian Frutiger 1968.

20.5 Morse code alphabet.

20.6 Barcode.

20.7 Vormgevers poster, designed by Wim Crouwel, 1968. Museum of Design, Zurich, Poster Collection. Photographer Franz Xaver Jaggy.

20.8 Design Quarterly #133, 'Does It Make Sense?', designed by April Greiman. Courtesy April Greiman.

20.9 Emigre magazine, vol.10, 1988. Emigre.

20.10 Emigre magazine, vol.11, 1989. Emigre.

20.11 Nike advertisement, designed by Neville Brody, 1992. Courtesy Research Studios.

20.12 'Graphic Arts Message Tokyo' poster, designed by Neville Brody, 1992. Courtesy Research Studios.

20.13 Walker Art Gallery corporate typeface, designed by Matthew Carter, 1994. Courtesy Matthew Carter.

20.14 Modern digital fonts.

20.15 Raygun cover issue 3, designed by David Carson, 1993. Courtesy Chris Ashworth.

20.16 Text page from Raygun. Courtesy Chris Ashworth.

20.17 Carl Cox album cover, F.A.C.T. Silver Edition, designed by Me Company, 1995. Courtesy Me Company.

20.18 'Echoes of Techno' poster, designed by Niklaus Troxler, 2000. Courtesy Niklaus Troxler.

20.19 Adidas poster, designed by Blue Source, 2001. Photography James Dimmock; art direction Blue Source.

20.20 Lecture poster for AIGA, Detroit, designed by Stefan Sagmeister, 1999. Courtesy Sagmeister Inc.

p.1 Amazon's Kindle DX, 2009. Getty Images.

p.2 Seadragon Apple iPhone app., 2008. Microsoft Live Labs.

p.3 Split photo portrait double. Patrick Cramsie.

15.10 Printed by permission of the Norman Rockwell Family Agency. Copyright © 1943 The Norman Rockwell Family Entities.

INDEX